ENGLISH SURNAMES SERIES

THE SURNAMES OF SUSSEX

ENGLISH SURNAMES SERIES

Edited by R. A. McKinley

Department of English Local History
University of Leicester

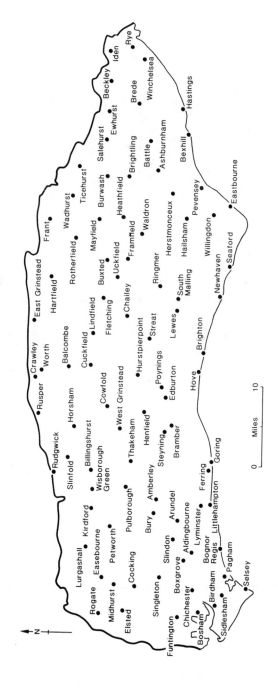

Sussex, showing some places mentioned in the text

ENGLISH SURNAMES SERIES

V
The Surnames of Sussex

by
Richard McKinley

LEOPARD'S HEAD PRESS

1988
Published by
LEOPARD'S HEAD PRESS LIMITED
2a Polstead Road, Oxford OX2 6TN

© Richard McKinley 1988

ISBN 0 904920 14 3

*This is the fifth volume in the
English Surnames Series
which is published for the
Marc Fitch Fund*

Printed in Great Britain at the
University Printing House, Oxford

Contents

		page
LIST OF MAPS		vii
ABBREVIATIONS		ix
ACKNOWLEDGEMENTS		xiii
INTRODUCTION		1
1.	The Rise of Hereditary Surnames in Sussex	29
2.	Locative Surnames	91
3.	Topographical Surnames	141
4.	Surnames Derived from Occupation, Status, or Office	221
5.	Surnames Derived from Personal Names	301
6.	Surnames Derived from Nicknames	361
7.	Surnames of Relationship, and Surnames of Unexplained Origins	423
Conclusion		429
INDEX		437

List of Maps

		page
1.	Sussex, showing some places mentioned in the text	*Frontispiece*
2.	The Sussex Rapes, 1332	89
3.	Ramified Surnames, 1524	90
4.	Medieval Instances of some Topographical Surnames	220

Abbreviations

Battle Custumals	S. R. Scargill-Bird, *Custumals of Battle Abbey* (Camden Society, New Series, vol. xli) (1887).
Boxgrove Chart.	L. Fleming, *Chartulary of Boxgrove Priory* (Sussex Record Society, vol. lix) (1960).
Cal. Pat.	*Calendar of Patent Rolls.*
Chichester Bishops' Acta	H. Mayr-Harting, *Acta of the Bishops of Chichester, 1075–1207* (Canterbury and York Society, vol. lvi) (1964).
Chichester Chart.	W. D. Peckham, *Chartulary of the High Church of Chichester* (Sussex Record Society, vol. xlvi) (1946).
Cottle, *Dict.*	B. Cottle, *Penguin Dictionary of Surnames* (1978).
Cowdray Archives	A. A. Dibben, *Cowdray Archives: A Catalogue*, vol. i (1960), vol. ii (1964).
De Lisle and Dudley MSS	*Report on the Manuscripts of Lord De Lisle and Dudley* (Historical MSS. Commission), 4 vols. (1925–42).
Fitzalan Surveys	M. Clough, *Two Estate Surveys of the Fitzalan Earls of Arundel* (Sussex Record Society, vol. lxvii) (1969).
Fransson, *Surnames of Occupation*	G. Fransson, *Middle English Surnames of Occupation* (1935)
Hastings Lathe C.R.	E. J. Courthope and B. E. R. Fermoy, *Lathe Court Rolls and Views of Frankpledge in the Rape of Hastings* (Sussex Record Society, vol. xxxvii) (1934).

Abbreviations

H.M.C. *Rye MSS.*	*Manuscripts of Rye and Hereford Corporations, Capt. Loder-Symonds, Mr E. R. Woodhouse, M.P. and others* (Historical MSS. Commission, 13th Report, appendix iv) (1892).
Inderwick, *Winchelsea*	F. A. Inderwick, *The Story of King Edward and New Winchelsea*, (1892).
Lane, *Suss. Deeds*	W. Budgen, *Abstracts of Sussex Deeds and Documents from the Muniments of the late H. C. Lane* (Sussex Record Society, vol. xxix) (1924).
Lewes Barony Recs.	A. J. Taylor, *Records of the Barony and Honour of the Rape of Lewes* (Sussex Record Society, vol. xliv) (1939).
Lewes Chartulary	L. F. Salzman, *Chartulary of the Priory of St. Pancras of Lewes*, vol. i (Sussex Record Society, vol. xxxviii) (1932); vol. ii (*ibid.*, vol. xl) (1935).
Löfvenberg, *Local Surnames*	M. T. Löfvenberg, *Studies on Middle English Local Surnames* (1942).
M.E.D.	H. Kurath and others, *Middle English Dictionary* (1956–).
Non. Inquis.	*Nonarum Inquisitiones in Curia Scaccarii* (Record Commission) (1807).
Norf. and Suff. Surnames	R. A. McKinley, *Norfolk and Suffolk Surnames in the Middle Ages* (1975).
P.N. Suss.	A. Mawer, F. M. Stenton and J. E. B. Gover, *Place-Names of Sussex* (1969).
P.R.O.	Public Record Office.
Reaney, *Dict.*	P. H. Reaney, *Dictionary of British Surnames* (1976).

Reaney, *Origins*	P. H. Reaney, *Origin of English Surnames* (1967).
Rec. Soc.	Record Society.
Robertsbridge Charters	Anon., *Calendar of the Charters and Documents relating to Robertsbridge Abbey* (1873).
Robertsbridge Surveys	H. D'Elboux, *Surveys of the Manors of Robertsbridge, Suss. and Michelmarsh, Hants., and of the Demesne lands of Halden in Rolvenden, Kent, 1567–70* (Sussex Record Society, vol. xlvii) (1946).
Rubin, *Suss. Phonology*	S. Rubin, *Phonology of the Middle English Dialect of Sussex* (1951).
S.A.C.	*Sussex Archaeological Collections*
Surnames of Lancs.	R. A. McKinley, *Surnames of Lancashire* (1981).
Surnames of Oxon.	R. A. McKinley, *Surnames of Oxfordshire* (1977).
Suss. Custumals, vol. i	W. D. Peckham, *Thirteen Custumals of The Sussex Manors of the Bishop of Chichester* (Sussex Record Society, vol. xxxi) (1925).
Suss. Custumals, vol. ii	B. C. Redwood and A. E. Wilson, *Custumals of the Sussex Manors of the Archbishop of Canterbury* (Sussex Record Society, vol. lvii) (1958).
Suss. Custumals, vol. iii	A. E. Wilson, *Custumals of the Manors of Laughton, Willingdon and Goring* (Sussex Record Society, vol. lx) (1962).
Suss. Fines, vol. i	L. F. Salzmann, *Abstract of the Feet of Fines relating to the County of Sussex, from 2 Richard I to 33 Henry III* (Sussex Record Society, vol. ii) (1903).

Suss. Fines, vol. ii	L. F. Salzmann, *Abstract of the Feet of Fines relating to the County of Sussex, from 34 Henry III to 35 Edward I* (Sussex Record Society, vol. vii) (1908).
Suss. Fines, vol. iii	L. F. Salzmann, *Abstract of the Feet of Fines relating to the County of Sussex, from 1 Edward II to 44 Henry VII* (Sussex Record Society, vol. xxiii) (1916).
Suss. Indictments	J. S. Cockburn, *Sussex Indictments* (P.R.O.), vols. i and ii (1975).
Suss. Subsidy, 1524–5	J. Cornwall, *Lay Subsidy rolls for the County of Sussex, 1524–25*, (Sussex Record Society, vol. lvi) (1956).
Suss. Wills	W. H. Godfrey and R. Garraway Rice, *Transcripts of Sussex Wills so far as they relate to ecclesiological and parochial subjects, up to the year 1560* (Sussex Record Society, vols. xli, xlii, xliii, xlv) (1935–41).
Valor Eccl.	*Valor Ecclesiasticus temp. Henr. VIII* (Record Commission) (1810–34).
V.C.H. Suss.	*Victoria County History of Sussex* (1905–).
W. Suss. 1641–2	R. Garraway Rice, *West Sussex Protestation Returns, 1641–2* (Sussex Record Society, vol. v) (1906).
Wiston Archives	J. M. L. Booker, *The Wiston Archives: A Catalogue* (1975).

Acknowledgements

I have to acknowledge the assistance which has been given to me in the writing of this book by many people, who have given advice, and have provided me with information about Sussex, its history, and its surnames. The footnotes in the book record the many instances where I have been supplied with references, or other information. I must, however, acknowledge the more general help I have received from Dr Marc Fitch, who has made many valuable observations about the whole book. I have also been supplied with much information, especially from parish registers, by Mr Francis Leeson, of Ferring, whose extensive knowledge of Sussex genealogy and family history will be well known to many people.

The publication of this book, and the research carried out for it, and for the other volumes of the English Surnames Survey, has only been possible because of the generous and continuing support of the Marc Fitch Fund.

R.A.M.

Introduction

Sussex was for centuries geographically a somewhat isolated county. The difficult country of the Weald separated it from London, and from much of the rest of England. In the coastal region of East Sussex, communications with Kent were impeded by marshes, though to the west there was reasonably easy intercourse with south Hampshire along the coastal plain. These obstructions to easy passage persisted into the 18th century. It is not surprising, therefore, that Sussex surnames had over a long period their own distinctive characteristics. In some general respects, the history of surnames in Sussex differs from that in other counties. The development of surnames derived from first (or baptismal) names, for example, has a history in Sussex distinct from that of the midland or northern counties, and even to some extent from that of the other counties in the south-east.[1] Where surnames derived from place-names are concerned, those surnames occurring in Sussex were for long predominantly those from Sussex place-names, and surnames from place-names outside the county only appear in limited numbers. There are a number of surnames, of various types, which so far as can be seen originated solely in Sussex. Although at all periods from the years immediately after the Conquest onwards, there was some influx of surnames from outside, it was not until the 19th century that shifts in population became large enough to alter significantly the general nature of surnames in the county.

One feature of minor place-names in Sussex for centuries has been the great number of holdings, detached farms and other minor localities which had names derived from the surnames of owners or tenants. Examples of locality names formed from surnames in this way can be found in most if not all parts of England, but in Sussex the formation of place-names from surnames has long been especially common. As early as the 13th century many examples can be found, and at the present day, an inspection of the Ordnance Survey map for almost any part of Sussex will reveal many instances of farms, woods and so forth with names derived from surnames which have been well established in the county over a long period. Not only do many surnames which originated in Sussex during the medieval period still survive in the county, and still form a major part of the body of surnames in Sussex, despite the population movements of the last two centuries, but a great number of Sussex surnames have left their mark on the place-names of the Sussex landscape.

DEFINITION OF TERMS

Although much work has been carried out on the history of surnames by both genealogists and linguistic scholars, there is no set of terms used in such studies which is generally known to and accepted by all the varied groups of people who for one reason or another are interested in investigations into the development of English surnames, and it is therefore necessary to set out the principal terms used. For the purposes of this work, surnames have been divided into six main categories:

(1) Locative surnames. These are surnames derived from the names of specific places, such as, for example, in Sussex such surnames as Worthing, Lindfield, Arundel, Steyning etc. Surnames from the names of small hamlets, or from lost places, have been included in this category.

(2) Topographical surnames. These are surnames from words for features of the landscape, whether natural or man-made, such as, for example, surnames like Ford, Bridge, Style, Wood and so forth. Surnames such as Bridger, Fielder or Fenner have been included here, and so have surnames such as Bridgeman, Wellman, etc.

(3) Occupational surnames. These are surnames such as Baker, Chapman, Cooper, Goldsmith, etc. Surnames from status or rank, such as Freeman, Burgess, Cottar, or Franklin, for instance, have been included in this category, as have surnames from offices, such as Beadle, Reeve, or Hayward, and surnames from high ecclesiastical or secular ranks, such as Bishop, Abbot, Prior, Duke, Earl, Sheriff and so forth.

(4) Surnames from Personal Names. These are surnames derived from first or 'baptismal' names, including surnames such as Godwin, Gregory, Gilbert, etc., and including surnames such as Peters, Roberts, Williams etc., formed from first names with a genitival 's', and surnames such as Williamson, Robertson, Harrison etc.

(5) Surnames derived from Nicknames, including surnames from physical characteristics, Long, Brown, Sheepshank, Joliff, etc., names from birds or animals, such as Jay, Fox or Beaver, and a great variety of names originally bestowed as nicknames and derived from habits, commonly used expressions, and so forth, such as Godesmark, Wardew or Milksop.

(6) Surnames or Relationship. These are surnames from terms of relationship, such as Couzens, Uncle and so on. A few names from terms connected with relationships, such as Bastard or Filderoi, have been included here.

It is much easier to draw up a list of categories into which surnames can be divided than it is to decide how to classify each of a large body of surnames. While it is clear that a great many surnames fall into one or other of the categories just set out, there remain a substantial number which are difficult to assign. Some surnames have more than one possible origin, and in individual cases there is often not enough evidence to make it feasible to decide between the various possibilities. In some instances it is uncertain if surnames are derived from the names of specific places, and so ought to be classified as locative, or if they are really topographical, and when dealing with a surname such as, for example, Bridger, it is difficult to be sure if it is a topographical name, from residence beside a bridge, or if it is really an occupational name. Further, some surnames of the nickname type are closely connected with occupations. Besides such issues, which raise points about just how surnames should be classified, there are a certain number of surnames of which the origins have defied elucidation. This is true of but a small minority of surnames, but the number is larger than might be gathered from some reference works on the subject. Some surnames of which the origins are not known may be alien ones, but this is unlikely to be true of all of them.

In attempting to decide upon the origin of surnames, writers on the subject have often relied, in doubtful cases, upon the presence before individual surnames of prepositions or articles. Up to c. 1400, and even occasionally later, prepositions, or the definite article, are quite frequently prefixed to surnames or bye-names erroneously in original sources. During the 13th and 14th centuries in particular, a period when many surnames were being formed and becoming hereditary, examples of this are very numerous, both in Sussex, and in other counties. There are, for instance, many cases of the French definite article being used with locative surnames, some of them surnames derived from French place-names, but some of them ones from English place-names. In the Sussex subsidy for 1327, for example, the names le Burdeville, le Wancy, le Gundeuille and le Bauent are all listed, though in fact these are all locative surnames, from French place-names.[2] The article can be found similarly with locative surnames from English place-names, in such cases as, for example, le Lychepole, or le Bromham.[3] There are, in the same way, instances of surnames or bye-names derived from personal names with the definite article attached in error, such as, for example, le Jewdewyne or le Ketel.[4] The preposition 'de' is also at times prefixed wrongly to surnames from personal names, so that forms such as, for instance, de Gundewyne can be found.[5] Many other examples could be given of cases where 'le' or 'de' are attached in error to surnames or bye-names in various categories. It is consequently rash to rely very much on the presence of a preposition, or the definite article, before any name as a reliable piece of evidence about origins.

The use of counties as the basic units for carrying on the Surnames Survey is inevitable, because a high proportion of the records which have to be used are drawn up county by county. Sussex, fortunately, is a fairly well demarcated area geographically. Even so, it is of course the case that county boundaries are not in themselves a complete barrier to the migration of surnames. It is generally not feasible to pursue systematically the history of surnames which have originated in Sussex, but have subsequently spread outside the county, though at points it has seemed useful to make some comments upon the spread of some Sussex surnames beyond the county boundary. It has also been thought useful at times to point to characteristics which Sussex surnames have in common with those in other south-eastern counties. In general, however, it has been necessary to confine this study within the limits of the county's borders.

Most of this work is concerned with the discussion of Sussex surnames category by category, but there are several topics which cut across the usual division of surnames into types, as set out above. One of these is the whole question of the development of stable, hereditary surnames. This is a matter which requires treatment at some length, and it has therefore been made the subject of a separate chapter. There are, however, several issues which affect the history of Sussex surnames generally and which will best be dealt with here.

INFLUENCE ON SURNAMES OF THE PATTERN OF LANDOWNING.

Medieval Sussex is notable for the fact that some of the largest landowners in the county also held large estates outside the county. The de Warenne family, who were lords of Lewes Rape, held much land in other parts of England, including Surrey and East Anglia. The D'Aubigny family, who were Earls of Arundel for much of the 12th and 13th centuries, were also large landlords in East Anglia, and the Fitzalan family, who were Earls of Arundel from the late 13th century, also held lands in the Welsh Marches. The Percy family, lords of the Honour of Petworth in West Sussex, were great landowners in the north of England, with large estates in Yorkshire and Northumberland. The Archbishops of Canterbury, whose Sussex holdings included the two extensive manors of South Malling and Pagham, were landowners elsewhere, notably in Kent. In addition, from the late 11th century to the early 13th, a number of Sussex landholders, including some below the status of tenant in chief, held land in France. These tenurial connections raise the question of whether the surnames to be found in Sussex were significantly affected by the movement of tenants, or estate officials, into the county from lands held outside it by lords who were landowners both in Sussex and elsewhere.

Some Sussex sub-tenants listed in 1086, or mentioned in the county during the late 11th or early 12th centuries, had locative names which indicated that they came from the parts of Normandy where the tenants-in-chief, under whom they respectively held, had lands. This development has been discussed in the *Victoria County History of Sussex*,[6] and need not be considered further here. Many of the surnames concerned are dealt with in the following chapter. It may, however, be noted here that in the period after the Conquest tenurial links in Normandy were of some significance in the establishment of some locative names, from French place-names, in Sussex. There is some evidence at later periods for movement between the Sussex lands of some major landholders, and the lands of the same magnates in other parts of England, but most of the evidence suggests that the direction of movement was out of Sussex, rather than into it. For instance, in a list of tenants in 1301 on the Norfolk manors of Mileham and Beeston, both belonging to the Fitzalan family, there are a number of serfs with rare surnames or bye-names, which also occur in Sussex. The name Crede, probably from Crede Farm in Bosham, is given at Mileham in 1301, and occurs in Sussex in the 13th century and later.[7] Pesecod, a 'nickname' type surname, existed at Mileham in 1301, is found later on the Fitzalan estates in Sussex, survived in that county to be quite numerous in West Sussex in the 17th century, and in several forms (Peasegood, Pescud) is still a Sussex surname at the present time.[8] Another rare surname Pypelor, was that of a serf at Beeston in 1301, and can be found in Sussex during the 13th and 14th centuries (the origin of the name is 'poplar').[9] The name Whitlok is listed in 1301 at both Mileham and Beeston, but it existed in the 13th century in Sussex at places where the Fitzalan family held lands, and it appears at a later date on the Fitzalan estates in Sussex. It should be said, however, that this particular name occurs elsewhere in both Norfolk and Sussex during the 13th and 14th centuries.[10] On the Battle Abbey manor of Brightwalton (Berks.), the rare surname Godeshalf existed in the late 13th century. This is a surname which had been present in Sussex earlier.[11] There is also evidence for some interchange of tenants between the Percy estates in Sussex, and the same family's lands in other counties. Richard (or Richeman) Calle (there is some inconsistency in the way in which his first name is given), was a tenant on the Percy estate at Petworth, and also on the Percy lands in Yorkshire. At one time he also held land at Foston (Leics.), where the Percys were lords of the manor.[12] Calle witnessed charters of members of the Percy family, and acted as an attorney for them, and he may have been an estate official. He was living in the mid 13th century, and seems to have been a Yorkshireman by origin. Calle does occur as a surname or bye-name in West Sussex rather later.[13] In a parallel instance, several persons named de Bigenor (de Bigenouer etc.) who were probably all related, and whose name was from either Bignor in Sussex, or from Bigenor Farm, near Egdean, appear in Norfolk as witnesses to deeds relating to Lewes Priory estates in that county.[14] The name does occur in Sussex.[15]

The number of instances where there are grounds for suspecting that movement had taken place between Sussex and other English regions, through links of landownership, are, however, small. Though it is obviously possible that the sources do not reveal the full facts about the matter, it is unlikely that the defects of the evidence account for the very small number of examples which can be detected. There are in fact sources which should make it possible to discover such interchanges between Sussex and other regions if they had happened on any great scale. The 14th and 15th century surveys of the Fitzalan estates, inside and outside Sussex, for example, give much evidence about the free and unfree tenants on the family lands.[16] The chartulary of Lewes Priory, which covers holdings both in Sussex and Norfolk,[17] gives a good deal of information about the priory's tenants in both counties, and the Percy Chartulary[18], though it has no very great amount of information on the family lands in Sussex, does contain the names of many tenants on the family estates in the north, which can be compared with the names of the inhabitants of Petworth and other Sussex holdings of the Percys. It seems fair to conclude from this that although the links set up by land-owning between Sussex and estates in other English regions led at times to movement both in and out of the county, such movements were occasional, and were not sufficiently numerous to have much effect on the body of surnames in use in Sussex. This is all the more notable because the connections between Sussex and some other counties in terms of landowning were so strong. Apart from the tenants-in-chief, whose holdings within and outside Sussex have already been mentioned, there were many sub-tenants, mostly families of knightly rank, who held fiefs both in Sussex and elsewhere. In many cases these were families which were enfeoffed with lands both inside and outside the county between the Conquest and about 1150. In Sussex during the 12th and 13th centuries, there was an exceptionally large number of landowners who were also holders of lands outside the county, not just in adjoining counties, but in many cases, in relatively distant parts of England, yet these circumstances had little discernible influence on the surnames existing in Sussex.

NAMES OF ALIENS

As Sussex is a maritime county it is not surprising that considerable numbers of aliens from France and the Low Countries settled there at various periods. Many aliens resident in the county can be found listed in the 15th century alien subsidies, the 1524–25 subsidy returns, and the patent rolls. The wars of religion in France during the 16th century led to many Frenchmen coming to inhabit south coast ports such as Rye (though many of them were probably not permanent residents), and at later periods there were settlements of Huguenots and others. It might be thought that the substantial flow of alien names into the county would have had a noticeable influence upon the surnames to be found there, and that the Sussex ports in particular would have been much affected, but in fact this is not the case. This may be due to some extent to the fact that some foreigners settling in Sussex did not have hereditary surnames, and this is likely to have been true of some settlers from the Low Countries, and it is no doubt also true that some people who appear in such sources as alien subsidies were not permanent settlers in Sussex, but the main factor appears to have been the process of Anglicisation to which foreign names were subjected.

The most striking characteristic of the surnames or bye-names listed in the 15th century alien subsidies for Sussex is the small number of names which could be recognised as not being English. For instance, a list of Flemings living in Sussex in 1449 records some with surnames or bye-names from personal names, such as Andrew, Saier, Johnson, Williamson and Peter; from occupations such as Taillour, Barbor, Furbour, Wever, Sherman or Cowper; from place-names such as Bukherst; or from topographical terms such as Lake or Halle.[19] A few people in the list can be recognised as foreign because they have surnames or bye-names from their country of origin; there are, for instance, five persons named Ducheman and one named Flemmyng. It must be suspected, however, that these were bye-names bestowed upon the men concerned after their settlement in England, rather than alien surnames brought into the country by immigrants. Several of those listed could be recognised as aliens because they had Christian names not generally used in England at that time; the first names Hans, Cornelis, Levyngfolle, Derik, Isebrond and Herman all occur, for example. There are one or two examples of men with occupational names which are English linguistically, but which were not usually found in England at the time as natives' surnames, such as Hardwareman or Organmaker. In the 1449 list a total of 49 people are listed. Out of these 17 had surnames or bye-names which do not appear to be English, including those named Flemmyng or Ducheman. The majority of those concerned, therefore, had names which were not detectably alien, and which, supposing they became hereditary and persisted in the county, would not establish a body of new surnames of outside origin in Sussex. This does not necessarily mean that there would be no effect at all upon the local surnames. Some of those listed had names formed from a personal name with the suffix -son (Johnson, Williamson, etc), and immigration may have led to an increase in Sussex of surnames of that type, originally scarce there.[20]

The names found in the 1449 list are typical of aliens' names in the 15th century alien subsidies for Sussex, and of the names of foreigners living in the county which can be found in other sources such as the patent rolls. Many aliens appear in these sources with surnames or bye-names which seem entirely English. There are a few examples of aliens with names which are not only English, but which are found in Sussex, or in the south-eastern counties generally, but which are not usually found in other parts of England, and which have a distinctly local appearance. These include, for example, occupational names such as Repyer[21], or topographical names such as Compe.[22] There is no reason to suppose that the position in Sussex was exceptional. It has not been possible to examine the alien subsidies for the whole country, but those for some other counties have been investigated, and the names of aliens granted letters of denization, recorded on the patent rolls, have been examined, and the position about 15th century aliens' names in Sussex seems to resemble fairly closely that in other parts of England.

A good general view of the surnames of aliens in Sussex in the early 16th century can be obtained from the subsidy returns of 1524 and 1525.[23] About 300 persons are listed as aliens in the 1524 returns, and some fresh names of aliens appear in 1525. Out of the aliens listed in 1524 and 1525, rather less than half had surnames or bye-names which could be English in origin. This is a considerably smaller proportion than in the 15th century alien subsidies, and it does seem that 16th century lists of aliens contain a smaller proportion of people whose names had been thoroughly Anglicized.[24] Even so, some of the aliens recorded in 1524 and 1525 had surnames or bye-names which appear to be locative names from English place-names, such as Exetter or Hacford;[25] from occupations, such as Feryman, Clerke, Knyght, Glasier or Lokear;[26] from topographical terms, such as Style or Corner,[27] or from personal names such as Nicholas, Davye, Robard or Johnson.[28] Some aliens in the 1524–25 subsidy returns are not given surnames or bye-names at all, but it is doubtful if this was because they did not have such names. Both in Sussex and in some other counties, the assessments for the subsidy at those dates sometimes list taxpayers, usually servants, without surnames, some of them aliens, some English.

Precisely what processes were at work in modifying aliens' names into English forms is not altogether clear. It is probable that foreigners with occupational surnames or bye-names who settled in England replaced their original names with English ones which were more or less literal translations, which would not be difficult to do in the case of occupational names. It would also not be difficult to replace alien surnames or bye-names from personal names with cognate forms from English personal names. It is also possible that names from topographical terms could have been translated into English without too much difficulty. Such developments, however, do not explain how aliens come to appear with locative names derived from English place-names. It is possible that such names could have been acquired in England, but it also seems likely that such cases are the result of alien surnames having been assimilated to English place-names which were phonetically somewhat similar. Unfortunately it is not normally possible to discover what surnames or bye-names aliens who occur in such sources as subsidy returns had before coming to England, so that it is not possible to compare the original forms of the names concerned with the Anglicized versions. It seems likely that in some cases aliens adopted English surnames which were those of their employers. Thomas Wynder, an inhabitant of Hastings in 1439–40, had an alien servant called Colyn; it seems likely that Colyn was the same person as the Colett atte Wyn, an alien, mentioned at Hastings at the same time.[29] (In Sussex, surnames formed from a topographical term with -er, such as Wynder, are often used interchangeably with names formed from the topographical term in question with atte).[30] There may have been other such cases which cannot now be traced, especially since examples of servants acquiring surnames from their masters are known in other connections.[31]

During the second half of the 16th century considerable numbers of aliens came into Sussex for various reasons, but many of them seem to have merely sojourned in the county temporarily. Many aliens, mostly Frenchmen, resided at Rye under Elizabeth I, and formed a distinct community there. Some certainly lived in Rye for long periods, but many were refugees, usually Protestants, from the wars of religion in France, and many of these returned to France after dwelling in Rye for varying periods. In general, the surnames of aliens living in Rye during the second half of the 16th century do not seem to have been Anglicized, but there may have been cases where foreigners in the port adopted English surnames to replace their original ones. In 1574–75, for example, a French surgeon living at Rye, and resident in the town since 1572, was described as John Preston alias Dabredin. This looks very much as if he was acquiring a locative surname of a purely English character.[32]

Apart from aliens who settled in the Sussex ports, permanently or temporarily, as merchants or as refugees from war or persecution, there were a considerable number of aliens engaged in the iron-founding and glass-making industries in Sussex during the 16th century. In many cases, however, these too appear not to have been permanent residents in the county. Aliens were employed in the Sussex iron founding industry from the end of the 15th century, and during the first half of the 16th, foreigners, mostly French, were employed in the Wealden iron works in some numbers, but this does not seem to have left a permanent mark on the surnames in use in that part of Sussex. This was perhaps partly due to the fact that some of those concerned did not settle permanently in the county, but it must also have been partly due to the surnames of many of them having become assimilated to English ones. A list of aliens employed in the Wealden iron industry who were granted letters of denization in 1544, nearly all from northern France, mentions some men with surnames which would appear purely English if it was not known that they were the names of foreigners, such as Bennett, Harrison, Holmes, Lenarde or Tyler, though there were others with surnames which were clearly alien.[33] During the second half of the 16th century some immigrants were also employed in the glass industry in north Sussex, and in the late 16th and early 17th centuries, there were communities of immigrant glass workers at some places in the north, such as Wisborough Green and Petworth. However, many of the alien glassmakers moved away from Sussex after about 1620. One or two surnames brought into Sussex by immigrant glass makers survived in the county for some time, such as that of the Bungar or Bongard family, but the impact on the general body of Sussex surnames caused by the migration into the county of aliens during the 16th century seems to have been very small.[34]

This discussion of aliens' surnames omits the substantial number of surnames, derived from French place-names, which first appear in Sussex between the Conquest and about 1250. Some of these survived, ramified to varying degrees in Sussex, and in some cases are still there at the present day. Many of these surnames are discussed in Chapter I.

It is difficult to find examples of surnames of aliens which first appear in Sussex during the 15th or 16th centuries, and which subsequently persisted there and ramified. The only clear instance of such a surname which has been discovered is the name Lasher. The first known example of the surname in Sussex is in 1439–40, when Laurence Lassher, an alien at Rye, was listed in a subsidy.[35]

RATIOS OF SURNAMES IN DIFFERENT CATEGORIES

The method of dividing surnames into different categories has already been set out. In considering the surnames of the county, and the distinctive local characteristics which they display, it is obvious that one point to be examined is the way in which surnames are divided between the categories, and how the situation in Sussex compares with that in other regions of England. Some evidence for such comparisons can be obtained by dividing into the appropriate categories the surnames or byenames found in Sussex subsidy rolls of various dates, and comparing the results with those from subsidy returns for other counties of about the same dates. This method has its defects, for subsidies do not list the poorest parts of the population, and as there are grounds for thinking that, at least up to about 1500, there were significant differences between social classes in regard to the types of surname used, the names given in the subsidies may not represent a fair sample of those in use by the whole population, at least where medieval assessments are involved. Although this factor has to be taken into account, and indeed in any work on medieval surnames it has to be born in mind that the surnames of some classes are very badly represented in the sources, the subsidy returns do provide the best means of making comparisons between the different parts of England. In order to show how Sussex compares with other counties, figures have been compiled for a number of counties, showing how surnames or bye-names found in some 14th century subsidies are divided into categories. Considerations of space have made it necessary to limit the number of counties for which figures are given, but statistics for some other counties, not included in the tables below, have been compiled. Some figures for a number of counties have been published by Dr P. H Reaney.[36] The figures given below have been divided into categories on a different basis from that used by Dr Reaney, to correspond with the method by which surnames have been discussed in this work, and in other publications of the survey of English surnames, and consequently differ in some respects from those calculated by him.

The columns in the two following tables are for surnames or bye-names, found in each of the sources used, in the following categories:

1. Locative names
2. Topographical names
3. Occupational names
4. Surnames and bye-names from personal names.
5. Nickname type surnames or bye-names.
6. Names of relationship.
7. Names of uncertain or unknown origin, and others not in the above categories.

In compiling statistics from medieval sources, individuals who are listed without any surnames or bye-names at all have been excluded from the calculations. The figures given are for numbers of individuals, per 1,000 persons listed in each source. They are not statistics for numbers of different surnames.

Table 1[37]

	1	2	3	4	5	6	7
Sussex, 1332	217	259	179	149	116	6	74
Bucks., 1332	235	149	211	255	67	10	73
Dorset, 1327	151	162	210	193	163	21	100
Kent, 1334/5	268	188	147	223	119	7	48
Lancashire, 1332	523	148	149	32	67	3	78
Oxfordshire, 1327	191	69	241	245	94	19	141
Suffolk, 1327	135	110	231	285	119	5	115
Surrey, 1332	246	179	244	143	87	22	79
Warws., 1332	301	108	225	213	76	12	64

The figures in the table are for a selection of counties in the main regions of England, and they are for a period when most of the taxpayers listed in subsidy returns had surnames or bye-names, though small numbers do appear in the sources without bye-names at all. The figures are also for a period when the great majority of people either had names which were not hereditary, or had ones which had not been hereditary for very long. The statistics given ought, therefore, to show what the position was region by region, at a time when surnames were still being formed, and when the distribution of surnames or bye-names had not been disturbed by migration to any great extent. As the table shows, there were considerable differences, even between counties in the same region. The main point here is how Sussex compares with other counties. The most noticeable feature of Sussex surnames is the very high proportion of topographical names, higher than in the adjoining counties of Kent and Surrey, and much higher than in any of the other counties for which information has been given in the table. In fact, similar evidence has been collected for a considerable number of counties, not in the table, but no other county has been found with a proportion of topographical surnames which is as high as that in Sussex. Sussex has rather fewer names in most of the other categories than do the other south-eastern counties, but this is probably just the consequence of the high proportion of topographical names. It is never easy to account for such differences between counties or regions. Somewhat different naming habits seem to have prevailed in the various English regions. Locative surnames, for instance, were more common in most northern counties. In Sussex, topographical names were much less common, proportionately, in Chichester and the Sussex boroughs than they were in the county as a whole. In the subsidies for 1296, 1327 and 1332, the proportion of topographical names in Chichester and the boroughs was about half that for the county as a whole.[38] It is also the case that aristocratic or knightly landholders in Sussex very rarely had topographical names during the 12th, 13th and 14th centuries. It consequently seems that topographical names in medieval Sussex were mostly those of the lesser free tenants or of bondmen. Serfs in Sussex certainly had a high proportion of topographical names. In a list of the serfs of several Sussex landowners, assessed in 1296, 28% of those mentioned had topographical names.[39] Among serfs mentioned in a series of custumals of the Bishop of Chichester's Sussex manors, drawn up between the late 13th century and the late 14th, nearly a third of those listed had topographical names.[40]

Serfs and small free tenants were classes which acquired hereditary surnames at a relatively late period, though perhaps rather earlier in Sussex than in most parts of England. In some regions, members of the same classes tended to acquire surnames derived from personal names. In Lancashire, small free tenants and bondmen often acquired surnames formed from a personal name with -son (Williamson, Robertson, etc.),[41] and this was perhaps true of the north of England as a whole. In the south Midlands and the south-west, many people in the same classes acquired surnames formed from a personal name with a genitival '-s' (Roberts, Williams, etc).[42] Both these types of personal names were scarce in Sussex during the Middle Ages,[43] and it seems probable that people of the social classes who, in some parts of the country, acquired surnames from personal names, of one of the two types just mentioned, in Sussex often acquired topographical surnames. As is often the case with regional characteristics of surnames, it is not easy to see what the cause of this development was. It does not seem to be connected with the local pattern of settlement, and it must be considered as due to local habits of forming surnames, which can be observed to have existed in various parts of England, without it being possible to assign any cause for them. There do seem to have been local practices in such matters which were in the nature of fashions.

SURNAMES AND SOCIAL CLASS

It has been stated in the preceding section that topographical surnames were not evenly distributed throughout the different social classes. In fact, during the period when hereditary surnames were being formed, marked differences are apparent in at least some regions between social classes in the types of surnames acquired. It has been pointed out elsewhere in connection with other counties that during the period when most surnames were formed, roughly 1100–1400, there were noticeable differences between social classes in the types of surnames each class acquired.[44] It is not necessary to repeat here what has been said on the subject about other counties. So far as Sussex is concerned, there are several points to be made. One is the fact that during the 13th and 14th centuries, serfs' surnames or bye-names included a particularly high proportion of topographical names. Some evidence about this has already been mentioned. Other evidence about serfs' names shows the same characteristic. For instance, out of 35 bond tenants listed at Wiston about 1300, 13 (or more than a third) had topographical names.[45] (Some serfs here were listed without bye-names, and these have been excluded from the figures.) Beyond this, it is also the case that serfs had an exceptionally high proportion of surnames or bye-names of the nickname type.[46] In contrast to these features of bondmen's names, at the other end of the scale the families of knightly or aristocratic landholders in the county had an exceptionally high proportion of surnames derived from place-names. In a list of Sussex tenants holding by knight service, 1242–43, just under 70% had locative names.[47] Most of these were surnames which were already hereditary. Tenants by knight service were a small group, though one which included all the really large landowners in the county. In an attempt to obtain evidence about a wider body of property owners, the names of the parties to fines levied about property in Sussex, 1190–1249, have been analysed.[48] More than 53% had locative names. The value of property conveyed by fines varied considerably of course, but this method of conveyance was not generally used for lands of very small value, so that parties to fines were normally people involved in property transactions of some substantial worth. The factors which led to landowners having a high proportion of locative surnames are better discussed in dealing with the forces behind the evolution of hereditary surnames.[49] This characteristic of landowners' names was not confined to Sussex. These figures can be compared with those for all taxpayers in the 1332 subsidy, already given.

The points just made deal with all the differences between the names of the various social classes which can be clearly established in Sussex. It would be wrong to lay much stress on differences of a few per cent which can be seen between the names of people in different classes or different levels of tax assessment, in such sources as subsidy rolls. Once surnames become hereditary, it is to be expected that, even with a limited degree of social mobility, the differences in the surnames of the various classes would in time be obliterated. Some impression of how far this process had gone by the mid 15th century can be gained from the names of those persons in Sussex implicated in Cade's revolt in 1450.[50] In the great majority of cases the ranks or occupations of those involved are given, so that it is possible to see how the surnames of the various sections of society compared. So far as locative surnames were concerned the position was (taking the descriptions of occupations etc., given in the source as being correct, and without attempting to check against other information) as follows:

Occupation, etc.	Total persons in each class	No. of persons with locative names	Percentage with locative names
Husbandmen	81	10	12
Yeomen	109	31	28
Labourers	73	13	18
Artisans	52	9	17
Gentlemen	22	6	27
Others and persons with occupations not given	88	13	15

Obviously in 1450 there was still a considerable difference between classes where locative names were concerned, with the more prosperous classes, gentlemen and yeomen, having a much higher proportion of locative names than the rest. Despite the fact that by 1450 much of the

Introduction

population must have had hereditary surnames for a century or more, distinctions still survived between classes, if rather less marked than earlier. Even in the 16th century, difference still survived. As an example of what the position was, the surnames of taxpayers in Bramber rape in the 1524 subsidy have been examined. In each place in the rape the name of the person with the highest assessment has been noted.[51] Out of these highest taxpayers, no less than 40% had locative surnames. This compares with 16% for all the taxpayers listed.

Apart from the position about locative surnames, there is no significant difference either in 1450 or in 1524, in regard to the character of the surnames born by the different classes. Where locative surnames were concerned, however, the differences were evidently persistent.

SOME REMARKS ON PHONETICS AND ORTHOGRAPHY

This work is not the appropriate place for a discussion of the phonetics of the Sussex dialect at any period,[52] but it may be useful here to make some observations about phonetics and spelling in so far as they bear upon the development of surnames. Some surnames appear in original sources in a number of very different forms, and this can be confusing unless the phonetics of the local dialect are kept in mind.

One phonetic development is the tendency for an initial 'f' to be voiced to 'v'. (This is not confined to Sussex, but can be found in other southern counties).[53] Some Sussex surnames consequently occur with an initial 'f' in some examples and an initial 'v' in others. For instance, the Sussex place-name Vinehall, in Mountfield,[54] has given rise to a surname which appears frequently in East Sussex during the 13th and 14th centuries as Finhagh, de Fynhagh, etc. The surname was already fairly common in East Sussex by 1400, with most instances being near Mountfield.[55] During the 14th century the form Vynagh was also used.[56] Forms with both initial 'f' and initial 'v' persist during the 15th century, with sometimes the name of a single individual being given in both forms.[57] In the 16th century, by which time the surname had become widespread in Sussex, the usual forms were Vynall, Vinall or Vynawe.[58] The surname persists in Sussex during the 17th and 18th centuries, usually in the form Vinall.[59] Vinall is still a common Sussex surname. Or, to take another example, the place-name Vinnetrow in North Mundham, earlier Feningetrowe, etc.,[60] is the origin of a surname which appears variously as Fyntrewe, Venitroe, Vennetree, etc.[61] The topographical surname Fairhall, not from any identifiable place-name, which is given in the 1332 subsidy as atte Fayrehale, appears later in a variety of forms, Fairhall, Fyrral, Verral, Virroll, Farrall and so forth.[62] Some of these forms, such as Fairhall, Fairall, Farrall, Verrall and Verrell have survived and now are to be found frequently in Sussex. In the 16th and 17th centuries the names of a single individual are often given in a confusing number of differing forms. Many other examples could be given where surnames in different categories are found at times with an initial 'f', at times with an initial 'v', and instances are frequent where the surname of one person is given sometimes with one initial consonant, sometimes with the other. In a few cases initial 'v' develops further into 'w'. For example, the surname Fining, derived from one of several places so named, appears also as Wynyng.[63] Instances where initial 'f' has developed into 'v', and less frequently into 'w', will be found in several chapters.

One further characteristic of Sussex surnames which needs to be mentioned is the tendency for the vowels used in any one surname to vary very greatly. Some variations can be explained in terms of sound changes in the Sussex dialect,[64] and in any part of England it is possible to find instances where the spelling of surnames is occasionally erratic, and this is true for any period up the 19th century, but in Sussex the variations in the vowels used in surnames appears to be more frequent than in most other regions, and to persist more often into relatively late periods, so that some surnames show a range of variant forms in the 16th, 17th and 18th centuries. It is not clear how far such variants are purely orthographic, and how far they reflect pronunciation. Out of many examples which could be given, the surname now usually spelt Strudwick, a common one in Sussex at the present day, and derived from Strudgwick in Kirdford, appears during the 16th and 17th centuries as Stradwick, Stridwicke, Strodewyke and Strudwick.[65] Similar variations occur in the name in Surrey at the same period.[66] The surname Brodnex, from a lost place in East Sussex, occurs in the 15th century as Bradenex, Brednex and Brodnex.[67] The surname Brickden (from one of several place-names in East Sussex), is given in the 16th century variously as Brakden, Brekden and Brokeden, though earlier the usual spelling was Brikeden, and although it seems probable that all the 16th century references concern members of one family.[68] Or, turning to occupational surnames, a single name occurs variously as Fruter, Fretour, le Friter and Frytour,[69] while another, derived from the office of beadle, appears during the 16th and 17th centuries as Bedell, Bidle, Bodle and Buddle.[70] The surname Dauber occurs also as Dubber, Dober and Daber,[71] and another Sussex occupational name is given as Dender, Dinder, Dunder, Thonder and Thunder.[72] The degree of variation found in vowels, even at fairly late periods, seems to be greater in Sussex than in other English counties outside the south-east. At times this makes it very difficult to be certain about the origin of some surnames. For example, it is difficult to be sure whether the surname Tapper, found in West Sussex in the 16th century, is a variant of the surname Tupper (or Topper), found in the same area in the same period and earlier.[73] Or, to give another example, the surname Bellingham, found in Sussex from the 15th century onwards, could be derived from Bellingham (Greater London), or possibly from Bellingham (Northumberland), but it is difficult to be sure that it is not from the Sussex place-name Billingham, (in Udimore).[74] Both Bellingham and Billingham exist in Sussex at the present time, but there are other possible origins for Billingham.

A feature of Sussex surnames and bye-names, observable from the 13th century onwards, is the tendency for names which normally have a terminal 'e' to occur in forms with terminal 'y', 'ey', or, less frequently, 'ie' or 'ee'. In many cases the names of single individuals appear, at times with a terminal 'e', at other times with a terminal 'y' or 'ey'. At least as late as the 17th century, it is still possible to find instances where the surname of one person is given sometimes with a terminal 'e', sometimes with 'y'. The results of this development can still be seen in Sussex today, when many surnames which would normally be expected to end in a final 'e' in fact end in 'y'. A few examples can be found during the second half of the 13th century. For instance, the topographical name Trendle or Trendell occurs in one 13th century example as Trendlee. This was at Nyetimber in Pagham, not far from the topographical feature from which the name was probably derived.[75] In another case, William Wylye, a taxpayer at or near Wiston in 1296, appears to be the same person as William atte Wyle, who was holding land in the area rather later. The surname atte Wyle persisted in that part of Sussex, and was probably hereditary there.[76] Similarly, the nickname type surname Legge occurs sometimes as Leggy. Robert Leggy, a taxpayer in 1296 at Imberhorne in East Grinstead, is the same person as Robert Legge, a taxpayer at East Grinstead in the 1327 subsidy. There seems to have been a family at East Grinstead in the 13th and 14th centuries whose name appears sometimes as Legge, sometimes as Leggy.[77] During the 14th and 15th centuries there are a number of further instances. William Julle, for example, a bond tenant at West Dean (West Sussex), early in the 14th century, is listed as William Jully in 1332. There seems to have been a family of serfs at and near West Dean with a name which is given sometimes as Julle, sometimes as Jully.[78] Apart from such cases, where the name of one individual appears in two forms, there are others where the two different forms occur at the same place, in such a way as to suggest that both forms were being used by a family with a hereditary surname. For example, the names le Bone and Bonye both existed as surnames or bye-names among the unfree tenants of South Malling manor in the 14th century.[79] The name Bonee is found in the same area in the 13th century, and Boneye appears there later in the 14th century.[80] The surname Cobbe, a fairly common Sussex surname derived from a nickname, existed in and around Icklesham in the 14th and 15th centuries, and in the 15th century the name Cobey appeared in the same area.[81] The name Pratte or Prat existed at Ticehurst in the 15th century, and the name Praty existed there at the same period.[82] The surname de la Mote or Mot was present at Sedlescombe in the 14th century, and was then common in that part of the county; later in the same century the name Motay occurs at Sedlescombe, and it survived there in the 15th century, and was still in the same part of Sussex in the 16th.[83] The name Motte also appears at Salehurst in the 15th century, and Motey existed at the same place in the same period. At Salehurst the form Moteys also occurs, apparently formed from Motey with an inorganic 's'.[84] There are also some doubtful cases. The name Lotty, found in the 15th century, may be a form of atte Lote, a topographical name fairly common in Sussex,[85] and Bondy, found at Chichester about 1360, may be a form of Bonde, another surname quite common in the county.[86] It seems likely that the surname Mori, Mory or Moury, found in Sussex from the late 13th century, is a form of atte More, a common and widespread surname in the county from the 13th century onwards. Morey and Moorey are still well established Sussex surnames at the present.[87]

Even during the 16th and 17th centuries, the surname of a single individual sometimes appears in both forms, with a terminal 'e', and with a terminal 'y' or 'ey'. For example, Nicholas Staple, a Litlington yeoman, also occurs, in 1597, as Stapley.[88] John Bode, a 16th century inhabitant of Hastings, is also given as John Boddy.[89] John Henle, a taxpayer in the Henhurst Hundred in 1524, is listed in 1525 as John Henly (a surname from one of the places called Henley, perhaps from Henley in Frant).[90] In this last instance, the form Henle may be a case of hyper-correction. In the same source, the Christian name Henry is sometimes spelt Henre.[91] In the 1524–25 subsidy, also, the topographical surname Wyske or Wiske (earlier atte Wiske or atte Wyseke, probably meaning 'at the meadow') is given sometimes as Wyske, sometimes as Wysky.[92]

The tendency for a terminal 'e' to become 'y' or 'ey' in Sussex complicates any study of the origins of surnames in the county. To give but one example, the surname Hony or Honey is often taken to be a nickname type surname in origin, and this may be correct in some cases, but in Sussex it may well be a form of the topographical surname Hone.[93] It must be presumed that spellings ending in 'y' reflect the phonetics of the local pronunciation of surnames. No attempt has been made to examine the situation in adjoining counties.

One other development which affects surnames in all the main categories and which should be mentioned here, is the tendency of some surnames to acquire a final 's' or 'es'. This development affects a considerable number of surnames, and cases can be found at relatively late periods, such as the 16th and 17th centuries, where the surnames of particular families are found in two forms, sometimes with a terminal 's' or 'es', sometimes without. This is not confined to Sussex, and the situation in some other counties has been discussed elsewhere.[94] This development is one which occurred in many parts of England, probably over most of the country, and it is one which operated over a long period, at least from the 14th century to the 17th. It has yet to be comprehensively studied, and the factors behind it are obscure. It is often in practice difficult to distinguish cases where a surname has acquired a final 's' or 'es' at some fairly late period from names which have a plural or genitive termination. This issue is discussed below in connection with surnames derived from personal names.[95]

DEVELOPMENT OF FRENCH NAMES FOUND IN SUSSEX

One characteristic of medieval Sussex surnames is the relatively large number of names which are French linguistically. Many surnames or bye-names appear in the county from the Conquest onwards which are derived from French place-names, and it must be supposed that these names either originated in France, or were acquired by Frenchmen after their settlement in England. In addition, occupational names which are French linguistically occur in some sources, notably in subsidy rolls, but it must be suspected that these were frequently the result of the clerks who drew up the documents in question having translated Middle English occupational names, used in speech, into French. Possibly some surnames or bye-names in other categories, such as topographical names, may also have been translated similarly.[96] It is, however, difficult to suppose that all or most of the French surnames or bye-names which are to be found in medieval Sussex can be explained on these lines, especially since some French surnames, apart from those derived from place-names, persisted as hereditary names in the county over long periods. This raises the question of whether such surnames always arose in France, and were present in England as a result of immigration, or whether some at least of the names concerned developed in England.

It is difficult to discover just how far the French language was understood or spoken in any one county during the 12th and 13th centuries, when most of the surnames or bye-names under consideration first appear in Sussex, and it is difficult to know what the position was about the knowledge of French among the different social classes. Some evidence suggests that in 12th century Sussex there was still a body of landholders who regarded themselves as specifically French, and not English. A charter of the Earl of Arundel *c.* 1160–76, was addressed to all his men, French and English, and especially those of Arundel Honour.[97] In about 1167 a Geoffrey Wastel was granted land in Sussex, and it was provided that it should descend to his heirs only if they were born of a 'normannigena' wife.[98] Such evidence suggests that in the second half of the 12th century there were landholders in Sussex who still thought that their status as Frenchmen and not Englishmen, was significant, and presumably they were people who regarded French as their mother tongue. However, no similar evidence has been discovered for the 13th century.

The constant trade across the Channel between the South Coast ports and France must have led to many mariners, merchants and so forth having some knowledge of French, and this may have led to some surnames which were linguistically French coming into existence in Sussex ports. It also seems possible that some Englishmen resident in the ports, and engaged in trade across the Channel, acquired French bye-names, originally in French ports, and subsequently became known by these names in England. This may explain the presence in the coastal parts of Sussex of people with surnames or bye-names such as *Anglicus*, Engleys, Engleterre, Engelond, etc.[99] It is likely that such names were bestowed in France, either on Englishmen who visited France frequently, or resided there for a time, or on Frenchmen who traded with England and in some cases settled here. Janyn English, a Frenchman resident in Sussex in 1443, was probably an example of this.[100] The surname Trenchmere, discussed later,[101] is an instance of a linguistically French surname which arose in a Sussex port during the late 12th century.

Another circumstance which suggests that linguistically French surnames in fact arose in England, is that serfs sometimes had French surnames or bye-names. For instance, the names Cachelow,[102] Belefaunte,[103] Belamy,[104] Bonsire,[105] Blanchard,[106] le Cras,[107] and le Ray[108] were all surnames or bye-names of serfs. It would perhaps be possible for Frenchmen to settle in England, and later to accept, or be forced into, servile status, but this could only have happened exceptionally, and cannot account for all the instances of serfs with French names. Personal names introduced after the Conquest had by the late 12th century become common in all social classes, and it is not therefore surprising that in the 13th and 14th centuries, some bondmen can be found with surnames from such personal names, but many serfs had French names in other categories. In a few cases surnames or bye-names which are given in French are obviously translations of Middle English names; for instance, the name le Ray or le Roy was in some cases a translation, made by clerks drawing up subsidy rolls, of 'King'.[109] However, not all French names of serfs can be explained as translations, particularly as some of them survived over long periods, and were evidently hereditary. It seems probable that in most cases those bondmen's surnames or bye-names which were French linguistically arose in England, despite the fact that unfree tenants are unlikely to have understood French. Possibly a few French phrases may have been understood by the unfree population. Possibly at times French soubriquets may have been bestowed on serfs by French speaking lords or bailiffs.

Beyond this, the number of surnames or bye-names, French linguis-

Introduction

tically, and derived from nicknames, to be found in Sussex is so large that it seems unlikely that they can all be the result of immigration, or of Middle English names being translated. A total of 175 French surnames or bye-names in the category have been found in Sussex before 1500, and even in a county where much immigration from France is to be expected, this figure seems too large for all the names concerned to have been brought in by migrants.[110].

It seems probable that some surnames which were French linguistically did develop in Sussex, even among sections of the community which are unlikely to have understood French. It is impossible to say how common this was, but it is unlikely that it was very rare.

The number and variety of surnames to be found in England during the 12th and 13th centuries are very great, and indeed the strongest impression left by examining the surnames and bye-names in use in almost any English county for the period between about 1100 and 1350 is simply that the number of names in existence was enormous. It is very exceptional during that period to find cases where a single township was dominated by, say, three or four surnames, or where surnames in any one category formed a majority of the names in use. This impression is reinforced if the limitations of the source material are borne in mind. It is unlikely that even the most diligent and comprehensive search through all the available sources would produce a list of half the inhabitants of any English county at any one date during the period 1100–1350. It is impossible to say how far the general picture we have of medieval surnames and bye-names might be modified if fuller information could be obtained, though the fact that when more complete, but still not exhaustive, information becomes available in the 16th and 17th centuries, the general impression of English surnames does not change greatly, suggests that the body of surnames and bye-names given in medieval sources is reasonably representative, however incomplete. It must, however, be reckoned that some surnames not recorded until after 1500 had existed from an earlier period, but were not documented before the 16th century.

The method adopted in this volume, and in the other volumes of the Surnames Survey, of considering surnames category by category, is intended to provide a framework within which the vast, and at first sight shapeless, mass of surnames and bye-names, to be found in any county, can be dealt with in an orderly fashion, thus enabling the general lines of surname development to be perceived.

Any work dealing with medieval surnames or bye-names has to face some difficulties caused by the variant forms for individual names given in the original sources. It is a common experience to find instances where the name of a single individual is given in several forms, each of which differs considerably from any of the others. Some of these variations are due to surnames or bye-names being badly mangled by scribes in spelling names which were unfamiliar to them. This is particularly the case with legal or administrative documents drawn up at Westminster, which must often have been written by clerks unfamiliar with the provincial names with which they were dealing. Many examples can be found in Sussex where scribes have spelt surnames or by-names erratically. For instance, many taxpayers in the county, listed in the 1327 lay subsidy, are also given again in the 1332 subsidy. A comparison of the two sources shows how some names become distorted in the subsidy rolls. For example, Robert Beaumond, listed at Parham and Greatham in 1332, is given as Robert Blamond in 1327;[111] Robert Barye, listed at Shoreham in 1332, appears as Robert Larie in 1327;[112] and Michael a Lyde, the bearer of a rare topographical name, listed at Horsham in 1332, is given as Michael Aside in 1327.[113] Many similar examples can be found, both in the two subsidy rolls just mentioned, and in other sources. Some instances are mentioned in later chapters. The existence of variant forms of surnames, sometimes the product of scribal errors, necessarily complicates research, and at times makes it very difficult to be certain about the origin of some surnames.

References

[1] See p. 318.
[2] *3 Suss. Subsidies*, p. 139, 145, 147, 159
[3] *Boxgrove Chartulary*, p. 193; *Lewes Chartulary*, vol. i, pp. 100, 101, 152.
[4] *3 Suss. Subsidies*, pp. 131, 294.
[5] *Chichester Chart.*, p. 156. For further examples, see p. 162.
[6] *V.C.H. Suss.*., vol. i, pp. 377–80. See also remarks by J. H. Round in *S.A.C.*, vol. lxxi, pp. 104–5.
[7] *Fitzalan Surveys*, pp. 38, 40; *Suss. Custumals*, vol. ii, pp. 4, 10, 98, 99, 101, 126, 137; *P. N. Suss.*, vol. i, p. 58; Reaney, *Dict.*, p. 88; *3 Suss. Subsidies*, pp. 169, 183, 197.
[8] *Fitzalan Surveys*, pp. 37, 147; Lane, *Suss. Deeds*, p. 19; *Suss. Subsidy, 1524–5*, p. 31; *W. Suss. 1641–2*, pp. 35, 61, 93, 94, 115, 125, 148; *Wiston Archives*, p. 117; *Feudal Aids*, vol. v, p. 165. And see p. 404.
[9] *Fitzalan Surveys*, p. 42; *3 Suss. Subsidies*, pp. 46, 176, 290; *Chichester Chart.*, p. 350; *Non. Inquis.*, p. 382.
[10] *Fitzalan Surveys*, pp. 40, 41, 137, 141, 142; *3 Suss. Subsidies*, pp. 69,

80, 143; *Suss. Custumals*, vol. ii, p. 116; Inderwick, *Winchelsea*, p. 159; B. Selten, *Early East-Anglian Nicknames: Bahuvrihi Names*, (1975) pp. 42–3; P.R.O. S.C. 11/877.

[11] *Battle Custumals*, p. 58; *3 Suss. Subsidies*, p. 62; D. M. Stenton, *Great Roll of the Pipe for the 8th Year of King John*, (Pipe Roll Soc., vol. lviii) (1942), p. 63; *Lewes Chartulary*, vol. ii, p. 67.

[12] M. T. Martin, *Percy Chartulary*, (Surtees Soc., vol. cxvii) (1911), pp. 1, 7, 15, 16, 45–8, 67–9, 87, 88, 90, 134–5, 390, 429.

[13] *S.A.C.*, vol. lxxxiv, p. 61; L. Fleming, *Hist. of Pagham*, (1949), vol. i, p. xxxvi; *3 Suss. Subsidies*, pp. 129, 252. The same man also seems to occur in Lancs.: J. Jönsjö, *Studies on Middle English Nicknames: I, Compounds*, (1979), p. 151.

[14] J. H. Bullock, *Norfolk Portion of the Chartulary of the Priory of St Pancras of Lewes*, (Norf. Rec. Soc., vol. xii) (1939), pp. 13, 53, 55, 56, 62, 65, 66, 69, 71.

[15] *Lewes Chartulary*, vol. ii, p. 65; *Lewes Barony Recs.* pp. 37, 43, 48; *3 Suss. Subsidies*, pp. 19, 151.

[16] *Fitzalan Surveys*.

[17] *Lewes Chartulary*; Bullock, *op. cit.*

[18] M. T. Martin, *op. cit.*

[19] P.R.O. E. 179/270/10.

[20] See p. 326.

[21] P.R.O. E. 179/235/2.

[22] *Ibid.*, and see p. 172.

[23] *Suss. Subsidy, 1524–5.*

[24] See e.g. the list given in *Cal. Pat., Edward VI*, vol. iii, pp. 248–52.

[25] *Suss. Subsidy, 1524–5*, pp. 97–99.

[26] *Ibid.*, pp. 22, 97, 164–5.

[27] *Ibid.*, pp. 97, 164.

[28] *Ibid.*, pp. 97, 130, 164.

[29] P.R.O. E. 179/235/2.

[30] See p. 158.

[31] Reaney, *Origins*, pp. 306–7.

[32] H.M.C. *Rye MSS.*, pp. 1, 40–41, 47, 50, 51, 62, 63, 78, 85, 87–90, 111, 125.

[33] E. Straker, *Wealden Iron*, (1931), p. 47; L. Williams, "Alien Immigrants in Relation to Industry and Society in Tudor England", *Proceedings of the Huguenot Soc. of London*, vol. xix, pp. 164–5; W. Page, *Letters of Denization, 1509–1603*, (1893), pp. 10, 20, 22, 66, 73, 74, 97, 106, 111, 116, 119, 125, 145, 148, 152, 171, 173, 181, 200, 202, 209, 223, 233, 236, 237, 249.

[34] G. H. Kenyon, *Glass Industry of the Weald* (1967), pp. 14–15, 124–145.

[35] P.R.O. E. 179/235/2; and see p. 269.

[36] Reaney, *Origins*, p. 22.
[37] The sources used: *3 Suss. Subsidies*; A. C. Chibnall, *Early Taxation Returns* (Bucks. Rec. Soc.) (1946); A. R. Rumble, *Dorset Lay Subsidy Roll of 1327*, (Dorset Rec. Soc., no. vi) (1980); H. A. Hanley and C. W. Chalklin, "Kent Lay Subsidy of 1334/5", in F. R. H. Du Boulay, *Documents Illustrative of Medieval Kentish Society*, (Kent Archaeological Soc., vol. xviii) (1964); J. P. Rylands, "Exchequer Lay Subsidy Roll", *Miscellanies Relating to Lancs. and Chesh.*, vol. ii (Lancs. and Chesh. Rec. Soc., vol. xxxi) (1896); P.R.O. E. 179/161/9; Anon., *Suff. in 1327* (Suff. Green Books, vol. xi) (1906); Anon., *Surr. Taxation Returns* (Surr. Rec. Soc, vol. xi) (1922, 1932); W. F. Carter, *Lay Subsidy Roll for Warws., for 6 Edw. III* (Dugdale Soc., vol. vi) (1926).
[38] *3 Suss. Subsidies*, pp. 35, 50–51, 66–68, 82, 109, 152–3, 183, 202, 225–29.
[39] *Ibid.*, pp. 102–5.
[40] *Suss. Custumals*, vol. i, pp. 4–11, 13–31, 33–9, 42–52, 54–61, 71–86, 88–92, 106–122. And see p. 13.
[41] *Surnames of Lancs.*, pp. 322–24.
[42] *Surnames of Oxon.*, pp. 216–9, 224–32.
[43] See pp. 318, 325.
[44] *Norf. and Suff. Surnames*, pp. 141–49; *Surnames of Lancs.*, pp. 442–3; *Surnames of Oxon.*, p. 68.
[45] *S.A.C.*, vol. liii, pp. 150–5. On the similar position in Oxon., see *Surnames of Oxon.* pp. 43, 199–200. And see p. 12.
[46] See pp. 105, 385, 397.
[47] *Book of Fees*, vol. ii, pp. 688–93.
[48] *Suss. Fines*, vol. i, *passim*.
[49] See pp. 52.
[50] *S.A.C.*, vol. xviii, pp. 17–36.
[51] *Suss. Subsidy, 1524–5*, pp. 59–85. The highest taxpayer in each place, however assessed, has been taken.
[52] See S. Rubin, *Phonology of the Middle English Dialect of Suss.* (1951).
[53] *Ibid*, p. 222; M. F. Wakelin and M. V. Barry, "Voicing of Initial Fricative Consonants in Present Day Dialectal English", *Leeds Studies in English*, (New Series) (1968) vol. ii, p. 62.
[54] *P. N. Suss.*, vol. ii, p. 476.
[55] *3 Suss. Subsidies*, p. 46, 206, 318, 333; *Hastings Lathe C. R.*, pp. 3, 4, 11, 12, 13, 14; *De Lisle and Dudley MSS.*, vol. i, pp. 131, 135, 147; *Non Inquis.*, p. 372; *Suss. Fines*, vol. iii, p. 202; *S.A.C.*, vol. xviii, p. 25.
[56] *3 Suss. Subsidies*, pp. 177, 291.
[57] E. Searle, *Lordship and Community*, (1974), pp. 365, 370; *De Lisle*

and *Dudley MSS*, vol. i, p. 153; *Robertsbridge Charters*, pp. 140, 142, 144.

[58] *Suss. Subsidies, 1524–5*, pp. 86, 90, 91, 104, 107, 129, 133, 153, 155, 156, 161, 162.

[59] *Wiston Archives*, pp. 48, 96; *S.A.C.*, vol. xxv, p. 131; *W. Suss. 1641–2*, pp. 95, 147; C. H. Wilkie, *St Andrews, Edburton, Suss.: Copy of the Parish Register Book, 1558–1673*, (1884), p. 31; P. S. Goodman, *Parish Register of Cowfold*, (Suss. Rec. Soc., vol. xxii) (1916), *per indice*.

[60] *P. N. Suss.*, vol. i, p. 75.

[61] *Suss. Subsidy, 1524–5*, p. 33; *W Suss. 1641–2*, pp. 35, 199; *3 Suss. Subsidies*, p. 128; H. A. Hanley and C. W. Chalklin, *op. cit.*, p. 86.

[62] *3 Suss. Subsidies*, p. 294; *S.A.C.*, vol. lviii, pp. 7, 20, 91; H.M.C., *Rye MSS*, pp. 24, 28; *Suss. Subsidy, 1524–5*, pp. 103, 104, 131, 132; *W. Suss. 1641–2*, p. 67; R. Garraway Rice, *Parish Register of Horsham*, (Suss. Rec. Soc., vol. xxi) (1915), pp. 32, 45, 274, 278; G. W. E. Loder, *Parish Registers of Ardingly*, (Suss. Rec. Soc., vol. xvii) (1913) *per indice*. And see pp. 188–89.

[63] *P. N. Suss.*, vol. i, pp. 39–40; *3 Suss. Subsidies*, pp. 76, 238, 259; *Non. Inquis.*, p. 362. See also the details of the name Fennell, or Venell, pp. 189–90.

[64] See Rubin, *op. cit.*, especially pp. 19–20, 27–8, 61–64,

[65] *Suss. Subsidy, 1524–5*, pp. 40, 41, 48; *W. Suss. 1641–2*, pp. 23, 30, 47, 48, 67, 90, 108, 109, 110, 115, 118, 120, 159, 195–6. And see p. 120.

[66] C. A. F. Meekings, *Sur. Hearth Tax, 1664*, (Surr. Rec. Soc., vol. xvii) (1940), pp. 146, 147.

[67] *Hastings Lathe C.R.*, pp. 54, 120, 121, 130, 132, 150, 151, 196.

[68] *Suss. Subsidy, 1524–5*, pp. 104, 129, 138, 139, 142; *Non. Inquis.*, p. 379; *Hastings Lathe C.R.*, pp. 30, 117; *P. N. Suss.*, vol. ii, pp. 353, 406, 478.

[69] See p. 251.

[70] See p. 261.

[71] See p. 262.

[72] Inderwick, *Winchelsea*, pp. 164, 207; *Wiston Archives*, p. 31; F. Hull, *op. cit.*, pp. 3, 4, 5, 10, 17, 20, 33; *Feudal Aids*, vol. v, p. 148; *3 Suss. Subsidies*, pp. 23, 104, 192; P.R.O. E. 179/225/5; E. 179/225/12. And see p. 263.

[73] *Suss. Subsidy, 1524–5*, pp. 22, 36, 37, 41, 45. And see p. 273.

[74] F. Hull, *op. cit.*, pp. 96, 103; *Suss. Fines*, vol. iii, pp. 281, 304; *Suss. Subsidy, 1524–5*, pp. 44, 53, 67, 106; *V.C.H. Suss.*, vol. vii, pp. 160, 207, 275–6, 279; P.R.O. E. 179/191/378, m. 1; *P. N. Suss*, vol. ii, 517.

[75] L. Fleming, *History of Pagham* (1949), vol. i, p. xl. And see p. 198.

[76] *3 Suss. Subsidies*, pp. 56, 57, 157, 158; West Suss. Record Office, E.P. VI/19A/1, m. 2. The surname is a form of atte Welle. See *Wiston*

Archives, p. 207. Wiley, Willey and Wyle survive as Sussex surnames to present.

[77] *3 Sussex Subsidies*, pp. 34, 202, 313; *Lewes Chartulary*, vol. i, p. 77.
[78] *Fitzalan Surveys*, pp. 28, 29; *3 Suss. Subsidies*, pp. 98, 242.
[79] *Suss. Custumals*, vol. ii, pp. 91, 125, 136.
[80] *Lewes Barony Recs.*, pp. 49, 53.
[81] *3 Suss. Subsidies*, pp. 213-4, 325; *Chichester Chart.*, p. 251; *S.A.C.*, vol. liii, p. 50; P.R.O. E. 179/225/5; E. 179/228/112.
[82] East Suss. Record Office, Dunn MSS, 1/19, 2/9.
[83] *Hastings Lathe C.R.*, pp. 117, 147; *Suss. Subsidy, 1524-5*, pp. 10, 151; *3 Suss. Subsidies*, p. 218.
[84] *Robertsbridge Charters*, p. 146; *Robertsbridge Surveys*, pp. 30, 56; *Hastings Lathe C.R.*, p. 144.
[85] *S.A.C.*, vol. ii, p. 322.
[86] *Chichester Chart.*, p. 222.
[87] *3 Suss. Subsidies*, pp. 26, 71, 83, 114, 157, 162, 185; *Suss. Fines*, vol. ii, p. 169; *S.A.C.*, vol. lxxxix, p. 159; *Non. Inquis.*, p. 351.
[88] Lane, *Suss. Deeds*, p. 112.
[89] F. Hull, *op. cit.*, p. 358; J. E. Ray, *op. cit.*, p. 33.
[90] *Suss. Subsidy, 1524-5*, p. 150.
[91] *Ibid.*, pp. 157, 158.
[92] *Ibid.*, pp. 45, 61; *3 Suss. Subsidies*, p. 185; *P.N. Suss.*, vol. i, p. 38; P.R.O. S.C.11/877; M. T. Löfvenberg, *Studies on Middle English Local Surnames* (1942), p. 233; *Suss. Wills*, vol. iii, p. 187.
[93] See p. 192.
[94] *Surnames of Lancs.*, pp. 207-10; *Surnames of Oxon*, pp. 49-51, 226-7.
[95] See p. 324.
[96] For an example, see p. 363.
[97] H. E. Salter, *Eynsham Chartulary* (Oxfordshire Hist. Soc. vol. xlix) (1907), vol. i, p. 82. Compare F. M. Stenton, *Documents Illustrative of the Social and Economic History of the Danelaw* (1920), pp. 33, 280, 336-7, 339, 356, 365, and *Somerset Rec. Soc.*, vol. xxxv, p. 57.
[98] *Boxgrove Chart.*, p. 155. Contrast the statements made about the difficulty of distinguishing between French and English in the late 12th century, in C. Johnson, *Dialogus de Scaccario* (1950), p. 53.
[99] *3 Suss. Subsidies*, pp. 63, 235; *Lewes Barony Recs.*, pp. 11, 19; *Lewes Chartulary*, vol. i, p. 163; *Boxgrove Chart.* pp. 62, 84; *Chichester Chart.*, pp. 82-83, 133; *Suss. Fines*, vol. iii, p. 297.
[100] *Hastings Lathe C.R.*, p. 35. See also H.M.C., *Rye MSS*, p. 30.
[101] See p. 407.
[102] *Suss. Custumals*, vol. i, pp. 10, 12.
[103] *Fitzalan Surveys*, p. 20.
[104] *3 Suss. Subsidies*, p. 103.

[105] *Fitzalan Surveys*, p. 128.
[106] *Suss. Custumals*, vol. i, pp. 48, 49, 111; vol. ii, pp. 91, 125.
[107] *Ibid.*, vol. i, pp. 75, 93.
[108] *Ibid.*, vol. i, p. 15.
[109] *3 Suss. Subsidies*, pp. 84, 124, 237, 242; *Suss. Custumals*, vol. i, pp. 12, 15; *Non. Inquis.*, p. 360.
[110] On the question of French surnames in England, see C. Clark, 'Certains éléments français de l'anthroponymie anglaise du Moyen Age: essai methodologique', *L'Onomastique, Témoin de L'Activité Humaine* (1985), pp. 259–67.
[111] *3 Suss. Subsidies*, pp. 147, 262.
[112] *Ibid.*, pp. 152, 227.
[113] *Ibid.*, pp. 153, 228.

CHAPTER 1

THE RISE OF HEREDITARY SURNAMES IN SUSSEX

In any discussion of the history of surnames in Sussex, one essential point to establish at the start is when hereditary surnames arose in the county. The evolution of hereditary surnames in England varies from one region to another, and within any region there are differences in this respect between one social class and another. It is necessary, therefore, to discover what the position was in Sussex in order to provide a framework within which the history of the county's surnames can be discussed. Hereditary surnames have to be distinguished from bye-names. Bye-names, in the sense in which the term is used in this work, were not hereditary, and frequently they were not stable, for one person might be known in the course of his or her life by several different bye-names. The only reliable way of showing that a surname was hereditary is through genealogical investigations into the history of individual families, to find out if the family had a name which was transmitted through several generations, for a sufficiently long period for the name to be recognisably hereditary. Normally, a name may be considered hereditary if it has been inherited through three successive generations, though cases do occur where a surname existed in a family for several generations, and was to all appearances hereditary, but was then abandoned, and replaced by another.

No example can be found of a hereditary surname in Sussex before 1066. At the time of the Conquest, some Norman aristocratic families had surnames which had already been inherited by one or two generations.[1] Out of the small number of lay tenants in chief for Sussex, mentioned in Domesday, two were the bearers of surnames which were to survive in the county for centuries. These were William de Warenne and William de Braose. In 1086 William de Warenne was the lord of most of the Rape of Lewes, and also of much land outside Sussex. The history and pedigree of his family has been discussed in published works at some length, and need not be recapitulated,[2] for what is in question here is the extent to which landowners in the county had hereditary surnames in the 11th century. William de Warenne, the Domesday tenant, and eventually first Earl of Surrey, was the son of Rodolfus de Warenne, a land holder in western Normandy.[3] William had an elder brother, another Rodolfus, who inherited lands in Normandy. William is given the name de Warenne in contemporary documents, including charters issued by himself.[4] The later use of the surname by William's descendants is complicated by his creation as Earl of Surrey at some unknown date, perhaps 1088. In consequence his son and heir, another William, often appears in documents of his own time with a title. The usage concerning titles was loose during the 11th and 12th centuries, and the younger William (second Earl of Surrey) occurs under various styles, 'William de Warenna comes Sudrie', 'Willelmus de Warenna comes', or 'Willelmus comes de Warenna'.[5] It seems reasonable to conclude from this that the second earl was using de Warenne as a hereditary surname. The surname is from a hamlet called Warenne (Seine Maritime).[6] The second earl was succeeded, at his death probably in 1138, by his son, another William (third Earl), who used the style 'Willelmus comes de Warenna', or, less frequently 'Willelmus de Warenna Comes'.[7] It might be difficult to say whether such usages can be taken as evidence of a hereditary surname being in use, but the third earl had two brothers, Ralph and Rainald (or Reginald), and both used the surname de Warenne.[8]

William, third Earl of Surrey, died in 1148, leaving as heir a daughter, Isabel, who married twice. It is difficult to say if she ever made use of what can properly be described as a surname. She is referred to in charters as Isabel 'Comittissa Warennie', but this is a title rather than a surname.[9] However, her son by her second husband was mentioned as William de Warenne before his succession to the earldom.[10] After his succession (as sixth Earl of Surrey) he used such styles as 'Willelmus de Warenna comes Surregie' or 'Willelmus comes Warennie'.[11] In this case the surname descended through a female, a course found in other cases during the 12th and 13th centuries where estates descended through heiresses.[12] It is not necessary to pursue the history of this well-known family further, so far as the senior branch is concerned. The Earldom of Surrey, with large estates in Sussex and elsewhere, descended to successive members of the family until the 14th century.

Junior branches of the family did not ramify greatly. Rainald (or Reginald) de Warenne, brother of the 3rd earl, held land in Sussex, and was sheriff of the county.[13] Rainald had a son, William de Warenne, who held land in Sussex and other counties in the late 12th century, and who died in or before 1209, when his land descended to a female heir,[14] so that the surname became extinct in this branch of the family. It does not seem that any other younger branch of the family was established in Sussex.

In 1086 William de Braose was the lord of much land in Bramber rape. The family name was derived from a French place-name, Briouze (Orne), where William and his successors continued to hold land for some time after the Conquest.[15] Willaim's father is known to have been named Philip, but it is not clear if Philip used the name de Braose,[16] and it must be doubtful if the name was hereditary before the Conquest. A Gosbert de Braiosa, mentioned in connection with Briouze under William I, may have been related to William,[17] and in that case the name may have been hereditary for a generation by 1066. William de Braose I was succeeded, on his death in about 1093–96, by his son Philip, who also used the surname de Braose.[18] Philip in turn was succeeded by his son, William de Braose II, who continued to use the surname de Braose.[19] It is not necessary to trace further the history of this major landed family in its senior branch, which continued to hold lands in Bramber rape, and other estates outside Sussex, until 1326, when the lands descended to female heirs.[20] It is, however, clear that the family had a hereditary surname which traced back to William de Braose who was granted lands in Sussex and elsewhere by William I.

Several younger branches of the de Braose family existed in Sussex. One branch held lands at Chesworth, near Horsham, Bidlington, near Bramber, and elsewhere in the county, during the 14th and early 15th centuries. The male line of this branch seems to have become extinct in 1418.[21] Another branch, of which the connection with the senior line is uncertain, was in possession of Wiston manor in the 14th and early 15th centuries. In 1357 a Peter de Braose had a grant of Wiston manor, and other lands in the same part of Sussex, from the king. The grant was made with a remainder to Peter, son of Thomas de Braose (of Chesworth).[22] This suggests that the Peter who obtained the grant in 1357 was related to the Chesworth branch of the family. The branch of the family which held Wiston, however, died out in the male line in 1426.[23] Several other persons named de Braose, Brewes, etc., can be found in Sussex during the 13th and 14th centuries,[24] but the connection of these individuals with the senior line of the family has not been discovered. So far as can be seen from the available sources, the family's surname did not survive in the county after the 15th century.

In fact both the de Warenne and de Braose families were major landowners in the county, without their surnames having become part of the surviving nomenclature of Sussex, and without either family having ramified very much. In this there is a contrast with the surnames of some families who were landholders in the county on a lesser scale. Apart from William de Warenne and William de Braose, none of the other lay tenants in chief of 1086 had surnames which survived in the county for any length of time. Roger de Montgomery, the lord in 1086 of much land in Chichester and Arundel rapes, was the son of an earlier Roger,[25] who is not definitely known to have used the name de Montgomery, which was almost certainly first assumed by the younger Roger. The younger Roger acquired an earldom in Sussex, and, subsequently, the Earldom of Shrewsbury, and he appears in Domesday Book simply as Earl Roger, without any bye-name being given. Earl Roger, at his death in 1094, was succeeded in his English lands by one of his sons, Hugh, who at times used the name de Montgomeri, though he often appears without any surname or bye-name.[26] Hugh had a (presumably younger) brother, Arnulf, who was known as Arnulf de Montgomeri.[27] Hugh died in 1098, and was succeeded by his elder brother, Robert, usually referred to in contemporary documents as Robert de Bellême ('de Bellismo').[28] (Robert was the count of Bellême, where he had inherited lands). It may be added that Hugh and Robert had two further brothers who survived into adult life, Roger (at one time a major landholder in the north of England), who was usually known as Roger the Poitevin (*Pictavinus*) and who had married the heiress to estates in Poitou, and Philip, known as Philip *gramaticus*.[29] It is clear from this evidence that the family of Earl Roger de Montgomery had not acquired a hereditary surname which was fully stable, and which was descending to all the members of the family. The position about the family name was still fluid, as might be expected at this early period. Robert de Bellême forfeited his English possessions, including those in Sussex, in 1102, but the history of the bye-names used by his family must be kept in mind when considering what the position was about the surnames of the larger landowners in Sussex during the late 11th and early 12th centuries.

A landowning family named de Montgomery existed in Sussex during the 14th century, and later. No connection has been traced between this family, and Roger de Montgomery who was holding land in Sussex and elsewhere in 1086.

Two other large landholders in Sussex in 1086, the Count of Eu and the Count of Mortain, are listed in Domesday under their titles, without any surnames or bye-names being given, and it does not appear that either of them came from a family then possessed of a hereditary surname. Two other lay tenants in chief in Sussex at the same date, Odo of Winchester and Eldred, were both relatively small landholders in the county. It is probable that the Eldred who was holding in Sussex in 1086 was the same person as the Eldred brother of Odo listed in the Hampshire Domesday,[30] and that Odo of Winchester and Eldred were brothers. In the 12th century the holdings of both Odo and Eldred came into the hands of families who do not appear to have been descended from either of them.[31]

The forfeiture in 1102 of Robert of Bellême's English possessions left his lands in the king's hands. The honour of Arundel, which included most of the Sussex lands once held by Earl Roger de Montgomery, passed eventually to Henry I's widow, Queen Adeliza, who married as her second husband William de Aubigny.[32] William was the son of an earlier William de Aubigny, who was holding land in Norfolk about 1092-95[33], and was granted further estates in that county by Henry 1.[34] The elder William was himself the son of Roger de Aubigny, living late 11th century, who was the son of an earlier William de Aubigny, living in the middle years of the same century.[35] The family name was therefore hereditary by the time of William de Aubigny, the husband of Queen Adeliza. William had an uncle, *Nigellus* de Aubigny, who was granted lands at Montbrai (Manche), and whose descendents used the surname Mowbray. The surname Daubigny was, therefore, not entirely stable in the first half of the 12th century.[36] The William de Aubigny who was the husband of Queen Adeliza, after having possessed briefly the earldom of Lincoln, was granted an earldom in Sussex. Earl William used various styles, included those of Earl of Arundel, Earl of Chichester, and Earl of Sussex.[37] His successors generally used the style of Earls of Sussex or Earls of Arundel. In this case too it is not necessary to follow the history of a well-known family further. The de Aubigny family retained the earldom, with estates in Sussex and other counties, until 1243, when the family lands passed to female heirs. The family surname was derived from Aubigny (Manche).[38] It usually appears in contemporary sources in a Latinised form, as *de Albini, de Albineia, de Albiniaco*, etc. In one instance the name appears as Daubeni, about 1096.[39]

Although the de Aubigny family was one of great importance in Sussex for more than a century, the family surname did not proliferate in the county to any great extent. A younger branch of the family was established in Bedfordshire, and a family named de Aubigny, holders of land from the Earl of Arundel at Hinton Daubeny (Hants.) from 1244 seem likely to have been another junior branch,[40] but the surname did not occur frequently in Sussex. A William Daubeni is listed as a taxpayer at Bignor, Coldwaltham, and Houghton in 1296. Judging from his assessment he was not a man of any great wealth. The surname survived at Bignor.[41] Richard Daubeny, listed at Rudgwick and Dunhurst in 1327, may have been related to William, but no connection has been traced,[42] and it is not known if either man belonged to the family who were Earls of Arundel. A John Daubenay or Daubene, living at Chichester in the late 14th and early 15th centuries, cannot be linked to anyone else of the name.[43] It is very doubtful whether the surname persisted in Sussex after 1500. Neither Daubeny, nor variants such as Dabney, can be found in the Sussex part of the 1524–25 subsidy.[44]

After the death of Hugh de Aubigny, in 1243, his lands were divided, and Arundel castle, with other Sussex holdings, fell to John Fitzalan.[45] The history of the Fitzalans, one of the most important of English aristocratic families, is well known. The family was descended from Alan, son of Flaald, who was holding land in Shropshire under Henry I, and who was a Breton by origin. It is not easy to say when the family acquired a hereditary surname. William and Walter, sons of Alan son of Flaald, were both referred to in their own lifetimes as '*filius Alani*', but this may have been merely a description of their parentage. However, William's son and heir, another William (and ancestor of the Fitzalans who later acquired Arundel) also appears as William '*filius Alani*', and in his case it must be supposed that the Latin phrase was a translation of his surname, which was in the process of becoming hereditary. The younger William's descendants usually appear in the 13th century with the description '*filius Alani*', and this must be a Latinisation of the surname Fitzalan. The family consequently already had a hereditary surname when John Fitzalan obtained Arundel and the other Sussex lands.[46]

The families which have already been mentioned were the most important aristocratic families to hold large estates in Sussex during the period between the Conquest and 1300. The families of de Warenne, de Braose, de Aubigny, and rather later Fitzalan, in particular, were all closely linked with the county for long periods, although all held large estates outside Sussex, too. Their surnames did not, however, ramify in Sussex in the way in which the names of some lesser, but more local, families did. Nevertheless, the existence of several very important families with large estates in the county, and in possession of hereditary surnames, must have had some influence on the attitudes of families of rather less wealth and standing towards the acquisition of hereditary surnames.

Hereditary Surnames of Knightly Families

It is obviously more difficult to trace the growth of hereditary surnames among the large body of middle ranking landholders than it is to deal with the few, and relatively well-documented, noble families. One source of difficulty at the start is that in Domesday the surnames or bye-names of sub-tenants are often omitted. This both makes it difficult to identify individuals in some cases, and means that in many cases Domesday does not provide evidence about the forms of names in use in 1086. In the Sussex Domesday the great majority of sub-tenants are listed without any surnames or bye-names at all, and usually by their personal names without any addition. It is not even easy to say what the total of sub-tenants in the county was in 1086, for when among the sub-tenants listed one personal name is found in several different places, perhaps dispersed geographically, and perhaps on the fiefs of more than one tenant in chief, it is sometimes difficult to be sure whether a single sub-tenant is involved, or several. Some light can be thrown upon such problems by other late 11th century sources, and from examining the holdings of sub-tenants as they existed at later periods, but such evidence is not sufficiently comprehensive to clear up all the problems. It is, therefore, not possible to make firm statements about, for instance, the proportion of sub-tenants who had hereditary surnames by 1086. Despite these difficulties, however, it is possible to produce some evidence about the extent to which hereditary surnames were developing among sub-tenants in the late 11th century.

Among the 1086 sub-tenants in the Sussex part of Domesday, there are, excluding tenants in chief who also appear as sub-tenants, nine with locative surnames or bye-names, William de Cahainges, Robert de

Hastinges, Ralph de Caisned', Robert de Cruel, William de Sept Mueles, Geoffrey de Floc, Robert de Olecumbe, William de Wateuile, and Robert de St. Leger.[47] Several of these men bore names that were to be prominent in the county for many years. Out of the sub-tenants just mentioned, William de Cahainges, whose name was from Cahagnes, near Bayeux (Calvados) was the founder of a family of which the members were major landholders in Sussex for two centuries, with the surname de Cahainges (de Kaienes, de Keynes, de Caines, etc.).[48] In this case the name of a sub-tenant in 1086 survived as a hereditary surname. No evidence has been found to show whether the surname was hereditary in Normandy before the William of 1086. The place-name Horsted Keynes preserves the family surname in Sussex, but although branches of the family were established in other counties, the surname does not seem to have survived in Sussex.[49] Robert de Hastinges was a tenant of Fécamp Abbey, with lands probably at Hastings. It is interesting to see that by 1086 he had already acquired a bye-name from his English possessions, but so far as can be discovered his name did not survive as a hereditary surname. The surname de Hastings does occur at Hastings, and at places nearby, during the 12th and 13th centuries, but it has not been possible to connect the later bearers of the name with the Robert of 1086. However, individuals named de Hastings appear from the early 12th century. Ingerannus de Hastingis witnessed several Norman charters early in the century,[50] Raimbert of Hastings is mentioned in connection with Hastings in 1106, Wiliam son of Robert de Hastings appears in Sussex in 1130–31, and Robert son of Ralph of Hastings occurs several times under Henry I. This Robert, who was still alive about 1128, is very unlikely to be the same person as the 1086 tenant, but was probably the Robert fitz Ralf, mentioned at Hastings in 1106.[51] It seems possible that some or all of these men may have been descended from the Robert de Hastings of 1086, but no pedigree can be established. Further people named de Hastings existed at Hastings later in the 12th century, but no connected pedigree can be drawn up linking them with any of those mentioned above, and it must remain an open question if the Domesday sub-tenant was the first of a line which had the name de Hastings as a hereditary surname, or not. Ralph de Caisned' was the ancestor of the de Cheney, or de Chesney, family. The family's surname is probably from le Quesnay (Seine-Maritime).[52] In 1086 Ralph was an important sub-tenant of William de Warenne both in Sussex and in Norfolk. No evidence has been found to prove whether or not the family's name was hereditary in Normandy before the Conquest. The family's name is found during the Middle Ages in a great variety of forms, de Caisneto, de Kainneto, de Chenei, de Cheyni, Cheney, Cheyne, Chenne, *de Querceto*, etc. Ralph, the 1086 tenant, was succeeded by a son, Ralph *de Querceto*,[53] and the younger Ralph was succeeded in turn by his son, John de Chaisneto (de

Caisneto, etc.).[54] This family, therefore, had a hereditary surname, descending from the Domesday sub-tenant. It is not necessary to pursue the history of this important family further. The family's surname ramified considerably in Sussex and in other counties. Although some of the persons who appear in medieval Sussex with surnames such as de Caisneto, de Chesney, etc., cannot be proved to be descended from the Domesday sub-tenant, it does seem probable that all the people who occur in Sussex with such surnames, and later with surnames such as Chesney, Cheney, Chenne, etc. were descended from the Ralph of 1086. Even if some of those concerned were, in fact, members of families with different origins, it is clear that the descendants of the Domesday sub-tenant did multiply in Sussex, and that this is one case, out of a number, where the surname of a landholding family proliferated in the county.[55]

Robert de Cruel had a bye-name derived from Criel-sur-Mer (Seine-Maritime).[56] The Sussex lands held by Robert de Cruel were later in the hands of holders not known to be descended from him,[57] but the name de Criol does occur in Sussex in the 12th and 13th centuries, though no connected pedigree can be traced from the Domesday sub-tenant.[58] The de Criol family survived as landowners in Kent.[59] Despite the difficulty of establishing a complete pedigree, it seems likely that this is another case where the name of the Domesday sub-tenant survived as a hereditary surname. It is uncertain if the surname Creall or Cryell, found at Hastings in the 15th and 16th centuries, is derived from de Criol, or whether it is from the Sussex place-name Cralle.[60]

Neither William de Sept Mueles nor Geoffrey de Floc passed on their names to any descendants in Sussex, so far as can be seen. The name *de Septemmolendinis*, which is a Latinised form of de Sept Mueles, existed in Normandy in the 12th century, and may have been hereditary there.[61] Robert de Olecumbe had a bye-name from Ulcombe (Kent). Ulcombe was held in 1086 by the Count of Eu, who was Robert's overlord in Sussex. Presumably Robert was, or had been at some time before 1086, a sub-tenant there. It is interesting that by 1086 Robert, presumably from his name a Frenchman, had already acquired a bye-name from an English place-name, but so far as can be seen he did not pass on his bye-name to any descendants. The name de Ulecumbe does occur in Sussex during the 13th century, but there is no known connection with the Robert of 1086, and the name was probably re-introduced into the county by migration from Kent.[62] William de Wateville, whose name was probably from Watteville (Eure), is not known to have been succeeded in his English lands by anyone with the same name.[63] A Robert de Watevill was holding land in Sussex by military tenure in 1197, and during the 13th and 14th centuries a family called de Watevill, probably Robert's descendants, were holding land at Billingshurst and elsewhere in Sussex.[64] It has not, however, been possible to trace any connection between these later de

Watevills, and the William of 1086, and it seems possible that the surname was brought into the county again from Normandy, perhaps by a family not related to the Domesday sub-tenant, especially as the later de Watevills were not holding lands held by William in 1086. Robert de St. Leger (whose name was probably from Saint Leger-aux-Bois, Seine-Maritime), is not known to have left any descendants, and the Sussex lands held later by the St. Leger family do not seem to have included the land held by Robert at Bexhill in 1086. The St. Leger family who held lands in Sussex and other counties from the 12th century were descended from a William de St. Leger (*de Sancto Leodegario*), who gave land at Broomhill to Battle Abbey, under Henry I.[65] William de St. Leger may have been the William (not given any bye-name) who was a subtenant in 1086 with lands in Wartling, Dallington, Hollington, Cortesley, and elsewhere, for these holdings were later held by the St. Leger family.[66] William de St. Leger's heir was Clarembald, whose relationship to William is unknown, and who is not known to have had any surname or bye-name,[67] but in the mid 12th century William de St. Leger's Sussex lands were being held by Rainald (or Reginald) de St. Leger.[68] Rainald had a brother, William de St. Leger,[69] another brother Thomas, and a third brother Godard.[70] It is not clear if Thomas or Godard used any surname, but Thomas may be the Thomas de St. Leger found in Normandy c.1160,[71] and listed as holding land in Sussex in 1166.[72] Rainald had a son, Geoffrey de St. Leger, who is not known to have left any issue.[73] The family possessions in Sussex descended to John de St. Leger, son of the Thomas de St. Leger (1166) already mentioned, and then to John's son, another Geoffrey de St. Leger, who was living under King John.[74] It is not necessary to pursue further here the history of the St. Leger family, who continued to be large landowners in Sussex and elsewhere,[75] but it is clear that the family had a hereditary surname from the early 12th century, and possibly from the William of 1086, though a complete pedigree cannot be traced. It was sometimes the case, however, in the 12th century that landed families had a hereditary surname which descended in the senior branch, but was not always used by junior branches, and there is an instance of this in the St. Leger family. In the late 12th century a William de St. Leger (probably the William who was a, presumably younger, brother of Rainald de St. Leger) had two sons, Roger de Swokenerse and William de Sokenerse, who were successive holders of Socknersh manor (in Brightling).[76] It is probable Socknersh had been sub-infeudated to William de St. Leger, as a younger son, and had then descended successively to his sons, who acquired a bye-name from the manor they held.

Apart from these 1086 sub-tenants with locative names, some sub-tenants in Sussex are listed in 1086 with surnames or bye-names in other categories. Several sub-tenants are given descriptions from ecclesiastical orders or ranks, such as *clericus, presbiter,* or *canonicus*,[77] but it seems probable that these were designations from positions in the Church actually held, rather than surnames or bye-names of any kind. At later periods, surnames from ecclesiastical ranks or offices are found frequently in most parts of England, and seem to have usually originated as nicknames,[78] but there is no evidence that any of the Sussex sub-tenants of 1086 had bye-names of such a type, or that any of the descriptions from clerical ranks or offices found in the Sussex Domesday became hereditary surnames. A few other bye-names derived from occupations or offices do occur among the Sussex sub-tenants; Robert *coquus*, Hugh *Arbalistarius*, Gilbert *vicecomes*, and William *miles* are cases of this.[79] It seems likely, however, that these, too, were derived from positions held in 1086 by the sub-tenants in question. Gilbert *vicecomes*, for example, seems likely to have been sheriff of Pevensey Rape.[80] No evidence has been found that any of these bye-names from office or occupation became hereditary. One Domesday sub-tenant in 1086, Roger Daniel, had a bye-name derived from a personal name.[81] Daniel was a fairly common surname in Sussex from the 13th century onwards, but it has not been possible to show any genealogical connection between the 1086 sub-tenant, and any of the later bearers of the name. Humphrey Flamme, a minor sub-tenant at Chichester in 1086,[82] had a bye-name, which was probably from a nickname, but in his case also the name cannot be shown to have been hereditary.

It would appear from this evidence that there were some 1086 sub-tenants with locative names which were transmitted to their descendants, and became hereditary, but that so far as can be seen from the evidence this was not true about sub-tenants with bye-names of other types. This leaves the question of how many sub-tenants there were who possessed bye-names or surnames, but who are given in the Sussex portion of the Domesday survey merely under their personal names. The fragmentary nature of the evidence available for the names of landholders in the late 11th and early 12th centuries makes it impossible to be sure how many such cases there were in the county, but some sub-tenants mentioned in the Sussex Domesday without surnames or bye-names can be identified with persons known from other sources to have had names which were, or became, hereditary. One of these, the de Pierrepoint family (*de Petroponte*, Perpond, etc) may have had a surname which was hereditary in France before the Conquest. The Godfrey, not otherwise named, who held land in 1086 from William de Warenne at Harpingden (in Piddinghoe), Ovingdean, Aldrington, and East Chiltington, and the Robert, also not further named, who held land from de Warenne at 'Herst' (now Hurstpierpoint), Westmeston, and East Chiltington, were probably the same persons as the Godfrey and Robert *de Petreponte*, who were de Warenne's tenants in Suffolk.[83] In the late 11th century Godfrey *de Petroponte* gave a hide to Lewes Priory at Aldrington, which was held in 1086 by 'Godfrey'.[84] Godfrey *de Petraponte*, his son William, and Robert *de Petraponte* all witnessed a charter to Lewes Priory, about 1100.[85] The William, son of Godfrey, just mentioned, was probably the William *de Petroponte* who gave land at Rottingdean, perhaps about 1100, to the priory; this land had probably formed part of Godfrey's estate of Ovingdean.[86] At some date after 1059, a Robert *de Petroponte* and his son Godfrey made a grant to the Norman abbey of Tréport. It seems possible that Robert and his son Godfrey were the Robert and Godfrey who were sub-tenants in both Sussex and Suffolk in 1086, but it has been suggested that the Robert who made a grant to Tréport may have been the father of the Robert of 1086[87]; if this were so, and it is impossible to be certain, then the Godfrey and Robert of 1086 would have been brothers, and would have been using a surname which had descended to them from their father. It is not possible to trace a complete pedigree of the Pierrepoint family during the 12th century, but it is clear that some of the lands held in 1086 by Robert *de Petroponte* in Sussex descended to other persons of the same surname,[88] and there is no doubt that there was a hereditary surname descending from the two sub-tenants of 1086, and possibly from a generation earlier.

A similar case is that of the family of Savage (*Silvaticus, Salvagius, le Sauuage*). In 1086 a certain Robert, not otherwise named in Domesday Book, held lands in Broadwater, Durrington, Worthing, Lancing, Ashington, Buncton, and Sompting, all from William de Braose as tenant in chief.[89] In the 13th century most of these lands were in the hands of the Savage family.[90] A Robert *Salvagius*, or *Silvaticus*, or *Silvatinus* was a witness to several late 11th century charters granted by members of the de Braose family,[91] and it is probable that he was the Robert who was a sub-tenant of William de Braose in 1086. In 1150 a Robert *Salvagius*, no doubt a member of a later generation of the family, was holding land at Durrington in demesne.[92] Several individuals named Robert *Salvagius* or Robert *le Sauuage* are mentioned in Sussex in the 12th and 13th centuries; it would seem that there were several men with the same first name, who held the family lands successively.[93] In this case a surname, derived from a nickname, was borne by a Domesday sub-tenant, and survived as a hereditary name among his descendants. The surname Savage has survived in Sussex, but the name is one which was widespread from an early date, and it is impossible to say if any descendants of the Savage family who were medieval landowners can still be found in the county.

It seems likely that the de Buci family had a surname which had been that of a sub-tenant in 1086. The early history of the family was discussed in detail by William Farrer, who concluded that a 1086 sub-tenant, Ralph, who held land at Shermanbury and Kingston-by-Sea was the ancestor of the de Buci family. It is not clear if Ralph himself ever used the name de

Buci, but a Robert de Buci, who occurs during the first half of the 12th century, seems likely to have been Ralph's son and heir. From this Robert the family had a hereditary surname.[94] The family surname was probably derived from Boucé (Orne).[95] A Robert de Buci was a tenant in chief in 1086, with holdings in the East Midlands, but no connection has been traced between this Robert and the Sussex family, despite the coincidence of the names.

The de Dive family were also prominent landowners in Sussex over a long period, and can be traced back to Domesday sub-tenants. The Boselin who held at Pevensey, under the Count of Mortain, in 1086, has been identified as Boselin *de Diva* and the William who held at Alfriston from the count has been identified as Boselin's son, William *de Diva*. Boselin had a brother, Hugh *de Diva*, who is mentioned under that name in a charter of 1056–57, so that the name *de Diva* was in use before the Conquest by the family.[96] It is not possible to trace a complete pedigree of the de Dive family during the late 11th and 12th centuries, but a succession of individuals named *de Diva* continued to hold lands in East Sussex, and it is reasonable to deduce that this represents the survival of a family with a hereditary surname.[97] The family continued to be landowners in the county during the 13th and 14th centuries. The family's surname was derived from Dives-sur-Mer (Calvados).

The 1086 sub-tenants mentioned above all had names which were transmitted to their descendants, and which became hereditary surnames in Sussex. Lack of sources for Normandy in the period before the Conquest makes it difficult to be sure how frequently such names were already hereditary in France before 1066, but it is unlikely, from what is known about the development of hereditary surnames in Normandy, that many of the names involved had been hereditary for long, if at all, before 1066.[98] It seems clear that some Sussex sub-tenants of 1086 did not have either surnames which were already hereditary, or bye-name which were passed on to their descendants to become hereditary surnames. The *Tezelinus* who held land in Perching and Fulking in 1086, for example, was succeeded by his son, who is named as William son of Techeline, without any bye-name.[99] No further descendants are known, but it is evident that there was no hereditary surname in the 11th century.

A similar case is that of *Aluredus* who was a tenant of the Count of Mortain at Pevensey and elsewhere in Sussex, and who also held lands from the count in other shires. Though given no bye-name in the Sussex Domesday, he occurs in the Lewes Chartulary as *Aluredus pincerna*,[100] a bye-name from his position as the count's butler. The son and heir of *Aluredus pincerna* was William usually mentioned as William son of *Aluredus*, and William was succeeded in turn by his son, Richard, referred to as Richard son of William son of *Aluredus*, or Richard son of William of Pevensey, or Richard son of William.[101] It is not necessary to pursue the history of the family further,[102] but in this case a Domesday sub-tenant and his descendants were without a hereditary surname during the 11th and 12th centuries. In another example, the Gilbert who was a sub-tenant at Clapham, near Worthing, in 1086, and who is not given any bye-name in Domesday, occurs elsewhere as Gilbert de Cleopeham, a bye-name from his English holding, and as Gilbert *de Sancto Audeono*, a name presumably from his place of origin in Normandy (probably St. Owen-sur-Maire, Orne). Clapham, and other lands in the same part of Sussex, were later held by a family named St. Owen (*de Sancto Audeona*, de Seyntoweyn, etc.), who were still landowners in that part of the county in the 15th century, and who must have been the heirs of the Gilbert of 1086.[103] In this case a hereditary surname seems to have been emerging in the late 11th century. Evidently the 1086 sub-tenant had a bye-name which was not altogether stable. The case is interesting as showing how Normans could acquire bye-names from their possessions in England within a short period after the Conquest.

It is impossible to say what proportion of Domesday sub-tenants possessed hereditary surnames, or bye-names which later developed into hereditary surnames. Obviously there was no uniformity in the matter. If the evidence for the late 11th century was more complete, it might be possible to show that rather more of the 1086 sub-tenants had hereditary names than can now be seen to be the case, but even allowing for this it remains clear that some important sub-tenants were without hereditary surnames in 1086, and that in some cases their descendants were without such surnames for several generations.

In the late 11th and early 12th centuries a number of landholding families appear in Sussex with hereditary surnames, some of which were to have a long history in the county. In some of these cases it is clear that families did not acquire hereditary names until after about 1100, but in others the start of hereditary names cannot be traced, and it is possible, especially where surnames are derived from French place-names, that there may be instances where the beginnings of surnames date back either to the period immediately after the Conquest, or to before 1066. In Sussex there were a number of knightly families in the 12th and 13th centuries with surnames from French place-names, in addition to the Domesday tenants in chief and sub-tenants already mentioned. One such was the family of Pointell. Robert *de Punctello* was mentioned as a man of William de Braose, in Normandy, probably in 1093, and William de Puintel witnessed a charter of Philip de Braose concerning Bramber and Sele (in Upper Beeding).[104] It has been supposed that the surname Pointel is derived from a personal name, or from a nickname,[105] but in the above two examples the name is clearly from a place-name. The place in question is Pointel (Orne), which is near Briouze.[106] Ralph Pointel witnessed a deed concerning lands in Sussex and Normandy in 1160,[107] and Adam Puntel was holding lands in East Dean (West Sussex) and Garston in 1199–1200.[108] About 1220 Robert Pointel possessed land in Offington (which was in the de Braose Rape of Bramber), and subsequently during the 13th and 14th centuries a succession of persons named Pointel appear as holders of land at Offington.[109] Though no pedigree can be drawn up, it seems from this evidence that there was a family named Pointel in Sussex, with a hereditary surname, from at least 1160, and that the hereditary name probably goes back to the late 11th century. The surname ramified to some extent in the county, and in the late 13th and 14th centuries it appeared at several places near Offington.[110] The surname occurs in the 14th century at East Dean, where Adam Puntel had held land, as the name of serfs.[111] It was also the name of a cottar at Preston (near Hove) in the late 13th century.[112] Instances of serfs having the surnames of local landholding families are known from other parts of England, and these are further examples of the phenomenon, which is not easy to explain, though such serfs may have been the illegitimate issue of landowners.[113] The name Pointel or Pyntel also existed from the late 13th century around Seaford,[114] but so far as can be seen the people found with the surname in that part of the county were not connected with the family who held land at Offington.

The family of Scotney has been said to be descended from Walter son of Lambert, a sub-tenant in 1086 of the Count of Eu at Sedlescombe and Crowhurst, but no adequate evidence has been adduced for this, though the Scotney family were Walter's successors in title at both places.[115] A Lambert de Scoteigny, who was holding land from the Bishop of Lincoln (not in Sussex) about 1160 and later, and who was a tenant in chief in Kent in 1166, seems to have been related to the Sussex Scotney family. Other persons named Scotney, etc., held land in Lincolnshire, including Peter de Scotney, who may be the same person as the Peter who held land in Sussex.[116] The use of the first names Walter and Lambert by the Scotney family might suggest a connection with Walter son of Lambert, but hardly amounts to proof of descent from him. The surname Scotney is from Étocquingny, near Eu (Seine-Maritime).[117] An *Inguerranus de Esscotengiis* witnessed a charter of Henry, Count of Eu (the lord of Hastings Rape), in 1106, concerning Hoo. Ingelram de Scoteney, perhaps not the same man, at some date before 1140 gave land to St. Mary's, Hastings, which had been founded by one of the Counts of Eu.[118] Ingleram was probably the same person as the *Engerranus de Scoteni* who witnessed several Norman charters of John, Count of Eu, about 1150.[119] Walter de Scoteigni was holding land at Sedlescombe and at Hazelhurst in Ticehurst, about 1180.[120] Walter was already holding land in Sussex in 1170.[121] Walter was succeeded by his son, Peter de Scoteigni, who in 1211–12 was holding nine knights' fees in Sussex with the duty of serving as the standard bearer of the Count of Eu.[122] Peter's descendants continued to hold land in East Sussex.[123] It seems likely that the Scotney family acquired the lands of Walter son of Lambert, early in the 12th century, under circumstances that cannot now be discovered.

In this case a hereditary surname existed from before 1140, and perhaps from the early 12th century, though it is not known how or when the Scotney family acquired lands in England. The execution of Walter Scoteney in 1259, and the consequent forfeiture of his lands, brought to an end the history of the family as major landowners in Sussex,[123] but the surname survived in the county. It had already ramified to some extent by the early 13th century; a Thomas and William de Scoteigni are mentioned in 1212, and a Henry de Scotiniis witnessed a deed concerning Sedlescombe in about 1216.[125] Three persons named de Scoteney were among the inhabitants of Winchelsea in 1292, and in 1327/8 a Benedict Scoteney was a taxpayer at Udimore.[126] These places are near Sedlescombe, but the surname also appeared in West Sussex. A William Scoteney held land at his death about 1260 at Rumboldswyke, near Chichester.[127] A Richard Scoteney is mentioned at Chichester in 1357, and a William Scoteny was a taxpayer at Parham and Greatham, in West Sussex, in 1327/8.[128] No connected pedigree can be traced to link all these individuals together, but it is often difficult to trace younger branches of landholding families in the Middle Ages. Though the surname Scotney has never become common, it has survived to the present day in Sussex, and in the Portsmouth area of Hampshire, just outside Sussex.

The Scotney and Pointel families both had surnames derived from French place-names. There are some other families of landholders in Sussex with surnames, derived also from French place-names, which were hereditary from the first half of the 12th century. The history of many of these families has already been discussed in print, and need not be examined in detail here. One important family, that of de Laigle (usually Latinised as *de Aquila*) became tenants in chief in East Sussex under Henry I. The family's surname was derived from Laigle (Orne).[129] Gilbert *de Aquila* was granted lands in the county by Henry I. The family already had a hereditary surname by Gilbert's time.[130] Gilbert's descendants continued to be tenants in chief in Sussex until the 13th century, and continued to use the family's hereditary surname. This is usually given in contemporary sources in the Latinised form *de Aquila*, but occasionally vernacular forms such as del Egle can be found.[131] In this case the family had a hereditary name before it acquired Sussex lands in the early 12th century. The de Clere family held lands at Atlingworth, in Sussex, with lands in Hampshire and Yorkshire, from the 12th century. The family was established in Sussex by about 1140, and the surname was hereditary at least from that period onwards. The name de Clere did exist in Normandy before the Conquest, and it may have been hereditary from the 11th century. The surname is probably from Cleres (Seine-Maritime).[132] A surname variously spelt Clere, Clare, or Cleares (with an inorganic 's') existed in Sussex during the 15th, 16th, and 17th centuries, but it is not possible to link these later examples with the landowning family found in the 12th and 13th centuries, and there was evidently some new migration into the county, for one of the 16th century persons named Clere was an alien.[133] The le Fleming (Flameng, *Flandrensis*, etc.) family of Pulborough had a hereditary surname from the first half of the 12th century.[134] There are no grounds for thinking that all those who are found in Sussex with the name Fleming are connected with this family. Individuals with the name, who cannot be linked with the landowning family, oocur in the county during the 12th and 13th centuries, and some of those called Fleming noted in the county at later periods were aliens, and presumably immigrants from Flanders.[135] Ancel *de Fraelvilla*, who was holding land at Playden early in the 12th century, and who was a benefactor of Battle Abbey, was the son of Richard *de Fraevilla*, and the grandson of Robert *de Fraelvilla*. Roger *de Freelvilla*, living in 1170, was probably Ancel's son. The family name is from Freulleville (Seine-Maritime), where Ancel held lands.[136] A family named Friville (*de Freivill'*, de Frollouill, Fryvill, etc.), who appear as witnesses to charters of the Earls Warenne, in Sussex and elsewhere, from *c.* 1130 onwards, and who were holding land in the Brighton area from the late 12th century, and probably earlier, have no connection that has been traced with the family who held land at Playden. It seems clear, however, that the Friville family had a hereditary surname from the first half of the 12th century.[137] The de Hautrive family (*de Alta Ripa*, Dautryve, later usually Dawtrey), from Hautrive (Orne), were also established in Sussex before 1150. Robert *de Alta Ripa* appears as a witness to charters concerning West Sussex from about 1140, and his son, William *de Alta Ripa*, obtained a grant of lands belonging to the Honour of Petworth.[138] The family continued to hold lands in West Sussex, and the surname later ramified considerably in the county.[139] The de Plaiz family of Iford had a hereditary surname from the early 12th century. Ralph de Plaiz gave Iford church to Lewes Priory. He was succeeded by his son, Hugh de Plaiz. The de Plaiz family acquired lands held in 1086 by Hugh son of Golda, but it is not certain if they were related to him in any way.[140] Though the pedigree in the late 12th century is not altogether clear, Iford and other Sussex lands remained in the hands of the de Plaiz family during the late 12th, 13th and 14th centuries.[141] In this case, too, there was a hereditary surname from the first half of the 12th century. The de Vilers family, who held the manor of Treyford from the 12th century, were a younger branch of a Lancashire family, which had a hereditary surname from the early 12th century, and perhaps from the late 11th.[142] The family's surname is from a French place-name, not identified.[143]

The position about the de Haye family, whose surname was derived from La Haye-du-Puits (Manche), is not altogether clear. Robert *de Haia* acquired lands in West Sussex, at some date before 1105.[144] His Sussex estates included Hunston. Robert's father, Ranulf, is not known to have used the name *de Haia*. Robert's grandfather was Richard, who was presumably living in the middle or late 11th century, and who may be the Richard *de Haia* mentioned in a later confirmation.[145] It is possible, therefore, that Robert *de Haia* had a hereditary surname which went back to the 11th century, but this is uncertain. Robert had a son, also a Richard de Hai.[146] This Richard had a nephew, Ralph *de Haia*.[147] It would appear from this that the *de Haia* family had a hereditary surname, at least by the first half of the 12th century. From the late 12th century the manor of Hunston was held by a family named Hai or Hay. It has been suggested that this family was related to Robert *de Haia*. Although this is probable, there is no proof of it.[148] The later surname Hay has more than one origin, and is in most cases not connected with the family under discussion here.[149]

All the families just mentioned had surnames derived from French place-names, and all had hereditary surnames established in Sussex before about 1150. Besides the families mentioned, there were several others, with surnames from French place-names, who held land in Sussex, but which also had large holdings elsewhere, more important than their Sussex lands, such as the families of de St. John or de Crevequer, for example. There were also some families with surnames from French place-names, with surnames already existing from before *c*. 1150, who are not found in Sussex until a later period, such as de Wancy or de Bavent, for instance. Were more evidence available for the late 11th and early 12th centuries, both in England and in Normandy, it might well be possible to trace rather more names back to before *c*. 1150, and to establish that there were more hereditary surnames in existence by that date than appears from the very limited evidence that there is. However, it is clear that by the mid 12th century there were already in Sussex quite a number of landed families with surnames from French place-names. These must either have been formed in France, or they must have developed and become hereditary in England while the links between the families in question, and their places of origin across the Channel, were still known, and probably while the families concerned retained possession of their lands in France.

There were, in addition, a smaller number of knightly families with surnames, hereditary by about the mid 12th century, which were surnames of the nickname type, and which were French linguistically. One of these was the Aguillon family, descended from Manasser Aguillon, living about the middle of the 12th century. Manasser had three sons, and during the late 12th and early 13th centuries the surname ramified in Sussex. The pedigrees of the different branches of the family cannot be disentangled with certainty. The name Aguillon also occurs in

Yorkshire, on the estates of the Percy family. As the Percys also held lands in West Sussex, where the Aguillon family were landowners, the presence of the name in Yorkshire may be due to this tenurial connection.[150] The meaning of the surname is 'sting', as in an insect's sting. The occasional use of the Latin word *aculeus* to translate the surname shows that it was understood in this sense by contemporaries in the 12th century.[151]

The family of Tartcurteis (Talecurteys, Tardcorteys, etc)., appears to have had a hereditary surname from the early or mid 12th century, though the early stages of the pedigree are not clear. A William Tarcortais occurs about 1150. In 1166 he was a tenant by knight service of the Bishop of Chichester.[152] Adam Talcurtes, who was holding the manor of Wyckham (in Steyning) in 1228, claimed then that the manor had long been held by his ancestors. This is a vague phrase, but Adam had been in possession of land at Wyckham under Richard I, and it is probable, in view of the rarity of the name, that he was a descendant of William Tarcortais.[153] Adam was succeeded at Wyckham by Philip Talcurtes, who appears with him in 1230, and who was probably his son.[154] Various persons named Talcurtes, etc., who occur in the part of Sussex around Wyckham in the late 13th and the 14th centuries are likely to have belonged to the same family, though no pedigree can be traced.[155] The surname also existed in the 13th century on the Percy estates in Yorkshire.[156] The surname signifies 'slow courteous' no doubt originally a nickname for an ill-manered individual.[157] Another surname derived from an uncomplimentary nickname is one which appears in Sussex in the 12th century as Malfet, Malfed, or Malfei. A William Malfed or Malfeth made grants to Lewes Priory, and witnessed several charters concerning the priory, in about 1130–50.[158] William was succeeded in his lands, at Chiddingly and elsewhere in East Sussex, by his son, another William Malfed, and then by his grandson, a third William, who was in possession of the family holdings early in the 13th century.[159] The family continued to be landholders in Sussex and elsewhere, and the surname later ramified considerably in the county. The name underwent changes at a relatively early date, which obscure its origin. The third William, just mentioned, appears early in the 13th century, as William Maufe, and his father and grandfather are mentioned in 13th century documents with their names in the same form.[160] During the 13th and 14th centuries Maufe is the most commonly found form of the family's surname, though other forms, such as Maufai, Maifai, Malfe, and Mafey appear.[161] All the persons who appear in Sussex with the name Maufe during the Middle Ages appear to be members of this landowning family, and it is evident that in Sussex at least the surname Maufe is derived from a name which occurs in the late 12th century as Malfeth, Malfei, etc. As the family concerned also held land in Northamptonshire, it seems likely that the instances of the surname Maufe found in that county have the same origin.[162] It has been suggested that the surname Maufe is derived from the Middle English *maugh* ('relative by marriage'),[163] but this is not the case in Sussex, and probably not in at least some other counties. Maufe has not been found as a surname in medieval Lancashire, though that is a county where surnames formed from compounds of *maugh* were more common than in most parts of England. On the other hand, forms such as Morfey or Morphew, which are said to be developments of Malfet, etc., have not been found in Sussex.[164] From the 12th century forms found in Sussex, it seems probable that the surname Maufe is from 'mal fait', 'ill made.'[165] As is often the case with surnames of the 'nickname' type, the circumstances in which the name arose remain unknown.

One or two other knightly families may have had surnames of the nickname type which were French linguistically, and which went back to the first half of the 12th century. The Sansaver family may be such a case. Ralph Sansaver, who was living *c*. 1170 and later, held lands in West Sussex which had been held by his father, William, in 1135. Ralph's grandfather, Hugh, had also held lands in West Sussex.[166] There is, however, no evidence that either Hugh, or William, though Ralph's ancestors, used the name Sansaver, and the beginnings of the name in Sussex remain uncertain.[167] Sansaver occurs as a bye-name in Norfolk early in the 12th century, but no relationship can be established between the individuals concerned in that county, and the Sussex family.[168] Another family with a surname of the 'nickname' type was that of le Count (le Conte, le Cunte, *Comes*). As no members of the family were counts or earls, the surname is evidently one of the numerous class of surnames, derived from high lay or ecclesiastical ranks, which originated as nicknames.[169] It has been supposed that the family was descended from a Domesday sub-tenant, but there is no proof of this.[170] A Simon *Comes* witnessed a deed of Philip de Braose, about 1096, and a Simon *Comes*, probably not the same, but likely to be the son of the earlier Simon, witnessed a charter about Bramber, in 1125–47.[171] The Simon of 1125–47 presented a William *Comes*, presumably a relative, to the church of Southwick.[172] Early in the 13th century the lands which had been held by Simon (1125–47) were in the hands of a descendent, John le Cunte, said to be Simon's grandson.[173] In this case there was a hereditary surname from the first half of the 12th century, and possibly from the end of the 11th. The family survived as landowners in Sussex during the 13th century, and it is probable that the persons who appear in the area around Bramber in the 14th century with the surname Counte or Conte were in fact descendants of this family.[174] A family named Hose (or Husse), whose surname may have been a nickname, had a hereditary surname from before 1100.[175]

It would be unwise to assume that such surnames must have originated in France, for surnames which were linguistically French might arise in

England.[176] It must be suspected, however, in the case of names which are found in England in the late 11th or early 12th centuries, and which are French linguistically, that they did originate in France. In this connection it is significant that Simon *Comes* (of *c*. 1096) was the witness to a charter for a Norman monastery, and that the surnames Aguillon and Malfet both existed in northern France.[177] One or two other families with hereditary surnames (derived from names which are French) going back to before 1150 appear in Sussex at later periods, though not found in the county until after the mid 12th century. For instance, the family of Haringod (Herigaud, Heringaud, Harengod, etc.), whose name was of the type in question,[178] and who were descended from a Domesday sub-tenant holding in Kent,[179] held land in Sussex from the late 12th century.[180]

There were thus some knightly families in the first half of the 12th century with hereditary surnames derived from French place-names, and a smaller number of such families with hereditary surnames which were French linguistically, but not derived from place-names. The relatively high proportion of families with hereditary surnames derived from French place-names is significant in considering the factors which led to families acquiring hereditary surnames in the first place. It was already the case, however, before the middle of the 12th century, that some knightly families were coming to have surnames from the names of places in England where they had landed possessions. It has been pointed out above that in 1086 there were already instances in Sussex of sub-tenants with bye-names from English place-names.[181] During the period between Domesday and the mid 12th century more such instances appear.

Some examples of such families can be given. One of these was the Poynings family, long prominent in Sussex and in national affairs. In 1086 Poynings, with Pangdean and other Sussex lands, was held from William de Warenne by William son of Rainald, who also held from de Warenne in Norfolk. Rainald (presumably dead by 1086), must be the same person as the Rainald son of Renner son of Reidi, who gave the tithes in Pangdean to Lewes Priory.[182] Rainald is also referred to (at a later date) as Rainald de Puninges.[183] By *c*. 1140 Poynings and Pangdean were in the hands of Adam de Poynings.[184] Adam's descendants were later holding land from the Earls de Warenne in Norfolk.[185] Though Adam was the successor of William son of Rainald, there is no proof that he was William's descendant. William, and his father Rainald, were clearly without a hereditary surname. Adam was succeeded by his son, another Adam de Poynings. The elder Adam also had other sons, William and John, probably the John de Poynings who occurs as a charter witness.[186] The younger Adam was succeeded in turn by his son, Michael de Poynings. There is no need to consider here the family's later history, which has been discussed in print in several works.[187] In this case a landed family, possibly descended from a Domesday sub-tenant, acquired a hereditary surname which originated before the mid 12th century.

Another case is that of the family which took its name (de Essete, de Excete, etc.), from Exceat, in West Dean (East Sussex). This family, exceptionally, was descended from a pre-Conquest tenant. In 1086 Chollington, Sherrington, Exceat and Frog Firle were held by Haiminc, who had held the same lands (together with Rottingdean, which he had lost after the Conquest), under the Confessor.[188] His son appears, early in the 12th century, as Richard *filius Hemmingii*, Richard *filius* Hemming de Essete, and Richard de Exsete.[189] Richard was succeeded in turn by his son William, who is mentioned as William son of Richard de Esset, William de Esseta or de Esete.[190] In this instance a family which was English in origin had adopted after the Conquest both first names, such as Richard and William, which had been brought in by the invaders, and the practice of using a hereditary surname, derived from the name of a place which was, presumably, the family's principal residence. Though a pedigree cannot be traced further, persons named de Exsete, de Essetes, etc., appear as holders of land at Exceat and other places nearby during the 13th century, and were probably the descendants of Richard de Exsete.[191]

Another family which acquired a locative surname from an English place-name during the first half of the 12th century was that of Echingham. This family, too, was perhaps descended from a Domesday sub-tenant. In 1086 a considerable estate was held in Hastings Rape by Reinbert, from the Count of Eu. Reinbert's heir was a certain Drogo, whose relationship to Reinbert is not known.[192] Drogo was probably the same person as Drogo de Pevensel (Pevensey), who is mentioned in Sussex under Henry I.[193] Simon de Echingham, the first person known to have used that name, is also mentioned as Simon son of Drogo.[194] It has been presumed that Simon must have been the son of Drogo of Pevensel. This is probable, but there is no proof of it, and as the name Drogo (Dru, Drew) was fairly common in the 12th century, the assumption is not altogether safe. Simon de Echingham was succeeded, in or shortly before 1167, by his son, William de Echingham, and William in turn by his son, another Simon de Echingham.[195] The Echingham family remained in possession of Etchingham, and other lands in East Sussex, for many years subsequently.[196] In this case also, a family which was probably descended from a Domesday sub-tenant acquired during the 12th century a hereditary surname from an English place-name.

It would be possible to deal with more cases of knightly families from Sussex who possessed hereditary surnames going back to before the mid 12th century, but space would not permit a detailed consideration of all the early medieval landholding families in the county, and in any case the incomplete nature of the evidence for the period from 1086 to *c.* 1150 makes it impossible to form any precise view of what proportion of knightly families in Sussex had hereditary surnames by *c.* 1150. There were certainly some which did not. For much of the 12th century Midhurst and other Sussex lands were held by a family, later known as de Bohun, from St. Georges de Bohun (Manche), which for most of the century did not use a surname or bye-name.[197] However, in addition to the families already discussed, there are others in Sussex with hereditary surnames which go back to before the mid 12th century. There are also, as already mentioned,[198] some families, with surnames derived from French place-names, whose names cannot be traced back in Sussex to before c. 1150, but who are known to have existed, with hereditary surnames, in other counties from before that date. In addition, some knightly families with surnames from French place-names can be found in Sussex during the second half of the 12th century, and the early 13th, which have not been discovered in the county earlier, but which may have existed there, with hereditary surnames, from an earlier period. These include such families as that of Bassoch, of Sedlescombe (with a surname from a French place-name),[199] a name that long survived in East Sussex; de Covert, another surname which has persisted in Sussex over a long period;[200] de Cressi, a family who held Rottingdean (and much land outside Sussex[201]); de Crevequer, a family who held lands in East Sussex and Kent from c. 1155;[202] de Scardeville (later Scarfield) a name present in Sussex from the 13th century, and one which later proliferated in the county in several variant forms;[203] de St. George, a family which held land at Didling, Dumpford, and elsewhere in West Sussex, from the 12th century;[204] or de Tregos (de Tresgos, Treisgoz, etc.), a family which appears in Sussex from the middle of the 12th century, which held land at and near Goring, and which had a surname which ramified in Sussex later,[205] and still survives there.

The general impression left by examining the evidence for the pedigrees of many Sussex knightly families, and from reading the manorial descents set out in the topographical volumes of the *Victoria County History of Sussex*, is that the majority of knightly families in the county already had hereditary surnames by the late 12th century. The proportion of such families which had hereditary surnames traceable to before the mid 12th century seems to be higher than in most other counties, though this may owe something to the fact that there is more evidence for Sussex for the period from 1086 to c. 1150 than there is for some other parts of England. The impression is also gained that the proportion of knightly families with surnames from French place-names is higher than in many other parts of the country, though in the absence of detailed studies for all the other counties it is difficult to be certain about this. It is not easy to support these rather general remarks with precise statistics from any source, but some conclusions can be drawn from an examination of the *Cartae* of 1166 for Sussex. These list tenants-in-chief, and their sub-tenants holding by knight service. The record of the *Cartae* for Sussex is incomplete, but it is likely that it provides a reasonably representative sample.[206] There is the further complication that it is not certain that all the sub-tenants listed were living in 1166. 90 sub-tenants are listed in all; out of these, 18 have surnames or bye-names derived from French place-names, and 31 have surnames or bye-names from English place-names; 8 are listed merely by their first names, without any bye-names at all, and 11 are listed as the son of some other person, without any bye-names. These figures, however, exaggerate the number of those without bye-names. The Avenel mentioned as a sub-tenant of the Earl of Arundel, for example, was a member of a family with the surname Avenel, which probably dated back to the late 11th century.[207] This evidence suggests that by 1166 it was already unusual for tenants by knight service to be without any bye-name or surname.

It is possible to gain some further information on the general position about the surnames of knightly families in Sussex from the evidence collected by Sir William Farrer about the history of fiefs forming part of the Honour of Arundel in Sussex. Farrer's work does show what the circumstances were about hereditary surnames in respect of most of the families holding from the honour by knight service, though there are some fiefs where the circumstances are uncertain. Out of the tenants holding directly or indirectly from the honour by knight service c. 1200, 27 belonged to families with surnames which by that date were either already hereditary, or were transmitted to the descendants of the holder at that time, and which became hereditary. Only 3 were from families which did not have surnames either hereditary already, or passed on to the descendants of the then tenant.[208] Ecclesiastical bodies have been excluded from these figures, and so have cases where the evidence is too scanty for the position to be clear. Lands held from the honour, but outside Sussex, have also been excluded. It is unlikely that the knightly tenants of this particular honour were markedly different in their use of surnames from families of the same class in the county, holding from other lords. This evidence, therefore, suggests that by the end of the 12th century a large majority of knightly families in Sussex either already had hereditary surnames, or had acquired names which were to be hereditary subsequently.

It would be wrong to imply that the knightly class in Sussex was a group with lands and interests confined to that county, with no significant connections elsewhere. In fact, many tenants by knight service in Sussex held lands in other counties. During the 12th century both the Earls of Arundel and the Earls de Warenne had large estates in other counties besides Sussex, notably in East Anglia. Many tenants by knight service of the Honour of Arundel in Sussex also held from the Earl of Arundel outside the county, and many tenants holding from the Earls de Warenne in Sussex also held from the same earls elsewhere, mostly in Norfolk. There were, too, knightly families which held some land in Sussex, but had the bulk of their estates elsewhere. Further, during the 12th century some Sussex landowners continued to hold lands in Normandy, and some of them appear as grantors of, or witnesses to, charters executed in that province.[209] Despite these links, however, it is not the case that the growth of hereditary surnames among the knightly class in Sussex was precisely the same as in all other parts of England. The position in some other southern counties was probably similar to that in Sussex, though the development of hereditary surnames among the class in question was perhaps rather more advanced in Sussex than in at least some other counties in the south of England.[210] Development in East Anglia was probably rather later than in Sussex, and in the north of England later still. The writer's impression, after a preliminary but necessarily incomplete investigation, is that the position in the adjoining counties of Kent and Surrey was much the same as in Sussex, but more research on those two counties than it has been possible to undertake for this work would be needed to substantiate such a conclusion fully. More detailed comparisons, in fact, will not be possible until studies have been made of many more counties.

Although the evidence about the names of some knightly families in Sussex is not so complete as might be wished, in general it is possible to form a reasonably accurate view of the evolution of hereditary surnames among that class, but it is much more difficult to arrive at any conclusion about the factors which fostered the process. The issue is a significant one, because it appears that the growth of hereditary surnames among the knightly families of the country, together with that among the much smaller body of tenants in chief, was a major influence in bringing about the adoption of hereditary surnames by other classes of the community at later periods. The high proportion of surnames, among this class, which were in the period between 1086 and about 1200 derived from place-names, either in France or in England, provides an indication of at least one of the forces at work. Normally, if a landed family, in the period up to about 1200, had a surname derived from a place-name, whether the place concerned was in France or England, the place in question was one where the family involved held land. There was, therefore, a close connection between the surnames of landed families, and their territorial possessions, and it must be supposed that one reason for the adoption by such families of hereditary surnames was to stress the hereditary nature of their title to their land holdings.[211]

This was probably the most important single cause for the acquisition of hereditary surnames by landed families. Such hereditary names had begun to appear in Normandy before the Conquest.[212] No doubt the geographical proximity of Sussex to Normandy, which must have made it relatively easy for landed families to maintain contact across the Channel, helped to encourage the growth of hereditary surnames in the county at an earlier

The Rise of Hereditary Surnames in Sussex

period than in some other parts of England. It is not easy to discern what other forces may have been at work. A small number of landed families had surnames which were in origin nicknames, such as Aguillon or Talcurtes, for example. It is generally very difficult to discover what circumstances gave rise to any surname of such a type. It is possible that surnames of the type may in some cases have been bestowed as a nickname upon some notable individual, and have been retained by descendants of the person concerned as a matter of family pride in ancestry. As against this, such surnames are sometimes unflattering, at least in their literal meaning (though they may have had some more favourable significance for contemporaries which eludes research). Where nickname type surnames were derived from terms for physical characteristics, the characteristics in question might have been hereditary for several generations, and this may have favoured the development of hereditary surnames in a few instances. It is possible that the main factor behind the growth of hereditary surnames, where landowning families were concerned, was a desire to signal the hereditary nature of their tenure, strengthened in some cases by a wish to emphasise descent from some renowned ancestor.

There are, of course, many landowning families which have existed in Sussex at one period or another, including some which still survive in the county, which have not been discussed here. Many of these are mentioned in later chapters. Here it is intended only to deal with those families whose history helps to illustrate the development of hereditary surnames in the county.

The landholding families in any county inevitably tend to be the section of the population which is best documented during the Middle Ages. Information about the surnames or bye-names of other classes is very scanty for any period before 1200, and even after that date it is often difficult to discover the position regarding the surnames of some parts of the population. One basic fact about the history of surnames is that some classes are very badly represented in the source material for any time before the appearance of parish registers in some numbers during the 16th century. It is, despite these obstacles, possible to say something about the rise of hereditary surnames among some other sections of the community in Sussex.

HEREDITARY SURNAMES OF BONDMEN

Although the legal position of serfs was lowly, the evidence for their surnames and bye-names given in such records as manor court rolls and the custumals makes it possible to discover something about the history of their surnames from the 13th century onwards. In fact the position about bondmen is rather clearer than it is about some other classes which ranked higher. In legal theory bondmen were a clearly demarcated class. In practice, the situation is complicated by such factors as the occupation by freemen of villein land, the leasing of free holdings to serfs, and the failure at times of such documents as custumals to make it clear whether some groups of tenants were free or unfree.

Nothing can be said about the surnames or bye-names of serfs in Sussex before the 13th century. One of the few sources to throw any light on the subject is a list of small tenants, possibly free, possibly unfree, at Brighton, in 1147. Some of these were holding a virgate each, others were cottars.[213] The list gives only one of the tenants a bye-name at all (*palmarius*).[214] Information about serfs' names is scanty for England generally during the 12th century, but such evidence as there is suggests that before the 13th century serfs rarely had surnames or bye-names of any kind. It is probable that this was the case in Sussex, but in the absence of fuller information it is impossible to be sure.

When more facts become available after 1200, they indicate that bondmen were acquiring hereditary surnames during the 13th century. It is possible to find a number of instances where bond families adopted or received hereditary names in the course of the century. For example, about the middle of the century John de la Quarer' ('of the Quarry') was a bondman of Sele Priory, probably at Bramber. He was the son of William de la Quarer', who was presumably living during the first half of the 13th century. John in turn had at least two sons, John (the younger), and Henry de la Quarer'; Henry was a useful servant to the priory, and in 1270 he was manumitted. The surname survived in the same area in the 14th century.[215] At Battle, a family with the hereditary surname of Hamond was descended from Hamo, a customary tenant who was living in 1252.[216] At Amberley, Daniel Hoel, or Howel, a villein living in the late 13th century, died in or before 1307, leaving as his heirs William Howel and Walter Howel; Daniel also had a sister Isabel Howel; the surname Howel survived at Amberley during the 14th century.[217] Gilbert *cinerarius* (probably 'charcoal burner'), who was granted as a serf to Robertsbridge Abbey, about 1240, was the son of Robert le Coliere, who was living in the early 13th century.[218] Other instances where unfree families had hereditary surnames during the 13th century could be given. There are also many cases where scarce surnames persist among the serfs in one locality in such a way as to show that a hereditary surname existed, even if no connected descent can be traced. For instance, the surname Merewine, from a personal name, persisted at Bosham for a long period during the 13th century.[219] The surname Wolvyn, also from a personal name, was that of a villein at Ferring in the late 13th century. It survived there, and in the adjoining parish of Goring, into 14th century. The surname persisted at Ferring in the 16th century, and it was still in the same part of Sussex in the 17th.[220] About 1250 the name le Mew ('gull') was borne by serfs at

Boxgrove; the name already existed there about 1220, and it persisted at Boxgrove into the 14th century.[221] Le Mist, or le Myst, was the name of several bond tenants at Mayfield, about 1285. The name survived at Mayfield into the 14th century, and was still there in 1377.[222] The name is a nickname from the word 'mist', but the circumstances which gave rise to it are unknown. Perhaps it was a nickname for one with short, or 'misty', sight. In all these cases the persistence of rare names over a period in one locality suggests strongly that the names in question were hereditary, even though connected pedigrees cannot be traced.

All this evidence tends to show that bondmen were acquiring hereditary surnames during the 13th century, but it is difficult merely from individual examples, such as those cited above, to tell, even approximately, what proportion of the unfree population acquired hereditary names in the course of the century. When unfree tenants are found in 13th century sources for Sussex, it is unusual for them not to have surnames or bye-names of some kind. For example, out of 43 serfs mentioned in three Sussex fines from the end of John's reign, and the early years of Henry III, all but five have surnames or bye-names of one sort of another; the five remaining are each described as the son of some other persons.[223] The 1296 subsidy roll for Sussex lists 252 serfs (described as such), belonging to several lords.[224] Out of all these, 2 are described merely as the son of some other person, one is listed only by his first name, and 2 are widows who appear to be without bye-names (several other widows are listed under what seem to be their deceased husbands' bye-names). The rest all have surnames or bye-names of some sort. The 1296 lists include a fair number of women, nearly all of whom have surnames or bye-names. Some surveys of the Fitzalan family's estates, made in 1301, list many unfree tenants on a number of Sussex manors. The great majority of the serfs listed have surnames or bye-names; a few are mentioned simply as the son of some other person, and there are a few widows who are listed by their first names only.[225]

Some further information about serfs' names can be gained from cases where two successive rentals or surveys, made at different dates, exist for a single manor. For instance, two surveys exist for the East Sussex manor of Willingdon, made in 1292 and 1296. The manor was in the queen's hands at the time. As might be expected from the short time between the two surveys, many tenants are listed in both, but there are a number of cases in which tenants listed in 1292 had been replaced by others, by 1296. In 1292 there were 54 customary tenants on the manor, including some with quite large holdings, and including several women. By 1296, 10 of these had been replaced by others with the same surnames. One tenant holding in 1292 had been replaced, in or before 1296, by his heir, who is not named in the 1296 survey. In two other cases tenants in 1292 had been replaced in 1296 by new tenants with names indicating a link with those of

1292: Reynold le Pottere, of 1292, had been succeeded by 1296 by Simon Renaud, whose bye-name was clearly from his predecessor's (probably his father's) first name, and Thomas de Lem, of 1292, had been replaced in 1296 by William Goldyng de Lem. This last case was probably one in which a surname had still not become stable. As against this evidence that serfs' names at Willingdon were hereditary at the time, 7 customary tenants listed in 1292 had by 1296 been succeeded by others whose names had no connection with their predecessors. In none of these instances, however, is there evidence that the 1296 tenant was related at all to the predecessor of 1292, and it is likely that they were cases of tenants having died without heirs, or possibly of tenants having fled from the manor.[226]

Similar evidence can be obtained by comparing the names of customary tenants listed at Wellingham, Norlington, Goat and Middleham, Ashton, and Southerham, as given in a rental of 1305–6,[227] with the corresponding lists of customary tenants given in a custumal of 1285.[228] Out of the customary tenants in 1305, 46 were either the same persons as the tenants listed in the custumal, or the widows of men listed in the custumal; in 12 cases tenants listed in the custumal had been succeeded in their holdings, in 1305, by persons with the same surname, and in 17 cases tenants mentioned in the custumal had been replaced, in 1305, by persons with different surnames; one tenant in 1305 had no surname or bye-name. Where tenants mentioned in the custumal had been replaced, in 1305, by tenants with different surnames, there is not, in any case, evidence that the tenant in 1305 was related to the previous tenant of the same holding, and it is probable that in most at least of these instances the tenants listed in the custumal had been succeeded by incomers not related to the earlier tenants. One fact which suggests that this was the case is that in two holdings at Southerham, the tenants listed in the custumal had been replaced, by 1305, by a tenant with the significant name of Niweman.

It would seem from this evidence that hereditary surnames were common among unfree tenants by the end of the 13th century, though not universal. There were still at that period serfs without bye-names at all. There are some indications that in the late 13th century serfs on some manors may have been acquiring surnames for the first time. At Wadhurst, in 1285, there are many bond tenants with surnames or bye-names derived from minor localities at which the bondmen in question had their holdings.[229] Many of them had holdings which included areas of coppice. It seems possible that at Wadhurst there were in the late 13th century some holdings which had been recently assarted, and occupied by bondmen, who derived bye-names, which in some cases became hereditary, from the names of the localities where their new holdings were. This seems all the more probable because the place-names concerned are mostly not known to have existed before the late 13th century.[230] Lists of bondmen on Sussex manors in the late 13th or early 14 centuries show few people without surnames or bye-names, though it is often not possible to tell what proportion had hereditary names.[231]

It is difficult to arrive at any accurate figure for the proportion of serfs with hereditary surnames at any date, but it seems that by about 1300 hereditary surnames were already common among serfs in Sussex. Possibly about half of all unfree families may have possessed such names by 1300. In late 14th and 15th century sources, serfs in the county are usually given surnames or bye-names, and it is probable that by the late 14th century it was general for serfs to have hereditary surnames. A customal of Streatham manor, drawn up in 1374, shows that many unfree tenants then were occupying holdings which had been previously held by one, or often two, previous tenants with the same surnames, and it is a reasonable assumption that these were instances of unfree holdings descending in families with hereditary surnames. Evidently in some cases new surnames were still being formed at Streatham in the late 14th century; Ralph Walklyn, an unfree tenant, was in 1374 holding land held formerly by Walkelyn atte Broke, and it is probable that Ralph was Walkelyn's son, with a bye-name derived from his father's first name.[232] There may have been many variations between manors, and Streatham was not necessarily typical of all places in Sussex. Even in the early 15th century, occasional examples can be found of unfree tenants who do not appear to have had any surnames or bye-names.[233] As was the case with other classes, the acquisition of hereditary surnames by bondmen was spread over a long period, and the chronology cannot be ascertained very precisely.

SURNAMES OF SMALL FREE TENANTS

It is not easy to say what the position was at any date about the hereditary surnames of the varied and numerous body of lesser freeholders in the county. Individual examples can be found from a relatively early period of families belonging to that class with hereditary surnames, but individual cases give little idea of what the general position was for the social class as a whole, and the defects of the source material make it difficult to devise any method of estimating what proportion of the class had hereditary surnames by any particular date.

Some families of small freeholders had hereditary surnames from the 12th or early 13th centuries. This can be seen, in some cases from the pedigrees of individual families, in some cases from the persistence of rare surnames in particular localities, in a way which suggests that a hereditary surname existed. For example, the surname Merle persisted from the 12th century to the 14th at West Firle;[234] The name le Foghe (le Fogh, le Fohe) must have been hereditary at Aldrington from the late 12th century, for John le Foghe of Aldrington, living about 1240, was the son of William le

Foghe, and the grandson of John le Foghe (who was presumably living in the late 12th century); the name persisted in the same part of Sussex in the late 13th century;[235] the name atte Setene (de la Setene, de Seton, etc.), existed at Pagham from about 1200 as the name of a family of freeholders.[236] These cases, and a few others which might be cited, show that hereditary surnames were at any rate not unknown among the lesser free tenants in the late 12th and early 13th centuries, but even allowing for the limited quantity of source material available at this relatively early period, the number of instances in which hereditary surnames can be found is small, and it must be supposed that hereditary surnames were then exceptional among the social class under discussion. There are a considerably larger number of examples from the middle and late 13th century. For instance, the surnames Flote,[237] Shoesmith,[238] and Napper,[239] all seem to have been hereditary from the middle or late 13th century. The surname Earl was hereditary at Midhurst from the late 13th century. The surname, like others derived from high offices, was probably a nickname in origin.[240] The topographical surname Marays was hereditary at Rackham from the mid 13th century, and survived in that part of the county into the 14th century.[241] The surname Cley was hereditary in the Manwood in the mid 13th century.[242] The surname Turgis, from a personal name, was hereditary in a family of freeholders at Up Waltham and Boxgrove from the mid 13th century.[243] A considerable number of other instances could be cited, and it is clear that hereditary surnames were becoming common among free tenants during the second half of the 13th century. Even where the descent of a hereditary surname cannot be traced, the persistence of many rare surnames among the freeholders in one particular township strongly suggests that the names in question were hereditary.[244]

Such evidence, even if a large number of examples are taken into account, gives at best a very general impression of how the development of hereditary surnames was taking place. In an attempt to obtain some more definite evidence, a comparison has been made between the taxpayers listed in the subsidies for 1296, 1327, and 1332, for six townships in different parts of the county, Aldingbourne, Elsted, Storrington, Ticehurst, Streat, and Rustington.[245] There are differences between the three successive subsidies in the proportion of the population covered by each, and in particular the number of taxpayers listed in 1296 is in most places considerably less than the numbers given in 1327 and 1332. As would be expected from the short time between the 1327 and the 1332 subsidies, many persons appear as taxpayers in both, but the long period elapsing between the 1296 subsidy, on the one hand, and those for 1327 and 1332 on the other, makes it possible to use the subsidies to provide some evidence about the continuity of surnames in the county. In the six townships, in 1296, very few taxpayers were without surnames or bye-

The Rise of Hereditary Surnames in Sussex

names. The only examples are two men at Ticehurst, who are each mentioned merely as the son of some other person. Besides these, at Rustington the rector of that place is listed simply as such, without any name being given,[246] and in several townships earls are mentioned by their titles. All these persons have been excluded from calculations for the table set out below. The figures in the table are for numbers of surnames or bye-names found in the three subsidies for each of the six townships. They are not figures for numbers of individuals. Some difficulties have arisen because the writers of the subsidy rolls have occasionally made errors in the spelling of proper names. If two subsidy rolls which are close together in time, such as those for 1327 and 1332, are examined together, it is at points obvious that there are cases where the name of a taxpayer occurs in both subsidies, but where in one of them it has been wrongly spelled. In some cases, this can be confirmed from references to the same individuals in other sources. One consequence of such scribal errors is that it is sometimes uncertain whether a given surname or bye-name occurs in two successive subsidy rolls or not.

Survival in six Sussex townships of surnames or bye-names listed in the 1296 subsidy, in the subsidies for 1327 and for 1332.

Township	No. of names, 1296	No. of names, found 1296, still present in same township, 1327	No. of names, found 1296, still present in same township, 1332
Aldingbourne	11	5	2
Elsted	13	2, & 2 doubtful	1, & 2 doubtful
Storrington	20	5	5, & 1 doubtful
Ticehurst	26	10	10
Rustington	28	13, & 1 doubtful	11, & 3 doubtful
Streat	24	14	11

In considering these figures, it has to be borne in mind that even if hereditary surnames had been universal in 1296 in Sussex, the passage of time between 1296 and 1327, or 1332, would have led to some changes in the nomenclature of a township, through migration, or through the extinction of some families as a result of deaths. It is doubtful if in this case migration was an important factor. Had there been a great deal of movement in or out of the townships being studied here, this should have led to some of the rarer surnames or bye-names found in 1296 in each of the six townships being found, in the two later subsidies, outside the township in which the names in question appear in 1296, but in other townships nearby. In fact this is not usually the case. The rarer surnames or bye-names found in 1296, which do not appear again in the same townships in 1327 or 1332, do not occur in 1327 and 1332 in adjoining townships, or in other nearby townships. The presence in adjoining townships of surnames or bye-names which were common, and widely distributed throughout the county at the period cannot be considered significant in this connection. It is of course true that the persistence of a name in one locality might not be due to the existence of a hereditary surname, for it is always possible that a bye-name might develop independently on more than one occasion in a single place, but is unlikely that this would happen very frequently. Taking all these considerations into account, the evidence does show that there was a sufficient degree of continuity in the names in use to suggest that perhaps half of those listed as taxpayers in 1296 had hereditary surnames. Taking all six townships together, and counting the doubtful names as instances where names found in 1296 did not survive to 1327, just over 40% of the names listed in 1296 appear again in 1327 in the same townships. The taxpayers in the subsidy rolls varied greatly in wealth and status. Some can be indentified as landowners of some importance, while some may have been serfs, though none is noted as such in the subsidies. Most, however, must have been free tenants with only moderate resources, and assessments do suggest that this was the case.

Some other evidence leads to the same conclusion. A comparison has been made between free tenants on the manor of South Malling, at Wellingham, Norlington, Ashton, and South Malling, as listed in a custumal of 1285, and the names of free tenants at the same places as given in a rental of 1305–6.[247] Out of the free tenants listed in 1285, 45 were listed, again, in 1305–6, 15 had by 1305 been succeeded by another tenant with the same surname or bye-name (and it must be supposed that in such cases the 1285 tenant had been succeeded by an heir with the same, hereditary, surname), 11 had been succeeded by tenants with a different surname or bye-name, and the successors of 7 cannot be traced in 1305–6. Allowing for the fact that it would be expected that some tenants might die without heirs, and that some would alienate their holdings and leave the manor, this suggests that on South Malling manor a high proportion of free tenants had hereditary surnames by the late 13th century.

All this evidence indicates that by about 1300 it was already very common for small free tenants to have hereditary surnames, though it is not possible to give any precise figure for the proportion with hereditary names by that date. During the 14th century, when the facts about the names of people in that class can be ascertained, it is usually found that their surnames were hereditary.[248] One piece of evidence for this is the almost total disappearance after about 1300 of cases where individuals have what are obviously from the sources bye-names, perhaps of a temporary or unstable character. During the 13th century there are many instances in Sussex of persons who are described as "called" (*dictus*) by some bye-name. At Winchelsea in 1292, for example, several men with such bye-names were listed, Pote *dictus* Chepman, Herbertus *dictus* Brouning, or Thomas *dictus* Boun Mounger, for instance.[249] Before about 1300 people from the class of small freeholders appear in the sources from time to time with bye-names given in this fashion.[250] No instances have been found after 1300 among that class, though there are a few instances during the 14th century in Sussex among the clergy.

On the other hand, there are during the 14th century many instances in Sussex of persons from the class of small free tenants having hereditary surnames, including names in all the main categories of surname. For instance, the surname Maydekin (a surname of the nickname type) was hereditary at Broomhill, near Rye, from the early 14th century;[251] Godesole was hereditary around Burwash from the 14th century;[252] the locative name Willesham was hereditary at Ashburnham from the late 14th century;[253] and Catteslond (from Catslands Farm, in Henfield) was a hereditary name at Streatham, in Henfield, from the 14th century.[254] A further indication that hereditary surnames were becoming general among small free tenants in the 14th century is the presence in 14th century subsidy rolls of cases where a single surname was the name of several people in the same township. There are a good many instances in the Sussex subsidy roll for 1332. For instance, there were in 1332 5 taxpayers named Swyft at Lancing, 6 named de Posterne or atte Posterne at Brede, 6 named de Wyke at Udimore, and 6 named Cade at Wadhurst and Mayfield.[255] Judging from their assessments these people all seem likely to have been small free tenants. It seems likely that such groupings of persons with a single surname or bye-name represent the ramification locally of a family with a hereditary surname. Even allowing for the fact that the subsidy does not list all inhabitants, but only taxpayers, so that there were very probably further individuals with the surname in question living but unlisted, it would not take very long for a hereditary surname to multiply to the point at which a family had half a dozen representatives in one township. Such a result could be produced in a generation or two, so that the surnames in question need not have been hereditary for very long before 1332.

It seems probable that by the end of the 14th century most small free tenants in Sussex had hereditary surnames, but such surnames were not universal. Even in the late 14th century, occasional examples can be found of individuals without hereditary surnames.[256] Such instances are, however, rare, and the general impression left by the considerable number of cases in which families of smaller freeholders can be shown to have had hereditary surnames in the 14th century, and by the many examples of surnames persisting among that section of the population in one township, during the same period, is that hereditary surnames had become generally used by small freeholders by the late 14th century at the latest.

It is much more difficult to say what the position was, at any time during the Middle Ages, about the surnames of those parts of the rural population who were neither serfs nor free tenants, such as domestic servants, landless labourers, and possibly sub-tenants of villeins or of small free tenants. The appearances of such people in medieval records are scarce and sporadic, so that it is seldom possible to trace pedigrees for families belonging to those classes. In the late 14th century poll tax returns for Sussex, many persons, male and female, who are noted as 'servants' (*servientes*) are listed without any surnames or bye-names at all.[257] A few examples can be found in other sources of about the same date of servants who are mentioned without surnames or bye-names.[258] It does not appear, however, that it was usual at the time for servants or labourers to be without bye-names at all, for the Sussex poll tax returns list many people described as *laborator, servus,* or *serviens* who are given surnames or bye-names.[259] In general, such persons as labourers or domestic servants are so badly represented in the source material as to make it impossible to come to any firm conclusion about the development of hereditary surnames among those classes. In the Sussex lay subsidy for 1524–5, there are still some persons listed as taxpayers who are not given any surnames or bye-names.[260] The taxpayers concerned mostly have low assessments, and some are described in the subsidy returns (which do not give occupations in most cases) as 'servant' or 'labourer'. Similar examples of people without surnames or bye-names, and with low assessments, can be found in the subsidies for other counties of about the same date.[261] It is impossible to be sure if these are cases where people did not have bye-names at all, even in the early 16th century, or if they are due to the subsidy returns simply omitting the surnames or bye-names of a small number of lowly individuals. It seems possible that even in the 16th century there were still persons without any settled bye-names, but if so such cases were rare.

Some further information about the hereditary surnames of parts of the rural population, especially craftsmen and artisans, can be gained from considering how far occupational surnames or bye-names coincided with occupations actually being pursued. It is not always safe to conclude that an occupational surname must be hereditary if it does not correspond with the trade or craft that the bearer of the name was in fact practising; people could change their occupations, or follow more than one occupation, sometimes seasonally. However, where there are many instances of occupations actually pursued being the same as the occupational surnames or bye-names of the persons involved, it must be probable that the occupational names concerned were not in general hereditary. Considering rural areas alone, and leaving aside the town population for discussion later, many instances can be found in Sussex during the late 14th and the 15th centuries of individuals with occupational names which were from the occupation which the persons in question were in fact practising. During the same periods, however, there are many cases where people with occupational names were not pursuing the occupations from which their names were derived. Unfortunately subsidy records do not give occupations consisently, so that it is not possible to use them systematically to test how far occupations correspond to occupational surnames or bye-names, but it is possible from other 14th and 15th century sources to collect very many examples where the trades or crafts being followed by persons with occupational names are given. There are also some instances where it may be inferred that an individual's occupation was the same as that from which his name was derived.[262] All the instances, where people with occupational surnames or bye-names have occupations which are stated, or can be deduced, form a variety of sources, for Sussex in the late 14th and 15th centuries have been collected; when this is done, it can be seen that cases where people with occupational names had occupations which were the same as those from which their names were derived were more numerous than those where people had occupational names which were different from the occupations actually being pursued by the persons in question. Of course in some cases the fact that occupations happened to correspond with surnames or bye-names might be no more than a coincidence. It is also true that there may have been examples where both an occupation, and a surname, had descended in one family for several generations. Even allowing for these possibilities, however, the correspondence between the names and occupations actually being followed seems so great that it can only be explained by accepting that, even during the late 14th and 15th centuries there were many craftsmen and artisans who still had bye-names which were derived from their own occupations, and which had not been inherited.

The facts about the surnames of some sections of the medieval population remain elusive, and it is often difficult to discover any details about the surnames of some classes. When surnames are found in the county for the first time at some relatively late period, such as the late 15th century, or the 16th, this may be due in some cases to migration from other areas, and in a few cases it may be due to entirely new surnames having arisen at a late date, but in many instances it must be caused by surnames having existed for a period of time without having been noted in any extant record.

HEREDITARY SURNAMES OF TOWNSPEOPLE

Some information can be obtained about the development of hereditary surnames in the city of Chichester, and in the larger Sussex towns.

At Chichester, some of the inhabitants possessed hereditary surnames in the 13th century. The surname Lardener was hereditary in the city from early in that century.[263] So were the surnames Scutt (or Scute) (probably a nickname),[264] and Squibb.[265] Squibb occurs as a surname long before it is evidenced as a word in general use, and it is not clear what it originally meant. Obviously it cannot have meant a firework when used in the 13th century.[266] The surname de Twaincherch (from a Chichester place-name) was hereditary in the city from the late 12th century.[267] The surname Doneghton (from the place-name Donington) was hereditary there from the late 13th century.[268] Besides such examples, where hereditary descent can be demonstrated, there are other cases where surnames persisted in the city over a long period, in such a way as to suggest that they had become hereditary there. The name Pricklove ('prick wolf'), for instance, persisted at Chichester from the mid 13th century, and was certainly hereditary there in the 14th.[269] The occupational name Sherer, a rare one in Sussex, existed in the city from the late 13th century to the 17th.[270] All the names mentioned above are those of families which owned property in Chichester, and it seems from this somewhat fragmentary evidence that the more prominent families in the city often had hereditary surnames during the 13th century, though it is impossible to say how common this was, even for families at that level. What the position was about those inhabitants of the city who were lower down the social scale it is also impossible to say, though it is unlikely that they were slower to adopt hereditary surnames than the small free tenants in rural areas. The wills of Chichester inhabitants show that surnames were generally hereditary there in the 15th century.[271]

The evidence for the other Sussex towns is no more adequate. At Winchelsea, also, some families had hereditary names in the 13th century. The surname Andrew was hereditary there in the 13th century, derived from the personal name of Andrew of Winchelsea, who was apparently living about 1200.[272] The surname Alard is said to have been derived at Winchelsea from the first name of a certain Alard who was living in the port in the late 12th century. In fact, the genealogical evidence does not prove this, but the surname was certainly hereditary at Winchelsea in the 13th century. By about 1290 the surname was already numerous there, and it later became widespread in the neighbouring parts of Sussex, very probably through the spread of one family with a hereditary surname.[273] These cases, and a few others where surnames survived over a period at Winchelsea, suggesting that they may have been hereditary, concern families who held property in the port. It is impossible to say anything about the hereditary surnames of other sections of the town's population, then or later.

Evidence about the rise of hereditary surnames in the other Sussex towns is even scantier. It is possible to find a few cases where families at Lewes or Battle had hereditary surnames from the 13th century, but these all concern families which seem to have been people of some standing, and tell us nothing about the rest of the population. It is in fact not possible to say more than that in the 13th century some, but probably not all, of the wealthier townspeople belonged to families which by then had hereditary surnames.

Some other issues concerning the rise of hereditary surnames remain to be explored.

DOUBLE NAMES

In a small number of instances, there occur in Sussex persons mentioned with two bye-names or surnames, given consecutively, such as, for example, John Fuller Coventre (Hawkesborough Hundred, 1443),[274] John a Neston Passhele (Catsfield, 1434),[275] Ralph de Blukefeld *de querceto* (South Malling, c. 1265),[276] William Berewerthe atte Byrchette (Ticehurst, 1436),[277] or John Pistor Witegrom (Winchelsea, 1292).[278] In some cases it is probable that an additional name has been added in order to distinguish one individual from another with the same personal name and bye-name. This is probably the case where a topographical term has been added, as in the example of William Berewerthe, or as in the examples of several persons with double names listed at Winchelsea in 1292, where the second name is a topographical term.[279] In other cases what appears to be a nickname has been added, perhaps also to prevent confusion where two individuals with the same personal name and surname or bye-name existed in the same community. This was probably the case with John Pistor Witegrom, mentioned above, especially since, as might be expected, there were other men named Pistor (presumably for 'Baker') at Winchelsea at the time.[280] Another inhabitant of Winchelsea at about the same period was Gervase Alard Frendekyn.[281] Gervase belonged to a family which already had a hereditary surname.[282] He was sometimes referred to as Gervase Alard, sometimes as Gervase Alard Frendekin, sometimes as Gervase Frendekyn. Alard was a common surname at Winchelsea in the late 13th century, and about 1290 there were at least two men named Gervase Alard in the port, so that the distinguishing mark of an added nickname may have been needed.[283] Sander de Brokexe *longus* and Alexander de Brokexe *curtus*, both inhabitants of Winchelsea in 1292, were obviously a further example of two men with the same personal name and bye-name, living in the same place, and needing to be distinguished by additional nicknames.[284]

A moderate number of double names has been found in Sussex during the 14th and 15th centuries. At no time were such double names used for more than a small minority of people. Some of the forms which have been found are Latinised, but allowing for this, it may be suspected that the double names are the forms actually used in speech when it was necessary to mark out one individual from another by bestowing an added nickname. This is a usage which could hardly have arisen in a community where most people did not have hereditary surnames, or at least bye-names which had acquired a good deal of stability. Where people had no hereditary surnames or fixed bye-names, double names would have been unnecessary, for individuals could have been distinguished one from another simply by the bestowing of new bye-names, whether of the nickname type, or of other categories.

In some northern counties, individuals can be found with two bye-names in 'son' such as, for example, William Robynson Dobson, or Henry Jakkeson Jankynsone.[285] No examples of such double names have been discovered in Sussex, and that type of double name seems to have been exclusively a northern phenomenon. Another type of double name is that formed by a 'group genitive'. Four examples have been found in Sussex; William Jonesservant Wilton, noted at Chichester, in 1403, and the servant of John Wilton, esquire;[286] John Jonesservant de Avesford, and Henry Jonesservant de Stanbourne, both mentioned in connection with disturbances at Goring, in 1331;[287] and Thomas Jonesservant Bukke, at Horsham, in 1401.[288] Such instances can be found in other counties, but were not common anywhere.[289] 'Group genitives' involve the use of a construction which existed in Middle English, but which is lacking in Modern English. William Jonesservant Wilton signifies 'William, servant of John Wilton', and similarly John Jonesservant de Avesford means 'John, servant of John de Avesford'. It does not seem that such names can ever have become hereditary surnames, and it is unlikely that they were even bye-names with any stability. In most if not all cases, these names must be taken as simply descriptions, used in particular instances, and not as bye-names in constant use.

SURNAMES OF MARRIED WOMEN

The origin of the convention whereby married women habitually take their husband's surnames, and discard the surnames used before marriage, has been discussed elsewhere.[290] It was suggested that the convention developed gradually, that it was first adopted by aristocratic or landed families, and that during the 12th, 13th, and 14th centuries the usages about the surnames or bye-names of married women were very flexible. The Sussex evidence shows that the position in the county was not significantly different from that elsewhere. Women are mentioned in medieval sources much less frequently than men, so that the evidence for their names, and the customs connected with married womens' names, is bound to be incomplete, but there is enough to show that in Sussex, as in other counties, usages were for long very variable.

Before 1200, the evidence all concerns the wives of men who were landholders of some standing. There are one or two 12th century cases of wives using the same surnames or bye-names as their husbands,[291] but there are more instances where wives were using different surnames or bye-names from their husbands.[292] How unsettled the practice was at this time can be seen from the case of Rainald de Meiniers and his wife Matilda, who was the daughter of an East Sussex landowner, Ingelram de Fressenville. Rainald and his wife were living in the late 12th century and the beginning of the 13th. Matilda is mentioned sometimes as Matilda de Meiniers, sometimes as Matilda de Fressenville. She even possessed two seals, presumably in use consecutively, one with the legend *Sigill(um) M. de Fressenvilla*, and one with the legend *Sigill(um) Matildis de Meiniers*.[293] During the 13th century landowning families' usage regarding the surnames of married women was still unsettled. There are examples both of married women having different surnames from their husbands, often surnames inherited from the wives' fathers,[294] and there are examples of married women with the same surnames or bye-names as their husbands, though this seems to have been less common.[295] There is some 13th century evidence for people in other classes, which shows that a similar lack of rigid conventions prevailed. There are some cases among serfs and small free tenants of wives having the same surnames or bye-names as their husbands,[296] and there are examples, rather more numerous, of wives using surnames or bye-names different from those of their husbands.[297] It seems evident that up to 1300 at the earliest, there were no fixed rules about the surnames used by married women. In the 14th century there was still some variation in practice, at any rate among serfs and small freeholders, where it is possible to find cases both of wives having the same surnames or bye-names as their husbands, and of them having different names.[298] Conventions do not appear to have been settled until the 15th century, when, so far as can be seen from the not very copious material available, it was usual for married women to use the same surnames as their husbands.[299] A few cases occur in the 16th century of wives with surnames which were not the same as those of their husbands, but these all seem to involve foreigners resident in Sussex.[300]

It does not appear that the position as regards married womens' surnames was significantly different in Sussex from that in other parts of England, and as far as can be seen from investigations made so far, the development of conventions about married womens' names was more or less uniform throughout the country.

RAMIFICATION OF THE SURNAMES OF SOME LANDED FAMILIES

Some surnames seem each to have originated with one single family, and to have subsequently ramified. Other surnames clearly arose in a large number of different places, independently, and must from the first have each been the name of many separate families. The defects of the genealogical information existing for the Middle Ages, especially where obscure families were involved, frequently make it difficult to be sure whether a given surname originated with one family or not. It is almost always impossible to link together genealogically all the bearers of one surname, past and present, even in examples where there are strong grounds for thinking that a surname has in fact originated with one family. In later chapters the history of many surnames which have multiplied in Sussex is discussed, and it is suggested in some cases that surnames have originated with a single family in each case. There are, however, a group of surnames which were each originally the name of a landed family, and which have all ramified in the county in a similar manner. It has seemed worthwhile to deal with these surnames together at this point. Some of them belonged to families which have been mentioned earlier in this chapter. It is not suggested that the surnames of landed families all ramified in the county. There were certainly important landowning families which existed in the county during the Middle Ages whose surnames became extinct there. The surnames of some landed families, however, including some families established in the county before 1300, have ramified notably in Sussex, and are still to be found there at the present day. It is intended here to examine the history of some of these.

Bassock

The surname Bassock (de Basoches, de Basochiis, etc.) is derived from a French place-name, though it has not been possible to discover from which of several possible places the family came. The beginnings of the surname in England have been briefly mentioned above.[301] The first member of the family to be found in Sussex was William de Basochiis, who is mentioned in the county from about 1160 onwards.[302] The name had existed earlier in Normandy, but the persons so named who occur there cannot be connected with the Sussex family.[303] William was followd by Adam de Basoches, probably his son, and Adam in turn had two sons, Alfred de Basokes, who was holding land in East Sussex early in the 13th century,[304] and Robert, known as Robert de Basoches or Robert de Sedlescombe.[305] (The use of an Old English personal name by a family of French origin is interesting, but not unique.) Robert obtained a grant of land at Sedlescombe about 1210.[306] Subsequently the family, whose landed possessions were never very great, seems to have declined in importance. Much of its land at Sedlescombe was alienated to the abbeys of Battle and Robertsbridge, and by 1320 at the latest the family seems to have lost all its holdings there.[307] Two of the family, John and Laurence Basok, were executed in 1303.[308] Despite this, the surname survived in Sussex. From the late 13th century onwards it occurs in East Sussex as the name of people who seem to have all been small free tenants.[309] Three men named Basock are listed as taxpayers in the Sussex lay subsidy for 1524–5, all in East Sussex,[310] and the name occurs in other 16th century sources for the east of the county.[311] During the 17th century the surname existed at Horsham and Cocking.[312] In this case the name of a landed family survived in the county, and ramified to some extent, despite the family's loss of its original status, by, apparently, the end of the 13th century.

Covert

The Covert family (de Covert or de Cuvert, sometimes given in medieval sources as le Covert) was already established in Sussex as a landholding family of some importance in the 13th century. The connection of the family with Sussex may go back before 1200, as a Richard de Cuvert was a witness to a Devon charter granted by William de Braose, a tenant in chief in Sussex, in 1157.[313] Claims put forward in some pedigrees that a member of the Covert family fought at Hastings have not been substantiated.[314] The surname is from a French place-name, or topographical term, but it has not been possible to identify any particular place from which the family originated.[315] A Richard le Covert was involved in a lawsuit about Sussex property in 1233.[316] He is unlikely to have been the Richard earlier mentioned. Richard was succeeded by his son, William de Covert, or del Covert, who was holding two knights' fees at Sullington and Broadbridge, near Horsham, under Henry III, besides other lands in Sussex, and in Surrey.[317] The frequent use of the form le Covert for the family's name in medieval sources is one instance, out of many, of the misuse of the definite article before surnames. The family name was clearly hereditary from the the 13th century onwards, whatever the position may have been earlier. The Coverts continued to hold Sullington and Broadbridge for many years. The reversion of Sullington was alienated to the earl of Arundel in the 14th century, but Broadbridge was still being held by the family in the 16th century.[318] The pedigree of the family has been discussed in print, and need not be set out here.[319] The family descent during the first half of the 15th century is not altogether clear, but from about 1470 a William Covert (died 1494), was in possession of a large Sussex estate, including Slaugham, which became the main family seat, Twineham, and other lands in Sussex and Surrey.[320]

During the late 15th and 16th centuries the family ramified considerably. Branches were established at Woodmancote, Cuckfield, Boxgrove, and in Kent, and one 16th century member of the family had many illegitimate children who took the name of Covert.[321] The senior branch of the family, the Coverts of Slaugham, died out in the male line in 1679, but other branches of the family survived as landowners in Sussex in the 18th century.[322]

Early in the 16th century the surname Cover appears in Sussex.[323] This surname still survives in the county to the present day. Cover is generally said to be an occupational name, and in fact the bye-name le Coucrer can be found in Sussex in the 13th century, and this might be the origin of Cover in the county.[324] In view of the existence of Covert over a long period in Sussex, it may be conjectured that Cover, which does not appear in the county until a relatively late period, is there a late form of Covert, but this cannot be proved.

Dawtry

The surname Dawtry is derived from a French place-name, Hautrive (Orne). In sources written before *c.* 1400, the name usually appears in a Latinised form (*de Alta Ripa*), and it is not easy to be sure what the vernacular form was. The form de Alteriue occurs in the 12th century, and the form Hautriche in 1296.[325] Dautre and Dawtrey were usual forms in the late 14th and 15th centuries.[326]

Robert *de Alta Ripa* and William his son occur as witnesses to several mid and late 12th century Sussex deeds. Robert was evidently a landholder in Sussex.[327] Robert's son, William *de Alta Ripa*, is said to have married a sister of Jocelin, the brother of Henry I's second wife, and lord of the Honour of Petworth, and William was certainly granted land in Sussex by Richard de Perci, to whom the honour descended.[328] In the 13th century members of the Dawtry family were holding land from the Percy family in Yorkshire.[329] The family lands in Sussex were held by individuals named William *de Alta Ripa* from some date towards the end of Stephen's reign until about 1247. One man cannot have been holding the family lands for the whole of this period, and it must be supposed that there were at least two, and probably three, Williams holding the Sussex estates in succession.[330] It is, however, clear that the family already had a hereditary surname during the 12th century. During that period there were already younger sons who were using the surname *de Alta Ripa*; Robert *de Alta Ripa*, who witnessed charters at the end of the 12th century, was a son of the William *de Alta Ripa*, who was living about 1190, and Joscelin *de Alta Ripa*, a canon of Chichester, who is known to have been a nephew of Jocelin the queen's brother, may have been a son of the William *de Alta Ripa* who was the son of Robert.[331] It is, however, generally very difficult to trace the descendants of younger sons in the 12th century, even if they belonged to established knightly families. The *de Alta Ripa* or Dawtry family remained landowners in Sussex for a very long period of time. Early in the 14th century the lands of the senior branch passed with an heiress to another family,[332] but other branches remained holding land at Up Waltham, Aldsworth, Fittleworth, and elsewhere.[333] The family were still important landowners in Sussex in the 18th century. Branches of the family were established in Hampshire,[334] and the family held land in Yorkshire during the 13th and 14th centuries.[335] The family's surname had already ramified to some extent by the end of the 13th century; four members of the family are listed as taxpayers in the 1296 subsidy, all in the west of the county; three of these had assessments which show that they were substantial landowners, but the fourth had a low assessment which indicates that he was probably a small free tenant.[336] Subsequently the surname multiplied considerably in the county, leaving aside the branches of the family which were established in other counties. In the Protestation Returns, 1641–42, which cover West Sussex but not East, there are seven persons named Dawtry, Dawtreye, etc., listed.[337] The surname still survives in Sussex at the present day, usually in the forms Dawtry or Daughtery.

In this case a surname, established in Sussex by, at the latest, the mid 12th century, has survived in the county to the present, and has ramified considerably. It must be regarded as extremely probable that all the persons named Dawtry etc., in Sussex, together with some in other counties, share a common ancestry.

Scarfield

The early history of the de Scardeville family in Sussex has already been mentioned.[338] From the late 13th century members of the family were landowners at Lavant, where they were holding land in the 17th century.[339] In the 15th century the family also held land by knight service at Singleton, which adjoins Lavant, and early in the same century William Scardevyle inherited from his mother some land at Broadbridge, near Bosham.[340] Land in Bosham was still held by one of the family in 1700.[341] Some branches of the family were landowners on a moderate scale during the 13th, 14th, and 15th centuries, but already in the late 13th and early 14th centuries there were de Scardevilles holding land in the Selsey area who seem to have been no more than free tenants with very limited possessions.[342] In the 16th century the surname still existed in the part of Sussex where it had been present since before 1300. In the subsidy of 1524–25, there are eight taxpayers named Scardevile (or Skardevile, etc.) listed at East Lavant; several others are listed at nearby places, such as Funtington and East and West Ashling.[343] In the subsidy the surname is confined to the south-west part of West Sussex, where it is first found in the 13th century. Other 16th century sources show the surname still surviving in the same area, but not elsewhere in Sussex.[344] The surname dispersed somewhat during the 17th century, when it appears in the north of West Sussex, at Kirdford, and further east than earlier in the southern part of West Sussex, at Poling, Ferring, Angmering, and Lyminster, all places close together. The West Sussex Protestation Returns list 18 persons named Scardevile, etc., which was probably the whole number of adult males with the name in West Sussex at that time.[345] No evidence has been found for the name in East Sussex before 1700.

Until after 1500 the surname usually appears as Scardevile or Skardevile. Forms such as Skardefeld, and Skarvile appear during the 16th century, but forms such as Scardevile continued to be used all through the 16th and 17th centuries, beside forms such as Scardefield.[346] The form Scardefield was in use in West Sussex during the 18th century.[347] The surname still survives in Sussex at the present day, though no longer limited to any one part of the county. The usual forms to-day are Scarfield and Scardifield. There seems no serious doubt that all the persons who appear in Sussex named Scarville, de Scardevile, Scarfield, etc., share a common descent, and are all descended from the 13th century landed family.

References

[1] On the surnames of Norman nobles before the Conquest generally, see J.C. Holt, *What's in a Name? Family Nomenclature and the Norman Conquest* (1982), pp. 13, 14.

[2] C.T. Clay, *Early Yorks. Charters* (1949), vol. viii, pp. 1–26.

[3] *Ibid.*, vol. viii, pp. 1, 2; L.C. Loyd, "Origin of the Family of Warenne," *Yorks. Archaeological Journal* (1934), vol. xxxi, pp. 98–103.

[4] C.T. Clay, *op. cit.*, vol. viii, pp. 54, 55, 56, 57; H.W.C. Davis, *Regesta Regum Anglo-Normannorum* (1913), vol. i, pp. 21, 27, 40, 41, 48, 49, 52, 57; J.H. Round, *Calendar of Documents Preserved in France* (1899), p. 141.

[5] C.T. Clay, *op. cit.*, vol. viii, pp. 66, 67, 70, 71, 73, 74, 75; H.W.C. Davis, *op. cit.*, vol. i, p. 83; C.H. Haskins, *Norman Institutions* (1960), p. 287.

[6] L.C. Loyd, "Origin of the Family of Warenne", *Yorks. Archaeological Journal* (1934), vol. xxxi, p. 111.

[7] C.T. Clay, *op. cit.*, vol. viii, pp. 12–13, 82–95; Round, *op. cit.*, p. 74.

[8] C.T. Clay, *op. cit.*, vol. viii, pp. 10, 26, 76, 78, 81, 84, 85, 87, 93–5, 97–8; *Lewes Chartulary*, vol. ii, p. 19.

[9] C.T. Clay, *op. cit.*, vol. viii, pp. 116–8, 121, 128, 129.

[10] *Ibid.*, vol. viii, pp. 116-8.
[11] *Ibid.*, vol. viii, pp. 129–36; *Lewes Chartulary*, vol. i, p. 49.
[12] See, e.g., *Surnames of Oxon.*, pp. 181–4.
[13] C.T. Clay, *op. cit.*, vol. viii, pp. 26, 28; *Lewes Chartulary*, vol. ii, pp. 21, 41.
[14] *Ibid.*, vol. i, pp. 53, 55; vol. ii, p. 50; C.T. Clay, *op. cit.*, vol. viii, pp. 33–4.
[15] J.H. Round, *Calendar of Documents Preserved in France* (1899), vol. i, pp. 395–6; L.C. Loyd, *Origins of Some Anglo-Norman Families* (Harleian Society, vol. ciii) (1951), p. 20.
[16] Round, *loc. cit.*
[17] Round, *op. cit.*, p. 398.
[18] *Ibid.*, p. 39; W. Dugdale, *Monasticon Anglicanum* (1830), vol. vi, 1083; J. Hunter, *Magnum rotulum scaccarii, vel magnum rotulum pipae, anno tricesimo-primo regni Henrici primi* (1833), p. 72.
[19] *Lewes Chartulary*, vol. ii, p. 71; *Great Roll of the Pipe for the 31st year of Henry II* (Pipe Roll Soc., vol. xxxiv) (1913), p. 169.
[20] *V.C.H. Suss.*, vol. vi, part i, p. 4; I.J. Sanders, *English Baronies* (1960), p. 108.
[21] *S.A.C..*, vol. x, pp. 139–40; vol. liv, p. 166; *3 Suss. Subsidies*, p. 154; *Cal. Pat., 1441–46*, p. 391; *V.C.H. Suss.*, vol. vi, part i., p. 206.
[22] *Cal. Pat., 1354–8*, p. 651.
[23] *V.C.H. Suss.*, vol. vi, part i, p. 261; *S.A.C.*, vol. liv, pp. 165–67.
[24] *S.A.C.*, vol. lxxxiii, p. 44; *Non. Inquis.*, p. 367; *V.C.H. Suss.*, vol. vii, p. 207.
[25] J.C. Holt, *What's in a Name? Family Nomenclature and the Norman Conquest* (1982), p. 14.
[26] H.W.C. Davis, *op. cit.*, vol.i, pp.55, 103; J.H. Round, *op. cit.*, p.446; M. Chibnall, *Ecclesiastical History of Orderic Vitalis* (1972), vol. iii, pp. 136, 138.
[27] Round, *op. cit.*, p. 447.
[28] H.W.C. Davis, *op. cit.*, vol. i, pp. 27, 31, 46, 47, 50, 55, 89; M. Chibnall, *op. cit.*, pp. 100, 138.
[29] H.W.C. Davis, *op. cit.*, vol. i, pp. 55, 84; M. Chibnall, *op. cit.*, vol. iii, pp. 138, 140; J.F.A. Mason, 'Roger de Montgomery and his sons', *Trans. Royal Historical Soc.*, 5th series, vol. xiii, pp. 13–23.
[30] *Victoria County History of Hants.*, vol. i, pp. 427, 509.
[31] *V.C.H. Suss.*, vol. iv, pp. 63, 85.
[32] On the descent of the honor, see W. Farrer, *Honors and Knights' Fees* (1925), vol. iii, pp. 5–7.
[33] H.W.C. Davis, *op. cit.*, vol. i, p. 95.
[34] H. Hall, *Red Book of the Exchequer* (1896), vol. i, p. 397.
[35] *Complete Peerage*, vol. ix, p. 366, and sources there cited.
[36] *Ibid.*, vol. ix, pp. 336–67; J.H. Round, *op. cit.*, p. 2.

[37] J.H. Round, *Geoffrey de Mandeville* (1892), pp. 319–20; H.A. Cronne and R.H.C. Davis, *Regesta Regum Anglo-Normannorum* (1968), vol. iii, pp. 12, 34, 62, 70, 74, 98, 103, 184, 208, 271, 326.

[38] L.C. Loyd, *Origin of Some Anglo-Norman families* (Harleian Soc., vol. ciii) (1951), p. 7.

[39] H.W.C. Davis, *op. cit.*, vol. i, p. 97.

[40] W. Farrer, *Honours and Knights' Fees*, vol. iii, pp. 78–9; *Calendar of Charter Rolls, 1226–52*, pp. 280, 381.

[41] *3 Suss. Subsidies*, p. 73; *Fitzalan Surveys*, p. 136.

[42] *Ibid.*, p. 147.

[43] *S.A.C.*, vol. xxiv, p. 67; vol. lxxxix, p. 127, see also West Suss. Rec. Office, E.P. VI/19A/1, m.4d.

[44] The surname Dauborne occurs in West Suss., 1642 (*W. Suss. 1641–2*, pp. 119, 130), but is unlikely to be a variant of Daubigny.

[45] *Cal. Pat., 1232–47*, p. 408; *Calendar of Close Rolls, 1242–47*, pp. 249–51.

[46] J.H. Round, *Studies in Peerage and Family History* (1970), pp. 115–146; H.A. Cronne and R.H.C. Davis, *Regesta Regum Anglo-Normannorum* (1968), pp. 145–6, 173, 303; *Book of Fees*, vol. i, pp. 144, 539-41; *Curia Regis Rolls*, vol. x, p. 270; *Rotuli Hundredorum*, vol. ii, pp. 76–77; D.M. Stenton, *Great Roll of the Pipe for the 9th Year of Richard I* (Pipe Roll Soc., vol. xlvi) (1931), pp. 156–8; D.M. Stenton, *Pleas before the king or his justices* (Selden Soc., vol. lxxxiii) (1967), p. 96.

[47] *V.C.H. Suss.*, vol. i, pp. 388, 391, 392, 396, 397, 405, 438.

[48] L.F. Salzman, "William de Cahagnes and the Family of Keynes", *S.A.C.*, vol. lxiii, p. 180.

[49] Surnames such as Caine, Kayne, etc., have a different origin.

[50] J.H. Round, *Calendar of Documents Preserved in France* (1899), vol. i, pp. 81, 524.

[51] J. Hunter, *Magnum rotulum scaccarii, vel magnum rotulum pipae, anno tricesimo-primo regni Henrici primi* (1833), p. 68; H.A. Cronne and R.H.C. Davis, *op. cit.*, vol. ii, pp. 27, 53, 76, 218, 243.

[52] L.C. Loyd, *op. cit.*, p. 27.

[53] *Lewes Chartulary*, vol. i, pp. 17–18, 38.

[54] *Ibid.*, vol. i, p. 153; vol. ii, pp. 28–9, 46, 47, 61; *S.A.C.*, vol. lxv, pp. 22–3.

[55] L.F. Salzman, "Sussex Domesday Tenants", *S.A.C.*, vol. lxv, pp. 20–53; J.H. Round, "Early Sheriffs of Norf.", *English Historical Review*, vol. xxxv (1920), pp. 482-4; *V.C.H. Suss.*, vol. iv, pp. 23, 58–9; vol. vii, p. 114.

[56] L.C. Loyd, *op. cit.*, p. 36.

[57] *V.C.H. Suss.*, vol. ix, p. 127.

[58] *Lewes Chartulary*, vol. i, p. 152; *S.A.C.*, vol. xxiv, p. 3.

[59] *Calendar of Inquisitions Post Mortem*, vol. i, pp. 190, 214–5; vol. iii, pp. 168–9; vol. iv, p. 102; F.R.H. Du Boulay, *Lordship of Canterbury* (1966), pp. 333, 388.

[60] *P.N. Suss.*, vol. ii, p. 469; F. Hull, *Calendar of the White and Black books of the Cinque Ports* (1966), pp. 122, 154. De Cralle occurs as a surname in 14th century Suss. at Warbleton, in which parish Cralle lies: *Non. Inquis.*, p. 392.

[61] J.H. Round, *Calendar of Documents Preserved in France* (1899), pp. 64, 82. The name Floc occurs in Suss., 1296 (*3 Suss. Subsidies*, p. 33), but this may be an error for Flot.

[62] *De Lisle and Dudley MSS.*, vol. i, p. 61.

[63] W. Farrer, *Honors and Knights' Fees* (1925), vol. iii, p. 339.

[64] *Suss. Fines*, vol. i, p. 95; vol. ii, pp. 134, 137, 154; D.M. Stenton, *Great Roll of the Pipe for the 9th year of Richard I* (Pipe Roll Soc., vol. xlvi) (1931), p. 223.

[65] E. Searle, *Chronicle of Battle Abbey* (1980), p. 120. Roger de St. Ledger, who quit – claimed land at Bexhill, c. 1190 (*Chichester Chart.*, p. 85) probably inherited this land from his grandmother, Mabel de Bixle. On the origins of the surname, see Loyd, *op. cit.*, p. 90; W. Dugdale, *Monasticon Anglicanum* (1821), vol.iii, p. 247.

[66] *V.C.H. Suss.*, vol. ix, pp. 84, 137.

[67] E. Searle, *loc. cit.*

[68] *Lewes Chartulary*, vol. i, pp. 149, 150, 153; J.H. Round, *Calendar of Documents Preserved in France* (1899), p. 64; *V.C.H. Suss.*, vol. ix, p. 137.

[69] *Lewes Chartulary*, vol. i, pp. 150, 153.

[70] *Ibid.*, vol. i, p. 153.

[71] Round, *loc. cit.*

[72] H.Hall, *Red Book of the Exchequer* (1896), vol. i, p. 202.

[73] *Great Roll of the Pipe for the 23rd Year of Henry II* (Pipe Roll Soc., vol. xxvi) (1905), pp. 189, 191.

[74] *De Lisle and Dudley MSS.*, vol. i, p. 68; H. Hall, *op. cit.*, vol. ii, p. 554.

[75] *V.C.H. Suss.*, vol. ix, p. 137.

[76] *Ibid.*, vol. ix, p. 229; *De Lisle and Dudley MSS.*, vol. i, p. 46; *Book of Fees*, vol. ii, pp. 659, 670; *Suss. Fines*, vol. i, p. 81.

[77] *V.C.H. Suss.*, vol. i, pp. 390, 393, 396, 397, 399, 402, 407.

[78] See p. 234.

[79] *V.C.H. Suss.*, vol. i, pp. 396, 397, 407, 444.

[80] *V.C.H. Suss.*, vol. i, p. 352.

[81] *V.C.H. Suss.*, vol. i, p. 397.

[82] *Ibid.*, p. 421.

[83] *Victoria County History of Suffolk*, vol. i, pp. 536, 537.

[84] *Lewes Chartulary*, vol. i, p. 40.

[85] *Ibid.*, vol. i, p. 31; J.H. Round, *Ancient Charters* (Pipe Roll Soc., vol. x) (1888), p. 7.

[86] *Lewes Chartulary*, vol. i, p. 12; C.T. Clay, *Early Yorks. Charters* (1949) vol. viii, pp. 65, 71.

[87] J.H. Round, *Calendar of Documents Preserved in France* (1899), p. 80; *S.A.C.*, vol. xlii, p. 81.

[88] *V.C.H. Suss.*, vol. vii, p. 175; *S.A.C.*, vol. lxxxii, p. 87.

[89] *V.C.H. Suss.*, vol. i, pp. 447, 448, 449, 450.

[90] *Book of Fees*, vol. ii, p. 689; *Suss. Fines*, vol. i, pp. 10, 121; vol. ii, pp. 25, 63, 121; *V.C.H. Suss.*, vol. i, p.379.

[91] J.H. Round, *Calendar of Documents Preserved in France* (1899), pp. 396, 398, 401; L.F. Salzman, *Chartulary of Sele* (1923), p. 3.

[92] H. Mayr-Harting, *Acta of the Bishops of Chichester, 1075–1207*, p. 110.

[93] *Ibid.*, p. 185; *Lewes Chartulary*, vol. ii, p. 38, 71, 105; *Chichester Chart.*, pp. 87, 351; D.M. Stenton, *Great Roll of the Pipe for the 6th year of Richard I* (Pipe Roll Soc. vol. xliii) (1928), p. 229; P.M. Barnes, *Great Roll of the Pipe for the 16th year of John* (Pipe Roll Soc., vol. lxxiii) (1962), pp. 164, 165; *S.A.C.*, vol. cv, pp. 76–83; L.F. Salzman, *Chartulary of Sele* (1923), pp. 4, 48, 81.

[94] W. Farrer, *Honors and Knights' Fees*, (1925), vol. iii, pp. 351-2.

[95] *S.A.C..*, vol. lxi, p. 142.

[96] *V.C.H. Suss.*, vol.i, p. 380; D.C. Douglas, *Domesday Monachorum* (1944), pp. 37-8; *English Historical Review*, vol. xxix, p. 353; J.H. Round, *Calendar of Documents Preserved in France* (1899), p. 159; *Lewes Chartulary*, vol. i, pp. 75, 138.

[97] *Ibid.*, vol. i, pp. 75, 130, 138, 161; *Chichester Chart.*, p. 45; *V.C.H. Suss.*, vol. iv, p. 59; D.M. Stenton, *Great Roll of the Pipe for the 10th year of Richard I* (Pipe Roll Soc., vol. lxvii) (1932), p. 228.

[98] J.C. Holt, *What's in a Name? Family Nomenclature and the Norman Conquest* (1982), pp. 13, 14.

[99] *V.C.H. Suss.*, vol. i, pp. 439, 440; *Lewes Chartulary*, vol. i, p. 13. Tesselyn occurs as a surname in Suss., 1296; *3 Suss. Subsidies*, p. 63; *S.A.C.*, vol. liii, p. 162.

[100] *Lewes Chartulary*, vol. i, p. 75; J.H. Round, *Calendar of Documents Preserved in France* (1899), pp. 435, 437.

[101] H. Hall, *Red Book of the Exchequer* (1896), vol. i, p. 204; *Lewes Chartulary*, vol. i, p. 74; *Great Roll of the Pipe for the 11th Year of Henry II* (Pipe Roll Soc., vol. viii) (1887), p. 92; J. Hunter, *Magnum rotulum scaccarii, vel magnum rotulum pipae, anno tricesimo-primo regni Henrici Primi* (1833), p. 68.

[102] See L.F. Salzman, 'Some Domesday Tenants', *S.A.C.*, vol. lvii, pp. 162.

[103] W. Dugdale, *Monasticon Anglicanum* (1830), vol. vi, part. ii, p. 1083;

104 V.C.H. Suss., vol. i, p. 379; vol. vi, part i, p. 11; Round, op. cit., p. 401–3; T.D. Hardy, Rotuli de Oblatis et Finibus (Record Commission) (1835), pp. 175, 182; L.C. Loyd, op. cit., p. 91.
104 Round, Calendar of Documents Preserved in France (1899), pp. 400, 401.
105 Reaney, Dict., p. 277.
106 V.C.H. Suss., vol. i, p. 378. See also B.A. Lees, Records of the Templars in the 12th Century (1935), p. 239.
107 De Lisle and Dudley MSS., vol. i, p. 33.
108 Suss. Fines, vol. i, p. 7.
109 Ibid., vol. i, p. 100; vol. ii, p. 126; Boxgrove Chart., p. 85; 3 Suss. Subsidies, pp. 63, 276.
110 Ibid., pp. 62, 66, 138, 160, 163, 254, 273; S.A.C., vol. xii, p. 31.
111 3 Suss. Subsidies, p. 98; Fitzalan Surveys, pp. 31, 34.
112 Suss. Custumals, vol. i, p. 83.
113 Surnames of Oxon., pp. 204–6.
114 3 Suss. Subsidies, pp. 45, 48; S.A.C.., vol. xviii, p. 35.
115 V.C.H. Suss., vol. ix, p. 278.
116 H. Hall, op. cit., vol. i, pp. 32, 39, 56, 75, 170, 385; vol. ii, p. 697; I.J. Sanders, Feudal Military Service, (1956), p. 20; see also I.J. Sanders, English Baronies (1960), p. 82; F.M. Stenton, Documents Illustrative of the Social and Economic History of the Danelaw, pp. 113, 355.
117 Loyd., op. cit., pp. 96–97.
118 Chichester Chart., p. 301; Round, op. cit., p. 134.
119 Ibid., p. 82; Loyd, op. cit., pp. 96–97; W. Dugdale, Monasticon Anglicanum (1830), vol. vi, part iii, p. 1470.
120 De Lisle and Dudley MSS., vol. i, pp. 38, 39.
121 Great Roll of the Pipe for the 16th Year of Henry II (Pipe Roll Soc., vol. xv) (1892), p. 138.
122 H. Hall, op. cit., vol. ii, p. 623; V.C.H. Suss., vol. ix, p. 278; C.F. Slade, Great Roll of the Pipe for the 12th Year of John (Pipe Roll Soc., vol. lxiv) (1951), p. 59.
123 V.C.H. Suss., vol. ix, p. 278.
124 Ibid., vol. ix, p. 79; Calendar of Close Rolls, 1261–64, pp. 54–5, 142.
125 De Lisle and Dudley MSS., vol. i, p. 71; P.M. Barnes, Great Roll of the Pipe for the 14th year of King John (Pipe Roll Soc., vol. lxviii) (1955), p. 86. See also Suss. Custumals, vol. ii, pp. 116, 134.
126 Inderwick, Winchelsea, pp. 160, 161, 187, 215; 3 Suss. Subsidies, p. 211.
127 Calendar of Inquisitions Miscellaneous, vol. i, p. 182.
128 3 Suss. Subsidies, p. 148; S.A.C., vol. lxxxix, p. 125; Suss. Fines, vol. iii, p. 139.
129 Loyd, op. cit., p. 52.
130 M. Chibnall, Ecclesiastical History of Orderic Vitalis (1973), vol. iv,

pp. 48–50, 200, 204, 224; J.H. Round, *Calendar of Documents Preserved in France* (1899), pp. 218, 225; I.J. Sanders, *English Baronies* (1960), pp. 136–137; C. Johnson and H.A. Cronne, *Regesta Regum Anglo-Normannorum* (1956), vol. ii, p. 188.

[131] *Chichester Chart.*, pp. 28, 45; *Suss. Fines*, vol. i, pp. 45, 69, 71; *Lewes Chartulary*, vol. i, pp. 159, 160; *Great Roll of the Pipe for the 17th year of Henry II* (Pipe Roll Soc., vol. xvi) (1893), p. 130.

[132] *Lewes Chartulary*, vol. ii, pp. 37, 46, 50–53; *Curia Regis Rolls*, vol. iv, p. 62; *V.C.H. Suss.*, vol. vii, p. 258; W. Farrer, *Early Yorks. Charters* (1914), vol. i, pp. 480–81; W. Farrer, *Honors and Knights' Fees*, (1925), vol. iii, p. 355.

[133] *Suss. Subsidy, 1524–5*, pp. 28, 32, 33, 44, 101; P.R.O. E.179/225/50, m. 30; E.179/191/378,mm.1,3d; *W. Suss, 1641–2*, pp. 28, 59, 74, 89, 96, 125, 137, 163, 200.

[134] W. Farrer, *Honors and Knights' Fees* (1925), vol. iii, pp. 33–4; *Boxgrove Chart.*, p. 35; *Lewes Chartulary*, vol. i, pp. 121, 144–5.

[135] *Suss. Fines*, vol. ii, p. 37; *3 Suss. Subsidies*, pp. 57, 61, 93, 116, 214, 272, 325; D.M. Stenton, *Great Roll of the Pipe for the 6th year of Richard I* (Pipe Roll Soc., vol. xliii) (1928), p. 231; *Suss. Subsidy, 1524–5*, pp. 110, 122; P.R.O. E.179/270/10.

[136] J.H. Round, *Calendar of Documents Preserved in France* (1899), pp. 80, 81, 134; E. Searle, *Chronicle of Battle Abbey* (1980), p. 120; *V.C.H. Suss.*, vol. i, p. 377; Loyd, *op. cit.*, p. 44.

[137] *Lewes Chartulary*, vol. i, pp. 61–3, 97; vol. ii, pp. 25, 45–7, 57, 63, 65; *Suss. Fines*, vol. ii, p. 52; *V.C.H. Suss.*, vol. vii, pp. 213, 228, 231; C.T. Clay, *Early Yorks, Charters* (1949), vol. viii, pp. 78, 82, 87, 92, 99, 114, 158.

[138] *Lewes Chartulary*, vol. ii, pp. 74–77, 117; *Chichester Chart.*, p. 121.

[139] W. Farrer, *Honors and Knights' Fees* (1925), vol. iii, 91–2. And see p. 70.

[140] Farrer, *op. cit.*, vol. iii, pp. 334–5; *Lewes Chartulary*, vol. i, pp. 23, 62; vol. ii, pp. 37, 75; *Complete Peerage*,vol. x, pp. 535–6.

[141] *V.C.H. Suss.*, vol. vii, pp. 54, 95, 96; *Lewes Barony Recs.*, p. 69; *Suss. Fines*, vol. i, p. 3; vol. ii, p. 25.

[142] *V.C.H. Suss.*, vol. iv, pp. 30–31; W. Farrer, *Honors and Knights' Fees* (1925), vol. iii, p. 52; *Surnames of Lancs.*, pp. 13–14.

[143] Loyd, *op. cit.*, p. 111.

[144] J.H. Round, *Calendar of Documents Preserved in France* (1899), pp. 328–9.

[145] *Ibid.*, pp. 328–9, 331.

[146] W. Farrer, *Honors and Knights' Fees* (1925), vol. iii, p. 56.

[147] *Ibid.*; *Boxgrove Chart.*, p. 35.

[148] *Ibid.*, pp. 18, 19, 26, 30, 45, 50, 62; *V.C.H. Suss.*, vol. iv, pp. 156–7.

[149] Reaney, *Dict.*, p. 170. And see p. 191.

[150] *S.A.C.*, vol. lxix, pp. 45ff; M.T. Martin, *Percy Chartulary* (Surtees Soc., vol. cxvii) (1911), pp. 109, 111, 116, 135.

[151] M.T. Morlet, *Etude D'Anthroponymie Picarde* (1967), p. 198; W. Farrer, *Honors and Knights' Fees* (1925), vol. iii, p. 72; H.E. Salter, *Eynsham Chartulary* (Oxford Historical Soc., vol. xlix) (1907), vol. i, p. 82; *Two Chartularies of the Augustinian Priory of Bruton and the Cluniac Priory of Montacute* (Somerset Rec. Soc., vol. viii) (1894), p. 84.

[152] L.F. Salzman, *Chartulary of Sele* (1923), p. 82; H. Hall, *Red Book of the Exchequer* (1896), vol. i, p. 199 (given as William Parcertes.)

[153] *V.C.H. Suss.*, vol. vi, part i, p. 229; F.W. Maitland, *Rolls of the King's Court in the Reign of Richard I* (Pipe Roll Soc., vol. xiv) (1891), p. 4.

[154] *V.C.H. Suss.*, vol. iv, part i, p. 229; L.F. Salzman, *Chartulary of Sele* (1923), pp. 16, 80; *Close Rolls of Henry III, 1227–31*, p. 324; C. Robinson, *Great Roll of the Pipe for the 14th year of Henry III* (Pipe Roll Soc., vol. xlii) (1927), p. 240.

[155] L.F. Salzman, *op. cit.*, pp. 61, 62; *V.C.H. Suss.*, vol. iv, p. 28; *3 Suss. Subsidies*, pp. 61, 167, 281; *Non Inquis.*, p. 390.

[156] M.T. Martin, *op. cit.*, pp. 13, 474; *Feudal Aids*, vol. vi, p. 47.

[157] J. Jönsjö, *Middle English Nicknames* (1979), vol. i, p. 175. Some land at Woodmancote was called Talcourteys, 14th Century, probably from the surname: *Calendar of Inquisitions Post Mortem*, vol. xvi, p. 144.

[158] *Lewes Chartulary*, vol. i, pp. 117–8, 123, 131, 135, 138, 157–8; J. Hunter, *op. cit.*, p. 171; *S.A.C.*, vol. xi, p. 75.

[159] *Curia Regis Rolls, 15–16 John*, pp. 198–9, 293; *S.A.C.*, vol. lvii, pp. 173–4; *Lewes Chartulary*, vol. i, pp. 73, 75, 82.

[160] *Curia Regis Rolls, 11–14 John*, p. 248; *Curia Regis Rolls, 15–16 John*, p. 293; *Chichester Chart.*, p. 350; *Suss. Fines*, vol. i, p. 51.

[161] See, e.g., *ibid.*, vol. i, pp. 9, 51; vol. ii, pp. 98, 129; *3 Suss. Subsidies*, pp. 21, 24, 186, 190, 202, 210, 321; *Chichester Chart.*, pp. 151, 163, 175, 214, 350, 351; *De Lisle and Dudley MSS.*, vol. i, pp. 115, 128; *Suss. Custumals*, vol. iii, p. 24; *Book of Fees*, vol. ii, p. 691; *Curia Regis Rolls, 11–14 John*, p. 248; *Cal. Pat., 1258–66*, p. 333; *Calendar of Inquisitions Miscellaneous*, vol. i, pp. 276, 321. The name has sometimes been printed Mause, in error: *Feudal Aids*, vol. v, pp. 131, 137, 138, 144; *Placita De Banco* (P.R.O. Lists and Indexes, xxxii) vol. ii, pp. 663, 667.

[162] Reaney, *Dict.*, p. 243; *Feudal Aids*, vol. v, p. 144.

[163] Reaney, *Dict.*, p. 236; B. Cottle, *Penguin Dictionary of Surnames* (1978), p. 239.

[164] Reaney, *Dict.*, p. 243–4; P. Erlebach, *Die Zusammengesetsten englischer Zunamen franzosischer Herkunft* (1979), p. 88.

[165] J. Jönsjö, *Middle English Nicknames* (1979), vol. i, p. 127; A. Dauzat, *Dictionnaire Etymologique Des Noms de Famille* (1951), p. 408.

[166] *Curia Regis Rolls, 7–8 John*, p. 129; *Lewes Chartulary*, vol. ii, p. 109.

[167] A Gildewin son of Sanzaver occurs, early 12th century, but this is probably an error for Gildewin son of Savaric: *Lewes Chartulary*, vol. ii, p. 84.
[168] Farrer, *Honors and Knights' Fees* (1925), vol. iii, pp. 154–55.
[169] See p. 234.
[170] *V.C.H. Suss.*, vol. i, p. 379.
[171] J.H. Round, *Calendar of Documents Preserved in France* (1899), p. 401; L.F. Salzman, *Chartulary of Sele* (1923), p. 4; see also B.A. Lees, *op. cit.*, p. 228.
[172] *Curia Regis Rolls, 7–8 John*, p. 4. William *Comes* is said to have been Simon's brother: *V.C.H. Suss.*, vol. vi, part i, p. 180.
[173] *Curia Regis Rolls, 7–8 John*, pp. 4, 39; *V.C.H. Suss.*, vol. vi, part i, p. 180; Salzman, *op. cit.*, pp. 5, 48.
[174] *Ibid.*, pp. 62, 67; *Lewes Chartulary*, vol. ii, pp. 67, 69, 72; *Book of Fees*, vol. ii, p. 689, 1204, 1239, 1257; *Non. Inquis.*, p. 369; *3 Suss. Subsidies*, pp. 81, 121, 125; P.R.O. E.179/189/42,m.23; *Suss. Fines*, vol. i, p. 25; vol. ii, p. 69.
[175] See p. 267.
[176] See the case of Trenchmere, p. 407; and see p. 19.
[177] M.T. Morlet, *op. cit.*, pp. 281, 430.
[178] *Ibid.*, p. 155.
[179] D.C. Douglas, *Domesday Monachorum* (1944), p. 48; *Victoria County History of Kent*, vol. iii, pp. 258, 269.
[180] *De Lisle and Dudley MSS.*, vol. i, pp. 37, 48, 58.
[181] See p. 35.
[182] *Lewes Chartulary*, vol. i, p. 13.
[183] W. Dugdale, *Monasticon Anglicanum* (1825), vol. v, p. 14.
[184] *Lewes Chartulary*, vol. i, pp. 28, 30.
[185] *Rotuli Hundredorum*, vol. i, p. 461; W. Rye, *Short Calendar of the Feet of Fines for Norf., for the Reigns of Richard I, John, Henry III, and Edward I* (1885), p. 116; *Feudal Aids*, vol. iii, pp. 427, 447, 493, 542.
[186] *Lewes Chartulary*, vol. i, pp. 30, 56, 62, 64; vol. ii, pp. 29, 125; C.T. Clay, *Early Yorks. Charters* (1949), vol. viii, p. 93.
[187] W. Farrer, *Honors and Knights' Fees* (1925), vol. iii, pp. 327–31; *Complete Peerage*, vol. x, p. 656; *S.A.C.*, vol. xv, p. 5; vol. lii, p. 1.
[188] *V.C.H. Suss.*, vol. i, p. 371.
[189] J.H. Round, *Calendar of Documents preserved in France* (1899), p. 511; *S.A.C.*, vol. xl, pp. 76–77; *Lewes Chartulary*, vol. i, pp. 122, 159, 160; W. Dugdale, *Monasticon Anglicanum* (1830), vol. vi, part ii, p. 1091.
[190] *Lewes Chartulary*, vol. i, pp. 109, 122, 139.
[191] *Suss. Fines*, vol. ii, p. 13, 24, 35, 98, 127; J. Hunter, *Rotuli Selecti* (1834), p. 252; *Lewes Chartulary*, vol. i, p. 150; *Catalogue of Ancient Deeds*, vol. iii, p. 53.

192 *3rd Report of Royal Commission on Historical MSS.* (1872), p. 223; E. Searle, *Lordship and Community* (1974), p. 210; *V.C.H. Suss.*, vol. ix, p. 212.

193 C. Johnson and H.A. Cronne, *Regesta Regum Anglo-Normannorum* (1956), vol. ii, p. 243; J. Hunter, *Magnum rotulum scaccarii, vel magnum rotulum pipae, anno tricesimo-primi regni Henrici primi* (1833), p. 69.

194 *Lewes Chartulary*, vol. i, pp. 108, 109, 158–9; *Great Roll of the Pipe for the 5th year of Henry II* (Pipe Roll Soc., vol. i) (1884), p. 60; *3rd Report of the Royal Commission on Historical MSS.* (1872), p. 224.

195 H. Hall, *Red Book of the Exchequer* (1896), vol. i, p. 202; vol. ii, p. 554; *Lewes Chartulary*. vol. i, pp. 108, 109; *Great Roll of the Pipe for the 12th year of Henry II* (Pipe Roll Soc., vol. ix) (1888), p. 90; *De Lisle and Dudley MSS.*, vol. i, p. 35.

196 E. Searle, *op. cit.*, p. 210; *V.C.H. Suss.*, vol. ix, p. 212.

197 *Ibid.*, vol. iv, p. 77; W. Farrer, *Honors and Knights' Fees* (1925) vol. iii, pp. 65–6; *Herald and Genealogist*, vol. vi, pp. 429–36.

198 See p. 45.

199 On the place-names possibly involved, see F. de Beaurepaire, *Les Noms des Communes et Anciennes Paroisses de L'Eure* (1981), p. 61; *V.C.H. Suss.*, vol. ix, p. 278.

200 The family appears to have been established in England by c. 1150 or shortly after: J.H. Round, *Calendar of Documents Preserved in France* (1899), p. 461. On the origin of the name, see Dauzat, *op. cit.*, p. 159.

201 The surname is probably from Cressy, (Seine-Maritime).

202 The surname is from Crèvecouer, (Calvados).

203 A place called Scarvilla, mentioned about 1160, is probable the place from which the surname is derived; Round, *op. cit.*, p. 160.

204 *V.C.H. Suss.*, vol. iv, p. 34; *S.A.C.*, vol. lv, pp. 29, 30.

205 The surname is from Troisgotz (Manche): Loyd, *op. cit.*, p. 106. There are localities in Cornwall called Tregoss and Tregoose, and when Tregos, Tregoose, etc., occur as surnames in south-west England, the derivation is probably from one of the Cornish place-names. The surname occurs in Essex from 1130, but the connection between the Essex and Suss. families is uncertain: *S.A.C.*, vol. xciii, pp. 34–58.

206 H. Hall, *Red Book of the Exchequer* (1896), vol. i, pp. 198–204.

207 *Ibid.*, vol. i, p. 201; W. Farrer, *Honors and Knights' Fees* (1925), vol. iii, pp. 49–50.

208 *Ibid.*, vol. iii, pp. 16–100.

209 See the instances of members of Suss. knightly families appearing as grantors or witnesses to deeds printed in J.H. Round, *Calendar of Documents Preserved in France* (1899).

210 On Oxfordshire, see *Surnames of Oxon.*, pp. 12–13.

211 See the remarks made in J.C. Holt, *What's in a name? Family*

[212] *nomenclature and the Norman Conquest* (1982), and F. Barlow, *William Rufus* (1983), p. 164.
[212] Holt, *op. cit.*, pp. 13–16.
[213] In Suss. in the 13th century some cottars were free, some unfree.
[214] *Lewes Chartulary*, vol. ii, p. 46. See also *Curia Regis Rolls, 7–8 John* (1929), p. 234, for a family of Suss. serfs without a hereditary surname, early 13th century.
[215] L.F. Salzman, *Chartulary of Sele* (1923), pp. 70, 71, 87, 93; *3 Suss. Subsidies*, p. 274.
[216] E. Searle, *Lordship and Community* (1974), p. 440.
[217] *Suss. Custumals*, vol. i, p. 45; West Suss. Record Office, EP. VI/19A/1,mm.2d,4; the surname was derived from a personal name: L.F. Salzman, *Chartulary of Sele* (1923), p. 78.
[218] *De Lisle and Dudley MSS.*, vol. i, pp. 42, 88, 95.
[219] *Suss. Fines*, vol. i, p. 47; *3 Suss Subsidies*, p. 92.
[220] *Suss. Custumals*, vol. i, p. 73; *3 Suss. Subsidies*, pp. 68, 142, 264; *Suss. Wills*, vol. ii, p. 154; *Suss. Subsidy, 1524–5*, p. 49; *W. Suss. 1641–2*, p. 111.
[221] *Boxgrove Chart.*, pp. 70, 125, 183; *3 Suss. Subsidies*, pp. 96, 97, 126, 249.
[222] *Suss. Custumals*, vol. ii, pp. 51, 53, 59; *3 Suss. Subsidies*, pp. 199, 310; *S.A.C.*, vol. xcv, p. 49.
[223] *Suss. Fines*, vol. i, pp. 34–5, 45, 47.
[224] *3 Suss. Subsidies*, pp. 43, 92, 102–5.
[225] *Fitzalan Surveys*, pp. 4, 7–8, 10–15, 16–21, 26–28, 28–34.
[226] *Suss. Custumals*, vol. iii, pp. 26–30, 33–36.
[227] *Ibid.*, vol. ii, pp. 124–5, 127–8, 130, 131.
[228] *Ibid.*, vol. ii, pp. 90–91, 97, 100–01, 104–5, 108–9. Some groups of cottars, listed in 1285, are not included in 1305, and have been ignored in the comparison.
[229] *Ibid.*, vol. ii, pp. 37–39. The position at Mayfield was similar: *ibid.*, vol. ii, pp. 51–2, 62–3.
[230] *P.N. Suss.*, vol. ii, pp. 385–7.
[231] See, e.g., *Suss. Custumals*, vol. i, pp. 33–9, 42–8, 48–52, 54–6, 79–86; vol. ii, pp. 13, 18–21, 23–4, 24–5, 51–3, 60, 61, 64–6, 67–9, 73–4, 79–83; L. Fleming, *History of Pagham* (1949), vol. i, pp. xxxiv–xxxvi; *S.A.C.*, vol. liii, pp. 150–55; *Battle Custumals*, pp. 19–21, 26–7, 32, 33, 34, 53; *Fitzalan Surveys*, pp. 4, 7–8, 10–15, 18–21, 26–31.
[232] *Suss. Custumals*, vol. i, pp. 106–122.
[233] *Fitzalan Surveys*, p. 156.
[234] See p. 370.
[235] *Lewes Chartulary*, vol. ii, p. 134; *3 Suss. Subsidies*, p. 49. The surname is presumably derived from a nickname, but its meaning is not clear. It is probably from an adjective meaning "streaked, variegated" (?from clothing worn).

[236] L. Fleming, *op. cit.*, vol. i, pp. 26, 27, 38, 87, 142, 147–9; *S.A.C.*, vol. xii, p. 37; *3 Suss. Subsidies*, p. 86; *Calendar of Close Rolls, 1369–74*, p. 76. On the meaning of the name, see *P.N. Suss.*, vol. ii, pp. 561–2, and M. Löfvenberg, *Studies on Middle English Local Surnames* (1942), p. 183.

[237] See p. 243.

[238] See p. 245.

[239] See p. 252.

[240] *Lewes Chartulary*, vol. ii, p. 82; *Cowdray Archives*, vol. ii, p. 331; *Catalogue of Ancient Deeds*, vol. iii, p. 37. And see p. 234.

[241] *Chichester Chart.*, p. 238; *3 Suss. Subsidies*, pp. 75, 150, 262.

[242] *Chichester Chart.*, pp. 36, 96, 141; *S.A.C.*, vol. li, p. 46.

[243] *Boxgrove Chart.*, pp. 85, 178, 185; *Chichester Chart.*, pp. 18, 66, 186, 247; *Suss. Custumals*, vol. i, p. 141; *De Lisle and Dudley MSS.*, vol. i, pp. 24, 25; *Suss. Fines*, vol. ii, p. 276. A Domesday sub-tenant in the area was called Turgisius, but there is no evidence to link him to the 13th century family.

[244] See, e.g., the surnames Stacker, atte Wynde, Hone, Soundry, Thele, Wisk. See below, pp. 171, 192, 196–7.

[245] *3 Suss. Subsidies*, pp. 10, 51–2, 69, 74, 84, 95, 113, 128–9, 142–3, 146, 178–9, 220, 237, 252–3, 259–60, 264, 292, 332.

[246] *Ibid.*, pp. 10, 69.

[247] *Suss. Custumals*, vol. ii, pp. 85–8, 99–100, 100–104, 111–2, 123–4, 126–7, 129, 135.

[248] See the comments made in E. Searle, *Lordship and Community* (1974), p. 330.

[249] Inderwick, *Winchelsea*, pp. 167, 174, 207.

[250] E.g. Richard de Sengeltone, called Poltreuyesch, c. 1300 (*Chichester Chart.*, p. 186); Adam called le But, 1291 (*S.A.C.*, vol. lxxxii, p. 131); William called Crul, 1212–22 (*Boxgrove Chart.*, p. 70); Joan called Noble (*S.A.C.*, vol. lxxxii, p. 128); William called Testard, 1279 (*ibid.*, vol. lxxxii, p. 129).

[251] *De Lisle and Dudley MSS.*, vol. i, p. 129; *Hastings Lathe C.R.*, p. 126.

[252] See p. 400.

[253] *Hastings Lathe C.R.*, pp. 37, 126, 127, 193.

[254] *Suss. Custumals*, vol. i, p. 105; *P.N. Suss.*, vol. i, 216.

[255] *3 Suss. Subsidies*, pp. 276, 309, 322, 323.

[256] See e.g., William de Loughteburgh, son of Richard Calf: *Chichester Chart.*, p. 372.

[257] See e.g., P.R.O. E./179/189/42,mm.1, 2, 16.

[258] *Hastings Lathe C.R.*, p. 119.

[259] P.R.O. E./179/189/42,mm, 12, 12d, 21, 22, 28.

[260] *Suss. Subsidy, 1524–5*, pp. 35, 36, 37, 41, 43, 44, 45, 48, 65, 68, 70, 78, 87, 90, 91, 98, 130, 132, 135, 137, 154, 155, 156, 159.

[261] *Surnames of Oxon.*, pp. 29–30; *Norfolk and Suffolk Surnames*, p. 21.
[262] E.g., William Wodeward (1395) is mentioned in connection with transporting 500 faggots: *Hastings Lathe C.R.*, p. 43; William Smyth (1473) tenanted a smithy: P.R.O. S.C.11/653; John Taillour (1443–5), was buying woollen cloth: *Hastings Lathe C.R.*, pp. 93–4; John Chesman (1373–4), was employed in a dairy: *S.A.C.*, vol. liv, p. 159.
[263] *Chichester Chart.*, p. 18; *Boxgrove Chart.*, p. 91; *Suss. Fines*, vol. i, pp. 30, 115; vol. ii, p. 3; *S.A.C.*, vol. li, pp. 48, 49.
[264] *3 Suss. Subsidies*, p. 109; *Chichester Chart.*, pp. 95, 111, 116, 152; *S.A.C.*, vol. li, pp. 44, 58; *Boxgrove Chart.*, p. 189.
[265] *Chichester Chart.*, pp. 140, 152, 153.
[266] Cottle, *Dict.*, p. 356.
[267] *Chichester Chart.*, pp. 83, 84, 132, 136.
[268] *S.A.C.*, vol. lxxxix, p. 119. The surname is from Duncton (Suss.), or Donnington (Suss.), or possibly from a place-name outside Suss.
[269] *Chichester Chart.*, pp. 18, 23, 164, 286; *S.A.C* vol. v, p. 241; vol. xxiv, p. 69; vol. lxxxix, pp. 120, 124, 126–7; vol. xcvi, p. 26; *Suss. Fines*, vol. ii, pp. 74, 130; *3 Suss. Subsidies*, p. 82.
[270] *Suss. Fines*, vol. ii, p. 130; *S.A.C.*, vol. xxiv, p. 68; vol. lxxxix, pp. 130, 134; vol. xcviii, p. 67; *W. Suss. 1641–2*, p. 54.
[271] *S.A.C.*, vol. lxxxvii, pp. 4ff.
[272] Inderwick, *Winchelsea*, pp. 187, 207, 215; *De Lisle and Dudley MSS.*, vol. i, pp. 76, 93–4, 97, 99, 109, 111, 112; *Suss. Fines*, vol. ii, pp. 32, 42.
[273] Inderwick, *Winchelsea*, pp. 166, 171, 176, 180, 182, 187, 190, 192, 198, 204, 213, 214; E.B. Fryde, *Book of Prests of the King's Wardrobe, 1294–5* (1962), p. 111; *Placita de Banco* (P.R.O. Lists and Indexes, no. xxxii), vol. ii, p. 658; *Chichester Chart.*, p. 286; *De Lisle and Dudley MSS.*, vol. i, pp. 76, 109, 117, 126, 128, 145; *S.A.C.*, vol. li, p. 126ff; vol. lxxxviii, p. 25.
[274] *Hastings Lathe C.R.*, pp. 24, 25, 92.
[275] *Ibid.*, p. 197.
[276] *Lewes Chartulary*, vol. i, p. 66.
[277] *Hastings Lathe C.R.*, p. 138.
[278] Inderwick, *Winchelsea*, p. 168.
[279] *Ibid.*, pp. 159, 172, 174.
[280] *Ibid.*, pp. 181, 191.
[281] Fryde, *op. cit.*, p. 111; *S.A.C.*, vol. li, p. 136.
[282] See p. 64.
[283] Fryde, *op. cit.*, pp. 107, 108, 111; *De Lisle and Dudley MSS.*, vol. i, p. 109; Inderwick, *Winchelsea*, pp. 166, 180, 198.
[284] *Ibid.*, pp. 189, 197. De Brokexe is from a Suss. place-name: see *P.N. Suss.*, vol. ii, p. 511.
[285] *Surnames of Lancs.*, pp. 325–6; Reaney, *Dict.*, p. xix.

286 S.A.C., vol. xcv, p. 53.
287 Cal. Pat., 1330–34, p. 128; E. Ekwall, *Studies on the Genitive of Groups in English*, p. 44.
288 Ibid., p. 30; Cal. Pat., 1399–1401, p. 458.
289 Ekwall, op. cit., pp. 26–40, for examples.
290 *Surnames of Oxon.*, pp. 181–191.
291 E.g., Maud de Dive, wife of William de Dive: *Lewes Chartulary*, vol. i, p. 130.
292 E.g., Emma de Falesia, wife of Gilbert de Sartilleio (*Boxgrove Chart.*, p. 64); Agnes de Falesia, wife of Hugh de Gundevilla (ibid., p. 71); Awis de Gurnaio, wife (or ?widow) of Roger de Clere (*Lewes Chartulary*, vol. ii, p. 53.
293 *Robertsbridge Charters*, pp. 4, 36, 37.
294 E.g., Olive Tyrel, daughter of Thomas Tyrel, and widow of Roland de Acstede, (*S.A.C.*, vol. lxxxiii, p. 45); Christina de Grashurst, (Grashurst in Icklesham) wife of Simon Sperling le Hunte (E. Searle, *Lordship and Community*, (1978), p. 144); Mabel de Walilonde, daughter and heiress of Robert de Walilonde, and wife of Stephen de Barmlinge (*Robertsbridge Charters*, pp. 60, 61, 63–4; *De Lisle and Dudley MSS.*, vol. i, pp. 86–7); Mabilia de Yerceneselle (Yorkshire Hill), wife of William de Eillesford (ibid., vol. i, p. 65; Juliana de Drictneselle (Drigsell near Robertsbridge) wife successively of Simon de Padiham and of Ralph de Turtellescumbe (ibid., vol. i, p. 64; *Robertsbridge Charters*, pp. 25, 26).
295 E.g., Margaret de Bodiham, wife of Henry de Bodiham (*De Lisle and Dudley MSS.*, vol. i, p. 66); Isabella de la Beche, widow of Philip de la Beche (*Lewes Barony Recs.*, p. 4); Lucy de Blancmoster, daughter of Reynold de Clifton, and wife of Gaudin de Blancmoster (*Suss. Fines*, vol. i, p. 102; vol. ii, p. 44; *Chichester Chartulary*, pp. 174, 352); Alice de Kaynes (Cahaignes) wife of Richard de Kaynes (*Suss. Fines*, vol. ii, p. 61, 96).
296 E.g., Denise la Wise, widow of a serf called le Wise (*Suss. Custumals*, vol. ii, p. 104;) Maud Germayn, widow of a cottar called German (ibid., vol. ii, pp. 107, 110); Gunnora le Caysere, widow of a serf called le Casiere (ibid., vol. ii, pp. 48, 51, 54).
297 E.g., Alice de Hildershurst, wife of Stephen Whatman (M.T. Martin, *Percy Chartulary* (Surtees Soc., vol. cxvii) (1911) pp. 396, 400); Matilda de Wogham, wife of Robert Russell (*Lewes Barony Recs.*, pp. 12, 30); Rose de Suttone, wife of Robert de Shobeham (*Lewes Chartulary*, vol. ii, p. 116).
298 E.g., Alice Bordon, wife of Gilbert Stacy (*Chichester Chart.*, p. 248); Agnes Sparwe, wife of Gilbert Herry, nief (*Suss. Custumals*, vol. i, p. 117); Isabel Tranchemier, widow of Robert Trenchemer (*Lewes Chartulary*, vol. ii, p. 54); Alice Goushurde, widow of Ralph Goushurde

(West Suss. Record Office, E.P. VI/19A/1,mm.4, 5); Alice atte Huth, widow of Robert atte Huth (*ibid.*, m.4).

[299] E.g., Joan Danyell, wife of Thomas Danyell (*Hastings Lathe C.R.*, p. 153); Gillian Ryman, widow of John Ryman (*S.A.C.*, vol. lxxxix, p. 146); Alice Walshe, widow of Ralph Walshe (*ibid.*, vol. lxxxvii, p. 4); Potencia Pakyn, widow of Jn. Pakyn (East Suss. Record Office, Glynde MSS., 1032, mm.2, 5d).

[300] H.M.C., *Rye MSS.*, pp. 22, 36.

[301] See p. 50.

[302] *Lewes Chartulary*, vol. ii, pp. 147, 152; *De Lisle and Dudley MSS.*, vol. i, p. 33; *Great Roll of the Pipe for the 14th year of Henry II* (Pipe Roll Soc., vol. xii) (1890), p. 196.

[303] J.H. Round, *Calendar of Documents Preserved in France* (1899), p.. 215.

[304] *De Lisle and Dudley MSS.*, vol. i, p. 62.

[305] *Ibid.*, vol. i, pp. 76, 77, 82.

[306] *V.C.H. Suss.*, vol. ix, p. 278; *Suss. Fines.*, vol. i, p. 108.

[307] *Calendar of Inquisitions Miscellaneous*, vol. ii, p. 102; *De Lisle and Dudley MSS.*, vol. i, p. 86.

[308] E. Searle, *op. cit.*, p. 160.

[309] *Suss. Custumals*, vol. i, p. 97; *Hastings Lathe C.R.*, p. 115.

[310] *Suss. Subsidy, 1524–5*, pp. 127, 133, 147.

[311] *Suss. Wills*, vol. iv, p. 281; E. Straker, *Buckhurst Terrier* (Suss. Record Soc., vol. xxxiv) (1934), p. 84.

[312] W.H. Challen, *Parish Register of Cocking, 1558–1837*, p. 45; R. Garraway Rice, *Parish Register of Horsham* (Suss. Record Soc., vol. xxi) (1915), pp. 29, 43, 44, 386.

[313] J.H. Round, *Calendar of Documents in France* (1899), p. 461.

[314] *S.A.C.*, vol. xlvi, p. 171.

[315] A. Dauzat, *op. cit.*, p. 159.

[316] *S.A.C.*, vol. xlvi, p. 172.

[317] *Suss. Fines*, vol. i, pp. 85, 89, 129; vol. ii, pp. 20, 43, 60. Broadbridge was a detached portion of Sullington parish; *Calendar of Close Rolls, 1242–47*, p. 112; *Book of Fees*, vol. ii, p. 690.

[318] *S.A.C.*, vol. xlvi, p. 177–8; *S.A.C.*, vol. xxii, p. 155.

[319] *S.A.C.*, vol. xlvi, p. 170ff; vol. xlvii, p. 116ff; vol. xlviii, p. 1ff. And see the pedigree printed *ibid.*, vol. xlvii, p. 144.

[320] *Ibid.*, vol. xlvii, p. 178–80; *Suss. Wills*, vol. iv, p. 132; *V.C.H. Suss.*, vol. vii, pp. 100, 159, 183, 190; *Wiston Archives*, p. 203.

[321] *S.A.C.*, vol. xlvii, pp. 120–128; *Suss. Wills*, vol. i, pp. 181, 291.

[322] *S.A.C.*, vol. xlviii, p. 5; *V.C.H. Suss.*, vol. iv, pp. 62, 129, 161.

[323] *Suss. Wills*, vol. iii, pp. 153, 175; *Suss. Subsidy, 1524–5*, p. 37.

[324] Reaney, *Dict.*, p. 86; *3 Suss. Subsidies*, p. 43; *Suss. Fines*, vol. i, p. 52.

[325] *Lewes Chartulary*, vol. ii, p. 74; *3 Suss. Subsidies*, p. 88; Reaney, *Dict.*, p. 97. And see p. 44.
[326] E.g., *Suss. Wills*, vol. i, p.167; vol. iii, p. 293; *Chichester Chart.*, pp. 249, 251; *De Lisle and Dudley MSS.*, vol. i, pp. 26–7; Lane, *Suss. Deeds*, p. 24. Forms such as Dawtrey given in secondary works for earlier dates are often translations of Latinised forms given in original sources.
[327] *Lewes Chartulary*, vol. ii, pp. 74, 75, 76, 77, 117; W. Farrer, *Honors and Knights' Fees* (1925), vol. iii, p. 91; M.T. Martin, *op. cit.*, p. 406; J.H. Round, *Calendar of Documents Preserved in France* (1899), p. 510.
[328] *Chichester Chart.*, pp. 87, 88; M.T. Martin, *op. cit.*, p. 406; W. Farrer, *op. cit.*, vol. iii, p. 24.
[329] M.T. Martin, *op. cit.*, pp. 42, 97, 131; *Feudal Aids*, vol. vi, p. 47.
[330] W. Farrer, *op. cit.*, vol. iii, p. 91.
[331] *Chichester Chart.*, p. 87; *Lewes Chartulary*, vol. ii, p. 114; *Boxgrove Chart.*, p. 37; M.T. Martin, *op. cit.*, p. 405; W. Farrer, *op. cit.*, vol. iii, p. 24.
[332] *Ibid.*, vol. iii, pp. 92–3.
[333] *V.C.H. Suss.*, vol. iv, pp. 115, 128, 174, 216; *Chichester Chart.*, pp. 249, 251; *De Lisle and Dudley MSS.*, vol. i, pp. 26, 27; *Suss. Wills*, vol. i, pp. 167, 292; vol. iii, pp. 206, 293; *S.A.C.*, vol. lxxxix, pp. 127, 129; *Feudal Aids*, vol. vi, p. 523.
[334] *Wiston Archives*, pp. 36, 143.
[335] M.T. Martin, *op. cit.*, pp. 42, 50, 97, 123, 131, 185, 421; *Feudal Aids*, vol. vi, pp. 47, 113, 127, 128, 145.
[336] *3 Suss. Subsidies*, pp. 76, 77, 88, 89, 96.
[337] *W. Suss, 1641–2*, p. 11, 93, 137, 138, 141, 142, 180.
[338] See p. 50.
[339] *Suss. Custumals*, vol. ii, p. 16; *Non. Inquis.*, p. 359; J.E. Ray, *Suss. Chantry Records* (Suss. Rec. Soc., xxxvi) (1931), p. 197; *W. Suss. 1641–2*, p. 113; *Suss. Subsidy, 1524–5*, pp. 23, 30, 31; *S.A.C.*, vol. lxxvii, p. 101.
[340] *Fitzalan Surveys*, p. 169; *V.C.H. Suss.*, vol. iv, p. 185.
[341] Lane, *Suss. Deeds*, p. 20; *Suss. Wills*, vol. i, pp. 169, 293.
[342] *3 Suss. Subsidies*, pp. 132, 247; L. Fleming, *History of Pagham* (1949), vol. i, p. 28; *Suss. Custumals*, vol. i, pp. 139, 140.
[343] *Suss. Subsidy, 1524–5*, pp. 21, 23, 25, 28, 30, 31, 33.
[344] *Suss. Wills*, vol. ii, p. 204; vol. iii, pp. 85, 87; vol. iv, p. 337; *V.C.H. Suss.*, vol. iv, p. 185; *S.A.C.*, vol. lxxvii, pp. 99, 101; L. Fleming, *op. cit.*, vol. i, p. lxxv.
[345] J.E. Ray, *op. cit.*, p. 197; *S.A.C.*, vol. xlii, p. 115; *W. Suss. 1641–2*, pp. 13, 15, 19, 54, 68, 87, 110, 112, 113, 116, 121, 133, 169, 175, 193;

E.W.P. Penfold, *First Book of the Parish Registers of Angmering* (Suss. Rec. Soc., vol. xviii) (1913), pp. 36, 39, 47, 49.

[346] See sources cited in notes 343–5, above, and also *Suss. Indictments*, vol. i, pp. 8, 19; *Suss. Wills*, vol. i, pp. 169, 293.

[347] Lane, *Suss. Deeds*, p. 20; *S.A.C.*, vol. lxvii, p. 197.

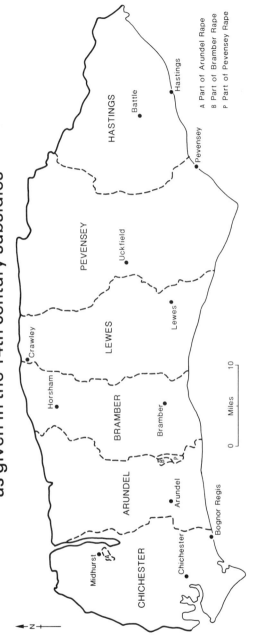

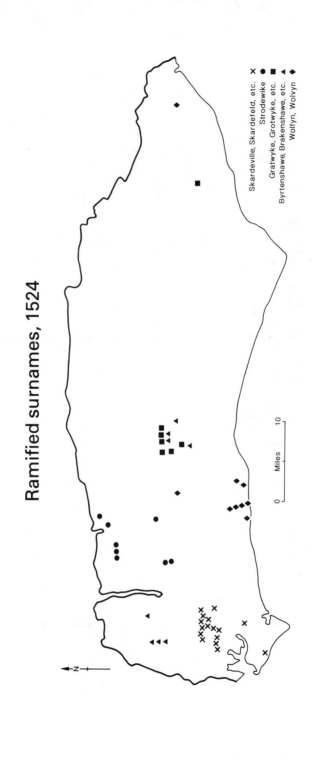

CHAPTER 2
LOCATIVE SURNAMES

Locative surnames are here defined as surnames derived from the names of specific places, as distinct from surnames derived from general topographical terms for features of the landscape. The limitations of the sources for the period between the Conquest and the middle of the 12th century means that there is little evidence for that time. Some individuals, and some families, with locative surnames or bye-names can be found in Sussex during that period, but the names in question mostly belong to aristocratic or knightly families, and many of them have already been discussed in the preceding chapter. It is impossible to say how far locative surnames were prevalent among other sections of the population at the time, but it is unlikely that hereditary surnames were at all common outside the class of larger landholders.

After the mid 12th century the information available becomes increasingly copious, and is less confined in terms of social class, though the surnames or bye-names of some sections of the community still remain very sparsely documented. Between about 1150 and 1350 very many locative surnames or bye-names occur in Sussex. There are many instances in which a locative name has been found as the name of a single individual, and it is likely that the majority of locative names discovered during this period were not hereditary. The names of all the Sussex towns, and those of most villages of any size in the county, gave rise to locative surnames or bye-names at this time, but there are also a very large number of surnames or, more frequently, bye-names, derived from small hamlets, farms, or other minor localities, including some from settlements which are now lost. Many of the locative surnames or bye-names to be found in the county before about 1350 have not been discovered there subsequently. No doubt this is partly because many of them were not hereditary, but it is likely that some surnames which were already hereditary in the early 14th century disappeared because of the heavy population losses which were experienced from the middle of the century onwards.

The great majority of the locative surnames or bye-names found in Sussex during *c.* 1150 to 1350 are ones which could originate from the names of places in the county. In some cases derivation from places outside the county is possible, but there are not a great number of names which can be said with certainty to be from the names of places outside Sussex. There are a certain number of surnames or bye-names from

French place-names, but most of these are the names of land-owners, and most of them also are names which appear in Sussex between the Conquest and the mid 12th century. Where surnames or bye-names from French place-names are not traceable as those of landholders, they are usually to be found in towns, and are likely to have been the names of merchants. The surnames of Sussex give no indication of any large scale movement into the county from outside during the period up to 1350.

These general statements are based upon an examination of the very numerous locative surnames and bye-names to be found in a wide range of sources for Sussex history for the period between the Conquest and about 1350. Though a very large number of locative names have been found, there is no possibility of discovering all those in use in the county at any one date, and any statements made about the character of the locative names in the county at any point during the Middle Ages must be subject to the reservation that there are sections of the population which are badly represented in the sources. However, in an attempt to show what the nature of the locative names in use in Sussex were at one date, the surnames and bye-names in this category given in the 1332 lay subsidy for the county have been analysed.

SUSSEX LOCATIVE NAMES IN 1332

The 1332 subsidy return for Sussex contains the names of just under 1500 persons with locative surnames or bye-names.[1] There are some disadvantages in using evidence from lay subsidies for the study of locative surnames.[2] It is often impossible to be sure if individuals were normally resident in the townships where they were assessed for the subsidy. Some persons are listed in the subsidy returns at more than one place, but it is impossible to be sure how often this occurs, and how many instances where one individual appears to be listed more than once are in fact due to the presence in the county of more than one person with the same Christian name and surname. With landowners of some importance, whose estates can often be traced, it is sometimes possible to be certain that one individual is listed at more than one place in a subsidy, but with more obscure people the position is usually not clear. It is consequently not possible to say how many persons are listed more than once in the 1332 subsidy. A further complication is that surnames or bye-names are sometimes badly mis-spelt in subsidy returns. In the case of the Sussex 1332 subsidy, this can at points be detected by comparing the 1332 returns with those of the subsidy for 1327, for many people occur as taxpayers in both. For example, William Pikewoll, listed at Ewhurst (in Shermanbury) in 1332, is listed at the same place in 1327, as William Pitknolle; his surname or bye-name was probably from the place-name Picknoll or Pyteknolle (now Parkminster) nearby.[3] Nichola de Hertherugg, listed at

Kingston by Sea in 1332, is listed in 1327 at the same place as Nichola de Hautyngtot.[4] Peter de Harpeyng, listed at Rodmell in 1332, is listed at the same place as Peter de Harpeting in 1327; his name was probably from Harpingden (formerly Herbertinges, Harpetinges) in the nearby township of Piddinghoe.[5] Some surnames which have been mangled in the 1332 subsidy can be corrected by referring to the 1327 subsidy, and some taxpayers listed in 1332 can be found in other sources, but it is impossible to check all the locative names in the 1332 subsidy against other evidence.

Though such considerations reduce the value of subsidy returns as evidence for locative names, and though subsidies do not list the whole population, it remains the case that subsidy returns still provide a more complete view of the locative names present in medieval Sussex at any one date than any other single source. Out of the just under 1500 individuals with locative surnames or bye-names in the 1332 subsidy, about 140 had names which were derived from places outside England. Many of these were members of landed families, which had existed in Sussex since the late 11th or early 12th centuries. Among the surnames derived form French place-names which appear in the 1332 subsidy, for instance, are de Cheney, de St. Leger, de Pierrepoint, de Dive, and de Haute Rive, all the surnames of landed families established in the county before 1150.[6] Other names which are found in the 1332 subsidy are Bassock, de Bohun, de Cressi, de St. George, de Scardeville, de Tregos, and de Covert, all those of landed families established in Sussex, which have not been found in the county before about 1150, and all surnames already discussed.[7] Other landowning families mentioned in 1332 with surnames from place-names outside England are de Burdeville, de Camoys, de Caumbray, de Bavent, Daundeville, de Gundeville, and de Wancy.[8] Most of these families were established in Sussex before 1200, and others, though not appearing in the county until a later time, had existed in other counties during the 12th century. The 1332 subsidy also contains the names of a few other major landed families, such as those of Percy or Mowbray, who had estates in Sussex, but whose main possession lay elsewhere. The presence of these surnames in 1332 is obviously not evidence of alien immigration into Sussex in the period immediately preceding the date of the subsidy, and many of the surnames or bye-names from place-names outside England found in Sussex in 1332 are those of families known to have been holding land in England before *c*. 1200. If such surnames or bye-names are left aside, the number of locative names derived from outside England is small, less than 30 surnames or bye-names, borne by a total of 65 individuals. This is out of a total of about 6,800 taxpayers in all listed in the subsidy, and is few considering the proximity of Sussex to France, and the presence in the county of ports engaged in trade across the Channel. Some of the locative names from outside England were derived from the names of regions or provinces; there were, for example, 2 persons named

Braban (from Brabant), 4 named Bret or le Bret, a name which when found in Sussex was probably from Brittany, one named Burgayn (from Burgundy), 3 named Champenays (from Champagne), 2 named Flemyng, 16 named le Frensh, le Frenssh, etc., 3 named Petevyne or Peytevyn (from Poitou), and 2 named Picard or Pycard (probably from Picardy, though other origins are possible).[9] If surnames known to be those of established landed families are left on one side, and the distribution of the remaining locative names originating outside England is examined, then it can be seen that the surnames or bye-names in question are widely distributed throughout the county, and not, as might perhaps be expected, concentrated at the main Sussex ports. It is true that there are a good many such names in the coastal area of West Sussex, but this merely reflects the fact that there are a large number of taxpayers listed in that area. Presumably, the presence of a good many locative surnames of foreign origin in the county was due to people having migrated across the Channel into Sussex ports in the course of trade, but if so, the immigrants (or their descendants) must have dispersed into the rural parts of the county.

In the 1332 subsidy there are listed 926 taxpayers with surnames or bye-names which could be derived from places in Sussex (though in some cases origin from places outside the county is also a possibility). Some names were those of more than one individual, and the 926 had between them 648 names. There is no infallible method of detecting which names are locative ones, but the subsidy returns have been carefully searched, and the figure just given are unlikely to be inaccurate by more than a few names. It is impossible to be certain what proportion of these names were already hereditary by 1332, but the probability is that most of them were either not hereditary, or had been hereditary for only one or two generations.

A large majority of the locative names which could be from Sussex place names were listed in the 1332 subsidy at or near to the places from which they could be derived. There were some taxpayers with surnames or bye-names which could be derived from more than one place in the county (and which in some cases, could also be from places outside Sussex). In such cases, where a taxpayer had a surname or bye-name which could be derived from the name of the place at which he was assessed, it has been assumed that his name was derived from the place-name in question. For example, the surname or bye-name de Kyngeston was that of three taxpayers in the 1332 subsidy, and it could be from any of the four places named Kingston in Sussex, or possibly from one of quite numerous places named Kingston outside the county.[10] However, one of the taxpayers named de Kyngeston was assessed at Kingston in Ferring, and the other two at Kingston near Lewes,[11] and it has therefore been assumed that the three persons concerned had names derived from those of the places where they were assessed. It is reasonable to suppose that such an assumption is sound in the great majority of cases, though it is always possible that in a few instances coincidentally an individual assessed at a place from which his surname or bye-name could have been derived in fact had a surname or bye-name from some other place with the same, or a very similar, place-name. Where, however, in the 1332 subsidy, a taxpayer had a name which could have been derived from more than one place in Sussex, and was not assessed at a place from which his name could be derived, then the taxpayer in question has been omitted from the figures that follow. There were a total of 107 taxpayers, with between them 52 names, in the 1332 subsidy, who have been omitted from the figures given below for this reason.

The figures are based on the further assumption that, where an individual listed in the subsidy had a locative surname or bye-name which might be derived either from a Sussex place-name, or from a place-name in some other county, then the surname or bye-name in question was from a Sussex place-name, and not from the name of some place outside the county. It is probably that this assumption, too, is justified in the great majority of instances, though not in all. A considerable number of the people listed in the 1332 subsidy can be found in other sources, and it is often clear from evidence other than the subsidy returns that taxpayers had property where they were assessed, and are likely to have resided in the townships where they are listed in the subsidy. The larger landowners, many of whom were assessed in several different places, were of course an exception to this, but they were not very numerous, and in most cases they belonged to families which are well known, and can be readily identified. In a minority of cases, it can be seen from sources other than the 1332 subsidy that taxpayers listed in 1332 had hereditary surnames by the time of the subsidy, and in many such cases it can be seen that families with hereditary locative surnames had resided for two or three generations at the places from which their surnames were derived. It seems very probable, therefore, that where taxpayers in 1332 had locative surnames which might be derived either from a Sussex place-name, or from a place-name in some other county, in the great majority of such cases the locative names in question were derived from Sussex place-names. This is all the more likely to be true because there is no indication, either from locative names in the whole body of source material for Sussex, or from evidence of other types, that there was any large scale migration into the county in the period preceding the date of the subsidy.

If the locative names recorded in the 1332 subsidy are examined on the basis of the assumptions set out above, and if the 107 individuals who, as already mentioned, had locative names which might be derived from more than one place name within Sussex, are left on one side, then it can be seen that in 1332 the majority of taxpayers with names which could be from Sussex place-names were still assessed, and probably in most cases still resident, at or very near to the places from which their names could be derived. Subtracting the 107 persons just mentioned, there were in 1332 819 individuals with locative names which could be from Sussex place-names, and these had between them 595 separate names (treating spelling variants of any given name as a single name). Out of these, however, 19 persons, with 19 names between them are assessed in the subsidy in hundreds, but not in individual townships; these people cannot be located in any area smaller than the hundred in which they are assessed, and have consequently been left out of the calculations. Out of the rest (800 persons with 576 names), 296 individuals, with 215 names, were in 1332 assessed at places from which their names could have been derived, or were assessed in townships or boroughs[12] within which there existed localities from the names of which their surnames or bye-names could be derived. For instance, in the subsidy five men, all named de Sedelescomb or de Sedelescombe are listed at Sedlescombe, and have been included in the 296 individuals just mentioned; also listed at Sedlescombe is a John de Chitelesbirch, whose name is from Chittlebirch, in Sedlescombe, and John has also been included in the 296.[13] Or, to give another example, two men named de Brakepole are listed at Patcham; their name is from Brapool, in Patcham, and both have therefore been included in the figure of 296.[14] A further 277 individuals, with 205 names, were listed in the subsidy outside the vills within which the places from which their names were derived lay, but within five miles of the places from which their names were derived. 227 individuals, with 156 names, were assessed in 1332 more than five miles away from the places from which their names were derived. Some of the taxpayers in the last group were only a little more than five miles distant, but there were a considerable number of instances where individuals were listed at places remote from the localities which gave rise to their names, sometimes at opposite ends of the county.

The distribution of locative surnames or bye-names in 1332 does not indicate any distinct pattern of movements in Sussex during the preceding period, and there is no sign in this evidence of large scale migration from one part of the county to another. It might perhaps have been expected, for example, that there would be many taxpayers in the Weald with names from place-names in the southern townships of the county, because of movement into the Weald where assarting was going on, but this is not the case. Even making allowance for the fact that many names in 1332 were not hereditary, and were newly derived from the places at which taxpayers were resident in 1332, the evidence from locative names suggests that there had been no very large scale movement into any particular district within the county in the years before 1332, but that there had been a limited amount of migration, mostly over quite short distances, without there being any general drift of population in any single direction.

The figures given above show that a large majority of people in the subsidy with locative names from Sussex places were still at or near the places from which their names were derived, but to some extent the impression of immobility given by these figures is misleading. The statistics given take no account of persons with surnames or bye-names from Sussex place-names who were living entirely outside the county. The only way to form any estimate of how much migration there was out of the county would be to search the subsidy returns for the whole country, so far as these are available, and note those persons with locative names from Sussex place-names. Such an exercise would not only be very laborious, but it might well be inconclusive, for there would be many cases where it was impossible to be certain if surnames or bye-names were from localities in Sussex, or in other counties. However, an examination has been made of the 1334/5 subsidy for Kent,[15] and of the Surrey subsidy for 1332,[16] in order to discover how many taxpayers are recorded in these two counties, bordering on Sussex, with surnames or bye-names which are derived from Sussex place-names. There are inevitably some instances where surnames or bye-names could be from Sussex place-names, but could also be from place-names outside the county. Excluding such instances, which are very uncertain evidence for migration, the number of persons in either Kent or Surrey with names which can be reliably derived from Sussex place-names is small. In Kent, in 1334/5, there were a few taxpayers with names from Sussex towns; there were, for example, at least 2 named Arundel, 7 named Bataille, Batayle, etc. (probably from Battle), 2 named Winchelse or Wynchelese, and one named de Lewes.[17] There are a few individuals with names from places in Sussex near the Kent border, such as Echyngham (from Etchingham),[18] Farnthe (from Frant),[19] Idenne (from Iden),[20] Jardeherst, from Yardhurst in Mayfield,[21] Maghefeld, from Mayfield, Mapelhurst (probably from Maplehurst in Ore),[22] or Bougeselle (probably from Bugsell, in Salehurst).[23] There were a limited number of people with names from places in other parts of Sussex, such as Courthope (from Courtup in Nuthurst, or Curtehope in Laughton; Courthope, Curthup, etc., is an East Sussex surname in the 14th century, and later),[24] Flecchynge (from Fletching),[25] or Ponyghe and Ponyng (from Poynings).[26] The total number of taxpayers in Kent in 1334/5 with names which can be confidently derived from Sussex place-names is small. There are a further number of persons with names which are likely to be from Sussex place-names, but which might, alternatively, be from place-names in other counties; the surnames or bye-names Findone, Fisschebourne, and Southewyk, for example, which occur in the Kent subsidy, are likely to be from the Sussex place-names Findon, Fishbourne, and Southwick, but there are places in other counties from which all three could be derived.[27] Even allowing for the probability that many of the surnames or bye-names in the Kent subsidy which might be from Sussex place-names, or might be from place-names in other counties, were in fact from Sussex, there is no evidence for any large scale migration from Sussex into Kent in the period before the 1334/5 subsidy.

The position in Surrey, as shown by the 1332 subsidy for that county, was similar. A few Surrey taxpayers in 1332 had names from places in the north of West Sussex, such as Bylinghurst (from Billingshurst), Hertynge (from Harting), Stedham, or Troton (from Trotton). Some of the people with these names were assessed in south-west Surrey, and though outside Sussex had not moved far from the localities from which their surnames or bye-names were derived.[28] There are a few other taxpayers in Surrey with names from places in other parts of Sussex, such as Aldingbourne, Bosham, Gravetye, Isenhurst, and Wigperry,[29] but the total number of persons listed in the Surrey 1332 subsidy with names which can be derived from Sussex place-names is very small, and fewer, in proportion to the total number of taxpayers than in the Kent 1334/5 subsidy. Again, there is nothing to suggest any migration on more than a very small scale between Sussex and Surrey.

It has not been possible to make a more extensive search for locative surnames or bye-names derived from Sussex place-names in similar sources for other English counties, but the number of locative names from Sussex which have been found in searching subsidy rolls in other counties for various purposes has been very small. A few Sussex locative names were present at London in the 13th and 14th centuries.[30] A scattering of examples has been found in more distant parts; the name Helnaked (from Halnaker) appears in Dorset in 1327,[31] Manewode (from the Manwood district south of Chichester) in Essex at the same date,[32] and Arundel and Bosham in Devon in 1332.[33] A more extensive search than it has been possible to make would no doubt produce further instances of locative surnames originating in Sussex in various parts of England during the 13th and 14th centuries, but it seems unlikely that such examples would be very numerous. The detailed work that has been carried out in other counties for the Surnames Survey has not revealed any substantial number of Sussex locative names in the counties which have been examined. No doubt the geographically rather isolated position of Sussex, cut off as it was by the difficult country of the Weald from easy communication with the counties to the north, was one reason for the absence of any large number of migrants from Sussex in other parts of England.

A rather more complete view of migration into Sussex from other parts of England can be formed from the evidence of the 1332 subsidy for the county. It has already been pointed out that the number of locative names from places outside England in the 1332 subsidy was small, and that many of the names concerned were those of landed families which had been present in Sussex since before 1200. There are just over 400 persons with locative surnames or bye-names from places outside the county in the

1332 subsidy. This figure excludes names which might be derived from places inside Sussex, but which might alternatively be from places outside the county. The figures is rather less than half the number of taxpayers with locative names which could be from Sussex place-names, but it would be unwise to deduce from this that the proportion of the county's population which was made up of migrants from other counties was rather less than half the proportion made up of persons born in Sussex. Apart from the fact that some locative names had been hereditary in the county for several generations by 1332, it is probable that people who moved away from their places of origin were particularly likely to acquire locative names when they settled elsewhere. It would, therefore, be unsafe to base any precise estimate of the scale of migration into Sussex on this figure, and the number of taxpayers with locative surnames from outside the county is a small proportion of the total of about 6,800 listed in the subsidy. Nevertheless, the number of locative names from outside the county is sufficient to show that in the period before 1332 Sussex was not so isolated as to prevent immigration from other parts of England on a scale which was more than negligible.

Persons with locative names from outside Sussex in 1332 were not particularly concentrated in any one part of the county, nor were they especially numerous in the Sussex ports. On the contrary, they were widely distributed throughout the county. This evidence from the 1332 subsidy agrees with that from other Sussex sources for the 13th and 14th centuries, which show locative surnames or bye-names from outside Sussex present in many parts of the county, but not particularly common in any one area. It is not possible to identify in all cases the places from which locative names from outside the county originated. Names such as, for example, Assheby, Bromlegh, or de Walecot occur, which in the absence of direct evidence about places of origin might be from any one of a number of places,[34] and besides such instances there are many locative names which could be from more than one locality. It is, therefore, not possible to assign all the locative surnames or bye-names found in 1332 to individual counties. There are eleven persons with names from the name of the county of Kent[35] (Kent, Kentish, and Cantays), and there are a further 23 with names which could be from places in Kent, though in several cases a derivation from places in other counties is possible. The names concerned here are Badelesmere (from Badlesmere), Cobeham (from Cobham in Kent, or the place of the same name in Surrey) (2 persons so called), Copeshurst (probably from Copperhurst) (two persons so called), Douere (from Dover), Herterugg (from Hartridge) (two persons so called), Ledes (probably from Leeds in Kent), Lyndregg (probably from Lindridge, near Lamberhurst and very near to the Sussex border, but again there are other possible origins), Mene (possibly from the Mean in Kent), Parstepe (from Pastheap), Polton (from Poulton in

Kent, or from one of the places so called in other counties), Renefeud (from Renville), Sevenok (from Sevenoaks), Sidyngebourn (from Sittingbourne), Sodyngton, Sotiton and Sotyngton (all probably from either Shoddington or Shottenden), Wateryngbury (from Wateringbury), Wenbregg (from Win Bridge on the Kent-Sussex boundary), and, doubtfully, Wykyng, said to be from Wickens, near Cowden and very near to the Sussex border.[36] Some of these are listed at places in East Sussex near to the Kent border, such as Ewhurst, Guestling, Wadhurst and Mayfield, Brambletye, or Brede,[37] but other appear in West Sussex, at for example Petworth, Tillington, Chichester, East Preston, and Crimsham.[38] It is of course impossible to detect all the migrants from Kent who are listed in the 1332 subsidy, but the evidence from locative names indicates that there had been a considerable movement (impossible to quantify accurately) into Sussex from Kent in the period before 1332.

It is impossible to tell with any certainty how long all the Kentish names had been established in Sussex before 1332. Names derived from the county of Kent (Kent, Kant, Kentish, Kenteys, etc.) appear frequently in Sussex during the 13th century.[39] In fact these names can be found during the 13th and 14th centuries in most southern counties, and were widely distributed in England at that period and later. Of the surnames from places in Kent, Copeshurst,[40] Renefeud, and Wykyng are all listed in the 1296 subsidy, at or very near the places where they appear in 1332,[41] and it is likely that these were the hereditary surnames of families established in Sussex already during the 13th century. Renefeud existed from the late 12th century in the area of Sussex where it is found in 1332.[42] Of the rest, Cobeham existed in East Sussex in the 13th century;[43] Douere was present in the county in the same period;[44] Ledes was the name of a family in Sussex from the late 12th century;[45] Sevenok also existed in Sussex in the 13th century.[46] This evidence suggests that many of the Kentish names found in 1332 were already established in Sussex by 1300.

There is a similar body of surnames or bye-names from places in Surrey in the 1332 Sussex subsidy. There are 14 persons in the subsidy with names which could be from Surrey place-names, though in some instances they could be derived, alternatively, from places in other counties. Most of the 14 were assessed in West Sussex, but they were not concentrated in the part of Sussex just south of the Surrey border. The surnames, or bye-names, in question are Chuddingfold (two taxpayers so named) (from Chiddingfold); Croyden (from Croydon); Lechemere (possibly from Latchmere in Surrey); Merewe (two persons so named) (from Merrow near Guildford); Mulesy (from Molesey); Pipperham (from Pepperhams near Haslemere); Pokeford (from Pockford near Chiddingfold); Pollyngfold, Polyngefold, and Polyngfold (three persons in all) (from Pollingfold); Purlye (probably from Purley in Surrey, though again there are places in other counties from which the name might be derived); and Sprakeligh (from Spreakley near Frensham).[47] Surnames or bye-names which could be derived from places in Sussex or in Surrey, have been excluded from this list, and have been dealt with in the discussion of names derived from places in Sussex. For instance, the surname or bye-name Reygate, that of two taxpayers in 1332, could be from Reigate (Surr.), but it could also be from Rogate (Suss.);[48] similarly Ferncumbe, also the name of two taxpayers in 1332, could be from Farncombe, near Godalming (Surr.), but it might be from Varncombe, in Pyecombe (Suss.).[49] Both names have, therefore, been included in the category, already dealt with, of names which could be from Sussex place-names. In fact, the early Sussex examples of the surname or bye-name Ferncumbe are around Varncombe,[50] though the early instances of Reygate are not closely concentrated around Rogate.

Some of the names from Surrey place-names, like some of the Kentish names, had a long history in Sussex. The name Chiddingfold, in various forms, was present in Sussex in the 13th century, and continued there after 1332;[51] the early references are all at or near Midhurst, and probably concern a single family there with a surname hereditary from at least the late 13th century. The name Lechemere, in a number of forms (Lachemere, Lashmer, etc.), also existed in Sussex in the 13th century; the name survived at and near Albourne from the mid 13th century until the 19th, and must have been hereditary there, but there are examples of the name in other parts of the county, which may not be connected with the family resident at Albourne.[52] The name Merewe (Merowe, Merwe, etc.) occurs in the area around West Grinstead and Steyning from the late 13th century, so that it, too, was hereditary; the first person of the name found there was a steward of William de Braose, the principal landowner in that part of Sussex, and may have been an estate official brought into the county from elsewhere, as such functionaries tended to be more mobile than most sections of the population. The name also occurs, from the mid 13th century, at and near Boxgrove, very probably as the name of a separate family. The name survived into the 15th century in both areas.[53] The possession by Boxgrove Priory of land at Merrow accounts for the presence of the surname around Boxgrove.[54] Pollingfold was a surname or bye-name in several parts of Sussex during the 13th century, but does not seem to have survived in the county after the 14th.[55] Purlye, too, was a name present in Sussex during the 13th century, and the surname Pearly or Perly, fairly widespread in Sussex in the 17th century, was probably a later form of the name. The surname persisted in the Selsey area from the 13th century to the 17th.[56] The names from Surrey in the Sussex 1332 subsidy, therefore, like those from Kent, were not by any means all recent arrivals in Sussex in 1332.

Surnames or bye-names from places in Kent and Surrey can be found in Sussex during the 14th and 15th centuries in a variety of sources, apart from the 1332 subsidy. Some of these are names, like Sevenok, for instance, listed in 1332, while others are not to be found in Sussex until a later date. Many of the names in question survived in Sussex into the 16th century and later, and some of them are still present there today. Evershed, for example, a surname from a minor place in Surrey, situated just north of the Surrey-Sussex boundary, was a surname in both Surrey and Sussex in the 14th century. By the 17th century it had ramified considerably in Sussex, though it is not possible to trace a pedigree connecting the Eversheds found in Sussex in the 14th century with those living there in the 17th. The Sussex parishes where the name occurs in the 17th century are just south of the Surrey border. Evershed is still found in numbers in Sussex at the present day.[57] Dorking was a surname in the southern part of West Sussex during the 13th, 14th and 15th centuries, and its survival in one area shows it was hereditary. It persisted in the same area in the 17th century, and the surname is still in Sussex at the present day.[58]

There are a limited number of surnames or bye-names in 1332 which could be from place-names in the remaining county bordering on Sussex, Hampshire. Possible names from Hampshire in 1332 are Burhunte (two persons so called), from Boarhunt; the name persisted in Sussex, mostly in the east of the county, from the early 13th century, and it survived at Denton, evidently hereditary, from the 13th century to the 15th;[59] Capenor (three persons so called), from Copnor, a name present in Sussex from the 13th century to the end of the 14th;[60] Chillonde, from Chilland;[61] Clanefeld, from Clanfield;[62] Ichene, from one of the places called Itchen;[63] Iddesworth (two persons so named), from Idsworth, a name which survived at Pulborough from 1332 until the 15th century;[64] Lidhouk or Lydhouk, from Liphook;[65] Medested, Medsted, or Mested (two taxpayers in all), from Medstead, the name during the 14th and 15th centuries of a knightly family with lands in both East and West Sussex;[66] Mucheldeuere, from Micheldever;[67] Tysted, from East or West Tisted;[68] Walkeford, possibly from Walkford; this may be the origin of the surname Wakeford, present in West Sussex in the 15th century, and numerous there in the 17th;[69] Wakeford is still a Sussex surname at the present day, and not rare; and Wincestr' and Wynchestr' (two taxpayers in all), from Winchester, a name which not surprisingly existed in Sussex from *c.* 1100, and which remained a surname in the county into the 17th century.[70] The surnames or bye-names from Hampshire place-names found in Sussex in 1332 were not particularly concentrated in parts of Sussex bordering on Hampshire. Some in fact were in East Sussex. On the other hand, most of the Hampshire places concerned lay in the east of that county, not far from the Sussex border. Only Walkford is in the west of Hampshire. Boarhunt, Copnor, Clanfield, Idsworth, Liphook, and East and West Tisted are all within ten miles on the Sussex boundary, and Medstead is only slightly more distant.

Apart from names from places in the counties bordering on Sussex, the 1332 subsidy lists a number of taxpayers with surnames or bye-names from places in parts of England further away. Few of the surnames or bye-names concerned were at all numerous in Sussex in any period. Out of such names listed in 1332, many have, in each case, been found as the name of a single individual. Some of these were probably not hereditary in 1332. Leaving aside Kent, Surrey, and Hampshire, there is no one county, or region, from which more than a few names recorded in 1332 could be derived, and there is no evidence to suggest a large migration into Sussex from any distant part of England. It may be said further that, although many surnames cannot be connected exclusively with any particular area in origin, and although many surnames were widely distributed in England from an early period, there are a certain number of surnames which were in origin confined to limited areas, and an examination of the surnames or bye-names listed in the 1332 subsidy, other than locative names, does not disclose any grounds for supposing that there had been any substantial movement into Sussex in the period preceding the date of the subsidy. All the evidence from the subsidy, both from the locative names and from names in other categories, suggests that there had been only a relatively small amount of movement into Sussex, that most if it was from the adjoining counties, and that migration from more distant regions involved movement by individuals whose places of origin were very scattered.

A few of the names from more distant counties found in 1332 were those of landowning families, who had acquired estates in Sussex, but who originated elsewhere. Examples are Leukenor, from Lewknor (Oxon.), a family which acquired much land in Sussex, mainly by marriage, from the 13th century, which continued to be major landowners in the county in the 17th, and which ramified into several branches in Sussex;[71] Bassyngeboun, from Bassingbourn (Cambs.), a knightly familiy who were landowners in Sussex and elsewhere during the 13th and 14th centuries;[72] and Pelham, generally said to be from one of the places called Pelham in Hertfordshire, and the name of a family who were important landowners in Sussex from the late 13th century.[73] For the rest, there are some names which are from places in Northamptonshire, such as Badeby, from Badby,[74] or Haryngworth, from Harringworth.[75] There are a few names from places in other Midland counties, such as Boseworth, from one of the two places in Leicestershire called Bosworth, a surname which has survived in Sussex to the present,[76] Poulesworth, from Polesworth (Warws.), a surname which gave rise to a minor Sussex place-name,[77] or Stiltone, from Stilton (formerly Hunts., now Cambs.).[78] There are a few names from the west of England, such as Devenyssh, from the county of Devon, a surname which persists in Sussex at later periods, but which is a widespread one in England generally, so that not too much significance can be attached to its occurence in Sussex over several centuries,[79] Excetr', from Exeter,[80]

Dymmok, from Dymock (Glos.), a surname which continued in Sussex during the 14th and 15th centuries, and which still survives there today,[81], Godmanneston, from Godmanstone (Dorset), a surname which persisted in the same part of Sussex in the form Godmeston,[82] Icoumbe, from Iccombe (Glos.),[83] Tokenham, from Tockenham (Wilts.),[84] and Wilteschyre and Wylcher, from Wiltshire, a name established in West Sussex from the 13th century, one which survived at and around Petworth from the 14th century to the 18th,[85] and in various forms is still in Sussex at the present day. There are a few names from Yorkshire place-names, such as Bonwyk, from Bonwick (North Yorks.), a surname present in the Horsham area from the 14th century to the 17th, which must have been hereditary there from the early 14th century, and which in the forms Bonwick and Bonnick is still quite numerous in Sussex at the present time,[86] Ingmanthorp, from Ingmanthorpe (West Yorks.), a surname which persisted for some time in the Goring area, and was probably hereditary there,[87] and Mildeby, from Milby (North Yorks.), present in the district around Chichester from at least the mid 13th century, and evidently hereditary there.[88] There are also a few names from East Anglia and Essex, such as Dallyng, from Field Dalling or Wood Dalling (Norf.),[89] Nereford, from Narford (Norf.),[90] or Stistede, from Stisted (Ess.).[91]

Some of the surnames just mentioned have survived in Sussex to the present day, and in some cases have ramified in the county to become fairly numerous there. Others which seem to have established themselves in the county, and to have been hereditary, did not survive there into the 16th century. Some of the surnames which seem to have been hereditary in the county have not been found after the middle of the 14th century, and probably disappeared as a result of the population losses of that period. Many surnames or bye-names from places outside Sussex have been discovered as the names of single individuals only, and even allowing for the gaps which exist in the source material for medieval surnames, it is probable that many of the surnames or bye-names from place-names outside the county found both in the 1332 subsidy, and in other medieval sources, were brought in by the migration into the county of single individuals, and in many cases never became hereditary there.

The evidence from the 1332 subsidy does not indicate any sizeable movement from other parts of England into Sussex. The factors which led individuals or families to migrate to Sussex from widely scattered parts of England can only be conjectured. In some cases a part may have been played by the connections of landownership. Field Dalling was held from the de Warenne family, who were large landowners in East Sussex,[92] and Harringworth was held by a branch of the Zouche family, who held land in West Sussex.[93] The presence of some names from places in Yorkshire may owe something to the fact that the Percy family, which held the

Honour of Petworth in Sussex, were also the holders of much land in Yorkshire.

Lay subsidy records suffer from the defect that they do not list the poorest sections of the community. Some unfree tenants are listed in subsidies, but there were some serfs too poor to pay tax, and there were other classes, such as the sub-tenants of villeins, landless labourers, and household servants, who are also likely to have been below the tax threshold, though as the 1332 subsidy does not usually list occupations, it is impossible to be sure how far down the social scale the list of taxpayers extends. The evidence from the subsidy cannot in this respect be satisfactorily supplemented by using other sources, for the classes which are insufficiently represented in the subsidy tend to be those which appear very sparsely in records of other types. It has to be accepted that the names of some parts of the medieval population very largely elude research. So far as locative names are concerned, it would be rash to assume that those sections which were too poor to be taxed directly must have been less mobile than the more affluent classes.

Though there is no adequate means of remedying these limitations on the general scope of medieval sources, such information as is available from material other than subsidies for locative surnames in Sussex up to c. 1500 does not suggest that the 1332 subsidy is misleading in the picture it gives of locative names in the county. The surnames or bye-names of very many Sussex bondmen can be discovered from sources such as manor custumals. It is to be expected that bond tenants would be more static than freemen, since serfs were bound to their native manors, even though it was not rare for them to quit the manors to which they belonged, legally or otherwise. The proportion of locative surnames or bye-names among unfree tenants in Sussex was low. The serfs listed in custumals for a number of Sussex manors held by the Bishop of Chichester, drawn up in the second half of the 13th century, and the 14th century, had locative names in only 14% of cases.[94] This compares with 21% for all the people listed in the 1332 subsidy, which includes some unfree tenants. A total of 45 locative names are to be found among the unfree tenants on the bishop's manors in the source just mentioned, including some borne by more than one person. 34 of the locative names concerned could be from Sussex place-names. Out of these 15 (just over 44%) could have been derived from places which were in the same township as the manors to which the serfs bearing the names in question belonged, and a further 10 (more than 29%) could have been derived from places within five miles of the manors to which the serfs concerned belonged. In some instances the surnames or bye-names in question might be derived from place-names further afield, but for bondmen, who were normally tied to a particular manor, there is a strong case for assuming that their locative surnames or bye-names were much more likely to be from localities within the manors to which serfs were attached, than from more distant places. 9 of the locative names concerned could be from places in Sussex, but more than five miles from the manors to which the serfs concerned belonged. There were a further 9 locative names from places outside Sussex, but in other parts of England. In addition the names le Frensch and le Irysse, or Yrisse, occur as the surnames or bye-names of serfs. These may indicate that there are a small number of unfree tenants of French or Irish origin, but it is impossible to be sure that such names were not at times bestowed as nicknames.

Some parallel information can be obtained about the unfree tenants on the Archbishop of Canterbury's large manor of South Malling, which included land not only in South Malling, but in some other East Sussex townships, about 1285.[95] The bondmen listed on the manor at that date included 51 individuals with locative names, and these had between them 36 names. Out of these, 9 individuals, with 7 names, had surnames or bye-names which could have been derived from more than one place-name in Sussex, and in none of these instances was there sufficient reason for preferring any one of the possible sources. The 7 names in question have consequently been omitted from the figures which follow. After eliminating these, there remain 29 names, borne by 42 persons; 15 names (those of 26 individuals) could be derived from places in the township within which the bearers of the names in question were listed in the custumal. (Some of the surnames or bye-names concerned were from minor locality names within the manor of South Malling, which are not given in the *Place-Names of Sussex*. For instance, the surnames or bye-names de Cornerlye, de Bayregg, de Alerdynden, de Betesfeud, de Leneslye, de Everesfeud (later Eversfield), and de Iardherst (later Yardhurst), are all from minor place-names within the manor.)[96] A further 6 names (those of 9 individuals), could be from places within 5 miles of the townships where the bearers of the names concerned were listed, and there were 4 names (those of 3 individuals), which could be from places in Sussex, but more than 5 miles from the townships where the bearers of the names in question were listed. Besides these cases, there were 4 names, those of 4 persons, from places outside Sussex. There were thus 25 names in all from places in Sussex (not counting those which might be from more than one place in the county, and which consequently have had to be omitted from the figures), and of these, 60% were from places in the same townships as those where the bearers of the names were tenants, and 24% were from places within 5 miles.

In considering this evidence, it must be remembered that the custumal from which the South Malling serfs' names were taken dates from the late 13th century, and is therefore from a period earlier than the 1332 subsidy. There is consequently less chance that the South Malling names, as compared with those in the subsidy, had been hereditary for any length of time, and this may partly account for the fact that such a high proportion of them were still at or near to the places from which they originated. There would have been less time for names to migrate after becoming hereditary. Even allowing for this factor, however, it seems probable from the evidence about serfs' names just set out, that unfree tenants were less likely to migrate in the late 13th and early 14th centuries than were, on the average, the sections of the population who appeared as taxpayers in 1332.

Serfs' names can be discovered, at least where some manors are concerned, from such sources as custumals and manor court rolls, but there remain some classes of people whose names it is difficult to examine at all. When fuller information becomes available in the 16th century, it can be seen that there were then in the county many surnames which have not been found there before 1500. This is true both of locative surnames, and of surnames in other categories. Some of the surnames in question had already ramified in Sussex to some extent by the early 16th century, and are consequently unlikely to have arrived in the county after the beginning of the century. It is probable that there was in medieval Sussex a body of surnames which were not recorded in any source before 1500, but which appear in the county during the 16th and 17th centuries. These include some locative surnames derived from places in Sussex.

The locative names to be found in the 1332 Sussex subsidy have been analysed above. A very large number of locative surnames or bye-names existed in the county during the Middle Ages, and it is not possible to discuss in detail all the material. However, in general the evidence shows that there was no large influx of locative names from outside the county in the period before 1500, and that although some locative names (mostly ones derived from Sussex place-names) ramified to a moderate degree in the county, there are no cases of particular locative names increasing very greatly in number, nor are there any instances of townships where a single locative name was the surname of the majority of the inhabitants. Out of all the surnames or bye-names derived from places outside Sussex which occur in the county before 1500, a small minority survived there into later periods, including a few which proliferated, to a modest extent, in Sussex. These include one or two surnames which were widely dispersed throughout England as a whole by 1500, such as Kendal (usually from Kendall in Cumbria, though there are other possible origins), and Pomfrett (from Pontefract, West Yorks.). Kendal occurs in Sussex during the 14th century, has persisted there ever since, and is still quite a numerous surname in Sussex at the present day. There is no reason to suppose that all those named Kendal who lived in the county at various periods were related, and in fact there seems to have been migration into Sussex of people named Kendal at various periods.[97] Pomfrett, in various forms, existed in Sussex from the 13th century, and was still there in the

16th and 17th, but again it seems unlikely that all those so named in the county belonged to the same family.[98] Both these names occur in Kent, and other south-eastern counties, in the 14th century and later.

Apart from names which were widely distributed nationally, the majority of locative names which survived in Sussex from the Middle Ages into the 16th century and later were derived from places in other counties of the south-east. There are a small number of surnames from more distant parts of England which can be found in Sussex before 1500, survive in the county into later periods, and in some cases have persisted there to the present time. The surname Bellingham, for example, probably from Bellingham (Northumberland) or Bellingham (Greater London), first occurs in Sussex about the 15th century, at Rye. This was probably a case of migration into a port as a result of coastal trade. Thomas Bellyngham, at Rye in 1486, acquired land in central Sussex, his descendants acquired further estates in the same area, and during the 16th and 17th centuries the name Bellingham proliferated in that part of Sussex to some extent. It still exists in the county.[99] The surname Colebrook, or Colbrook, probably from one of the places in Devon called Colebrook, appears at Maresfield in the 14th century. From the 15th century to the 18th it survived in the area around Midhurst, and by the 16th century had already multiplied in that part of Sussex considerably. It is still in the county today.[100] The surname Crosby, from one of the places called Crosby or Crosbie in the north of England, or, perhaps, in Scotland, existed in Sussex in the 14th, 15th and 16th centuries, and still survives in the county.[101] Gilby (probably from Gilby, Lincs.) occurs in the 14th century at Streatham, near Henfield, as the name of a bondwoman. No connection can be traced with any of the later persons so named who appear in Sussex, but from the 15th century the name Gylby or Gilby was present in Goldspur Hundred (in East Sussex on the Kent border) and in one or two parishes just outside the hundred. The name survives, as Gilby or Gilbey, in Sussex now.[102] The surname Seagrave, or Segrove, probably from Seagrave (Leics.), was present in Sussex during the 15th century, persisted there in the 16th and 17th centuries, and still exists in the county at the present time.[103] The surname appears to have originally belonged in Sussex to a single family, living in the Pulborough and Billingshurst area, but the surname is one which was already widely distributed in England by the 16th century, and there may have been further migration into Sussex by persons with the surname at periods after 1500. The surname Trowell, which occurred in Sussex in the 13th century, and still survived there in the 16th, is generally said to be from Trowell (Notts.), and this may be its correct derivation in some cases, but in the early Sussex instances it appears as Truell or Trouel, and this suggests that it may be in origin here a French occupational name, and not locative. Though there are 13th century examples of the name in Sussex, forms with a preposition (de Trowell, etc.) have not been found in the county.[104]

A limited number of surnames derived from place-names outside Sussex have therefore entered the county in the centuries before 1500, and survived there for long periods, often down to the present time, and have been part of the county's nomenclature for many years. Many of the surnames which have survived can be seen to have persisted in Sussex from the 15th century, or in some instances earlier, but it is generally impossible to be certain whether or not there has been further migration into the county, bringing more families with some of the surnames in question. During the 19th and 20th centuries there was much movement into Sussex from other parts of the United Kingdom, mostly to the growing coastal resorts, and many surnames which were by then well established in other parts of the country were brought into Sussex, and in some cases multiplied there. It would consequently be wrong, when dealing with a surname such as, for instance, Kendal, Gilby, or Seagrave, to assume that because the surname in question has been present in the county from, perhaps the 15th century or earlier, all families with the surname must have been established in Sussex over the same length of time.

SUSSEX LOCATIVE SURNAMES IN 1524–5

The assessments for the lay subsidy granted in 1523 list a higher proportion of the population than do most Tudor taxation returns, and those for Sussex provide a good general view of the locative surnames present there during the earlier part of the 16th century. Sussex assessments for this subsidy were made in 1524 and 1525. The locative surnames listed in the assessments for the Rape of Lewes in 1524 have been analysed. Lewes Rape forms the western part of East Sussex. The returns analysed include those for the borough of Lewes.[105] There were rather more than 1850 taxpayers in the rape.

In 1524 subsidy returns for Lewes Rape, there are 339 individuals with locative surnames, and these persons had between them 210 surnames. Most locative names listed in the rape were the names in each case of a single individual. The position is the same taking the subsidy returns for the whole of Sussex. It is, however, the case, both in Lewes Rape, and in Sussex as a whole, that there were in 1524 a small number of locative names which had by that date ramified considerably, and were noted in the subsidy (which of course did not list all the inhabitants of the county) as the surnames of more than a few people. These more numerous locative names were in a few instances dispersed geographically, so that there were some locative names which appeared in a number of widely separated places. It is more common, however, when dealing with any of the more frequently occurring locative names, to find that each name was fairly concentrated in its distribution, with all or most examples of any one name being listed in a single township, or in two or three neighbouring townships. This, too, is true both of Lewes Rape, and of other parts of Sussex. It is reasonable to suppose that, where surnames were concentrated in this way in the 16th century, all the bearers of each name are likely to have been related. In cases where a surname appears in the subsidy as widely dispersed, however, and where perhaps, too, it can be seen from other sources that the name in question had been for some time much dispersed, inside Sussex and in some cases outside the county as well, it would obviously be unwise to assume that all those discovered with the name in the subsidy were related. This is especially the case when dealing with surnames which could originate from more than one place-name.

Among those taxpayers with locative surnames in Lewes Rape in 1524, there were 195 individuals with names which could be from Sussex place-names (though in some cases their surnames might, alternatively, be derived from place-names outside the county). These 195 people had between them 111 surnames. It is unfortunately not possible to use all the names concerned for calculations about the distances between the places from which surnames originated, and the places at which surnames occurred in 1524, so as to make a comparison with the figures already given for the 1332 subsidy. There were, out of all those listed in the rape with locative surnames, 72 taxpayers, with 41 surnames between them, who were not listed in any township, but who were listed merely under the hundred in which they were taxed. As in 1332, these individuals have been omitted from the calculations made about the bearers of locative names. There were in the rape in 1524 a further 45 persons, with 16 locative surnames between them, who had surnames which could be derived from more than one place-name in Sussex. These, too, have been excluded from the figures. After subtracting these two groups, there remain 78 taxpayers, with 54 locative surnames between them. Out of these, only 2 persons, with 2 separate surnames, or rather less than 3% of the 78 individuals, were listed in 1524 in the townships in which the place-names from which their surnames could be derived were situated. 12 individuals, with 12 surnames, that is, just over 15% of the 78 taxpayers, were listed in townships which were within five miles of the townships in which the place-names from which their surnames could be derived were situated. The remaining 64 taxpayers, with 40 surnames among them, that is, about 82% of the whole 78, were listed in 1524 in townships which were more than 5 miles from the townships in which the place-names from which their surnames could have been derived were located.

There is a contrast between these figures for 1524, and those given earlier for 1332. This can be seen if the figures for the two subsidies are set out in percentages.

These figures given below are for numbers of individuals not for numbers of surnames. The method employed to produce these figures has its imperfections. In the case of both subsidies, considerable numbers of

	1332	1524
Taxpayers listed in same townships as places from which surnames derived	37%	3%
Taxpayers listed in townships within 5 miles of places from which surnames derived	35%	15%
Taxpayers listed in townships more than 5 miles of places from which surnames derived	28%	82%

taxpayers with locative names have had to be excluded either because they were listed under hundreds, and not under townships, or because their names could be derived from more than one place-name in Sussex. The method also involves assuming that where a surname or bye-name could be from a place-name in Sussex, it was in fact so derived, even if there are alternative possible derivations from place-names outside the county. This assumption is likely to have been true in the majority of cases, but is improbable that it was true in all. There is the further consideration, already discussed, that subsidy assessments do not cover the whole population. Both in 1332 and 1524 the poorest sections of the community were omitted, and it is impossible to tell how differently the evidence might appear if the names of the whole community could be discovered for either date. Even making full allowance for these factors, however, it seems improbable that the position about locative surnames as revealed by the subsidy evidence substantially misrepresents the situation, as it was at either date, regarding the locative names in use by the population of Sussex. Although for the 1524 subsidy calculations have only been made for Lewes Rape, an inspection of the 1524 assessment for the remaining rapes does not suggest that the position in the rest of the county, outside Lewes Rape, was significantly different. A separate study of locative names in one part of West Sussex has produced similar results. The fact that in 1524 a very much smaller proportion of taxpayers was assessed at or near to the places from which their surnames could have been derived than in 1332 is not surprising, though it does show that there had been a great deal of movement among the population in the intervening two centuries. It is likely that by 1524 much of the Sussex population had surnames which had been hereditary from the 14th century, and there were some families with names which had been hereditary from the 12th or 13th. In many cases surnames must have been hereditary for five or six generations, and in some instances for more. Such a passage of time would allow several consecutive moves of habitation by any of the families involved.[106]

It seems probable that the degree of movement between 1332 and 1524 shown by locative names is typical of Sussex surnames in general. Locative surnames often arose when people moved away from their places of origin and settled elsewhere, and because of this it is unsafe to regard such names when found in relatively early sources like the 1332 subsidy as a reliable guide to the amount of migration in the community as a whole. In the first half of the 14th century many names were either not hereditary, or had been so for only a short period, and some of the locative names listed in 1332 are likely to have originated when the bearers of them, listed in 1332, left their native settlements to reside elsewhere. By the 16th century, however, these considerations are unlikely to have been applicable to any great extent, because of the length of time for which at least most surnames had been hereditary. It therefore seems probable that the evidence from locative names is a fairly accurate indication of the degree of migration which had taken place within Sussex in the 200 years or so between 1332 and 1524.

In the 1524 assessments for Lewes Rape, there are 144 taxpayers with locative names not derived from place-names in Sussex, with 99 surnames among them. These are surnames from place-names inside England. In addition, there were 34 individuals with surnames from places or regions outside England, and these had 18 surnames between them. 9 of these persons were noted in the subsidy as aliens, and so must have been themselves migrants into England. Out of the locative surnames from within England, but outside Sussex, noted in the rape in 1524, only 15 also appear anywhere in Sussex, inside or outside Lewes Rape, in the 1332 subsidy. It is obviously not possible to say what proportion of the locative surnames from places outside Sussex had been present in the county since the 14th century, or any later period. However, a comparison has been made between the locative surnames from outside Sussex, in Lewes Rape in 1524, and an index drawn from a large number of printed and manuscript sources for Sussex. Out of the surnames listed in 1524 from places outside the county, 6 have been found there between 1066 and 1200, 17 have first been found in the county during the 13th century, 6 have first been found there during the 14th, and 11 have first been found in the 15th. A further 2 have been first found in Sussex between 1500 and 1524. These are figures for numbers of surnames, not for numbers of individuals. There are thus 42 names in all which were those of taxpayers in 1524, and which are included in the index for some period before that date. This is less than half the number of locative names from places outside Sussex given, but within England, in the 1524 subsidy. It has not been possible to compile an index comprehending all possible sources for Sussex surnames for the period before 1524, and a more complete search through the material than it has been possible to make might well produce medieval examples of a few more names, but it is unlikely that the evidence provided by the existing index is seriously misleading. It is also the case that some surnames which have been found in Sussex at relatively early periods, such as the 13th century, have in some cases not been found

Locative Surnames 113

in Sussex again before 1524. This may be because some families declined in status, and for a time disappeared from the sources but it is possible that some names were brought into the county in the 12th or 13th centuries, died out there, and were subsequently re-introduced, before 1524. Many of the surnames from places outside Sussex which appear in the 1524 assessments, and which have not been found for any period before the subsidy in the index just mentioned, were in 1524 each the name of a single individual, and most of these names which occur in the subsidy as each that of one person have not been found in the county after 1524 either, though here again a fuller investigation, especially through parish registers, would no doubt produce some additional information. A few surnames which appear in 1524, and which have not been found in Sussex before 1500, have survived in the county, and in some cases have proliferated there. For example, the surname Byrtenshawe is in the 1524 assessment as the name of four taxpayers, all at or near Henfield. The surname Brakonshawe, Brekenschawe, or Bretinsha, which appears in 1524 in other parts of Sussex, appears to be a variant of the same surname.[107] The name is derived from Birkenshaw (West Yorks.),[108] and had existed in both West Yorkshire and Lancashire before 1500. The surname survived in Sussex in various forms, which perhaps reflect confusion in dealing with a surname from a distant region (Burtenshaw, Beconsawe, Buttenshaw, Buttinger, Burtinshall, etc.) during the 16th, 17th, and 18th centuries, and still survives in Sussex today.[109] This is one of the few surnames from places remote from Sussex to have survived and ramified in the county. Such cases are, however, exceptional. It is probable that many of the surnames, listed in the 1524 assessment, which appear there once only, and which have not been discovered in other Sussex sources, were usually the names of single individuals, who had migrated into the county before the date of the subsidy, and who either later left Sussex, or who died without leaving male heirs to carry on their surnames.

The locative surnames from place-names outside Sussex in the section of the 1524 subsidy for Lewes Rape do not suggest that there had been any large scale migration into the county in the period between 1332 and 1524. This is in fact true of the locative surnames found in 1524 in the whole of Sussex. In the whole county, a considerable number of locative surnames are given in the subsidy. Some of these are surnames which have not been found in Sussex before the reference in the subsidy, others are names which have been discovered in Sussex between 1500 and 1524, but not before 1500. Of course some of these may well have been present in the county earlier, especially as the sources for the 15th century are not good. Some of the surnames which have been found in Lewes Rape for the first time in 1524 are from place-names in adjoining counties, such as Chittinden, from Chittenden (Kent),[110] or Ricford, probably from

Rickford (Surr.), near Guildford, a name which occurs as that of six persons in Sussex in the 1524 subisdy.[111] There are a further small number of surnames in the rape from place-names in adjoining counties which do occur in Sussex before 1524, but which have not been found there before the 15th century, such as Holibone, from Holybourne (Hants.) or Hollingbourne (Kent);[112] Markewike, from Markwick (Surr.), which was the surname of eight taxpayers in Lewes Rape in 1524, and of several more in other parts of Sussex;[113] this surname had been established in the Lewes area from the early 15th century, appears in West Sussex early in the 16th, probably having spread there from the Lewes district, persisted in both East and West Sussex during the 17th century, and survives today as one of the more common locative surnames in Sussex;[114] or Wigmore, possibly from Wigmore (Kent), though there are place-names in more distant counties which could have given rise to the surname; the name has first been found in Sussex early in the 16th century.[115]

There are a small number of surnames derived from place-names in counties further from Sussex, which are either surnames found in Sussex for the first time in 1524, or which occur in Lewes Rape in 1524, and have not been found anywhere in Sussex before the 15th century, and so are likely to have been brought into the county through migration during the 15th or early 16th centuries. Such surnames include, for example, Brabroke, from Braybrooke (Northants.),[116] a surname which has not been found in the county before 1524, Byrtenshawe, already mentioned,[117] Bredon, from one of the places in Worcestershire called Bredon, or from Breedon (Leics.), a surname which first appears in Sussex during the 15th century, and another name which has survived in the county to the present,[118] Cheverell, from one of the Wiltshire places named Cheverell,[119] also a surname first found in Sussex in the 15th century,[120] Dacre, from one of the places called Dacre in Cumbria or Yorkshire, a surname for which the first known instance in Sussex is in 1524,[121] Otley, from Otley (Suff.), or Otley (West Yorks.), a surname first discovered in Sussex during the 15th century, and one which has persisted in the county to be numerous there at the present time,[122] Puggesley, from Pugsley (Dev.), a name for which the 1524 reference is the first known in Sussex,[123] Segrave, already mentioned,[124] or Somarsall, from one of the places called Somershall in Derbyshire.[125] The places from which these surnames originated (and others from more remote parts of England, occuring in 1524) are very scattered. It is probable that some of the surnames involved arrived in Sussex after a succession of movements from the localities where they originated, but that there were some instances of migration into Sussex directly from distant regions of England. Some evidence for this can be obtained from the history in Sussex of the surname Bradshaw, which first appears there early in the 16th century, at and around Chichester. The people who occur with the surname all seem to have been related. From the will (1539) of James Bradshaw it can be discovered that he was baptised at Eccles (Greater Manchester). In this case the Bradshaws had probably migrated directly from Lancashire to Sussex. Their surname was probably derived from Bradshaw (Greater Manchester), which is no great distance from Eccles.[126] The name Bradshaw was in the Chichester area in the 17th century.[127] It still exists in Sussex to-day, and there are now many examples of it in the county, but since Bradshaw is now, and has been at least since the mid 19th century, a numerous surname, and one widely distributed in England, especially in the north, it is obviously likely that there have been further movements of the surname into Sussex since the 16th century.

It is exceptional to find evidence of this sort for the migration of surnames in the 16th century. In most cases surnames appear in Sussex without any indication of why their bearers moved into the county, and it is usually impossible to be sure how long a name has been in the county at the time when it was first recorded in sources now extant. Even in a relatively well documented period like the 16th century, it is possible for a surname to exist in any county for some considerable time before being noted in any source now available, and this is even more true of earlier centuries. If, however, the evidence for Sussex locative names from the 1524–25 subsidy returns for the whole county, and from other material for the 16th century, is considered, there is still no cause to suppose that there was any large scale movement into the county from any quarter during the century. In addition, if surnames in other categories, apart from locative names, are taken into account, there is no substantial number of surnames which could be considered, on any grounds, as having originated outside Sussex. For example, it is pointed out in a later chapter that very few surnames formed from a personal name with suffix '-son' (Robinson, Williamson, etc.) originated in Sussex, and that such surnames were rare in the county before 1500.[128] In the 1524–5 subsidy such surnames were still only a very small proportion of the total number of names, though rather more common than in previous periods. The general conclusion from this evidence must be that the whole body of surnames in use within Sussex had still, even as late as the 16th century, not been very much affected by migration from outside.

From the late 16th century onwards the material for the study of surnames becomes increasingly copious. In particular, a large number of parish registers has survived, which provides a great deal of evidence about the surnames in use, and about the genealogy of families bearing some surnames. It is not possible to analyse this large body of source material in detail here, especially since no more than a small proportion of it is available in print. It has, however seemed worthwhile to consider the evidence about locative surnames from the Protestation Returns of 1641–42.

WEST SUSSEX LOCATIVE SURNAMES IN 1641–42

The Protestation Returns ought to have included all the male population over the age of eighteen, and although they do not appear to be completely comprehensive, they list the great majority of the adult male inhabitants of the areas for which the returns are extant. The returns for West Sussex have survived,[129] but those for East Sussex have been lost. In the West Sussex returns, out of just under 13,000 men, there are listed 897 persons with locative surnames which could be derived from Sussex place-names. Some of them might, alternatively, be from places outside the county, but many of the surnames concerned had already been present in the county for centuries before 1642, and it is likely that in the great majority of cases the surnames in question were derived from Sussex places. The 897 individuals had 219 surnames between them. Though the majority of the surnames under discussion occur in 1642 as each the name of one person, some of the locative surnames had ramified considerably. The number of individuals with locative surnames from places outside the county, but in England, was considerably larger; there were 1,243 persons with such surnames, with between them 436 different surnames. There were many fewer surnames from places outside England, 151 individuals with locative surnames from places or regions, etc., outside England, with between them 49 surnames. In compiling these figures, spelling variants have not been counted as separate surnames. Some surnames which might be derived from specific place-names, but which seem more likely to be topographical, have been excluded from the totals.

It would not be useful, in dealing with a relatively late period like the 17th century, to discuss how far those surnames which seem likely to have originated in Sussex had moved from their points of origin. In fact, in 1642 there are some cases, of which examples are discussed below, where surnames were closely clustered around their places of origin, but this was exceptional. In West Sussex in 1642, there were nearly as many surnames which could be from place-names in East Sussex as there were surnames which could be from West Sussex. It is also the case that in 1642 there were more persons in West Sussex with surnames from outside Sussex than there were persons with surnames which could be from places in the county, east or west. This is hardly surprising, for by the 17th century most surnames had been hereditary for several centuries, leaving time for a good deal of movement.

Though there is a larger proportion from places outside Sussex in 1642 than in earlier sources such as the 1332 or 1524 subsidies, there is still nothing to suggest any very large scale movement from any one country or region into West Sussex. Many of the surnames from places outside Sussex, listed in 1642, had by that date already been in Sussex for long periods. This is especially true for surnames which occur in 1642 as each the names of more than one individual. For instance, the surnames Badbye, Bonnick, Dimucke (or Dymmook), Leedes, Leucknor, Pearley (or Perly), Pelham, Renfield, Wakeford, and Wilshire, all found in 1642, are names given in the 1332 subsidy for Sussex.[130] Other surnames found in 1642 which had been present in Sussex already before 1500, and which have already been mentioned, were Colbrook, Dorcking, Eversed (Evershed), Kendall, and Seagrave.[131] Further surnames from the 1642 returns which existed in Sussex before 1500 include Catrik, from Catterick (North Yorks.) a name which existed in Sussex from the 15th century, and which occurs frequently there during the 16th and 17th,[132] Farnefold, a surname which appears from the 13th century in Sussex, variously spelt as Farnfold, Farnfeld, or Farnford (all these forms concerning a single family at Steyning), and which possibly is from a Hampshire place-name,[133] Gilforde, from Guildford (Surr.), a surname existing in Sussex since the 13th century,[134] Madgwick, a surname of which the origin has not been identified, but which in various forms (de Megwik, Magicke, Magewike, etc.) existed in West Sussex from the 13th century, had become common there by the 17th, and still survives in Sussex,[135] or Markwick, a surname of a landowning family in East Sussex from the 15th century, and one which has become numerous in the county, probably by the ramification of the one family.[136]

The presence in West Sussex in 1642 of very many surnames from place-names outside Sussex was therefore not due to any sudden influx of migrants from outside the county. Apart from the surnames just mentioned, many of the locative names from outside Sussex listed in 1642 had appeared in the county during the 16th century, and indeed many of them occur in the 1524 and 1525 subsidy returns. The 1642 returns do contain some locative surnames from places outside Sussex which do not appear in the 1524 or 1525 subsidy assessments, many of them names not found in the county before 1642. Where such new locative names are concerned, in the great majority of instances each surname is found in 1642 as the name of one person, and given the comprehensive nature of the 1642 evidence, it is unlikely that there were other males with the surnames in question residing in West Sussex who escaped listing. Some locative surnames which were in West Sussex in 1642, but which have not been found anywhere in Sussex until after 1524, were from adjoining counties, such as, for example, Dartnall, or Dartnole, from the name of a lost place in Kent, near Penshurst, a surname which was present in Sussex from the late 16th century, and is still one of the county's more frequently found locative surnames,[137] Edsoll or Edsawe, from High Edser (Surr.), a name which existed in the north of West Sussex from the mid 16th century, in an area not far from its place of origin, which was already numerous in West Sussex by 1642 and which still persists in Sussex today,[138] Porchester, from Portchester (Hants.),[139] and Wikenden, from a lost place in Kent,[140] another surname which has survived in Sussex.

The majority of locative surnames from outside Sussex, however, found in 1642, but not in 1524 or earlier, were from more distant parts of England. Their places of origin were scattered, and it is probable that many of them had reached Sussex after experiencing a series of migrations. During the 16th and 17th centuries, and occasionally earlier, instances can be found of Londoners buying property in Sussex. As London over a long period tended to draw in migrants from many different parts of England, movement from the capital into Sussex probably accounted for some of the locative names which appear in the county during the 16th and 17th centuries. In 1642 there are some surnames derived from places in the north of England, not found in Sussex until after 1524, such as for instance Antrobus, from Antrobus (Chesh.),[141] Battersbee, from Battersby (North Yorks.), Fishwick (probably from Fishwick (Lancs.),[142] Holyroyd, from the name of a locality in West Yorkshire,[143] Heptonstall, also from a West Yorkshire place-name,[144], Henshaw (from one or other of several places in the north of England), the surname of four persons in the West Sussex Protestation Returns, the name of a family already established in Sussex in the late 16th century, and a surname which still survives in the county,[145] Oldham, from Oldham (Greater Manch.), or Parre, probably from Parr (Merseyside), a surname of which there are many instances in Sussex at present,[146] though there is a possibility that Parre in Sussex has an alien origin.[147] There is, however, only a sprinkling of such names in 1642, and their origins in the north are not concentrated in any one district, so that it does not appear that there was substantial migration from any one part of northern England. There are a certain number of names from counties in the south and south-west of England, not immediately adjoining Sussex, such as, for instance, Bevestock, from Baverstock (Wilts.),[148] Bodicote, from Bodicote (Oxon.),[149] or Mougridge or Mugeregg, from Mogridge (Dev.),[150] another surname from outside Sussex which has multiplied there, and there are a few surnames derived from place-names in various parts of the Midlands, such as Grooby, from Groby (Leics.),[151] or Harborough, from one of the places so called in Leicestershire or Warwickshire.[152] These surnames, too, do not indicate any sizeable movement into Sussex from any other region of England.

The surnames mentioned in the 1642 returns which were derived from places outside England include a number which had been in Sussex for several centuries by that date. These included names which had been those of important medieval landholding families, such as Bassocke,[153] Covert,[154] Scarfield, Scardeville, or Scarvill, already the name of 18 men in West Sussex in 1642,[155] Tregose, Tragoose, or Treagoose, the name of 8 men in West Sussex in the returns,[156] Bowne (Bohun),[157] or Dawtry, the name of 7 persons in 1642.[158] Some of the other surnames involved are ones which had been widely distributed in England well before the 17th century, such as Mortimer, Montague, or Nugent. Others still, such as Callaway,[159] Tracie,[160] or Tervell,[161] were ones which had been present in Sussex for centuries before 1642. The second half of the 16th century saw the appearance in Sussex of many Frenchmen, often refugees from the wars of religion, but these were mostly to be found in the ports, and it is likely that many were only temporary residents in England. The number of new surnames from places outside England in 1642 is certainly small, and there are very few surnames in any category in the West Sussex Protestation Returns which are French in origin, and which cannot be found in Sussex in 1524 or earlier. It is possible that the position would look rather different if the Protestation Returns had survived for East Sussex, as during the late 16th century there were numbers of French people in East Sussex ports such as Rye or Hastings.

The very full list of male inhabitants provided by the Protestation Returns makes it possible to see how some locative surnames had ramified in West Sussex by 1642. Some such names had become quite numerous by that date, while still remaining geographically concentrated, so that a few of the more common surnames were each confined to a small area. It is reasonable to assume in such cases that each of the surnames concerned was that of a single family. Examples can be found both among surnames derived from Sussex place-names, and among those from place-names outside the county. For instance, the surname Baxshell, from Paxhill in Lindfield,[162] was the name of five men in 1642, all at Henfield. The surname existed at Lindfield in the 13th and 14th centuries, and it probably became hereditary there.[163] It is obviously likely that all those with the name listed in 1642 belonged to one family. In the forms Backshall and Backshell the surname survives in Sussex to the present day, and has ramified considerably. 23 persons named Boxall are listed in 1642, all in the area around Kirdford. The surname is probably from a lost place, Boxholte, in Kirdford.[164] The surname occurs, as Boxolle, Boxhole, and Boxsoll, in the same district in 1524. This surname, too, was probably that of a single family in 1642. It has subsequently multiplied greatly, and survives, as Boxall and Boxell, as a very numerous surname in Sussex. The surname Gratwick is from the place-name Greatwick, in Cowfold. It was the surname of 27 men in 1642, so that it was one of the names found more frequently in the West Sussex Protestation Returns.[165] In 1642, seven of the persons so named were still at Cowfold; the remainder were mostly still in nearby parishes in the Adur valley. The surname had existed around Cowfold from early in the 14th century. By the 16th, members of a family called Gratwick, from Cowfold, were acquiring lands in East Sussex, and the surname proliferated considerably there, though the lack of any returns for 1642 for East Sussex makes it impossible to compare the position there with the west. The surname still survives in Sussex.[166] Grumbridge or Grombridge (from Groombridge in Withyham)[167] was the name of 11 men in West Sussex in 1642, 10 of them at Horsham, and the remaining one at Billingshurst nearby.[168] This distribution of the name leaves little doubt that one family was involved. The surname had been established at Horsham since the 16th century.[169] It still survives in Sussex. Another numerous surname in 1642 is one which appears variously as Strudwicke, Stradwick, and Stridwicke (from Strudgwick in Kirdford).[170] This surname had already multiplied to some extent in West Sussex by 1524, when 8 people with the name (given then in the form Strodwyke or Strodewyke), were assessed for the subsidy.[171] The surname was then concentrated in the north of West Sussex, with none of the instances in the subsidy very far from Kirdford, and it is likely that all those with the name were related, and that the surname had remained in the area where it originated. In 1642, 29 men with the surname were listed in the Protestation Returns. 12 of these were at Kirdford, and most of the rest were in nearby parishes. 2, however, were at Chichester, where the surname was already present in 1628–29.[172] By the 17th century the surname had also spread across the county boundary into Surrey, with some instances still quite close to Kirdford.[173] This surname, too, has ramified, and is now one of the more common locative surnames in Sussex.

It can be seen from this evidence that by 1642 some surnames were already ramifying, and most of the names which were multiplying in the 17th century are ones which have survived to be among the more common locative surnames in Sussex at the present time. The point should be made that, although locative surnames are a major category of surname, individual locative names are rarely as numerous as are, for instance, some of the more common surnames derived from occupations or from personal names. Some of the ramified surnames just mentioned were still in 1642 closely grouped near the places from which they originated, but this was not always the case. As can be seen, some of the surnames concerned, though ones which had proliferated in West Sussex, were derived from places in the east of the county. There were, also, in 1642 some examples of surnames from place-names outside Sussex which had increased in numbers considerably. For instance, the surname Betsworth, from Betchworth (Surr.), was the name of 28 people listed in West Sussex in 1642, mostly in the north west of the county; many of these seem to have been members of a landowning family which was established in that part of Sussex during the 16th century. The surname was also then present in the adjoining part of Hampshire.[174] It has persisted in Sussex to the present day. Duffield (from either Duffield, Derbys., or Duffield, North Yorks.) a surname widely disseminated in England by c. 1500, was present at East Grinstead from the beginning of the 16th century, and multiplied considerably there and in the adjoining parishes. Almost certainly all the people named Duffield at East Grinstead belonged to the same family, though it is not possible to connect all of them genealogically. By 1642 the surname had spread into West Sussex, and there were 6 persons so called in the Protestation Returns. Though it is possible that there had been fresh migration into Sussex by people named Duffield during the 17th century, it is obviously probable that the presence of the surname in West Sussex was due to the dispersal of one family from East Grinstead.[175] This surname, too, has persisted in Sussex in several forms (Duffield, Duffill, Dutfield), and is now relatively common there. These surnames each seem to be a case of a single family ramifying in the period before 1642, so that some surnames were by that date already increasing considerably. As against such examples of ramyfing names, the great majority of surnames from places outside Sussex listed in 1642 appear in the returns as each the name of a single individual. Where names which could be derived from place-names in Sussex are concerned, the proportion of surnames which are listed in 1642 as the names of more than one person is greater, but even so the majority of the surnames involved each occur as the name of one man.

Some of the surnames just discussed might be seen to be more dispersed in their distribution in 1642 if the Protestation Returns had survived for East Sussex, so that the surnames there could be studied with as much information as is available for West Sussex, and if it had been possible to make a full search through some other 17th century sources, such as in particular parish registers, not only for Sussex, but for the adjoining counties as well. County boundaries do not in themselves create barriers to movement, and one or two of the surnames discussed above were to be found not only in Sussex, but in areas just across the boundary. An extensive search through records for other counties would take more time than results might justify, and it would probably not change the impression, given by the Protestation Returns, that by 1642 some locative surnames had already proliferated greatly, mainly by the ramification in West Sussex of individual families. This process can be seen from the 1642 evidence, and many of the surnames which were ramifying in 1642 have since increased substantially in numbers in Sussex. However, the growth in numbers of some locative surnames in Sussex in the 17th century was on a modest scale compared to the corresponding growth which was taking place in the same period in some parts of northern England, such as south Lancashire or the West Riding of Yorkshire, and the number of surnames concerned was much fewer than in those northern parts. No doubt demographic factors partly account for the difference. Sussex did not experience a growth of population by natural increase on the same scale as parts of Lancashire and Yorkshire during the 16th and 17th centuries.

CIRCUMSTANCES UNDER WHICH LOCATIVE SURNAMES AROSE

Some locative surnames were originally those of landholding families, which acquired surnames from the names of their principal places of residence, or from some other important part of their estates. The significance of this for the early development of hereditary surnames has already been discussed, and examples of surnames in Sussex which arose in this way have been given.[176] Families of large landholders were, however, but a small fraction of the population, and surnames acquired under such circumstances cannot account for more than a small minority of the locative surnames which can be found. Many more locative surnames arose when individuals left their native settlements and migrated elsewhere, to become known by the place-names of the settlements which they had left. Many of the locative names which occur in Sussex during the 12th and 13th centuries, but which were derived from places outside the county, probably originated in this way. It is problematical whether bye-names from villages in remote regions of England would have become established in Sussex, where the place-names from which such bye-names were derived would probably be unknown, but it is difficult to be sure what the position was about this. When people with names from villages in distant counties are found in Sussex, it is generally not possible to be certain if the names in question were already hereditary when first found in Sussex, so that migrants into the county arrived with names which were already well established, or if the names in question came into existence when a stranger from some village far removed settled in the county, and acquired a fresh bye-name from his former place of residence. It is also the case that tenurial connections may have meant that the names of villages in counties some way from Sussex were better known there than might be expected. During the 12th and 13th centuries, for instance, the D'Aubigny and De Warenne families were both large landholders in Sussex and in Norfolk, while the Percy family, who held the Honour of Petworth in Sussex, held great estates in the north of England.[177] An examination of an index of locative surnames or bye-names found in Sussex between 1066 and 1500, compiled from a large number of printed and manuscript sources, shows that during the 12th and 13th centuries there were fewer surnames or bye-names in the county which were from villages or hamlets in regions for which tenurial links of the kind just mentioned did not exist, but this may mean no more than that there was little migration into Sussex from some of the more distant parts of England.

Though some locative surnames originated when people moved from their native settlements to reside elsewhere, neither this, nor the acquisition by landholding families of surnames from the names of places where they had estates, can explain the origin of all the locative names to be found. During the 13th and 14th centuries, when small free tenants and bond tenants were in many cases acquiring hereditary surnames, there are many examples of individuals from both those classes having locative surnames or bye-names from the names of places where they were tenants, and where, it must be supposed, they normally lived. From the large number of examples to be found it must be supposed that a considerable proportion of locative surnames originated in this way. There are no reasons for supposing that the position in Sussex was significantly different from that in other parts of England, for similar examples can be found in other counties.[178] This raises the question of why people who were not substantial landholders came to possess surnames or bye-names from the names of places at which they resided.

In some cases it is clear that such locative names arose from the names of very small settlements. Some hamlets may have been so small that they were originally each occupied by a single family, in some cases by a single family of unfree tenants, and consequently the family involved might easily take its name from the settlement where it lived. Some evidence that locative surnames developed in this way can be found in a late 13th century custumal of South Malling manor, which extended into several townships, including some in the Weald. Some unfree tenants of the manor had names from very small localities. For example, several bond tenants with the name of de Eueresfeud held land at Eversfield, a small settlement apparently near Mayfield.[179] This is the origin of the surname Eversfield, which existed in East Sussex in the 14th, 15th, 16th, and 17th centuries, and which has survived in Sussex to the present day.[180] In this case the tenants named Eueresfeud, who are likely to have been all related, seem to be the only tenants at Eversfield. Several similar cases can be found in the same custumal: Matthew de Crouherst was the sole tenant of land listed at Crowhurst,[181] Christine de Alderdynden, a bondwoman, was the only tenant listed at Alderdynden,[182] at Stanleygh (apparently in Mayfield) the only tenants listed were two named de Stanleygh,[183] and at Alkesford (in Withyham), the only tenant listed was Henry de Arkesford.[184] It seems likely that in all these cases unfree tenants were acquiring surnames or bye-names from small localities where they were the sole tenants of one particular manor, and where they may have been the only inhabitants. There are many further instances in the same custumal of unfree tenants or small free tenants with names from small localities where they were holding land, but where they were not the only tenants. For example, at Gillridge (in Withyham), one tenant, out of three listed, was named de Gelderegg', at Greenhurst (in Buxted) one of the tenants was named de Grenherst, and at Hempstead (in Framfield) two tenants were named de Hemsted.[185] In such cases certain tenants may have been the chief or, where new small settlements had been established, the earliest inhabitants of some localities.

Such developments probably explain how some locative surnames arose among bondmen and small free tenants, but there are early instances of locative names which do not seem to be explicable on such lines. For instance, in the 1296 subsidy the name Gestlyng appears at Guestling, the name Wyltyng at Wilting, the name Hodlegh at Hoadley Wood (in Ticehurst), and the name Gadebergh at Gateborough.[186] None of the taxpayers concerned seems to have been a large landowner, and judging from the assessments all of them seem to have been persons of no particular wealth. These examples have been taken from one source, but many instances can be found in 13th century Sussex in other evidence, from a period when names were mostly not hereditary, or had only been hereditary a short time, so that it is unlikely that drastic changes in the status of the people with such names had occurred since the names originated. Precisely why such surnames arose is not clear, but in at least some cases the origin of such surnames may be linked to the morphology of the villages where the surnames concerned developed. It may perhaps be that the families with such locative names originally lived at the core of each village, and were the chief or perhaps the only inhabitants there, while the rest of the village population lived in a somewhat dispersed way. It is not usually possible to tell whereabouts in a village any particular family lived, and where most villages are concerned it is difficult to obtain any information about the exact way in which houses, crofts, etc., were arranged. Even in nucleated villages, settlement was not necessarily entirely compact. The existence of many topographical surnames derived from the position of houses or holdings in villages (Townsend, Streetend, Bynorthetown, atte Church, atte Cherchestygele, etc.) shows that surnames were often formed from the location of houses, etc., and if more was known about the shape of individual villages, and the location within them of the residences of the people known to us only from such sources as subsidy returns, some points about the origins of both locative and topographical surnames might be explained.

USE OF PREPOSITIONS WITH LOCATIVE NAMES

One notable feature of the body of Sussex surnames in use during the Middle Ages, and to a lesser degree later periods, is the large number of topographical surnames and bye-names in existence, and the high proportion of the population with such names. It is, however, not always easy to separate surnames from specific places from those which are from features of the topography. The presence of a preposition, or a preposition and definite article, such as 'atte' or 'de la' before a surname or bye-name has sometimes been used as a criterion for distinguishing locative names from topographical ones.[187] There are a few Sussex locative names from place-names, which were those of major settlements, which appear at times with prepositions and definite articles. For example, during the 13th and early 14th centuries persons with surnames or bye-names from the place-name Rogate sometimes occur with their names in the form de la Rogate.[188] During the 13th century, the definite article was sometimes prefixed to the place-name.[189] The article was not used consistently where surnames or bye-names were concerned, and even the name of a single individual was given sometimes with the article, sometimes without it.[190] The bye-name ate Niwewyke (from Newick) has been found once, *c.* 1320, and the surname or bye-name atte Worthe has been found several times; in one or two cases 'worth' may not be used to refer to any place-name, but one instance refers to the village of Worth, which was a major settlement, and in another instance the surname or bye-name involved was from Worth Farm in Little Horstead.[191] There are a rather large number of examples where 'atte' or 'de la' is prefixed to minor place-names, for instance, atte Birchenestie[192] (from Bursteye Farm in Ardingly), atte Blakelond (from Blackland Copse, in Henfield),[193] atte Bokholte (from one of the places called Buckholt in East Sussex, or possibly from Buckwell in Ashburnham),[194] atte Finnyng (or atte Wynyng) (probably from Fyning in Rogate),[195] or ate Haneholte (from, probably, the locality now called Harlot's Wood, in Northiam).[196] The fact that most early instances of the surnames mentioned occur at or very near the place-names concerned does show that the surnames are from Sussex place-names, at least when they occur in the county. There is, however, an obvious difficulty in drawing a clear distinction between surnames or bye-names from such minor localities, and names derived from topographical terms pure and simple. When dealing with the names given to minor localities of such a sort, it is generally impossible to be sure at what period the names applied to them ceased to be phrases used casually, and perhaps interchangeably with others, and hardened into place-names with a stable character. Very few of the minor locality names just mentioned can be shown to have existed before the 13th century. The examples of surnames or bye-names with 'atte' which have just been given (from minor locality names) come from the 13th or 14th centuries. At those periods the meaning of the place-names in question would still be understood. This would also be true of place-names belonging to major settlements such as Rogate or Newick.

Besides such cases, there are some instances of surnames which occur frequently as topographical ones being at times derived from the names of particular localities. For instance, the topographical name Field (atte Feld, de la Feld), was in at least one case derived from the name of a specific locality, Field Place in Goring.[197] In other similar cases, the same name appears to have been derived from Field Place, at Warnham, and from a locality called la Felde at Whatlington.[198] Or, to take another example, the topographical name at Knelle or de Knelle was in some instances derived from a minor place-name, Knelle in Beckley.[199] The existence of such examples makes it difficult to draw a rigid distinction between locative surnames and topographical ones, and there are individual cases where it is difficult to be sure whether a surname is derived from the name of some specific locality or not. Topographical names were presumably derived in most cases from residence at, or connection with, some particular spot, but not from an actual place-name.

Many locative names which appear in Sussex at one period or another have not been discussed in this chapter. Before the 18th century, the majority of the locative surnames in the county were ones derived from Sussex place-names, though some surnames from place-names outside the county, including some from outside England, became established in Sussex, and in some cases proliferated there. At the present day, the telephone directories covering Sussex show that there are many surnames from place-names in the county still persisting there. The surnames Anstee (or Anstey), Arundel, Balcombe (or Baulcombe), Bathurst, Battle, Billingshurst and Billinghurst, Chatfield, Crawley, Crowhurst, Eversfield, Farncombe, Gosden, Gratwick, Grinstead, Hastings, Lindfield, Nutley, Sedgewick, Shelley, Singleton, Strudwick, Tickner,[200] and Washington, for example, are all surnames which could be from Sussex place-names, though in some cases they could all have alternative origins, and all names which have survived in Sussex to the present day as the surnames of more than one or two people. There are, of course, now many locative surnames in Sussex which are from the names of places outside the county, and these include a large number of surnames which have been brought into the county after c. 1800. For example, surnames derived from places in Lancashire, and today quite numerous in Sussex, include Aspinall, Bamber, Bardsley, Bickerstaff and Bickersteth, Clegg, Clitheroe, Cowlishaw, Dewhurst, Fishwick, Greenhalgh, Pendlebury, Pendleton, Pickup, Scarisbrick, and Winstanley. Lancashire is one of the more populous counties, and it is one which has long been rich in locative surnames, with a high proportion of the population having names in that category, but similar, if shorter, lists could be drawn up of surnames, now present in Sussex, from each of many English counties.

There are many other Sussex locative surnames which have interesting histories. Scotland, which has the appearance of a locative name, and is a surname which appears in Sussex from the 13th century, is derived from a personal name, which was present in Sussex c. 1100, and which existed in Kent at the same period.[201] The surname Rigden is usually said to be from the personal name Richard, but in the 13th century it occurs in Sussex in the form de Riggeden, which suggests that it was, at least in some cases, derived from a place-name, though the place in question has not been located.[202] The surname Crop (despite the occurence of occasional instances of le Crop), is from a minor Sussex place-name, Creep Wood in Penhurst.[203] Another surname, which might appear from late forms to be locative, but of which the origin has defied elucidation, is Gibbridge. The name occurs in that form in the 17th century, but it is found earlier in Sussex, in the 15th and 16th centuries, as Geberissh, Gybbrishe, Guybberishe, Gebryge, etc. The 15th and 16th century examples of the surname are all in the more westerly part of West Sussex, but are there somewhat scattered, though all might concern one family. The word 'gibberish', in the sense of 'unintelligible language' is uncertain in its origins, and is not evidenced before the 16th century. Unfortunately no instances of the surname is known in Sussex before 1449, though it is found earlier elsewhere, and its origins remain unknown.[204]

Even considering surnames derived from Sussex place-names alone, and disregarding surnames from places outside the county which have entered it at various periods, the total number of locative surnames in Sussex is too great for discussion of each individual name to be feasible at all. Many surnames still surviving in the county are derived from the names of major settlements, and have origins which are recognisable without too much difficulty even from the modern forms of the surname concerned. A great many more locative surnames, however, are derived from the names of very small places, including some now long since lost through depopulation, or in a few cases through coastal erosion. It is not possible to say with any certainty how many places in Sussex gave rise to locative surnames, for there are too many instances of surnames which could be derived from more than one place-name, including many which might be from a place-name in Sussex, but which might alternatively be from a place-name elsewhere. Some indication of how many locative surnames or bye-names developed in Sussex can be gained from examining the locative names which are derived from the names of localities in Lindfield parish. Lindfield is a fairly large parish containing a number of minor settlements, but it is fairly typical of the parishes in the northern half of Sussex. Those in the southern part of the county tend to be smaller, and to have fewer minor localities. The surname Lindefeld occurs in Sussex in the 13th century; it has persisted in the county to the present, and is now numerous there. The surname Linfield, which was already established there in the 17th century, is probably also from Lindfield in most cases when it is found in Sussex, though there are other possible sources; it too is now common there.[205] Badhurst in Lindfield may have given rise to the bye-name Badeherste, which existed in Sussex in the 12th century, but that name could be from Bathurst in Warbelton, or Bathurst in Battle.[206] Beckworth in Lindfield is possibly the origin of the bye-name de Becworth, which is listed in East Sussex in 1332, though the place-name is not recorded until later.[207] Buxshalls in Lindfield is one possible origin of the surname which occurs as de Bokeselle, de Bokesull, etc., and the name de Bokesulle is listed at Lindfield in the 1296 subsidy, but there are other possible sources for the surname, including Bugsell, in

Salehurst, where the name also occurs from the 13th century, and the derivation of the surname when it appears at later periods must be uncertain.[208] Cockhaise in Lindfield was the origin of a, probably hereditary, name at Lindfield and elsewhere in East Sussex, Cokkehese, etc., in the late 13th and 14th centuries, but the surname does not seem to have survived.[209] Goddenwick, another minor locality in Lindfield, was the origin of a bye-name, for which a single instance has been found.[210] Gravelye is a minor place-name in Lindfield which is not recorded before the 16th century, but the surname or bye-name de Grauele existed at and near Lindfield from the early 13th century, and Gravely has survived as a Sussex surname.[211] The surname or bye-name de Henfeld existed at Lindfield in the 14th century, and is likely to have been from Henfield Wood, in Lindfield, but there is another Henfield in Sussex, and when the surname occurs at later periods it is impossible to be sure of its origin.[212] Keysford in Lindfield gave rise to a bye-name, Carleford or Carlesford, which existed in the 13th and 14th centuries near Lindfield, but which does not seem to have survived.[213] Noven Farm, at Lindfield, may be one origin of the name ate Novene, which is recorded near Lindfield in the 14th century, but the name could have other origins.[214] Paxhill is the origin of the surname Baxshell, already mentioned, which has survived in Sussex.[215] Pegden gave rise to a bye-name, de Peghedenn or de Pehedenn, but this has not survived unless it has been absorbed by the surname Peckden, which has another source.[216] Plummerden in Lindfield is another place-name not evidenced before the 16th century, but the bye-name or surname de Plumeresden or de Plummerdene existed at and near Lindfield in the 14th century, and the surname persisted in Sussex.[217] Walstead in Lindfield is the origin of the surname Walksted or Walsted, which appears in the 13th century near Lindfield, and which survived in the county.[218] There are several minor place-names in Lindfield which did not give rise to surnames or bye-names so far as can be seen from the sources which have been examined, but it has to be remembered that the evidence for medieval surnames is very incomplete.

Many of the larger Sussex parishes, and especially those in the more northerly part of the county, produced a crop of surnames or bye-names from minor place-names, much in the way in which Lindfield did. The total number of locative names from Sussex place-names which existed at one period or another was consequently very large. It included many which did not persist, and probably there were many which were never hereditary at all, but even so, the number which survived into the 16th century, and which can be found in such sources as the 1524 and 1525 subsidy returns, remains very great. So far as can be seen from sources such as subsidy returns, which allow something of a general impression to be gained of the distribution of surnames and bye-names throughout the county, no one part of Sussex was especially prolific in locative surnames.

Locative Surnames 129

The large parishes in the north of the county each contained many minor place-names, and gave rise to a correspondingly large number of surnames, but it does not seem that taking the northern part of the county as a whole, it originated noticeably more locative surnames than the south, and the widespread acquisition of locative names by all sections of the population was a feature of Sussex nomenclature from at least the 13th century onwards.

References

[1] Printed in *3 Suss. Subsidies*, pp. 225-333.
[2] P. McClure, "Patterns of Migration in the Later Middle Ages: the evidence of English Place-Name Surnames", *Economic History Review*, 2nd series, vol. xxxii (1979), 167-82.
[3] *3 Suss. Subsidies*, pp. 167, 281; *P.N. Suss.*, vol. i, p. 211.
[4] *3 Suss. Subsidies*, pp. 167, 281.
[5] *Ibid.*, pp. 170, 284; *P.N. Suss.*, vol. ii, p. 325.
[6] *3 Suss. Subsidies*, pp. 232, 240, 246, 247, 293, 319, 320, 331. On the history of these families, see pp. 35, 37, 38, 40, 70.
[7] *3 Suss. Subsidies*, pp. 239, 246, 247, 253, 256, 257, 263, 264, 265, 272, 315, 323. And see pp. 50, 68, 69, 71.
[8] *3 Suss. Subsidies*, pp. 227, 237, 238, 240, 250, 255, 257, 259, 262, 263, 268, 270, 272, 274, 276, 278, 288, 297, 301.
[9] *Ibid.*, pp. 225, 228, 232, 238, 242, 247, 262, 265, 271, 272, 273, 275, 277, 280, 281, 285, 286, 291, 292, 293, 295, 299, 301, 312, 325, 332, 333.
[10] *P.N. Suss.*, vol. i, pp. 168, 209, 245; vol. ii, p.310.
[11] *3 Suss. Subsidies.*, pp. 265, 283.
[12] The term "borough" is employed here in its usual sense. Some Sussex townships, and some manors, were divided into units called "borghs", but the term "borough" is not used here for such units.
[13] *3 Suss. Subsidies*, p. 329; *P.N. Suss.*, vol. ii, 525.
[14] *Ibid.*, vol. ii, p. 294; *3 Suss. Subsidies*, p. 287.
[15] H.A. Hanley and C.W. Chalklin, "Kent Lay Subsidy Roll of 1334/5", in F.R.H. Du Boulay, *Documents Illustrative of Medieval Kentish Society* (Kent Archaeological Soc., vol. xviii) (1964).
[16] *Surr. Taxation Returns* (Surr. Record Soc., vol. xi) (1922, 1932), pp. 1-94.
[17] Hanley and Chalklin, *op. cit.*, pp. 72, 75, 80, 83, 87, 119, 121, 132, 138, 155, 158.
[18] *Ibid.*, pp. 146, 147, 148.
[19] *Ibid.*, p. 118.
[20] *Ibid.*, p. 106.

[21] *Ibid.*, p. 94; *Suss. Custumals*, vol. ii, pp. 52, 70.
[22] Hanley and Chalklin, *op. cit.*, p. 120; *P.N. Suss.*, vol. ii, p. 505.
[23] *Ibid.*, vol. ii, p. 438; Hanley and Chalklin, *op. cit.*, p. 141.
[24] *Ibid.*, p. 152; *P.N. Suss.*, vol. i, p. 231; P.R.O. S.C.11/877; E. 179/225/1; *Hastings Lathe C.R.*, pp. 8, 118; *Robertsbridge Charters*, p. 125; *3 Suss. Subsidies*, p. 309.
[25] Hanley and Chalklin, *op. cit.*, p. 119.
[26] *Ibid.*, pp. 98, 167.
[27] *Ibid.*, pp. 99, 128, 130, 160.
[28] *Surr. Taxation Returns* (Surr. Record Soc., vol. xi) (1922, 1932), pp. 3, 8, 24, 33, 62, 78, 81.
[29] *Ibid.*, pp. 11, 12, 41, 84, 88.
[30] Reaney, *Origins*, p. 351.
[31] A. Rumble, *Dorset Lay Subsidy Roll of 1327* (Dorset Record Soc., vol. vi) (1980), p. 29.
[32] J.C. Ward, *Medieval Essex Community: The Lay Subsidy of 1327* (1983), pp. 52, 56.
[33] A.M. Erskine, *Devonshire Lay Subsidy of 1332* (Devon and Cornwall Record Soc., new series, vol. xiv) (1969), pp. 13, 15, 24, 32, 33, 57, 102. See also *ibid.*, p. 114. (Robert Rede of Winchelsea, at Plymouth), and *Book of Fees*, vol. ii, 766.
[34] *3 Suss. Subsidies*, pp. 292, 308, 324.
[35] *Ibid.*, pp. 245, 253, 260, 264, 266, 300, 308, 309, 310, 328.
[36] *Ibid.*, pp. 225, 234, 235, 242, 245, 250, 257, 258, 265, 275, 279, 280, 281, 291, 293, 299, 303, 307, 311, 313, 316, 318, 322, 326, 328.
[37] *Ibid.*, pp. 310, 313, 322, 325, 328.
[38] *Ibid.*, pp. 225, 245, 257, 258, 265.
[39] *Chichester Chart.*, pp. 111, 127–8, 158; *Suss. Fines*, vol. ii, p. 67; *Boxgrove Chart.*, p. 185; *Suss. Custumals*, vol. ii, pp. 3, 20, 23, 24, 33, 44; *3 Suss. Subsidies*, pp. 82, 94; *Battle Custumals*, p. 53.
[40] As Copereshurst. A place called Copshurst in Suss., probably near Kirdford, is mentioned in about 1405 (*Fitzalan Surveys*, p. 111), but seems unlikely to be the origin of the name found in 1332. The 1296 form shows the link with the Kent place.
[41] *3 Suss. Subsidies.*, pp. 35, 64, 75, 77, 78.
[42] *Lewes Chartulary*, vol. i, pp. 75, 77, 88, 130.
[43] *Suss. Custumals*, vol. ii, p. 42.
[44] Inderwick, *Winchelsea*, pp. 159, 179; *Great Roll of the Pipe for the 3rd year of Henry III* (Pipe Roll Soc., vol. lxxx) (1976), p. 143.
[45] *De Lisle and Dudley MSS.*, vol. i, p. 41; *S.A.C.*, vol. liv, pp. 40–43.
[46] *Lewes Chartulary*, vol. i, p. 87; vol. ii, p. 48.
[47] *3 Suss. Subsidies*, pp. 226, 232, 237, 243, 249, 250, 255, 258, 259, 262, 268, 274, 299, 326.
[48] *Ibid.*, pp. 297, 311; *P.N. Suss.*, vol. i, p. 38.

[49] *Ibid.*, vol. ii, p. 288; *3 Suss. Subsidies*, p. 287.
[50] *Non. Inquis.*, p. 385; *Suss. Wills*, vol. iii, p. 328; *3 Suss. Subsidies*, pp. 41, 287.
[51] *Ibid.*, pp. 93, 115, 125; *S.A.C.*, vol. xx, p. 10; *Lewes Chartulary*, vol. ii, pp. 82, 83, 90; *Cowdray Archives*, vol. i, pp. 5, 6.
[52] *3 Suss. Subsidies*, pp. 49, 79, 165, 167; *Suss. Custumals*, vol. i, p. 109; *Suss. Fines*, vol. i, p. 58; *Suss. Wills*, vol. iii, p. 24; *Chichester Chart.*, p. 198; C.H. Wilkie, *St. Andrew's, Edburton, Suss.: Copy of the Parish Register Book, 1558–1673* (1884), pp. 22, 23, 25, 26, 28; P.S. Godman, *Parish Register of Cowfold, Suss., 1558–1812* (Suss. Record Soc., vol. xxii) (1916), pp. 88, 105, 110, 111, 113, 158, 228; *Suss. Subsidy, 1524–5*, pp. 89, 90. The surname Lashmar, in Sussex at the present day, is probably a form of Lechemere.
[53] *3 Suss. Subsidies*, pp. 121, 126, 160, 161, 162; *Suss. Fines*, vol. ii, pp. 64, 165; vol. iii, pp. 83, 115, 119, 240; *Non. Inquis.*, p. 386; *Suss. Custumals*, vol. iii, p. 41; *Feudal Aids*, vol. v, pp. 152, 160, 164; *Fitzalan Surveys*, p. 112; *Chichester Chart.*, p. 241; *S.A.C.*, vol. lxxxii, p. 30; West Suss. Record Office, Wiston MSS., 5234(2); *Boxgrove Chart.*, pp. 41, 42, 70, 135, 137.
[54] *Boxgrove Chart.*, pp. 18, 39, 101, 107–12.
[55] *Sussex Fines*, vol. ii, p. 51; vol. iii, p. 9; *S.A.C.*, vol. lxxxii, p. 132; vol. lxxxiv, pp. 68, 69; *Rotuli de Quo Warranto* (1818), p. 752; *3 Suss. Subsidies*, pp. 127, 151.
[56] *Ibid.*, p.132; *Suss. Fines*, vol. ii, pp. 80, 141; *Boxgrove Chart.*, p. 144; *Chichester Chart.*, p. 59; *W. Suss. 1641–2*, pp. 13, 19, 66, 85, 121, 122, 150, 165, 180; P.R.O. E.179/191/378, m. 2.
[57] *Placita de Banco* (P.R.O. Lists and Indexes, no. xxxii) (1963), vol. ii, p. 662; P.S. Godman, *op. cit.*, pp. 80–83, 87, 145, 201, 223; W.H. Challen, *Parish Register of Cocking, 1558–1837* (1927), p. 119; *W. Suss. 1641–42*, p. 188; Cottle, *Dict.*, p. 130; J.E.B. Gover, A. Mawer, and F.M. Stenton, *Place-Names of Surr.*, (1934), p. 276.
[58] *Suss. Fines*, vol. i, p. 40; *Non. Inquis.*, p. 365; *Fitzalan Surveys*, pp. 123, 125; *S.A.C.*, vol. lxxvii, p. 4; vol. lxxxix, p. 142; *W. Suss. 1641–2*, pp. 202.
[59] *3 Suss. Subsidies*, pp. 23, 196, 244, 305; *Suss. Fines*, vol. i, p. 84; vol. iii, p. 25; *Feudal Aids*, vol. v, p. 166; *S.A.C.*, vol. xviii, p. 27; vol. lxxxiii, p. 48; *Lewes Chartulary*, vol. i, p. 83.
[60] *3 Suss. Subsidies*, pp. 290, 319; *Lewes Barony Recs.*, p, 74; *Hastings Lathe C.R.*, p. 129; *Suss. Custumals*, vol. ii, p. 42. Capenor (Surr.) is probably derived from the surname: J.E.B. Gover, A. Mawer, and F.M. Stenton, *Place-names of Surr.* (1934), p. 303. Copner is usually said to be a nickname (Reaney, *Dict.*, p. 82; Cottle, *Dict.*, p. 99), but the early references in Suss. are de Capenor.
[61] *3 Suss. Subsidies*, p. 324.

[62] *Ibid.*, p. 225.
[63] *Ibid.*, p. 330.
[64] *Ibid.*, pp. 225, 260; *Fitzalan Surveys*, p. 107.
[65] *3 Suss. Subsidies*, pp. 245, 251.
[66] *Ibid.*, pp. 254, 256, 288, 301, 302; *Non.Inquis.*, p. 393; *Lewes Chartulary*, vol. i, pp. 170, 181; *Feudal Aids*, vol. v, p. 143; *V.C.H Suss.*, vol. vii, p. 225; *Suss. Fines*, vol. ii, p. 197; vol. iii, pp. 41, 95, 117; *Placita de Banco* (P.R.O. Lists and Indexes, xxxii) (1963), vol. ii, p. 667; East Suss. Record Office, Glynde MSS., 997.
[67] *3 Suss. Subsidies*, p. 276.
[68] *Ibid.*, p. 284.
[69] *Ibid.*, p. 295; *S.A.C.*, vol. lxix, p.116; *W. Suss. 1641–2*, pp. 35, 58, 64, 68, 73, 74, 81, 89, 96, 97, 116, 119, 120, 127, 136, 138, 157, 201.
[70] *3 Suss. Subsidies*, pp. 268, 328; *Lewes Chartulary*, vol. i, pp. 14, 33, 132; *Suss. Wills*. vol. iv, 418; *Suss. Fines*, vol. i, p. 16; vol. ii, p. 33; Inderwick, *Winchelsea*, p. 168; *S.A.C.*, vol. lxxxix, p. 126; *Wiston Archives*, p. 383; *Chichester Chart.*, p. 130, 241; *W. Suss. 1641–2*, pp. 104, 153, 161.
[71] *3 Suss. Subsidies*, p. 306; on the family, see *V.C.H. Suss.*, vol. iv, p. 24; *S.A.C.*, vol. lxiii, p. 201.
[72] *3 Suss. Subsidies*, pp. 165, 279; *Lewes Chartulary*, vol. i, p. 1; *Non. Inquis.*, pp. 386, 396; *Wiston Archives*, p. 53; C.F. Slade, *Great Roll of the Pipe for the 12th year of John* (Pipe Roll Soc., vol. lxiv) (1951), p. 59; W. Farrer, *Honors and Knights' Fees*, vol. iii, pp. 201–2.
[73] *3 Suss. Subsidies*, p. 330; *S.A.C.*, vol. xxiv, p. 5.
[74] *3 Suss. Subsidies*, p. 71 (or from Badby, Northumberland).
[75] *Ibid.*, p. 321.
[76] *Ibid.*, p. 291; *Suss. Wills*, vol. iv, 347; *Suss. Subsidy, 1524–5*, p. 46.
[77] *3 Suss. Subsidies*, p. 330; *P.N. Suss.*, vol. ii, p. 462.
[78] *3 Suss. Subsidies*, p. 303.
[79] *Ibid.*, p. 253; *Suss. Wills*, vol. i, pp. 31, 40, 236; vol. ii, p. 302; *V.C.H. Suss.*, vol. iv, p. 177; *Suss. Fines*, vol. iii, p. 99; P.R.O. E.122/147/21; *Fitzalan Surveys*, p. 156.
[80] *3 Suss. Subsidies*, p. 234.
[81] *Ibid.*, p. 293; *Lewes Barony Recs.*, p. 64; *Lewes Chartulary*, vol. ii, p. 115; *S.A.C.*, vol. xviii, p. 30.
[82] *3 Suss. Subsidies*, p. 272; *Fitzalan Surveys*, p. 134; P.R.O. E.179/189/42, m. 19.
[83] *3 Suss. Subsidies*, p. 237.
[84] *Ibid.*, p. 273.
[85] *Ibid.*, pp. 71, 145, 150, 266, 268; *Non. Inquis.*, p. 370; *Suss. Wills*, vol. iii, pp. 103, 176, 297; *S.A.C.*, vol. lxxxii, p. 133; vol. lxxxix, pp. 121, 159, 161; vol. xcv, pp. 45, 48; Lord Leconfield, *Sutton and Duncton Manors* (1956), pp. 25, 39; Lord Leconfield, *Petworth*

Manor in the 17th Century (1954), p. 81; *Suss. Subsidy, 1524–5*, pp. 39, 128;*W. Suss. 1641–2*, pp. 62, 68, 80, 138, 143, 194.

[86] *3 Suss. Subsidies*, p. 278; *Suss. Subsidy, 1524–5*, pp. 112, 118, 123, 136;*W. Suss. 1641–2*, p. 104; *Wiston Archives*, pp. 294–5; *Suss. Fines*, vol. iii, pp. 35, 94, 188, 199. The Suss. place-name Bonswick is probably derived from the surname: *P.N. Suss.*, vol. ii, p. 348.

[87] *3 Suss. Subsidies*, pp. 142, 267; *Suss. Fines*, vol. iii, p. 96; West Suss. Record Office, EP. VI/19A/1, m. 5.

[88] *3 Suss. Subsidies*, p. 246; *Suss. Custumals*, vol. ii, pp. 16, 18; *Suss. Fines*, vol. ii, pp. 15, 65, 73; *S.A.C.*, vol. lxxxiv, p. 63; *V.C.H. Suss.*, vol. iv, p. 63; *Lewes Chartulary*, vol. ii, p. 64, 66. (A date of *c.* 1170, given *ibid.*, vol. ii, p. 6, for John de Mildeby, may be too early.)

[89] *3 Suss. Subsidies*, p. 274; Reaney, *Dict.*, p. 93.

[90] *3 Suss. Subsidies*, p. 289.

[91] *Ibid.*, pp. 304, 311; see also *Lewes Barony Recs.*, p. 56.

[92] *Feudal Aids.*, vol. iii, p. 420; *Book of Fees*, vol. ii, p. 905. And see p. 4.

[93] *Feudal Aids*, vol. iv, pp. 26, 44.

[94] *Suss. Custumals*, vol. i, pp. 4–11, 13–31, 33–9, 42–52, 54–61, 65, 71–78, 79–86, 88–95, 106–122. And see p. 12.

[95] *Ibid.*,vol. ii, pp. 37–9, 40–46, 51–61, 64–69, 73–4, 79–83, 88, 90–94, 96, 98, 100, 104, 107, 111–13.

[96] *Ibid.*, vol. ii, pp. 37, 38, 39, 42, 51, 52, 70.

[97] *Chichester Chart.*, p. 269; *Suss. Wills*, vol. i, p. 309; vol. iii, p. 291; vol. iv, p. 263; *V.C.H. Suss.*, vol. iv, p. 135; *Suss. Fines*, vol. iii, p. 290; *Wiston Archives*, p. 96; *S.A.C.*, vol. xxi, p. 69; vol. xxii, p. 123; vol. liv, p. 162; Lane, *Suss. Deeds*, p. 1; *Feudal Aids*, vol. v, p. 163; A. Dale, *Fashionable Brighton, 1820–1860*, p. 129; J.E. Ray, *Suss. Chantry Records* (Suss. Record Soc., vol. xxxvi) (1931), p. 194.

[98] *Lewes Chartulary*, vol. i, p. 99; Lane, *Suss. Deeds*, p. 130; *Suss. Indictments*, vol. i, pp. 9, 10; *De Lisle and Dudley MSS.*, vol. i, p. 26; P.S. Godman, *op. cit.*, p. 109.

[99] *Suss. Fines*, vol. iii, pp. 281, 304; *Suss. Wills*, vol. i, pp. 11, 243; vol. ii, p. 257; vol. iii, pp. 179, 239; *V.C.H. Suss.*, vol. vii, pp. 160, 207, 275–6, 279; F. Hull, *op. cit.*, pp. 96, 103; *Wiston Archives*, p. 205; *Suss. Subsidy, 1524–5*, pp. 44, 53, 67, 106; *W. Suss. 1641–2*, pp. 53, 55, 138; W.H. Challen, *op. cit.*, p. 55; C.H. Wilkie, *op. cit.*, pp. 31–35, 68; P.R.O. E.179/191/378, m. 1; E.179/191/380.

[100] *Non. Inquis.*, p. 377; *Feudal Aids*, vol. v, p. 165; *Suss. Wills*, vol. i, p. 291; vol. iii, p. 216; *Cowdray Archives*, vol. i, p. 16; vol. ii, p. 242; *V.C.H. Suss.*, vol. iv, pp. 5, 150; *S.A.C.*, vol. xx, pp. 15, 16, 17, 28; vol. xxiv, p. 82; *Suss. Subsidy, 1524–5*, pp. 7, 96, 111, 164; *W. Suss. 1641–2*, pp. 8, 73, 74; W.H. Challen, *op. cit.*, pp. 81, 102; R. Garraway Rice, *Parish Register of Horsham* (Suss. Record Soc.

vol. xxi) (1915), pp. 25, 142, 149, 160, 222, 231, 372, 380; P.R.O. E.179/191/378, m. 1; Reaney, *Dict.*, p. 79.

[101] *Suss. Wills*, vol. iv, p. 395; *Suss. Indictments*, vol. i, p. 11; *V.C.H. Suss.*, vol. iv, p. 150; *S.A.C.*, vol. liv, p. 93; vol. lxxxii, pp. 136, 137.

[102] *Suss. Custumals*, vol. i, p. 119; F. Hull, *op. cit.*, pp. 168, 225, 228; *Suss. Fines*, vol. iii, p. 296; *Hastings Lathe C.R.*, pp. 74, 148; *Suss. Subsidy, 1524–5*, p. 157; P.R.O. S.C.11/649, m. 2.

[103] J.E. Ray, *op. cit.*, p. 182; *Wiston Archives*, pp. 142, 144, 277; *Suss. Wills*, vol. iii, p. 107; *W. Suss. 1641–2*, pp. 109, 118; *Suss. Subsidy, 1524–5*, pp. 47, 93; P.S. Godman, *op. cit.*, pp. 44, 45, 129.

[104] *Lewes Barony Recs.*, pp. 8, 27; *Cal. Pat. 1330–34*, p. 128; *Suss. Wills*, vol. i, p.151; vol. iv, p. 422; Dauzat, *op. cit.*, p. 579; Reaney, *Dict.*, p. 355; Cottle, *Dict.*, p. 390.

[105] *Suss. Subsidy, 1524–5*, pp. 86–107.

[106] See the discussion of the locative names listed in 1524 in another part of Sussex by Mr. F. Leeson, "The Development of Surnames: Locative Surnames in West Suss." *Genealogists' Magazine*, vol. xvi (1971), pp. 536–46.

[107] *Suss. Subsidy. 1524–5*, pp. 7, 14, 69, 70, 71, 86.

[108] Reaney, *Dict.*, p. 36.

[109] *P.N. Suss.*, vol. ii, p. 314; *W. Suss. 1641–2*, pp. 17, 18, 67; *Suss. Wills*, vol. i, pp. 1, 292;; vol. ii, p. 124, 307; *S.A.C.*, vol. ix, pp. 74, 81, 83, 84; vol. xxiv, p. 104; vol. xxv, p. 132; vol. xxxvi, p. 31; vol. xlii, p. 114; vol. lviii, pp. 7, 8, 19; *V.C.H. Suss.*, vol. iv, p. 24; *Wiston Archives*, pp. 49, 280, 398, 414; Lane, *Suss. Deeds*, p. 131; *Suss. Indictments*, vol. i, pp. 34, 47, 82; P.S. Godman, *op. cit., per indice*; W.C. Renshaw, *op. cit., per indice*; R. Garraway Rice, *op. cit.*, p. 357.

[110] *Suss. Subsidy, 1524–5*, p. 97; J.K. Wallenberg, *Place-Names of Kent* (1934), p. 319.

[111] *Suss. Subsidy, 1524–5*, pp. 36, 41, 45, 95, 97. The name might possibly be from Rickford (Somers.).

[112] *Feudal Aids*, vol. v, p. 152; *Suss. Fines*, vol. iii, p. 286; *S.A.C.*, vol. xviii, p. 29; vol. cvi, p. 100.

[113] *Suss. Subsidy, 1524–5*, pp. 19, 25, 93–5, 103, 128.

[114] *W. Suss. 1641–2*, p. 32; Lane, *Suss. Deeds*, pp. 48, 49, 56, 103; *P.N. Suss.*, vol. ii, p. 388; *S.A.C.*, vol. xviii, p. 29; *Suss. Fines*, vol. iii, pp. 286, 298; *Feudal Aids*, vol. v, pp. 152, 165; *V.C.H. Suss.*, vol. vii, pp. 87, 236; *Suss. Wills*, vol. i, pp. 68, 168, 259; vol. ii, p. 255; vol. iii, pp. 102, 119, 263; vol. iv, p. 341.

[115] *Suss. Subsidy, 1524–5*, pp. 35, 128; *Suss. Wills*, vol. i, p. 108; vol. iv, p. 3; Wallenberg, *op. cit.*, p. 130.

[116] *Suss. Subsidy, 1524–5*, pp. 99, 118.

[117] See p. 113.

[118] *Suss. Subsidy, 1524–5*, p. 92; *Suss. Wills*, vol. iv, p. 152; *Chichester Chart.*, p. 200; East Suss. Record Office, Glynde MSS., 1032, m. 1.
[119] An alternative source of the surname might be Keverall (Cornw.), and the name may be occupational in some cases; Reaney, *Dict.*, pp. 71–2; J.E.D. Gover and others, *Place-Names of Wilts.*, pp. 238–9.
[120] *Suss. Subsidy, 1524–5*, p. 101; J.E. Ray, *op. cit.*, p. 42; *Hastings Lathe C.R.*, p. 168; *Suss. Wills*, vol. i, p. 125; vol. ii, p. 331; *Cowdray Archives*, vol. i, p. 7.
[121] *Suss. Subsidy, 1524–5*, p. 99.
[122] *Ibid.*, pp. 96, 100; *Suss. Wills*, vol. ii, p. 220; vol. iii, p. 119.
[123] *Suss. Subsidy, 1524–5*, p. 96.
[124] See p. 108.
[125] *Suss. Subsidy, 1524–5*, pp. 68, 88.
[126] *Valor Eccl.*, vol. i, p. 295; *Suss. Wills*, vol. i, pp. 30, 74, 266, 286; vol. ii, pp. 30, 221; vol. iv, pp. 185, 195; J.E. Ray, *op. cit.*, p. 16; *S.A.C.*, vol. lxxvii, p. 98; vol. lxxxix, p. 149.
[127] *W. Suss. 1641–2*, p. 155; L. Fleming, *History of Pagham* (1949), p. 190.
[128] See p. 325.
[129] *W. Suss. 1641–2*.
[130] *Ibid.*, pp. 11, 13, 19, 20, 35, 38, 58, 62, 64, 66, 68, 73, 74, 80, 81, 88, 89, 91, 93, 96, 97, 100, 104, 110, 116, 119, 121, 122, 126, 127, 136, 138, 143, 150, 157, 165, 176, 177, 194, 201; and see pp. 99–104.
[131] *W. Suss. 1641–2*, pp. 8, 73, 78, 98, 109, 118, 125, 126, 188, 198, 202; and see pp. 102, 107–8.
[132] *W. Suss. 1641–2*, p. 22; *Hastings Lathe C.R.*, p. 167; *Wiston Archives*, pp. 71, 72; *Suss. Wills*, vol. i, pp. 198, 199.
[133] *W. Suss. 1641–2*, p. 87; J.E. Ray, *op. cit.*, p. 79; *S.A.C*, vol. lix, p. 84; vol. xcviii, p. 63; vol. liv, p. 167; *Wiston Archives*, pp. 30, 203; Lane, *Suss. Deeds*, p. 84; *V.C.H. Suss.*, vol. iv, pp. 213, 231; *Suss. Wills*, vol. i, p. 64; vol. iv, p. 161; *De Lisle and Dudley MSS.*, vol. i, p. 25; *Suss. Fines.*, vol. iii, pp. 240, 248, 266, 276; P.R.O. E.122/35/3; *Fitzalan Surveys*, p. 107.
[134] *3 Suss. Subsidies*, pp. 71, 72, 99; *V.C.H. Suss.*, vol. iv, p. 95; *Boxgrove Chart.*, p. 147; *Suss. Fines*, vol. ii, p. 182; *Suss. Wills*, vol. i, p. 167; vol. iii, p. 194; *De Lisle and Dudley MSS.*, vol. i, p. 155; *W. Suss. 1641–2*, p. 35; East Guldeford (Suss.), is a place-name derived from the surname: *P.N. Suss.*, vol. ii, pp. 529–30.
[135] *Suss. Custumals*, vol. ii, p. 8; *Fitzalan Surveys*, p. 137; *Suss. Wills*, vol. iii, p. 64; vol. iv, p. 378; *V.C.H. Suss.*, vol. iv, pp. 124, 230; W.H. Challen, *op. cit.*, pp. 16, 21, 28, 30-32, 34, 59; P.S. Godman, *op. cit.*, pp. 50, 51, 120, 208, 253; P.R.O. E.179/189/42, m. 21d; E.179/191/378, m. 2; *W. Suss. 1641–2*, pp. 47, 63, 65, 85, 109, 130, 147, 201.

[136] *Ibid.*, p. 32; *Feudal Aids*, vol. v, pp. 152, 165; *Suss. Fines*, vol. iii, pp. 286, 298; *S.A.C.*, vol. xviii, p. 29; *Suss. Wills*, vol. i, pp. 68, 69, 168, 259; vol. iii, pp. 102, 119, 263; vol. iv, p. 341; Lane, *Suss. Deeds*, pp. 48, 49, 56, 103; *P.N. Suss.*, vol. ii, p. 388; *V.C.H. Suss.*, vol. vii, pp. 87, 236.

[137] *W. Suss. 1641–2*, pp. 131, 159; *Buckhurst Terrier*, p. 35; P.S. Godman, *op. cit.*, pp. 5, 141, 221; Reaney, *Dict.*, p. 110.

[138] *Suss. Wills*, vol. i, p. 294; vol. iv, pp. 35, 377; Lord Leconfield, *Petworth Manor in the 17th century* (1954), pp. 63, 91; *S.A.C.*, vol. v, p. 260; vol. lxix, p. 135; *Wiston Archives*, pp. 17, 209, 211, 260, 265; Reaney, *Dict.*, p. 114; *W. Suss. 1641–2*, pp. 84, 85, 101, 180, 181, 189.

[139] *Ibid.*, p. 175.

[140] *Ibid.*, p. 81; Reaney, *Dict.*, p. 382.

[141] *W. Suss. 1641–2*, p. 153.

[142] *Ibid.*, p. 171. Fishwick survives as a surname in Suss.

[143] *Ibid.*, p. 137; G. Redmonds, *Yorks.: West Riding* (1973), pp. 202, 207.

[144] *W. Suss. 1641-2*, p. 159.

[145] *Ibid.*, pp. 12, 47, 53, 172; *V.C.H. Suss.*, vol. iv, p. 213; *S.A.C.*, vol. ix, p. 73; Lane, *Suss. Deeds*, p. 142; *Wiston Archives*, p. 107; P.R.O. E.179/191/380.

[146] *W. Suss. 1641–2*, pp. 100, 141.

[147] Paul van parr, an alien, is listed in Suss., 1456–7; P.R.O., E.179/189/94a.

[148] *W. Suss. 1641–2*, p. 50.

[149] *Ibid.*, p. 41.

[150] *Ibid.*, pp. 31, 141, 153; Reaney, *Dict.*, p. 242.

[151] *W. Suss. 1641–2*, p. 159.

[152] *Ibid.*, p. 190.

[153] *Ibid.*, pp. 29, 100. And see p. 68.

[154] *W. Suss. 1641–2*, p. 77. And see p. 69.

[155] *W. Suss. 1641–2*, pp. 13, 15, 19, 54, 68, 87, 110, 112, 113, 116, 133, 169, 175, 193. And see p. 71.

[156] *W. Suss. 1641–2*, pp. 11, 70, 156, 171.

[157] *Ibid.*, p. 113.

[158] *Ibid.*, pp.11, 93, 137, 138, 141, 142, 180.

[159] *Ibid.*, pp. 12, 56, 57, 113; *3 Suss. Subsidies*, p. 135; P.R.O. E.179/191/380.

[160] *W. Suss. 1641–2*, pp. 52, 110; *S.A.C.*, vol. lxxxvii, p. 7; *Non. Inquis.*, pp. 368, 387; *Valor Eccl.*, vol. i, p. 300; *Suss. Fines*, vol. i, pp. 33: vol. ii, pp. 105, 125; *Chichester Chart.*, pp. 149, 172, 173, 176; *3 Suss. Subsidies*, p. 137.

[161] *W. Suss. 1641–2*, p. 116; *Boxgrove Chart.*, pp. 41, 135; *Suss. Fines*, vol. ii, p. 104; *Lewes Chartulary*, vol. ii, p. 65.

[162] *P.N. Suss*, vol. ii, p. 342. The name has been derived from Backshells

in Billinghurst, but the place-name appears to be a late one, derived from the surname: *ibid.*, vol. i, p. 150; Reaney, *Dict.*, p. 19.

[163] *W. Suss. 1641–2*, pp. 95, 96; *3 Suss. Subsidies*, p. 52, 181, 295.

[164] *W. Suss. 1641–2*, pp. 110, 119, 120, 125, 126, 130, 137, 163, 180; *P.N. Suss.*, vol. i, p. 103. Alternative sources of the surname might be Buxshalls, in Lindfield (*ibid.*, vol. ii, p. 340) or Bugsell in Salehurst (*ibid.*, vol. ii, p. 458).

[165] *Ibid.*, vol. i, p. 210; *W. Suss. 1641–2*, pp. 18, 22, 27, 39, 43, 67, 68, 90, 95, 98, 100, 110, 124, 131, 151, 152, 153, 181.

[166] *3 Suss. Subsidies*, pp. 167, 281; *Suss. Fines*, vol. ii, p. 210; vol. iii, pp. 254, 269; J.E. Ray, *op. cit.*, p. 74; *Suss. Custumals*, vol. i, p. 110; *V.C.H. Suss.*, vol. vii, pp. 105, 235; *S.A.C.*, vol. lx, p. 34; vol. lxii, pp. 139, 140; P.R.O. E.179/191/378, m. 1; *Suss. Subsidy, 1524–5*, pp. 60, 69, 70, 116, 118, 138.

[167] *P.N. Suss.*, vol. ii, p. 371.

[168] *W. Suss. 1641–2*, pp. 32, 98–101.

[169] *S.A.C.*, vol. lxix, p. 141; R. Garraway Rice, *Parish Register of Horsham* (Suss. Record Soc., vol. xxi) (1915), *per indice*.

[170] *P.N. Suss.*, vol. i, p. 107. The surname occurs in the 15th cent.: West Suss. Record Office, EP. VI/19A/1, m. 15d.

[171] *Suss. Subsidy, 1524–5*, pp. 40, 41, 48. See also G.H. Kenyon, *Glass Industry of the Weald* (1967), pp. 45, 111, 112, 119.

[172] *W. Suss. 1641–2*, pp. 23, 30, 47, 48, 67, 90, 108, 109, 110, 115, 118, 120, 159, 195, 196; P.R.O. E.179/191/380.

[173] Information from Mr. L.A. Strudwick of Worthing; C.A.F. Meekings, *Surr. Hearth Tax, 1664* (Surr. Record Soc., vol. xvii) (1940), pp. 146, 147.

[174] *W. Suss.1641–2*, pp. 11, 46, 56, 60, 63, 65, 80, 105, 115, 117, 119, 126, 144, 163, 180, 183, 184; *V.C.H. Suss.*, vol. iv, pp. 5, 23–25, 36, 63–4; C.R. Davey, *Hants. Lay Subsidy, 1586* (Hants. Record Soc., vol. iv) (1981), pp. 49, 50. The surname existed in Surr. in the 17th century: Meekings, *op. cit.*, p. 16.

[175] *W. Suss. 1641–2*, pp. 54, 76, 80, 104, 174; *Suss. Subsidy, 1524–5*, p. 137; *S.A.C.*, vol. lxix, p. 121; vol. cix, pp. 25, 26; *Suss. Fines*, vol. iii, p. 301; J.E. Ray, *op. cit.*, pp. 184–5; *Suss. Wills*, vol. ii, p. 222; R.P. Crawfurd, *Parish Register of East Grinstead* (Suss. Record Soc., vol. xxiv) (1917), *per indice*.

[176] See pp. 48, 49, 52.

[177] See pp. 29, 32.

[178] See *Surnames of Oxon.*, p. 71.

[179] *Suss. Custumals*, vol. ii, pp. 48, 49, 51.

[180] *V.C.H. Suss.*, vol. vii, pp. 89, 105, 134; *Hastings Lathe C.R.*, p. 140; *3 Suss. Subsidies*, pp. 199, 310; *Suss. Subsidy, 1524–5*, pp. 94, 126, 136.

[181] *Suss. Custumals*, vol. ii, p. 38. The place concerned may be Crowhurst in Burwash.
[182] *Ibid.* The place concerned has not been located, but seems to have been in Wadhurst.
[183] *Ibid.*, p. 52.
[184] *Ibid.*, p. 62.
[185] *Ibid.*, pp. 62, 63, 70. And see p. 62.
[186] *3 Suss. Subsidies*, pp. 3, 5, 11, 16.
[187] G. Kristensson, *Studies on Middle English Topographical Terms*, pp. 9–10.
[188] *3 Suss. Subsidies*, p. 85; *Suss. Fines.*, vol. iii, p. 13; *S.A.C.*, vol. lxxxiv, p. 60; vol. lxix, p. 113.
[189] *P.N. Suss.*, vol. i, p. 38.
[190] *Suss. Fines*, vol. i, p. 20; *Calendar of Charter Rolls*, vol. ii, p. 169.
[191] Lane, *Suss. Deeds*, p. 98; *Lewes Chartulary*, vol. i, p. 112; *3 Suss. Subsidies*, p. 182; *S.A.C.*, vol. xii, p. 34; *Suss. Fines*, vol. iii, p. 26; *P.N. Suss.*, vol. ii, p. 349.
[192] *Lewes Barony Recs.*, pp. 36, 40; *P.N. Suss.*, vol. ii, p. 252.
[193] *Ibid.*, vol. i, p. 219; *3 Suss. Subsidies*, p. 55.
[194] *Ibid.*, pp. 26, 28, 30, 204, 209; *Suss. Fines*, vol. iii, p. 187; *S.A.C.*, vol. xcv, p. 47; P.R.O. S.C.11/877; *P.N. Suss.*, vol. ii, pp. 474, 478, 491; M.T. Löfvenberg, *Studies on Middle English Local Surnames* (1942), p. xl.
[195] *P.N. Suss.*, vol. i, pp. 39–40; *3 Suss. Subsidies*, pp. 76, 259; Löfvenberg, *op. cit.*, p. 64.
[196] *3. Suss. Subsidies*, p. 218; *P.N. Suss.*, vol. ii, p. 524.
[197] *Suss. Custumals*, vol. iii, p. 41; *P.N. Suss.*, vol. i, p. 169.
[198] *De Lisle and Dudley MSS.*, vol. i, p. 59; *P.N. Suss.*, vol. i, p. 239.
[199] *Hastings Lathe C.R.*, pp. 120, 132, 174; *P.N. Suss.*, vol. ii, p. 528.
[200] Probably from a minor locality near Wisborough Green: *Suss. Custumals*, vol. i, p. 70. Possibly from Tugmore in Hartfield: *P.N. Suss.*, vol. ii, p. 369.
[201] *Suss. Custumals*, vol. i, pp. 12, 15; *3 Suss Subsidies*, p. 275; *Lewes Chartulary*, vol. i, p. 13; W. Stubbs, *Memorials of St. Dunstan* (Rolls Series) (1874), p. 143. The name of Scotland Farm, Steyning, is probably from the surname, but see *P.N. Suss.*, vol. i, p. 238.
[202] P.M. Barnes, *Great Roll of the Pipe for the 16th year of John* (Pipe Roll Soc., vol. lxxiii) (1962), p. 165; E.P. Ebden, *Great Roll of the Pipe for the 2nd year of Henry III* (Pipe Roll Soc., vol. lxxvii) (1972), p. 20; P.M. Barnes and others, *Great Roll of the Pipe for the 3rd year of Henry III* (Pipe Roll Soc., vol.lxxx) (1976), p. 137.
[203] *Non. Inquis.*, pp. 372, 378, 403; *S.A.C.*, vol. lxxxii, pp. 120, 130; P.R.O. S.C.11/663; S.C.11/666; *P.N. Suss.*, vol. ii, p. 477.
[204] *S.A.C.*, vol. lxxvii, p. 99; vol. lxxxix, p. 161; H.M.C., *Rye MSS.*,

pp. 149, 155; *V.C.H. Suss.*, vol. iv, p. 78; *Suss. Wills*, vol. i, p. 151; vol. ii, p. 84; vol. iii, p. 217; vol. iv, p. 404; *Cowdray Archives*, vol. ii, pp. 278, 336; *W. Suss. 1641–2*, p. 185. On the history of the name, see Reaney, *Origins*, p. 225.

[205] P.M. Barnes and others, *Great Roll of the Pipe for the 3rd Year of Henry III* (Pipe Roll Soc., vol. lxxx) (1976), p. 144; *W. Suss. 1641–2*, pp. 52, 67, 85, 90, 104, 131, 197.

[206] *Chichester Bishops' Acta.*, p. 73; *P.N. Suss.*, vol. ii, pp. 469, 496.

[207] *Ibid.*, vol. ii, p. 340; *3 Suss. Subsidies*, p. 330.

[208] *Ibid.*, p. 52; *Suss. Fines*, vol. ii, p. 26; *De Lisle and Dudley MSS.*, vol. i, pp. 116, 129, 132, 138; *P.N. Suss.*, vol. ii, pp. 340–1, 458.

[209] *Ibid.*, vol. ii, p. 341; *3 Suss. Subsidies*, pp. 104, 294–5, 305; P.R.O. S.C.11/639.

[210] *Lewes Barony Recs.*, p. 77.

[211] *3 Suss. Subsidies*, pp. 52, 105, 294; *Suss. Fines*, vol. i, p. 24; *Suss. Subsidy, 1524–5*, p. 89; *Placita de Banco* (P.R.O. Lists and Indexes, xxxii) (1963), vol. ii, p. 662; *Lewes Barony Recs.*, p. 79; *P.N. Suss.*, vol. ii, p. 341. The surname Gravene, in Suss. in the 14th century, may have the same origin (*Hastings Lathe C.R.*, pp. 3, 5, 14, 114).

[212] *P.N. Suss.*, vol. ii, p. 342; *3 Suss. Subsidies*, pp. 180, 294; *Suss. Custumals*, vol. i, p. 100; *S.A.C.*, vol. xviii, p. 25; *Suss. Subsidy, 1524–5*, p. 59.

[213] *3 Suss. Subsidies*, pp. 32, 196.

[214] *Ibid.*, pp. 179, 293; *P.N. Suss.*, vol. ii, p. 342.

[215] See above, p. 119.

[216] *3 Suss. Subsidies*, pp. 52, 179, 293.

[217] *Ibid.*, pp. 180, 294, 295; *Suss. Subsidy, 1524–5*, p. 104.

[218] *Lewes Barony Recs.*, pp. 36, 42, 48; *Lewes Chartulary*, vol. ii, p. 62; *P.N. Suss.*, vol. ii, p. 343; *3 Suss. Subsidies*, p. 311; *Suss. Subsidy, 1524–5*, p. 147.

CHAPTER 3
TOPOGRAPHICAL SURNAMES

It is intended here to use the term 'topographical surnames' to denote those surnames which are derived from words for features of the landscape, whether natural or manmade. Such surnames (or bye-names) as, for example, Hill, Down, and Brook, or Bridge, Mill and Field, will be included in the category. So too will names formed from a topographical term with the addition of a suffix, such as Brooker, Fielder, Hillman, or Bridgeman. Topographical surnames now occur in all parts of England, and from the 12th century onwards they can be found in all regions of the country. They are, however, exceptionally common in Sussex, where they form a higher proportion of the total body of surnames in use than is the case in most other counties. The topographical surnames which have appeared in Sussex at one period or another are unusually numerous and varied. It is not easy to devise a satisfactory method of measuring the difference which existed during the Middle Ages between the surnames present in one English county, and those present in other parts of the country. One possible method is to make use of the lay subsidy rolls as a means of comparing surnames in one county with those in others. This method has the advantage that the subsidy rolls, with certain exceptions, are drawn up county by county, and do list the names of large numbers of the inhabitants in each. The subsidy rolls for Sussex and for some other counties have been analysed to discover what the proportion of topographical surnames is in the source used for each county, and the statistics are set out in the table, printed in the Introduction.[1]

These figures make it possible to compare the position in Sussex with that in a number of other counties, some in the south east, and contiguous to Sussex, some situated in other regions of England. Statistics could be given for some further counties, but to do so would not significantly modify the impression given by the figures in the table. It is clear from these that Sussex had a much larger proportion of persons with topographical surnames or bye-names than any of the other counties examined. Two neighbouring counties, Kent and Surrey, have smaller, but still relatively high proportions of topographical names, and such names were evidently distinctly more common in south-eastern England than in other regions. The high proportion of topographical names in the Sussex 1332 subsidy is not an exceptional feature of that particular source. In the 1327 subsidy for the county, 26% of the individuals listed have topographical surnames or bye-names, and in the Sussex 1296 subsidy roll, the figure is 23%.[2]

During the 14th century, to which the figures cited relate, there were still many families which lacked hereditary surnames, and indeed it is still possible to find instances of people who do not appear to have had surnames or bye-names at all. Even at later periods, however, the proportion of topographical surnames was higher in Sussex than in most other counties. One feature of the evolution of surnames in England is that between about 1350 and 1500 there was in most parts of the country an increase in the proportion of the total population which had surnames derived from personal names (that is, what are usually called 'first' or 'Christian' names), surnames such as Godwin, Williams, or Johnson, for example. The development of such surnames in Sussex is discussed in another chapter. One consequence of the rise in the proportion of surnames which are derived from personal names is that the proportion of surnames which belong to other categories tends to diminish. It is therefore not surprising that both in Sussex, and in most other counties, the ratio of surnames that are derived from topographical terms, out of the total body of surnames in use, is less in the 16th and 17th centuries than in the 14th. In fact, if a comparison is made between the lay subsidy rolls for the first half of the 14th century, and taxation returns for the 16th and 17th centuries, together with other sources for the same periods which list the names of large numbers of the population, such as the 1522 'Military Survey', or the 1641-42 Protestation Returns, it will be found that in most counties the proportion of topographical names is greater in the first half of the 14th century than at later periods. This is in fact true in Sussex, where the proportion of topographical surnames in the 1524-25 subsidy rolls is just over 15%.[3] Though less than the figure for 1332, this is greater than the proportion for most English counties in 16th and 17th century sources.

The topographical surnames and bye-names which appear in Sussex during the Middle Ages are very numerous. Some of these which were widespread in the county, were the names of many individuals, and have survived there to the present day. Many others are found as the names of two or three persons only, probably never became hereditary in most cases, and have often not survived. Among the rare topographical names which occurred in the county, for example, were atte Hahewood[4] (probably 'the wood in the hedge or enclosure'), ate Haneholte[5] ('cock-bird wood'), atte Haseling[6] ('hazel copse'), atte Hauekfeld or de Hauekfeld[7] ('open land frequented by hawks'), atte Haycroft[8], atte Heghehecche[9] ('high gate'), atte Heldele[10] ('glade or wood on a slope'), ate Hethdone[11] ('heath down'), atte Highegate[12] ('gate by the landing place'), ate Holegrove[13] ('grove in the hollow'), atte Holirode[14] (probably 'at the Holy Rood', that is, at the cross), atte Holstrete[15] ('hollow road'), atte Homwerthe[16] ('homestead by the manor house'), atte Homwode[17] ('home wood'), atte Horse[18] ('horse island'), atte Hoseland[19] (?'brushwood land'), atte Hoste[20] ('at the inn'), Hunderherst[21] ('under the wood') and Hunderlith[22] ('under the slope'). These are all names beginning with one letter of the alphabet. They have been chosen from a large number of topographical surnames or bye-names found in Sussex before 1500, each of them borne by a few individuals, and most of them probably never hereditary. A few of these may have been brought into the county by migration, but there are no definite reasons for supposing that any of the rare topographical names which occur in Sussex during the medieval period originated outside the county, and the probability must be that practically all of them arose there. More than 300 rare topographical names can be found in Sussex before 1500 which do not appear to have survived into the 16th century in the county. Many of these appear as the name of one individual, others as the names of three or four persons. Though 300 is a large number of names, it is unlikely that the figure is entirely comprehensive. Some new topographical names can be found in Sussex during the 16th century which have not been found there earlier. In a few cases these are the names of persons who are known to have migrated into the county from elsewhere, and in some other cases the names concerned are ones which are common in other, sometimes distant, parts of England, and may well be those of migrants. It seems likely, however, that many of the topographical surnames, which appear in the county for the first time in the 16th century, are ones which had existed there earlier, but which have not been recorded in extant sources. It is necessary to bear in mind, when considering such issues, that the names of some sections of the medieval population are very badly documented.

The use of topographical surnames or bye-names was, therefore, very common in medieval Sussex, more so perhaps than in any other English county, and the number of such names to appear in the county was very large. While some of the names which have become extinct are interesting for various reasons, it is those which became hereditary, and have survived, which are most important for consideration here.

The topographical surnames and bye-names in use during the Middle Ages vary considerably from one region of England to another. Within each region there are differences between counties, and within counties there are often smaller districts where the topographical names in use had distinctive characteristics. Some of the observable differences between regions, counties, and smaller areas are explicable in terms of the phonetics or vocabulary of local dialects, and others are connected with the landscape and geology of particular parts of the country. Some instances where less common topographical names occur frequently in one limited area appear to be due to the ramification of individual families, a process which over several generations can make a hitherto rare name quite numerous in one particular sub-division of a county. There remain, however, some features of the distribution of topographical names which do not seem to be due to any of these factors. Where topographical names are concerned (and indeed where some other categories of surnames are involved, too), there were evidently habits or practices in the formation of surnames and bye-names which were confined to individual counties or regions. There must be a link between the methods used to form surnames in each part of the country, and local habits of speech in the vernacular. Many surnames, however, originated in the 12th or 13th centuries, and for those relatively early periods it is often difficult to obtain adequate information about local usages in spoken Middle English. It is difficult to be sure how 12th century patterns of speech among the serfs or small free tenants of East and West Sussex may have influenced the development of surnames in each of those areas. It is, however, possible to observe what the main characteristics of surnames evolution were in each county, and in some cases to detect the existence within counties of smaller areas which were distinguished by some features from other parts, where surnames were concerned. A search through the medieval source material for almost any county will reveal something of the local nature of the topographical names in use there. In Sussex, it is easy to point out topographical surnames which are common in the county, but which are scarce, or lacking, in other parts of England, and it is also possible to pick out certain more general characteristics which distinguish Sussex topographical surnames from those of other counties, or which in some cases mark off the topographical surnames of south-eastern England from those in other regions. It is, however, not easy to set out the evidence for this concisely in statistical form. It is possible to use sources such as taxation returns, which list large numbers of people county by county, as evidence for the distribution of certain topographical surnames. This method of proceeding has its imperfections, which have already been discussed.[23] Some evidence drawn from such material is set out in the two tables below, one dealing with evidence from late 13th century and 14th century sources, the other dealing with 16th and 17th century evidence. By the early 14th century a substantial proportion of the Sussex population had acquired hereditary surnames, but the evolution of surnames in the county was incomplete. By the 16th century almost all families in Sussex appear to have had hereditary surnames, and it is unlikely that any significant number of new surnames arose in the county after 1500. Considerations of space have made it necessary to restrict the number of surnames dealt with to a small selection and to use evidence from a few counties only. The counties chosen are spread through various English regions, but for comparative purposes counties adjoining Sussex have been included.

The distribution of surnames, as shown by a combination of medieval sources, is never clear cut. The evidence is of course defective in that it is never possible to recover the names of all, or even the great majority, of

Table 1. Incidence of some topographical surnames or bye-names in medieval sources for selected counties.

Numbers of individuals per 10,000 persons listed in each source.

Surnames	Dorset 1327[24]	Kent 1334/5[25]	Lancs. 1332[26]	Oxon. 1278/9[27]	Suff. 1327[28]	Surr. 1332[29]	Suss. 1332[30]	Warws. 1332[31]	Worcs. 1327[32]	Yorks. 1301[33]
Ash (inc. Dash and Nash)	21	18	0	20	0	26	34	7	19[40]	2
Aldret (inc. Naldret)	0	0	0	0	0	2	5	0	0	0
Birchett (inc. Birkett)	0	1	0	0	0	24	7	0	0	0
Brook	22	46	8	40	48	27	46	13	8	8
Brooker	1	0	0	0	0	9	5	6[39]	0	0
Brookman	0	1	0	0	0	0	0	0	0	0
Combe	12	23	0	14	0	38	24	6	0	0
Down	15	23	0	11	0	24	24	4	0	0
Downer	2	0	0	0[34]	1	0	0	0	0	0
Field	0	12	12	17	6	27	34	1	0	0
Mott	0	5	5	3[35]	2[36]	2	7	1	0	0
North	11	1	4	14	6	9	13	0	0	0
Oak (inc. Noak)	5	22	0	4	0[37]	16	12	1	4	1[41]
Perye	5	7	0	21	4	21	11	4	15	1
Perryer	0	0	0	0	0	0	0	0	0	0
Perryman	0	2	0	0	0	2	1	1	0	0
Sande	1	1	0	0	0[38]	31	9	0	0	0
Sole	0	26	0	0	0	2	11	0	0	0
Tye	0	3	0	0	7	14	34	0	0	3
Towne	1	7	0	0	0	0	11	6	5	0

Table 2. Incidence of some topographical surnames in 16th and 17th century sources for selected counties.

Surnames	Numbers of individuals per 10,000 persons listed in each source.								
	Dorset 1662-4[42]	Salford Hundred 1642[43]	Oxon. 1665[44]	Salop. 1672[45]	Suff. 1524[46]	Surr. 1664[47]	Suss. 1524[48]	Wilts. 1576[49]	Worcs. 1603[50]
Ash (inc. Dash and Nash)	5	2	17	15	4	6	14	15	37
Aldret (inc. Naldret)	0	0	0	0	0	0	1	0	0
Birchett (inc. Birkett)	0	0	0	0	2	10	11	0	0
Brook	5[51]	48	9	15	24	1	44	10	31
Brooker	0	0	0	1	0	7	12	0	0
Brookman	1	0	0	0	0	0	0	2	0
Combe	30	0	1	0	0	0[58]	5	10	0
Down	11	0[53]	0[55]	4	1	5	6	24	0
Downer	0	0	3	0	0	1	6	0	0
Field	3	4	9	3	6	21	16	2	39
Mott	0	0[54]	0	1	4	2	7	2	0
North	0	0	23	1	1	3	0	7	0
Oak (inc. Noak)	7	0	3	4	3	1	3	2	0
Perye	3	0	5	7[56]	4	7	1	17	33
Perryer	0	0	0	0	0	3	2	2	0
Perryman	0	0	0	0	2	1	1	0	0
Sande	0[52]	0	0	1	0	0	1	0	0
Sole	0	0	0	0	0	1	6	0	0
Tye	0	0	1	1[57]	5	2	10	0	0
Towne	0	2	8	0	1	1	0	0	0

any county's inhabitants at any date during the Middle Ages, but apart from this, there are factors which from the start blur the pattern of distribution. One is that surnames (unlike place-names, for example) are migratory. At no time during the Middle Ages was the population entirely static. Even serf families, whose movements were subject to restrictions not applying to the free population, show a degree of mobility in some areas. When surnames appear in a county such as Sussex, which are very rare there, but which are common in some distant region of England, it must often be suspected that they are the names of migrants into the county, but it is very often impossible to find evidence either to prove or to disprove such suspicions. A second factor is that once surnames become hereditary, distribution is liable to be affected by the growth of families. The ramification of a few families, all bearing one particular surname, can multiply the number of individuals with that name considerably over the course of a few generations. If all or most of those concerned remain in one area, and do not migrate, a surname can by this means become very common in one district. Some Sussex families already have hereditary surnames during the 12th century, so that by the early 14th century, when sources such as subsidy rolls are available, they may have been ramifying for four generations, or even more.

These considerations inevitably mean that the original distribution of surnames is obscured to some degree, even at an early period. The total effect of such factors is, however, very limited, and the main outlines of English surname distribution which can be already discerned during the 13th and 14th centuries, can still be found in the 16th and 17th centuries and indeed in many counties still survived, little impaired, into the 19th.

Evidence of the type set out in the two tables printed on adjoining pages has been collected for a much larger number of surnames than it has been possible to include, and statistics have been compiled for some further counties, which have been excluded for reasons of space. On the basis of this information and of much other material for the history of topographical surnames in Sussex, some observations can be made about the character of Sussex names in this category. There are two major types of topographical surname which were from an early date much more common in the south-east of England than in other regions, and which were rather more common in Sussex than in other south-eastern counties. These are surnames formed from a topographical term with the suffix -er added (Bridger, Fielder, Crowcher, etc.), and surnames composed of a topographical term with -man added (Bridgeman, Hillman, Crossman, etc.). Some individual names in each of these two groups have been taken at times to be occupational, and indeed it is not always easy to distinguish between occupational and topographical surnames in some cases. Both these types of surname, those in -er, and those in -man, are discussed separately below. If names of these two types are left on one side, there are certain other distinctive features of Sussex topographical names.

There are few surnames in this category which were at any period entirely confined to Sussex, or which seem likely to have originated in the county solely, without having arisen independently elsewhere. The surname Leyne or Layne is derived from a term, not exclusive to Sussex[59], for a stretch of arable, said to have in Sussex dialect the more restricted significance of a tract of arable land lying below the Downs. Leyne occurs as an element in field-names in several Sussex townships, all of them lying near the scarp slope of the South Downs.[60] The only places where the surname (de la Leyne, ate Layne) has been found is, however, at Sidlesham (south of Chichester, and some distance from the Downs), and at Chichester. The individuals who appear with the name were nearly all bondmen.[61] From the facts that the surname occurs in a single area and among people mostly of one class, it must be suspected that it was the name of one family, probably one that was hereditary from the time of its first appearance in the source material, in the late 13th century. The surname does seem to be one which originated in Sussex, and not elsewhere.

Another surname which seems clearly to be exclusively Sussex in origin is Pallant (ate Palente, de Palenta). The surname first occurs in the first half of the 13th century, and all the early bearers of it were people connected with Chichester.[62] The name is derived from that of a district in the south east of Chichester, known as the Pallant from the 13th century onwards. The surname was still present in West Sussex in the 17th century.[63] It has been suggested by reputable authorities that the name Pallant arose from the possession of palatine rights by the Archbishop of Canterbury in the Pallant. This cannot be correct, as the archbishop did not have palatine rights there, and no instances have been produced to show that the quarter of Chichester concerned was ever referred to as a palatinate in the Middle Ages, even in error. What the archbishop did possess in that quarter of the city was a court for his own tenants, and an ecclesiastical peculiar, a jurisdiction of quite a different nature. Further, the surname Pallant occurs rather earlier than the first known use of the term "palatinate" for an area of jurisdiction in England,[64] and presumably the place-name was in use still earlier.

Several other topographical surnames, all rare, seem likely to have originated in Sussex only. The name Sparre (atte Sparre, de la Sparre) first appears in the 13th century. All the early instances are found in the northern part of West Sussex, around Petworth, Billingshurst, and Wisborough. The surname is derived from a word which probably had the meaning in this context of 'enclosure', and in the 14th century holdings called la Sparre already existed at both Billingshurst and Wisborough. The surname is probably derived from one, or perhaps both, of these. The Old English 'spaer' is found as an element in several place-names in the same part of Sussex, but not elsewhere in the county. It also occurs as an element in a few place names in other counties. Possible the term remained in use in one limited area in Sussex, with the sense of 'enclosure'. The fact that the early distribution of the surname is so concentrated makes it likely that the name was that of one family.[65] A few rare bye-names compounded with the same element, such as de Lutemannesparr' and Wydesparre occur in the same part of Sussex during the early 14th century.[66] Similarly the name Whamm (atte Whamme, atte Whame, etc.), which occurs from the 13th century onwards, has been found in early instances in a single area, around Bexhill in East Sussex.[67] This name, which means 'in the corner', or 'in the small valley', was probably that of a single family, too. Another surname, the early instances of which are rather more dispersed, is Leem (de la Leme, Aleem, a Leme, de Lem, etc.; probably with the meaning 'loam'). This too seems likely to be a surname which orginated in Sussex exclusively. Some medieval examples of the surname occur at and near Willingdon, near Eastbourne, but others are found in the north of the county, at Warnham and in East Grinstead parish.[68] The name was still in Willingdon in the 16th century.[69] This seems to be entirely a Sussex name in origin. The surname Thele (atte Thele, etc.) is one which is confined so far as early instances are concerned to one part of Sussex. Its history is discussed below. Other surnames which seem likely to have originated in Sussex, and not in any other county, are Costedel, Eightacre, Forbench, Furlonger, Soundry, Waterer and Wister. All these are considered later in this chapter.[70]

These are instances of rare topographical surnames which seem to have originated exclusively in Sussex. In some cases the surnames in question arose from topographical terms which were probably not in use outside the county during the period when hereditary surnames were being formed. There are, however, some more common topographical surnames which were much more frequent in Sussex than elsewhere, and in these instances it is often difficult to explain the early distribution of the names concerned either on the basis of dialect, or on grounds of the county's topography. The distribution of some of the surnames in question has been set out in the two tables above. It can be seen that there are some surnames which in this latter group are very much more common, proportionately, in Sussex and in one or two adjoining counties, such as Surrey or Kent, than in other parts of England. These include, for instance, the names Aldret, Birchett, Sande, Sole, and Tye (with the variant forms of these names.) In addition, there are several further surnames, (Combe, Field, Down, Oak and Towne, for example), which were widely distributed, but which were distinctly more numerous in Sussex and the adjoining counties than in other regions. Most of the names in this further group are ones which, like Field or Towne, are derived from words which were not limited in use to south-east England.

In some cases circumstances can be found which may explain why several of the surnames in this group were exceptionally common in Sussex and adjoining counties. The surname Field, for instance, is derived from 'field', the original significance of which was 'stretch of open country', but which by the time surnames were being formed was being used for open fields of arable in contrast to woodland or hill country.[71] This is a term which might be commonly employed in a county like Sussex, where there were large areas of forest with tracts of arable land interspersed with woodland. Combe is found as a place-name element much more frequently in the south, and especially the south-west, of England, than in other regions.[72] In the case of some of the other surnames involved, however, it is not easy to see why they should be more common in Sussex, and in some instances in contiguous counties as well, than elsewhere. The distribution of some of the surnames involved is not readily explicable either in terms of local dialect, or of the county's geography. It must be assumed that there were local or regional practices in the formation of surnames which influenced the situation. In view of the rich crop of topographical names to be found in Sussex, it is not surprising that some names in that category were exceptionally common in the county.

The statements just made about the incidence of certain surnames in different parts of England are based primarily on the evidence given in the preceding tables, but in fact similar evidence has been collected for other counties, not mentioned in the tables,[73] and for some counties a great variety of source material has been examined. Evidence of a similar kind to that presented in the tables has been collected for many further topographical surnames and from this it can be seen that there were other names in that category which were much more common in Sussex in proportion to the whole body of surnames in use, than in most English regions. In many cases these were names which were generally common throughout South-East England. Among the names which were especially frequent in Sussex during the 14th century, on the basis of this evidence, were Gravett ('at the Grove'), and See (or Sea), both of which occur frequently in Sussex during the Middle Ages, and which were present, though less common, in Kent and Surrey, but which were scarce, or lacking, in most parts of England. It would be expected that the distribution of a surname such as See would be coastal. Some Sussex examples of the name are found at places inland, and it has been suggested that, because of this, the name must in these inland examples have had the meaning of 'at the pool', rather than 'at the sea'.[74] This view ignores the fact that the bearers of surnames or bye-names were mobile, and that even at early periods, surnames or bye-names do not always occur at the places where they originated. In fact, in one or two cases the Sussex individuals who have been cited as examples of the name See originating inland appear to be men who had earlier inhabited places on the coast. One person who has been cited in this connection, Philip atte

See, is listed at Ripe, an inland township, in 1332, but he is probably the same as the Philip atte See, recorded at Goring-on-Sea in 1327/8; William atte See, mentioned at Horstead Keynes, inland, in 1332, is probably the same as the William atte See, who occurs in the same year at Denton (adjoining Newhaven), a place where several other persons named atte See are found.[75] The great majority of medieval Sussex instances of the name in fact occur on the coast, or very near to it.[76] Many of the medieval examples are at and near Eastbourne, where the name still existed in the 16th century.[77] The surname occurs during the Middle Ages in Kent, and, infrequently, in some other south coast counties. It seems to be lacking in some other maritime areas. No medieval examples are known from Norfolk or Suffolk, for instance, and it has not been discovered in Lancashire during the same period, though a large collection of surnames has been made for that county.

Of other topographical surnames, the names Gate, Hease or Hese ('in the brushwood'), and Mott were all more common in Sussex, and in Kent and Surrey adjoining, than elsewhere, though they all appear in other counties as well. A few rarer surnames seem to have been rather more common in Sussex than elsewhere, but not much significance can be attached to this. Such a result could be produced by the ramification of one family over several generations.

A comparison between the two tables above shows that there was a large measure of continuity in the distribution of the surnames listed. One factor which complicates the comparison between medieval sources and those for the 16th and 17th centuries, is that the surnames of some families acquire an inorganic final '-s or '-es'. This development is disucssed elsewhere.[78] The transition to forms with an '-s' or '-es' termination took place in the surnames of some families as early as the 14th century, but occurred more frequently during the 16th century, and the first half of the 17th, than either earlier or later. In the tables above, surnames with an '-s' or '-es' termination have not been included in the total for surnames without such endings. Names such as Downes or Sandes, for example, have not been included in the figures for Down or Sande. This situation does affect comparisons between the two tables to some extent. For instance, the surname Down does not occur in the source used for Oxfordshire names in the 17th century, though it is found in that county earlier, but the name Downes does appear in the 17th century source. Where this factor seems likely to have a bearing on comparisons between the two tables, the relevant points have been indicated in footnotes. The tables show how much continuity there was between the distribution of surnames as it was in the 14th century, and as it was two or three centuries later, when the changes just described are taken into account. The inclusion of many more surnames would not have materially altered the impression made by the tables as published.

It is also true that some topographical surnames which were numerous and widespread in some English regions from the 13th century, when the available sources first begin to provide adequate information about surnames, were either completely absent, or very rare, in Sussex. This situation still persists in the 16th and 17th centuries. It is obviously difficult to demonstrate the negative fact that certain names are absent from the county, or only appear in a few instances, but is is possible to take some measure of how some topographical names, common in parts of England, are absent from Sussex, or very scare there, even at a relatively late period by examining the material for West Sussex surviving among the 1641–2 Protestation Returns.[79] (The corresponding returns for East Sussex are missing). Many topographical surnames which occur very frequently in some regions are absent entirely from the West Sussex returns. The names Booth, Clough, Cragg, Crabtree, Edge, Fell, Milne, Ridding, Rilands, and Scoles, for example, are all lacking, though all are names common in the north-west of England. Similarly, the names Childerhouse, Damm, Gap and Nabb, all of which are common in East Anglia, are lacking in the West Sussex returns. All these names which are absent from the West Sussex Protestation Returns are either not found at all in the medieval sources for the whole of Sussex, or appear in those sources as the names of one or two individuals only. Some other topographical names which are common in parts of England occur in the West Sussex returns as the names of but one or two persons; the names Carr, Orchard, Platt, and Townsend are instances of this. These names, too, are either absent, or very scarce, in medieval Sussex evidence.

The evidence considered above all relates to individual surnames. From these facts it is clear that while some elements of the distribution of topographical surnames can be explained on grounds of local dialect, or of the topography and landscape of counties and regions, there are other elements which are not readily explicable on such grounds. The appearance of some surnames in certain counties, but not in others, is no doubt due to the use of terms for some features of the landscape being restricted to certain regions, counties, or even smaller areas. There are, however, some broad types of surname, within the category of topographical names, which are numerous in some counties, but are scarce or absent, in medieval sources, in others. Two such types were from an early time more numerous in Sussex, proportionately, than in most other counties. These are surnames composed of a topographical term with the suffix -er added (Bridger, Fielder, Weller, etc.), and those composed of a topographical term with -man added (Bridgeman, Hillman, Wellman, etc.).

TOPOGRAPHICAL SURNAMES WITH THE SUFFIX -ER

Topographical names with the -er suffix have been numerous in Sussex from the 13th century onwards. It is difficult to be sure what the position was before about 1200 because of lack of evidence, and because of the extent to which Latinised forms of surnames were used during the 12th century. It is readily observable that there were many counties in which such surnames were very few, and there seem to have been regions of England where such names did not originate at all, but the distribution of surnames of this type has not been systematically studied. Such names were excluded from Löfvenberg's major work on English topographical surnames.[80] They were dealt with briefly by Fransson in an excursus to his work on occupational names.[81] Some surnames in this category have at times been thought to be occupational.[82] There are some surnames or bye-names formed from a place-name with the -er suffix added, but surnames of this type have always been few in number. Most, and probably all, such names originated in the south-east of England; a small number can be found in Sussex, and some appear to have originated in the county. The evolution of surnames formed from a place-name with -er is obviously parallel to that of names formed from a topographical term with -er, and by considering both types together a clearer view of both developments can be obtained.

Very few surnames of the type under consideration have been formed from compound topographical surnames. A list given by Fransson[83] of topographical names in -er found in a large number of counties, including Sussex, has five which are formed from compound surnames or bye-names. One of these, Ashburner, which does appear in Sussex, was considered by Fransson as being probably an occupational name. Three others, Berlondere and Rysebrigger, for both of which Fransson cites Surrey instances only, and Redlondere, for which a Sussex instance is cited, are all probably derived from place-names. The small group of surnames or bye-names formed from place-names with -er is considered below. The remaining compound name in Fransson's list, Mulgatere, is known from a single example, at Horsham, from 14th century Sussex. Mulgate did exist as a bye-name, at Ashfold in Sussex, at that period.[84] Mulgatere seems to be the single clear instance of a surname or bye-name in -er being formed from a compound topographical name in Sussex, and no certain examples have been found from other parts of England. Some topographical surnames which are compounds were relatively common in medieval Sussex, Freeland, Moorcroft, Penfold, Stanstreet, Townsend, or Watergate, for example, but none of these gave rise to forms in -er.

It was pointed out by Fransson that topographical surnames or bye-names with the -er suffix have not been discovered in any part of England before 1200, and in fact no instances have been found in Sussex before that date, though the amount of source material in print is now much fuller than when Fransson wrote. There are, however, dangers in arguing from the absence of evidence in such a case. During the 12th and 13th centuries, topographical names are frequently given in written sources in

Latinised forms, often by the translation of the Middle English terms, which were presumably used in speech, into Latin terms which had the same literal meaning. During the second half of the 13th century, topographical terms in -er occur in large numbers in Sussex, and at the same period, Latinised forms of topographical names continue to be common, but very few Latinised forms have been found which are clearly translations of vernacular names in -er. It consequently seems possible that forms in -er are concealed under Latinised forms, not recognisable as being translations of such forms, during the 12th century. It is also true that the names which appear in 12th century sources are predominantly those of landowners, who tended to have a smaller proportion of topographical names among their surnames than did other classes. These considerations make it difficult to be certain that no topographical names in -er existed during the period before 1200. In view, however, of the absence of any examples of such names during the 12th century, and the paucity of examples during the first half of the 13th, it seems probable that such names did not arise before the 13th century, either in Sussex or elsewhere.

Two examples of names of this type have been found in Sussex in 1200-1250. These are, firstly, Barrer, which occurs as the name of one individual in East Sussex c. 1230, in an area where the name atte Barre existed in the same century.[85] The same individual is also mentioned under the name Barre.[86] His name is also given in the Latinised form *Barrarius*, one of the few cases where a Latinised form of a topographical name in -er can be detected.[87] *Barrarius* looks like a translation of an occupation name, which shows how difficult it may be to discover topographical names in -er in the 12th century, when Latinised forms are common. The second example is the name le Heser, which appears in East Sussex, again as the name of one person, c. 1240.[88] The first element of the name is a word which means 'brushwood', or 'land covered with bushes'.[89]

During the second half of the 13th century topographical names in -er become much more numerous in Sussex. The two examples from before 1250 both come from East Sussex, and although the instances which have been found for the years 1250–1300 occur in both the east and west of the county, they are rather more numerous in the east. In the Sussex subsidy returns for 1296, there are rather less than 50 persons with surnames or bye-names in this category. There are a few cases where it is uncertain whether names ought to be included in this type or not, and there are several individuals about whom it is uncertain where in the county they were assessed. Leaving aside these doubtful examples, there are 26 persons with topographical names in -er in East Sussex, against 15 in West Sussex. In 1296 the number of tax-payers was about the same in East Sussex as in West Sussex.[90] The 1296 subsidy returns are the most copious single source for surnames in Sussex during the late 13th century, but examples in other sources of names of the type under discussion are rather more common from East Sussex than from West. This evidence indicates that topographical names in -er arose in East Sussex rather earlier than in the west, and were at first more numerous there. The difference between the two parts of the county was, however, not very marked, and in any case there are no grounds for supposing that names of this type originated exclusively in East Sussex. Fransson lists such names for the period before 1300 from other counties, including several, such as Somerset, Norfolk, and Huntingdonshire, which are not near to Sussex,[91] though his investigations were confined to ten English counties, and drew on a limited range of sources.

During the 14th century, topographical surnames in -er become more common. They do not seem to be especially numerous, in proportion to the population, in any one part of the county. Such names remained relatively rare during the 14th century and are markedly less common than the corresponding names without the -er suffix. In the 1332 subsidy returns for Sussex, for example, there are twelve instances of Bridge (Bregg, Brugg, etc), but 3 of Bridger (Brugger, etc.); 32 cases of Brook (Brok, Brouk), and 4 of Brooker (Broker, etc.); 8 cases of atte See, and one of Seer; and 4 cases of atte Street, but 2 of Streeter (Streter).[92] The increasing frequency of names in this category, and the appearance during the 14th century of some names in -er which have not been discovered in Sussex before 1300, show that more and more families were acquiring names of the type. The names Bircher, Bourner, Churcher, Fielder, Forder, Grover, Holter, Hyder, Lincher, Stapler, Streeter, Waterer, and Winder, for example, have all been found in Sussex for the first time during the 14th century.[93]

Between about 1400 and the early 16th century topographical names in -er multiplied considerably and came to form a larger proportion of the topographical surnames in use in Sussex. In some cases surnames in -er became more numerous than the corresponding names without the suffix. In the Sussex subsidy returns for 1524–25, for example, there are 40 persons named Bridger (Bregger, Brygger), but 4 named Brygges, and none named Bridge, etc; 10 named Hooker (Hoker), but one named Hook (Houke); 8 named Stapler, but one named Staple; and 34 named Weller, but 3 named Wells or Atwell.[94] Not all topographical names in -er increased in the same proportion. In 1524–25 there are, for instance, 6 individuals named Forder, but 20 named Forde; 7 named Gater, against 18 named Gate, and one named Agates; and 7 named Fielder (Felder), but 18 named Field (Felde).[95] It is, however clear that between about 1400 and the early 16th century many topographical names in -er increased at a greater rate than did topographical names without the suffix. There are a few cases where the increase of names in -er appears to be due to the proliferation of a single family. By 1524–5, for instance, the surname Holter had become more numerous than Holt, but out of the seven persons named Holter listed in the subsidy of 1524–25, 6 are listed together at Lewes, and it must be suspected that all belonged to one family.[96] However, it obviously cannot be the case that families with names with the -er suffix were as a group markedly more prolific than families with surnames not in that category, and it seems clear that during the 15th century a considerable number of families must have acquired surnames in -er, either by coming to possess hereditary surnames for the first time during the century, or through families with topographical surnames without the suffix having their names modified by the addition of -er, so that, for instance, a name such as atte Bridge became Bridger, and so forth. Since the forms of topographical names were often interchangeable, so that individuals with names such as Ford, Field, etc., were sometimes known, alternatively, as Forder, Fielder, etc.,[97] it seems possible that such modifications took place, even at a relatively late period. Whatever the precise nature of the development, which is difficult to trace because of deficiencies in the 15th century material, it is clear that during the later Middle Ages topographical surnames in -er increased to a greater extent than did other topographical names. During the 16th and 17th centuries some topographical surnames in -er were very numerous in Sussex. In the 1641–42 Protestation Returns, for example, there are listed in West Sussex 53 men named Bridger, 19 named Brooker, 17 named Crowcher, 20 named Downer, 20 named Feilder or Filder, 24 named Furlonger or Vurlonger, 34 named Streater or Streeter, and 15 named Weller.[98]

In Sussex, topographical surnames or bye-names in -er may have arisen earlier in the east of the county than in the west, but they soon became widely distributed throughout the county. It is not easy to discover the medieval distribution of such names throughout England, without undertaking a very wide ranging search through medieval sources. Some remarks about the distribution of such names were made by Fransson, who stated that such names were confined to the south of England and to the East Midlands.[99] These observations apparently applied to the period up to 1350. Fransson stated that such names did not occur in the West Midlands, but he cites some instances from Worcestershire, and a few such names can be found in Oxfordshire during the Middle Ages.[100] Fransson examined sources for ten counties, but these did not include Kent, a county important for the history of names of the type under discussion. The position in Sussex obviously ought to be compared to adjoining counties. For Surrey, a general view of the distribution of names of the type being considered can be gained from the 1332 subsidy returns for the county.[101] This record was compiled at a time when topographical names in -er were already becoming numerous, but when few of them can have been hereditary for a long time, so that it should show a distribution of such names before it had been much affected by population movement. In 1332, names of this type were very unevenly spread in Surrey. The three hundreds of Reigate, Blackheath, and Wotton, in the Wealden district of south Surrey, and bordering on Sussex, each had a fair number of such names, and Godalming Hundred, in the south-west corner of Surrey, and also bordering Sussex, had rather fewer. There is no certain example of a name of this type in the return for Tandridge Hundred, which occupies the south east part of Surrey, though this adjoins Sussex, too. The hundreds in the northern and central parts of Surrey have merely a scattering of such names.

In Kent, by contrast, topographical surnames or bye-names in -er seem to have been less common, in proportion to the whole body of names recorded, in the Weald. The Kent lay subsidy returns for 1334/5[102] show that very few such names were then to be found in the parts of Kent bordering on Sussex. Names of the type were then proportionately more common in East Kent than in the west of that county. It is also apparent from the 1334/5 subsidy returns that names of the kind under discussion were at that date distinctly less common proportionately in Kent, than in Sussex. As regards other counties, Fransson cites a moderate number of 13th and 14th century cases from Hampshire, a smaller number from Somerset and Essex, and scattered instances from several Midland and eastern counties. There can be no certainty that surnames or bye-names originated in the areas where they occur in such sources as, for instance, subsidy rolls, and it must be suspected that where but a few examples of such names are to be found in any county, this is the result, not of the names having originated in the county concerned, but of such names having been brought in by migration. It seems likely that topographical surnames in -er did not arise at all in the north of England. No certain examples of such names have been found in Lancashire before 1500, despite a search through a great variety of sources for that county.[103]

It is to be noted, however, that surnames formed from a place-name with the -er suffix (a type of surname clearly parallel to names formed from a topographical term and -er) do occur in the North Midlands, and examples can be found in Yorkshire, though not before the 16th century.[104]

Significance of Surnames Formed from a Topographical Term and -er

It sometimes has been supposed that surnames such as Bridger, Comber, Hyder, Hiller, and so forth are derived from occupations. It is possible to conceive of occupations which might give rise to at least some names of this type; Bridger, for example, might possibly denote a person employed to maintain a bridge, or to collect tolls on it; occupational origins have been suggested, credibly, for Comber and Loder; and with a name such as Hyder, which must be derived from the holding of land measuring a hide, it is impossible to be sure whether it is a topographical name, or one derived from status. Indeed, in such a case, it is unrealistic to draw a clear cut boundary between surnames of different categories, for it is seldom possible to say just how surnames were acquired. It is, however, very difficult to think of occupations which could have given rise to many of the names in this group. Names such as Bourner, Crowcher, Forder, Greener, and so forth are difficult to derive from any occupations. It is, further, the case that, though such surnames and bye-names are very numerous in Sussex, and are to be found in a great variety of sources, not a single instance has been discovered, in the evidence collected for this work, of anyone bearing a name of this type being described as having an occupation from which his or her name could be derived.

There is, on the other hand, much evidence to show that such names were topographic. During the 13th and 14th centuries, there are instances of individuals whose surnames or bye-names are given sometimes in a form with an -er suffix, sometimes in a form without the suffix. For example, Robert atte Linch, listed as a taxpayer at Madehurst in 1327/8, is listed as Robert Lyncher at the same place in 1332;[105] Walter atte Barre, a taxpayer at Merston in 1296, appears at the same place in 1327/8 as Walter le Barrer;[106] and several further instances can be found in the late 13th and early 14th century subsidies for Sussex.[107] Rather earlier, John de la Walle, who occurs as a tenant of Lewes honour in 1266, is also mentioned as John le Wllere.[108] The interchangeability of forms with and without the -er suffix persisted as late as the 16th and 17th centuries. Thomas Hope, a taxpayer in Robertsbridge Hundred in 1524, is given as Thomas Hopper in 1525.[109] George Athoth ('at the heath') who held land at Wivelsfield in the 17th century, was also known as Hother.[110] Forms in -er were used in Sussex as equivalent to forms of topographical surnames without the -er suffix over a long period.

In addition, the early distribution of some names in -er provides evidence that such names were topographic, and not occupational. This is best seen by examining the distribution of some rare names. For example, the scarce name Lotyer appears in 1296 in Flexborough Hundred. In 1296, 1327/8, and 1332 the name atte Lote occurs at Chyngton, in that hundred (which is quite a small area, of three parishes).[111] The name atte Lote is derived from a word signifying a share. In some places it was the practice to divide meadowland annually by lot between the tenants of a manor, and the name probably derives from residence near land alotted in this way.[112] The name Pendere was present in Beckley parish from the late 14th century onwards, and in the 15th century it appears at other places in the same part of Sussex; the name Pende also occurs in Beckley, and at other places in the same area. Pende is derived from a word meaning 'inclosure', often used for a close where stray animals were impounded.[113] During the 15th century the name Shamler occurs at Chichester, and in the Manwood area to the south of the city, but it has not been found elsewhere in Sussex before 1500. The name atte Shamele, or de la Shamele, was present at Chichester, and in the area south of the city, from the 13th century. (Atte Shamele also occurs at Wartling, in East Sussex, in the 13th and 14th centuries). A locality called le Shamell, in Birdham south of Chichester, may have given rise to the surname. The literal meaning of 'shamele' is 'bench' or 'stool'. It was perhaps used topographically in the sense of a ledge, possibly for the old cliff line which survives in the Selsey area inland.[114] The name Shamler, in the form Shambler, still existed near Chichester in the 17th century.[115] The rare name atte Wysshe appears at Eastdean (East Sussex) during the 13th and 14th centuries, and is probably derived from a locality in Eastdean; the name le Wyssere occurs at Denton, a few miles away. Atte Wysse signifies 'at the damp meadow'.[116] Many similar cases could be given and it is clear that in many instances the distribution of surnames in -er is closely connected with that of the corresponding names without the suffix. It does not seem that the similarities between the distribution of names in -er, and the distribution of names without it, can be explained merely on grounds of the topography of the various parts of the county. Though the topographical names just discussed are all rare, they are derived from words which could have been used for features of the landscape in many parts of Sussex.

Locative Surnames in -er

Surnames or bye-names formed from place-names with the -er suffix are closely linked with names formed from topographical terms with -er. There is no part of England where surnames formed from a place-name and -er have ever been at all general. In Sussex, and in the other southeastern counties, they are much less frequent than surnames formed from a topographical term and -er. In Sussex, the only surnames or bye-names from a place-name with -er which have been discovered before 1500 are Cressweller, not found before 1400, from one of the places called Cresswell or Creswell;[117] Kolhoker, from Colhook Common in North Chapel;[118] Glyndere, from Glynde in East Sussex;[119] Redlondere, from one of the places called Redland or Redlands, of which there are several in Sussex;[120] and two doubtful instances, le Campyner, possibly from one of the places in France called Campagne, or from Champagne,[121] and Harberner, perhaps from the place-name Harborne or Harbourne.[122] Besides these, the name Berlondere, from Burlands Copse in Ifield, occurs at Byfleet, in Surrey.[123] Out of all these, only Cressweller is known to have become hereditary. After 1500, some further names of the type occur in Sussex. Some of them are derived from place-names in the county, and probably existed there before 1500, even if not recorded in the available sources. During the 16th century the names Burbridger, Cressweller, Rombrydger or Rumbryger, Risbrigger or Rusbridger, and Ryponder,[124] all appear in Sussex. Of these, Burbridger may be from the lost place in West Sussex which gave its name to Burbeach Hundred.[125] Rombrydger, etc., may be from a lost place, Rumbridge, which formerly existed in West Sussex, near West Wittering. The surname is said to go back to the 15th century.[126] The place concerned has probably been destroyed by coastal erosion. The name Redbridger, which occurs in the 16th century, is a scribal error for Rombrydger.[127] Risbrigger may be from Rice Bridge, in Bolney, as has been suggested, but the late appearance of the surname in Sussex makes it quite possible that the surname originated outside Sussex, and was derived from a place-name elsewhere, such as Ridgebridge (Surr.), Risebridge (Surr.), or Risebridge (Ess.) This is all the more likely because the surname occurs in Surrey from the 13th century, long before it has been found in Sussex.[128] Ryponder is probably from one of the places called Ripon, with an inorganic 'd'. A few other surnames which occur in Sussex during the 16th century are doubtful cases. Lidgater, or Ludgater, which occurs in Sussex at the end of the 15th century, and is an established and fairly widespread name in the county during the 16th and 17th centuries, is probably a topographical surname, which has arisen from the name atte Lidgate ('at the swing gate'). Atte Lidgate was present in the coastal area of West Sussex during the 13th and 14th centuries, and Lidgater or Ludgater (the two forms were interchangeable) occurs in that area during the 16th century.[129] The names Durdener and Hanshoter each appear in 16th century Sussex as the name of a single individual. If these two names belong in the category under discussion, which is doubtful, they are likely to have originated outside Sussex, and to have been introduced by migration. However, during the 17th century the -er suffix was at times added occasionally to surnames which were normally without it. William Hilldrooper, for instance, a 17th century inhabitant of Chichester, was the occupier of a holding called Hidroop's, and John Trusweller, an Aldingbourne yeoman at the same period, was also known as John Truslow.[130] If Lidgater is left aside, the only surnames in the category which survived in Sussex into the 17th century as established local names were Cressweller (which became Crassweller) and Risbridger, or Rusbridger.

Surnames formed from a place-name with the -er suffix were always rare, both in Sussex, and elsewhere. At no period did they form more than an insignificant proportion of the locative names in use in Sussex, and the same situation appears to have existed in other parts of England, so far as can be seen from the sources for other counties which it has been possible to examine. It must be supposed that such names arose from a habit of using names formed from a place-name with -er to refer to the inhabitants of a particular place, rather as the term Londoner is used at the present day, or more probably, to refer to persons who had migrated away from some particular place. No case has been found in Sussex of a surname in this category occurring at the locality, from the name of which the surname in question was derived. The same seems to be true of surnames of the type in other counties.[131] It is also the case that many surnames of this type found in Sussex are derived from the names of places outside the county. The Sussex places from which such surnames arose seem mostly to have been very small. Where locative surnames without the -er suffix are concerned, it is quite common to find a surname present at the place from which it is derived, and it is clear that persons with locative surnames (without -er) often resided at the places from which their surnames arose. It seems likely that locative names in -er were acquired by people who moved away from their native towns or villages.

Origins of some surnames in -er

There has sometimes been confusion between occupational surnames, and surnames formed from a topographical term and -er. Where some surnames are concerned it is impossible to be certain about precise origins. The origins of some Sussex surnames can, however, be considered.

Dicker

The name Dicker has two different origins in Sussex. During the 13th and 14th centuries the surname or bye-name atte Dyker or atte Diker occurs. In the 13th century there was a large stretch of waste land called the Dicker, in the parishes of Chiddingly, Arlington, and Hellingly. At the same period, some land at Hartfield was called Dyker. There was also some land at Eastbourne called the Dicker, though this name is not evidenced before the 19th century. The medieval references to the name atte Dyker, etc., all occur in the area around Chiddingly, Arlington, and Hellingly.[132] The meaning of the word 'dicker' in this connection is uncertain. The name Dykerman, which occurs in East Sussex, not far from Chiddingly, Arlington, and Hellingly, from the late 13th century onwards, was probably formed from the name atte Dyker with the suffix -man added.[133] From the late 13th century the name le Dykere appears in Sussex. Most of the references to it relate to two places, Billingshurst, and Denton (near Newhaven).[134] The definite article is used too consistently with names at both places for its use to be merely a scribal error. Le Dykere could be an occupational name, from the work of cutting dikes, but in view of the frequency with which surnames formed from a topographical term and -er are found in Sussex, it seems more probable that le Dykere has been formed from 'Dyke' with the suffix added. The name ater Dyke or de la Dike does occur in Sussex during the 13th century.[135]

Already in the 14th century names such as Dicker or Diker appear, without any preposition or article prefixing them.[136] It is generally impossible to be certain about the origin of such names, and it is still more difficult to be certain of the origin of Dicker when it appears as a surname at later periods.

The surname Dicker is a clear instance of a name which developed within a single county from two different origins, and this despite the fact that the name was always uncommon. During the 13th and 14th centuries, articles and prepositions were very often attached to surnames or bye-names erroneously. There are many examples of this among Sussex topographical names. For instance, John and Thomas le Flode, who are listed as taxpayers at Washington in 1332, are obviously the same persons as Thomas atte Floude and John de Floude, listed at Findon, a parish contiguous to Washington, in 1327/8;[137] a taxpayer at Ecclesden is listed as William in the Hale, in 1296, William atte Hale, in 1327/8, and William le Halgh, in 1332;[138] Peter atte Sundre ('at the sundered or cut off land'), who was a taxpayer in 1296, occurs earlier as Peter le Sundre. He held land at Yapton, in an area where the name atte Sundre was in use for much of the 13th and 14th centuries, probably as the hereditary surname of one family.[139] In the case of Dicker, however, the surname plainly had two different origins in Sussex. Dicker survived as a surname, and was still in use in Sussex during the 16th century,[140] but it is impossible to be certain about the origin of the surname when it appears at such a relatively late period.

Elmer

The surname or bye-name Elmer is found in Sussex from the 13th century.[141] It might appear that this is a name formed from Elm with the -er suffix, but this origin is unlikely. Names such as atte Elm, atte Nelm, etc., were very few in Sussex. The two examples which have been found in the county before 1500 are both in East Sussex.[142] The plural form Elmys or Elmes occurs in West Sussex from the 16th century onwards, but all the individuals concerned seem to have belonged to one family, and the name's presence in Sussex may be due to migration from Surrey, where Elmes occurs from the 14th century.[143] There is a locality called Elmer Farm, at Middleton-on-Sea, West Sussex. In the late 13th century the name De Elmer or De Elmere occurs in West Sussex at places not far from Middleton, but distant from any known examples of atte Elm, etc.[144] This is clearly a locative name, and the origin of Elmer, which appears in West Sussex from the late 13th century. The surname was still present in the coastal parts of West Sussex in the 17th century,[145] and it survives in the county to the present day.

Flasher and Flusher

The earliest instance of the name Flasher which has been found in Sussex dates from 1332, when John atte Flassher was a taxpayer at Sullington.[146] The presence of a preposition in this case is no doubt an error, due, as in some similar cases, to confusion caused by the use of two forms, with and without the -er suffix, for the name of a single individual. John atte Flasshe, who is mentioned in 1366 in connection with land at Buncton, near Sullington, was probably from the same family as John atte Flassher.[147] Both Flasher and atte Flasshe are derived from the Middle English 'flasshe', a swamp or pool. Forms such as Flacher continue to appear after 1500,[148] but in the 16th century and later the most common form was Flusher. In the 1524 subsidy returns Flusher occurs at Thakeham, a parish contiguous to Sullington, and at other places in the same part of Sussex, though by the date the surname had spread to other areas of the county too.[149] In the 17th century Flusher was still present at West Chiltington, which adjoins Sullington and Thakeham, at Pulborough, which borders on West Chiltington, and at Horsham not far away.[150] In this case a rare topographical surname survived from the 14th century into modern times in one part of the county. It seems probable that all the persons named Flasher or Flusher who occur in Sussex share a common ancestry, though it is not possible to prove this genealogically. No early examples of Flasher or Flusher are known to the present writer from other counties, and it is possible that Flusher is a surname which developed in Sussex only.

The related surname Flashman, familiar from *Tom Brown's Schooldays*, has a similar origin. Some association of the surname with the later colloquial use of the term 'flashy' may give it an appropriate ring of villainy, but its origin is topographical.

Grevatter

The name Grevatter (Grevetour, Grevatour, etc.) has arisen from the topographical name atte Grevette or atte Gravette (from a diminutive of the Middle English word for grove), which had a markedly regional distribution, being most common in Sussex and Surrey, with some further early examples in Hampshire.[151] The earliest examples of Grevatter which have been found in Sussex occur in the manor of Amberley, where the name was present in the late 14th century. Richard and Walter Grevatour, who were tenants of the manor in 1370–73, were the same persons as Richard and Walter atte Grevette, who were tenants at the same date, and earlier.[152] The name atte Grevette had been present at Amberley from the early 14th century, and had existed at Parham, which adjoins Amberley, in the 13th.[153] At the beginning of the 15th century Grevatour appears as a name at Midhurst, where atte Grevette had been present from the 13th century.[154] Grevatour has sometimes been given, erroneously, as Grenatour in printed editions.

Furlonger

The surname Furlonger probably arises from the use of the term 'furlong' for a division of the open fields. The bye-name atte Forlange, probably from this sense of the word, occurs at Withyham, in north-east Sussex, in 1327/8.[155] The first appearance of Furlonger in Sussex is in 1450, when it was the name of two husbandmen at Shipley.[156] Although the name may have existed for some time before appearing in any of the sources which have been examined, it seems likely that Furlonger is one of the names in -er which did not arise before 1400. In the 1524-5 subsidy returns, Furlonger occurs at a number of places, most of them, however, in the north of West Sussex, around Shipley.[157] It must be suspected that this is due to the dispersal of one family bearing the name, originating at Shipley. In the 17th century Furlonger was still present at Shipley, and at other places in the same part of the county, though by that period it had become fairly widespread in West Sussex.[158] In some of these 17th century sources the name is given as Vurlonger.

Again, it must be thought probable that all the persons named Furlonger or Vurlonger who are found in Sussex were descended from the Furlongers who were living at Shipley in the mid 15th century. In this case, too, no early instances are known from other counties, and the name may have originated solely in Sussex.

Hammer

The name Hammer or Hamer occurs in Sussex from the late 13th century onwards.[159] No evidence has been found to show that the name is an occupational one, with the meaning 'hammerman', despite the importance of the iron industry locally. The name Atte Hamme was common in Sussex from the 12th century,[160] and the word Hamme appears as a field name at many places in the county.[161] This leaves little doubt that Hammer, or Hamer has been formed from 'hamme' (with the meaning of 'damp ground near a stream', or 'water-meadow') with the -er suffix. The surname Hamer is in some instances derived from a Lancashire place-name,[162] but none of the medieval Sussex references is in the form de Hamer, which would be expected at least in some cases if the surname in the county was from a place-name. There may, on the other hand, have been some confusion at an early date between Hammer and the occupational surname Haneper, which develops into Hamper. The name Hammer occurs at Lancing in 1296. In 1332 the name Haneper is found at the same place, and at Sompting, an adjoining parish.[163] Hammer still existed as a surname at Lancing in the the 16th century.[164] The bye-name Handhamer, found once only, at Horsham in 1296, may be occupational, but it may, alternatively, be an error for, or a variant of Haneper, which in the form Hamper occurs at Horsham later.[165]

Hopper and Hoper

Hopper is usually said to be an occupational name, with the meaning of 'cooper'.[166] In Sussex, however, the surname atte Hope was common from the 13th century.[167] Atte Hope is derived from a topographical term meaning 'enclosed land', especially enclosed land in marshes. The surname atte Hope occurs in connection with Hope, a locality in Beckley parish, in the valley of the eastern Rother. From the mid 13th century the name Hopper occurs in Sussex, mostly in the east of the county.[168] In the 14th century, the name Hoper appears. There seems no doubt that Hopper and Hoper are alternative forms of the same name. Richard Hoper, listed as a taxpayer in Barcombe Hundred in 1332, was the same person as Richard le Hoppere, listed in the same hundred in 1327/8.[169] As late as the 16th century the forms Hope and Hopper were still sometimes interchangeable. Thomas Hope, a taxpayer in Robertsbridge Hundred in 1524, is also listed as Thomas Hopper.[170] During the 16th century the surname Hope was at times spelt Hoppe; Robert Hope and John at Hope, who were taxpayers in 1524, at East Guldeford, not far from Beckley, were named in 1525 as Robert Hoppe and John Hoppe.[171] It seems clear from this evidence that in Sussex Hopper and Hoper are both derived from the topographical term Hope, though the same is not necessarily true of the surname Hopper when it appears in other parts of England.

During the Middle Ages most examples of Hopper and Hoper found in Sussex were in the east in the county, but a few appear in the coastal part of West Sussex.[172] In the 1524-25 subsidy returns, however, Hopper is confined to East Sussex, mostly to the area around Beckley. The form Hoper does not occur in the 1524-25 returns.[173] Instances of Hopper and Hoper which have been found in Sussex during the late 15th century are also all in the Beckley area.[174] In the Protestation Returns for West Sussex there are no examples of Hoper or Hopper. It seems likely that the surname died out in West Sussex, and that the families which preserved the surname in East Sussex derived their names from the locality called Hope in Beckley.

Lemmer

It has been held that the surnames Lemmer and Lemm are both derived from an Old English personal name, and Sussex examples have been cited in this connection.[175] The proposed derivation from a personal name may be correct in some instances, but there is evidence that in Sussex both surnames were usually, and probably always, topographical. The circumstances in other parts of England may be have been different. In Sussex the name de la Leme, de Lem, or A Leem occurs from the late 13th century onwards. This name is clearly topographical. Its meaning is uncertain, but it is probably derived from a term for a locality with loamy or clayey soil. A locality called Leamland existed at Horsted Keynes in the 15th century and later, and in the 13th century a place called la Leme existed at Aldrington. The topographical term in question, whatever its precise meaning, was consequently in use in Sussex. There are in medieval Sussex occasional instances of the name Lem occurring without any preposition, but little significance can be attached to this. The use of prepositions such as 'atte' or de la' is not consistent in medieval sources. Thomas Lem (1296) who has been cited as an example of a person whose surname was derived from a personal name, was a taxpayer at Brambletye, which is near Horstead Keynes, and his surname was probably derived from the locality called Leamland already mentioned. The surname de Lem, a Leme, etc., occurs as Willingdon from about 1270 onwards, and was still present there in the 16th century., This is probably a case of a hereditary surname surviving in one place from the 13th century.[176] It is, however, doubtful if it safe to deduce from this, as has been done, that a place-name Leme must have existed at Willingdon, as the surname may have been brought into Willingdon by migration.

The name Lemmer has first been found in Sussex in 1332, when it occurs at Nutley and Maresfield. These places are very close to Horsted Keynes. It seems reasonable to suppose that Lemmer is here formed from the topographical term Leme with the -er suffix, and is not derived from a personal name. The name survived in Sussex in the forms Leamer and Leymer.[177]

Lyger

The name Lyger or Ligier, which occurs in Sussex during the 13th and 14th centuries, has been included by both Fransson and Rubin among surnames formed from a topographical term with -er.[178] The first element of the name is the word 'leah', signifying variously 'glade in woodland', 'pasture', 'meadow'. The surname derived from the same element without the -er suffix is now usually spelt Lea, Lee, or Legh. It is very common in Sussex from the 12th century, in varying forms, de la Lye, atte Lee, ater Legh, de la Lea, etc.[179] There is accordingly nothing surprising in finding a form in -er in the county. The early Sussex examples of Lyger etc., nearly all appear in the area south east of Chichester, though there is an isolated case at East Grinstead.[180] At the same period, however, the surnames Legard and Legar, which are derived from personal names were present in much the same part of the county.[181] There is no reason to doubt that Lyger and Legard were in origin distinct, but it is difficult to say where later forms such as Leghere, Legyer, and Ledger belong,[182] though some at least of these seem likely to be topographical. Legard was still present in the area around Chichester in the 16th century,[183] but no form has been found after 1500 which appears to be clearly topographical.

Marker

Some doubts have been expressed about the possibility of Marker being a topographical surname,[184] but although the name probably has more than one origin, it is clear that in some Sussex examples the name is topographical. The name atte Merke, or de la Merke, was present from the late 13th century at Easebourne, in West Sussex, and at Rotherfield, in East Sussex. Several persons of the name are mentioned at each place, and it is probable that there were by the late 13th century two families, each with a surname by then hereditary, one at Easebourne and one at Rotherfield. The name le Merk, which appears at Midhurst, very near to Easebourne, in 1284, must be an error for de la Merke. Marker, Mirkare, or Merkare is a name which developed from atte Marke, etc. John de Mirkare, who occurs at Easebourne in 1327/8, is listed as John de la Merke at the same place in 1296, and as John atte Mirk there in 1332.[185] The name Marker or Mirker also occurs during the 14th century at Beckley and at Slindon, neither of which is particularly near to Rotherfield or Easebourne. Atte Merke signifies 'at the border'. Beckley and Rotherfield both abutt the boundary between Kent and Sussex. Easebourne is near a detached part of Hampshire, and Slindon is on the boundary between Chichester and Arundel rapes. Alternatively, however, the West Sussex examples of Marker, etc., might be derived from the locality now known as Marker Farm, on Thorney Island.[186]

Perryer

Perry (atte Perye, atte Purie, atte Pyrye, etc) ('at the pear tree') has been a numerous and widespread surname in Sussex from the 13th century onwards. It has also been a common name in some other counties over a long period. Names formed from atte Perye, etc, such as Peryer, Purier, etc., occur from the early 14th century in Sussex. In many cases the origin of such names is clear, but some forms such as le Perur or Perour have been held to be occupational names,[187] with the meaning of 'quarrier'. Although it is at times difficult to be certain about origins, it is doubtful if any of the forms which appear in Sussex are occupational. John le Perour, listed at Bidlington in 1327/8, has a name which might be occupational, but he appears to be the same person as John atte Purye, who is mentioned at Wiston, very near to Bidlington, in 1296, and as John Purie, at Wiston about 1300.[188] Most of the examples of Perour, Puriere, Peryer, etc., which had been found in Sussex before about 1350 come from one part of the county; instances can be found at Wiston, at Bidlington, and at Pulborough, a short distance north west of Wiston. At Wiston there was a succession of customary tenants during the 14th and 15th centuries named Puryere, etc., probably all of them belonging to one family. The surname atte Purie occurs frequently at Wiston during the same period, and some tenants who are named Puryere appear to be given the name atte Purie, alternatively, on some occasions.[189] The fact that the various forms, such as Perour, Periere, Puryere, etc., occur in early examples in the same limited area of the county suggests strongly that a single name is involved, and not two different names, one occupational, and one topographical. Though this seems to be the case in Sussex, the name might have different origins elsewhere.

At the end of the 14th century the surname Perryer, etc. appears in Aldingbourne, and during the first half of the 15th century it is also found at Horsham, Penhurst and Netherfield. At all four places, however, the name atte Perye, etc., occurs, before the mid-14th century.[190] This would suggest that the name Perryer, etc., arose separately at each place, and that its presence at each of the four places was not due to migration from the area around Wiston and Pulborough. If this was so, it seems likely that Perryer in some cases evolved from atte Perye during the early 15th century. Perryer was still present in Sussex in the 16th and 17th centuries, though it was uncommon.

Reder

The surname Reder (Reader, etc.) is usually said to be an occupational one, derived from the craft of thatching with reads. Some early examples of the name are to be found in Norfolk, where thatching with reeds was commmon, and in East Anglia the name was probably occupational.[191] In Sussex, however, the name atte Rede was widespread from the 13th century. Atte Rude, or de la Rude, appears to be another form of the same name. There are several possible origins for the name Rude, or Rede, the history of which is discussed elsewhere.[192] The first example which has been found of Reder in the county is in 1402, at Midhurst. Later Reder occurs at Pevensey, where there was a family so named in the late 15th and 16th centuries.[193] During the 16th century the surname, though not common, was present at a number of places in Sussex, not concentrated in any one part of the county.[194] The name de Rude or de la Rude existed at Midhurst from the 13th century, and it also existed at Easebourne, nearby. At Midhurst there was in the 14th century a croft called Jonhane Rude, which may have given rise to the name de Rude at that place.[195] De la Rude also appears at Pevensey in the 13th century, and atte Rede, etc., was quite a common name in the area inland from Pevensey during the 14th and 15th centuries.[196] These connections make it likely that in Sussex Reder has been formed from atte Rede, etc., with the -er suffix. The surname Reder also occurs in Kent, and may have the same origin there as in Sussex, since atte Rede also occurs in Kent.

Ryer

The name Ryer first occurs in Sussex in Whalesborne Hundred (which comprised an area on the coast, around Brighton) in the late 14th century. During the 13th and 14th centuries, the surname atte Rye or de la Rye was present in the same part of the county, and it seems likely that Ryer was formed from atte Rye with -er. Ryer was always a rare name, but it survived, and still existed in East Sussex during the 16th century.[197] It is unlikely that the surname is connected with the Sussex place-name Rye; the surname atte Rye is probably topographical, meaning 'at the island' or 'at the low-lying land'.

Sherter

The name Sherter or le Shurtare has first been found in Sussex during the 14th century. The name is to be connected with the bye-name atte Shurte, which occurs at Petworth in 1296. In this connection Shurte probably means 'detached piece of land'. The early examples of Sherter which have been discovered in Sussex all come from the coastal region in the west of the county. The name occurs at and near Chichester, and also at Atherington, on the coast.[198] The individual who appears at Atherington was probably a glazier. During the 13th and 14th centuries the names atte Schurte and Shurtare both occur in Surrey, at and near Chiddingfold, which is only a short distance from the Sussex border. Many of those named Shurtare who lived in the Chiddingfold area were engaged in glass making, but it is uncertain if there was any link between the Chiddingfold glass makers, and the John Sherter of Atherington.[199] During the 15th century the name Shurtare developed into Shorter in some cases in the Chiddingfold area, and in the adjoining parts of north west Sussex.[200] In the subsidy returns for 1524-25, Shorter occurs at Chichester, and at Westergate, a few miles to the east; it also occurs at Rogate and Harting, in the north west of Sussex, and not far from Chiddingfold.[201] There is little doubt that the persons named Shorter who occur in north west Sussex in the 16th century were descended from the the people named Shurtare or Shorter who occurred earlier in the Chiddingfold area, and in north Sussex, and it must be very probable that all those named Shurtare or Shorter who are to be found in the south west of Surrey and the north west of Sussex with names Shertare or Shorter belonged to one family. Whether the appearance of the name Shorter at and near Chichester in the 16th century is due to Shurtare having developed, independently, into Shorter in that part of Sussex, or whether it is due to migration into Chichester from north west Sussex or the Chiddingfold district of Surrey, must be doubtful. In the 1641-2 Protestation Returns, Shorter occurs around Chichester, and also in the north west of Sussex.[202]

There may have been some confusion during the 15th, 16th, and 17th centuries between the name Shorter, and another surname, Shotter (Shotcher, Shotyer, etc.), which was fairly common at those periods both in north west Sussex, and in the south west of Surrey. The two surnames seem, however, to be distinct in origin.[203] Shorter is said to have developed from the name Shorthose, but this has not been found in Sussex.

Slutter

Slutter appears to have been originally formed from the rare topographical name atte Slutte, which occurs in Sussex during the late 13th and early 14th centuries, at Ifield and in Horsham and West Grinstead,[204] and which probably had the meaning of 'at the muddy place'.[205] The earliest reference to Slutter which has been found in Sussex is in 1428, when the name occurs at Coombes,[206] not very far from West Grinstead. During the first half of the 16th century, Slutter occurs at West Grinstead, at Coombes, and at several other places in the same part of the county. The name also occurs at Lewes.[207] The name Slytter, which occurs in Ringmer Hundred, close to Lewes, in 1524-5, is probably a form of Slutter.[208] During the 16th century, Slutter seems to have become assimilated to the much better known name Slater. Edward Slutter, a tenant of land at Thakeham, near West Grinstead, in the mid 16th century, is also mentioned as Edward Slater.[209] Slutter occurs in Sussex in the late 16th and early 17th centuries, but has not been found there subsequently.[210] Slater, on the other hand, has not been found in Sussex before 1500. In the 1524-5 subsidy returns, Slater only appears in the area around West Grinstead and Coombes,[211] and it seems likely that the examples of Slater which occur in this area during the 16th century were all due to developments from Slutter. In the 1641-42 Protestation Returns, Slater was still present in the area around West Grinstead and Coombes, and it also existed at West Tarring, on the coast and adjoining Broadwater, where Slutter occurs during the 16th century.[212] Possibly some of the instances of Slater which appear in Sussex during the 16th and 17th centuries may be due to migration into the county, but it seems likely that Slater in Sussex has largely developed from Slutter.

Topographical Surnames 171

Stacker

Stacker, or Staker, has generally been held to be an occupational name from the task of building haystacks (which would at best be a seasonal job). It has further been suggested that the name Stack derives from the same occupation. In Sussex, however, both Stack and Stacker (or Staker) are topographical in origin. The name atte Stak, or de la Stake, occurs in the late 13th and early 14th centuries at Sidlesham, south of Chichester, as the name of customary tenants. It also occurs near Bosham. It seems likely that it was the name of a single family. The form le Stak does occur, and might seem to support the view that Stack could at times have arisen from a nickname, but the man who appears as le Stak also appears as atte Stak, and the form le Stak is evidently one of the many cases where the definite article has been used in error.[213] In these instances the name de la Stak, etc., is from the word 'stake'.[214] In the 15th century the name Staker occurs at Yapton, not far from Sidlesham. In the 1524-25 subsidy returns, Staker occurs at Yapton, and at several adjoining places. There is an isolated example in East Sussex. The form Stakyar or Stakear occurs in the 16th century at times.[215] It must be suspected from the distribution of the name that all those named Staker, etc., in 16th century Sussex belonged to the same family. In the 17th century Staker was still present at and near Yapton.[216] The name Stawker, which occurs near Battle in the 16th century, is probably a variant of Stalker, which occurs in the same area at the same period.[217]

Wister

Wister is a rare surname, derived from the Sussex dialect word 'wist', a local term for a virgate. The earliest occurrence of Wister which has been found is at the end of the 13th century. The name was always scarce, and all the instances which have been discovered are in East Sussex. The name Awiste, derived from the same word, appears in the same part of the county.[218] This is almost certainly a surname which originated exclusively in Sussex.

Winder

The surname Winder has often been held to be occupational.[219] It is possible that this may be the origin in some areas, though no conclusive evidence has been produced for this. Winder is the name of several places in northern England, and in some instances, the surname is derived from one of the place-names concerned.[220] In Sussex, however, Winder has developed from atte Wynde. The name atte Wynde (probably 'at the winding path or street') ocurs in East Sussex from the late 13th century. The early examples all concern Wilting, (a small locality near Hastings) or its neighbourhood,[221] and it seems very probable that all the persons involved belonged to one family. During the 15th century the name appears at places not far from Wilting, such as Rye and Udimore. The name Wynne or atte Wyne, which occurs in the same part of Sussex from the late 14th century, is evidently a form of atte Wynde, the forms Wynne and Wynde being used for the name of one individual.[222] The name le Wyn, which existed at Chichester in the Middle Ages, has a different origin.

Wynder first appears in Sussex during the 14th century, at Whatlington and Winchelsea, both not far from Wilting. During the late 14th century and the 15th, the surname appears at Hastings, and at other places in the same part of Sussex, but it has not been found elsewhere in the county.[223] In the 16th century the name Wynder was still present in the same area, but it has not been found anywhere else in Sussex.[224] Wynder is clearly in this case a name formed from atte Wynde. In view of the fact that Wynder was confined in Sussex to a limited district of the county, it seems probable that this name, too, belonged to a single family, but it is not possible to connect all the individuals concerned genealogically.

There are several other surnames where it may be suspected that the origin is topographical, even though the names concerned have usually been classified as occupational. For instance, the name Willer (Willar, Wyliar, Wyllere), which occurs in Sussex from the 13th century, is usually said to be derived from an occupation, perhaps basket-making. However, the name atte Wille (atte Wylle, atte Wyle), occurs in the county as a variant of atte Welle, and it must be suspected that Willer has been formed from atte Wille with the -er suffix.[225] This is all the more so because most references to Willer, etc., occur in the part of Sussex where the form atte Wille was in use. Similarly, the name Whitcher (Whicchere, le Wuchere, Wycher, etc.), which is also generally held to be derived from an occupation, may well be derived from the name atte Wych ('at the wych elm'), but the derivation cannot be proved.[226] Borer is usually said to be an occupational name, but in Sussex the names atte Boure and Bourer were both present in the north of the county, at and around Horsham, and in this area Bourer eventually developed into Borer, though this development did not take place until the 17th century. The names atte Boure and Bowrer both occur, too, at Wittering and at Pagham nearby, in the 14th century, so that in this area also Bowrer seems to have originated from atte Boure. Binner, again, has been thought to be an occupational name, and the surname Binn (Byn, etc.) has been supposed to have the same significance as Binner. Sussex examples of both Binn and Binner have been cited in support of this view, but there are grounds for considering that both surnames are topographical. This question is discussed below.[227] Comper is usually said to have the meaning of 'companion' or 'comrade', but the surname or bye-name atte Compe

Topographical Surnames

('at the field') existed in Sussex from the 13th century, and it is possible that Comper has been formed from atte Compe with the -er suffix. The names atte Compe and Comper both existed from the 14th century at Findon and at Wartling. Waterer is another surname, apparently occupational, which was probably topographical in origin.[228] However, it is clear that topographical surnames in -er have been exceptionally numerous in Sussex over a long period.

Topographical Surnames with the suffix -man

Topographical surnames in -man have not been found in Sussex before 1200, and though it is impossible to be certain that some names of the type are not concealed beneath the Latinised forms frequently used for topographical names during the 12th century, it seems probable that such names did not develop until after 1200, either in Sussex or in other counties. Fransson, who investigated names of the type briefly in his work on surnames of occupation,[229] found no examples anywhere in England before 1250. In fact topographical names in -man begin to appear in Sussex[230] just after 1200, but they do not become at all common until the second half of the 13th century, and many names in the category are not evidenced until the 14th.

In view of the defects in medieval source material, it is always dangerous to argue too dogmatically from the absence of evidence for names of one particular type. Names of the type under discussion do not seem to have been, in the early stages of development, those of landowners, or other persons of wealth and standing, who would be likely to appear often in medieval sources. However, although these limitations in the evidence might explain the lack of references to some individual names, the lack of instances for a whole category of surnames is not explicable by such factors. It seems likely that topographical names in -man did not begin to arise in Sussex until about 1200, and that at first such names were scarce. It has not been possible to make a full investigation of the position throughout England, but judging from the material presented by Fransson, and by detailed work done on some other counties, names of the type arose in other southern and Midland counties at about the same period as in Sussex.

There seems to be no doubt that the significance of such names is topographical. As with names in -er, cases can be found where individuals with names in -man are mentioned with their names given in an alternative form which is clearly topographical. For example, William Loteman, who is listed at Chyngton in 1332, is also referred to as William atte Lote, at the same place and at the same date.[231] Similarly, John Trandleman, mentioned at Aldwick in 1327-8, is also referred to as John ate Trandle ('at the circle').[232] While such instances leave no doubt that surnames or bye-names formed with -man are topographical, it is difficult to see why topographical names in -man, and the corresponding group of names in -er, should have evolved side by side, in much the same regions, and at much the same period. It might be thought that there would be some shade of difference in meaning between the names in -er, and those in -man, but if this was so at the time when names of both these types were being formed, the nature of the difference cannot now be detected. It is not a question of either type being used exclusively, or mainly, in one limited area of the county. The 1296, 1327/8, and 1332 subsidy returns for Sussex show names in -er and names in -man present in all the main districts of the county. The two types are not separated in their geographical distribution in Sussex. Nor is the difference between the two types one of social or economic class. Judging by the subsidy rolls, and by such other evidence as there is, there was no perceptible difference in class or wealth between those with names in -er, and those with names in -man. Both types of name were borne by unfree tenants. Neither type of name occurs in early instances among the class of larger landowners, but this is because by the late 13th century, when names of both types first start to appear in numbers, most landowning families had already acquired hereditary surnames. Many topographical terms appear as the first element both of names in -er, and of names in -man, so that pairs of names, such as Brooker and Brookman, Bridger and Bridgeman, etc., constantly occur. A group of surnames exists which is composed of a place-name with the addition of -man. These, however, seem originally to have been confined to the north of England, and for reasons discussed below, are unlikely to throw any light upon the point at issue here. In Sussex, topographical names in -man do not seem ever to have been formed from compound topographical surnames or bye-names. A parallel duplication of forms existed in the case of some occupational surnames, as is shown by Fransson's well-known work on Middle English surnames of occupation. For example, Capiere and Capman occurred in the same area and at much the same period, so did Candeler and Candelman, Chapman and Chappere, and so forth,[233] without there being any obvious difference between the two types of name in meaning. It may be that during the 13th and 14th centuries, when many topographical surnames first arose, some difference in meaning separated the two types of name, so that Bridger signified something rather different from Bridgeman, Churcher something different from Churchman, and so on. It is, on the other hand, quite possible that there was no real difference in meaning between the two types of surname. Such a possibility is supported by the fact that surnames in -er were evidently at first regarded as interchangeable with surnames formed from topographical terms without the -er suffix, and that surnames in -man were also regarded as interchangeable in the same way. There are

Topographical Surnames

a few cases in which topographical terms appear as the first element of surnames in -man, but not as the first element of names in -er, but the elements in question do not form a group in any obvious respect.

Although a moderate number of topographical surnames or bye-names in -man can be found in Sussex during the second half of the 13th century, many such names are not evidenced in the county until after 1300. In all, 84 topographical surnames or bye-names in -man have been found in Sussex before 1600 in the sources which have been searched for this work. A fully comprehensive search, especially through local manuscript evidence, might perhaps reveal a few more. The total of 84 includes a small number which never became hereditary. Out of the 84, only 19 have been discovered in use in the county before 1300. Most of the remainder occur in the course of the 14th century, but there are 19 which have not been found until after 1500. Allowance must be made for the fact that 15th century sources for surnames are not good, and many surnames which have first been discovered in the 16th century probably came into existence earlier, during the preceding century. Even if this is so, however, it is evident that many topographical surnames in -man must have arisen after 1400, and that the number of such names in use must have increased significantly during the later Middle Ages. It is always possible that a few of the surnames which occur for the first time in Sussex during the 16th century may have been brought into the county by migration. None of these surnames, however, has a first element which does not occur in a topographical name in Sussex before 1500, and there is no sign of surnames appearing in the 16th century which contain topographical terms especially connected with English regions distant from Sussex. The part played by migration in the appearance of new topographical names in -man during the sixteenth century is likely, therefore, to have been slight.

Topographical surnames in -man, though more common in Sussex than in most parts of England, were never confined to that county. Within Sussex they were never limited to one area. In Kent, the subsidy returns for 1334-5 show that topographical names in -man, though fewer in proportion to the number of taxpayers listed than in Sussex, were then widely distributed throughout the country.[234] In Surrey, the 1332 subsidy shows that names of this type were fewer, proportionate to the number of persons listed, than in either Sussex or Kent, but such names were scattered through the county, and were not especially concentrated on the Sussex border.[235] It does not seem possible that the presence of such names in either Kent or Surrey could be due to migration from Sussex, and such names have obviously developed in each county. It is more difficult to say what the position was in other parts of England. Fransson cites a number of 14th century examples from Essex, sufficient to show that the type was by then established in the county, though not apparently very numerous.[236] In the 16th century, surnames of the type under discussion were nearly as common in Essex as in Sussex, judging from the Essex returns for the subsidy granted in 1523.[237] From the 13th century onwards, such names can be found in most parts of the south of England, the Midlands, and East Anglia, but so far as can be seen from the subsidy returns available in print for those regions of England, names of this type were more numerous in the south eastern counties of Kent, Sussex, Surrey, and Essex than elsewhere. In the north of England such names always seem to have been rare, though some instances can be found.

In the north of England there existed from the 13th century a group of surnames or bye-names formed from a place-name with the suffix -man. The surname Honickman is said to be from the place-name Honeywick (Suss.) but no examples of the surname have been found in the county, and it is very doubtful if surnames formed from a place-name with -man ever arose in the south of England. A possible alternative source of Honickman might be Hunwick (Durham).[238] It is in many cases doubtful whether such surnames were derived directly from place-names, or whether they were derived from already existing locative surnames, which had arisen earlier from place-names. It is doubtful, for example, if the surname Penkethman is derived directly from the place-name Penketh (the name of a village in Lancashire), so that the surname would have the meaning of 'the man from, or of, Penketh'; or whether the meaning of the surname is 'the man of the person named Penketh', Penketh being on this hypothesis a locative surname, derived at some earlier date from the place-name Penketh. In the case of some Yorkshire surnames evidence has been cited to show that the second hypothesis just stated is the correct one, so that, for example, Fentonman means 'the man (servant or vassal) of the person named Fenton'.[239] It is impossible to be certain if all surnames formed from a place-name with the suffix -man can be explained in this way. There does, however, seem sufficient evidence to make it necessary to exercise caution before concluding that surnames formed from a place-name and -man, a category of name which seems originally to have been confined to the north of England, have the same origin as surnames formed from a topographical term and -man, a category of surname which was more common in the south-east than elsewhere. The northern surnames formed from a place-name with -man ought to be considered as a separate category, different in geographical distribution, and probably different in origin too, from surnames formed from a topographical term and -man. The position about the origins of surnames from a place-name and -man, therefore, can not be used to throw light on the origins of the large group of surnames formed from a topographical term and -man.

A small number of surnames formed from a topographical term and -man do occur in the north of England. Dr. Redmonds, dealing

Topographical Surnames 177

specifically with Yorkshire surnames, has suggested that these arose in the same way as the name Fentonman has been shown to have originated, so that, for instance, in Yorkshire, the surname Bridgeman would mean 'servant of the man named Bridge'. The precise circumstances which gave rise to any individual surname often elude all research, but it may be suggested that in the north of England both surnames formed from a place-name and -man, and surnames formed from a topographical term and -man, both arose in the same way, so that in the north, Fentonman, Bridgeman, etc., meant 'the servant of the man named Fenton', 'the servant of the man named Bridge', and so forth. In the south eastern counties of England, however, surnames from a place-name and -man do not seem to have arisen, and surnames such as Bridgeman, etc., were clearly topographical. It seems probable that surnames from a topographical term with -man originated in different ways in different regions. It is important not to over-simplify the history of surnames, and to allow for differences between the various English regions.[240]

A few topographical surnames in -man need separate discussion.

Cherryman

Cherryman appears at first sight to be a surname of the type under discussion, but it is very doubtful if this is a correct view. The name has generally been thought to be occupational, but no early examples have been cited by the various authorities who have dealt with it. The first person of the name to be discovered in Sussex is Thomas Cheryman, mentioned at Horsham in 1571, but he seems to be the same person as Thomas Chyryam or Chyriam, who is listed several times in the Horsham parish registers rather earlier. During 1600-50 the name Cheriman or Cheryman also occurs at Pulborough, about ten miles from Horsham, and at West Chiltington, which adjoins Pulborough. In 1570 the name Cherian appears at Pulborough. This evidence indicates that, at least in Sussex, Cherryman evolved from Chyriam (or Chiryam, Cherian). The origin of Chyriam, etc., is uncertain.[241]

Loteman

Some remarks have already been made about the names atte Lote and Lotyer.[242] In the late 13th and early 14th centuries the name Loteman appears for the first time in Sussex, and it was then present in two areas, in East Sussex around Alciston, and in West Sussex at Wisborough. At the same time the name atte Lote occurs around Alciston (though it has not been found at or near Wisborough), and there is no doubt that Loteman has the same significance as atte Lote.[243] One individual who is mentioned at Wisborough, Walter Loteman, is also mentioned as Walter de

Lutmannesparr or Lotemanesparre ('Loteman's enclosure'). No doubt he held some enclosed land which, as so often in Sussex, derived its field-name from the surname of its holder.[244] In this instance the forms Loteman and Lutemann were evidently being used for the same individual.

In the late 14th century the name Loteman was still present in West Sussex, not far from Wisborough. In the 15th century the surname Lutman or Luttman occurs in the same part of Sussex, and Lutman, etc., survived around Wisborough in the 16th and 17th centuries. The name also appeared during the 16th and 17th centuries in some other parts of West Sussex, including Chichester, probably as a result of migration from the Wisborough area. The names Ludman and Lydman, which existed in West Sussex at the same period, seem to be forms of Lutman.[245] By the 17th century, Lutman had multiplied in West Sussex, especially in the more northerly part. On the other hand, the surname seems to have been absent from East Sussex during the 16th and 17th centuries. In this case Lutman seems clearly to have developed from Loteman. It seems possible that all the persons named Lutman, etc., who appear in West Sussex during the 16th and 17th centuries were descended from the Walter Loteman who was mentioned at Wisborough in 1332. This does not accord with the account usually given of the origins of the surname Lutman, which is generally said to be from Lytelman ('little man').[246]

At the end of the 13th century and during the 14th, the name Lyteman, or Liteman, occurs in East Sussex. Most examples are found in places lying just to the east of the area, around Alciston, where Lutman was present at the same period. No instances of Lyteman, or Liteman, have been found in Sussex after 1400.[247] Under these circumstances it seems doubtful if Lyteman was a form of Luttman, or not. In any case Lyteman, etc., does not seem to have survived.

Potman

The surname Potman probably had more than one origin. During the 13th century Poteman was in use as a first (Christian) name in Sussex. In the 12th and 13th centuries Poteman also appears as a first name in Kent. In both counties it was rare. No examples of Poteman as a first name have been discovered after 1300.[248] No positive evidence has been found to show that Poteman or Potman as a surname is derived from the first name concerned, but since Poteman occurs as a surname in an area of East Sussex when the first name also occurs, it seems possible that the surname arose from the first name. The origins of Poteman as a first name have not been satisfactorily explained.

In a few cases Potman may be an occupational name in Sussex. Stephen Poteman, who is mentioned at Brede in 1327/8, was probably the same person as Stephen Potter, mentioned there in 1332.[249] This is not conclusive, as it is not possible to be certain that a single person is involved in both references, but it seems likely that in this case Poteman was occupational. However, the usual surname derived from the work of pot-making, in Sussex and in other south-eastern counties, was Potter, which was quite a common name in Sussex from the 13th century onwards. It is not impossible for two surnames, both derived from the same occupation, to arise in the same part of the country, and indeed examples of such a development can be found, but it is unusual, and it must be doubtful if Potman is normally an occupational surname in Sussex.

The surname atte Potte (de la Potte, etc), appears in Sussex in the 13th century and later. Potte was also used as a field-name in Sussex. In particular, some land at Willingdon was known as le Potte, and this is in the area where Potman first occurs as a surname.[250] The meaning of Potte, when used topographically, was probably 'hole' or 'pit'.[251] In the late 13th and early 14th centuries, the surname or bye-name Poteman occurs at Willingdon, (near Eastbourne), at other places nearby, and at Brede, Udimore, and Rye, in the easternmost part of Sussex.[252] The name survived in those parts of the county into the 15th and 16th centuries.[253] The surname persisted in the same parts of the county over a long period without dispersing very much, and so far as can be seen without becoming noticeably more numerous. No occurences of the name have been found before 1600 either in West Sussex, or in the western part of East Sussex. Field and locality names such as Potman's Land, Potman's Farm, and Potmanshill, existing in the eastern part of the county, reflect the surname's long existence there.[254]

In view of the existence in Sussex of the name atte Potte, which was fairly common there over a long period, and in view of the existence within the county of numerous surnames formed from a topographical term with -man, it must seem probable that in Sussex the significance of Potman was topographical. Though an origin from the use of Poteman as a first name is possible, there is no positive evidence for it, and the use as a first name was very rare. The apparent use of Poteman as a synonym for Potter might have arisen, in the one case in which it is known, by accident from the existence together of two very similar names in one area, and though it is impossible to be entirely certain, a topographical origin seems much the most feasible.

There are, of course, many topographical names in -man which appear in Sussex, but which have not been discussed here. Some of these occur as the names of one or two individuals only, and were probably not hereditary. Others, such as Brookman, Bridgeman, Pyrieman, or Gateman, for instance, have been numerous and widespread in Sussex over a long period. In general, however, the topographical names in -man which have not been discussed do not present any especial difficulties concerning their origins or significance.

Surnames formed from a topographical term with either -er, or -man, were already numerous in Sussex by about 1300. During the later Middle Ages the proportion of the population with surnames of the two types appears to have increased, and during the 16th century the number of persons in the county with such surnames was very considerable, more perhaps in proportion to the total population than in any other county. Very few surnames in -er arose from compound topographical terms, and there are no certain cases where a surname in -man has been formed from a compound topographical term. Very few examples occur of the cardinal points being used as an element of a name in -er or -man. A few such names can be found, such as Westre or Southman, but instances are very scarce, and in none of them is it clear that the name became hereditary.[255] This is despite the fact that surnames formed from the cardinal points, or compounds formed from the cardinal points with other terms, are very common in Sussex. The number of topographical terms which have given rise to surnames or bye-names in -er or in -man is, however, very large, and very many topographical terms occur as the first element of names in both -er and -man. A few topographical terms which, used without a suffix, were common as topographical names in the county, do not appear as an element in topographical names in -er or -man. The surnames Bank, Eye, Hurne, and Mott, for example, were all quite common in medieval Sussex, but none of the four topographical terms which gave rise to those surnames has been found as an element of a surname in -er or -man in the county before 1600. However, if compound topographical terms, and terms from the points of the compass, are both left on one side, the remaining topographical terms which have not given rise to names in -er or -man do not seem to have any special characteristics which mark them out as a group. No doubt some surnames existed which failed to be recorded in any surviving source. It is evident that very many topographical terms were in use as elements of surnames in -er or -man in Sussex, and that it was not the case the names in -er or -man were formed from a small group of topographical terms with special characteristics.

The Surnames East, North, South, and West

The names East, North, South, and West were by the 13th century already present in many English counties. Although in some cases these names may have arisen through a person from one part of England migrating into a distant region (so that, for instance, a Southerner who settled in the north of England might be named South), it seems more likely that in most cases such names arose from the location of a person's house in the village where he lived, so that a man living at the north end of a village would be named North, and so forth. This seems all the more probable because, both in Sussex and elsewhere, some of those who appear with such names were bondmen, who were unlikely to have migrated over any distance. The very scattered distribution of all four names throughout England by an early date rules out any possibility that any of the four could have originated with a single family, and is indeed evidence of the influence of locality on topographical names.

It is therefore all the more surprising that in Sussex most of the examples found before 1400 for all four names come from one part of the county, the coastal district of West Sussex, lying between the Downs and the sea. There are a smaller number of cases from the part of the county lying to the north of the coastal area, but still in the south west portion of West Sussex.[256] Outside this area, there is an isolated example of North at Bishopstone in East Sussex, one individual named West mentioned in connection with Lewes Honour, a constable of Lewes Castle named North, and a few scattered instances of East, West, and North in the more northerly parts of West Sussex.[257] The distribution of the four surnames in question is more concentrated than this account would suggest, for a high proportion of the examples found before 1400 come from a limited area in south-west Sussex. A number of instances occur at Pagham and others at nearby places, such as Shripney or North and South Bersted, where there were lands belonging to the Archbishop of Canterbury's manor of Pagham. At Aldingbourne, in the same part of Sussex, the names East, North, South and West all occur in the 14th century. The number of places at which any of the four names appear during the 13th and 14th centuries is small considering the number of individuals involved. It does not seem likely that East, West, North, or South could have originated in Sussex as each the name of a single family. In the case of each name, the bearers included people of varying status; some were bondmen, others were freeholders. None of the four names occurs in one township, or only on one manor. This is not a case of four families having proliferated over a couple of centuries in one part of the county. It must be supposed, therefore, that the distribution of the four names in question was due to the use of North, South, East, and West as surnames being confined to one part of Sussex. The presence of dispersed examples in other parts of the county was very probably the result of migration. This is an example of the way in which certain usages in the formation of surnames could in one county be confined to quite a small area, even though the surnames involved also occurred in other parts of England.

During the 15th century rather more instances of the surnames under discussion can be found in East Sussex, and by the 16th century the original distribution had largely disappeared.[258] West, the most frequent of the four surnames in Sussex, was the name of a well-known landed family in the county. East, North, South, and West occur as elements in many compound topographical surnames in Sussex, but these are not concentrated in any one part of the county.

Apart from the distribution of the four surnames discussed above, it does not seem that the topographical surnames in any one part of Sussex have special characteristics which mark them out as different from those in the rest of the county. There are many topographical names, most though not all scarce ones, which so far as early references are concerned (before about 1400) are to be found in one restricted area of Sussex, and not elsewhere in the county. If, however, the topographical names to be found in any one part of Sussex are collected together, and considered as a group, no special peculiarities emerge which distinguish that group of names from the topographical names occurring in other parts of the county. In the case of some topographical names, all or nearly all the instances which can be found for any one name before 1400 are concentrated in a very limited area, and where some names are concerned, this concentration persists into the 16th and 17th centuries. This situation is produced by several factors.

The ramification of families is one of the forces which determine the spread of surnames. It has already been suggested that there were in Sussex some surnames which were originally each the name of a single family in the county, though some of the names in question may have originated independently in other counties. The genealogical evidence available for the Middle Ages is not usually sufficiently complete to enable the pedigrees of all the persons who appear with any one name to be traced, and it is generally impossible to find conclusive proof that all those who occur bearing one surname share a common descent. However, there are instances where the fact that all the early examples of a given surname are to be found within a very limited area, and in that area, within one particular social class, creates a strong presumption that all the bearers of the name in question were related. It has been suggested above that the names Leyne, Sparre, Whamm, Thele, Flasher, Furlonger, Stacker, Wynder, and Loteman were in Sussex each, probably, at first the name of a single family. Once a surname becomes stable and hereditary, its spread, the number of individuals who use it as a name, and even its survival, cease to be determined by linguistic considerations. Both the dispersal and the proliferation of hereditary surnames depend on genetic factors, on each family's position in life, which will affect its members' chance of survival, and on economic factors which may in some cases tend to promote migration, and in others to create conditions in which people tended to remain at or near their places of birth. Many of the more common topographical surnames have obviously not originated with one family, even within the single county of Sussex. The early instances of some topographical names are too widely dispersed in the county for that to be possible. The names Ash, Birchett, Bridge, Brook, Church, Combe, Comber, Crouch, Court, Dene, Denne, Fenn, Field, Ford, Frith, Gate, Gore, Hamme, Hatch, Hay, Hease, Heath, Held (and Hilde), Hide, Holme, Holt, Hook, Hurst, Legh, Marsh, More, Mott, Oak, Perry (and Pirie), Shaw, Sole, Staple, Stile, Stock, Stone, Towne, Tye, Welle, and Wood were all widespread in Sussex from an early date, and cannot have originated within a single family, even within the county's borders. There are, on the other hand, a number of surnames, not already mentioned, which seem likely to have originated in Sussex with one single family. These include Belchamber[259]; Delve, which appears in the 13th century at and near Lewes, and at and near Little Horstead, the persons who are found at Little Horstead being also holders of land at Lewes; the surname existed in the same part of Sussex later in the Middle Ages, and still persisted there during the 16th and 17th centuries;[260] Forapple (signifying probably 'assart, land newly cleared from forest'), which appears from the late 13th century at Glynde, South Malling, and Ringmer, three adjoining parishes in East Sussex, but which has not been found elsewhere in the county during the Middle Ages; the place-name Farables Shaw, in Glynde, is derived from this surname;[261] the name atte Posterne, or de Posterne, which has been found early in the 14th century at Brede; one of the individuals who occurs at Brede is also mentioned at Winchelsea, nearby, but apart from this, the surname has not been found elsewhere in Sussex before 1400;[262] the surname, however, arose independently in other counties; atte Sounde, which is a name first found in Sussex in 1296, at Beddingham; all the instances which have been found in the county before 1400 are at the same place, though the name occurs elsewhere in East Sussex later; the meaning of 'sounde' here was probably 'sea', or 'stretch of water'; Beddingham is on low ground near the Ouse, and in the 14th century there was an area there called the Sounde; part of Beddingham was subject to seasonal inundations during the 14th century, and the area called the Sounde may have been among the land so affected; in the 16th century there was a large seasonal lake at Beddingham, covering several hundred acres;[263] and Standbynorth, which has been found before 1500 only at Perching (near Fulking) where it occurs in the 13th and 14th centuries, and at Shoreham, not far away, where it is found in the 14th; during the 16th century it appears elsewhere in East Sussex; this is a rare topographical name which seems to have originated with a single unfree family at Perching.[264] These surnames are all ones which were rare in Sussex before c. 1500, though some of them, such as Belchamber, subsequently ramified in the county. In cases such as these, the distribution of surnames depends on the spread of individual families, and it is no use trying to detect linguistic factors behind the patterns of distribution which can be discovered in the 13th and 14th centuries.

The incidence in the county of some topographical surnames is naturally affected by the nature of the landscape, of the soil, of the vegetation, and by the nature and the extent of cultivation. A few of the rarer topographical surnames derive from one particular feature of the landscape. This was the case with Sounde, discussed above. Some more common names in this category appear entirely, or almost entirely, in one particular type of country. For instance, the name Aldret (atte Aldratte, ate Naldrette, ate Nelrette, Naldraate, etc.: given in a Latin form as *de Alneto*), signifying 'at the alder grove', occurs up to 1500 almost entirely in the wooded Wealden areas near the northern border of Sussex, though a few cases can be found in places rather further south, such as Amberley or Hurstpierpoint. Even during the 16th and 17th centuries, the surname was still largely concentrated in the same northern areas.[265] Forms such as Naldrett, Alderet, etc., appear as the names of localities in the same northern parts of Sussex.[266] The name atte Hese ('in the brushwood') has been found in medieval instances within the county in a single area, the Wealden part of East Sussex. No doubt its presence there was due to the heavily wooded nature of that district at the period when surnames were evolving.[267] The name atte Hese probably developed into Hayes in the same area later. The surname Frith (Fryth, Vrythe, etc.) is also mainly to be found in Sussex in the northern part of the Weald, though a few instances occur rather more to the south. The surname Frith is derived from a term originally applied to a stretch of woodland where there were exclusive hunting rights, and where game was protected.[268] The surname Gravett or Grevatt (from a word meaning 'grove' or 'copse') was until about 1500 confined in the county to the northern and central parts of West Sussex. The distribution of early instances suggests that there originally were three or four families of the name in Sussex, all in the west of the county. During the 16th and 17th centuries the surname became increasingly more dispersed in West Sussex. The name Gravett, etc., appears during the Middle Ages in Surrey (with some examples near the Sussex border) and in Hampshire, and is probably a name which arose in one region of England.[269] Naldrett, Hese, Frith and Gravett were all surnames which in Sussex were largely confined, so far as early instances are concerned, to the wooded northern parts if the county, and these are all woodland names. All four surnames, however, were too dispersed in the county at an early date for it to be likely that any one of them could have originated there in a single family.

One or two other names are linked, in a similar fashion, with the nature of the soil or the landscape in particular areas of the county. The surname Clay, for example, is one which is likely to arise where clay soil exists, but where it is not general. In a region where most of the surface soil is clay, residence on clay soils would hardly be sufficiently distinctive to give rise to a surname. In Sussex the name Clay (atte Claye, atte Clee) has been found before 1400 mostly in two areas; one of these is in a group of West

Sussex townships, lying just north of the scarp slope of the South Downs, Sullington, Thakeham, Washington, Storrington, Wiston, and Ashurst; these are in an area where some of the surface soil consists of gault clay, which has a reputation for being difficult to plough; the second area is near the coast, east and south of Chichester; here there is some Weald clay.[270] The early distribution of the name does appear to be linked to the geology of the county. On the other hand the name seems to be too dispersed for it to have originated with a single family.

The factors which lie behind the distribution of topographical surnames, from an early date, are therefore complex. Both the vocabulary and the phonetics of local dialect influence the topographical surnames which come into use in any one county. Besides this, the development of surnames, both topographical ones and those in other categories, can be affected by local or regional practices in the formation of surnames or bye-names, practices which must relate to local or regional habits of speech, in use at the periods when surnames were evolving. Once surnames became hereditary, however, other factors begin to operate. The survival, the spread, and the numbers of surnames then depend on the extent to which families with hereditary surnames ramify and disperse. Some surnames are so numerous, and so widely distributed, at an early period (say before about 1350), that it is obvious that each of them has arisen at a large number of separate places, and in a large number of families. In such cases the effect of the performance of any single family on the numbers or the distribution of a surname will be small. In contrast, where a surname has become hereditary in a single family, the extent to which that family multiplies, and spreads geographically, will decide the history of the surname in question. Instances where a surname becomes hereditary in a single family in the whole of England are uncommon, though there do appear to be examples. However, cases where in a single county, or even in a whole region, a surname became hereditary in just one family, are more numerous than has perhaps always been appreciated, and some instances from among Sussex topographical names have already been cited.

There is always the possibility that surnames from outside Sussex, either from other parts of England or from other countries, entered Sussex and were then rapidly assimilated to names already well established in the county. Such a development would be hard to detect, and may have happened in a few instances. This may occasionally have made it seem that surnames were ramifying more rapidly than was in fact the case.

Some of the topographical surnames occurring in Sussex need to be discussed individually.

Belchamber

It has been suggested that the surname Bellchamber is derived from the French place-name Bellencombre (Seine-Maritime). A William de Bellencumbr' was a witness to two charters granted by the Countess of Surrey to Lewes Priory, about 1165. As Bellencombre was held in the 11th century by the De Warenne family, who were lords of the Rape of Lewes, and who became Earls of Surrey, the appearance of the name de Bellencumbr' in connection with Lewes is not surprising. No link can be traced, however, between William and any of the people who later had the surname Belchamber (which is not found in Sussex until the late 13th century), and it is uncertain if he held land in Sussex, or had any real connection with the county.[271] The first person named Belchamber who has been found in Sussex is Richard Belechambr, or Belechombre; he was the tenant of a virgate at Slindon, and seems to have been dead by about 1285. Walter Belechambre is mentioned as possessing land at Kirdford, before 1334. These instances are both from West Sussex. Belchamber seems to have been a rare name in Sussex until the 16th century. It occurs at London in the 14th century, but seems to have been scarce in the country as a whole. Early in the 16th century Belchamber occurs at Petworth and Fittleworth, which adjoin Kirdford, and at several other places in West Sussex. Though the name had dispersed somewhat by the 16th century, it is probable that it survived in the county as the hereditary surname of a single family, at Kirdford, and spread to some extent during the 14th and 15th centuries. By the 17th century the surname was fairly common in West Sussex, though there are very few instances in the eastern half of the county. 27 persons named Belchamber are listed in 1642, in the Protestation Returns for West Sussex. The surname was present in Hampshire in the 16th century, possibly through migration from West Sussex. In this case a rare name multiplied to become widespread in West Sussex, with some occurrences in both Hampshire and East Sussex, probably through the proliferation of one family.[272]

It is conceivable that the name Belchamber derives from the work of bell ringing, but the name is not in the form which would be expected if it were an occupational one. Noise would make living in the bell chamber of a church very inconvenient. Room in the upper stories of church towers was sometimes leased out, probably for storage, and the name Belchamber may have been originally that of someone who tenanted room in a church tower for some such purpose.

Binn

It has been held that the name Binn (Byn, Byne) is occupational, and that it is from the trade of making bins, for grain, etc. Sussex instances have been cited as evidence of the name being used in this sense. The first examples which have been discovered in the county appear in the early 14th century, at Ewhurst and Tottingworth, both in the east of the county. In the late 13th century there was a field called La Binne, at Robertsbridge, close to Ewhurst, and the surname Binn, etc., which occurs in the same part of the county, is in all probability derived from this field name. Possibly the field name may have arisen from the presence in the field concerned of a bin or manger, but alternatively it is possible that the field name has the meaning of 'hollow'.

The surname or bye-name le Bynere existed in Sussex during the 13th and 14th centuries. The only place in the county at which it then occurs is Sompting, which is not near any of the known medieval instances of Binn, Byn, etc. It has been thought that Binner, etc., is an occupational name, and Sussex instances, from Sompting, have been cited in this connection. However, since Binn, etc., seems to have a topographical origin in Sussex, and since names formed from a topographical term and -er are very common in the county, it seems likely that here Bynere is a topographical name in -er.[273] In the 16th century the surname Byne still existed at and near Tottingworth, and also, at that late period, at Sompting. As has already been shown, during the 13th and 14th centuries there were many cases in Sussex of individuals having topographical surnames which occured sometimes with an -er suffix, but on other occasions without the suffix. Under these circumstances, it must be suspected that a family called sometimes Byne, sometimes Bynere, survived at Sompting from the 13th century to the 16th.[274] The name de Byne found in Sussex from the 12th century onwards, is derived from a locality near West Grinstead.

Costedell

The surname Costedell is one which has arisen in Sussex as the name of a single family, and it seems possible that there was a single family so named in the whole of England, though it is difficult to be sure of this without making a very extensive search through sources for the whole country. The name is derived from the Middle English word 'cotstedel', a term for some form of cottage, though the precise significance is uncertain.[275] The surname occurs from the late 13th century at Bolney, at Twineham, which adjoins Bolney, and at Wyndham nearby, as the name of a family. The surname was present at Bolney, and Twineham, during the 14th and 15th centuries. The family was still owning land at Bolney in the late 16th century, by which time the name was sometimes being spelt Costdell or Costell. Even in the seventeenth century the surname was still present in the same part of the county. It has not been found in any other part of Sussex before 1600, and although it has not been possible to make a comprehensive search, no early examples of the name are known from other counties. This does appear to be a case of a surname originating with one family in the 13th century, and surviving over a period of several hundred years in one part of Sussex, without dispersing very much geographically, and without increasing significantly in numbers. The name of Costell's Wood, in Lindfield, is from the family's surname.[276]

Eightacre

The surname Eghtacre or Eightacre occurs at Warbleton during the 15th century. In all probability the surname was derived from a field name, but the exact origin cannot be discovered. A field called the Crooked Eight Acres existed at Ambersham, but that is a place distance from Warbleton, and it is unlikely that this field name has any connection with the surname. Early in the 16th century the surname appears at Pevensey, which is not far from Warbleton, and later in the same century it appears at Streat, further to the west. It also occurs at one or two places near Pevensey. The form Aytakers appears in the late 16th century. This surname, too, seems to be one which originated in a single family, at Warbleton. It spread to some extent in East Sussex, but did not become at all numerous.[277]

Fairhall and Verall

The name Fairhall has first been found in Sussex in 1332, at Lindfield, in the form atte Fayrehale. There must be some doubt whether the second element in the name is the Old English *heall* ('hall') or *healh* ('nook' or 'corner of land'.). The surname occurs in East Sussex in the 16th century in forms such as Feyrall and Fyrrall, and during the 16th and 17th centuries it sometimes appears as Verral or Virroll. The evolution of such forms can be traced through parish register entries. Evidently, however, not all the individuals named Verral, etc. had surnames which had developed from Fairhall, as a Gilbert Verall, a Frenchman, was resident in Sussex in 1524. In Gilbert's case, the form in which his surname was given in England was probably the result of a French surname (possibly Feral) being assimilated into the form of an English surname already in use in the county. Despite this instance, it must be probable that a large majority of those who appear in Sussex during the 16th and 17th centuries with the name Verrall, or similar forms, had surnames which had evolved from Fairhall. Verall became a well established name in several Sussex parishes in the north central part of the county, around Lindfield where the name Fayrehale was found in the 14th century. In this case, too, a rare surname persisted in one area of Sussex for some centuries.[278] The surname survives in Sussex at the present in a number of variants, Fairhall, Fairall, Farhall, Farrall, Verrall, etc.

Fennell and Vennell

The early history of the surnames Fennell and Vennell is complicated by the occurrence in some medieval sources of names such as *de Venele* or *de Venella* as Latin translations of the vernacular atte Lane. Atte Lane was a fairly common name in Sussex during the Middle Ages, and in particular it persisted over a long period around Chichester. It is, however, usually possible to distinguish instances where *de Venella*, etc., is a Latin form for atte Lane, because frequently both Latin and vernacular forms can be found for the names of individuals or families. For example, Adam atte Lane, a customary tenant of Pagham manor in the late 13th century, is also mentioned as Adam *de Venella,* and Robert in le Lane, another tenant of the same manor, living in the late 13th and early 14th centuries, is also mentioned as Robert *de Venella*.[279] Similarly, Henry de la Venele, listed at East Harting in 1296, appears to be the same person as Henry in le Lane, listed at the same place in 1327/8.[280] If we eliminate instances where forms such as *de Venella*, etc., are clearly translations for atte Lane, then the only examples to be found in Sussex before about 1350 of names which could be the origin of the later Fennell or Vennell are some which appear in one area of East Sussex, around Wilmington. During the first half of the 14th century a name in the form atte Fenegle, Fenigle, or ate Fynegle occurs at Wilmington, and at Litlington, about two miles to the south.[281] Since the name was scarce, and all the known examples are found in the same small area, it must be suspected that all the individuals concerned were members of one family, but the relationship cannot be proved. The meaning of the name atte Fenegle, etc., is uncertain. It has been suggested that it is derived from the Middle English word 'fenecel', for the herb fennel.[282] Surnames derived from plants or herbs are rare (though Woodruff is an example), but fennel was cultivated for use in cookery, and might have given rise to a surname, perhaps for someone who lived beside a plot where the herb was grown.

The name survived at Litlington during the late 14th and the 15th centuries. In the late 14th century it appears there in the form atte Feynel. During the 15th century the usual form at Litlington is atte Fenell or a Fenell. The fact that as late as the 15th century the preposition was still usually, though not always, employed shows that the name must have been topographical. The form Venell occurs, though rarely, in the 15th century, as the name of individuals whose surnames are also given in the form Fennell. The persons named atte Fenell, etc., who can be found at Litlington in the 15th century all seem to have been yeomen or husbandmen, and although no complete pedigree can be traced it is very probable that they all belonged to the same family.[283] Several individuals named atte Fenel or Venell who occur at Litlington also appear during the 15th century in connection with Westdean, Exceat, and Arlington, all places within a few miles of Litlington, and the surname may have been tending to disperse somewhat.[284] However, before 1500 the name seems to have been confined to the Litlington area, so far as Sussex was concerned.

During the 16th century, the surname Fenell or Venell still persisted at Westdean. Early in the century the name also appears at Pevensey, about 8 miles from Litlington, and rather later at Eastbourne, which is nearer Litlington. Forms such as a Fenell still occur after 1500. After about 1520 the name Fonell appears at Pevensey; this is evidently a development from Fenel, as the individuals who first appear named Fonell also appear with the name Fenell. The 1524-5 subsidy returns show that the surname Fenell or Fonell was by that date already quite numerous in East Sussex. Most of the persons with the name listed in the subsidy were still resident in the area around Litlington, and in that part of Sussex the surname had ramified considerably by 1524-25. Elsewhere, there are a few scattered instances of the name in the more easterly part of East Sussex, but there are none in the subsidy in the more westerly parts of East Sussex, or in West Sussex. Examples to be found in other 16th century sources are mostly from the Litlington area, too, and there are none from west or central Sussex.[285] In all probability, this surname originated with one family holding land at Wilmington and Litlington which did not disperse very much up to the 16th century, though it proliferated considerably.

During the 16th and 17th centuries the surname evolved into further forms. The variant Fonnels occurs, but this is no doubt an instance of the tendency for surnames to acquire an inorganic final 's', during the 16th century. Fonell developed further into Funell or Funnell. It has been suggested that Funnell in Sussex is from the French 'fournel' ('furnace'), or from a French place-name such as Fournal or Fournel, but this does not seem to be correct. One of the first instances of Funnell in Sussex is at Westham (near Pevensey), in 1553, at a place where Fenell occurs rather earlier. Forms such as Fernall and Furnell also seem, at least in Sussex, to be variants of Fennell; the first example of Fernell, etc., found in the county is in 1535, at Clapham (in Litlington), where Fennell had long existed.[286]

The surname Funnell subsequently became established in other parts of Sussex, as for instance at Cuckfield and Horsham. At the present time, Fennell, Vennell, and Vennells all survive as surnames in Sussex, though all are rather rare. Funnell, on the other hand, has multiplied greatly, and is now one of the county's more numerous surnames. It is in practice very difficult to be certain if any surname has originated exclusively in one part of England, but so far as can be discovered Funnell is a surname which originated only in Sussex.

Forbench

Forbench is a rare surname which so far as it has been possible to discover did not occur during the Middle Ages outside Sussex. Within the county it only appears before 1500 at Broadwater, near Worthing. In the 16th and 17th centuries it appears at several places in the southern part of West Sussex, mostly not far from Broadwater, but it remained a very rare name. The West Sussex Protestation Returns, which include a high proportion of the adult male inhabitants, list two persons with the surname. It seems likely that the surname originated with one family at Broadwater, and survived in West Sussex without increasing very much in numbers, though it did disperse geographically to some extent.[287]

The element 'bench' here may refer to a bench or seat, perhaps one placed in front of a house. It is, however, possible that the term is being used in the sense of 'bank' or 'ledge'.

Hay

The surnames Hay and Hey have several different origins, and in Sussex there was confusion between the names involved at an early period. A surname of the nickname type, le High or le Hay, existed in Sussex from the late 13th century. This is a name with the meaning of 'high, tall'. The Sussex examples of the name are scattered, and unlikely to have all been from a single family. Some of the instances may have been non-hereditary bye-names, but the name was hereditary in the case of a family at Guestling. No clear examples of this name have been found in the county after the mid-14th century.[288] Its disappearance is probably due to confusion with a topographical name.

A topographical surname or bye-name occurs in Sussex during the 12th, 13th and 14th centuries, in the forms atte Hegh, de la Hegh, atte Heye, de la Haye, and atte Heyghe. The form Haye, where it is preceded by a preposition, which is not always the case, is in the Sussex 13th and 14th century instances always given in the form 'de la Haye', not 'atte Haye'. De la Haye ought probably to be considered as a form which is linguistically French. In some cases, however, Haye is from a French place-name.[289] The meaning of atte Hegh, etc., is 'at the fence or hedge' or 'at the enclosure'. The French de la Haye would also mean 'at the hedge or fence'. During the 13th and 14th centuries the name atte Hegh, etc., appears at a considerable number of places in the county, and the references seem too dispersed for it to have been the name of a single family. The persons who appear with the name were of varying status, from knights and other substantial freeholders to customary tenants.[290] It is in some cases very difficult to separate the examples of this topographical name from those of two other surnames or bye-names which also occur in Sussex, the name atte Hegge ('at the Hedge'), and the name atte High ('at the high ground').[291] It seems likely that the surname Hay or Hey, as it appears in Sussex at later periods, was derived both from the nickname type surname discussed above, and from three different topographical names, atte Hegh, atte Hegge, and atte High.

Hone

Hone is a further example of a surname with complex origins. From the late 13th century onwards the name atte Hone occurs south of Chichester, at Wittering and Sidlesham. The name still existed at both places during the 14th century, and it was present at Sidlesham in the 15th. The persons named Hone, who are listed at Somerley (in Wittering) and at Chichester, in the subsidy rolls in 1524-5, were very probably descendants of the people named atte Hone who appear in the same area from the 13th century.[292] The persistence of the name in one part of the county over so long a period shows that it was hereditary, probably from the late 13th century, and the way in which the early references are concentrated geographically makes it probable that all those named atte Hone who are to be found in this part of Sussex shared a common descent. No instances of atte Hone or de la Hone have been found in any other part of Sussex. Atte Hone is clearly a topographical name, with the meaning of 'at the rock or stone'.[293] Besides the cases just cited, the name de Hony was present at Bexhill about 1250, and the name Hony, without any article or preposition, occurs at the same place during the 14th century. Sussex surnames with a final 'e' often possess alternative forms with a final 'y', and it is possible that de Hony is topographical, but it is also possible that it is derived from a Sussex place-name, Honey Bridge near West Grinstead. It has been suggested that John Hony, listed as West Grinstead in the 1332 subsidy had a bye-name from the place-name, but this seems doubtful. There is no positive evidence to link John with the place concerned. The name Hony appears at other places in East Sussex at the same period, and it is uncertain if John's bye-name is derived from a place-name at all.[294]

During the late 13th and early 14th centuries, the name le Hune, le Hone, or le Hony appears in Sussex. The references to this name are scattered, in various parts of the county, and it is unlikely that all those concerned can have been members of one family.[295] In these cases, the surname is probably derived from the use of the term 'honey' as a nickname.[296]

Besides the instances already mentioned, there are from the end of the 13th century many examples in Sussex of persons with the names Hone, Hony, Hune, or Huny, without any preposition or article. In such cases it is generally impossible to be certain what the origin of the name is. Where a surname has survived more or less continuously at one spot for a long period, as for instance at Wittering, it may be possible to be reasonably sure how the surname originated at that particular place. When, however, the surnames Hone or Honey appear at a relatively late period, such as the 16th century, it is generally impossible to be certain how they originate. Such names are probably in some instances topographic, arising from the earlier atte Hone; in some cases they have probably originated from the use of Honey as a nickname; and it is possible that some may be from the place-name Honey Bridge.

The Christian name Hunna, which was still in use in the 12th century, gave rise to a surname in some parts of England. Hunna has not been discovered in use as a first name in Sussex during the 12th, 13th and 14th centuries, when many surnames from personal names developed, and it is unlikely that the Christian name can have been the origin of any of the surnames which appear in medieval Sussex.[297]

The surname Honer, or Honner, which appears in Sussex during the 14th century, has sometimes been supposed to be from the trade of sharpening tools. However, in view of the frequency with which surnames formed from a topographical term and -er are found in Sussex, it seems probable that Honer and Honner, when they occur in the county, have been formed from Hone (in the topographical sense already discussed).[298] Honer is the name of a minor locality in Pagham, but forms such as de Honer have not been found, and it seems unlikely that the surname has originated from the place-name. Hone, Honey and Honney still survive as Sussex surnames. The surname Honess, still found in the county, has probably developed from Hone, with the addition of an inorganic 's'.

Jewery

The name atte Jewerye (or atte Giwerye) first appears early in the 14th century as the name of one person at Donnington, a short distance south of Chichester. During the 13th century there was a small Jewish community in the city, and although nothing is known about there having been any distinct Jewish quarter there, one may have existed.[299] The Jewish community in England ceased to exist with the expulsion of the Jews from England in 1290, but it is possible that after this time there was still a part of Chichester which was known as the Jewry from having been formerly inhabited by Jews. In 1369 Jewary occurs as a surname or bye-name at Horsham. No link has been traced between Horsham and the earlier references to the name at Donnington, but in view of the rarity of the name it seems likely that there was a connection.[300] The surname, though very scarce, survived, and was still present at Horsham in the 17th century. The Protestation Returns show the name, in the form Jure, or Jewre, at Horsham, and at several places in the north-west of the county.

The name was then fairly numerous at Midhurst. It seems probable that all those who appear in Sussex with the name Jewery, Jure, etc. shared a common descent from the individual who appears at Donnington in the 14th century.[301]

Lever

The surname Lever is in some cases derived from a place-name, but there is no evidence for this being the origin of any of the early examples of the name in Sussex. The early instances in the county are in the form atte Leuere, and this is a topographical name, 'at the reed or rush'. Most of the examples before 1500 of the surname are from one part of East Sussex, at Ore, Pett, and Fairlight, all places close together near the coast; a few cases occur a short distance from this area, for instance at Bucksteep (in Warbleton), but the distribution of the name is sufficiently concentrated to make it likely that all the persons named atte Leuere who appear in Sussex before 1500 belonged to one family. The surname was probably hereditary from the late 14th century, when it first appears. Early in the 16th century the name Lever was present at Pevensey, which is not far from the area around Ore. At the same period it also appears in West Sussex, probably as a result of the surname dispersing from the east of the county where it originated. As late as the 16th century the name is sometimes given in the form a Lever, so that the 16th century instances were clearly topographical, and not derived from one of the other possible origins of the surname. No early examples of atte Leuere are known from outside Sussex, and it seems likely that the surname, when it is topographical, originated solely in the county, and probably with a single family there. The surname Lever can have other origins. The name occurs in Lancashire, and is there derived from a Lancashire place-name.[302]

There may have been some confusion between Lever and two other surnames found in Sussex, Lower and Lewer. Both are usually said to be occupational names developed from *le ewer* (a French occupational term). It is, however, doubtful if either originated in this way in Sussex. The first instances which have been found for Lower in the county are at Amberley, in 1418-19, and during the 15th century atte Lowe occurs there, and in several nearby townships. It would appear from this that Lower developed from atte Lowe ('at the hill').[303] The origin of Lewer is uncertain. The name appears in Sussex in the 14th century, and in one instance it is in the form 'le Lewer'. This cannot have been formed from 'le Ewer', if the presence of the definite article can be relied upon as evidence. Since articles are sometimes prefixed to surnames in error, however, this is doubtful.[304] Lower and Lewer were both rare names in medieval Sussex, but both have survived in the county.

Reed

In Sussex during the 13th and 14th centuries, four separate forms occur, atte Rede (or atte Read), atte Ryde (or de la Ride), atte Rode, and atte Rude. Professor Löfvenberg, in his work on topographical names, apparently considered that atte Rede, atte Ryde, and atte Rude were all variant forms of one single name, though he was in doubt about the source of it, while he considered atte Rode to be a separate name, probably from an Old English word meaning 'clearing'.[305] There was, however, confusion at an early period between the different forms, with the names of individuals appearing in more than one variant. For example, Michael de la Rede, listed at Ringmer in 1327, must be the same person as Michael atte Rode, listed at the same place in 1332; and William de la Rode, mentioned in Easebourne Hundred at the end of the 13th century, was probably the same person as William atterede, mentioned in the same area in 1304.[306] A similar confusion of forms can be found in compounds; John ate Roddelond, listed at Selham in 1327/8, seems to be the same person as John atte Rued, listed there in 1332, and his name probably came from the land at Selham called Redelond; Richard atte Redelande, mentioned at Selham in 1363, may have belonged to the same family.[307] From this evidence, it seems that all four forms are variants of a single name. Its derivation is uncertain. Pieces of land called the Rede, the Rude, or Redeland existed at several places in East and West Sussex,[308] and the various forms of the name were widespread and numerous in the county, so that the name must be derived from a topographical term which was widely used, and which was a term for some feature of the landscape to be found in differing parts of the county. Of the various meanings which have been suggested as possible for the name, the meaning of 'clearing' or 'assart' is the one which seems most probable, though the term may have meant 'reed bed' in some cases.

The examples which have been discovered of the form atte Rude or de la Rude are almost all from West Sussex. Most of them are from the district around Midhurst.[309] The instances of the form atte Rude which have been found in East Sussex concern one individual, who was bailiff of Pevensey about 1265. The class of functionaries such as bailiffs was one of the more highly mobile sections of the community during the Middle Ages, and the presence of this one man in East Sussex may well be due to movement from the west of the county.[310] It has been suggested that forms such as atte Rude might be derived from an Old English word meaning 'rue'. This seems unlikely, as there are several examples in West Sussex of La Rude being used as the name for a field. These include two instances from the Midhurst district.[311] The form atte Rude also appears in parts of Surrey.[312] It was probably a form which was confined to a limited region, but an extensive investigation into counties other than Sussex would be needed to discover what the form's distribution was.

A surname or bye-name of the nickname type, le Rede ('the red'), was widely distributed in Sussex from the 13th century onwards. When dealing with later periods, such as the 16th and 17th centuries, it is not possible to distinguish between surnames which are derived from this name of the nickname type, and those which are topographical in origin. Forms which are clearly topographical, such as a Reede or at Ryde, still occur occasionally during the 16th century, but this is exceptional.[313]

Selde

The name Selde (atte Selde, *de Selda*) first appears in Sussex during the 13th century. The people who appear with the name before 1300 all seem to have been inhabitants of Chichester, and all the medieval examples of the surname which have been found in Sussex occur at or near to that city. In this case too it seems probable that all the persons with the name belonged to one family.[314] The surname was a rare one, but it survived, and was still present in West Sussex in the 16th century.[315] It has been suggested that the meaning of the name was 'hall, palace, or residence',[316] but the significance was probably 'stall' or 'shop'. The word was frequently used in that sense during the 13th century in deeds conveying property in Oxford. It does appear occasionally in deeds relating to property at Chichester, though in none of these cases is it clear precisely what the nature of a 'seld' in the city was.[317] The fact that the surname appears to have originated entirely in Chichester, and not in any of the rural parts of the county, supports this interpretation of its origin. From London experience this is almost certainly correct.

Soundry

The name de la Sondre was present at Yapton, near Bognor, early in the 13th century. There are other references to the name at the same place later in the century, and in the late 13th and early 14th centuries the name also occurs at Madehurst, Binstead, and Tortington, which immediately adjoin Yapton. During the 14th and 15th centuries, the name continues to appear at Yapton, and at Binstead, and it also appears at one or two other places in the same part of Sussex, such as Arundel and Amberley. No references have been found to the name in any other part of Sussex before 1500. In the 16th century the name occurs at Fishbourne, about nine miles from Yapton. It seems probable from the distribution of the surname that it originated with a single family at Yapton, and that all those who are found in Sussex during the Middle Ages with the surname shared a common descent. If this is so, the name must have been hereditary from the early 13th century. The surname was evidently very rare, but it survived. No early instances of the name have been discovered in other counties, and the surname may be one which was originally confined to Sussex. De la Sondre signifies 'at the sundered or cut off land'; probably this referred to land which had been detached from some large estate.[318]

Sinderford

Sinderford is another rare topographical surname which seems likely to have originated as the surname of a single family. The name occurs in the late 13th century at Isenhurst, and at Hawkhurst in East Hoathly, a few miles away, in the form atte Synderford. The surname is probably derived from a ford with a bottom laid with cinders or slag from iron works, but the ford in question has not been located. During the 14th and 15th centuries the surname was present at Cowbeech, near Herstmonceux, and not far from East Hoathly. It was still to be found in the Herstmonceaux area in 1524. Later in the 16th century it existed at Fletching, which is not far from East Hoathly and Isenhurst.[319] Although no connected pedigree can be traced for the surname, it was probably that of one family. If this was so, the surname was hereditary from the 13th century. The persons who appear with the name during the Middle Ages were small freeholders or customary tenants.

Thele and Tele

The name atte Thele ('at the plank bridge') has first been found in Sussex in the late 13th century. The surname occurs fairly frequently during the 14th century, but all the examples come from one part of the county, at and near Rudgwick, Slinford, and West Grinstead. It is probable that there was a single family so named, with a surname hereditary from the late 13th century. The name may have been derived from a bridge at Slinfold. No examples have been found from other parts of Sussex, and no early examples have been discovered outside the county. It seems likely that this is a surname which originated with one family in north Sussex. In the 16th century the surname Tele appears in the same part of Sussex. Although no pedigree has been traced, it is most probable that Tele here has arisen from the name Thele, present earlier in the same area. Tele is usually said to be a surname of the nickname type, from the species of wild duck called teal, and there is no reason to doubt that this is the correct derivation in some cases, but in Sussex Tele seems likely to have developed from atte Thele. This is another instance of a rare topographical surname which remained confined to one part of the county for several centuries.[320] The name of Theale Farm, at Slinfold, preserves the surname in the district where it originated. The names Teele, Teal, and Teale still survive in Sussex.

Trendle

The surname Trendle (Trandle, Trindle), is derived from an Old English word meaning a ring or circle. In Sussex a large circular earthwork, about five miles north of Chichester, is known as the Trundle, and field names such as Trendelgrof, Trendlefeild, and Trandilgrenes occur in the county. The name at Trendlee appears in the 13th century at Nyetimber, near Pagham. In 1327/8 John ate Trandle is listed as a taxpayer at Bognor Regis, a few miles from Nyetimber. He was probably the same person as John Trandleman, mentioned at the same date at Aldwick, between Bognor and Nyetimber. No other instances of the name Trandleman have been found, and it was probably employed in this case as an alternative to ate Trandle. Bognor, Aldwick, and Nyetimber are about ten miles from the Trundle, and the surname could be derived from the earthwork. However, a locality called Trandilgrenes existed in the manor of Pagham, which extended into Bognor and Nyetimber, and this was probably the origin of the surname. No examples of the surname have been found before 1500 in any other part of Sussex. The surname did, however, occur during the 12th century in Suffolk and during the 14th century in Kent, where it probably arose independently, and in Warwickshire.[321]

The word 'trendell' was in use in Sussex during the 15th century for a wooden circle carrying tapers or candles, and used to illuminate churches.[322] It is, however, unlikely that this is connected with the origin of the surname.

It is uncertain if the name ate Trandle, etc., was hereditary in any of the early examples cited above, but the name must have become so, for it survived in the county. The name was present in Sussex during the 15th and 16th centuries, mostly in the northern part. The places where it appears after 1400 are not near those where it was present during the 13th and 14th centuries, and it must be uncertain if there was any link between the persons named ate Trandle, etc., who occur near Pagham, and the later examples of the surname, which are found elsewhere in Sussex. During the 16th and 17th centuries the name was present for considerable periods in several Sussex parishes, including Horsham, Cuckfield, Ardingly, and Hurstpierpoint, but it never became at all numerous.[323]

In the 16th century the surname Trendle was at times given in the form Trunell or Tronell. John Trendle, mentioned in 1560, was apparently the same person as John Trunell and John Tronell.[324] The origin of the name Trunell (etc.) is, however, uncertain. It has first been found in Sussex during the early 13th century, at Findon. This is near the area where Trendle first appears as a surname or bye-name, and it is possible that from the start Trunell was a variant form of Trendle. This must be considered doubtful, especially as no forms such as atte Trunell have been found. It has been suggested that Trunell is a form of Thornhill, but the early examples found in Sussex do not support this view. During the 16th and 17th centuries Trunell was still present in West Sussex, mostly at places not far from Findon, where it had appeared in the 13th century.[325]

Topographical surnames formed from Christian names and from occupational surnames

At the present day there are many detached farms in Sussex which have place-names derived from the surnames of previous owners or occupiers. This situation has existed over a long period, and as far back as the 13th century many cases can be found where holdings were named from the surnames or bye-names of the existing tenants, or of earlier tenants. Examples of holdings having place-names derived from the surnames or bye-names of tenants can be found in most parts of England, but the practice of naming holdings in this way was more common in the south-east of England than in some other regions, and it was especially frequent in Sussex. It is to be expected that there would be some surnames derived from place-names which had originated in this way. The number of Sussex surnames which are so derived, is, however, very small. During the 14th and 15th centuries the name atte Stephenes occurs at Wiston, and at Amberley not far away. At Wiston, the name was certainly hereditary, and it is probable that this was also the case at Amberley. At Wiston the bearers of the name were unfree tenants. In this case the surname atte Stephenes was presumably from the place-name of a holding, and the place-name in question must have originated from either the Christian name, or bye-name, of some earlier holder.[326] Ate herrys occurs at Amberley in 1373, and at Robynes at Washington, in 1378-9. The names at Adamys and A James are to be found in Sussex during the 16th century, but no other examples have been discovered in the county before 1600. The name de Cockes, present at Amberley in the 14th and 15th centuries, is a doubtful case.[327]

Apart from surnames of this type, derived from the names of holdings, and where the place-names were derived from the Christian names or bye-names of earlier tenants, there are a few cases in Sussex of surnames or bye-names such as atte Prestes, atte Persones, A Webbys, and so forth. Such surnames are no doubt derived from residence, or employment, at houses, or perhaps land holdings, known as Priest's, Webb's, and so on. It is generally not possible to decide whether place-names such as Priest's, Webb's, etc., when applied to houses or holdings, originated from the positions or occupations of owners (or tenants), or whether they originated from the surnames of owners (or tenants). Surnames such as Priest or Parson sometimes originated as nicknames, and appear from an early date as the surnames or bye-names of people who were not clergy. The number of surnames or bye-names such as atte Prestes, A Webbys, etc., to be found in Sussex is small and many of the medieval examples seem not to have been hereditary.[328] The name atte Smythe, which occurs in Sussex from the early 14th century, is probably 'at the smithy', not 'at Smiths'.[329]

Once the proposition 'atte' (etc.) ceases to be used before names, it is very difficult to distinguish surnames which were originally atte Stephenes, at Adamys, and so forth, from surnames which are patronymics formed from a first name with a genitival 's' added.[330] In fact, in Sussex, 'atte', etc., remains in use before topographical surnames for a longer period than in most parts of England, possibly because the proportion of topographical surnames in the county was high. The preposition frequently appears before topographical surnames during the 16th century, and sometimes, though less often, during the 17th. This continuing use of the preposition at a relatively late period is a characteristic which Sussex shared with Surrey. The contrast with most other counties can readily be seen if Tudor subsidy rolls for various parts of England are compared. It is similarly impossible, once the preposition falls out of use, to separate surnames such as, for instance, A Webbys, from the surnames formed from an occupational term with a genitival 's'. In 1328, the name atte Someres occurs in East Easewrithe Hundred, in West Sussex. No other medieval references to this name have been found in Sussex, but in 1642 the name Somneres appears at Steyning, a short distance outside the hundred, and the name Sumners appears at Midhurst, rather more distant. It must be suspected that both these 17th century instances were survivals of the 14th century topographical name.[331]

A further difficulty is caused by the tendency of some surnames to acquire an inorganic final 's', often at a relatively late period, such as the 16th or 17th century. Early in the 16th century, for example, William at Redes was a tenant at Salehurst. He appears, however, to be the same person as William at Rede, mentioned earlier at the same place, and it is probable that his surname was derived from a parcel of land called the Rede, at Ewhurst, an adjoining parish.[332]

Cases such as these make it difficult to be certain about the origin of some surnames, especially those which occur after c.1500. When dealing with 16th and 17th century sources, it is sometimes impossible to be sure whether some names are derived from the place-names of houses or land holdings, or whether they are derived from first names, or occupational terms, with the addition of a genitival 's'. This in turn creates some difficulty in discovering how many Sussex surnames found in the 16th and 17th centuries are patronymics with a genitival 's', a type of surname which is noticeably scarce in the county during the Middle Ages.

There remain many topographical surnames which have occurred in Sussex, but which have not been dealt with in this chapter. Some of these are names which have been established in Sussex over a long period, and some, too, are names which have complex origins there, so that it can be difficult to be certain what the origin of some present day surnames really is. There is, for instance, the name which usually appears in medieval sources as atte Ree ('at the stream' or 'at the water'). This name occurs from the 13th century in a number of Sussex townships, mostly in East Sussex. One family of the name possessed land at Wivelsfield, and at one time held the manor there.[333] The name at Ree was still present in East Sussex in the 16th century, but at that period the name at times appears in the form At Trice. John at Ree (1525) is also mentioned as John at Trice.[334] However, though the surname Trice or Tryce originates in this way in some cases, the name de Tryse is mentioned in West Sussex in 1332, and this seems to be derived from a place name.[335] Further, from an early date, there was confusion between the name at Ree, and another topographical surname which was widespread in Sussex, atte Rie or atte Rye ('at the island' or 'at the piece of firm land in the marsh'). Michael atte Ree, for instance, a taxpayer at Ifield in 1327, is mentioned as Michael atte Rye at the same place in 1332.[336] There is the further complication that some persons appear in Sussex in the 12th and 13th centuries with the name de Rie or de Rye, and this surname is probably derived from a place-name, perhaps Rye, the Sussex port. To this it may be added that the name atte Eye, and the name Nye or Nie, are derived from the same source as atte Rie or Rye, and have the same meaning, and that it is difficult to be sure in some cases if the surname Atree is a form of Ree, or if the second element in the name is 'tree'. At the present day, Atree, Nye and Nie, Ree and Rea, Tree, and Trice, are all present in Sussex.

Similar complications about origins exist with other Sussex topographical surnames. The name atte Dene or de la Dene ('in the valley') was already quite numerous in Sussex during the 13th and 14th centuries, and at that early period the majority of instances of the name were on the South Downs. A separate, and less common, name at the same time was atte Denne, or atte Danne ('at the woodland pasture'). Even in the 13th century, there was confusion at times between the two names, with cases of the same individual being named sometimes Dene, sometimes Denne.[337] In addition, the name de Dene, which occurs in Sussex during the 12th and 13th centuries, is probably from one of the places called Dean, in Sussex or elsewhere, and the name le Dene, which is also present in the county, is derived from the ecclesiastical office of dean, either through the name le Dene, being acquired by holding a position as dean, or through the name being originally bestowed as a nickname. In view of the existence of these varied origins, it is generally not possible to say what the derivation of names such as Dean, Dene, Denne, and Dann is when they appear in the 16th century and later.

Examples such as these show how complicated the origins of even the more common topographical surnames can be. Sussex has for centuries been very rich in surnames in this category, and perhaps possesses a larger and more varied body of such names than any other. During the Middle Ages, and especially during the 13th and 14th centuries, a large number of topographical surnames or bye-names arose in Sussex which did not survive, and which in some cases never became hereditary.

References

[1] See p. 11.
[2] *3 Suss. Subsidies*, pp. 3-222.
[3] *Suss. Subsidy, 1524-5*.
[4] *3 Suss. Subsidies*, p. 66; Löfvenberg, *Local Surnames*, 87.
[5] *3 Suss. Subsidies*, p. 218; Löfvenberg, *op. cit.*, p. 92.
[6] *3 Suss. Subsidies*, pp. 117, 291; Löfvenberg, *op. cit.*, pp. 93-94. The bye-name is probably from Hazeldean near Cuckfield, near which the bye-name occurs.
[7] *3 Suss. Subsidies*, p. 76; Löfvenberg, *op. cit.*, p. 94.
[8] *3 Suss. Subsidies*, p. 253; Löfvenberg, *op. cit.*, p. 88.
[9] *3 Suss. Subsidies*, p. 47; Löfvenberg, *op. cit.*, p. 95. The bye-name has been connected with High Hatch Lane at Hurstpierpoint (*P. N. Suss.*, vol. ii, p. 275), but it occurs in another part of the county (at Crawley).
[10] *3 Suss. Subsidies*, p. 202; Löfvenberg, *op. cit.*, p. 96.
[11] *3 Suss. Subsidies*, p. 114; Löfvenberg, *op. cit.*, p. 99.
[12] *3 Suss. Subsidies*, p. 75; Löfvenberg, *op. cit.*, p. 101.
[13] *Lewes Barony Recs.*, p. 77; *3 Suss. Subsidies*, pp. 180, 294; Löfvenberg, *op. cit.*, p. 103. The bye-name is probably from Holgrove Wood, at Ardingly.
[14] *Lewes Chartulary*, vol. ii, pp. 82, 83; *3 Suss. Subsidies*, p. 93. Andrew atte Holirode, mentioned in 1309 and 1311, is probably the same person as Andrew de Cruce, mentioned in 1296 and 1327/8; Thomas Holerode, mentioned in 1296, is probably the same as Thomas le Cruchere, mentioned in the same year: *3 Sussex Subsidies*, pp. 84, 91, 119; *S. A. C.*, vol. xx, p. 7.
[15] *3 Suss. Subsidies*, pp. 6, 209; Löfvenberg, *op. cit.*, p. 103.
[16] *3 Suss. Subsidies*, pp. 299, 301; Löfvenberg, *op. cit.*, p. 106.
[17] *3 Suss. Subsidies*, pp. 34, 46, 47, 178, 202; *Lewes Barony Recs.*, pp. 45, 75; Löfvenberg, *op. cit.*, p. 106.
[18] *3 Suss. Subsidies*, p. 194; Löfvenberg, *op. cit.*, p. 108; possibly connected with Horsey (near Eastbourne) or with Horse Eye at Pevensey.

[19] *S. A. C.*, vol. xii, p. 39.
[20] *Hastings Lathe C.R.*, p. 43.
[21] *3 Suss. Subsidies*, p. 149.
[22] *Ibid.*, pp. 146, 260, 272. The surname might be from a Suss. place-name, Underley in Pulborough: *P. N. Suss.*, vol. i, p. 155.
[23] See p. 10.
[24] A. Rumble, *Dorset Lay Subsidy Roll of 1327* (Dorset Record Soc., No. VI) (1980).
[25] H. A. Hanley and C. W. Chalkin, "Kent Lay Subsidy of 1334/5", *Documents Illustrative of Medieval Kentish Society* (Kent Archaeological Soc., vol. xviii) (1964).
[26] J. P. Rylands, "Exchequer Lay Subsidy Roll", *Miscellanies Relating to Lancs. and Chesh.*, vol. ii (Lancs. and Chesh. Record Soc., vol. xxxi) (1896).
[27] *Rotuli Hundredorum* (Record Commission) (1818), vol. ii, pp. 688-877.
[28] Anon., *Suff. in 1327* (Suff. Green Books, vol. xi) (1906).
[29] *Surr. Taxation Returns* (Surr. Record Soc, vol. xi) (1922, 1932), pp. 1-94.
[30] *3 Suss. Subsidies*, pp. 225-334.
[31] W. F. Carter, *Lay Subsidy Roll for Warws.* (Dugdale Soc., vol. vi) (1926).
[32] F. J. Eld, *Lay Subsidy Roll for the County of Worcs.* (Worcs. Historical Soc., vol. ix) (1895).
[33] W. Brown, *Yorks. Lay Subsidy* (Yorks. Archaeological Soc. Record Series, vol. xvi) (1894).
[34] Examples of Downer occur in Oxon. later.
[35] The surname le Mote, which occurs, is not included.
[36] Some instances of the name Mottes occur, but are not included.
[37] The names Okes and Nokes, which occur, are not included.
[38] The name Sandys does occur.
[39] The form found in Warws. is Brocker.
[40] The name De Nesse, which occurs, is not included.
[41] The form which occurs is atte Ak.
[42] C. A. F. Meekings, *Dorset Hearth Tax Assessments 1662-64* (1951).
[43] House of Lords Record Office, Protestation Returns, Salford Hundred, Lancs., covers south-east Lancs. only.
[44] M. M. B. Weinstock, *Hearth Tax Returns, Oxfordshire, 1665* (Oxon. Record Soc., vol. xxi) (1940).
[45] W. Watkins-Pitchford, *Shropshire Hearth Tax Roll of 1672* (1949).
[46] Anon., *Suff. in 1524* (Suff. Green Books, no. x) (1910).
[47] C. A. F. Meekings, *Surr. Hearth Tax, 1664* (Surr. Record Soc., vol. xvii) (1940).
[48] *Suss. Subsidy, 1524-5*.

[49] G. D. Ramsey, *Two 16th Century Taxation Lists* (Wilts. Archaeological and Natural History Soc., vol. x) (1954).

[50] J. Amphlett, *Lay Subsidy Roll, 1603* (Worcs. Historical Soc., vol. xiii) (1901). Does not cover whole county.

[51] Brookes also occurs.

[52] Sandis occurs once.

[53] Downes occurs once.

[54] Mottes occurs twice.

[55] Downes occurs several times.

[56] Possibly a variant of Parry in Shropshire.

[57] Occurs as Tay.

[58] Combes occurs frequently.

[59] Löfvenberg, *Local Surnames*, p. 115, cites examples of the element in field names in other counties.

[60] *Ibid.*; *S. A. C.*, vol. c, p. 62; H. L. Gray, *English Field Systems* (1969), p. 443; *P. N. Suss,*, vol. ii, 310.

[61] Löfvenberg, *op. cit.*, p. 115; *3 Suss. Subsidies*, pp. 131, 132, 248, 312; *Suss. Custumals*, vol. i, p. 29; *Placita de Banco* (P.R.O. Lists and Indexes, no. xxxii), vol. ii, pp. 666, 667.

[62] *3 Suss. Subsidies*, p. 83; *S. A. C.*, vol. li, p. 43; L. Fleming, *History of Pagham* (1949), vol. i, pp. 42, 141; *Boxgrove Chart.*, pp. 127, 166; *Chichester Chart.*, pp. 119, 241, 242.

[63] *Cowdray Archives*, vol. ii, p. 248.

[64] *P. N. Suss.*, vol. i, p. 13; Reaney, *Dict.*, p. 261; J. W. Alexander, 'The Alleged Palatinates of Norman England', *Speculum*, vol. lvi, no. i, pp. 17-27.

[65] *P. N. Suss.*, vol. i, pp. 107, 135, 150; Löfvenberg, *op. cit.*, pp. 195-96; *3 Suss. Subsidies*, pp. 73, 75, 120, 148, 260; *Chichester Chart.*, p. 236; *Lewes Chartulary*, vol. ii, p. 66; *Wiston Archives*, pp. 33, 35, 37, 218, 287; A. H. Smith, *English Place-Name Elements*, vol. ii, p. 135.

[66] *3 Suss. Subsidies*, pp. 73, 120, 151.

[67] *3 Suss. Subsidies*, pp. 6, 209, 321; *Battle Custumals*, p. 23; Löfvenberg, *op. cit.*, p. 228; *Great Roll of the Pipe for the 3rd year of Henry III* (Pipe Roll Soc., vol. lxxx) (1976), p. 144.

[68] Löfvenberg, *op. cit.*, 119; *3 Suss. Subsidies*, pp. 35, 57, 190, 202, 302; *S. A. C.*, vol. xcvii, p. 23; vol. xcviii, p. 59; *Suss. Fines*, vol. ii, p. 71; *Robertsbridge Charters*, p. 96; Lane, *Suss. Deeds*, p. 98; *Suss. Custumals*, vol. iii, pp. 28, 34.

[69] *Suss. Subsidy, 1524-5*, p. 114. It has been suggested that some cases of the surname in Suss. are derived from a personal name (Reaney, *Dict.*, p. 214), but it is unlikely that the same name occurs, with two separate derivations, in the same area.

[70] See pp. 155, 164, 171, 187, 188, 191, 196.

[71] A. H. Smith, *English Place-Name Elements* (1970), vol. i., p. 167; M. Gelling, *Place-Names in the Landscape* (1984), p. 236.

Topographical Surnames 205

[72] Coombe and Tye are both terms in use in present-day Sussex dialect: W. D. Parish, *Dictionary of the Suss. Dialect* (1957), pp. 25, 147.
[73] See also the instances collected in Löfvenberg, *op. cit.*, for some counties, including Suss.
[74] Löfvenberg, *op. cit.*, p. 179.
[75] *Ibid.*; *3 Suss Subsidies*, pp. 142, 264, 298, 305, 306; *Non. Inquis.*, p. 376.
[76] See sources cited in note 75 above, and also *3 Suss. Subsidies*, pp. 120, 143, 191, 264, 302, 303, 305; Lane, *Suss. Deeds*, pp. 77, 147; *Battle Custumals*, p. 55; *Lewes Chartulary*, pp. 168, 170, 181; *Chichester Chart.*, pp. 5, 306; *Cal. Pat., 1321-24*, pp. 193, 275; *Cal. Pat., 1324-27*, p. 348; *Suss. Fines*, vol. iii, pp. 95, 150; *Suss. Custumals*, vol. ii, pp. 25; vol.iii, pp. 40, 41; *Fitzalan Surveys*, pp. 106, 122.
[77] *Suss. Subsidy, 1524-5*, p. 110.
[78] See p. 18.
[79] *W. Suss., 1641-2*.
[80] Löfvenberg, *op. cit.*
[81] G. Fransson, *Surnames of Occupation*, pp. 192-202.
[82] Löfvenberg, *op. cit.*, p. xxxv.
[83] Fransson, *op. cit.*, pp. 194-202.
[84] *Suss. Custumals*, vol. i, p. 55; West Suss. Record Office, E.P. VI/19A/1,mm. 3d, 9d; *Suss. Fines*, vol. iii, p. 103.
[85] *Suss. Fines*, vol. i, pp. 58, 68; vol. ii, p. 96; *Robertsbridge Charters*, p. 55; *S. A. C.*, vol. xii, p. 7; P. M. Barnes, *Great Role of the Pipe for the 16th year of King John* (Pipe Roll Soc., vol. lxxiii) (1962), p. 62.
[86] *De Lisle and Dudley MSS.*, vol. i, pp. 70, 83; Reaney, *Dict.*, p. 24.
[87] E. P. Ebden, *Great Roll of the Pipe for the 2nd year of Henry III*, (Pipe Roll Soc. vol. lxxvii) (1972), p. 19.
[88] *De Lisle and Dudley MSS.*, vol. i, p. 92.
[89] Löfvenberg, *op. cit.*, p. 98.
[90] *3 Suss. Subsidies*, pp. 3-105.
[91] Fransson, *op. cit.*, pp. 194-202.
[92] *3 Suss. Subsidies*, pp. 225-333.
[93] *Ibid.*, pp. 120, 129, 155, 181, 254, 273, 327; *Chichester Chart.*, p. 268; *Non. Inquis.*, pp. 372, 383, 403; *Wiston Archives*, p. 195; *S. A. C.*, vol. lxxxix, p. 126; vol. xcvi, p. 25; *Hastings Lathe C.R.*, pp. 3, 7, 120, 130, 131; Fransson, *op. cit.*, p. 198; West Suss. Record Office, EP. VI/19A/1, m.3d.
[94] *Suss. Subsidy, 1524-5, passim.*
[95] *Ibid.*
[96] *Ibid.*, p. 98.
[97] See p. 158.
[98] *W. Suss. 1641-2, passim*. See also the very numerous references to Streater in E. W. P. Penfold, *First Book of the Parish Registers of Angmering* (Suss. Record Soc., vol. xviii) (1913), *per indice*.

[99] Fransson, *op. cit.*, p. 193.
[100] *Ibid.*, pp. 196-200, 202; *Surnames of Oxon.*, pp. 51-52.
[101] *Surrey Taxation Returns* (Surr. Record Soc., vol. xi), no. xviii, pp. 1-64; no. xxxiii, pp. 65-94.
[102] H. A. Hanley and C. W. Chalkin, *op. cit.*, pp. 71-170.
[103] *Surnames of Lancs.*, p. 214.
[104] Reaney, *Origins*, pp. 201-202; G. Redmonds, *Yorks: West Riding*, pp. 65-66.
[105] *3 Suss. Subsidies*, pp. 136, 254.
[106] *Ibid.*, pp. 95, 127.
[107] See the examples given in Fransson, *op. cit.*, pp. 193-94. In several cases, however, Fransson's identifications of individuals seem doubtful.
[108] *Lewes Barony Recs.*, pp. 25, 31, 33.
[109] *Suss. Subsidy, 1524-5*, p. 151.
[110] Lane, *Suss. Deeds*, p. 142.
[111] *3 Suss. Subsidies*, pp. 23, 24, 192, 304.
[112] Rubin, *Suss. Phonology*, p. 67.
[113] *Hastings Lathe C.R.*, pp. 44, 125, 133, 148, 157-8; *S. A. C.*, vol. xcv, p. 48; *Suss. Fines*, vol. ii, p. 77.
[114] *Rotulorum Originalium Abbrevatio* (Record Commission), vol. i, p. 276; *3 Suss. Subsidies*, pp. 8, 208, 320; *Chichester Chart.*, pp. 116, 217-8, 248, 367; *S. A. C.*, lxxxvii, pp. 10, 11, 17; *Valor Eccl.*, vol. i, p. 295; Löfvenberg, *op. cit.*, p. 183. Compare the bye-name "ater Hokebench", found in Somerset: *ibid.*, p. 141. And see the mention of a "schamell" in the street, at Arundel, c.1405: *Fitzalan Surveys*, p. 120. See also the 2 pieces of land called Benches, at Wiston, 13th Century: L. F. Salzman, *Chartulary of Sele* (1923), p. 26.
[115] *W. Suss. 1641-2*, p. 76; E. W. D. Penfold, *First Book of the Parish Registers of Angmering*, p. 6; *Suss. Wills*, vol. i, p. 350; *Suss. Fines*, vol. iii, p. 295.
[116] *3 Suss. Subsidies*, pp. 23, 189, 302; *P. N. Suss.*, vol. ii, p. 418; Löfvenberg, *op. cit.*, p. 233.
[117] *S. A. C.*, vol. lxxxvii, p. 9; vol. lxxix, pp. 131, 143, 146, Kerswollere, found c.1405 (*Fitzalan Surveys*, p. 145) may be a form of Cresweller.
[118] *3 Suss. Subsidies*, p. 77; Reaney, *Origins*, p. 202; *P. N. Suss.*, vol. i, p. 114.
[119] Fransson, *op. cit.*, p. 197.
[120] *Ibid.*, p. 201; *P. N. Suss.*, vol. i, pp. 27, 88, 114; vol. ii, pp. 459, 466, 479; *Suss. Fines*, vol. iii, p. 103; *Fitzalan Surveys*, p. 123.
[121] *3 Suss. Subsidies*, p. 94.
[122] *Ibid.*, p. 181.
[123] Fransson, *op. cit.*, p. 194; *Surr. Taxation Returns* (Surr. Record Soc. vol. xi, no. xviii), p. 8.
[124] *Suss. Indictments*, vol. i, pp. 9, 37, 46; *S. A. C.*, vol. lxxxvii, pp. 20,

99; vol. lxxxix, pp. 147, 149; J. E. Ray, *Suss. Chantry Records* (Suss. Record Soc., vol. xxxvi) (1931), pp. 9, 15, 56, 159, 176; *Suss. Subsidy, 1524-5*, pp. 3, 4, 11, 18, 23, 32-3; *Valor Eccl.*, vol. i, pp. 304, 339; *Cal. Pat., Edward VI*, vol. ii, pp. 242-3.

[125] *P. N. Suss.*, vol. i, p. 205.

[126] *P. N. Suss.*, vol. i, p. 89; Reaney, *Origins*, p. 202. There is a place called Rumbridge in Hants.

[127] *Suss. Indictments*, vol. i, pp. 9, 46.

[128] Gover and others, *Place-Names of Surrey* (1934), p. 306; Reaney, *Origins*, p. 202; Reaney, *Dict.* p. 295.

[129] *S. A. C.*, vol. lxix, pp. 113, 114, 116; *P. N. Suss.*, vol. i, p. 136; C. Robinson, *Great Roll of the Pipe for the 14th Year of Henry III* (Pipe Roll Soc., vol. xlii) (1927), p. 244; *3 Suss. Subsidies*, pp. 237, 238, 241, 261, 233; *Suss. Subsidy, 1524-5*, pp. 30, 53, 57; Lane, *Suss. Deeds*, pp. 31, 54; *Wiston Archives*, pp. 153, 160; J. E. Ray, *op. cit.*, pp. 20, 37, 154; H.M.C., *Rye MSS.*, p. 68; P.R.O. E.179/190/268, m.2d; E.179/191/377, roll 6; E.179/191/410, m.5d; S.C.11/653; *Suss. Indictments*, vol. i, p. 82; *Chichester Chart.*, p. 56; *W. Suss. 1641-2*, pp. 21, 22, 26, 33, 62, 108, 113, 122, 135, 158, 165, 180; E. W. D. Penfold, *First Book of the Parish Registers of Angmering* (Suss. Rec. Soc., vol. xviii) (1913), *per indice*.

[130] *Cowdray Archives*, vol. i, p. 19; *S. A. C.*, vol. xxiv, p. 83. (Truslow probably originated as a nickname, see p. 387); J.E. Ray, *op. cit.*, pp. 25, 95; *Valor. Eccl.*, vol. i, p. 319.

[131] Reaney, *Origins*, p. 202.

[132] *Non. Inquis.* pp. 378, 403; *3 Suss. Subsidies*, pp. 26-28, 149, 184, 314; *Suss. Fines*, vol. ii, p. 39; *P. N. Suss.* vol. ii, pp. 439-40; Löfvenberg, *op. cit.*, p. 51; P.R.O. S.C. 11/877.

[133] *3 Suss. Subsidies*, pp. 50, 301.

[134] *Ibid.*, pp. 23, 149, 261; *S. A. C.*, vol. lxxxiii, p. 38; *Suss. Custumals*, vol. i, p. 100; *Fitzalan Surveys*, p. 146.

[135] *3 Suss. Subsidies*, p. 15; *Lewes Chartulary*, vol. i, p. 94.

[136] *S. A. C.*, vol. xii, p. 28; *Lewes Barony Recs.*, p. 54; *3 Suss. Subsidies*, p. 313.

[137] *Ibid.*, pp. 161, 269, 270.

[138] *Ibid.*, pp. 70, 142, 263.

[139] *Ibid.*, pp. 80, 136-7, 256; *S. A. C.*, vol. lxxxix, p. 160; *Boxgrove Chart.*, pp. 78, 88, 193; *Non. Inquis.*, p. 368; West Sussex Record Office, E.P. VI/19A/1, m.10d. And see p. 3.

[140] *Suss. Subsidy, 1524-5*, p. 136.

[141] *S. A. C.*, vol. xcv, p. 53; *Suss. Fines*, vol. ii, pp. 165, 174.

[142] *Chichester Chart.*, p. 195; Inderwick, *Winchelsea*, p. 183.

[143] *Suss. Subsidy, 1524-5*, pp. 11, 26; *Suss. Indictments*, vol. i, p. 42; Löfvenberg, *op. cit.*, p. 57; *Suss. Wills*, vol. ii, p. 319.

[144] *Chichester Chart.*, pp. 174-5; *Boxgrove Chart.*, p. 62; *Suss. Fines*, vol. ii, p. 170; *3 Suss. Subsidies*, pp. 80, 81, 131, 256; *Feudal Aids*, vol. v., p. 142; *Cal. Pat.*, *1324-27*, p. 348.

[145] *W. Suss.*, *1641-2*, p. 13.

[146] *3 Suss. Subsidies*, p. 272.

[147] *De Lisle and Dudley MSS.*, vol. i, p. 23; *Fitzalan Surveys*, p. 135.

[148] Lane, *Suss. Deeds*, p. 113.

[149] *Suss. Subsidy*, *1524-5*, pp. 19, 21, 66, 70, 89, 101, 137, 162; *S. A. C.*, vol. xlv, p. 44; *Suss. Wills*, vol. i, p. 81; vol. ii, p. 307; vol. iii, pp. 99, 263.

[150] *Wiston Archives*, p. 284; *W. Suss. 1641-2*, p. 142; R. Garraway Rice, *Parish Register of Horsham* (Suss. Rec. Soc., vol. xxi) (1915), p. 298. Flussher occurs at Chiltington, 1378-9: P.R.O. E. 179/189/42, m.15.

[151] Löfvenberg, *op. cit.*, p. 81; Reaney, *Dict.*, p. 154; *P. N. Suss.*, vol. i, p. 17.

[152] West Suss. Record Office, E.P. VI/19A/1, mm. 5, 9d, 10, 10d.

[153] *3 Suss. Subsidies*, pp. 75, 150, 262.

[154] *S. A. C.*, vol. xcv, p. 52 (printed Grenatour); *ibid.*, vol. xx, p. 4 (printed Grenette).

[155] *3 Suss. Subsidies*, p. 160.

[156] *S. A. C.*, vol. xviii, p. 24.

[157] *Suss. Subsidy*, *1524-5*, pp. 31, 40-42, 59, 60, 68-9, 74-5.

[158] *W. Suss. 1641-2*, pp. 17, 30, 52, 85, 118, 126, 129, 132, 137-8, 145, 153, 174, 195-6; *S. A. C.*, vol. xxiv, p. 80; vol. xli, p. 141; E. W. D. Penfold, *First Book of the Parish Registers of Angmering* (Suss. Rec. Soc., vol. xviii) (1913), pp. 5, 115; P.R.O., E. 179/191/378, m.3; E.179/191/410, mm. 10, 10d, 11, 11d.

[159] P.R.O. E. 179/189/42, m.20; *3 Suss. Subsidies*, pp. 16, 61, 211.

[160] *Ibid.*, pp. 94, 147, 163, 184, 185, 187, 216, 234, 260, 278, 297, 300, 302, 308-9, 328; *Great Roll of the Pipe for the 22nd Year of Henry II* (Pipe Roll Soc., vol. xxv) (1904), p. 205; *S. A. C.*, vol. liii, p. 163; *Suss. Custumals*, vol. i, pp. 23, 26; vol. iii, pp. 35, 44; *Chichester Chart.*, pp. 134, 271; East Suss. Record Office, Dunn MSS. 2/3, 2/4; *Feudal Aids*, vol. v, pp. 130, 131, 135, 165.

[161] *P. N. Suss.*, vol. ii, p. 559; *Suss. Custumals*, vol. iii, p. 56.

[162] *Surnames of Lancs.*, p. 153.

[163] *3 Suss. Subsidies*, pp. 61, 162, 276.

[164] *Suss. Subsidy*, *1524-5*, p. 78. And see p. 266.

[165] *3 Suss. Subsidies*, p. 68; *P. N. Suss.*, vol. i, p. 230. And see p. 245.

[166] Reaney, *Dict.*, p. 182; Cottle, *Dict.*, p. 187.

[167] See, e.g., *3 Suss. Subsidies*, pp. 12, 209, 215-6, 221, 295; *Robertsbridge Charters*, p. 50; *Hastings Lathe C.R.*, pp. 32, 53, 103-4, 114, 126, 130-31, 148, 150, 154-5, 177, 186, 205; *De Lisle and Dudley MSS.*, vol. i, pp. 89, 168.

[168] *Suss. Fines*, vol. ii, p. 160; *Battle Custumals*, p. 38; *3 Suss Subsidies*, pp. 30, 50, 67, 69, 103, 181-2, 203, 295; *Lewes Barony Recs.*, p. 4; East Sussex Record Office, Dunn MSS., 3/27; P.R.O., S.C. 11/877
[169] *3 Suss. Subsidies*, pp. 181, 295.
[170] *Suss. Subsidy, 1524-5*, p. 151.
[171] *Ibid.*, p. 160. On the Middle English pronunciation of Hope in Suss., see Rubin, *Suss. Phonology*, p. 68. See also *Hastings Lathe C.R.*, p. 146.
[172] See note 169.
[173] *Suss. Subsidy, 1524-5*, pp. 147, 156, 163.
[174] P.R.O. E. 179/225/50, m.29; East Suss. Record Office, Dunn MSS., 3/27; *Hastings Lathe C.R.*, p. 156.
[175] Reaney, *Dict.*, p. 214.
[176] *Suss. Custumals*, vol. iii, pp. 28, 34; Löfvenberg, *op. cit.*, p. 119; *P. N. Suss.*, vol. ii, p. 337; *Suss. Fines*, vol. ii, p. 71; *3 Suss. Subsidies*, pp. 35, 57, 190, 202, 302; *Hastings Lathe C.R.*, p. 27; *Suss. Subsidy, 1524-5*, p. 114; Lane, *Suss. Deeds*, p. 98; *S. A. C.*, vol. xcvi, p. 23; *Robertsbridge Charters*, p. 96; *Lewes Chartulary*, vol. ii, p. 134.
[177] *3 Suss. Subsidies*, p. 307; R. Garraway Rice, *op. cit.*, pp. 17, 25, 94, 99, 110, 120, 313, 329-30.
[178] Rubin, *op. cit.*, p. 177; Fransson, *op. cit.*, p. 199.
[179] Löfvenberg, *op. cit.*, pp. 117-8.
[180] *3 Suss. Subsidies*, pp. 79, 80, 138; *Lewes Chartulary*, vol. i, pp. 86, 87; *Non. Inquis.*, p. 380.
[181] *3 Suss. Subsidies*, pp. 96, 97, 123, 125; *S. A. C.*, vol. lxxxix, p. 122, 126; *Non. Inquis.*, p. 353; *Boxgrove Chart.*, pp. 32, 33, 68, 70, 76, 177, 178; and see p. 340.
[182] *S. A. C.*, vol. xxi, p. 46; vol. xcv, p. 50; *West Suss. 1641-2*, p. 33.
[183] *Suss. Subsidy, 1524-5*, pp. 25, 28, 30, 121. And see p. 340.
[184] Reaney, *Dict.*, p. 232.
[185] *3 Suss. Subsidies*, pp. 31, 101, 115, 120, 188, 239, 246; *S. A. C.*, vol. xx, p. 4.
[186] *Hastings Lathe C.R.*, pp. 119, 132; *3 Suss. Subsidies*, p. 120; *P. N. Suss.*, vol. i, p. 62.
[187] Reaney, *Dict.*, p. 270.
[188] *3 Suss. Subsidies*, pp. 56, 157; *S. A. C.*, vol. liii, p. 153.
[189] *Non. Inquis.*, p. 386; *S. A. C.*, vol. liv, pp. 156, 157, 175, 176, 177; West Suss. Record Office, Wiston MSS., 5233 (1); 5233 (2); 5234 (2); 5236 mm. 1, 3; 5237, m.5d; 5238.
[190] *Hastings Lathe C.R.*, pp. 6, 16, 28, 41, 129, 143; *Chichester Chart.*, pp. 248, 252; *Wiston Archives*, p. 84; *3 Suss. Subsidies*, pp. 18, 154, 207; *Suss. Custumals*, vol. i, p. 141.
[191] Reaney, *Dict.*, p. 292; Fransson, *op. cit.*, p. 179.
[192] Löfvenberg, *op. cit.*, pp. 162, 163. And see p. 195.

[193] S. A. C., vol. xlv, p. 174; vol. liii, p. 54; vol. xcv, p. 50. The form Rudere occurs, 14th cent., at Thakeham: P.R.O. E.179/189/42, m.9.
[194] Suss. Subsidy, 1524-5, pp. 4, 22, 37, 32, 116-7, 125; Valor Eccl., vol. i, p. 338; P.R.O. E.179/190/268, m.2.
[195] S. A. C., vol. xx, p. 4; Cowdray Archives, vol. i, pp. 5, 6; 3 Suss. Subsidies, pp. 116, 118.
[196] Chichester Chart., p. 165; 3 Suss. Subsidies, pp. 4, 27, 318, 324, 333; East Suss. Record Office, Glynde MSS., 1031; Hastings Lathe C.R., pp. 128, 193.
[197] S. A. C., vol. lxxvii, p. 256; vol. xcv, p. 49; 3 Suss. Subsidies, p. 43; Chichester Chart., p. 219.
[198] 3 Suss. Subsidies, p. 75; Chichester Chart., p. 247; S. A. C., vol. lxxxix, p. 131; De Lisle and Dudley MSS., vol. i, p. 4; Löfvenberg, op. cit., pp. 185-6. See also Fitzalan Surveys, p. 136; G. H. Kenyon, Glass Industry of the Weald, (1967), p. 31.
[199] Kenyon, op. cit., pp. 31, 115-7; J. F. Willard and H. C. Johnson, Surr. Taxation Returns (Surr. Rec. Soc., vol. xi, no. xviii), p. 9.
[200] Kenyon, op. cit., pp. 116-7; Fitzalan Surveys, p. 150.
[201] Suss. Subsidy, 1524-5, pp. 3, 13, 15, 26; see also R. Garraway Rice, op. cit., pp. 29, 31, 399; Suss. Wills, vol. ii, p. 267; vol. iii, p. 51; vol. iv, p. 337.
[202] W. Suss. 1641-2, pp. 72, 130, 163, 174, 183, 198.
[203] See p. 270; William Shottere, a 15th century Suss. cleric, is also referred to as William Shorter: C. Deedes, 'Extracts from the Episcopal Register of Richard Praty', in Miscellaneous Records (Suss. Rec. Soc., vol. iv) (1905), pp. 132, 192-4.
[204] 3 Suss. Subsidies, pp. 59, 65, 164, 274, 279; Suss. Custumals, vol. ii, p. 28.
[205] Löfvenberg, op. cit., p. 191; P. N. Suss., vol. i, p. 30.
[206] Feudal Aids, vol. v, p. 164.
[207] Suss. Subsidy, 1524-5, pp. 59, 62-3, 76, 86, 89, 99; Wiston Archives, pp. 38, 409; J. E. Ray, op. cit., pp. 25, 76, 83, 95, 142.
[208] Suss. Subsidy, 1524-5, pp. 128-9.
[209] J. E. Ray, op. cit., p. 76.
[210] Suss. Indictments, vol. i, pp. 77-78; R. Garraway Rice, op. cit., p. 117; Suss. Wills, vol. i, p. 11; P. S. Godman, op. cit., p. 25.
[211] Suss. Subsidy, 1524-5, pp. 60, 62, 67, 82; information on West Grinstead and Steyning parish registers from Mr. F. Leeson.
[212] Suss. Subsidy, 1524-5, p. 76; W. Suss. 1641-2, pp. 20, 23, 26, 36, 91, 98, 100, 101, 142, 153, 170, 176-7, 186.
[213] Suss. Custumals, vol. i, pp. 12, 24; Suss. Fines, vol. ii, p. 187; Chichester Chart., p. 177; Reaney, Dict., 330.
[214] Löfvenberg, op. cit., p. 196.
[215] S. A. C., vol. lxxxix, p. 162; Suss. Indictments, vol. i, pp. 2, 39, 50; Suss. Subsidy, 1524-5, pp. 55-7, 91.

[216] *W. Suss. 1641-2*, pp. 82, 185, 202; E. W. D. Penfold, *op. cit.*, pp. 19, 20, 22, 24, 30, 34, 54, 79, 83.

[217] *Suss. Indictments*, vol. i, pp. 14, 18; *Suss. Subsidy, 1524-5*, p. 155.

[218] *3 Suss. Subsidies*, p. 18; *Hastings Lathe C.R.*, p. 143; *Chichester Chart.*, p. 194.

[219] Reaney, *Dict.*, p. 386.

[220] Cottle, *Dict.*, p. 426; *Surnames of Lancs.*, pp. 108, 149-50.

[221] *3 Suss. Subsidies*, pp. 5, 212, 324; *Hastings Lathe C.R.*, p. 123; *S. A. C.*, vol. lxxiv, p. 71; Löfvenberg, *op. cit.*, p. 232.

[222] F. Hull, *Calendar of the White and Black Books of the Cinque Ports* (1966), pp. 55, 60, 68, 74, 75, 87; P.R.O. E.179/225/5; E.179/225/50, m.27. Some persons called atte Wyn were aliens: P.R.O. E.179/235/2. One of these was the servant of a Thomas Wynder. (*ibid.*). And see p. 9.

[223] F. Hull, *op. cit.*, pp. 72, 77; *Non. Inquis.*, pp. 372, 403; *S. A. C.*, vol. xcv, p. 57; *P. N. Suss.*, vol. ii, p. 533; *Robertsbridge Charters*, p. 145; P.R.O. E.179/235/2; *Hastings Lathe C.R.*, pp. 3, 7, 32, 150.

[224] *Suss. Subsidy, 1524-5*, pp. 111, 146; *Robertsbridge Surveys*, pp. 17, 19, 27, 63, 64.

[225] *3 Suss. Subsidies*, pp. 56, 57,142, 143, 157, 158, 236; *Wiston Archives*, pp. 142, 207; *Lewes Chartulary*, vol. i, pp. 100, 102; *Suss. Custumals*, vol. i, p. 87; Reaney, *Dict.*, p. 385; Rubin, *op. cit.*, p. 208; West Suss. Record Office, E.P. VI/19A/1, m.2; P.R.O. E.179/189/42, mm. 11, 25; *Fitzalan Surveys*, p. 135. On the form Wille, see A. H. Smith, *Place-Name Elements* (1970), vol. ii, p. 250.

[226] *Non. Inquis.*, p. 365; *S. A. C.*, vol. xxxii, pp. 6, 8; vol. lxxxix, p. 160; vol. xcv, p. 55; *3 Suss. Subsidies*, p. 68; Rubin, *op. cit.*, p. 55; *Fitzalan Surveys*, p. 29; P.R.O. E.179/189/42, m.25; *Hastings Lathe C.R.*, p. 67.

[227] *3 Suss. Subsidies*, pp. 62, 123, 162, 217, 218, 330; *Suss. Fines*, vol. i, p. 130; *Non. Inquis.*, p. 388; *Suss. Indictments*, vol. i, p. 2; *S. A. C.*, vol. li, p. 53; *Boxgrove Chart.*, p. 31; *De Lisle and Dudley MSS.*, vol. i, p. 14; *Robertsbridge Charters*, p. 75; Reaney, *Dict.*, p. 35; L. Fleming, *History of Pagham*, vol. i, pp. 57, 63, 87, xxxvii, lviii.

[228] Reaney, *Dict.*, p. 81; L. F. Salzman, *Cartulary of Sele*, pp. 23, 91, 94, 208; P. McClure 'Origin of the Surname Waterer', *Nomina* (1982), vol. vi, p. 92. And see p.149. See also *P. N. Suss.*, vol. ii, p. 483.

[229] Fransson, *op. cit.*, p. 203; see also Reaney, *Origins*, pp. 200-203.

[230] D. M. Stenton, *Great Roll of the Pipe for the 8th Year of King John* (Pipe Roll Soc., vol. viii) (1942), p. 63; A. M. Kirkus, *Great Roll of the Pipe for the 9th Year of John* (Pipe Roll Soc., vol. lx) (1946), p. 40.

[231] *3 Suss. Subsidies*, p. 304.

[232] *Ibid.*, p. 122; *P. N. Suss.*, vol. i, p. 54. See also Fransson, *op. cit.*, p. 203.

[233] Fransson, *op. cit.*, pp. 51, 55, 72-3, 116.

234 H. A. Hanley and C. W. Chalklin, "Kent Lay Subsidy of 1334/5", in *Documents Illustrative of Medieval Kentish Society* (Kent Archaeological Soc., vol. xviii) (1964), ed. F. R. H. Du Boulay, *passim*.
235 Anon., *Surrey Taxation Returns* (Surr. Record Society, vol. xi) (1922, 1932), pp. 1-94.
236 Fransson, *op. cit.*, pp. 204-7.
237 Based on an index to the returns for the 1523 subsidy, in the Essex County Record Office.
238 Fransson, *op. cit.*, pp. 203-8; G. Redmonds, *Yorks: West Riding*, pp. 50-52; *Surnames of Lancs.*, pp. 151-2; Reaney, *Origins*, p. 201.
239 Redmonds, *op. cit.*, pp. 50-52, 143-4.
240 *Ibid.*; *Surnames of Lancs.*, pp. 151-2.
241 Lane, *Suss. Deeds*, p. 132; *Suss. Indictments*, vol. i, p. 76; *W. Suss. 1641-2*, p. 141; E. A. Fry, *Calendar of Wills in the Consistory Court of the Bishop of Chichester* (1968), p. 74; R. Garraway Rice, *Parish Register of Horsham* (Suss. Rec. Soc., vol. xxi) (1915), pp. 5, 67, 71; Reaney, *Dict.*, p. 71; P.R.O. E.179/191/378, m.3.
242 See p. 158.
243 *3 Suss. Subsidies*, pp. 23, 29, 30, 43, 44, 192-3, 269, 303-5; *Battle Custumals*, pp. 32, 36.
244 *3 Suss. Subsidies*, pp. 73, 151, 269; Rubin, *op. cit.*, p. 161.
245 *Suss. Subsidy, 1524-5*, pp. 19, 41; *Valor Eccl.*, vol. i, p. 314; *Wiston Archives*, pp. 29, 70, 145; *S. A. C.*, vol. xxiv, p. 82; J. E. Ray, *op. cit.*, p. 198; *W. Suss. 1641-2*, pp. 56, 98, 100, 101, 102, 109, 112, 124, 138, 144-5, 164, 174, 184, 196; P.R.O. E.179/191/377, roll 6; E.179/191/410, part i, m.3d, part 2, m.11d, part 4, mm. 1, 6, 7; E.179/258/14, mm. 1d, 28d, 37; West Suss. Record Office, E.P. VI/19A/1, m.9; R. Garraway Rice, *op. cit.*, pp. 41, 44, 238, 242, 264; *Suss. Wills*, vol. iv, p. 378.
246 Reaney, *Dict.*, p. 216.
247 *3 Suss. Subsidies*, pp. 189-91; *Hastings Lathe C.R.*, pp. 10, 12, 127; Inderwick, *Winchelsea*, p. 161.
248 *P. N. Suss.*, vol. ii, p. 480; Inderwick, *Winchelsea*, p. 163; Reaney, *Dict.*, p. 279; Anon., "Inquisitions Post Mortem", *Archaelogica Cantiana*, vol. iii, p. 246. Pote also occurs as a first name in Sussex: Inderwick, *op. cit.*, p. 167.
249 *3 Suss. Subsidies*, pp. 210, 322.
250 *P. N. Suss.*, vol. i, p. 187; *Chichester Chart.*, pp. 104, 375; *3 Suss. Subsidies*, pp. 65, 147, 199, 256, 260; *Boxgrove Chart.*, pp. 116, 159, 164, 179, 193; *Wiston Archives*, pp. 37, 195; *Fitzalan Surveys*, pp. 120, 157, 164, 166; *V. C. H. Suss.*, vol. iv, pp. 104, 105; C. Robinson, *Great Roll of the Pipe for the 14th Year of Henry III* (Pipe Roll Soc. vol. xlii) (1927), p. 244.
251 Löfvenberg, *op. cit.*, p. 156.

[252] *3 Suss. Subsidies*, pp. 16, 22, 190, 203, 209-11, 314, 322; *S. A. C.*, vol. xcv, p. 46; *Non. Inquis.*, p. 373.

[253] *Suss. Subsidy, 1524-5*, pp. 119, 140, 162; Lane, *Suss. Deeds*, pp. 91, 104; F. Hull, *Calendar of the White and Black Books of the Cinque Ports*, pp. 75, 86; *Hastings Lathe C.R.*, pp. 35, 61, 125-6, 172; *S. A. C.*, vol. xviii, p. 28; vol. xxii, p. 121; vol. cvi, p. 99; *Valor Eccl.*, vol. i, pp. 333, 355; P.R.O. E.179/225/50, m.26; E.179/228/112; *Feudal Aids*, vol. v, pp. 149, 166; *Suss. Fines*, vol. iii, p. 42.

[254] *Chichester Chart.*, p. 199; *P. N. Suss.*, vol. ii, p. 486; *Hastings Lathe C.R.*, p. 154.

[255] *3 Suss. Subsidies*, pp. 221, 248. John Westres (1524) may have had a name formed from Westre with an inorganic 'S', in which case Westre may have become hereditary: *Suss. Subsidy, 1524-5*, p. 51.

[256] *3 Suss. Subsidies*, pp. 90, 95-7, 103-4, 110, 113, 115, 120-2, 124, 126-9, 130, 133, 135, 138, 141, 143, 232, 237, 244, 247-8, 250-3, 255-6, 264-6; L. Fleming, *History of Pagham*, vol. i, pp. 57, 63, xxxix, xliii; *Non. Inquis.*, pp. 351, 357, 359; *Hastings Lathe C.R.*, pp. 29, 33; *Boxgrove Chart.*, pp. 186-7; *Chichester Chart.*, p. 365; *Suss. Custumals*, vol. i, p. 35; vol. ii, pp. 13, 14, 16.

[257] *3 Suss. Subsidies*, pp. 113, 115, 337; *Non. Inquis.*, p. 387; *Suss. Custumals*, vol. i, p. 89; *Lewes Barony Recs.*, pp. 12, 18, 21; P.R.O. E.179/189/42, m.2d; *V. C. H. Suss.*, vol. vii, p. 20.

[258] *S. A. C.*, vol. xviii, p. 25; *Chichester Chart.*, pp. 203, 296-7; *Hastings Lathe C.R.*, pp. 29, 33; J. E. Ray, *op. cit.*, p. 165; Fleming, *op. cit.*, vol. i, p. 131; *Suss. Subsidy, 1524-5*, pp. 3, 9-10, 12, 16, 23, 25, 26, 32, 36-7, 42, 47, 52, 54, 56, 86-7, 90, 96-7, 100, 116-17, 124, 134, 158.

[259] See below, p. 186.

[260] *3 Suss. Subsidies*, pp. 33, 50, 183, 196, 229, 297; Lane, *Suss. Deeds*, p. 51; *Lewes Chartulary*, vol. i, pp. 103, 112-3, 129; *Valor Eccl.*, vol. i, p. 331; *Suss. Custumals*, vol. i, p. 87; *S. A. C.*, vol. xviii, pp. 27, 50; vol. xxi, p. 188; *Suss. Subsidy, 1524-5*, pp. 96, 99, 126-7, 136; P.R.O. E.179/258/15, m.9; E.179/258/18; East Suss. Record Office, Glynde, MSS., 1032, m.2; *Feudal Aids*, vol. v, p. 165; *Suss. Wills*, vol. ii, p. 194; vol. iii, pp. 7, 59.

[261] *3 Suss. Subsidies*, pp. 38, 309; *Suss. Fines*, vol. i, p. 99; East Suss. Record Office, Glynde, MSS, 1031; Löfvenberg, *op. cit.*, p. 68; *P. N. Suss.*, vol. ii, p. 353; *Suss. Custumals*, vol. ii, p. 103.

[262] *3 Suss. Subsidies*, pp. 210, 322; Inderwick, *Winchelsea*, p. 212.

[263] *3 Suss. Subsidies*, pp. 25, 181, 200, 201, 311; *Hastings Lathe C.R.*, p. 161; *S. A. C.*, vol. cix, pp. 97, 98, 100; Löfvenberg, *op. cit.*, pp. 205-6; East Suss. Record Office, Glynde MSS. 998, mm. 1, 10, 10d. The bye-name Soundere, found at South Malling, 1397 (*S. A. C.*, vol. xxi, p. 188) may have been formed from atte Sounde.

[264] *Lewes Chartulary*, vol. ii, p. 107; *3 Suss. Subsidies*, p. 104; *V. C. H.*

Suss., vol. vii, 203; S. A. C., vol. vii, p. 100; Suss. Subsidy, 1524-5, p. 142; F. Hull, op. cit., p. 205.

[265] 3 Suss. Subsidies, pp. 11, 61, 75, 147, 176, 180, 262, 269, 294; Abbrevatio Placitorum (Record Commission), p. 191; P. N. Suss., vol. i, p. 157; Wiston Archives, pp. 33, 144, 146-7; Suss. Fines, vol. ii, p. 183; S. A. C., vol. xxii, p. 154; vol. lvii, p. 192; De Lisle and Dudley MSS., vol. i, pp. 2, 3; Chichester Chart., pp. 213, 227, 258; Suss. Custumals, vol. i, pp. 55, 68; J. E. Ray, op. cit., pp. 22, 26, 69; Non. Inquis., p. 387; Suss. Subsidy, 1524-5, p. 48; W. Suss. 1641-2, pp. 30, 85, 91, 138, 145-7, 159, 187; P.R.O. E.179/191/378, m.3; West Sussex Record Office, E.P. VI/19A/1, mm. 5, 15; Fitzalan Surveys, pp. 107, 131; Suss. Wills, vol. iv, p. 36.

[266] Löfvenberg, op. cit., p. 1; P. N. Suss., vol. i, pp. 135, 157, 264; E. Straker, Buckhurst Terrier (Suss. Record Soc., vol. xxxix) (1934) p. 36.

[267] Suss. Custumals, vol. ii, p. 70; 3 Suss. Subsidies, pp. 33, 40, 178, 207, 219; Hastings Lathe C.R., pp. 12, 206; Lewes Barony Recs., pp. 28, 68; S. A. C., vol. xii, p. 25; Robertsbridge Charters, p. 121; Battle Custumals, pp. 38-9. William de la Hese occurs as a chantry priest at Pagham on the coast, but clerics were liable to move wherever they could find benefices, and William seems to have been linked with Salehurst, in north-east Sussex: L. Fleming, History of Pagham, vol. i, p. 87.

[268] 3 Suss. Subsidies, pp. 28, 31, 40, 146, 167, 188, 197, 204, 281, 300, 310, 315, 319; Hastings Lathe C.R., pp. 4, 14; Wiston Archives, pp. 33, 288; Robertsbridge Charters, p. 132; S. A. C., vol. lxxxiv, p. 76; Non. Inquis., pp. 356, 372; Suss. Custumals, vol. i, p. 120; vol. ii, pp. 49, 61, 73; Chichester Chart., pp.162-3, 269, 352; P.R.O. E.179/225/5; S.C. 11/877; Suss. Fines, vol. iii, p. 180.

[269] 3 Suss. Subsidies, pp. 60, 75, 101, 150, 262; Suss. Fines, vol. ii, pp. 14, 27; S. A. C., vol. xx, p. 4; vol. xxxvi, p. 33; vol. lxix, pp. 113-5; Suss. Custumals, vol. i, p. 55; J. E. Ray, op. cit., p. 159; Wiston Archives, p. 170; Suss. Subsidy, 1524-5, pp. 9, 47, 77, 80; W. Suss. 1641-2, pp. 21, 39, 49, 51, 56, 59, 73-5, 80, 83, 85, 90, 95, 126, 158, 180; P.R.O. E.179/191/378, m.2d; West Sussex Record Office, EP. VI/19A/1, m.5; Fitzalan Surveys, p.iii; Suss. Wills, vol. ii, pp. 97, 159; vol. iii, p. 219.

[270] Wiston Archives, pp. 195, 217; Non. Inquis., pp. 367, 388; S. A. C., vol. li, p. 46; 3 Suss. Subsidies, pp. 29, 129, 146, 156, 158, 259, 269, 271, 272, 274; Chichester Chart., pp. 36, 96, 141, 143, 344; De Lisle and Dudley MSS., vol. i, p. 24; West Suss. Record Office, EP. VI/19A/1, m.4; Suss. Fines, vol. iii, pp. 46, 120, 121; Calendar of Inquisitions Post Mortem, vol. viii, pp. 50-1.

[271] Lewes Chartulary, vol. i, pp. 57, 66; C. T. Clay, Early Yorks. Charters (1949), vol viii, p. 3.

[272] *Suss. Subsidy, 1524-5*, pp. 36, 42, 46, 50, 55, 64; *W. Suss. 1641-2*, pp. 40, 47, 50, 83, 104, 110, 129-30, 138-9, 149, 159, 165, 170, 175, 180, 186, 190; *S. A. C.*, vol. xli, p. 139; *Chichester Chart.*, p. 212; J. E. Ray, *op. cit.*, p. 37; Lord Leconfield, *Petworth Manor in the 17th Century* (1954), pp. 14, 79, 83; C. R. Davey, *Hants. Lay Subsidy Roll, 1586*, pp.92, 128; P.R.O. E.179/191/378, m.1d; W. C. Renshaw, *Parish Registers of Cuckfield* (Suss. Rec. Soc., vol. xiii) (1911), pp. 39, 112; R. Garraway Rice, *Parish Register of Horsham* (Suss. Rec. Soc., vol. xxi) (1915), pp. 22, 41, 234, 240, 381; Reaney, *Dict.*, p. 31; *Suss. Custumals*, vol. ii, pp. 5, 9; *Suss. Fines*, vol. iii, p. 147; *Fitzalan Surveys*, pp. 115, 148; *Suss. Wills*, vol. i, p. 227; vol. iii, p. 245.

[273] *S. A. C.*, vol. xcv, p. 46; *3 Suss. Subsidies*, pp. 62, 162, 217, 218; *De Lisle and Dudley MSS.*, vol. i, pp. 4, 5, 114; *Robertsbridge Charters*, p. 75; Reaney, *Dict.*, p. 35; *Suss. Indictments*, vol. i, p. 2.

[274] *Suss. Subsidy, 1524-5*, pp. 78, 147-9; *P. N. Suss.*, vol. i, p. 185.

[275] Löfvenberg, *op. cit.*, pp. 45-6. On some Wilts. manors, 13th cent., a *cotsetlum* was a type of customary holding; *Somerset Rec. Soc.*, vol. v, pp. 59, 137, 142-5.

[276] *Lewes Chartulary*, vol. ii, p. 62; *Suss. Fines*, vol. ii, p. 182; vol. iii, p. 264; *S. A. C.*, vol. ii, p. 321; vol. lviii, pp. 18, 19; *3 Suss. Subsidies*, pp.47, 178, 292; *Wiston Archives*, pp. 37, 203, 206, 278-80; *Suss. Indictments*, pp. 2, 3, 34; *Suss. Subsidy, 1524-5*, pp. 89, 90; *P. N. Suss.*, vol. ii, p.341; W. C. Renshaw, *op. cit.*, pp. 102, 104.

[277] *Hastings Lathe C.R.*, pp. 24, 141; *S. A. C.*, vol. xxv, p. 130; vol. xlv, p. 166; *Suss. Subsidy, 1524-5*, pp. 102, 104-5, 113; *Cowdray Archives*, vol. i, p. 110; W. C. Renshaw, *op. cit.*, pp. 9, 49, 53, 93, 97, 128, 178, 180, 183; *Suss. Wills*, vol. iv, pp. 331, 349; however, it is possible that Eightacre is from a Kent place-name: John de Eartakere, whose name was probably from Hardacre (in Preston Hundred, Kent), occurs in Kent, 1334-5 (Hanley and Chalklin, *op. cit.*, p. 84).

[278] *Suss. Subsidy, 1524-5*, pp. 103-4, 109, 127, 131-2; *S. A. C.*, vol. lviii, pp. 7, 20, 91; H. M. C., *Rye MSS.*, pp. 24, 28; *3 Suss. Subsidies*, p. 294; *W. Suss. 1641-2*, p. 67; G. W. E Loder, *Parish Registers of Ardingly* (Suss. Rec. Soc., vol. xvii) (1913), *per indice*, under Verall; R. Garraway Rice, *Parish Register of Horsham* (Suss. Rec. Soc., vol. xxi) (1915), pp. 32, 45, 274, 278; W. C. Renshaw, *op. cit.*, pp. 58, 61, 64, and *passim*; Löfvenberg, *op. cit.*, p. 60; *Suss. Wills*, vol. ii, pp. 81, 105, 181; *Suss. Fines*, vol. iii, pp. 258, 302.

[279] L. Fleming, *History of Pagham*, vol. i, p. xxxvi, p. 26; *3 Suss. Subsidies*, p. 122.

[280] *Ibid.*, pp. 83, 113.

[281] *Ibid.*, pp. 186, 315; *Non. Inquis.*, p. 376.

[282] Löfvenberg, *op. cit.*, p. 62; It has been suggested that Fennell has developed from Fitzneal (Erlebach, *op. cit.*, p. 91), but no evidence has been found for this.

[283] S. A. C., vol. xviii, p. 29; *Chichester Chart.*, pp. 250, 252; Lane, *Suss. Deeds*, pp. 25, 54, 91, 98, 105; *Suss. Fines*, vol. iii, p. 285.

[284] *Wiston Archives*, p. 6; Lane, *Suss. Deeds*, pp. 25, 91.

[285] *Suss. Subsidy, 1524-5*, pp. 109, 110, 112, 114-6, 124, 126, 152, 155; S. A. C., vol. xlv, pp. 164-7, 171, 176-8; *Suss. Wills*, vol. ii, pp. 18, 104, 105; vol. iii, p. 127; vol. iv, p. 431; F. Hull, *op. cit.*, pp. 143, 360.

[286] *Suss. Indictments*, vol. i, p. 64; J. E. Ray, *op. cit.*, p. 102; W. C. Renshaw, *op. cit.*, p. 134; R. Garraway Rice, *op. cit.*, p. 232; Reaney, *Dict.*, p. 136; Reaney, *Origins*, p. 60; *Suss. Wills*, vol. ii, p. 18; vol. iv, p. 431.

[287] *3 Suss. Subsidies*, p. 163; Lane, *Suss. Deeds*, p. 2; *Suss. Subsidy, 1524-5*, p. 31; *W. Suss. 1641-2*, pp. 36, 150.

[288] *3 Suss. Subsidies*, pp. 17, 122, 164, 318; S. A. C., vol. lxxxiv, 62; *De Lisle and Dudley MSS.*, vol. i, pp. 117, 119; E. Searle, *Lordship and Community* (1974), p. 162; *Rotuli Hundredorum* (Record Commission), vol. ii, p. 211.

[289] The form atte Haye is found in other counties: Löfvenberg, *op. cit.*, p. 87. See also L. C. Loyd, *Origin of Some Anglo-Norman Families*, (Harleian Soc., vol. ciii) (1951), p. 51.

[290] *3 Suss. Subsidies*, pp. 13, 17, 20, 23, 28, 50, 54, 58, 101, 117, 184, 201, 206, 318, 329; S. A. C., vol. xx, p. 11; vol. xlix, p.4; vol. lxxxix, p. 127; vol. xcv, p. 51; Inderwick, *Winchelsea*, p. 192; *Suss. Fines*, vol. i, p. 78; vol. ii, p. 150; L. Fleming, *History of Pagham*, vol. i, p. xxxix; *Lewes Chartulary*, vol. i, pp. 137-8; vol. ii, pp. 9, 11; *Suss. Custumals*, vol. i, p. 78; *Chichester Chart.*, pp. 88, 194, 247, 362; *Hastings Lathe C.R.*, pp. 10-12, 127.

[291] Löfvenberg, *op. cit.*, pp. 95, 100.

[292] *3 Suss. Subsidies*, pp. 89, 131, 247; *Chichester Chart.*, p. 247, 288; *Non. Inquis.*, pp. 357, 366; *Suss. Subsidy, 1524-5*, pp. 4, 32; *Suss. Wills*, vol. i, p. 369.

[293] Löfvenberg, *op. cit.*, 107.

[294] *Suss. Fines*, vol. iii, pp. 83. 159, 280; *3 Suss. Subsidies*, pp. 273, 326; *Chichester Chart.*, pp. 250, 358; *P. N. Suss.*, vol. i, p. 187; The place-name Hound (Hants.) seems unlikely to be the origin of de Hony in Suss., though it is possible.

[295] *3 Suss. Subsidies*, pp. 13, 183, 237.

[296] Reaney, *Dict.*, p. 181.

[297] Reaney, *Dict.*, p. 187.

[298] *Ibid.*, p. 181; *Suss. Subsidy, 1524-5*, pp. 16, 78; *3 Suss. Subsidies*, pp. 297, 308; *Fitzalan Surveys*, pp. 163, 165; *Suss. Wills*, vol. iv, p. 316.

[299] H. G. Richardson, *English Jewry under the Angevin Kings*, (1960), p. 15; *Chichester Chart.*, pp. 100, 101; J. M. Rigg, *Select Pleas, Starrs, and other Records* (Selden Soc., vol. xx) (1902), p. 69.

[300] *Wiston Archives*, p. 83.
[301] *W. Suss. 1641-2*, pp. 9, 81, 98, 125-27.
[302] *Hastings Lathe C.R.*, p. 128; *S. A. C.*, vol. xlv, p. 163; *Catalogue of Ancient Deeds*, vol. vi, p. 153; P.R.O. E.179/225/50, mm. 21, 26; E.179/228/112; *Suss. Subsidy, 1524-5*, pp. 66; *Feudal Aids*, vol. v, p. 149; *Suss. Fines*, vol. iii, p. 212.
[303] Reaney, *Dict.*, p. 119; *S. A. C.*, vol. xii, p. 31; vol. xviii, p. 24; vol. liv, p. 178; *3 Suss. Subsidies*, p. 156; West Suss. Record Office, EP. VI/19A/1, mm. 10, 11, 11d; Wiston MSS., 5237, m.5; 5233 (2); 5241, mm. 1,2.
[304] *3 Suss. Subsidies*, pp. 165, 168; see also *Battle Custumals*, p. 42; P.R.O. E.179/189/42, mm. 2, 2d.
[305] Löfvenberg, *op. cit.*, pp. 162-63, 167-68.
[306] *Suss. Fines*, vol. ii, p. 178; *S. A. C.*, vol. vi, p. 220; *3 Suss. Subsidies*, pp. 102, 197, 309.
[307] *Ibid.*, pp. 117, 241; *S. A. C.*, vol. lxix, pp. 114-5.
[308] *Ibid.*, vol. lxix, p. 115; *Lewes Chartulary*, vol. i, pp. 129, 130; vol. ii, p. 115; *Robertsbridge Surveys*, p. 49; *V. C. H. Suss.*, vol. iv, p. 56; *Suss. Custumals*, vol. i, p. 99; vol. ii, p. 124; vol. iii, p. 24. The last instance refers to an area of reed beds.
[309] *3 Suss. Subsidies*, pp. 53, 54, 116, 118, 132, 139, 239, 241, 248, 260, 272; *Chichester Chart.*, p. 204; *S. A. C.*, vol. xx, p. 4; vol. lxxix, p. 120; *Suss. Custumals*, vol. i, pp. 3, 12; *Cowdray Archives*, vol. i. p. 5; P.R.O. E.179/189/42, m.2d; *Lewes Chartulary*, vol. ii, p. 84.
[310] *Chichester Chart.*, p. 165; *Suss. Fines*, vol. ii, p. 52.
[311] *Cowdray Archives*, vol. i, p. 6; *Boxgrove Chart.*, pp. 34, 95, 161; *V. C. H. Suss.*, vol. iv, 56; *Suss. Custumals*, vol. iii, pp. 55, 74.
[312] Löfvenberg, *op. cit.*, p. 163.
[313] *S. A. C.*, vol. xlv, p. 168; *Suss. Subsidy, 1524-5*, p. 48.
[314] *S. A. C.*, vol. li, p. 62; *Chichester Chart.*, pp. 18, 83, 159; *Suss. Fines*, vol. ii, p. 26; *3 Suss. Subsidies*, p. 110.
[315] *Suss. Subsidy, 1524-5*, p. 65; R. Garraway Rice, *op. cit.*, p. 9.
[316] Löfvenberg, *op. cit.*, p. 180.
[317] *Suss. Fines*, vol. i, pp. 96-7. 116.
[318] Löfvenberg, *op. cit.*, pp. 206-7; *3 Suss. Subsidies*, pp. 80, 136-7, 256; *Non. Inquis.*, p. 368; *Chichester Chart.*, p. 206; *S. A. C.*, vol. lxxxix, p. 160; vol. xcv, p. 48; *Boxgrove Chart.*, pp. 78, 88,193; West Suss. Record Office, EP. VI/19A/1, m.10d; *Fitzalan Surveys*, p. 109.
[319] *3 Suss. Subsidies*, p. 28; *Hastings Lathe C.R.*, pp. 91, 127, 184; *Lewes Barony Recs.*, p. 68; E. Straker, *Buckhurst Terrier* (Suss. Rec. Soc., vol. xxxix) (1934), p. 63; *Suss. Subsidy, 1524-5*, p. 138; P.R.O. S.C.11/877.
[320] *Suss. Fines*, vol. iii, p. 9; W. Bolland, *Year Books of Edward II: 8 Edward II* (Selden Soc., vol. xxxvii) (1920), p.209; *Wiston Archives*,

p. 34; *Suss. Custumals*, vol. i, p. 68; *3 Suss. Subsidies*, pp. 65, 147, 160, 260-61, 273; *Chichester Chart.*, p. 235; *Suss. Subsidy, 1524-5*, p. 39; *P. N. Suss.*, vol. i, p. 160.

[321] W. F. Carter. *Lay Subsidy Roll for Warws.* (Dugdale Soc., vol. vi) (1926), pp. 22, 34, 35, 39; Löfvenberg, *op. cit.*, p. 214; *3 Suss. Subsidies*, p. 122; L. Fleming, *History of Pagham*, vol. i, pp. xl, 131; *P. N. Suss.*, vol. i, p. 54; Hanley and Chalklin, *op. cit.*, pp. 96, 110, 130; *Wiston Archives*, p. 209; Reaney, *Dict.*, p. 354; *Suss. Custumals*, vol. iii, p. 57.

[322] *S. A. C.*, vol. liv, pp. 89, 94, 96.

[323] *Suss. Subsidy, 1524-5*, pp. 90, 102, 132; *S. A. C.*, vol. lviii, p. 16; vol. xcv, p. 56; *Suss. Indictments*, vol. i, p. 9; W. C. Renshaw, *op. cit.*, pp. 4, 17, 99, 120, 204; R. Garraway Rice, *op. cit.*, pp. 5, 9; G. W. E. Loder, *Parish Registers of Ardingly*, (Suss. Rec. Soc., vol. xvii) (1913), p. 136; *Suss. Wills*, vol. ii, p. 81; vol. iii, p. 21.

[324] *Suss. Indictments*, vol. i, pp. 9, 40, 76.

[325] *Suss. Fines*, vol. i, p. 37; *Suss. Subsidy, 1524-5*, pp. 15, 20, 44, 57; *W. Suss. 1641-2*, pp. 19, 21; *V. C. H. Suss.*, vol. iv, p. 136.

[326] *S. A. C.*, vol. liv, pp. 157-8; West Suss. Record Office, Wiston MSS., 5235; 5236, mm. 1d, 2, 3; 5237, mm. 1, 1d, 2, 5; 5238; 5241, m.1; EP. VI/19A/1, mm 9d, 10, 11, 12.

[327] *Suss. Subsidy, 1524-5*, p. 43; J. E. Ray, *op. cit.*, p. 177; P.R.O. E.179/189/42, m.22; West Sussex Record Office, EP. VI/19A/1, mm. 9, 10, 11d, 12. As to at Herrys, a croft called the Herrye existed at Whatlington (distant from Amberley) in 1567: *Robertsbridge Surveys*, p. 132. Herry, or Harry, was a surname at Amberley in the 14th and 15th centuries: West Sussex Record Office, EP. VI/19A/1, mm. 6, 8d, 9, 10, 11d, 15d.

[328] *3 Suss. Subsidies*, pp. 150, 294; *S. A. C.*, vol. lxxxii, p. 134; *Suss. Subsidy, 1524-5*, p. 100; West Sussex Record Office, Wiston MSS., 5233 (1); 5236, mm. 1d, 3.

[329] Löfvenberg, *op. cit.*, p. 192; *3 Suss. Subsidies*, pp.198, 204, 308; *Suss. Indictments*, vol. i, p. 2; *S. A. C.*, vol. xcv, p. 47; *Suss. Fines*, vol. iii, p. 186.

[330] On these surnames, see pp. 318–324.

[331] *W. Suss. 1641-2*, pp. 126, 165; *3 Suss. Subsidies*, p. 150

[332] *Robertsbridge Surveys*, pp. 31, 49; *Robertsbridge Charters*, p. 143; *De Lisle and Dudley MSS.*, vol. i, p. 151. And see p. 195.

[333] Löfvenberg, *op. cit.*, p. 55; *S. A. C.*, vol. xxxv, pp. 33-35, 47; vol. lxxxiv, p. 74; vol. xlvi, p. 179; vol. liv, p. 159; P.R.O. E.179/189/42, mm. 4, 4d; *Lewes Barony Records*, p. 46.

[334] *Suss. Subsidy, 1524-5*, pp. 103, 131.

[335] *3 Suss. Subsidies*, p. 265.

[336] *Ibid.*, p. 164, 279.

[337] E.g., Amfred de Dene, or de Denne, or de Dane, and Walter de Dene, or de Denne; *Robertsbridge Charters*, pp. 10, 14, 29, 34, 54; *De Lisle and Dudley MSS.*, vol. i, pp. 44, 59.

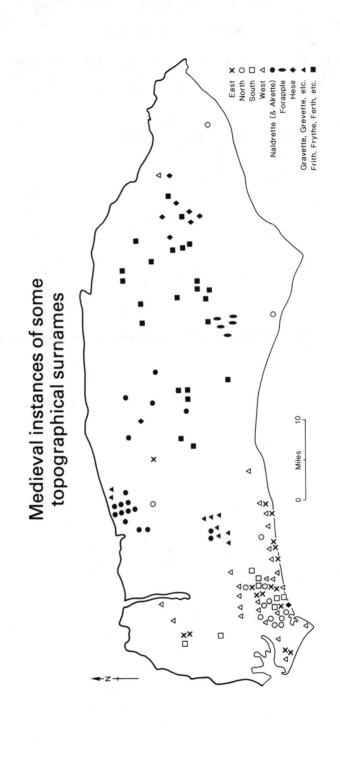

CHAPTER 4

SURNAMES DERIVED FROM OCCUPATION,
STATUS, OR OFFICE

It is in practice very difficult to draw a clear distinction between surnames derived from occupation, and those derived from office or status. It is not usually possible to discover the precise circumstances in which any surname arose, and it is difficult to formulate any logical set of rules for dividing occupational surnames from those derived from office; a name such as, for instance, Bailey might be considered as one derived from an office, but it might also be thought to be an occupational name. There is the further complication that some surnames derived from high ranks in state or church, King, Bishop, Earl, and so forth, seem to have originated as nicknames, a point discussed further below. It has, therefore, seemed best to treat all surnames from occupations, ranks, offices, or status together, without attempting to subdivide them. The whole category of surnames derived from occupation, rank, status, or office will be referred to as occupational names.

In medieval sources for Sussex, occupational surnames form about 18 to 20% of the whole body of surnames appearing. The figure for the 1327 Sussex lay subsidy is 19%, and for the Sussex 1332 lay subsidy 18%.[1] These figures are much the same as those for subsidy rolls of about the same date for most other English counties. The corresponding figures for most counties in the Midlands are rather higher, and those for most northern counties rather less, but in general there are no very marked differences between the various English regions in the proportion of surnames which are occupational ones.[2] A few counties, like Lancashire, for instance, have a lower proportion of occupational names, but this is exceptional. Subsidy rolls have defects as sources of information on surnames. In particular, the names of the poorer sections of the community are not given. However, an examination of a great variety of source material for medieval Sussex has not produced any evidence to indicate that the proportion of occupational names among the county's population as a whole was significantly different from that among the taxpayers listed in the subsidy rolls.

Some of the more common occupational surnames were already numerous and widespread in Sussex as early as the 13th century. Names such as Baker, Chapman, Carpenter, Cook, Cooper, Gardener, Smith, Taillor, and Tanner were already to be found in large numbers in the county before 1300. The distribution of some common occupational surnames, including those just mentioned, in the whole body of 13th century sources for Sussex, and in the early subsidy rolls for the county, such as those for 1296, 1327, and 1332,[3] is so scattered that there can be no possibility of any of the names in question having arisen in the county as the surname of a single family. Many common occupational names were in the 13th century already dispersed in most parts of the county, and had obviously arisen independently in many separate places. It is impossible to be certain if this situation already existed in the 12th century, as the sources for that period are not full enough to enable the distribution of surnames or bye-names to be accurately assessed. There is the further impediment that in 12th century sources occupational surnames or bye-names are very often translated from the vernacular into Latin, and it is difficult to be sure what vernacular forms are being translated by the Latin words found in the sources. To give one example, the Latin word *molendinarius* has the literal meaning of 'miller', but it is usually impossible to tell whether it is being used to translate the name Miller, or one of the other names which have the same significance, such as Milward or Milner, or some rare name such as Millgroom (which occurs in Sussex).[4] In any case, during the 12th century much of the population was probably without surnames or bye-names of any kind. It seems probable that from the period when surnames or bye-names first began to be at all general, some common occupational names were widely distributed, and were from the start the names of many separate families.

Some occupational surnames such as Smith, Baker, Taillor, and so forth are well known at the present day for being very numerous, and for occurring in all parts of England. This, however, tends to conceal the fact that some common occupational surnames were not evenly distributed over the whole country. Many such names were much more numerous (proportionately to the whole population) in some counties than in others. In the case of many surnames, this can be observed as early as the 13th century. In many instances, too, the main characteristics of the distribution detectable at that early period survived for centuries, sometimes until after 1800. This persistence is not surprising, for many features of surname distribution in England have tended to continue little changed for centuries. It has been pointed out elsewhere, in connection with Lancashire surnames, that Taylor, one of the most common occupational surnames taking England as a whole, was for long much more numerous, in proportion to total population, in Lancashire than in many other counties (one of which is Sussex). This was already true in the 14th century, and it was still true in the 16th and 17th.[5] The distribution of many other familiar occupational names was similarly uneven. This can best be seen by examining the occurrences of surnames in the lay subsidy rolls. One difficulty about using subsidy rolls for this purpose is that they do not list the poorer section of the population. This is a considerable disadvantage, because there are grounds for believing that in the 13th and 14th centuries there were substantial differences between the types of surnames used by the various social classes. There is a further difficulty that in subsidy rolls of the period under consideration here, occupational surnames or bye-names are often given in a Latin form.[6]

In the table following (Table I), the evidence from some late 13th and 14th century subsidy rolls is set out. The subsidy rolls are for a selection of counties, in various regions of England.[7] Some of the sources used are not complete for entire counties. The figures given are for the number of individuals with each of the occupational surnames (or bye-names) in the table, *per* thousand persons listed in each of the sources tabulated. Latin forms have been included in the figures in cases where there is no serious doubt concerning what vernacular name is represented by any particular Latin form. Where there is any serious doubt, the Latin forms have not been counted in the figures given in the table.

It is clear from the figures given in the table that some common occupational surnames occurred much more frequently in some counties than in others. Smith is notorious, out of all the occupational surnames found in England, for being extremely common. Many years ago H. B. Guppy, basing his findings on late 19th century directories, pointed out that Smith was very much more common, proportionately, in some parts of the country than in others.[20] The table shows that in the case of Smith, there was already much variation in the frequency of the name by the 14th century. Smith was then nearly three times as common in Oxfordshire as it was in Sussex, though the two counties are not particularly far apart. Differences on the same scale can be seen in the distribution of other very common occupational names, such as Baker or Taylor.

Though some of the names in the table occur much more frequently than others, none of them is sufficiently rare for it to be likely that it could be seriously affected by the proliferation of merely one or two families. Where very uncommon surnames are concerned, the consequence of one family ramifying considerably in one county could be that a rare name would become much more common in one area than elsewhere. Where more numerous surnames are concerned, however, the effect of a single family expanding would be much less marked. It is possible for individual families to proliferate, over a long period, to such a degree that names which were originally scarce become quite numerous in one part of the country. It seems certain, however, that each of the surnames listed in the table originated with a fair number of separate families. They were all too dispersed at an early period for any other explanation to be feasible. The distribution of the names shown in the table has been influenced by other causes. One factor is that occupational surnames form a much higher proportion of the whole body of surnames in use in some counties than in others. The fact that many occupational surnames, common in England as

Table 1. *Individuals bearing each of a selection of occupational names, per thousand persons listed in each source. Figures are given to the nearest .5*

	Dorset 1327	Kent 1334/5	Lancs. 1332	Leics. 1327	Oxon. 1327	Staffs. 1327	Suff. 1327	Surr. 1332	Suss. 1332	Warws. 1332	Yorks. 1327
Baker	3	6.5	1	1	3	2	2.5	6.5	5.5	1.5	3.5
Barker	0	.5[8]	1	1.5	.5	1	2.5	0	less than .5	.5	3
Carter	3	1	1.5	3.5	7	2.5	3	4	1.5	6	5.5[15]
Chapman	2	3	1	3.5	5	.5	4.5	5	2	2	3.5
Cook	3	3	3	less than .5	2.5	2	5	0	3	1	5
Cooper	.5	3.5	0	1.5	3	3	2.5	5	2	2	2.5
Fisher	.5	1	1	.5	2.5	1.5	.5	2	1.5	1.5	less[17] than .5
Hunt	2	1	1	1	2	1.5	1.5	1	3	2.5	less[18] than .5
Miller	.5	4.5	.5	0	1	0[19]	3	0	less than .5	3	0
Milward	3.5	.5	0	0	1[10]	.5	0	6.5	3	0	0[19]

Surnames Derived from Occupation, Status, or Office 225

Smith	.5	10.5	7	16.5	13	8	20	7	8	8	10
Spicer	6	.5	.5	1	.5	less than .5	3	0	.5	.5	1
Taylor	0	5	3.5	9	6	4	11	3.5	6.5	7	4.5
Tanner	4	0	2	4.5	.5	less than .5	0	1	0	2.5	1.5
Turner	3.5	.5	2	1.5	1.5	1	1.5	0	1	1	.5
Walker	1	1	2	0	0[13]	.5	0[11]	1	3	0	0
Ward	2.5	4	.5	0	2	1.5	1.5	3	1	1	less than .5
Webb	2	1.5	1	6	.5[14]	less than .5	.5[12]	.5	0	3	2
Webster	0	0[16]	0	0	.5	0	0	less than .5	.5	0	0
Wright	1	.5	.5	.5	1	.5	1	2.5	0[9]	less than .5	0

a whole, were relatively scarce in Lancashire, for example, is due mainly to occupational surnames forming a low proportion of the total number of names in use in the county.[21]

A more important factor is the markedly regional distribution of some occupational surnames during the Middle Ages. Even during later periods, many features of this regional distribution survived, though modified to a small degree by migration. This has affected the occupational surnames present in Sussex, as in other counties. Some surnames, such as Baker, Carter, Chapman, Cook, Smith, Taylor, or Turner, for example, were very widely distributed, as were the actual occupations from which the names in question were derived, but as the evidence set out in the table shows, even these very common and widespread surnames were by no means evenly distributed. Baker was much more common in Sussex, and Kent adjoining, than in most other parts of England, during the 14th century. Guppy, using evidence from late 19th century directories, found that Baker was still at that period exceptionally common, in proportion to the total numbers of persons listed in his sources, in Sussex, and that it was more common in Kent, Surrey, and Hampshire than in most parts of England.[22] Carter, on the other hand, was in the 14th century much less common, proportionately, in both Sussex and Kent, than in some other counties. By the 19th century, according to Guppy's findings, Carter had become about as common in Sussex (and in Surrey), as in most other counties, though the name remained relatively rare in Kent.[23] Smith and Taylor are both names which were proportionately much more numerous in some parts of England than in others. Both were relatively uncommon in Sussex during the 14th century. Judging from Guppy's evidence again, this was still the case in the late 19th century. Both surnames then formed a much smaller proportion of the total body of surnames in Sussex, and in Kent and Surrey, than in some other regions, such as the south-west Midlands.[24]

There were, therefore, considerable differences during the 13th and 14th centuries between one county and another in the frequency with which some common occupational surnames occurred. These differences, apparent from the time when adequate evidence for assessing the distribution of surnames first becomes available, tended to persist over long periods. Where such common surnames were concerned, the differences were ones between regions, rather than between individual counties. Generally, the situation in Sussex tends to resemble that in other south-eastern counties. There were differences between regions in the vocabulary of occupational terms in use, and this is part of the explanation for the regional differences which existed in the distribution of occupational surnames. The distribution of Baker, for example, is affected by the fact that in some regions the alternative name Baxter was the most usual surname derived from the trade of baking.[25] Walker is a name derived from the trade of fulling cloth, and was over a long period the usual surname from that trade in the north of England and the West Midlands, in which regions it became numerous.[26] The name gradually spread to other parts of England,[27] but it has not been found in Sussex before the 16th century, except for one isolated example. In the 1524–5 subsidy roll for the county, Walker appears as the name of eleven individuals, dispersed in both East and West Sussex, which suggests that the name had been established in the county for some time before that date.[28] The usual surname from the occupation of fulling to occur in the south-east was Fuller, which was a widespread name in Sussex from at least about 1200 onwards.[29] In the 1524 subsidy roll for Sussex, Fuller was still a much more numerous surname than Walker, and Guppy's evidence shows it as more common, proportionately, in Sussex than in any other county, in the late 19th century.[30] The other major surname derived from fulling, Tucker, is chiefly found in the south-west during the Middle Ages. One medieval instance of the name has been found in Sussex,[31] and it is probable that it was not an hereditary name in the county during the Middle Ages. In the 16th century it was still very uncommon there. The position about the surnames derived from the occupation of weaving is similar. In Sussex, and in the southern and south-eastern counties generally, the usual name derived from that occupation was Webb. Webb was a surname very frequently found in Sussex from the 13th century onwards, and existed in most parts of the county. In some places, such as at Chichester, or at Fairlight in East Sussex, it persisted over long periods, in a way which indicates that it was in those localities a hereditary surname. It was still a common name in Sussex in the 16th century. On the other hand Webster, though a surname frequently appearing in most northern counties and in East Anglia, has not been found in Sussex before 1500.[32] A third surname from the same occupation, Weaver, occurs in Sussex, chiefly in the east of the county, during the Middle Ages, but was much less common than Webb.[33]

Regional differences of this kind explain why some occupational surnames which are today very numerous occurred often in medieval Sussex, while other similarly numerous occupational names were absent from the county, or very scarce there. Obviously, however, there are some elements in the history of surnames in this category which cannot be so explained. The fact that some occupational names which are very widely dispersed throughout England from an early date, such as Carter, Chapman, Cook, Parker, Smith, or Taylor, for example, were proportionately much more plentiful in some counties than in others does not seem to be explicable on such grounds. It is unlikely that the relative frequency with which such surnames appear has any close connection with the numbers of people engaged in the particular trades from which the surnames in question are derived. It is in fact very doubtful if there is more than a very loose and general connection between the frequency with which any one occupational surname occurs, either locally, or taking England as a whole, and the number of individuals practising the occupation from which the surname arose. This question is discussed later in the chapter. It is, however, clearly improbable that (taking examples from the figures given in Table I) there were in the 14th century twice as many tailors, proportionate to the population, in Kent than there were in Sussex, though Taylor was a name twice as common in Kent as in the neighbouring county, or that there were at the same period twice as many smiths in Oxfordshire as there were in Dorset, or nearly three times as many as there were in Sussex, as would seem to be indicated by the frequency with which the surname Smith was to be found in those counties. Such variations in frequency were not limited to those occupational surnames which were extremely common, but can be found in many surnames of the type which existed in most parts of England, but which were not amongst the occupational names appearing most often. The names Fisher, Hunt, and Spicer, which have been included in Table I, may serve as examples, but other occupational names show similar variations in the frequency with which they occur, and could have been included in the table if space permitted.

There are consequently variations between counties, and between regions, in the frequency with which some occupational surnames occur, and these variations cannot all be explained by differences between one region and another in the vocabulary of occupational terms in use, or by the ramification of individual families. It further seems improbable that such fluctuations can be due to some trades or crafts being much more generally pursued in some parts of England than in others, though the lack of any reliable evidence about how many smiths, spicers, tanners, turners, etc., there were in any county or region makes it impossible to be sure about that point. There may have been characteristics of social organisation, not now readily perceptible from the available evidence, which made some occupations more distinctive in some regions than in others, and so more likely to give rise to surnames. It was when an occupation was distinctive, at least within a particular community, and when it marked a man out from the other inhabitants of his town or village, that it was likely to give rise to a surname. Activities which were pursued by a considerable part of the inhabitants of any place would be unlikely to be the origin of surnames. That this was so can be seen from the very small number of persons with names derived from any of the operations involved in arable farming, despite its importance. It is perhaps this factor which explains, for instance, why the name Smith was relatively less common in Sussex than in some other counties. Sussex had an active iron industry, and on some manors tenants were obliged to supply iron work, often a ploughshare each, annually as part of the rent and services which they owed.[34] In such a situation, the craft of smithing might be an occupation less clearly demarcated from others, and there may have been numbers of people involved in ironworking, who followed other occupations for part of the year. Other surnames from iron workings, such as Faber or Ferrour, were not common in Sussex.

In general, the distribution of the more common occupational surnames in Sussex, and the frequency with which they occur there, resembles that of the other south-eastern counties. Among the rarer occupational surnames, there are a few which seem likely to have originated in Sussex exclusively, and a few others which appear to have been confined at first to Sussex and one or two counties bordering on it. Some of these were rare names which occur as those of one or two individuals, were probably bye-names which never became hereditary, and do not seem to have survived to the present day. Instances of such bye-names are Bellower (probably the operator of the bellows at a forge or smithy),[35] Colebrener (charcoal burner),[36] Cornman (presumably a dealer in grain),[37] Criblur (flour sifter),[38] Jureman (possibly for a juror, but that is an unlikely source of an occupational name; as the name atte Jewerye occurs in the same area, this may be a topographical name),[39] Mulegrom (miller),[40] Organmaker (an alien),[41] Persevent (probably a poursuivant in the sense of a legal officer),[42] Quernbetere (a maker of hand querns),[43] Ripecherl (probably a labourer employed in reaping),[44] Trumpet (the bearer of the name was a trumpeter),[45] Wringar (possibly someone who pressed cheese),[46] and Wyldereve (a bailiff in charge of land in the Weald).[47] These, and some other bye-names which could be cited, seem to have been confined to Sussex, but all were very scarce, and so far as can be discovered they did not survive to become part of the general body of surnames in the county. Some other names, which appear to have originated in Sussex, and were not present in other counties at any early period, did survive the Middle Ages, and have persisted in the county. Among such surnames are Bender (probably a name for a bowman);[48] Fishman, probably a name for a fishmonger;[49] Shoker, possibly for a labourer who put up corn in shocks at harvest (though that must have been seasonal work), and a name which persisted from the 13th century at and near West Grinstead;[50] Axsmith, a surname found in the 14th century in north Sussex;[51] and Trussman (probably a name for a porter or baggage man).[52] So far as can be seen from the evidence which has been examined, these surnames originated exclusively in Sussex. All remained rare.

Besides these surnames there are a few others for which early references are confined to Sussex, to the adjoining counties of Kent, Surrey, and Hampshire, and to the city of London. Such names include Carker (probably meaning 'carrier'), which is found in both Hampshire and Sussex,[53] Gyser ('archer'), similarly found in Hampshire and Sussex,[54] Luter ('Lute player'), which occurs in Sussex and Kent, and at

London, and which in Sussex appears in the 16th and 17th centuries as Lutter and Loyter,[55] Roofer, which occurs in both Sussex and Surrey,[56] Steeper (for someone who steeped flax or cloth), a name which persisted over a considerable period at Horsham, and elsewhere, in the north of West Sussex,[57] and Vesseler (maker of cooking vessels?), the name of a landed family which was present from the 13th century in the north west corner of Sussex, and which also appears in Hampshire.[58]

These surnames were, so far as can be seen from the available evidence, originally peculiar to Sussex and a few other south-eastern counties. All were scarce, and even taken together, they do not amount to more than a small fraction of the occupational surnames or bye-names existing in England during the Middle Ages. In some instances it seems likely that these rare surnames were each borne by a single family. The way in which some surnames, such as Vesseler or Steeper mentioned above, are confined in early references to limited areas, strongly suggests this, though it is not possible to draw up detailed pedigrees for the bearers of such surnames. It might appear from what has been said that occupational names found in Sussex had little to distinguish them from the surnames in the same category found in other counties, and that even taking the south-east of England as a whole, the occupational surnames present in the region during the Middle Ages had few characteristics to separate them from names of the same type occurring in other parts of the country. This, however, is not the case. Though the occupational surnames which originated exclusively in Sussex were neither very numerous, or particularly important, some occupational names, apart from the names very common throughout England generally which have been discussed, were much more numerous and prominent in Sussex than in the country as a whole. One group of surnames for which this is true are those derived from terms denoting status, especially those denoting free or servile status.

SURNAMES DERIVED FROM TERMS FOR STATUS

Surnames such as Free, Fry, Freebody, Bond, and so forth can be found in most parts of England from the 12th century onwards. In Sussex, however, such surnames have been unusually common over a long period. In the 1332 subsidy returns for Sussex, for example, there are 22 taxpayers listed named Frye (Fray, Fryg, etc.) ('free'), and there are also 3 named Freman (or Fryman), and one named Frebody. There are also 3 persons named Frank (or Fraunk), which here probably has the meaning 'free', and 2 named Freeland (Frilond, Frylond), which is a topographical name in form, but is obviously linked to status.[59] By contrast, in the Kent subsidy returns for 1334/5, the names Frye (Free, Frey, etc.), Frebody, and Frank do not occur, and Friman appears once. Freland (or Friland)

Surnames Derived from Occupation, Status, or Office 231

occurs as the name of 4 individuals.[60] Or, to take two more distant counties, in the Lancashire lay subsidy returns for 1332, the names Fry (Frey, Free, Frie, etc.), Freebody, Freeman, Frank, and Freeland do not appear at all; in the Suffolk subsidy for 1327, there are 3 persons named Fre, one named Frebody, 7 named Freman, and 2 named Fraunch.[61] The Kent and Suffolk subsidies just cited each list more than 11,000 taxpayers, against about 6,800 in the Sussex 1332 subsidy. Outside subsidy rolls, other references to the name Frye (Free, Frie, Frig, Frey, etc.) are very numerous in medieval sources for Sussex, and appear in many parts of the county.[62] It is clear that Fry was a very common and widespread surname in Sussex from the 13th century onwards, and it remained so at later periods. The 1524–5 subsidy return for the county, for instance, lists 3 taxpayers named Fray, 3 named Fre, or Free, and 15 named Fry or Frye, all these being variant forms of one surname.[63] The 1642 Protestation Returns, which survive for West Sussex but not East Sussex, list 19 persons named Fry in the western half of the county.[64]

Other surnames with a similar significance are less numerous in Sussex, but still fairly common. The surname Frebody (Fribody, Freebody) appears in Sussex from the late 13th century onwards at Udimore, and at Guestling nearby. The medieval instances of the name which have been found in Sussex all relate to this area, and it seems likely that all the Sussex Freebodys belonged to a single family, which multiplied to a moderate extent in one part of the county.[65] The name survived in the same part of the county in the 16th century, though by that date it had become rather more dispersed in East Sussex, and in the 17th century it was still to be found not far from Udimore.[66] On the other hand no medieval or 16th century references to the name have been discovered in West Sussex. It does not appear in the 1642 Protestation Returns for that part of the county, which give a fairly full list of the adult male inhabitants of the area. The surname Freeman (Freman), by contrast, appears during the Middle Ages in both East and West Sussex. There are medieval instances of the name in the extreme east of the county, on the Kent border, where the name was still present during the 16th century. Very possibly these instances all concern one family with a surname hereditary from the 13th century. There are, however, many references to the name in other parts of the county during the Middle Ages, and later.[67] Frank (Fraunk, Fronk, etc.) was also widely distributed in Sussex from the 13th century onwards. A family holding land at Eastbourne had the hereditary surname of Frank from the 13th century, but there are other persons named Frank who appear elsewhere in Sussex, and were not linked to this family so far as can be seen from the evidence.[68] Fraunchomme, a much rarer name than any of those just discussed, has been found in a single instance in Sussex before 1500, at Broadwater. It occurs in the 16th century, in the form Francombe, not far from Broadwater, and may have survived as a hereditary name from its first appearance in the 14th century.[69]

None of the surnames mentioned above were peculiar to Sussex. Fry, Freeman, and Freebody all occur widely in England, and there is no reason to suppose that where these names occur elsewhere in the country, there must necessarily be any link with Sussex, even where, as in the case of Freebody, there are grounds for thinking that all the medieval examples in Sussex concern one family.

Surnames or bye-names derived from servile status are much less common than those from free condition. The only such name which was at all frequent in medieval Sussex was Bond (le Bond, Bound, Bownd, Bunde). Bond is a name which has more than one possible origin, but the frequent occurrence in Sussex of forms such as le Bond, le Bounde, etc., leaves little doubt that in Sussex the name is usually, and probably always, derived from unfree status. Bond (etc.) was already a widespread name in Sussex in the late 13th and early 14th century subsidy rolls,[70] despite the fact that serfs were less likely than freemen to be listed in subsidy returns. There are a considerable number of references to the name in other medieval sources for Sussex.[71] No other surname from a term for unfree status was at all common. The name Border existed in east Sussex from the 13th century, but the origin of the name is doubtful. All the medieval instances found in Sussex come from the area around Battle, and it is possible that they all concern one family.[72] The name Cotterel appears in Sussex from the late 12th century, and can be found in several parts of the county. The names Cotier, le Cotur, and Cotman occur in Sussex in a few instances, and it is not clear that they ever became hereditary in the county. These are all names derived from words for tenants holding cottages, often with a few acres attached. In Sussex such tenants were often unfree, but it is clear from custumals of Sussex manors that they were sometimes free.[73]

Two surnames from terms for unfree status which were more common in Sussex were Threle (Thrale, Threel, Threll, Thrule), and Carl (Karl, etc.). The name Threel occurs in the late 13th and early 14th centuries at Framfield, in East Sussex, at Billingshurst and Pulborough, two adjoining places in the north of West Sussex, at and around Combes, near Bramber, at East Dean (West Sussex), and at East and West Preston, on the coast in West Sussex. Some of the people so named were unfree at this early period, others were free.[74] Sussex instances of the surname in the later 14th century and the 15th are mostly from the northern part of West Sussex. In this area one family so named became landowners of some importance at Drungewick. Very possibly this family was descended from the persons named Threle or Thrule who appear earlier at Billingshurst and Pulborough, both of which are near Drungewick.[75] The name also occurs in Surrey in the 15th century, possibly having spread there from

Sussex.[76] From the fact that the early references to the name are very dispersed, it seems likely that the name originated in Sussex with several distinct families. The name survived in the county in the 16th and 17th centuries, but was then rare.[77]

The name Carl (Karl, le Kerl), was probably applied in most cases to bondmen, though its literal meaning did not necessarily imply lack of freedom, but many of those who appear with the name in early Sussex instances were unfree. During the 13th and 14th centuries the name occurs at a number of places in both East and West Sussex, and from the start it must have been borne by several families.[78] The name Cherl, which was also probably used for a bondman, occurs in East Sussex as the name of one individual, but does not seem to have become hereditary.[79]

Surnames derived from terms for a bondman were less numerous in medieval Sussex than those from words which denoted free status. Possibly surnames carrying the stigma of servility may have been disliked, and consequently sometimes discarded. It is also true that bondmen appear in medieval sources much less frequently than freemen, so that the evidence may not give an altogether accurate view of the number of surnames derived from terms for unfree status. Despite this, the number of names in Sussex derived from terms for servile condition is larger than in most counties.

The reason for the existence in Sussex of so many surnames from words for free or bond status is presumably that it was a county where both bondmen and small freeholders existed in sizeable numbers, and where a tenant's status was a matter of much significance. In Kent, serfdom had virtually ceased to exist by the 13th century, and questions of status would be less vital in a county where it was assumed that all tenants were free men. It is, therefore, not surprising that surnames derived from terms for status were much less common in Kent than Sussex.

One surname which has been held to be derived from a term for status is Evening. This has been said to be derived from the Middle English word 'evening', meaning 'an equal'.[80] The bye-name le Yqual, found at Midhurst in the late 13th century, is an example of a name with such a significance.[81] The origins of Evening are, however, different. Evening is a name which appears to have originated exclusively in Sussex, and no early instances of it are known from outside the county. In Sussex, the name occurs in the late 13th century, and in the 14th, at two places, Eastbourne and Preston (near Hove). It is uncertain if a single family is involved, or two separate ones.[82] As the same Christian names are found at both places, it seems probable that all the Sussex Evenings were related. However, a Philip de Aveninge, who was holding land at Eastbourne in 1231, seems likely to have been the ancestor of the Evening family there.[83] Philip's name was evidently derived from a place-name, probably Avening (Gloucestershire).

As early as the 13th century, instances can be found where persons with names derived from unfree status were in fact free.[84] Such cases presumably arose from serfs being emancipated. Examples are not numerous, but they are a reminder of how rapidly names derived from status or occupation could cease to indicate the rank or trade of the bearers. It is more surprising that there are also a few instances of persons with surnames or bye-names from terms for free condition who are mentioned as bondmen.[85] Presumably such cases arose from freemen having accepted unfree status in order to obtain holdings. In 13th century Sussex there are instances of men who were personally free becoming tenants of servile holdings, and freemen in such a position must have been in danger of being reduced to serfdom.[86]

NAMES DERIVED FROM HIGH LAY OR ECCLESIASTICAL OFFICE

There are a considerable number of surnames which are from high positions in the state (King, Prince, Duke, Earl, for example), or in the church (Bishop, Abbot, Pope, Cardinal, and so forth). Such surnames occur very widely in England, and have clearly not arisen from the holding of the high offices in question, but must have originated as nicknames, though it is generally not possible to discover what circumstances gave rise to them. Perhaps the possession of what passed for a royal or episcopal manner or bearing led to a villager being nicknamed King or Bishop, but this is no more than conjecture. In many cases it is clear that such surnames are not derived from the actual holding of high positions. Such names as, for example, Cardinal, which occurs in Sussex during the 13th century,[87] or Soweden ('sultan'), which occurs there in the 14th and the 15th, and was probably a name derived from a character in a play or pageant,[88] obviously did not originate in the actual holding of the offices concerned. The names of King, Bishop, and Abbot, all fairly common, are likewise clearly in the nature of nicknames. The same is true of surnames from the ranks of the lay nobility. The name Earl appears in several parts of Sussex during the 13th century, and later, but many of those who occur with the name were persons in humble positions, such as cottars or labourers, and none appears to have been of any rank or standing.[89] The name was still to be found frequently in the county during the 16th and 17th centuries.[90] There is no evidence that any of those concerned were in fact earls, or the descendants of earls. Duke was a less widespread name in medieval Sussex. It occurs in West Sussex from the early 13th century onwards. Most of the instances are in the southern part of Arundel Rape, and it seems possible that all the Sussex Dukes belonged to one family. The name has not been found in East Sussex before 1400.[91] The title of duke did of course not exist in England during the 13th century, though it must have been familiar to at least part of the population from the use of the titles of Duke of Normandy and Duke of Aquitaine as part of the royal style. It is, however, often difficult to distinguish between names from the title 'duke', and names from the word 'duck', and it is impossible to be entirely certain about the origin of some Sussex examples.[92] In the 16th century, there were still more instances of Duke to be found in the southern part of Arundel Rape than in any other single part of the county, but by that date the name was present in other parts of West Sussex, and it had also spread to East Sussex.[93] The name Count (Conte, le Cunte, Latin *Comes*) occurs in Sussex from the 12th century. Many of the instances concern a landed family which held land by knight service in the Shoreham area, but the name also appears during the 13th and 14th centuries elsewhere in Sussex.[94] Though there are a fair number of medieval examples of the name in the county, it seems to have become extinct there.

In cases of surnames or bye-names derived from terms for very high lay or ecclesiastical rank, it is usually possible to be certain that the names in question were not derived from the holding of the high offices concerned. This is the case with the names mentioned above. It is much more difficult to be sure what the position is where surnames have arisen from words for less exalted ranks or positions, such as for example Knight, Sheriff, or Justice, or from lesser grades in the church, such as Canon, Priest, Deacon, or Monk. In some 12th and 13th century examples, those who appear with Knight as a surname or bye-name were clearly actual knights. On the other hand, there are 13th century examples where persons named Knight were serfs, or freeholders with very small properties, and in these cases the name Knight may be from the term in the meaning of servant.[95] The uncertainty about the date when individual families first acquired their individual surnames makes it particularly difficult to be sure what the meaning of Knight was when the word gave rise to the name of any one family.

During the 14th and 15th centuries, when the surname Knight was widely distributed in Sussex, there are further instances of individuals named Knight who were clearly not of knightly rank, but no safe deductions can be drawn from evidence from relatively late periods. During the 12th and 13th centuries, only a minority of families (outside the class of large landowners) had hereditary surnames, and even where surnames were hereditary, they had usually not been so for long. Up to about 1300, therefore, it might be expected that surnames or bye-names derived from occupation, rank, or office would usually correspond to the actual ranks, occupations, or offices of those bearing such names, though this would obviously not be true in cases where bye-names or surnames were really in the nature of nicknames. From about 1300 onwards, the increasing number of hereditary surnames, and the increasing number of names which had been hereditary for several generations, would mean that, with even a limited amount of social mobility, and changes of occupation from one generation to the next, surnames from rank, occupation, or office would be less likely to correspond with actual ranks, occupations, or offices.

The position of the surname Sheriff, also a fairly common name in Sussex during the 13th and 14th centuries, is different from that of the names just discussed; the origins of the surname may have been influenced by the fact that, in addition to the sheriff of the county, a royal official, some at least of the Sussex rapes had sheriffs of their own, who were appointed by the lord of each rape, and who are therefore much less easily identified than the county sheriffs. Some persons who appear in Sussex during the 13th century with the name Sheriff were customary tenants, and so very unlikely to have been actual sheriffs, though they might have been descendants who had fallen in status.[96] There are, on the other hand, late 11th and 12th century instances where persons appear as Sheriff (or *Vicecomes*) who were the sheriffs of one or other of the Sussex rapes. In none of these cases, however, is it clear whether Sheriff is a bye-name, or simply a description of the posts held by the individuals concerned.[97] The latter is more likely, though in 11th and 12th century evidence it is usually impossible to be sure about such points. None of the people who appear in Sussex during the 13th and 14th centuries with the surname or bye-name of Sheriff can be proved to be the descendants of any of the earlier sheriffs of the rapes, and though it is generally difficult to establish descents from persons occuring in the 12th century or earlier, it is unlikely that the surname Sheriff is in any of the Sussex examples derived from an ancestor who was in fact a sheriff. It seems probable that usually, if not always, the name Sheriff originated as a nickname.[98]

It is, similarly, difficult to be certain about the origins of the surname Justice. The Sussex bearers of the name during the 12th and 13th centuries seem to have been small tenants of no great standing, but it is possible that they may have had some functions as lawmen.[99] There must also be doubts about the origins of the name Baron. The burgesses of the Cinque Ports were known as barons, and some Sussex instances of the name were in the Cinque Ports.[100] In such cases it is possible that the surname may have arisen from a rank actually held, though not from the status of a baron in the sense generally understood. The name was present at Ewhurst, near Hastings, from the 14th century to the 16th (so that it was probably hereditary there) and it could well have originated there as the name of someone who was a freeman of one of the Cinque Ports.[101] On the other hand, the name occurs in West Sussex, some distance from any of the Cinque Ports, during the 13th and 14th centuries, and was fairly widespread there. Baron was also the name of serfs, who cannot have been freemen of the Cinque Ports, and are unlikely to have been the descendents of such freemen.[102] The name Chamberlain is a similar case. Chamberlains were not necessarily royal officials. The bishops of Chichester had chamberlains. Lewes Priory had a chamberlain, and the men who witness the priory's charters with the name Chamberlain (*Camberlengus*, *Camerarius*, etc.) were no doubt the priory's own officials.[103] There were chamberlains on the Archbishop of Canterbury's manors of South Malling and Pagham in the 14th century.[104] It is, however, impossible to tell how many of the people who appear in medieval Sussex named Chamberlain held office as chamberlains (or were descended from such officials), or in how many instances the surname Chamberlain may have originated as a nickname. The name persisted at Heyshott over a long period during the 14th and 15th centuries, and so was probably hereditary there.[105]

There must be similar doubts concerning some surnames derived from ecclesiastical ranks. Bishop, Abbot, and Prior no doubt originated as nicknames. The surname Chancellor seems to have usually originated as a nickname. The persons who appear with the name in Sussex were customary tenants or small free tenants, where their status can be discovered, and there is no evidence that any of them held any position as chancellor, or were descended from any holder of such a position.[106] Canon was a rare name in medieval Sussex, but one man so called was a cottar, and none of the people who occur in the county during the Middle Ages were in fact canons, so far as can be seen.[107] Another rare surname in Sussex was Convers. This is derived from a term for a lay brother in a monastery (*conversus*), or, possibly, for a Jew converted to Christianity. The 13th and early 14th century instances of the name in Sussex are mostly from the area around Chichester, and probably concern one family, though at the end of the 14th century, and in the 15th, the name occurs at Ewhurst, on the Kent border.[108] Lay brothers ought to have been celibate, and the people who appear named Convers were evidently not lay brothers. It is therefore likely that the surname was originally a nickname.

Two more names from clerical orders are Priest (Prest), and Deacon (Dekne, etc.). Deacon was a very scarce name in Sussex during the Middle Ages, and the references to it seem to concern one individual.[109] Very probably it never developed into a hereditary surname within the county. Priest, on the other hand, was a fairly widespread surname in the county from about 1200 onwards. In some early instances it is difficult to be sure if Priest (or Latin forms such as *Sacerdos* or *Presbiter*) is a surname or bye-name, or a description of an individual's profession. However, some of the persons who can be found with the name of Priest (etc.) in the county during the 13th and 14th centuries have occupations, such as merchant, which were incompatible with being in priest's orders. In the case of Roger de Saleherste, 'called priest', who is mentioned *c.* 1260 'priest' was evidently a nickname.[110] It is impossible to be certain how frequently the surname Priest originated as a nickname, and how far it may have originated with families which were descended from ordained priests. In Sussex during the 12th and 13th centuries there are a number of references to men who are described as the sons of priests, and many examples can be found in other counties,[111] so it is possible that some families called Priest have surnames which have arisen through descent from priests.

Monk (Mone, le Moine, *Monachus*) was a numerous and widely distributed name in Sussex from the 13th century. It was borne by people of very varied position, from lords of manors and tenants by knight service, to villeins and cottars.[112] The name was still common in Sussex during the 16th and 17th centuries.[113] The persons with Monk as a surname or bye-name all seem to have been laity, from an early period, and the surname Monk probably always originated as a nickname. The name Dean is a less certain case. The modern name Dean is sometimes topographical, but in Sussex forms such as le Dene, le Dyen, le Doyn, and so forth are derived from the office of dean. Similar forms can be found in other counties.[114] None of the persons found with such names in Sussex can be certainly identified as a dean, and those who are listed in the subsidy returns appear, from their assessments, to have been laymen of no great wealth. It seems likely that the name Dean, too, originated in such cases as a nickname. The surname Chaplain (Caplain, Chaplin, Capelain, *Capellanus*) also seems to have been usually a nickname in origin. The term 'chaplain', or the Latin *capellanus*, was generally used during the Middle Ages for men who were in priest's orders, and who ought to have been celibate, though as has been remarked above, priests did at times have children. However, a number of persons named Chapelain, Capelain, etc., are listed in the 14th century Sussex lay subsidies. There is no indication that any of these were priests, though clergy do appear in lay subsidies, assessed on lay fees which they held; it consequently seems likely that these were all laymen. Walter Chapelayn, mentioned at Ferring in the late 13th century, was a villien, and consequently cannot have been a priest, and there are other cases of serfs named *Capellanus*, etc. The name Capelin (etc.) survived at Washington from the early 14th century for a long period, and was still the name of a yeoman family there in the 17th, so that it is probable that the name was hereditary there from the 14th century. Caplin, or Caplen, was a widespread surname in the county during the 16th and 17th centuries, especially in West Sussex.[115]

It seems likely that all these surnames from ecclesiastical ranks or offices were in origin nicknames, though it is impossible to be sure that this was so in all instances.

There must be doubts about the origin of some other surnames. The name Champion, or Campion, could have arisen from the legal procedure of trial by battle. In real property actions, the issue in dispute could be settled through trial by battle, and in such cases the parties to the action were each represented by a champion. Some religious bodies retained men to act as champions for them in such actions. Actual combats were infrequent, as disputes were very often settled by agreement before blows were in fact struck, so that the chances of a man surviving even a long career as a professional champion were better than might appear at first sight. The number of persons who can be found with Champion or Campion as a surname or bye-name, both in Sussex and elsewhere, however, seems greater than would be likely if the name originated solely with men paid to act as champions, for the number of such people must always have been small.[116] It seems possible, consequently, that in some instances the surname may have originated as a nickname.

The surname Squire is a similar case. The name could originate with persons who were in fact squires. However, out of 16 men listed with the name in the Sussex subsidy rolls for 1296, 1327/8, and 1332, there is only one[117] who has an assessment which indicates that he is likely to have been a squire; the others all have assessments which suggest that they were people with small resources.[118] None of the persons who appear with the name Squire in other medieval Sussex sources are men who were certainly squires.[119] In addition, nearly all the examples of the name found in the county before 1500 are from two areas, the borough of East Grinstead, and the north-west corner of the county. The one instance in the subsidy rolls which concerns a man who appears from his assessment to be an actual squire does not come from either of these areas.[120] From this evidence it seems probable that there were two families in Sussex, one at East Grinstead and one in the north-west of the county, which had the name Squire, and which had both acquired the name originally as a nickname.

A few other surnames which seem at first sight to be occupational are in fact nicknames in origin. The name Halfknight has been said to have arisen from the holding of half a knight's fee. The Sussex instances of the name all come from the Manwood area south of Chichester, and concern people who appear to be small freeholds tenants.[121] The same surname occurs in other counties as the name of serfs, or other persons who were clearly not tenants by knight service.[122] This must have been a nickname, probably of a derisory character. Similar names such as Halflord and Halfbond are found in some other counties. The name Halfknight existed at Southampton during the 13th and 14th centuries, and became hereditary there. Possibly the individuals with the name who appear in West Sussex may be linked with the Southampton family called Halfknight.[123] The rare surname Prince occurs in the 13th and 14th centuries in both East and West Sussex, and it still survived in the county during the 16th and 17th centuries.[124] This, too, must have been a nickname in origin. Pope, a widespread name in Sussex from the 13th century, must also have begun as a nickname, perhaps in some instances from the appearance of the Pope as a figure in pageants.

OCCUPATIONAL SURNAMES AND THE DISTRIBUTION OF CRAFTS AND INDUSTRIES

The distribution of many rarer occupational surnames tends to be very uneven. Where the less common occupational names are concerned, there are many instances of an individual name occurring quite frequently within a small area, but being absent elsewhere. This raises the question of whether this distribution of surnames corresponds more or less accurately with the distribution of occupations as it was about the period when occupational surnames were first being formed, or whether the distribution of surnames in the category ought to be attributed mainly to other factors. It has been pointed out above that where common occupational surnames are concerned, the distribution varies considerably from one county to another, and that this is unlikely to reflect at all precisely the way in which occupations were in fact distributed.[125] The history of some scarcer occupational surnames in Sussex may throw light upon the issue.

Surnames connected with the salt trade

In Sussex the most frequently occuring surname from the salt trade is Salter (Sealter, Selter, Silter, Syltere). In medieval Sussex salt was obtained by evaporating sea-water, and there were salt pans at many places on the coast. In 1086 some inland estates had salt works belonging to them, but these were probably situated on the coast, though attached to holdings inland.[126] If the distribution of occupational surnames, even at an early period in the evolution of hereditary surnames, corresponded reasonably closely with the distribution of occupations, it would be expected that in Sussex, most of the early instances of surnames linked with the salt trade would be found on or very near to the coast. In the Sussex subsidy returns for 1296, 1327/8, and 1332, the name Salter (Seltere, Syltere, etc.) occurs at twelve places. Out of these one is very near to the coast (Bilsham), and another (Leicester Liberty) included lands near the coast. The remainder were all situated inland, though these cases might have been dealers in salt, rather than producers. Another name connected with the salt trade, and found in the same subsidy returns, is le Salt, which appears twice at Chyngton, near the coast. The surname Salt is usually derived from the place-name Salt (Staffs.), but in this case it is clearly an occupational name.[127] No further references to the

Surnames Derived from Occupation, Status, or Office

name le Salt have been discovered in Sussex, but Salter (etc.) can be found frequently in medieval sources for the county. The name does appear at places on the coast, such as Winchelsea (where it occurs several times during the 13th century, though not in any of the subsidies mentioned above),[128] Bersted, where the name was present from the late 13th century and was probably hereditary, or Climping, and at places very close to the coast, such as Icklesham.[129] It also, however, occurs at places distant from the sea, such as Ticehurst or Kirdford, both of which are on the northern border of the county.[130] Even during the Middle Ages, therefore, the distribution of the surname Salter had little connection with the distribution of salt works. It must be concluded that the surname had quite rapidly become dispersed from its places of origin.

During the 16th and 17th centuries Salter was still a fairly numerous name in Sussex. In the 17th century it was still present at Horsham, where it already existed in the 13th century.[131]

Surnames from maritime occupations

There were in medieval Sussex several names derived from seafaring occupations. One of these is Cogger, a surname from the Middle English 'cogge', a type of ship,[132] though the name might be from the making of teeth for mill-wheels. Early references to the name (before *c.* 1350) in Sussex are often at places on or near the coast, such as Winchelsea, where five persons so named were listed among the inhabitants in 1292, Guestling, a short distance from the coast, where the name existed in the early 14th century, and Felpham, on the West Sussex coast. However, the name can also be found at Wadhurst, some distance from the sea or navigable water, where there were two cottars named le Coggere about 1285, and at Hoadley Wood, near Ticehurst, where the surname was present in the early 14th century.[133] Early instances of the surname are on or near the coast in the majority of cases but even so, the name was that of smallholders inland by the late 13th century. In the later Middle Ages the name occurs both on the coast, and inland.[134] The surname survived in Sussex to be still fairly common in the county during the 16th and 17th centuries. It was still present at and around Ticehurst in the 17th century, having probably existed there as a hereditary name since the 14th,[135] and it is still present in Sussex today.

The name le Cog occurs in a few examples in Sussex during the 13th and 14th centuries, sometimes at places where Cogger also appears.[136] Le Cog is probably an alternative for Cogger. The name Cogman, which has the same significance as Cogger, has been found once in the county, at Lewes, and probably never became hereditary.[137]

Several other surnames derived from seafaring existed in medieval

Sussex. The name Shipman was rare, and all the instances which have been discovered were at or very near to the coast.[138] The name Schepman, which has been found in one example in the county, probably had the meaning of 'shepherd'.[139] The surname Mariner (Maryner, Marner) occurs during the 13th and 14th centuries both on the coast, and inland. One early 14th century bearer of the name was a cotterell at Barnhorne, near Bexhill. This is very close to the sea, but obviously the individual concerned (in fact a woman), was not a mariner, though possibly the widow of one.[140] This surname survived in Sussex during the 15th and 16th centuries, and during the 17th Marner was quite a numerous name in West Sussex. By that period it was widely distributed, and was mostly found inland, though it still existed at Yapton, near the coast, where it had been present in the 13th century.[141] Another name, Sterman, has a long history in Sussex. Ketel Esterman was the holder of land in Chichester, at some date before 1094.[142] Possibly he may have been the helmsman of one of the king's ships. During the 13th century and the first half of the 14th, the name Sterman or Steresman occurs at a number of places in Sussex. The localities in question are all either on the coast, like Meeching (near the present Newhaven), or Atherington (a coastal village which has now largely been lost through erosion), or very near to the coast, like Coombes (in the Adur valley, near a river then navigable), or Horton (nearby, on the other side of the Adur).[143] Some doubts have been expressed about the significance of the name Sterman, and it has been suggested that the first element of the name might be 'steer' in the sense of 'bullock'.[144] However, in Sussex forms such as Steryngman and Steresman are found, and occur at the same places as Sterman. Both Steryngman and Sterman, for instance, occur at Horton.[145] It seems clear that Sterman, Steryngman, and Steresman are variant forms of the same name. Besides this, the fact that Sterman in early instances always appears on or near the coast leaves little doubt that it is a name linked with seafaring. Steer ('bullock') has been a well established name in Sussex over a long period, but it does not seem that 'steer' in that sense is generally the first element of Sterman in Sussex. Steersmen were probably a distinct class of seafarers; in 1170–71 the king paid for the services of 8 *gubernati* and 152 seamen from Sussex, and the *gubernati* were probably steersmen.[146] Stearman survives to the present as a Sussex surname.

A few other occupational names which appear in Sussex are less clearly linked with seafaring. The name le Botere or le Botre occurs at Winchelsea in the 13th century, but this is a name which could arise on rivers, etc., inland.[147] The name Segrom was present over a long period during the 14th and 15th centuries at Sidlesham and Appledram, both in the Selsey area, and both near the sea.[148] It is very probable that all the instances of the name found in Sussex concern a single family with a surname hereditary from at least the early 14th century. Apart from these Sussex examples, the only known medieval instance of the name is a single instance from the inland county of Worcestershire. The name's presence there might of course be due to migration.[149] The significance of the surname is doubtful; 'groom' is the second element in a number of occupational names, but it may mean 'sailor'. It seems possible, in view of the part of Sussex where the surname existed, that the name was connected with the maintenance of defences against the sea, though this is conjectural.

Another name of doubtful origins is Skypper, which was present in Sussex in the 15th and 16th centuries.[150] It has been suggested that this name signifies 'master of a ship', and this may be the origin in some cases. However, in the 16th century the name appears at Arundel, and earlier, during the 14th century, the names Skeppere and Skypard occur at Wiston, not far from Arundel. Skeppere and Skypard were variant forms of the same name; William Skypard also appears as William Skeppere (at Wiston, late 14th century).[151] The final 'd' in Skypard may be inorganic. It seems probable that the meaning of Skeppere and Skypard was 'basket maker', and that in Sussex Skypper developed from Skeppere. The form Skepper existed in the county in the 17th century,[152] and both Skipper and Skepper survive in Sussex.

One other surname connected with maritime activities is Shipwright (Sipwergte, Shipwerghte, Schipwerght). There are a few examples of this in Sussex during the 13th and 14th centuries. All are on or near to the sea. One late 13th century bearer of the name, John le Schipwerght, was a cottar at Cakeham, near Selsey, but he may have combined possession of a small-holding with some shipbuilding.[153] In this case, too, the instances of the name from Sussex were on the coast.

Galiot (galley sailor) is a rare name which occurs in Sussex and some other coastal shires. The early Sussex examples are all from the coastal part of central Sussex, at Brighton, Beeding, and Offington. In this area the name occurs in the late 13th century and the 14th.[154] Possibly all those so named may be members of one family. The name Galet appears in Sussex, inland, during the 13th century, and later.[155] The few instances which have been found are all in the Mayfield area, and may, again, all concern one family. While Galet might be a variant of Galiot, it seems more likely that it is a name of French origin.[156]

The name le Flote existed at Midhurst in the late 13th and early 14th centuries. In the 15th century the name Flote, without any article, appears at the same place, and it may be assumed from this that the name was hereditary there.[157] This could be an occupational name with the meaning 'sailor'. The name le Flotyere ('sailor') has been found in a single example in Sussex.[158] However, the topographical name ate Flote also existed in Sussex during the 14th century,[159] and since there are many cases of articles and prepositions being prefixed to surnames or bye-names erroneously, the significance of le Flote must be uncertain.

The evidence about names derived from maritime occupations shows that in early examples, up to about 1350, such surnames or bye-names usually occur on or very near to the coast. The distribution of the names Skypper and le Flote is best left on one side, as the origins of both are uncertain. The evidence from the distribution of Cogger, however, supposing that the name is usually from seafaring, demonstrates that in the case of some surnames there is sometimes no very close connection between the distribution of names, even where early instances are concerned, and the distributions of the occupations from which names are derived.

Surnames derived from ironworking

It might be expected that the important Sussex iron making industry would have left its mark on the county's occupational surnames, and that there would be a considerable number of surnames and bye-names connected with the iron industry, concentrated in the districts where iron manufacture was carried on. In fact that is not the case. The names Smith and Marshall were both already numerous in the county, and widely distributed there, in the 13th century, but though both these names arose from iron-working, they are not particularly connected with the production of the metal. Both are names which occur very widely in England, often in counties where iron was not produced. The surname Ferrer (Ferur, Ferour), though less frequently found than either of these two names, was still quite widespread in the county during the Middle Ages, and later. Early examples of Ferrer, (before about 1350) are not confined to any one area. Many instances can be found in the southern part of West Sussex, which is not a district where iron production was carried on, but which was one of the more densely populated parts of the county.[160] The name Forger existed in East Sussex from the early 14th century. It persisted at West Firle from that time onwards, and there was probably a family with a hereditary surname in that part of the county from the early 14th century. There are isolated instances of the name elsewhere in Sussex, but they cannot be linked with the distribution of iron smelting.[161]

None of the other surnames or bye-names found in Sussex which are connected with iron production are at all common. Bellowere (probably a name for a man who worked the bellows at a forge) has been found once, at Chichester, and is probably a bye-name which never became hereditary.[162] Blower, which probably has the same significance, though it may have been a name for a hornblower, occurs before 1350 in several parts of Sussex. At the end of the 13th century it appears at Crawley, and might be connected with iron production in that part of Sussex, but it also appears at the same dates and during the 14th century, at Kingston by Sea (near Shoreham), where it existed over a long period, and where it was probably a hereditary name from the late 13th century. Kingston was not an iron producing area. The name occurs elsewhere in Sussex during the 15th century, but its distribution then has no obvious link with that of the iron industry. The name survived in the county into the 16th and 17th centuries, and is still found there to-day.[163] The name Blome, said to be derived from a word for an iron ingot, and hence to be a name for a worker in the iron industry, has been found in Sussex from the 12th century onwards, but the name was rare, its distribution has no evident connection with that of the iron industry, and there is no indication that any of the persons so named were engaged in iron production.[164] The related name Bloomer, which existed in some northern counties during the 13th and 14th centuries, has not been discovered in Sussex before the 16th. It is then scarce, and all the examples which have been found at that period are at or near Beeding, and probably concern one family.[165] Possibly the presence of this surname in Sussex may be due to migration into the county. The name Handhamer, found in a single instance, is probably not connected with the iron industry. It appears to be a variant of the surname which is usually spelt Haneper or Hamper.[166]

None of the above names has a distribution clearly linked with that of the Sussex iron industry. The few other surnames which are connected with the making of metal articles, as distinct from iron smelting, do not show any clear link with what can be discovered about the distribution of the iron industry. Shoesmith is a rare surname, which occurs in 1296 near Mayfield, and its presence there might be linked with the iron industry. Shoesmith's Wood, near Wadhurst in the same part of the county, is a place-name not evidenced before 1600, but the surname existed at Wadhurst in 1386–7 and later. In the 16th century the surname still survived at Wadhurst, and also, in the form Showersmith, at Buxted, a parish which adjoins Mayfield, and it is likely that it had persisted, as a hereditary name, in the area from the late 13th century. However, during the 15th century, and later, the surname appears elsewhere in East Sussex.[167] It seems probable that this was at first the name of a single family in Mayfield parish, which was hereditary there, and gradually dispersed. To the extent that it first occurs in an iron working area, it is evidence for a connection between surnames and the distribution of occupations. Shoesmith had become a moderately common surname in East Sussex by the 16th century, probably by the proliferation of one family. The name Cutiller, or Cuteler ('cutler'), possibly for a vendor, rather than a maker, of knives, was present in East Sussex during the 13th centuries, but its distribution has no clear connection with the iron industry.[168] The form Coteler appears in various parts of the county, and this form has sometimes been supposed to have the meaning 'cutler'. However, in Sussex during the 14th century the word 'coteller' was used as a term for a class of small tenant, apparently with the same meaning as 'cottar'.[169] Axsmith was a rare name, which was present in north Sussex, near the iron smelting areas, in the 14th century, very probably as the name of one family, but it subsequently seems to have become extinct.[170] The surname Hammer, which was present in Sussex from the 13th century, is not occupational. It is, at least in Sussex, a topographical name, formed from the common topographical term 'hamme' with the -er suffix. Topographical surnames of this type have been common in the county over a long period.[171]

There is in fact in Sussex a notable scarcity of surnames or bye-names from iron smelting or forging, despite the importance of the iron industry in the county. Such surnames as can be found, which are connected with the industry, are in general not distributed in a way which is connected with the distribution of the industry. One reason for this may be that the growth of the iron industry did not occur until a relatively late time, so that when the industry started to become important in Sussex many families had already acquired hereditary surnames. The lack of detailed evidence about the industry's development makes it difficult to be certain about this. It is in any case clear that the existence of this major industry in the county has left surprisingly little trace among local surnames.

Where other trades or crafts in the county are concerned, there is no obvious link between the distribution of occupations, and that of the surnames derived from them. There are a small number of names connected with glass-making. The name Glaswright (Glaswyrthe, Glasewryth) has been found twice in the county before 1500, at Lewes about 1255, and at Kirdford (in an area important for glass manufacture) in 1380, as the name of a lessee of a glasshouse.[172] It must be doubtful if the name was ever hereditary in Sussex. The name Glasier has not been discovered in Sussex before the late 14th century, when it was present at Chichester. The name persists at Chichester during the 15th and 16th centuries, and was probably hereditary there. In the same century it occurs at Amberley, and Waldron, but it has not been found elsewhere in Sussex until after 1500.[173] In the 16th century the surname appears at various places in Sussex, not concentrated in any one part of the county.[174] The absence of early references to Glasier may be caused by the concealment of the name beneath a Latin form. The name *Vitrarius*, which has the literal meaning of 'glasier', occurs in Sussex during the 12th and 13th centuries, and some at least of those so named were certainly glasiers by trade. *Vitrarius* existed as a name at both Chichester, and at Southover by Lewes, in the 13th century, and it may at Southover be translating the vernacular name Glaswright, which appears at Lewes, while at Chichester it is probably translating Glasier, which was present in the city later.[175] Two men at Southover who are mentioned in one source with the name of *Vitrarius* are also mentioned with their names given in the French form le Verrer.[176] In this case le Verrer evidently has the

Surnames Derived from Occupation, Status, or Office 247

meaning of 'glasier', and is not, as might be supposed, a variant form of Ferrer. It is likely that here le Verrer, like *Vitriarius* at the same place, is translating Glaswright. During the later Middle Ages the main centre of glassmaking in Sussex was in the north of the county, but very few surnames derived from the glass industry occur in that area, probably, again, because glass manufacture there developed after most people in the county had acquired hereditary surnames.

One characteristic of English occupational surnames is the fewness of surnames derived from any of the operations of arable farming, despite its importance as an occupation. This is true both in Sussex, and in England as a whole. The main reason must be that so large a proportion of the population was engaged in arable cultivation that the occupations connected with it were not distinctive, and therefore did not usually give rise to surnames. This factor has to be borne in mind when considering how far surnames reflect the distribution of actual occupations. Where surnames have arisen from any of the activities of arable farming, there is generally some special reason. For example, the name Akerman occurs in West Sussex from the 13th century. Most of the 13th and 14th century instances come from places where there were lands belonging to the manor of Pagham, a large manor which extended into several townships. On this manor (and some others) akermen were a special class of tenant, who had the duty of ploughing for the lord of the manor every working day. They were in fact virtually full-time ploughmen.[177] The general paucity of surnames from arable farming is an indication of how impossible it is to estimate the importance of any occupation from the number of surnames derived from it.

In contrast to arable farming, there is a considerable number of surnames derived from herding livestock. No doubt this is because such work was often relatively specialised, with one or two individuals in each village being employed on particular tasks of herding. Much the most common of the names from pastoral husbandry is Shepherd (Sepherde, Schephurd, *Bercarius*). The Sussex subsidy returns for 1296, 1327, and 1332 show that the name was then already widely distributed in the county, though most of the instances are to be found in the southern part, and there are few in the High Weald area.[178] Numerous references in other sources for the 13th and 14th centuries confirm this distribution of the name, which probably coincides fairly closely with the actual distribution of sheep at the period.[179] Other names derived from herding stock are all much less numerous. Schepman, which has the same meaning as Shepherd, occurs at and near Bramber, and was probably not hereditary in the county.[180] The name Shepper (or Shepare), on the other hand, was probably not connected with sheep. This name appears at several places in Sussex during the 14th century, sometimes in the form Shupper. In the 13th century the feminine form Sheppestre also appears.

The name Shepper was rare, but it survived, and was still present in Sussex during the 17th century. The significance of the name is not clear, but it probably meant 'dressmaker'.[181]

There are a moderate number of names from cattle herding. The name Cowherd occurs at several places in Sussex, nearly all in the southern half of the county, during the Middle Ages. It survived in the county, and was still present, in the form Coward, during the 16th and 17th centuries.[182] Bullockherd first occurs in Sussex in the late 15th century as the name of a family holding land, at Highden and Washingham. The family continued to hold land of Amberley manor in the 16th century, and all the references to the surname during that period concern places near Amberley. After about 1550 the surname appears in the forms Bullocker or Bullaker. By the 17th century such forms had become usual, and the form Bullockherd had been lost. It seems very probable that all the persons with the name in Sussex, even as late as the 17th century, belonged to one family.[183] Oxherd occurs several times in West Sussex, and may have been a hereditary name at Selsey, but does not sem to have survived.[184] Oxman has been found once, and was probably a bye-name which never became hereditary.[185] Names such as le Bover or le Bovier can be found in Sussex during the 13th and 14th centuries, and may have the meaning of 'cattle herd', but the forms vary a good deal, and some at least may be variants of 'Bowyer'.[186] However, the surname Boverd, which was present in the county during the 16th century, was probably derived from Bover.[187] A few other names connected with cattle occur in one or two instances, and were probably not hereditary in the county. Bulshyne and Calverd ('calf herd') each appear once.[188] Bulman has not been found before the 16th century.[189] Le Vacher appears in one instance, and may be merely a translation of a Middle English name such as Cowherd.[190]

The reason for the existence of a fair number of surnames and bye-names from cattle herding no doubt owes something to the fact that on some Sussex manors there were tenants who held lands by the service of acting as oxherds.[191] Cattle herding was, therefore, a specialised occupation in some places. The relatively small number of names derived from the occupation may be deceptive, for the more general surnames of Herd and Herdman were probably often from cattle herding. Both were quite common names in the county during the Middle Ages, and were widely distributed.[192] The surname Steer probably originated as a nickname.

There are, similarly, some surnames derived from the care of horses. Coltherd and Coltman both occur once, and were probably not hereditary in the county.[193] Horsknave is a rare bye-name which has also been found in Sussex in a single example.[194] Horseman, on the other hand, survived for centuries in East Sussex. Most of the 13th and 14th century instances come from Alciston and the surrounding area, where the name was probably hereditary. Horseman was still present in the same part of the county during the 16th and 17th centuries, though it had not become at all numerous.[195] Horsekeeper is a scarce surname which has not been found in Sussex before the 16th century, and its presence in the county then may be due to migration.[196] Palfrey and Palfreyman were both rare in medieval Sussex, and the references to both are scattered. It is uncertain if either was hereditary in the county.[197] Stedman, by contrast, though at first a rare name in Sussex, survived over a long period at Horsham, where it was present early in the 14th century, and in the 16th and 17th centuries it was a well established surname there, and at other places in the same part of Sussex.[198] Stodherd is a name that has been found at and near Mayfield, but not elsewhere in Sussex though it occurs in other counties, and at Mayfield it seems to have been hereditary during the 13th century.[199] Studder, a rare name everywhere, has been found once as a bye-name in Sussex.[200]

In addition, there are a few surnames or bye-names from the work of herding other animals. Swynherde has been found once in the county, though the Latin form *Porcarius*, of which there are several examples in the 12th and 13th centuries, may perhaps be translating Swynherde.[201] The French le Porcher is mentioned in some Sussex sources for the 13th and 14th centuries, with most of the examples at or near Amberley. However, it is usually, and probably always, a translation of Pigherd. Robert le Porcher, who occurs at Amberley in the late 13th and early 14th centuries, is evidently the same as Robert Pighurde, who occurs at the same place at the same period, and William le Porcher, who occurs at Rackham, adjoining Amberley, about 1300, seems to be the same as William le Pigherde, listed at Amberley in 1306.[202] Gooseherd (Goshurde, Goushurde), appears as a name during the 14th century again at or near Amberley. It may have been hereditary in that area, though rare. The surname Gosset, which existed in the same part of Sussex during the 16th century, may be a development of Gooseherd; there are, however, other possible origins for Gosset, and it is to be noted that John Gossatt, listed as a Sussex taxpayer in 1525, was an alien. Gosset and Gossat may be French in origin, and were perhaps brought into the county by migration some time before 1525.[203] Gotherde has been found in a single instance in medieval Susex,[204] at Bury. There are references to goats being kept during the 13th century, sometimes in considerable numbers, at Slindon and Aldingbourne, both of which are near Bury. Again, it seems possible that the surname Goater or Goatcher, which was present in the same part of Sussex during the 17th century, and later, has evolved from Gotherde, but some of the forms in which Goater appears in the 17th century, such as Gauder or Gotier, suggest other origins.[205]

This considerable number of surnames derived from pastoral husbandry contrast with the very few surnames from arable farming. The reason for the contrast is no doubt that there were a number of specialised occupations connected with livestock rearing, which were sufficiently distinctive to give rise to surnames or bye-names. Many of the names from pastoral farming were rare, and some seem not to have been hereditary. This may be because some activities, goat herding for instance, were confined to limited areas in the county. The fact that so important an activity as arable farming gave rise to so few surnames shows how it is possible for there to be little connection between the extent and economic importance of any occupation, and the number of surnames derived from it. It is those occupations which were distinctive, in the sense that they were usually practised by a few persons in each village, which were most likely to give rise to surnames.

DISTRIBUTION OF SOME OCCUPATIONAL SURNAMES

It has been suggested above that some of the rarer occupational names may have originated in Sussex in a single family, and one factor which can obviously affect the distribution of names in the category is the ramification and spread of individual families. There are some surnames in the county which appear to have originated with a single family, or with two or three families, and which in some cases have proliferated considerably. Some examples will illustrate how such developments can affect the spread of occupational surnames in one county.

Canner

The name *cannarius* appears as that of a householder at Battle, about 1100. The Latin word *cannarius* normally means a reed-cutter, but it has been suggested that it is here translating the name Canner, and in view of the later presence at Battle of Canner, it seems almost certain that this is correct. Richard le Cannere is mentioned at Battle in the mid 13th century. A Richard le Cannere, very probably the same man, was holding property at Winchelsea in 1292. Perhaps he was a Battle resident who had taken the opportunity to acquire a holding at Winchelsea when that town was rebuilt. In 1332 the name Canner occurs at Frontridge, a short distance north of Battle. No medieval references to the name have been found in any other part of Sussex, and it seems extremely probable that all the persons so named belonged to a single family. It is probable that in this case the surname was hereditary from the early 12th century. The name means a maker of, or dealer in, cans. In this case, the surname seems to have existed in one area for several centuries without multiplying significantly. Despite its rarity, the surname survived in Sussex.[206]

Chaper

Chaper is a name for a dealer or trafficker. Apart from the Sussex evidence, there are medieval instances of the name in Surrey and Hampshire, and at London. In Sussex the early examples (before about 1350) are nearly all at or near Pulborough. One case occurs in 1292 at Winchelsea, in a different part of Sussex. Possibly, however, this may be due to a migrant moving in to Winchelsea, which had then just been rebuilt. The name continues to appear around Pulborough during the later Middle Ages. During the 16th and 17th centuries it was still present in the same part of Sussex, though rather more dispersed than at earlier periods. During those two centuries Chaper has not been found in Sussex outside the west of the county. The surname Chipper (or Chiper) which existed in one area of West Sussex, around West Tarring, during the 17th century, may be a variant form of Chaper. If this is so, the existence of Chipper in this coastal area of West Sussex is probably due to migration from the district around Pulborough. In this case, too, a surname persisted in one part of the county over some centuries. Although the genealogical links cannot be traced, it seems probable that this is a name which originated with a single family, and gradually became rather more dispersed in the course of time, without becoming spread generally throughout the county.[207] Chipper still survives in Sussex.

Fruter or Fretour

The name Fruter appears in Sussex as that of two customary tenants of the manor of Laughton, in 1292.[208] Laughton was a large manor, with lands extending into several townships, besides Laughton itself. In 1296 the name occurs at Ripe, which adjoins Laughton. The name survived at both Laughton and Ripe, and was still present at both places in the 15th century, having in all probability been hereditary from the late 13th.[209] Outside Laughton and Ripe, the only references to the name that have been found in medieval Sussex are in connection with the ownership of a house at Seaford, rather more than seven miles from Ripe, and in connection with Friston, near Seaford.[210] The name occurs during the Middle Ages as Fruter, Fretour, le Friter, and Frytour. It has the meaning of 'fruiterer', either a seller, or a grower, of fruit.[211] During the 16th century, the surname existed at Folkington, about four miles from Ripe, at South Heighton and Denton, near Seaford, and at Milton (in Arlington, near Ripe).[212] Within this imited area the name had become relatively numerous. This too seems to be an instance of a surname which had begun with a single family, in this case customary tenants, and had subsequently multiplied, but had spread to only a very moderate extent geographically.

Hoggesflesh

Hoggesflesh was probably a name for a pork butcher, though there is some possibility that it was a nickname in origin. The name occurs early in the 14th century at Easebourne, in north west Sussex. It has not been found elsewhere in the county before 1400.[213] In the early 16th century the surname was still present at Easebourne, where there is little doubt that it had been hereditary from the early 14th. By the early 15th century the name existed at Rogate (rather more than five miles from Easebourne) where it was by 1524 already a numerous name. The surname also occurred in the 16th century at Hardham, further from Easebourne, but still in the same part of the county. Up to this point the surname had not dispersed very much from its place of origin at Easebourne, though it had multiplied to some extent. Later in the 16th century the surname appears at Iping, a few miles from Easebourne, and, like Easebourne and Rogate, in the valley of the western River Rother, and at Cocking and Fernhurst, both near Easebourne. At the same period, however, the name appears farther afield, at Harting, which adjoins Rogate to the south, at Angmering, in the coastal area of West Sussex, and at Lewes, in the east of the county. It also occurs in 1586 at Petersfield, in Hampshire but not far from Rogate.[214] During the 17th century, Hoggesflesh continued to exist at places near to Easebourne, including Iping. It also appeared at several places close to Hardham, including Pulborough, Parham, Sullington, and Wiggonholt. The spread of the name in this area is probably due to the proliferation of one family from Hardham. It also persisted at Angmering, and it was present at places rather further from Easebourne, such as Beeding. The name spread from north-west Sussex to London. By the 17th century the surname had become fairly numerous. The West Sussex Protestation Returns list 13 persons so named (all adult males), and this does not include East Sussex.[215] Even as late as the mid-17th century, the surname was still largely concentrated in the northern part of West Sussex, where it first appears in the early 14th century. In all probability, this represents the gradual dispersion of a surname which originated, perhaps about 1300, with a single family. The surname still survives in north Sussex, though rare.

Napper

The history of Napper as a surname in Sussex is similar to that of the name last discussed. Napper is usually said to be a name for a person charged with the care of the napery or linen, but may have been from the trade of selling napery. The name first occurs in Sussex in 1296, at Stedham in the north west of the county. It can be found in Surrey earlier in the 13th century, but none of the Surrey instances are very near to the

Surnames Derived from Occupation, Status, or Office 253

Sussex border, and it is very doubtful if there is any link between the Surrey examples, and those in Sussex. During the 14th century the name continued to be present at Stedham, where it was probably hereditary from the late 13th century. Early in the 14th century it also appears at Racton, which is also in north west Sussex, but some distance from Stedham. It is possible that the individuals named Napper who occur at both places were related, but there is no certainty about this, and the surname may have originated with two distinct families. It has not been found in any other part of Sussex before 1350.[216] In the mid 14th century the name appeared at Petworth, which is in north west Sussex also, and about seven miles from Stedham,[217] and during the 15th century the surname occurs at Harsfold, a few miles further east than Petworth, and in one case at Brighton, which is more distant.[218] In the 16th and 17th centuries the surname can still be found at Petworth, and it was also present at several other places very near to Petworth, and at and near Harsfold. The surname still survived at places quite close to Stedham, such as Bepton, Heyshott, and Cocking. It does not seem to have persisted at, or very near to, Racton. However, during the same period, the surname also appears at places rather more distant from its origins. These include Rudgwick, Horsham, and Rusper, which lie to the north east of Harsfold and Petworth, and a scattering of places in West Sussex on or near the coast, such as Lancing, Oving, and Angmering.[219] The name does not seem to have spread to East Sussex during the 16th and 17th centuries. This is a case where a surname originated in the county with one or perhaps two families (though it arose independently in other parts of England), and which gradually multiplied and dispersed, until by the 17th century it existed in most parts of West Sussex.

These examples show how a surname, at first that of a single family, can in the course of time ramify until it spreads over an extensive area. This is a factor which must be borne in mind when considering the significance of the way in which surnames are distributed. Even by a relatively early date, such as the end of the 14th century, some surnames in Sussex had already been hereditary for long enough to allow a name which was originally that of one family to proliferate and disperse. Apart from the surnames which have just been examined, some others which have been discussed in this chapter in various connections seem likely to have originated with one family. Examples are the names Axsmith, Bulloker, Evening, Forger, Freebody, Galiot, Halfknight, Segrom, Shoesmith, Steeper, and Vesseler.[220] In all these cases, the spread and distribution of individual surnames appears to have depended on the way in which single families ramified and migrated. Such developments mean that over several generations, once surnames had become hereditary, the distribution of a surname can cease to have much connection with that of the occupation from which it is derived, and it would therefore be unsafe to rely on evidence from occupational surnames or bye-names as an indication of how occupations were distributed.

There are a considerable number of occupational surnames found in Sussex during the 16th and 17th centuries, which have not been discovered in the county before 1500. As medieval sources do not provide a comprehensive list of surnames for any date, and as there were some sections of the medieval population which do not generally appear in the extant records, it is rash to assume that because a surname has not been found in the county during the Middle Ages, it cannot have existed there. However, some occupational surnames which are not found in Sussex until after 1500 seem likely to have been brought in by migration. Some of these are names for which the known medieval examples are confined to other parts of the country. Examples of such surnames are quite numerous, but most of them have been found in Sussex as the names of no more than one or two persons. It is probable that their presence in the county was in most cases the result of migration into Sussex by single individuals. The surnames involved are too many to list in full, and many of them did not become permanently established in Sussex. Some examples can, however, be given.

Capper occurs as the surname of seven persons in the subsidy returns for 1524–25. Two of those so named were aliens. The name existed earlier in other parts of England, and in particular it was present in the 14th century in Hampshire, and in London in the form le Capeler. Its presence in Sussex during the 16th century was probably due partly to migration from elsewhere in England, and partly to the Anglicisation of the names of alien immigrants.[221] There does not seem to be any connection between Capper, and the surname Chaper, which survived over a long period in West Sussex.[222]

Fleshmonger first appears in Sussex at Chichester, during the 16th century. The first person so named to be found in the county was a clergyman, and Dean of Chichester. The migrations of clergy, which depended largely on the availability of benefices, were governed by factors different from those which affected the movements of lay people, and the appearance of the surname in Chichester may have been due simply to a clergyman having obtained a living there. However, the surname was fairly common in Hampshire during the 13th and 14th centuries, and probably migrated from that county into Sussex. Fleshmonger continued to exist as a surname at Chichester for many years, and was still there about 1670, but does not seem to have spread very much beyond the city.[223]

Leadbeater (Lidbetter, Lydbeter) was a common occupational surname in the north of England from the 13th century, but it has not been found in Sussex before 1500. It occurs at Washington, near Bramber, in 1524, and it still existed at the same place in the 17th century. From the late 16th century it was also present at Steyning, a few miles from Washington. The name persisted during the 18th and 19th centuries as that of a line of farmers and yeomen at Bramber, which adjoins Steyning, and Lidbetter is still a Sussex surname. In this case, too, it would appear that a surname migrated into the county in the 16th century, and persisted there over a long period, without increasing very greatly in numbers.[224]

Mower is another surname which has first been found in Sussex in the 1524 subsidy returns, and it also has survived in the county to the present day. Six persons with the name are listed in the subsidy, two of them at or near Petworth, the rest in East Sussex, mostly at places in the north east of the county, near the Kent border. The fact that by 1524 the name was already present at widely separated places in the county suggests that it had been in Sussex for some time, and the absence of earlier references to it there is probably due to the defects of the 15th century sources. The name had existed earlier in other counties, and in particular it had appeared at Bramley in Surrey (near Godalming), from where the name could easily have migrated to the Petworth area. The surname survived in the central part of Sussex in the 17th century. Some of the men who appear with the name in Sussex in the 16th century were domestic servants, who may have moved from place to place to find employment.[225]

Stringer is a name with a history in Sussex similar to that of Mower. The first evidence for the name which has been found in the county is in the 1524 Sussex subsidy. There Thomas Stringer is listed at several places, all in West Sussex, presumably because he held land at each. Two other men named Stringer are listed in the same subsidy, both in the south-east part of West Sussex, where Thomas Stringer occurs.[226] Later in the 16th century men named Stringer are mentioned at Horsham and at Slinfold, both further north in West Sussex.[227] In the 17th century, the name Stringer continued to exist in West Sussex. It appeared at Horsham, Slinfold, and other places in the same area, at Goring in the south east of West Sussex, near the instances noted in 1524, at and near Petworth, and elsewhere.[228] The name of Stringersland Farm, at Rudgwick near Slinfold, preserves the surname.[229] Stringer, probably a name for a maker of bow-strings, was a common surname in Yorkshire, it can be found in other northern counties, including Lancashire, and it was also found in south west England. Its presence in Sussex may be due to migration from one of those regions. It is today a frequently occurring name in Sussex.

Thrower, or Trower, is another surname which has not been found in Sussex before 1500, but which appears as a well established name in the county in 1524. In the subsidy for that year and for 1525, at least six persons named Trower are listed, dispersed in different parts of the county.[230] Some of those concerned were servants or labourers, and the others, judging by their assessments, were not people of any great wealth. The name Trower survived in Sussex in the 17th century. The name

Trewer, which appears in the 1642 Protestation Returns at Petworth, and at Kirdford adjoining Petworth, is evidently a variant form of Trower, which occurs in 1524–5 at River, near Petworth.[231] Trower, too, seems to be a surname brought into Sussex by migration, probably in the late 15th or early 16th centuries, which rapidly established itself in the county. Thrower or Trower was probably a name for a spinner who produced silk thread from raw silk. Thrower has survived in the county.

Walker is a surname from the occupation of fulling cloth. It had originally a markedly regional distribution, being quite a common name in northern England, and in the West Midlands, but being rare or absent in other regions, where other names from the same occupation, such as Fuller or Tucker, can be found. In Sussex, Fuller occurs as a surname in the 12th century, and was widespread by the 13th. One example of Walker occurs in Sussex c.1330, but apart from this, it has first been found in Sussex in the 1524 subsidy returns; in 1524 and 1525 it appears as the name of eleven persons, spread through both East and West Sussex. The surname at this date was already so dispersed as to make it unlikely that all the Walkers then in Sussex belonged to one family, and it seems probable that several families so named must have migrated into the county in the late 15th or early 16th centuries. One 16th century Walker in Sussex was a migrant from Herefordshire. There are parts of the county in 1524–5 where people named Walker are found closely grouped together (at and around Chichester, for example) in a way which suggests that all the individuals in the group might have shared a common descent, but it seems improbable that all the Sussex Walkers in the 16th century could be related.[232] Walker continued to be a widespread name in Sussex during the 17th century. Eight men so named are listed in West Sussex alone in the 1641–2 Protestation Returns, and the name also survived in East Sussex.[233]

In Sussex during the 13th and 14th centuries the name Waker occurs in a few instances. The name also occurs in Berkshire at the same period. This is a name either with the meaning of 'watchman', or one which was a nickname for someone, vigilant and it was in origin distinct from Walker.[234] The name was rare, and it is not clear if it was hereditary. During the 17th century, however, there are cases in which individuals named Walker have their names given occasionally in the form Waker or Wauker. In these circumstances it must be doubtful if the name Waker, which existed in West Sussex during the 17th century, is merely a form of Walker, or whether its existence is due to the survival of Waker in West Sussex from the 13th and 14th centuries.[235] Waker survives in Sussex, though rare.

The reason why a fair number of surnames are first found in Sussex in 1524, and appear then as names which are already those of more than just two or three persons, is that the 1524–5 subsidy returns provide a much fuller picture of the county's surnames than is available for the 15th century. It must be suspected that most of the names which are first discovered in 1524 had already by then existed in the county for some time, and had been able to ramify considerably by that date. It is always possible that some of the surnames which have been found for the first time during the 16th century had existed in the county from a much earlier period, but had not been mentioned in any of the sources which have been examined.

The surnames discussed above are examples of surnames which have not been discovered in Sussex before 1500, and which during the 16th and 17th centuries became established in the county, and in some cases ramified there considerably. There are many occupational surnames which occur in Sussex during the 16th and 17th centuries, but not earlier, as the names of not more than two or three individuals. Some of these were names of aliens. The Sussex subsidy roll for 1524–5, for example, lists aliens with the names of Berebruer, Capper, Feryman, Hatmaker, Jornyman, Phisicon, Poucher, and Wodetaller,[236] all of which are surnames not found in the county before 1500. Most of these names have a purely English appearance, despite being those of aliens. This is probably due to foreign surnames being translated literally into English, as was common with aliens' surnames in the 16th century. Wodetaller, for example, seems to be a translation for the French Taillebois.[237] Migration from overseas did, therefore, lead to the presence in Sussex during the 16th century of some new surnames which are English linguistically. It is possible to detect surnames brought into the county by foreign immigrants because aliens are distinguished as such in the subsidy returns, but it is not possible to discover migrants into Sussex from other parts of England in any systematic way. It must, however, be suspected that most of the instances where an occupational name appears in the county for the first time after 1500 are due to movement into the county from other English regions, rather than to surnames having existed in Sussex for a long period unrecorded. A few occupational surnames which occur in the county for the first time during the 16th century did proliferate to some extent there, and some examples have been given, but many occupational surnames which are found during the 16th century as the names of not more than two or three persons failed to survive, and left no permanent mark on the general body of Sussex surnames. This can be seen from the extant returns for the Protestation of 1641–42,[238] which give an almost complete list of the adult male inhabitants of the western half of Sussex. None of the eight names of aliens mentioned above (Berebruer, etc.) are listed in these returns. The great majority of the occupational surnames which appear in the Protestation Returns as those of more than a few men are either names which have been common in most parts of the country over a long period (Smith, Baker, Taillour, etc.), or names which were already established in Sussex before 1500, and which in many cases were more frequently found there than in some other counties, such as Banister, Bachelor, Beadle, Booker, Capron, Carver, Cheeseman, Collier, Fry, Marner, May, Roper, Stedman, Taverner, Tupper, and Washer, for example.

OCCUPATIONAL NAMES ENDING IN -ESTER

Many years ago Gustav Fransson discussed the group of occupational names of the same type as Baxter, Brewster, Webster, and so forth, and pointed out that in southern counties such names were predominantly borne by women, during the period 1100–1350. In Sussex, Fransson discovered eleven names of this type, ten of which were those of women, one that of a man.[239] A more extensive search through Sussex material than that made by Fransson has produced some further examples, but it remains the case that in Sussex such names were in the great majority of instances those of women up to 1350. Sixteen examples have been found where such names were those of women, two where they were those of men, and one where the sex was uncertain.[240] In considering these figures it must be remembered that women are badly represented in medieval sources, where the great majority of persons mentioned are men. In Sussex there are several instances where a name in -ester, borne by a woman, occurs, and where the corresponding name without that suffix also occurs either at the same place, or very near. For example, the name Kembestere, or Keymestere, appears at Amberley in the mid 14th century, as a woman's name, and Kember (a rare name in Sussex) appears at the same place as the name of men, both at the same period, and later.[241] Similarly, Dygestre occurs at Midhurst in 1296 as a woman's name, and Dyghere ('dyer') occurs as a man's name at the same place at the same date, and later.[242] La Fullestr' occurs at Uckfield about 1285 as the name of a woman who was the tenant of a fulling mill, and the widow of a fuller, and Fuller occurs at the same place at about the same date.[243] Such examples suggest that during the 13th and 14th centuries in Sussex forms in -ester were normally names of women.

Few if any of the names in -ester which can be found in Sussex before 1300 seem to have been hereditary. No single instance can be found in which it is possible to prove that one of the names in the category was hereditary, and most of the names of the type to be found in the county during the Middle Ages do not appear there during the 16th and 17th centuries. The probability is that, as such names were usually those of women, and as women did not normally transmit their surnames or bye-names to their descendants, names in -ester would be unlikely to become hereditary. There are instances where women did pass on their bye-names to their descendants, so that women's bye-names could become hereditary surnames. There are also cases in which feminine Christian names have given rise to hereditary surnames. Such instances were, however, exceptional. It is possible that names in -ester may have been used more frequently than is apparent from the surviving medieval sources, and that the general lack of information about women's names conceals the real extent to which names of the type were in use, but there seems to be no means by which the question can be cleared up.

Many of the occupational surnames which existed in Sussex are ones which were widespread in England generally, and which do not require any particular explanation, and many of the rarer names found in the county have been adequately explained in the standard reference works on surnames, such as those by Reaney, Fransson, and Thuresson, but there are some occupational surnames in Sussex which have origins that need to be elucidated. Some of these are names which were more common in Sussex than in most other parts of England.

Blaker

The name Blaker or Blacker is found in several counties during the Middle Ages. It is often, though perhaps not always, an occupational name, derived from the trade of bleaching. The name occurs in Sussex from the late 13th century, and the existence there of early forms such as le Blakere or le Blakyere show that it was an occupational name in the county.[244] The name persisted over a long period at and near Shoreham, where it was already present in the early 14th century. It still existed at Shoreham in the 17th century, and was during the 17th and 18th centuries the name of a landowning family at Portslade, nearby. The name still survived in the same part of Sussex in the 19th century.[245] Blaker also existed as a surname over a long period at Cuckfield, and in all probability was hereditary both there, and at Shoreham.[246] By the 16th century it had multiplied in the county to but a moderate extent; in the subsidy returns for 1524–5 there are ten persons named Blaker, listed, two at Cuckfield, and most of the rest in the southern part of central Sussex, probably representing the gradual dispersal of the name from Shoreham. (The name Blakyster occurs in 1524 at Warningcamp, in the same part of Sussex; it has not been found in the county earlier, but it may perhaps have originated with a female member of the Blaker family). Blaker appears in parish registers in the same part of the county during the later 16th century, and it still existed at Shoreham in the 17th, though by that period it had become more dispersed.[247]

During the 16th century there seems to have been confusion between Blaker and an orthographically similar name, Blaber. Blaber is in origin a surname of the nickname type with the meaning of 'blabberer'. The first known instance of Blaber in Sussex is at Cold Waltham, in 1494. This is not far from the area around Shoreham, where Blaker had long been an established surname, and there may have already by 1494 been some lack of distinction between the two names. In the subsidy returns for 1524–25, Richard Blaker, listed in Bexhill Hundred as a taxpayer in 1524, is given in 1525 as Richard Blaber.[248] In 1524–25 the names Blaker and Blaber both appear at Storrington, not far from Shoreham, and apart from the instance at Bexhill, all the examples of Blaber in the subsidy are in the same part of the county.[249] Blaber was quite a common surname during the 16th and 17th centuries at Angmering, which is also in the area, not far from Shoreham, where Blaker had long been present. At Cuckfield, Blaker and Blaber both occur as established surnames during the 17th century, and at Rye both Blaker and Blaber appear in the 16th century parish registers.[250] The evidence suggests that there was a good deal of confusion between Blaker and Blaber. It must be uncertain whether Blaber originated as a variant of Blaker, a development which would be difficult to explain phonetically. Blaber is now quite a common surname in Sussex.

Bode, Boad, and Body

The name le Bode appears during the 13th century in both East and West Sussex. It is derived from the Old English 'boda' ('messenger'). The name le Bodere, which has the same meaning, occurs in the county, mostly in places near the Kent border, during the same period. The two names seem to have been interchangeable, at least in some cases. Geoffrey le Bodere, who witnessed a number of documents relating to the east of Sussex in the mid 13th century, appears to be the same person as Geoffrey le Bode, who occurs in the same area at the same period.[251] No instances of le Bodere have been found after 1300, and the form seems to have disappeared in Sussex. The name Bode, however, remained during the 14th century both in the east of the county, and in the southern part of West Sussex.[252] The persistence of the name at one or two places, such as Walberton and Burpham, shows that it was by then hereditary.

Bode (or Boade) survived in Sussex, to be present there during the 16th and 17th centuries. In the 16th it existed in West Sussex, not far from the areas where it had been present in the 14th. The name also survived in the 16th century in the south east of the county, again in areas not far from where it had occurred in the 14th.[253] In the 17th century the Protestation Returns, and other sources, show Bode as a widespread name in West Sussex.[254] Bode is an example of a name which was never common in Sussex, but which persisted there from the 13th century, with no more than a moderate increase in numbers, though becoming more dispersed within the county. Though not exclusively a Sussex surname in origin, it perhaps came to occur more frequently in the county than elsewhere. Bode still survives in Sussex now, though rare.

The surname Body, now in various forms (Boddy, Boddey, Boddie, etc.) a much more common name in the county than Bode, seems in Sussex to be a form of Bode. Body occurs in 1327/8 at Sidlesham, near Chichester, not far from where some instances of Bode are to be found at about the same period. Body also appears in 1378–79 at Warminghurst, near Burpham, where Bode was probably hereditary. In the 15th century Body, or Boddy, was a surname in East Sussex, near the Kent border, where Bode had existed earlier, and in the 16th century Body appears at Hastings, and around Eastbourne, both places where Bode was present at the same period. In the 16th century also, Body still survived near Chichester.[255] It was suggested many years ago by H.B. Guppy that Body might be a form of Bode.[256] Guppy was not an authority on the etymology of surnames, and a different account of the origin of Body has been given by Reaney,[257] but it seems probable that Guppy was correct, at least as regards the origins of Body in Sussex. The distribution of the early instances of Body does suggest that Body was a form of Bode. In this connection the tendency of surnames in Sussex to acquire a terminal 'y' in place of 'e' has to be considered.[258]

Beadle, Boodle, and Bothel

In Sussex and some other southern counties beadles were a township or manorial officer (it is often not clear which), and the surname or byename Beadle, in various forms, occurs in the county from the 12th century onwards. By the late 13th century the name was already widespread and quite numerous in Sussex, and had become more common there than in most parts of England. Beadles usually seem to have been customary tenants, and those people who appear with the name Beadle (etc.) before about 1350 generally belonged to that class, in cases where their position can be ascertained.[259] The name was already so dispersed by about 1300 that it is not possible for it to have originated with a single family. During the 13th and 14th centuries the usual form of the name in Sussex was Bedel, and this form appears in both East and West Sussex. At the same period, however, the form Budel occurs in West Sussex.[260] Forms such as Bodill or Bodle have not been found before the mid 15th century, when Bodil occurs in East Sussex. During the 16th and 17th centuries Bodill and Bodle both existed in East Sussex.[261] Most of the instances of Bodle, etc., come from the area around Hailsham, and could concern one family, but there are examples from other parts of East Sussex. The form Bedel does occur in the Hailsham area during the 13th and 14th centuries. Boodle and Buddle both appear in West Sussex during the 17th century, having no doubt developed from Budel.[262]

The development of these forms seems clear. However, during the 13th and 14th centuries the name Bothell or le Bothel appears in Sussex, with most of the instances being in the east of the county. Bothel could be a topographical surname,[263] but forms such as atte Bothel have not been found in Sussex, while the form le Bothel occurs too frequently for the presence of the definite article to be put down as a scribal error.[264] In some cases Bothell or le Bothel appear at the same places as Bedel. For instance, Bedel and le Bothel both occur during the first half of the 14th century at Ecclesden and at Wartling.[265] Further, the place-name Bodlestreet Green, in Herstmonceux, is said to be connected with the surname of several individuals (not certainly related to each other), named le Bothel, living at Herstmonceux in the 13th and 14th centuries.[266] It seems probable, therefore, that Bothel was another form of Bedel. No instances of Bothell or le Bothel have been discovered in the county after 1400.

the surname existed in Sussex in the 16th and 17th centuries in various forms, Bedle, Bedell, Bodle, Buddle, Bidle, etc. and was quite a widespread surname in the county. The name survived for long periods at some places; it persisted, for example, at Findon and at Arlington from the 14th century to the 17th.[267] Biddle, Beedle, Beedell, Bodle, Bodill, etc., still exist in the county.

Conier

The surname Conier or Conyare is usually said to be a form of Coiner, and to be derived from the craft of striking coins. Sussex examples have been cited in support of this view.[268] It is, however, doubtful if this is the correct explanation of the name's origin. The surname existed at Chichester during the 13th century, and at Oving, just outside the city, in the 14th. Thomas le Conier, or le Cunier who witnesses documents relating to Chichester in the mid 13th century, was evidently the same person as Thomas le Coninger, who witnessed a deed about Fishbourne at the same period, and as the Thomas *Cunularius*, mentioned at Chichester about the same date. Coninger usually had the meaning of 'rabbit warren', but must here be a name for a man who had charge of a warren. The Latinised form cited confirms that this is the meaning in the case here considered. Evidently in Sussex Conier was a word for a warrener.[269]

Dauber, Dobber, and Dubber

Dauber is a surname from the work of building wattle and daub walls, which seems to have included plastering and whitewashing walls. Dubber is said to be a distinct name, derived from the work of trimming or repairing clothes.[270] However, in Sussex it is clear that Dubber was a form of Dauber. The name occurs in several forms, during the 13th and 14th centuries, Dauber, Daber, Dober, and Dubber, and these seem to have been interchangeable. Peter le Daber (near Lewes, 1266) is also mentioned as Peter le Daubur. Hugh Daber, who appears at Cliffe near Lewes in 1305–6, was probably from the same family.[271] William Dubbere (at Arundel, 1296) is also referred to as William le Dobur. Robert Dauber, (at Arundel, 1332), again probably came from the same family.[272] Peter le Dober, (at Crawley, in 1296) was probably the same person as Peter le Daber, at Worth, adjoining Crawley, in 1332.[273] It would appear from this evidence that in Sussex Dubber was a form of Dauber, though this may not have been the case in some other parts of the country.

Though the surname, in its variant forms, was always rare in Sussex, it did survive. During the 15th century it existed in the Lewes area, and it was still present in the same part of the county in the 16th, then in the form Dubber. The persistence of the surname around Lewes suggests that it had been hereditary in that area from the mid 13th century, though no connected pedigree can be established.[274] The form Dubber has survived in Sussex to the present time.

Dunder and Thunder

The name Thunder (Tunder, Toundour, etc.) first occurs in Sussex in the mid 13th century. Early instances of the name concern two areas, the city of Chichester, and the district around Seaford in East Sussex. The name has not been found elsewhere in the county before 1350. A William le Thundre, who held lands at Steyning and Bramber in the late 13th century, seems to be the same person as William le Tundur, who was an inhabitant of Chichester at the same period.[275] It is quite possible that there were just two families of the name in the county, one at Chichester, one in East Sussex. The name is derived from the trade of shearing cloth. The synonymous name Sherman seems to have been absent from Sussex until after 1400, though it occurs earlier in other counties. The name Sherer does appear in Sussex during the 13th century and later, at Chichester among other places, but that is a name which could be derived from sheep-shearing.[276]

After about 1350, Thunder seems to have died out in and near Chichester, but it survived in East Sussex, at places not far from the area around Seaford where it existed earlier.[277] During the 15th century forms such as Dunder and Dondir first appear. Thomas Thunder, a prominent townsman at Winchelsea, who was mayor of the port in 1435, has his surname given variously as Thunder, Thonder, Dunder, and Dondir.[278] A list of the inhabitants of Winchelsea in 1292 includes two persons named Dinder.[279] The origin of Dinder is obscure; possibly it is a form of Dunder, but that is very uncertain.

Although Thunder was always a rare surname in Sussex, it did survive in the county, and in the late 15th and 16th centuries it was found at

Chiddingly, which is not far from the area around Seaford.[280] le Thonderscrofth and Thunderyscrosse are recorded as field names at Chiddingly in the late 15th century.[281] In all probability the surname had persisted as a hereditary name in much the same part of the county since the late 13th century. A locality called Thunder's Hill still exists at Chiddingly. The surname also existed at Horsham in the 16th century.[282] Thunder and Dindar both survive today as rare Sussex surnames.

Eveske and Vesk

The surname Eveske and Vesk are French linguistically. It does not seem that either form was merely a translation of the English name Bishop. Bishop was a widespread name in Sussex during the 13th century, and thereafter, but no case has been found where one individual was mentioned both as Bishop, and as Eveske or Vesk. Evesque and Vesque both existed as surnames in France, and the presence of Eveske and Vesk in England may be due to migration from France, but it is possible that the names, though linguistically French, may have originated in England.[283] One Sussex instance concerns a Jew, Elias le Evesk (1259), and in that case Evesk is probably a translation of a Hebrew name, possibly Cohen.[284]

Ralph Leveque is mentioned in Sussex in 1203, but the evidence does not connect him with any particular place.[285] In the mid 13th century the name Eveske occurs at Steyning, and Vesk appears at the same place during the 14th century.[286] It is probable that the name was hereditary at Steyning from about 1240. In the 1296 subsidy Ralph le Eveske is listed as a taxpayer at Broadwater, where he was a landowner, and the name Vesk occurs at the same place during the 14th century. During the late 14th and 15th centuries, several persons named Vesk were the successive holders of land in Little Broadwater, which was a part of Broadwater manor.[287] It seems likely that the persons named Vesk or Eveske listed at Broadwater earlier were in fact dwelling at Little Broadwater. Very possibly the presence of the surname at Little Broadwater was due to migration from Steyning. During the 14th century the name Vesk, or Wesk, or Eveske, spread to other places, not far from Steyning and Little Broadwater. Master John Vesk, who held land at Little Broadwater in 1376, also held land at Wiston, which adjoins Steyning, and the name Vesk survived at Wiston in the 15th century.[288] A Ralph Vesk was a taxpayer in 1332 at Sompting, adjoining Broadwater. He may have been the same person as Ralph Vesk, mentioned at Broadwater a little later.[289] The name also occurs in the 14th century at places rather more distant from Steyning and Broadwater, such as Dunhurst and Petworth.[290] It seems probable that the surname originated with one family at Steyning, in the first half of the 13th century, and then gradually dispersed from there, mostly by migration further north into the Weald.

Though the surname was rare, it persisted in much the same part of Sussex into the 15th and 16th centuries. One family so named were of some importance as landowners in West Sussex. One of them, John Vesk, was a Sussex coroner, up to 1445, and was M.P. for Shoreham in 1447. He was probably the same as the John Vesk who acquired land at Pulborough in 1447. Other persons of the name, who were landowners in West Sussex in the 15th century, were probably related. Even during the 15th century, the places at which the surname appears, such as Pulborough or Arundel, though rather more distant from Steyning and Broadwater than the localities where the name had existed earlier, are still in the same part of the county.[291] This, too appears to be an instance of a surname which originated with a single family in the county, and which gradually dispersed.

Fagg and Fagger

The surname Fagg is said to be derived from a word meaning either a flat loaf, or a flat fish such as a plaice. The name has been discovered in Kent in 1202, which is earlier than any known example in Sussex, but there is no evidence that the name migrated into Sussex from the adjoining county. The name Fagg existed during the 13th century in other southern counties, but does not seem to have been present at any early period in any other English region. Forms such as le Fagg have not been found in Sussex, but le Fag' occurs in Kent.[292]

The name Fagg first appears in Sussex during the 13th century, at West Firle and at Bexhill.[293] In the 14th century William Fagg was a bond tenant at Streatham.[294] Besides these instances, the name Feg', probably a variant of Fagg, occurs in 1392 at Ewhurst, on the Kent border.[295] These four places are not close together, and there is no reason to believe that all the four invididuals were related, nor are there grounds for thinking that in any of these cases the name was hereditary. Fagg up to this point seems to have been a rare bye-name, found in a few scattered examples. William Fagg, who was holding land at Bolney in 1473, may have been connected with the William Fagg who was a bondman at Streatham near Bolney, but that is uncertain.[296] It is not until the 16th century that any clear hereditary surname can be found. John Fagg was a butcher at Rye under Elizabeth I. Very probably he may have been descended from one of the Faggs who lived in East Sussex at an earlier date, especially as the name Fagg existed at Brede, near Rye, in 1525, but that cannot be proved. The Fagg family remained prominent at Rye during the 17th century. Under Charles II one of them, Sir John Fagg, acquired a baronetcy, and purchased estates at Findon, Wiston, Albourne, and elsewhere. Sir John's family continued to be important landowners in Sussex during the 18th century, and the family proliferated into various branches.[297]

Fagg is a surname which cannot be clearly shown to have been hereditary during the Middle Ages, and the evidence available for its history at that period is fragmentary. Nevertheless, its survival into the 16th century shows that it must have become hereditary, probably in East Sussex. It subsequently became the surname of a landed family of some importance. The history of the name demonstrates the limitations that there are to the evidence for some surnames during the Middle Ages, and shows how dangerous it is to place any weight upon the absence of evidence. The name survives in Sussex.

A locality called Great Fagg exists near Rye. This place-name is not mentioned in the *Place-names of Sussex*, but it is presumably derived from the surname of the Fagg family of Rye.

Fagger, or Vagger, is a rare surname which is not connected with Fagg. Two persons named Vagger are listed in the 1296 subsidy, at Hove and at West Blatchington, two adjoining townships. During the 15th century Fagger was the name of a landed family at and around Steyning, which is inland but not far from Hove and West Blatchington. Although no link can be traced between this family, and the Faggers of 1296, the rareness of the surname, and the proximity of the localities concerned, suggest that there was a connection, and that the surname had been hereditary from the late 13th century. The name Fagger, or Vaggar, persisted at and near Steyning in the 16th and 17th centuries, and after 1500 it also appears at other places in West Sussex, such as Chichester and Horsham. The name Fugar, found at Arundel in the late 17th and early 18th centuries, was probably another variant.[298] Fagger may be from a Middle English word meaning 'flatterer', but it may be a variant of the name Fayre ("fair") which occurs at Streatham, near Steyning, in the 14th century.

Hamper

Subsidy returns for Sussex in 1327/8, 1332, and 1378–9, list taxpayers named Hanepere or le Henepere at Sompting (near Worthing). The name is also listed in 1332 at Lancing, which adjoins Sompting.[299] Although no connected pedigree can be traced, the persistence of an unusual surname at Sompting over a period suggests that it was hereditary there from the late 13th century. The name is French linguistically, meaning a maker of 'hanaps' or drinking vessels. Robert Haneper, listed at Sompting in 1332, was a villein of Fécamp Abbey (Seine-Maritime), in Normandy. The surname existed in northern France, and it is tempting to conjecture that its presence at Sompting was due to the abbey having brought over tenants from Normandy. However, the name can be found during the 14th century in other southern counties, including Kent and Essex, so such a theory might be unjustified.[300] It further seems possible that there may have been some confusion with the name Hamer or Hammer; in Sussex this is a topographical name, formed from the element Hamme with the 'er' suffix. Haneper and Hammer both existed at Lancing.[301] Apart from Sompting and Lancing, William Hanepers was a tenant at Amberley in 1306. He may perhaps have been the same person as William Haneper listed at Lancing in 1332.[302]

At a later stage Hanepere or Henepere developed into Hamper. The first known instance of the form Hamper in Sussex is at Horsham, in 1428. A Geoffrey Handhamer is listed at Horsham in the 1296 subsidy, and possibly his name, not otherwise evidenced, may have been a distortion of the unusual name Hanepere. Hamper survived at Horsham for a long period, and was still present there in the late 17th century.[303] There is still a Hamper's Lane at Horsham. During the 16th and 17th centuries Hamper was a fairly common surname in West Sussex. In the 1524 subsidy, there were already ten persons so named. Some of the 1524 instances were at places quite close to Sompting, such as West Tarring, Wiston, and Washington, but others were at places more distant, such as Petworth or Aldingbourne, and there were two individuals in East Sussex.[304] In the 17th century the surname still existed at Wiston, Washington, and West Tarring, and also at other places in the same area, such as Angmering, but it had spread further, to Easebourne in north west Sussex, for example.[305] The name survives in Sussex.

Hose, Huse, and Hussey

There has been much confusion about the origin of several surnames which are orthographically similar, and the difficulty of separating the names involved, one from another, is increased by the use, often inconsistent, in 12th and 13th century sources of Latinised forms such as *Hosarius, Hosatus,* and so forth.

A topographical name, atte Huse, or de la Huse, existed in Sussex during the 13th and 14th centuries and was quite widespread in East and West Sussex. This name is said to be a form of 'house'. Forms such as atte Huse or de la Huse have not been found after 1400 in Sussex, and it is impossible to say if this topographical name has contributed to the surname Hussey, which appears in the county later.[306] A second topographical name, atte Hose, also occurs in Sussex. This is a form of atte Hese ('at the brushwood'); William atte Hose, at Brightling, 1332, is the same person as William atte Hese, listed at the same place in 1327–28.[307]

From the 12th century onwards there was an important landed family in Sussex named Huse, or, later, Hussey. The family held the manor of Harting, other Sussex properties, and estates outside the county, some in Wiltshire and Berkshire. The family's surname was hereditary from the 12th century or perhaps the late 11th. It is not necessary here to deal in detail with the family's pedigree or history, as there are published accounts in other works.[308] What needs to be discussed are the origins and ramifications of the surname. 12th century sources usually give the surname in a Latinised form, as *Hosatus*. Robert *Hosarius*, mentioned as a Sussex landowner in 1130, was probably a member of the same family.[309] Apart from such Latin versions, the forms Huse and Hose were used during the 12th century, and during the 13th the most used form seems to have been Hose or le Hose, though Huse was also employed.[310] The name is given as Hosee in 1242–43, as Hosey in 1296, and frequently as Hussee or Husee in the 14th century.[311]

It is not easy to see the origin of a name which appears in such varying forms. The development of Hose or Huse to Husee or Hussey is understandable in terms of the history of Sussex surnames generally.[312] The Latin *Hosatus* ought to mean 'booted', and it is possible that this could be the significance of forms such as le Hose or le Huse. This may be the correct explanation but it does not account for the form *Hosarius* already mentioned, which should mean either 'hosier', or possibly, be a term for an officer of the king's buttery.[313] Since *Hosatus* is the most common early form the meaning 'booted' is the most probable. In that case the name would have been originally a nickname for someone whose boots were noteworthy in some respect.

The manor of Harting, and other Sussex lands, descended in the Hose, Huse, or Husee family until 1472, when the then owner of the lands died without male issue, leaving his estates to be divided among his daughters. Even after this, however, there were still members of the family in the male line surviving in Sussex, with the name Husee or Hussey, in the late 15th and 16th centuries.[314] In the 13th century several persons named le Hose are mentioned in different parts of Sussex. At least one of these was unfree, and another seems to have been a small free tenant.[315] Cases are known elsewhere of bondmen having the same name as local landed families, though the explanation for this is not clear.[316] In most cases there is no evidence that these names were hereditary, but in at least one instance the name became hereditary in East Sussex. Osbert Hose, or Hussee, is mentioned in connection with West Firle, possibly about 1150, but the date is doubtful. About 1200 Alexander Husar was holding land at Firle. Robert le Husyer, le Hosere, or le Hosier, who was living in 1296 and in 1316, but who was dead by 1327, held land at West Firle, and at Seaford not far away. Osbert le Huser, who witnessed a charter about East Grinstead c.1260, may be the same person as the Osbert Hose just mentioned.[317] Although no connected pedigree can be compiled, the continued existence of the surname at one place shows that the name was hereditary. It is unknown whether there was any relationship with the family which held Harting. In the case of the family at West Firle, the surname Hose developed into Hosier. As the family seem to have been landowners of some means, it is unlikely that they were in fact hosiers. It

Surnames Derived from Occupation, Status, or Office 269

is possible that the family were buttery officials, either of the king or of some magnate, and that this is the explanation of the surname, but there is no evidence of this.[318] What does seem to be clear is that the two surnames occur in what, so far as can be seen, were the same forms in the 12th century, but subsequently evolved differently.

The surname Husewif has in some cases developed into Hussey. Husewif does occur as a bye-name, at Chichester in the late 12th and early 13th centuries, but it does not seem to have been hereditary. Husewif also occurs as a woman's Christian name, both in Sussex and in Kent.[319] There is, however, no evidence that Husewif, either as a surname or a Christian name, contributed to the proliferation of the surname Hussey in Sussex.

In the 1524 subsidy, there are five persons named Hussey, all in the southern part of West Sussex. It is quite possible that these were all descendants of the family which held Harting earlier.[320] The name was present in the same part of the county during the 15th century.[321] Hussey still survived in West Sussex in the 17th century.[322] The name Hosier existed in the 16th century at Amberley, and in the 17th it appears both there, and at other places nearby, but there is nothing to connect these Hosiers in West Sussex with the family noted earlier at Firle.[323]

Lasher

Lasher is a surname which seems to have originated with an alien. The first person with the name to be noted in Sussex is Laurence Lasher, a foreigner living at Rye in 1439–40. During the 16th and 17th centuries the surname Lasher existed at Hastings, another of the Cinque Ports. Though no pedigree can be traced from Laurence, it is likely that the Lasher family who were living at Hastings were his descendants. The family was of some consequence at Hastings, and James Lasher was mayor there in 1590. Laurence's nationality is not known, but it seems probable that his name was an Anglicised version of the French Le Huissier or Lhuissier. The surname Lusher, which existed in the 17th century at Glynde, may be a form of Lasher.[324] Lusher still survives in Sussex.

Pilcher

Pilcher is a surname which has never been at all common in Sussex, but which seems to have been more common in the county than elsewhere in England. The name derives from the occupation of making or selling pilches, which were skin garments with the hair on the outside. The medieval instances of the surname which have been noted in the county were all in East Sussex, with most of them in the north east of the county, near the Kent border. In this area the surname occurs during the 13th and 14th centuries at Wadhurst, Mayfield, Maresfield, and Ticehurst. It is likely that all the individuals named Pilcher in this part of the county belonged to one family, of which the surname proliferated locally to a limited extent. However, the name also appears in other parts of East Sussex, at Lewes, Winchelsea, Laughton, and Newtimber (near Poynings), for example, so that it seems improbable that all the Sussex Pilchers were from a single family. There was a street called Pilecheerestrete at Lewes in the 12th century, which suggests that the trade was then well established there.[325] Early in the 15th century Pilcher occurs at Battle and the surname survived there during the 16th and 17th centuries. The name Pilter, mentioned at Sandlake near Battle in 1332, is probably an error for Pilcher.[326] In the 15th century, too, Pilcher was present at Westham, and it persists there in the 16th.[327] The surname was widely dispersed in the more easterly parts of East Sussex in the 16th century, but seems to have been lacking in West Sussex.[328]

The name Pulcher or Pullchare, of which there are two medieval examples in Sussex (both in the east), was evidently a variant of Pilcher; Richard Pilcher, of Upperton (near Eastbourne) 1430–31, is evidently the same as Richard Pulcher, of the adjoining parish of Westham.[329]

Portreve

A portreve was the principal officer of a town (usually a chartered borough). Portreve was always an unusual surname, but it did exist in several counties. The first person with the name who has been noted in Sussex was John le Portreve, who appears at Seaford and one or two other places in the vicinity, in the early 14th century. Other 14th century instances of the name are mostly at places not far from Seaford, such as Pevensey and Hailsham, and these may all concern one family, but the name also occurs at Icklesham, which is rather more distant, and it must be uncertain if all the Sussex Portreves were related.[330]

Though rare, the surname survived in East Sussex. In the 16th century it existed at Salehurst, and during the 16th and 17th centuries it was present at Rye. The form usually found after 1500 is Portriffe.[331] Rye is very close to Icklesham, though Salehurst is about nine miles away. Portreve persisted in East Sussex over a long period, without so far as can be seen proliferating to any noticeable extent.

Shotter and Shotcher

The name Shotter signifies someone who shoots, and was probably a name for a bowman.[332] The earliest examples of the name which have been found in Sussex are in the 14th century, at Linchmere, in the north west of the county, and on the Surrey border, and at Cocking, in the same area. The name was then in the form Schottere. It survived at Linchmere

Surnames Derived from Occupation, Status, or Office 271

over a long period, and Shotter was quite a numerous surname there in the 16th and 17th centuries.[333] It is probable that the surname was hereditary there from the 14th century. In the 16th century there was some confusion between Shotter, and the similar surname Shorter, which existed in the same part of Sussex, and across the border in south west Surrey, but which had a different origin.[334]

By the 16th century the name had begun to spread. In 1524 the name, in the form Shotyer, was present at Barlavington, some distance south of Linchmere, and it survived there in the 17th century.[335] After the mid 16th century the surname was sometimes spelt Satcher or Sacher. A family of tenant farmers, who held land at Petworth and Duncton, two places close to Barlavington, over a long period during the 16th and 17th centuries, had a surname which was given variously as Shotcher, Satcher, and Sacher.[336] Richard Shotcher, a 17th century resident of Angmering, is also referred to as Richard Sotcher, Satcher, or Sacher.[337] Early in the 17th century the name Satcher appears at Barlavington, no doubt as a development there from Shotter or Shotcher.[338] The 1641–2 Protestation Returns show that the surname had by that date ramified quite considerably in West Sussex. The returns list 31 men named Shotter, Shotcher, or Scotcher, mostly at places around Linchmere (where the name still survived in 1642), such as Fernhurst, Lodsworth, Easebourne, Lurgashall, and North Chapel. The name had also multiplied at Petworth, where 10 individuals lived. Besides this, however, the surname had spread to the southern parts of West Sussex, and men named Shotter are listed at Boxgrove, West Stoke, Warningcamp, and Poling.[339] As already mentioned, the surname also occurs during the 17th century at Angmering, close to Poling and Warningcamp. In 1642 Sacher is listed at Barlavington. The Protestation Returns give the name Saker at Horsham; this may be a further variant of the same surname, as Shoter existed at Horsham earlier.[340]

Shotter is a surname which probably originated in Sussex with a single family at Linchmere. The surname proliferated, until by the 17th century it had become quite numerous in West Sussex, and had dispersed considerably, though still most frequent in the north west of the county, where it first appeared. Sacher and Sacker are usually said to be from the occupation of sack-making, but in this case Sacher, at least, could be a variant of Shotter.

The name Shittere, which is mentioned at Annington (near Bramber) in 1378–79, probably had the same meaning as Shotter. Robert le Scheter, who appears in a Sussex assize roll for 1249, had what was probably another form of the same name. No other medieval references to this name have been discovered in Sussex, but it evidently survived, for in 1642 the name Shieter is listed in the Protestation Returns at Broadwater, quite close to Annington. The name Shuiter, listed in 1642 at West Stoke, may be another variant of the same name, but alternatively, it may be a variant of Sutor.[341]

Tapener

The surname Tapener, Taupener, or Tapner seems to have been confined originally to Sussex and Hampshire. It is derived from a word ('*taponnier*') of French origin, meaning a cloth worker. In England it may have been a term for a maker of some special type of cloth, but, if so, it is not clear what the speciality was. The first person with the name to be found in Sussex is Robert *tapinarius*, mentioned in 1202. Robert is described as 'of Southampton'.[342] Possibly he may have migrated into Sussex from Hampshire, where the name existed in the 13th century. From about 1240, several persons named le Tapiner or le Taupenyr were occupying land at Chichester. It cannot be shown that they were related, and it is uncertain whether there was a hereditary surname in the city at that time, or whether it is a case of several unrelated people having names from a craft which was presumably being practised at Chichester.[343] After the mid 13th century, the name spread from Chichester to villages nearby. Walter le Taupenyr, who held land in the city, acquired a house at Boxgrove, just outside Chichester, probably about 1250. The name still existed at Boxgrove in the 14th century, and had probably become hereditary there.[344] About 1300 the name appears at Appledram, and early in the 14th century at Hunston and Westbourne; these are villages near Chichester.[345] Later in the 14th century there are examples of the name in places further east, at Arundel, Broadwater, and West Tarring, all places in the southern part of West Sussex, but more distant from Chichester.[346] This has all the appearance of a name which existed at Chichester as that of a specialised craft (possibly imported from Southampton), and gradually dispersed into the surrounding rural areas. This would imply that the name had become hereditary, and detached from the actual exercise of the craft, probably by the late 13th century.

The name Tapene or le Tapene occurs during the 13th century in East Sussex, at Cliffe near Lewes and at Middleham, about a mile away.[347] This is probably another form of the same name, but it has not been possible to establish any link between the few men named Tapene, in East Sussex, and those named Tapiner, etc., in West Sussex. The name does not seem to have survived in East Sussex after about 1300. In the form Tapner the surname still exists in Sussex.

Topper and Tupper

The origins of the surnames Topper and Tupper are doubtful. Topper is said to be from wool or flax 'topps', and to be a name for someone who placed the tufts of wool or flax on the distaff. It is difficult to see this task giving rise to a distinct occupation, especially as in the Middle Ages spinning was largely carried on by women as a domestic industry, while the early instances of persons named Topper are all male. It has further been suggested that Tupper was from the occupation of ramming down earth.[348] Possibly Topper may be from the trade of dealing in wool tops.

In Sussex the names le Topere and le Tupere both appear together, at East Preston (in the coastal district of West Sussex) in 1321. Both were then the names of customary tenants. At that date there was a field at East Preston called le Tuperforlang, which suggests that the name was already well established there. In Sussex it is extremely common to find names of fields, holdings, farms, etc., which are derived from the names of owners or tenants, and this is probably such a case. As le Topere and le Tupere both occur together with one village, it is very probable that they are two variants of a single name.[349] The examples at Preston do not throw any light on the origins of the name, but in view of the frequency with which surnames formed from a topographical term with the suffix -er are found in Sussex, it may be suspected that Topere (or Tupere) is a name of that type, from 'topp' in the sense of the top of a hill or bank. Against this, however, no example of atte Topp as a surname has been found in Sussex.[350] The origin of the name must remain uncertain.

Tupper (or Topper) seems to have been a very rare name in medieval Sussex, and before 1500 it has not been found except at East Preston. It must, however, have survived, and ramified to some extent, for in the 1524–25 subsidy for the county there are six men named Tupper listed, at Bury and West Burton, which are inland from East Preston, and at Petworth, which is a short distance north of Bury. It is probable that this represents the dispersal of one family from Preston. In late 16th century parish registers Tupper is listed in many West Sussex parishes. In 1524 the name Tuppard appears in Robertsbridge Hundred (East Sussex). This is probably a variant of Tupper, but it might possibly be a form of Tupherd ('ram herd').[351] The more complete information about surnames provided by the 1641–42 Protestation Returns shows Tupper as a numerous surname in West Sussex; 26 men named Tupper were listed in this source, and this is probably the whole number of adult males in West Sussex with the surname. The surname was then numerous at and near Bury, but it was widely spread throughout West Sussex. Although all the 17th century Tuppers cannot be linked genealogically, there are indications that there were relationships between those who are listed in different parishes. In 1642, the Christian name Clement, then fairly rare, occurs among the

Tuppers at Bury, at Cocking further west (another place at which the surname was then numerous) and at Pagham. Unfortunately there is no similar source for East Sussex at the same period, but no examples of the surname are known from that part of the county in the 17th century.[352] Tupper remained a numerous surname at Cocking throughout the 17th and 18th centuries.[353]

Apart from the obscurity about the surname's origin, the history of Tupper in the county is of interest because it shows how a name could ramify and disperse. Tupper was always a scarce surname, taking England as a whole, and it is unlikely that migration into the county played any part in the development of the name in Sussex. It seems probable that the ramification of the name, observable in the 17th century, was due to the descendants of one family, from East Preston, multiplying.

Trott

Trott, or Trot, is a surname which, in contrast to Tupper, survived in one part of Sussex over a long period without increasing in numbers very significantly. The first example of the name which has been found in the county is at Warminghurst, in 1296. During the 14th century the name was still at Warminghurst, where it had probably become hereditary. It also appears then at Dishenhurst and Steyning, not far from Warminghurst, and at Mundham, south of Chichester. Possibly these instances might all concern one family.[354] However, at the same period the name can also be found at Burwash, in East Sussex, which is relatively distant.[355] The name survived in Sussex in the 15th century, but seems to have been rare.[356] In the 1524 subsidy returns, the surname is listed in the Chichester area, at Aldingbourne, North Mundham, and Selsey, but not elsewhere in Sussex.[357] The name must have been hereditary at Mundham since early in the 14th century. Trot does occur in East Sussex during the 16th century, and may perhaps have survived there too as a hereditary name from the 14th century.[358] The surname was still present during the 17th century at places in the district around Chichester, including Aldingbourne, where the name increased in numbers to some extent.[359]

Trott was probably a name for a messenger. The name Trotteman, which has the same significance, existed at Midhurst during the 13th and 14th centuries, but does not seem to have survived.[360] Trott itself was always an uncommon surname in Sussex, which survived over a long period, without ramifying to any noticeable extent. It is, however, at the present day fairly numerous in the county.

Washer

Among the surnames which were originally very rare in the county is Washer. This has first been found in Sussex in 1405, at Chichester, as the name of a former tenant, and in 1428, at Barpham (near Angmering) in the coastal part of West Sussex. The name could have existed from a much earlier date without being noted in any surviving record, but it is possible that it was a surname of relatively late origin in Sussex. A custumal of 1321 shows that on the manor of Barpham tenants' obligations included the duty of washing the lord's sheep. Tenants of East Preston manor, a few miles from Barpham, had the same duty, but so far as can be seen from the available sources, this was not a general obligation on Sussex manors. A similar duty existed in Hampshire before the Conquest.[361] It seems very probable that it was this duty of washing sheep which gave rise to the surname. The name Washer can be found in other counties, remote from Sussex, and may have other origins in other regions.[362]

Washer has not been discovered any where in Sussex, except at Barpham, before 1500. In the 1524 subsidy, however, nine persons so named are listed. Most of these were at places quite close to Barpham, such as Lancing, Sompting, Wepham, Clapham, and Parham, but one is rather more distant, at Sidlesham, south of Chichester.[363] Later in the 16th century there are examples of Washer at several places somewhat further from Barpham than Lancing, Wepham, etc., such as Southwick, Binstead, Eastergate and Warminghurst.[364] In the Protestation Returns for West Sussex (1642), 19 men named Washer are listed, at places including Lancing and Sompting, some other places quite near to Barpham, such as Goring, Burpham, Warningcamp, Storrington, and Findon, or Botolphs and Steyning, which are rather more distant, and also Horsham and Cowfold, further north and more remote from Barpham. Later in the 17th century Washer occurs at Chichester.[365]

Although no connected pedigree can be drawn up linking all the persons named Washer who can be found in Sussex, it seems extremely probable that all of them were the descendants of a single family, originating at Barpham, and that the surname ramified considerably. The 19 men named Washer listed in 1642 were probably the whole number of adult males with the surname then living in West Sussex. Unfortunately there is no equally comprehensive source for East Sussex for the same period, but no references to Washer have been found in that part of the county for the 17th century, and it may not have spread so far. It is also not possible to say how many Washers there may have been resident outside Sussex altogether by the 17th century who had origins tracing back to the county. Despite these reservations, the number listed in 1642 probably gives a reasonably accurate picture of how far the name had multiplied and spread by that date. It must be considered likely that this development was due to the gradual spread and increase of a single family. Though a rare name in England generally, Washer is now quite numerous in Sussex.

Some individual surnames have been discussed above because it has seemed necessary either to investigate their origins, which in some cases have not been adequately explained by the standard authorities, or to set out the evidence for the ramification and dispersal of some surnames, in order to throw light on the general history of surnames in Sussex. It has not been thought necessary to deal with the history within the county of the more common occupational names, which can be found very widely distributed throughout England from an early period, though something has been said about their relative frequency in the county. There remain many occupational surnames which were not generally common in England, but which have had a long history in Sussex, and which have in some cases been more numerous there than in other counties. A few of these have for various reasons been dealt with in other chapters, but there are many which for reasons of space it has not been possible to consider in detail.

Some occupational surnames which have for centuries been those of families in Sussex, and which have been found there more frequently than in many other parts of England, are given here in a list, with a few abbreviated comments. These will indicate in a condensed account, the position of each name in the history of the county's surnames, without filling the survey of Sussex occupational names with a mass of perhaps indigestible detail about individual surnames.

Bachelor: present in East and West Sussex from early 13th century, and for long survived at Brede, and in that area; from a Middle English word (a loan from Old French), 'bacheler' meaning a young, often landless, knight; despite this meaning, the name is found as that of families of very varied social status, some landowners, some serfs, and it may have originated as a nickname in some cases; remains a common Sussex name.

Banister: origins disputable;[366] very scarce in Sussex before 1500, though common in some other parts of England; later a fairly numerous name in the county.

Booker: widespread in Sussex during the 16th and 17th centuries, and later, up to the present day; in some cases at least derived from Bowker ('bleacher'), itself a common name in the county in 1200–1500; the only other county in which Bowker was at all common seems to be Lancashire.

Bolter and Boulter: from the occupation of sifting flour, or, possibly, of making bolts; a rare name nationally, but established in both East and West Sussex from the 13th century; the name is too dispersed from an early date for it to have originated with one family in the county; still quite common in Sussex, usually in the form Boulter; Bolterscombe in Ugborough is from the surname.

Caperon and Capron ('hood maker'): found in several parts of Sussex during the Middle Ages, but persisting especially in the north-west, around Midhurst; Capron and Caperon both survive in Sussex, though rare.

Carver: probably from the craft of carving wood or stone; a very rare name in the county before 1500, but one which later proliferated in north-west Sussex, probably through the increase of one family, and now more common in Sussex than in most parts of England.

Cheeseman: a surname widespread in Sussex from the 13th century, though more common in the east of the county; probably from the making of cheese from ewes' milk; for some reason not clear there have for long been markedly more people named Cheeseman in Sussex than elsewhere; possibly cheesemaking in Sussex may have been a more specialised occupation than in other regions; still very numerous in the county.

Collier: in Sussex, the name must be from charcoal burning; during the 13th and 14th centuries found mostly in the Wealden parts of East Sussex, though there are scattered references elsewhere in the county; the surname long survived in the same part of Sussex, though it spread to other areas and multiplied considerably.

Helier, Hellyer: from the craft of slating or tiling, and a name chiefly belonging to the south and south-east of England; present in Sussex from the 14th century, and for long survived around Eastbourne; now numerous in the county; occurs as the name of an alien in 15th century Sussex.

Ladd: the name is probably from the use of the word in the sense of 'servant', 'retainer'; found in Sussex mainly in the east, where it persisted over a long period, from the 13th century, though there are instances in other parts.

Man: similarly from the use of the word to mean 'tenant' or 'vassal', and generally in early instances the name of customary tenants or small freeholders; another surname now very common in Sussex.

Marshall: probably from the use of the word to mean 'smith'; the name was very common in Sussex from the 13th century, and in several forms (Mascold, Mascall, etc.) has remained so to the present.

Master, Moster, Muster, Maister: a name widely dispersed in Sussex in the 13th and 14th centuries, but then most common around Worthing, an area where it survived into the 16th and 17th centuries; possibly confused at a later period with the name atte Mostowe ('at the meeting place'), which existed in the 13th and 14th centuries not far from Worthing; now a rare name in Sussex; probably originally a name given to a freeholder of sufficient wealth to have labourers, etc., working his land.

May or Mey: a name with the meaning 'lad' or 'girl', probably used with the significance of 'servant' (compare Ladd); in 1525 the surname of an alien in Sussex, and in that case probably a French surname of the nickname type; May or Mey has been a fairly common surname in the east of the county from the late 13th century, evidently as the name of several different families, and it had ramified considerably by the 16th century; still a very common name in Sussex.

Millward, Millard, Mellward, Mulward: the most common surname in Sussex from the occupation of milling; existed in many places in the county during the 14th century, clearly as the name of many separate families; very widespread in the 16th and 17th centuries in forms such as Millard; still very common in Sussex, mostly in the forms Milward and Millard.

Reve, Reeve: originally mainly the name of customary tenants, who on many manors had the duty of filling the office of reve; very widely distributed in Sussex from the 13th century, but also common in many other counties; now very numerous in Sussex.

Roper: a scarce name in Sussex before 1400, with most of the early instances in towns; had become much more numerous by the 16th century, by which time there were a number of distinct families so called.

Sadler: survived from the 14th century in north-west Sussex around Midhurst; early references in the county are all from this area, and probably concern one family; still mostly in the Midhurst area in the 17th century; to-day widespread in Sussex, probably due to migration into the county since about 1800.

Soper, Saper, Sapper: found at many places in Sussex from the 13th century onwards, and evidently originating in the county with several separate families; by the 17th century had become one of the more numerous surnames in a few parishes, such as West Grinstead, but is now rare in the county.

Spicer: in the 13th and 14th centuries mostly found in towns, such as Lewes, Chichester and Winchelsea; another surname which clearly originated with several separate families in the county; more dispersed after about 1400, especially in East Sussex; at the present day fairly common in Sussex, but not noticeably more so than in some other counties.

Taverner: most early instances in Sussex concern one family, at Chichester, which acquired land around the city; in the 16th and 17th centuries there was a landed family so called with estates at Washington and Wiston, and most of the references in Sussex at those periods concern this family; however, the surname was widely distributed in England from an early date.

Thatcher, Thetcher, Theccer: from the 13th century more common in Sussex than in most other counties; widely scattered in early examples, evidently having originated in a number of separate families; by the 16th century the surname had become rare in West Sussex, but numerous in East Sussex; still one of the more common occupational surnames in the county.

Ward: ('watchman' or 'guard'); first found in Sussex in the 12th century, and in the 13th present in several different areas, such as East Dean (West Sussex) and Ewhurst (East Sussex), and so likely to have originated as the name of several distinct families in the county; already a very common and widespread name by the 16th century.

Warner: in early instances usually le Warenner or le Wariner (a name for a man in charge of rabbit warrens, a useful source of food on some medieval estates); dispersed throughout Sussex from the 13th century, but especially persistent in the Selsey area, perhaps a district exceptionally favourable for warrens.

Wheeler (wheelwright): a rare name in Sussex before 1500, and mostly found in the west of the county; ramified considerably by the 16th century, still mostly in West Sussex; now very numerous in West Sussex, probably partly as a result of recent migration.

Workman, Werkman: possibly a nickname for someone ambidextrous, but no evidence for this significance has been found in Sussex; early instances in Sussex probably all concern two families, one tenants on South Malling manor, one living near Chichester; always a rare name in Sussex, and in England as a whole, but has survived in the county.

Whitbread: (a name for a baker); a rare name, but one which in Sussex originated with three apparently unconnected families, one around Seaford, an area where the surname survived into the 16th century, one in the district near the Kent border, and one in central Sussex around Wiston, where the surname long persisted as that of yeomen; though scarce, the name has survived in Sussex.

References

[1] *3 Suss. Subsidies*, pp. 109–333.
[2] The figures here differ from those in Reaney, *Origins*, p. 22. It is not clear if Dr Reaney included surnames derived from terms for status in his figures.
[3] Printed in *3 Suss. Subsidies*.
[4] *Ibid.*, p. 128.
[5] *Surnames of Lancs.*, pp. 272–73.
[6] See above, p. 10.
[7] The sources used are: A. Rumble, *Dorset Lay Subsidy of 1327* (Dorset Record Soc., no. vi) (1980); H. A. Hanley and C. W. Chalklin, 'Kent Lay Subsidy of 1334/5', in *Documents Illustrative of Medieval Kentish Society* (Kent Archaeological Soc., vol. xviii) (1964), ed. F. R. H. Du Boulay; J. P. Rylands, 'Exchequer Lay Subsidy Roll', in *Miscellanies Relating to Lancs. and Chesh.* (Lancs. and Chesh. Record Soc., vol. xxxi) (1896), vol. ii; W. G. D. Fletcher, 'Leics. Lay Subsidy, 1327', *Associated Archaeological Socs. Reports and Papers*, vols. xix, xx; P. R. O. E. 179/161/9 (Oxon. lay subsidy, 1327); G. Wrottesley, *Exchequer Lay Subsidy Roll, 1327* (Collections for a History of Staffs., vol. vii) (1886); Anon., *Suff. in 1327* (Suff. Green Books, no. ix) (1906); Anon., *Surr. Taxation Returns* (Surr. Record Soc., vol. xi, no. xviii, (1923), and no. xxxiii (1931), pp. 64–94); *3 Suss. Subsidies*, pp. 225–334; W. F. Carter, *Lay Subsidy Roll for Warw.* (Dugdale Soc., vol. vi) (1926); J. Parker, 'Lay Subsidy Rolls, I Edward III', in *Miscellanea* (Yorks. Archaeological Soc. Record Series, vol. lxxiv) (1929).
[8] The form that occurs in the source is Berker.
[9] The name 'Carpentar' does occur. This is probably for the Latin *carpentarius* which could be a translation of Wright.
[10] See *Surnames of Oxon.*, pp. 122–23.
[11] *Ibid.*, p. 149.
[12] *Ibid.*, p. 148.
[13] *Norf. and Suff. Surnames*, p. 53.
[14] *Ibid.*, pp. 40–41.
[15] The references in this source are all in the Latin form *carectarius*.
[16] The Latin *textor* occurs, but it is uncertain what it translates.
[17] Occurs in the Latin form *piscator*.
[18] Occurs in the Latin for *venator*.
[19] The Latin form *molendinarius* occurs, but it is uncertain which vernacular name is being translated.
[20] H. B. Guppy, *Homes of Family Names* (1968), pp. 551–2.
[21] *Surnames of Lancs.*, p. 249.
[22] Guppy, *op. cit.*, pp. 451–2.

Surnames Derived from Occupation, Status, or Office

[23] *Ibid.*, p. 466.
[24] *Ibid.*, pp. 551–2, 558.
[25] Fransson, *op. cit.*, p. 61.
[26] *Ibid.*, p. 101; *Surnames of Lancs.*, pp. 253–4.
[27] *Surnames of Oxon.*, pp. 149–50.
[28] *Suss. Subsidy, 1524–5*, pp. 3, 27, 33, 94, 95, 102, 116, 128, 147, 149. And see p. 225.
[29] See, e.g., *3 Suss. Subsidies*, pp. 75, 77, 99, 101, 116, 138, 154, 184, 239, 258, 277; *Suss. Custumals*, vol. ii, pp. 32, 40, 80, 82; *Chichester Chart.*, pp. 91, 114, 115.
[30] *Suss. Subsidy, 1524–5*, pp. 6, 8, 19, 31–33, 65–6, 72, 81, 102–3, 105, 112, 123, 127, 134, 145, 147–50, 164; Guppy, *op. cit.*, p. 488.
[31] Fransson, *op. cit.*, p. 101.
[32] *Ibid.*, pp. 87–88; *Feudal Aids*, vol. v, p. 166; *Hastings Lathe C.R.*, pp. 26, 113, 124, 126, 132, 134, 155, 185, 187; *3 Suss. Subsidies*, pp. 7, 16–7, 26, 28, 41, 93, 102, 113, 115, 125, 146, 153, 172, 185, 187, 194, 199, 201, 208, 237, 249, 259, 287, 300, 302, 312, 323; *Non Inquis.*, pp. 364, 384, 390, 403; *S.A.C.*, vol. xxiv, p. 69; vol. lxxxvii, pp. 9, 22; vol. lxxxix, p. 143; vol. xcvi, p. 26; *Chichester Chart.*, pp. 255, 374; *Suss. Subsidy, 1524–5*, pp. 3, 7, 21, 25, 43, 45, 92, 96, 102, 103, 128–30, 133–4, 137, 159; *Wiston Archives*, p. 97; P.R.O. E. 179/225/50, m. 21; E. 179/228/112; S.C. 11/877; E. 179/189/42, mm. 22, 28; E. 179/189/94; *Suss. Fines*, vol. iii, p. 256; *Fitzalan Surveys*, pp. 128, 158.
[33] *Suss. Subsidies*, pp. 13, 18, 33–4, 39, 115, 199, 310; *Hastings Lathe C.R.*, pp. 31–2, 117, 126, 177; *S.A.C.*, vol. xcvi, p. 27; *Suss Custumals*, vol. i, p. 81; vol. ii, pp. 48, 71; P.R.O. E. 179/225/50, m. 28; E. 179/270/10; *Suss. Fines*, vol. iii, p. 263; *Fitzalan Surveys*, p. 153.
[34] *Suss. Custumals*, vol. ii, pp. 8, 13, 29, 85, 112, 137–8; vol. iii, pp. 32, 33.
[35] *S.A.C.*, vol. lxxxix, p. 118.
[36] *Robertsbridge Charters*, p. 137. The Latin *Cinerarius* (*ibid.*, p. 10), probably translates Colebrener.
[37] Inderwick, *Winchelsea*, pp. 174, 184.
[38] Fransson, *op. cit.*, p. 59; *Suss. Fines*, vol. i, p. 87. A Robert le Cribelere was murdered at Nottingham, about 1290, but his residence is unknown: *Calendar of Close Rolls, 1288–96*, p. 162.
[39] B. Thuresson, *Middle English Occupational Terms* (1950), p. 144; *3 Suss. Subsidies*, p. 119. And see p. 193.
[40] *3 Suss. Subsidies*, p. 128; Thuresson, *op. cit.*, p. 195.
[41] P.R.O. E. 179/270/10.
[42] *Boxgrove Chart.*, p. 195.
[43] *Chichester Chart.*, p. 104; some land at Chichester was called Quernbites, probably from this bye-name. See also Thuresson, *op. cit.*, p. 235; *Chichester Bishops' Acta*, p. 122.

[44] *Non. Inquis.*, p. 403; Inderwick, *Winchelsea*, p. 180. Compare the bye-name Ripreue; Thuresson, *op. cit.*, p. 102.
[45] *S.A. C.*, vol. xcvi, p. 33. The name Trumpeter, which occurs later (*Suss. Indictments*, vol. i, p. 37), may be a later form of Trumpet.
[46] *3 Suss. Subsidies*, p. 143; Fransson, *op. cit.*, p. 67.
[47] *3 Suss. Subsidies*, pp. 69, 143.
[48] *Ibid.*, p. 122; *Hastings Lathe C.R.*, p. 116; Reaney, *Dict.*, 31. A Peter Bender (probably English) is mentioned in connection with Gascony, in 1227. His place of origin is unknown: *Calendar of Liberate Rolls, Henry III* (1916), vol. i, p. 32.
[49] *Hastings Lathe C.R.*, p. 167; Thuresson, *op. cit.*, p. 88.
[50] *3 Suss. Subsidies*, pp. 64, 160, 273; J. E. Ray, *Suss. Chantry Records* (Suss. Record Soc., vol. xxxi) (1931), p. 21.
[51] *Chichester Chart.*, p. 227; *Suss. Custumals*, vol. i, p. 68; *Suss. Fines*, vol. iii, p. 254.
[52] *3 Suss. Subsidies*, p. 129; Reaney, *Dict.*, p. 356.
[53] *Ibid.*, p. 65; *Lewes Chartulary*, vol. i, p. 179.
[54] *S.A.C.*, vol. lxxvii, p. 256; Fransson, *op. cit.*, p. 176.
[55] West Suss. Record Office, EP. VI/19A/1, m. 10d; Reaney, *Dict.*, p. 223; *Suss. Subsidy 1524–5*, p. 98 (this reference is to an alien); *W. Suss. 1641–2*, pp. 42, 90, 115.
[56] *Robertsbridge Charters*, pp. 47–8; *Suss. Indictments*, vol. i, p. 29; Thuresson, *op. cit.*, p. 237.
[57] *3 Suss. Subsidies*, pp. 114, 153, 228, 238; *S.A.C.*, vol. lxix, p. 139; Fransson, *op. cit.*, p. 110.
[58] *Feudal Aids*, vol. v, p. 141; *Suss. Fines*, vol. ii, p. 184; vol. iii, pp. 45, 73; *Boxgrove Chart.*, p. 44; *Lewes Chartulary*, vol. ii, pp. 73–4; *3 Suss. Subsidies*, pp. 85, 114; *Non. Inquis.*, 350; Fransson, *op. cit.*, p. 140; M. T. Martin, *Percy Chartulary* (Surtees Soc., vol. cxvii) (1911), p. 465; *V.C.H. Suss.*, vol. iv, pp. 4–5.
[59] *3 Suss. Subsidies*, pp. 225–333.
[60] H. A. Hanley and C. W. Chalklin, *op. cit.*, pp. 71–170.
[61] Anon., *Suff. in 1327* (Suff. Green Books, no. ix) (1906); J. P. Rylands, "Exchequer Lay Subsidy Roll", in *Miscellanies Relating to Lancs. and Chesh.* (Lancs. and Chesh. Record Soc., vol. xxxi) (1896), vol. ii.
[62] See, e.g., *Suss. Custumals*, vol. i, pp. 41, 89, 136–7; vol. ii, pp. 2, 10, 48, 54, 59, 64, 102, 129; vol. iii, pp. 38, 41–2, 45–6, 56–61; *Suss. Fines*, vol. i, pp. 53, 100, 131; vol. ii, pp. 81, 91, 130, 163, 174; *Non. Inquis.*, pp. 354, 356, 359, 367, 382–3, 403; *S.A.C.*, vol. lxxxvii, p. 14; vol. lxxxix, pp. 120, 122; vol. xcv, p. 51; vol. xcvi, p. 24; *Chichester Chart.*, pp. 194, 219; *Great Roll of the Pipe for the 10th Year of Richard I* (Pipe Roll Soc., vol. xlvii), p. 225; P.R.O., E. 179/189/42, m. 26d; E. 179/225/5; E. 179/225/50, m. 40; S.C.

Surnames Derived from Occupation, Status, or Office 283

11/663; E. Suss Record Office, Glynde MSS., 1031; W. Suss. Record Office, EP. VI/19A/1, m. 15. Other references are too numerous to list.

63 *Suss. Subsidy, 1524–5*, pp. 17, 19, 29, 31, 33, 35, 43, 61, 128, 130, 157.

64 *W. Suss. 1641–2*, pp. 35, 39, 52, 64, 73, 78, 88–90, 93, 137, 150–51, 163, 199, 200.

65 *3 Suss. Subsidies*, pp. 16, 211, 322; *Hastings Lathe C.R.*, pp. 135, 147; P.R.O. E. 179/225/12; E. 179/225/5.

66 *Suss. Subsidy, 1524–5*, pp. 115, 161; Lane, *Suss. Deeds*, p. 94; *Wiston Archives*, p. 392; H.M.C., *Rye MSS.*, p. 202; P.R.O. S.C. 11/649, m. 2; *Suss. Wills*, vol. iv, p. 94.

67 *S.A.C.*, vol. lxxxii, p. 128; vol. lxxxiv, p. 76; *Wiston Archives*, p. 35; *Non. Inquis.*, p. 368; *Suss. Custumals*, vol. ii, p. 17; L. Fleming, *History of Pagham*, vol. i, p. 62; J. E. Ray, *op. cit.*, p. 27; *Lewes Barony Recs.*, pp. 23, 33; *3 Suss. Subsidies*, pp. 81, 121, 135, 221, 245, 254, 332; *Hastings Lathe C.R.*, pp. 148, 188; *Suss. Subsidy, 1524–5*, pp. 2, 47, 101, 103, 126, 131, 137, 146, 150–1, 154; P.R.O. E. 179/191/378, mm. 2d, 3; *Fitzalan Surveys*, pp. 109, 123; *Suss. Wills*, vol. i, pp.236, 322; vol. iii, p. 317.

68 *Boxgrove Chart.*, p. 30; *S.A.C.*, lxxxiii, p. 36; J. E. Ray, *op. cit.*, pp. 28, 34, 152; *Feudal Aids*, vol. v, pp. 131, 145, 146; *Non. Inquis.*, p. 358; F. Hull, *Calendar of the White and Black Books* (1966), pp. 115, 124, 155, 180; *Suss. Fines*, vol. ii, pp. 105, 186; *Suss. Custumals*, vol. ii, pp. 103, 126, 129; *Lewes Barony Recs.*, pp. 9, 77; *3 Suss. Subsidies*, pp. 37–8, 41, 83, 176, 193, 227, 337, 305.

69 *Non. Inquis.*, p. 389; *Suss. Subsidy, 1524–5*, p. 91.

70 *3 Suss. Subsidies*, pp. 39, 51, 64, 71, 77, 89, 103, 110, 164, 187, 232–4, 275, 307, 316.

71 *Suss. Custumals*, vol. ii, pp. 58, 76, 80, 92–3; vol. iii, p. 71; *Non. Inquis.*, p. 374; *Boxgrove Chart.*, pp. 122, 144, 184, 193; F. Hull, *op. cit.*, p. 123; *Robertsbridge Surveys*, p. 180; *Lewes Chartulary*, vol. i, p. 115; *Wiston Archives*, p. 207; P.R.O. E. 179/182/42, m. 14d; *Fitzalan Surveys*, pp. 136, 137, 166.

72 Reaney, *Dict.*, 39; *Feudal Aids*, vol. v, p. 149; *3 Suss. Subsidies*, pp. 18, 64, 69, 206, 317, 328; E. Searle, *Lordship and Community* (1974), pp. 151, 396, 412; E. Suss. Record Office, Dunn MSS., 1/5, 20/6; *Suss. Fines*, vol. iii, pp. 30, 36; *S.A.C.*, vol. lxxxiii, p. 42.

73 *3 Suss. Subsidies*, pp. 5, 56, 141, 265, 309; *Lewes Chartulary*, vol. i, pp. 142, 143; J. E. Ray, *op. cit.*, pp. 29, 145; *Boxgrove Chart.* p. 194; *De Lisle and Dudley MSS.*, vol. i, p. 59; D. M. Stenton, *Great Roll of the Pipe for the 7th Year of Richard I* (Pipe Roll Soc., vol. xliv) (1929), p. 241; D. M. Stenton, *Great Roll of the Pipe for the 10th Year of Richard I* (Pipe Roll Soc., vol. xlvii) (1932), p. 228; *Suss. Custumals*, vol. ii, pp. 40, 53, 64, 72–3, 79, 92, 97, 101, 112.

[74] *Suss. Custumals*, vol. ii, pp. 67–8, 70, 73–4; *Robertsbridge Charters*, p. 131; *3 Suss. Subsidies*, pp. 146, 156, 260, 265; *Suss. Fines*, vol. ii, p. 154; *Fitzalan Surveys*, p. 34.

[75] *Chichester Chart.*, p. 251; *Suss. Custumals*, vol. i, p. 70; *S.A.C.*, vol. lvii, p. 215; *Wiston Archives*, pp. 34–5, 203, 242; W. Suss. Record Office, EP. VI/19A/1, m. 11; *De Lisle and Dudley MSS.*, vol. i, pp. 4, 5; L. Fleming, *History of Pagham*, vol. i, p. 62 (printed Chrele); *Suss. Fines*, vol. iii, pp. 269, 286, 293; *Fitzalan Surveys*, p. 108.

[76] Thuresson, *op. cit.*, p. 52. One instance occurs at Dunsfold (Surr.), not far from Drungewick.

[77] *Suss. Subsidy, 1524–5*, p. 139; *W. Suss. 1641–2*, p. 118.

[78] *3 Suss. Subsidies*, pp. 26, 62, 94, 230; *Suss. Custumals*, vol. i, pp. 79, 116, 139; vol. ii, pp. 67, 70, 73, 106; L. Fleming, *History of Pagham*, vol. i, p. 41, p. xlii; *Chichester Chart.*, p. 349; P.R.O. SC.11/877.

[79] *Suss. Custumals*, vol. ii, pp. 132–3; Thuresson, *op. cit.*, p. 51.

[80] Reaney, *Dict.*, p. 119.

[81] *S.A.C.*, vol. xx, p. 6.

[82] *3 Suss. Subsidies*, pp. 21, 173, 191, 287, 303; *Feudal Aids*, vol. v, pp. 131, 145–6; *Suss. Custumals*, vol. i, p. 81; *Lewes Barony Recs.*, p. 54; *Lewes Chartulary*, vol. i, p. 170; *S.A.C.*, vol. lxxxiii, p. 36.

[83] *Suss. Fines*, vol. i, p. 73. The name de Avening occurs in Gloucs.: M. Chibnall, *Charters and custumals of the Abbey of Holy Trinity, Caen* (1982), pp. 27, 79.

[84] *Suss. Custumals*, vol. ii, pp. 58, 80, 93; *Suss. Fines*, vol. ii, p. 154.

[85] *Suss. Custumals*, vol. ii, p. 54.

[86] *Ibid.*, vol. ii, pp. 40–46, 53–59, 64–5, 73–4, 79–83, 93, 101, 105.

[87] Inderwick, *Winchelsea*, p. 206; *Suss. Fines*, vol. i, p. 102.

[88] *S.A.C.*, vol. xviii, p. 29; *De Lisle and Dudley MSS.*, vol. i, p. 167; P.R.O. E. 179/182/42, m. 21d.

[89] *3 Suss. Subsidies*, pp. 5, 15, 36, 49, 57, 101, 115, 154, 173, 181, 199, 269, 290; *Suss. Custumals*, vol. ii, p. 43; E. Searle, *op. cit.*, p. 148; *Non. Inquis.*, p. 392; *Catalogue of Ancient Deeds*, vol. iii, p. 37; Inderwick, *Winchelsea*, pp. 194, 207; *Hastings Lathe C.R.*, pp. 7, 120, 132, 139, 162; *S.A.C.*, vol. xviii, p. 26; P.R.O., E. 179/189/42, m. 4; E. 179/225/50, m. 27.

[90] *Suss. Subsidy, 1524–5*, pp. 72, 95–6, 98, 121, 145, 159; *W. Suss. 1641–2*, pp. 93, 148; P.R.O. E. 179/191/267; E. 179/191/410, part 4, mm. 10, 12; part 5, mm. 1, 2; E. 179/258/21, p. 13.

[91] East Suss. Record Office, Dunn. Mss., 20/6, 20/8; *3 Suss. Subsidies*, pp. 70, 79, 99, 101, 118, 135, 141, 254, 257, 263; *Non. Inquis.*, p. 361; *S.A.C.*, vol. xii, p. 44; *Wiston Archives*, p. 84; B. E. Harris, *Great Roll of the Pipe for the 3rd Year of Henry III* (Pipe Roll Soc., vol. lxxx) (1976), p. 144; L. Fleming, *History of Pagham*, vol. i, p. lix;

L. F. Salzman, *Chartulary of Sele* (1923), pp. 44, 75; P.R.O. E. 179/182/42, mm. 19, 19d.

92 Reaney, *Dict.*, p. 109.

93 F. Hull, *op. cit.*, p. 186; *Suss. Wills*, vol. ii, p. 11; vol. iv, pp. 347, 421; *Suss. Subsidy, 1524-5*, pp. 2-5, 22, 44-6, 71, 76, 90, 93, 100, 156, 160; R. Garraway Rice, *Parish Register of Horsham* (Suss. Record Soc., vol. xxi) (1915), *per indice*.

94 *Ibid.*, pp. 81, 121, 125, 245; *Chichester Chart.*, p. 299; *Lewes Chartulary*, vol. ii, pp. 27, 67, 69, 72; *Book of Fees*, vol. ii, pp. 689, 1204, 1239, 1257; *Suss. Fines*, vol. i, p. 25; vol. ii, p. 69; P. M. Barnes, *Great Roll of the Pipe for the 16th Year of John* (Pipe Roll Soc., vol. lxxiii) (1959), p. 166; C. Robinson, *Great Roll of the Pipe for the 14th Year of Henry III* (Pipe Roll Soc., vol. xlii) (1927), p. 240; *V.C.H. Suss.*, vol. vi, part i, pp. 176, 180; *Curia Regis Rolls*, vol. iv, pp. 4, 39; P.R.O. E. 179/182/42, m. 13; L. F. Salzman, *Cartulary of Sele* (1923), pp. 4, 5, 48, 62, 77.

95 *Lewes Chartulary*, vol. ii, pp. 74, 80, 100, 102; *Suss. Custumals*, vol. ii, pp. 107, 113, 115, 131, 133.

96 *Suss. Custumals*, vol. i, p. 89; vol. iii, p. 30.

97 *Lewes Chartulary*, vol. i, pp. 12, 33, 92, 96, 119, 121, 132; *3rd Report of the Royal Commission on Historical MSS* [c.-673] (1872), Appendix, p. 223; *V.C.H. Suss.*, vol. i, p. 352; vol. vii, p. 1.

98 Reaney, *Dict.*, p. 317, leaves the origin of the name unclear.

99 *Suss. Custumals*, vol. i, pp. 97-8; *De Lisle and Dudley MSS.*, vol. i, p. 36; *Robertsbridge Charters*, p. 3; *3 Suss. Subsidies*, p. 80. Compare *Surnames of Oxon.*, p. 201.

100 P.R.O. E. 179/225/50, m. 28; P.R.O. SC. 11/663.

101 *3 Suss. Subsidies*, p. 329; *Hastings Lathe C.R.*, pp. 30, 118, 170; *Robertsbridge Surveys*, pp. 36, 42, 45-6.

102 *Suss. Custumals*, vol. i, pp. 97, 118; vol. ii, pp. 3, 62, 64; *3 Suss. Subsidies*, pp. 26, 39, 57, 88, 98-9, 120, 122, 124-5, 140, 156, 185, 232, 242, 244, 247, 270, 308; *Chichester Chart.*, pp. 132, 376; *Lewes Barony Recs.*, p. 55; *S.A.C.*, vol. li, p. 55; D. M. Stenton, *Great Roll of the Pipe for the 8th Year of King John* (Pipe Roll Soc., vol. lviii) (1942), p. 63; *Fitzalan Surveys*, pp. 26, 27.

103 *Lewes Chartulary*, vol. i, pp. 121, 130, 132, 138, 145, 161, 175, 177; vol. ii, pp. 52, 66, 80, 100, 125; *Chichester Bishops' Acta*, pp. 91, 92, 96, 106.

104 L. Fleming, *History of Pagham*, vol. i, pp. 61, 62; *P. N. Suss.*, vol. ii, p. 356.

105 *Feudal Aids*, vol. v, p. 156; *Suss. Fines*, vol. ii, p. 172; *3 Suss. Subsidies*, pp. 118, 241; *V.C.H. Suss.*, vol. iv, p. 61; M. T. Martin, *Percy Chartulary* (Surtees Soc., vol. cxvii) (1911), p. 364.

106 *3 Suss. Subsidies*, pp. 77, 94, 134, 139; *Suss. Custumals*, vol. i, p. 22; vol. ii, pp. 39, 65, 87.

[107] *Ibid.*, vol. i, p. 74; *3 Suss. Subsidies*, pp. 67, 130, 135, 180; W. Stubbs, *Great Roll of the Pipe for the 12th Year of Henry II* (Pipe Roll Soc., vol. ix) (1888), p. 92. The Anfridus Canon' in the last reference may in fact have been a canon.

[108] *3 Suss. Subsidies*, pp. 97, 125; *S.A.C.*, vol. xxiv, p. 68; *De Lisle and Dudley MSS.*, vol. i, p. 149; *Robertsbridge Charters*, p. 138; *Suss. Fines*, vol. iii, p. 48.

[109] *3 Suss. Subsidies*, pp. 185, 316; *Placita de Banco* (P.R.O. Lists and Indexes, vol. xxxii), vol. ii, p. 662.

[110] *3 Suss. Subsidies*, pp. 15, 37, 62–3, 70, 77, 86, 123, 136, 148, 153, 219, 228, 243, 254, 330; *S.A.C.*, vol. lxxxii, p. 134; vol. xcvi, p. 24; Inderwick, *Winchelsea*, p. 202; *Robertsbridge Charters*, p. 78; *Lewes Barony Recs.*, pp. 17, 19, 21; E. Searle, *op. cit.*, p. 465; *Non. Inquis.*, p. 370; *Suss. Custumals*, vol. i, pp. 38, 52; vol. ii, p. 136; *Lewes Chartulary*, vol. ii, pp. 44, 100, 103; *Battle Custumals*, pp.22.

[111] *Lewes Chartulary*, vol. ii, pp. 5, 30, 103; *Boxgrove Chart.*, pp. 65, 156, 165; *Catalogue of Ancient Deeds*, vol iv, p. 70; *Suss. Custumals*, vol. ii, p. 81; *Robertsbridge Charters*, pp. 74, 137. And see Henry le Personeson, evidently son of the parson of Iping; *Placita de Banco* (P.R.O. Lists and Indexes, vol. xxxii), vol. ii, p. 671; see also the case of the vicar of Mundham, alleged to have two wives: W. W. Shirley, *Royal Letters, Henry III* (Rolls Series), vol. i, p. 277.

[112] *Suss. Fines*, vol. i, p. 9; vol. ii, pp. 75, 84, 146; *Suss. Custumals*, vol. i, p. 84; vol. ii, p. 42; *Books of Fees*, vol. ii, p. 1414; C. F. Slade, *Great Roll of the Pipe for the 12th Year of King John* (Pipe Roll Soc., vol. lxiv) (1951), p. 59; *3 Suss. Subsidies*, pp. 34, 47, 51, 56, 58–9, 64, 67, 110, 128, 131, 135, 154, 162, 164, 202, 231–2, 250, 252, 255, 276, 279, 312–3, 317–8, 325; P.R.O. E. 179/189/42, mm. 20, 28; *V.C.H. Suss.*, vol. iv, pp. 168–9; *Fitzalan Surveys*, pp. 17, 157.

[113] *Suss. Subisidy, 1524–5*, pp. 30, 59, 62, 65–6, 93, 97, 104–5, 109, 132; *W. Suss. 1641–2*, pp. 31, 37–8, 41, 61, 77, 136, 145, 165, 170.

[114] *S.A.C.*, vol. lxxxix, p. 139; *Cowdray Archives*, vol. ii, p. 362; *3 Suss. Subsidies*, pp. 89, 117, 126, 130, 241.

[115] *3 Suss. Subsidies*, pp. 156, 165–6, 173, 212, 221, 225, 280, 287, 323, 328; *S.A.C.*, vol. xviii, p. 24; vol. lxix, p. 135; *Wiston Archives*, p. 221; J. E. Ray, *op. cit.*, p. 77; *Lewes Barony Recs.*, p. 24; *Suss. Custumals*, vol. i, p. 75; *Suss. Fines*, vol. i, p. 80; *Chichester Chart.*, p. 168; *Suss. Subsidy, 1524–5*, pp. 24, 26–9, 31–2, 39, 72, 84, 102; *W Suss. 1641–2*, pp. 10, 23, 60–1, 74, 76, 105, 108–9, 119–21, 129–30, 176, 180, 189, 190; *Fitzalan Surveys*, pp. 15, 18, 29.

[116] Inderwick, *Winchelsea*, pp. 170, 195; *Hastings Lathe C.R.*, pp. 116, 119, 132; *Chichester Chart.*, p. 166; *3 Suss. Subsidies*, pp. 127, 136, 186, 221, 316; West Suss. Record Office, EP. VI/19A/1, mm. 9d, 10; P.R.O. E. 179/225/50, m. 52; Reaney, *Dict.*, p. 69.

Surnames Derived from Occupation, Status, or Office

[117] *3 Suss. Subsidies*, p. 66.
[118] *Ibid.*, pp. 35, 78, 85, 113, 114, 202, 229, 237, 238.
[119] *Non. Inquis.*, p. 363; P.R.O. SC. 11/666.
[120] See notes 117, 118, and 119 above.
[121] *Suss. Custumals*, vol. i, p. 140; *3 Suss. Subsidies*, p. 90.
[122] *Surnames of Oxon.*, p. 202; *Surnames of Lancs.*, p. 284; Reaney, *Dict.*, p. 163.
[123] *Catalogue of Ancient Deeds*, vol. ii, pp. 387, 398, 399; *Curia Regis Rolls, 15–16 John*, pp. 29, 42.
[124] *Boxgrove Chart.*, p. 140; *Hastings Lathe C.R.*, p. 123; *Chichester Chart.*, p. 357; *Battle Custumals*, p. 9; *3 Suss. Subsidies*, pp. 190, 302; *Suss. Subsidy, 1524–5*, p. 11; *W. Suss. 1641–2*, p. 168.
[125] See pp. 227.
[126] *Boxgrove Chart.*, pp. 57, 74, 171; P.R.O. S.C. 11/663; *V.C.H. Suss.*, vol. i, pp. 395, 396, 399, 408, 416, 417, 418, 428, 436, 444, 445.
[127] *3 Suss. Subsidies*, pp. 23, 31, 33, 36, 59, 68, 79, 81, 192, 198.
[128] Inderwick, *Winchelsea*, p. 165; *Lewes Chartulary*, vol. i, p. 151; *De Lisle and Dudley MSS.*, vol. i, p. 117.
[129] L. Fleming, *History of Pagham*, vol. i, pp. 62, 209; *S.A.C.*, vol. lxxxix, p. 159; *Non. Inquis.*, p. 351.
[130] *Chichester Chart.*, p. 212; East Suss. Record Office, Dunn MSS., 1/15; *Fitzalan Surveys*, p. 109.
[131] *3 Suss. Subsidies*, p. 68; *Suss. Subsidy, 1524–5*, pp. 5, 15, 18, 23, 25, 163; *W. Suss. 1641–2*, pp. 33, 98, 131, 191, 198; R. Garraway Rice, *Parish Register of Horsham*, pp. 35, 129, 134, 140, 204, 206, 215, 219, 222, 366–9, 372, 374.
[132] Reaney, *Dict.*, p. 79.
[133] *3 Suss. Subsidies*, pp. 213, 220, 254, 310, 325; Inderwick, *Winchelsea*, pp. 171, 199, 203, 207; *Suss. Custumals*, vol. ii, p. 43.
[134] *S.A.C.*, vol. liii, p. 52; vol. xcv, p. 54; vol. cvi, p. 100; *Hastings Lathe C.R.*, p. 176; *Suss. Fines*, vol. iii, p. 39; *P. N. Suss.*, vol. ii, p. 443.
[135] "Parish Registers of Ticehurst, 1559–1843" (transcript at Society of Geanealogists), pp. 63, 74; *Suss. Subsidy, 1524–5*, pp. 93, 142, 143, 149; *W. Suss. 1641–2*, p. 20; *Robertsbridge Surveys*, pp. 92–4; *Suss. Indictments*, vol. i, p. 17; E. Straker, *Buckhurst Terrier* (Suss. Record Soc., vol. xxxix) (1934), p. 73; P.R.O. E. 179/190/266; E. 179/258/20, p. 19; *Suss. Wills*, vol. i, p. 80; vol. ii, p. 296; vol. iii, p. 135; vol. iv, p. 232.
[136] *Suss. Custumals*, vol. ii, p. 34; *3 Suss. Subsidies*, pp. 68, 152.
[137] *Lewes Chartulary*, vol. ii, p. 5.
[138] *Hastings Lathe C.R.*, p. 133; *3 Suss. Subsidies*, p. 19; Thuresson, *op. cit.*, p. 83.
[139] *3 Suss. Subsidies*, p. 56.
[140] *Ibid.*, pp. 80, 136; *Battle Custumals*, p. 22.

[141] *S.A.C.*, vol. xxxii, p. 7; *Suss. Subsidy, 1524–5*, p. 36; *W. Suss. 1641–2*, pp. 9, 10, 65, 83, 89, 105, 110, 123, 125–7, 155, 165, 171, 197, 202; *Wiston Archives*, p. 251; P.R.O. E. 179/235/2.

[142] H. W. C. Davis, *Regesta Regum Anglo-Normannorum* (1913), vol. i, pp. 91, 112.

[143] *3 Suss. Subsidies*, pp. 44, 56, 59, 80, 164, 170, 279, 285; L. Fleming, *Hist. of Pagham*, vol. i, p. xlii.

[144] Reaney, *Dict.*, p. 332; Thuresson, *op. cit.*, p. 84.

[145] See references cited in note 143; and P.R.O. E. 179/182/2, m. 6.

[146] *Great Roll of the Pipe for the 17th Year of Henry II* (Pipe Roll Soc., vol. xvi) (1893), p. 128.

[147] Inderwick, *Winchelsea*, pp. 159, 178, 184.

[148] *3 Suss. Subsidies*, pp. 132, 203, 247; *Non. Inquis.*, p. 365; R. F. Hunnisett and J. B. Post, *Medieval Legal Records*, p. 372; *Suss. Custumals*, vol. i, p. 12.

[149] Thuresson, *op. cit.*, p. 85; Reaney, *Dict.*, p. 310.

[150] *Suss. Subsidy, 1524–5*, p. 149; *H.M.C., Rye MSS.*, p. 37; *P. N. Suss.*, vol. ii, p. 385; *Feudal Aids*, vol. v, p. 149.

[151] *S.A.C.* vol. liv, pp. 156–9, 173, 175; West Suss. Record Office, Wiston MSS. 5236, m. 1; Thuresson, *op. cit.*, p. 83; P.R.O. E. 179/189/42, m. 23.

[152] Reaney, *Dict.*, p. 322; Lane, *Suss. Deeds*, p. 100.

[153] *Lewes Chartulary*, vol. i, p. 151; *3 Suss. Subsidies*, p. 137, 254; *Suss. Custumals*, vol. i, pp. 10, 11. See also B. E. Harris, *Great Roll of the Pipe for the 3rd Year of Henry III* (Pipe Roll Soc., vol. lxxx) (1976), p. 143; *V.C.H. Suss.*, vol. iv, p. 202.

[154] *3 Suss. Subsidies*, pp. 58, 163, 278, 288; *S.A.C.*, vol. xcv, p. 49; P.R.O. E. 179/182/42, m. 18.

[155] *Suss. Custumals*, vol. ii, p. 64; *Suss. Subsidy, 1524–5*, p. 126; *Hastings Lathe C.R.*, pp. 3, 5, 14, 25, 61, 97; *Suss. Custumals*, vol. ii, p. 54.

[156] A. Dauzat, *Dictionnaire Etymologique Des Noms de Famille et Prénoms de France* (1951), p. 275.

[157] *Lewes Chartulary*, vol. ii, p. 83; *S.A.C.*, vol. xcv, p. 51; *3 Suss. Subsidies*, p. 93.

[158] Thuresson, *op. cit.*, p. 85; Reaney, *Dict.*, p. 130.

[159] *Non. Inquis.*, p. 378.

[160] *Ibid.*, p. 376; *3 Suss. Subsidies*, pp. 70, 94, 123, 126, 134, 226, 229, 237, 243, 247, 250, 264; *S.A.C.*, vol. x, p. 109; E. Searle, *Lordship and Community*, pp. 125, 425; *Suss. Fines*, vol. i, p. 97; *Boxgrove Chart*, pp. 158, 174; *Suss. Custumals*, vol. ii, p. 99; West Suss. Record Office, EP. VI/19A/1, mm. 3d, 4.

[161] *Chichester Chart.*, p. 194; *S.A.C.*, vol. xviii, p. 27; vol. xxii, p. 118; *Suss. Fines*, vol. iii, p. 274; *Fitzalan Surveys*, p. 29.

Surnames Derived from Occupation, Status, or Office 289

[162] See note 35 above.
[163] *V.C.H. Suss.*, vol. vii, p. 183; *Suss. Fines*, vol. iii, pp. 12, 196; *Suss. Wills*, vol. iv, p. 284; *Hastings Lathe C.R.*, p. 141; *3 Suss. Subsidies*, pp. 47, 60, 167; *S.A.C.*, vol. xx, p. 147; J. E. Ray, *op. cit.*, p. 33; East Suss. Record Office, Dunn MSS., 8/3; P.R.O. E. 179/189/42, m. 3; Fransson, *op. cit.*, pp. 143–4; P.R.O. E. 179/182/42, m. 10.
[164] *Chichester Chart.*, pp. 125, 157, 243; *S.A.C.*, vol. xviii, p. 29; J. H. Round, *Great Roll of the Pipe for the 24th Year of Henry II* (Pipe Roll Soc., vol. xxvi) (1906), p. 90; Reaney, *Dict.*, p. 39; *Chichester Bishops' Acta*, p. 75.
[165] J. E. Ray, *op. cit.*, p. 83; *Suss. Subsidy, 1524–5*, pp. 70, 72; Reaney, *Dict.*, p. 39; Fransson, *op. cit.*, p. 144; *Suss. Wills*, vol. i, p. 109.
[166] *3 Suss. Subsidies*, p. 68. And see p. 165.
[167] *Ibid.*, p. 9; E. Straker, *Buckhurst Terrier* (Suss. Record Soc., vol. xxxix) (1934), p. 82; Fransson, *op. cit.*, p. 144; *P. N. Suss.*, vol. ii, p. 387; *Suss. Subsidy, 1524–5*, pp. 100, 111, 124–5, 136, 140–41; P.R.O. E. 179/191/410, part 5, m. 9; East Suss. Record Office, Dunn MSS., 16/9; *Surnames of Lancs.*, p. 283, *Suss. Wills*, vol. i, p. 126; vol. iv, p. 83; *Suss. Fines*, vol. iii, p. 193.
[168] *Suss. Custumals*, vol. ii, p. 111; *S.A.C.*, vol. lxx, p. 117; *Robertsbridge Charters*, p. 110; *3 Suss. Subsidies*, pp. 50, 171.
[169] *Non. Inquis.*, p. 370; *S.A.C.*, vol. lxxxix, p. 130; P.R.O. E. 179/225/5; East Suss. Record Office, Glynde MSS., 997; Fransson, *op. cit.*, p. 153.
[170] *Chichester Chart.*, p. 227; *Suss. Custumals*, vol. i, p. 68.
[171] See p. 164.
[172] *Suss. Custumals*, vol. i, p. 86; G. H. Kenyon, *Glass Industry of the Weald* (1967), pp. 25, 31.
[173] *Chichester Chart.*, p. 221; *S.A.C.*, vol. lxxxvii, p. 8; vol. lxxxix, p. 146; West Suss. Record Office, EP. VI/19A/1, mm. 11. 12; *P.N. Suss.*, vol. ii, p. 407.
[174] *Ibid.*, vol. ii, p. 473; *Suss. Subsidy, 1524–5*, pp. 26, 63, 97, 125, 147, 155; *Robertsbridge Surveys*, p. 81; *Suss. Wills.*, vol. i, pp. 206, 348; vol. ii, p. 312; vol. iii, p. 30.
[175] *Lewes Chartulary*, vol. i, p. 180; *3 Suss. Subsidies*, p. 51; *Chichester Chart.*, p. 105; *Great Roll of the Pipe for the 19th Year of Henry II* (Pipe Roll Soc., vol. xix) (1895), p. 30; J. Glover, *Place-Names of Suss.* (1975), p. 131.
[176] *3 Suss. Subsidies*, p. 51; *Lewes Chartulary*, vol. i, pp. 96, 104.
[177] L. Fleming, *History of Pagham*, vol. i, pp. 34, xlii, xliv; *3 Suss. Subsidies*, pp. 89, 125, 128, 129, 236, 245, 249, 251–2; *Suss. Custumals*, vol. ii, p. 13; *Suss. Fines*, vol. iii, p. 181.
[178] *3 Suss. Subsidies, passim.*
[179] *S.A.C.*, vol. lxxv, p. 129–135; vol. lxxxii, p. 132; vol. lxxxiv, p. 72;

E. Searle, *Lordship and Community*, p. 267; *Non. Inquis.*, pp. 354, 362, 378; *Suss. Custumals*, vol. i, pp. 93, 100; vol. ii, pp. 3, 8, 67, 71, 73, 92, 101, 103, 105, 125, 129, 137; *Robertsbridge Charters*, p. 38; *Boxgrove Chartulary*, pp. 95, 184; *Lewes Barony Recs.*, pp. 26–7, 33, 39, 45–7; *Battle Custumals*, pp. 31, 35, 55; West Suss. Record Office, EP. VI/19A/1, mm. 3d, 4, 10; P.R.O. S.C. 11/877; E. 179/189/42, mm. 3, 4, 12, 19d; *Placita de Banco* (P.R.O. Lists and Indexes, no. xxxii), vol. ii, p. 660.

180 *3 Suss. Subsidies*, p. 56; L. F. Salzman, *Chartulary of Sele* (1923), p. 77.

181 Franson, *op. cit.*, p. 112; *Suss. Custumals*, vol. i, p. 83; vol. ii, pp. 43, 53, 105; *Lewes Chartulary*, vol. i, p. 178; Lane, *Suss. Deeds*, p. 38; P.R.O. E. 179/189/42, m. 9; *3 Suss. Subsidies*, pp. 81, 125, 127, 275.

182 *3 Suss. Subsidies*, pp. 38, 120, 125, 157, 197, 231, 258, 271; Rubin, *Suss. Phonology*, pp. 156, 210; E. Searle, *Lordship and Community*, p. 331; *Suss. Custumals*, vol. ii, p. 76; *Suss. Subsidy, 1524–5*, p. 137; *W. Suss. 1641–2*, pp. 136, 138, 169, 191, 196; W. Suss. Record Office, EP. VI/19A/1, m. 1d; Wiston MSS., 5233(2); 5234(1); 5237, m. 2.

183 *Chichester Chart.*, pp. 243, 252, 253; *S.A.C.*, vol. cxvii, p. 173; *Wiston Archives*, p. 39; J. E. Ray, *op. cit.*, pp. xxxii, pp. 137, 139; *Suss. Subsidy, 1524–5*, pp. 41, 46; *W. Suss. 1641–2*, pp. 152–3; P.R.O. E. 179/191/380; *Suss. Wills*, vol. iv, p. 310; B. Danielson and R. C. Alston, *Works of William Bullokar* (1966), vol. i, pp. x, xi.

184 *Suss. Custumals*, vol. i, pp. 15, 19; West Suss. Record Office, Wiston MSS., 5233(2); *Fitzalan Surveys*, p. 140.

185 West Suss. Record Office, Wiston MSS., 5235.

186 *3 Suss. Subsidies*, pp. 48, 54, 79, 144, 156–7, 170, 175, 218, 329; *De Lisle and Dudley MSS.*, vol. i, pp. 77, 137; Thuresson, *op. cit.*, pp. 59–60; *Fitzalan Surveys*, pp. 128, 139, 170; L. F. Salzman, *Chartulary of Sele* (1923), pp. 30, 41.

187 *Suss. Indictments*, vol. i, p. 15.

188 *Boxgrove Chartulary*, p. 178; *S.A.C.*, vol. xcv, p. 57.

189 *Suss. Subsidy, 1524–5*, p. 130; E. Straker, *Buckhurst Terrier* (Suss. Record Soc., vol. xxxix) (1934), p. 24.

190 L. Fleming, *History of Pagham*, vol. i, p. xlix. Vacher was a Suss. surname in the 19th century: *V.C.H. Suss.*, vol. iv, pp. 128, 224.

191 *Suss. Custumals*, vol. ii, pp. 118, 138.

192 *Ibid.*, vol. i, p. 15; vol. ii, pp. 87, 123–4; *Non. Inquis.*, p. 379; *3 Suss. Subsidies*, pp. 23, 34, 37, 44, 49, 71, 99, 111, 144, 178, 197, 233, 266–7, 293, 304; *Suss. Fines*, vol. i, p. 55; *S.A.C.*, vol. vi, p. 215; vol. xcv, p. 54; P.R.O. E. 179/225/5; E. 179/225/12; E. 179/189/42, m. 12.

193 *Non. Inquis.*, p. 362; Rubin, *Suss. Phonology*, p. 210.

194 *Wiston Archives*, p. 375.

195 E. Searle, *Lordship and Community*, p. 329; Lane, *Suss. Deeds*,

Surnames Derived from Occupation, Status, or Office

p. 109; *S.A.C.*, vol. xviii, p. 27; *Battle Custumals*, p. 35; *3 Suss. Subsidies*, pp. 29, 48, 324, 329; *Suss. Subsidy, 1524–5*, p. 117; P.R.O. S.C. 11/639; *V.C.H. Suss.*, vol. vii, p. 228.

[196] *Suss. Subsidy, 1524–5*, pp. 106, 107, 129.

[197] *S.A.C.*, vol. xii, p. 41; vol. xcvi, p. 34; *3 Suss. Subsidies*, pp. 28, 83, 139, 165, 258, 280; P.R.O., E. 179/189/42, m. 20; *Fitzalan Surveys*, pp. 122, 133, 149.

[198] *3 Suss. Subsidies*, pp. 53, 153, 158, 272; *Wiston Archives*, p. 83; *Fitzalan Surveys*, p. 135; *S.A.C.*, vol. i, p. 33; vol. xli, p. 144; vol. lxxxiv, p. 80; *Suss. Subsidy, 1524–5*, pp. 51, 65; *W. Suss. 1641–2*, pp. 67, 81, 101, 106–8, 118, 147, 159, 187, 195–6, 202; R. Garraway Rice, *Parish Register of Horsham* (Suss. Record Soc., vol. xxi) (1915), pp. 42, 87, 96, 270, 281, 302, 383, 396–7; P. S. Godman, *Parish Register of Cowfold, Suss., 1558–1812* (Suss. Record Soc., vol. xxii) (1916), pp. 1, 97–99, 125, 163, 171–2; P.R.O. E. 179/189/42, m. 11.

[199] Thuresson, *op. cit.*, p. 111; *3 Suss. Subsidies*, p. 36; *Suss. Custumals*, vol. ii, pp. 49, 50, 52, 56, 58; Rubin, *Suss. Phonology*, p. 210; *Suss. Fines*, vol. iii, p. 226.

[200] Thuresson, *op. cit.*, p. 112; *3 Suss. Subsidies*, p. 43.

[201] *Ibid.*, pp. 62, 156; *Lewes Barony Recs.*, p. 14; C. Clark, "Battle c. 1100; an anthroponymist looks at an Anglo-Norman new town", *Proceedings of the Battle Abbey Conference* (1979), vol. ii, p. 39.

[202] *3 Suss. Subsidies*, pp. 141, 150, 262, 264, 268; *Suss. Custumals*, vol. i, p. 65; West Suss. Record Office, EP. VI/19A/1, mm. 1d, 2.

[203] *Suss. Subsidy, 1524–5*, pp. 30, 131; *3 Suss. Subsidies*, p. 146; West Suss. Record Office, EP. VI/19A/1, m. 4, 5; A. Dauzat, *op. cit.*, p. 299; *Non. Inquis.*, p. 390; *Fitzalan Surveys*, p. 133; Reaney, *Dict.*, p. 152.

[204] *3 Suss. Subsidies*, p. 268.

[205] R. Garraway Rice, *op. cit.*, p. 42; *West Suss. 1641–2*, pp. 80, 142; Lane, *Suss. Deeds*, p. 35; *Suss. Custumals*, vol. ii, p. 5; *Chichester Chart.*, p. 61; *Wiston Archives*, p. 232.

[206] E. Searle, *op. cit.*, p. 125; Inderwick, *Winchelsea*, p. 198; R. E. Latham, *Revised Medieval Latin Word List* (1965), p. 67; *3 Suss. Subsidies*, p.332; C. Clark, "Battle c. 1100: an anthroponymist looks at an Anglo-Norman new town", in *Proceedings of the Battle Abbey Conference* (1979), vol. ii, p. 40; W. H. Challen, *Parish Registers of Cocking, 1558–1837* (1927), p. 96.

[207] *Ibid.*, pp. 146–7, 158, 271; Inderwick, *Winchelsea*, p. 212; *S.A.C.*, vol. liii, p. 162; vol. lxix, p. 116; *Wiston Archives*, p. 34; *Chichester Chart.*, p. 202; *Hastings Lathe C.R.*, p. 128; *Suss. Subsidy, 1524–5*, p. 12; *W. Suss. 1641–2*, pp. 86, 87, 175, 190; P.R.O. E. 179/189/42, mm. 2, 8; Reaney, *Dict.*, p. 70; *Suss. Wills*, vol. i, p. 355; vol. ii, p. 115; vol. iii, p. 170; *Fitzalan Surveys*, pp. 102, 127.

[208] P.R.O. S.C. 11/877.

[209] *3 Suss. Subsidies*, p. 26; *S.A.C.*, vol. xviii, p. 25; vol. xcv, p. 55. See also *Feudal Aids*, vol. v, p. 148; Lane, *Suss. Deeds*, p. 104.

[210] *Suss. Fines*, vol. ii, p. 146; *Feudal Aids*, vol. v, p. 166.

[211] Fransson, *op. cit.*, p. 70.

[212] *Suss. Subsidy, 1524-5*, pp. 111, 120, 121; *Suss. Wills*, vol. i, pp. 37, 158; vol. ii, pp. 77, 189, 301; vol. iv, p. 356.

[213] *3 Suss. Subsidies*, pp. 116, 239.

[214] *Fitzalan Surveys*, p. 139; C. R. Davey, *Hants. Lay Subsidy, 1586* (1981), p. 19; *Suss. Subsidy, 1524-5*, pp. 9, 13, 48; *Suss. Indictments*, vol. i, pp. 24-5, 58; *S.A.C.*, vol. xcv, p. 65; E. W. D. Penfold, *First Book of the Parish Registers of Angmering* (Suss. Record Soc., vol. xviii) (1913), pp. 14, 17, 21, 23, 26, 29, 39, 120, 121; *Suss. Wills*, vol. ii, pp. 31, 149; and information about parish registers for Fernhurst and Angmering from Mr F. Leeson.

[215] *W. Suss. 1641-2*, pp. 27, 105, 114-5, 120, 134, 141, 173, 184, 194; P.R.O. E. 179/191/377, roll 6; E. 179/191/378, m. 3; E. 179/191/410, m. 8d; *S.A.C.*, vol. lxiv, p. 74; information about parish registers for Angmering and Pulborough from Mr F. Leeson; A. E. Marshall, 'Parish Registers of Lodsworth, Suss., 1557-1736' (Transcript at Soc. of Genealogists).

[216] *3 Suss. Subsidies*, pp. 99, 112, 116, 233, 240; Thuresson, *op. cit.*, p. 121.

[217] *S.A.C.*, vol. xcv, p. 48; L. F. Salzman, *Ministers' Accounts of the Honour of Petworth* (Suss. Record Soc., vol. lv) (1955), pp. 25, 40.

[218] West Suss. Record Office, EP. VI/19A/1, m. 11; *Suss. Fines*, vol. iii, pp. 235, 236.

[219] *Suss. Subsidy, 1524-5*, pp. 25, 40-42, 48, 78; *W. Suss. 1641-2*, pp. 8, 10, 28, 41, 97, 118, 138-9, 145-7, 196; *S.A.C.*, vol. xxv, p. 36; *Wiston Archives*, pp. 100, 147-8, 156; Lord Leconfield, *Sutton and Duncton Manors* (1956), p. 81; E. W. D. Penfold, *op. cit.*, pp. 16, 19-22, 24-5, 28, 31, 33-5, 37-8, 55, 57-60, 62, 68, 130; R. Garraway Rice, *op. cit., per indice*; P.R.O. E. 179/191/378, mm. 1, 1d; W. H. Challen, *op. cit.*, pp. 28-32, 34-38, 40; *Suss. Wills*, vol. i, p. 298; vol. iii, p. 295; vol. iv, pp. 36, 379.

[220] See pp. 229, 231, 233, 239, 243-5, 248.

[221] *Suss. Subsidy, 1524-5*, pp. 3, 36, 37, 81, 99, 129, 154; Fransson, *op. cit.*, p. 116; *W. Suss. 1641-2*, p. 189.

[222] See p. 251.

[223] W. D. Peckham, *Acts of the Dean and Chapter of the Cathedral Church of Chichester*, (Suss. Record Soc., vol. lii) (1952), pp. 3, 23; *Valor Eccl.*, p. 298; *S.A.C.*, vol. xxiv, p. 82; J. E. Ray, *op. cit.*, p. 89; *W. Suss. 1641-2*, p. 49; Fransson, *op. cit.*, p. 74; H. Johnstone, *Churchwardens' Presentments* (Suss. Record Soc., vol. xlix) (1949), pp. 32, 114, 120.

[224] P. S. Godman, *Parish Register of Cowfold, Suss., 1558–1812* (Suss. Record Soc., vol. xxii) (1916), p. 154; *Surnames of Lancs.*, p. 268; *Suss. Subsidy, 1524–5*, p. 64; *W. Suss. 1641–2*, pp. 189–90; *Wiston Archives*, pp. 40, 67–9, 271; C. S. Wilkie, *St Andrews, Edburton, Suss.: Copy of the Parish Register Book 1558–1673* (1884), pp. 19, 24; *Suss. Wills*, vol. iv, p. 310; Fransson, *op. cit.*, p. 141; E. W. Cox, "A complete transcript of the Parish Register of Steyning, Suss.: Burials, 1565–1925" (at Society of Genealogists), pp. 23, 27, 35, 36, 40, 43, 44, 48, 50, 51, 61.

[225] *Suss. Subsidy, 1524–5*, pp. 36, 48, 100, 134, 136, 148; *W. Suss. 1641–2*, pp. 27, 96, 188; *S.A.C.*, vol. cxvi, p. 10; *Surr. Taxation Returns* (Surr. Rec. Soc., vol. xi) (1922), p. 23.

[226] *Suss. Subsidy, 1524–5*, pp. 13, 46, 53, 67, 80.

[227] *Suss. Indictments*, vol. i, p. 15; J. E. Ray, *op. cit.*, p. 21; R. Garraway Rice, *op. cit., per indice; Suss. Wills*, vol. iv, p. 141.

[228] *Ibid.; W. Suss. 1641–2*, pp. 72, 138–9, 145, 152–3, 159, 179; Lord Leconfield, *Petworth Manor in the 17th Century* (1954), p. 5; P.R.O. E. 179/191/378, m. 2d; P. S. Godman, *Parish Register of Cowfold, Suss.* (Suss. Rec. Soc., vol. xxii) (1916), *per indice; V.C.H. Suss.*, vol. iv, p. 83.

[229] *P. N. Suss.*, vol. i, p. 158.

[230] *Suss. Subsidy, 1524–5*, pp. 37, 42, 81, 66, 100, 142. See also J. E. Ray, *op. cit.*, p. 144.

[231] *W. Suss. 1641–2*, pp. 110, 137; P.R.O. E. 179/258/14, m. 28d.

[232] *Suss. Subsidy, 1524–5*, pp. 3, 27, 33, 94–5, 102, 106, 116, 128, 147, 149; *Suss. Wills*, vol. i, p. 105; vol. ii, p. 218; vol. iii, pp. 47, 124; L. F. Salzman, *Chartulary of Sele* (1923), p. 103.

[233] *W. Suss. 1641–2*, pp. 97, 104, 151, 157, 170; G. H. Kenyon, *Glass Industry of the Weald* (1967), p. 130; *Cowdray Archives*, vol. ii, p. 244; *H.M.C., Rye MSS.*, p. 150; P.R.O. E. 179/191/380.

[234] *Suss. Fines*, vol. i, p. 52; *3 Suss. Subsidies*, p. 135; Reaney, *Dict.*, p. 368.

[235] *W. Suss. 1641–2*, pp. 54, 118, 157; R. Garraway Rice, *op. cit.*, p. 326.

[236] *S.A.C.*, vol. cii, p. 40; *Suss. Subsidy, 1524–5*, pp. 12, 3, 154, 22, 98, 110, 4, 144.

[237] *Ibid.*, pp. 144. And see p. 7.

[238] *W. Suss. 1641–2*.

[239] G. Fransson, *op. cit.*, pp. 41–45.

[240] *3 Suss. Subsidies*, pp. 66, 81, 93, 119, 125, 133, 149, 203; Inderwick, *Winchelsea*, p. 183; *Suss. Custumals*, vol. i, p. 83; vol. ii, pp. 20, 53, 59, 75; Rubin, *Suss. Phonology*, p. 84; P.R.O. S.C. 11/877; East Suss. Record Office, Dunn MSS., 3/6; West Suss. Record Office, EP. VI/19A/1, mm. 2d, 3, 3d, 4; *Suss. Fines*, vol. iii, p. 96; *Fitzalan Surveys*, p. 29.

[241] West Suss. Record Office, EP. VI/19A/1, mm. 3, 3d, 4, 7, 10, 11, 12, 15.

[242] *3 Suss. Subsidies*, p. 93; *Cowdray Archives*, vol. i, p. 5.

[243] *Suss. Custumals*, vol. ii, pp. 75–6, 80, 82.

[244] Reaney, *Dict.*, p. 36; Fransson, *op. cit.*, p. 108; *S.A.C.*, vol. x, p. 109; *Suss. Custumals*. vol. ii, p. 112.

[245] J. E. Ray, *op. cit.*, pp. 194, 198; *S.A.C.*, vol. x, p. 109; *Wiston Archives*, pp. 113, 123–4; *W. Suss. 1641-2*, p. 154; *V.C.H. Suss.*, vol. vi, pp. 37, 109, 135, 152–3.

[246] *2 Suss. Subsidies*, p. 177; *Suss. Subsidy, 1524-5*, p. 86; *Suss. Wills*, vol. ii, p. 53; W. C. Renshaw, *Parish Registers of Cuckfield* (Suss. Rec. Soc., vol. xiii) (1911), pp. 3, 5, 12, 16, 19, and *passim*.

[247] Information on parish registers from Mr F. Leeson; *W. Suss. 1641-2*, pp. 91, 154; *Suss. Subsidy, 1524-5*, pp. 46, 55, 59, 80, 86, 92, 140; *V.C.H. Suss.*, vol. iv, p. 144.

[248] *Suss. Subsidy, 1524-5*, pp. 140, 141; West Suss. Record Office, EP. VI/19A/1, m. 15. The name Blobbere, perhaps a variant of Blaber, occurs at Winchelsea, 1292: Inderwick, *Winchelsea*, pp. 171, 178. See also *Suss. Wills*, vol. iv, p. 330. Blobbere occurs in Kent, 1334–5: Hanley and Chalklin, *op. cit.*, p. 99.

[249] *Suss. Subsidy, 1524-5*, pp. 45–6, 50, 78. See also *W. Suss. 1641-2*, pp. 21, 148.

[250] W. C. Renshaw, *Parish Registers of Cuckfield* (Suss. Record Soc., vol. xiii) (1911), pp. 3, 5, 12, 16, 19, 22–4, 27, 45, 49, 50, 101–2, 105, 109–10, 113, 136, 145, 153, 159, 193, 196; E. W. D. Penfold, *Parish Registers of Angmering* (Suss. Record Soc., vol. xviii) (1913) *per indice*, and information about Rye parish registers from Mr F. Leeson of Ferring; *Suss. Wills*, vol. i, p. 41; vol. iv, p. 330.

[251] *Suss. Custumals*, vol. i, p. 49; Inderwick, *Winchelsea*, p. 163; *Robertsbridge Charters*, pp. 57, 62, 64–5, 71; *De Lisle and Dudley MSS.*, vol. i, p. 78; *3 Suss. Subsidies*, pp. 56, 103; L. F. Salzman, *Chartulary of Sele* (1923), pp. 41, 86.

[252] *3 Suss. Subsidies*, pp. 103, 135, 144, 250, 255, 265; *Non. Inquis.*, p. 354; *Chichester Chart.*, p. 194.

[253] *Suss. Wills*, vol. iii, p. 80; vol. iv, p. 160; *Suss. Subsidy, 1524-5*, pp. 31, 63, 109; J. E. Ray, *op. cit.*, p. 33.

[254] W. H. Challen, *Parish Register of Cocking 1558-1837* (1927), p. 48; *W. Suss. 1641-2*, pp. 43, 59, 110, 141, 195, 197; *S.A.C.*, vol. xcviii, p. 76; Lord Leconfield, *Sutton and Duncton Manors* (1956), p. 95; P.R.O. E. 179/191/377, roll i, m. 1.

[255] *Suss. Wills*, vol. ii, p. 71; F. Hull, *Calendar of the White and Black Books of the Cinque Ports* (1966), p. 358; J. E. Ray, *op. cit.*, p. 33; *Feudal Aids*, vol. v, p. 151; P.R.O. E. 179/189/42, m. 9; *3 Suss. Subsidies*, p. 131; *Suss. Subsidy 1524-5*, pp. 22, 110, 114, 119.

[256] H. B. Guppy, *Homes of Family Names* (1968), p. 287.
[257] Reaney, *Dict.*, p. 40.
[258] See p. 17.
[259] *Boxgrove Chart.*, p. 194; *Battle Custumals*, p. 26; C. Clark, "Battle c. 1100: an anthroponymist looks at an Anglo-Norman new town", *Proceedings of the Battle Abbey Conference*, (1979), p. 35; *Suss. Custumals*, vol. i, pp. 11, 19, 21, 33, 56, 81, 85, 91–2; vol. ii, pp. 9, 29, 113; vol. iii, pp. 29, 36; *S.A.C.*, vol. xlii, p. 93; *3 Suss. Subsidies*, pp. 22, 31, 41, 46, 71, 104; P.R.O., S.C. 11/877; E. 179/189/42, m. 14.
[260] *Boxgrove Chart.*, p. 195; *3 Suss. Subsidies*, pp. 161, 228, 254, 260, 263; *S.A.C.*, vol. lxxxix, p. 159; vol. xcvi, p. 24; Rubin, *op. cit.*, p. 98. One instance occurs at Pyecombe, which is in the west portion of East Sussex: *3 Suss. Subsidies*, p. 290. Thomas le Beedel (1301) has been linked, rather uncertainly, with Bedales in Lindfield (*P. N. Suss.*, vol. ii, p. 344). On the phonology, see Rubin, *op. cit.*, p. 107.
[261] *Hastings Lathe C. R.*, pp. 68, 71; *Suss. Subsidy, 1524–5*, pp. 104, 112, 116, 129, 148; *S.A.C.*, vol. ix, p. 74; vol. lxvi, p. 111; Lane, *Suss. Deeds*, pp. 50, 51, 100; E. Straker, *Buckhurst Terrier* (Suss. Record Soc., vol. xxxix) (1934), p. 41; L. F. Salzman, *Parish Register of Glynde*, (1924), pp. 32–5, 50, 53; *Suss. Wills*, vol. i, p. 79; vol. ii, pp. 296, 302; vol. iv, pp. 24, 281.
[262] *W. Suss. 1641–2*, pp. 82, 134.
[263] Löfvenberg, *op. cit.*, p. 19.
[264] *3 Suss. Subsidies*, pp. 7, 8, 22, 70, 142, 159, 208, 263, 272, 320; *Non. Inquis.*, p. 371; *Hastings Lathe C.R.*, p. 126; *S.A.C.*, vol. xxii, p. 117; vol. xxxviii, p. 137; *P. N. Suss.*, vol. ii, p. 480.
[265] *3 Suss. Subsidies*, pp. 71, 142, 208, 263; *Non. Inquis.*, p. 371.
[266] *P. N. Suss.*, vol. ii, p. 480.
[267] *3 Suss. Subsidies*, p. 161; P.R.O. E. 179/189/42, mm. 14, 14d; *W. Suss. 1641–2*, pp. 10, 82, 83, 97, 134, 143, 157, 183; *Suss. Subsidy, 1524–5*, pp. 9, 10, 28, 70, 74, 84, 104, 106, 109, 112, 116, 123, 130–1, 147–8, 152–3, 160–1; Lane, *Suss. Deeds*, pp. 50, 51, 100; *S.A.C.*, vol. ix, p. 74; vol. xxii, p. 117; vol. lxvi, p. 111; J. E. Ray, *op. cit.*, pp. 5, 85; *Robertsbridge Surveys*, pp. 45, 47; *Suss. Wills*, vol. ii, p. 233; vol. iii, pp. 188, 202.
[268] Reaney, *Dict.*, p. 82; Fransson, *op. cit.*, pp. 134–5.
[269] *Chichester Chart.*, pp. 99, 113, 115, 125, 127; *3 Suss. Subsidies*, p. 128; *S.A.C.*, vol. li, p. 62; *Boxgrove Chart.*, p. 177.
[270] Reaney, *Dict.*, p. 96, 108; Fransson, *op. cit.*, pp. 113, 176.
[271] *Suss. Custumals*, vol. ii, p. 134; *Catalogue of Ancient Deeds*, vol. iv, p. 138; *Lewes Barony Records*, p. 28.
[272] *3 Suss. Subsidies*, pp. 81, 226.
[273] *Ibid.*, pp. 47, 291; see also *Suss. Fines*, vol. iii, pp. 108, 127, 151.
[274] *Suss. Subsidy, 1524–5*, p. 91; *Feudal Aids*, vol. v, pp. 152–3, 161.

275 *S.A.C.*, vol. lxxxix, p. 120; vol. xcviii, p. 66; *Chichester Chart.*, pp. 194, 241; *Suss. Fines*, vol. ii, pp. 119, 120; *3 Suss. Subsidies*, pp. 23, 82, 104, 192, 201, 304, 312; Fransson, *op. cit.*, p. 104; *Calendar of Close Rolls, 1302-7*, p. 117.

276 *Ibid.*, p. 103; *Suss. Fines*, vol. ii, p. 130; *S.A.C.*, vol. xxiv, p. 68; *3 Suss. Subsidies*, p. 246.

277 *Feudal Aids*, vol. v, p. 148; *S.A.C.*, vol. xii, p. 36; P.R.O., E. 179/225/5; E. 179/225/12; *Suss. Fines*, vol. iii, pp. 163, 251, 257, 275-6.

278 *Suss. Wills*, vol. iv, p. 362; F. Hull, *Calendar of the White and Black Books of the Cinque Ports* (1966), pp. 3, 4, 5, 10, 17, 20, 33; *Calendar of Close Rolls, 1441-47*, p. 353.

279 Inderwick, *Winchelsea*, pp. 164, 207.

280 *Suss. Subsidy, 1524-5*, p. 123.

281 *P. N. Suss.*, vol. ii, p. 400.

282 R. Garraway Rice, *Parish Register of Horsham* (Suss. Record Soc., vol. xxi) (1915), p. 40.

283 M.-T. Morlet, *Étude D'Anthroponymie Picarde* (1967), p. 210; A. Dauzat, *Dictionnaire Étymologique Des Noms de Famille* (1951), p. 242. And see p. 19.

284 *S.A.C.*, vol. cxvi, p. 399.

285 D. M. Stenton, *Great Roll of the Pipe for the Fifth Year of King John* (Pipe Roll Soc., vol. liv) (1938), p. 196.

286 *3 Suss. Subsidies*, pp. 66, 152, 227; *Suss. Fines*, vol. i, pp. 127, 132; vol. iii, p. 51; *S.A.C.*, vol. xii, p. 31; L. F. Salzman, *Chartulary of Sele* (1923), pp. 41, 59, 60.

287 *S.A.C.*, vol. liii, p. 149, vol. liv, p. 171-3; *P. N. Suss.*, vol. i, p. 193; *3 Suss. Subsidies*, pp. 62, 162; *Non. Inquis.*, p. 389; Little Broadwater is said to have been in Nuthurst: *P. N. Suss.*, vol. i, p. 193. This does not agree with *V.C.H. Suss.*, vol. vi, p. 72.

288 West Suss. Record Office, Wiston MSS., 5234(1); 5241, mm. 1, 2; *Suss. Fines*, vol. iii, p. 152.

289 *Non. Inquis.*, p. 389; *3 Suss. Subsidies*, p. 276.

290 *Ibid.*, p. 262; *Suss. Fines*, vol. ii, p. 92.

291 *Cal. Pat. 1441-47*, pp. 172, 246; *Feudal Aids*, vol. v, p. 152; *S.A.C.*, vol. xxxi, p. 104 (where the name is printed Vest); vol. xcviii, p. 64; *Wiston Archives*, pp. 16, 142, 153, 204.

292 Reaney, *Dict.*, p. 121; H. A. Hanley and C. W. Chalklin, *op. cit.*, p. 154.

293 *Chichester Chart.*, p. 357; *3 Suss. Subsidies*, p. 25.

294 *Suss. Custumals*, vol. i, p. 108.

295 *Hastings Lathe C.R.*, p. 117.

296 *S.A.C.*, vol. xlvi, p. 179.

297 H.M.C. *Rye MSS.*, pp. 23, 60, 69; *Wiston Archives*, pp. 1, 2, 97-99, 140, 151-2, and see pedigree, p. xiv; F. Hull, *op. cit.*, pp. 294-95,

302; *V.C.H. Suss.*, vol. vi, part 1, pp. 26, 134, 240; *Suss. Subsidy, 1524–5*, p. 160.

[298] P. S. Godman, *Parish Register of Cowfold, Suss., 1558–1812* (Suss. Record Soc., vol. xxii) (1916), p. 11; *V.C.H. Suss.*, vol. vi, part 1, p. 228; *Suss. Subsidy, 1524–5*, pp. 33, 70; *Chichester Chart.*, p. 252; *Suss. Indictments*, vol. i, pp. 31, 46; *S.A.C.*, vol. xxxiii, p. 271; vol. xcv, p. 54; *Wiston Archives*, pp. 27, 28, 65, 142, 298; R. Garraway Rice, *Parish Register of Horsham* (Suss. Record Soc., vol. xxi) (1915), p. 201; *W. Suss. 1641–2*, pp. 90, 152, 158, 165; Lane, *Suss. Deeds*, pp. 12, 159; *3 Suss. Subsidies*, pp. 41, 42; C. H. Wilkie, *op. cit.*, pp. 13, 17, 18; C. W. Cox, 'Complete Transcript of the Parish Registers of Steyning, Suss. Burials, 1565–1925' (Transcript at Society of Genealogists), pp. 1, 46, 56, 58, 63; information on parish registers for Ashurst and West Grinstead, from Mr. F. Leeson.

[299] *3 Suss. Subsidies*, pp. 162, 276; P.R.O. E. 179/189/42, m. 21.

[300] M. T. Morlet, *Étude D'Anthroponymie Picarde* (1967), p. 150; Fransson, *op. cit.*, p. 140; Hanley and Chalklin, *op. cit.*, p. 82.

[301] *3 Suss. Subsidies*, pp. 61, 276.

[302] West Suss. Record Office, EP. VI/19A/1, m. 2.

[303] *3 Suss. Subsidies*, p. 68; *S.A.C.*, vol. lxix, p. 145; *P.N. Suss.*, vol. i, p. 230; R. Garraway Rice, *op. cit.*, p. 40.

[304] *Suss. Subsidy, 1524–5*, pp. 24, 35, 50, 62, 64, 80, 90, 115; *Suss. Wills*, vol. i, pp. 24, 288; vol. iv, p. 310.

[305] *W. Suss., 1641–2*, pp. 61, 75, 121, 153, 170, 172, 175–6, 189, 197; Lane, *Suss. Deeds*, p. 1; E. W. D. Penfold, *op. cit.*, pp. 35, 37, 82; P.R.O. E. 179/191/378, m. 3d; F. Leeson, "Development of Surnames," *Genealogists' Magazine*. (1970), vol. xvi, p. 415; *Suss. Wills*, vol. i, pp. 24, 228; vol. iv, p. 310.

[306] *3 Suss. Subsidies*, pp. 29, 45–7, 89, 113, 120, 177; Rubin, *Suss. Phonology*, p. 156; P.R.O. E. 179/189/42, m. 3; *Calendar of Close Rolls*, 1377–81, p. 123.

[307] *3 Suss. Subsidies*, pp. 207, 319; Löfvenberg, *op. cit.*, p. 98.

[308] W. Farrer, *Honors and Knights' Fees* (1925), vol. iii, pp. 83–86; *V.C.H., Suss.*, vol. iv, pp. 13–15; *Victoria County History of Wilts.*, vol. vii, p. 201; V. Gibbs and others, *Complete Peerage*, vol. vii, p. 3; *S.A.C.*, vol. ix, p. 46.

[309] H. A. Cronne and R. H. C. Davis, *Regesta Regum Anglo-Normannorum* (1968), vol. iii, pp. 116, 292, 369; H. Hall, *Red Book of the Exchequer*, (1896), vol. i, p. 202; J. Hunter, *Magnum rotuli scaccarii vel magnum rotulum pipae, anno tricesimoprimo Henrici primi* (1833), p. 72; *Boxgrove Chart.*, p. 35; *Suss. Fines*, vol. i, p. 1.

[310] J. H. Round, *Calendar of Documents Preserved in France* (1899), p. 204; D. M. Stenton, *Great Roll of the Pipe for the 7th year of Richard I* (Pipe Roll Soc., vol. xliv) (1929), p. 37; *Suss. Fines*, vol. i,

[311] p. 111; vol. ii, pp. 66, 117, 135; *Chichester Chart.*, pp. 85, 221; *Lewes Chartulary*, vol. ii, p. 89; *3 Suss. Subsidies*, p. 83.
[311] *Ibid.*, pp. 236, 237, 260; *Feudal Aids*, vol. v, pp. 141–2; *Non. Inquis.*, pp. 350, 364, 370; *Suss. Wills*, vol. i, p. 56.
[312] See p. 17.
[313] R. E. Latham, *Revised Medieval Latin Word List* (1965), p. 229.
[314] *V.C.H. Suss.*, vol. iv, p. 15; vol. vii, p. 158; *Suss. Wills*, vol. iv, pp. 140, 400.
[315] *Suss. Custumals*, vol. ii, pp. 81, 105; *3 Suss. Subsidies*, p. 103.
[316] *Surnames of Oxon.*, pp. 204–5.
[317] *Lewes Chartulary*, vol. i, pp. 77, 138, 178; vol. ii, p. 10; *Feudal Aids*, vol. v, p. 130; *Chichester Chart.*, pp. 5, 192; *Placita de Banco* (P.R.O. Lists and Indexes, xxxii), vol. ii, p. 666; *3 Suss. Subsidies*, p. 25; Fransson, *op. cit.*, p. 115; *Curia Regis Rolls, 5–7 John*, p. 195; *Suss. Fines*, vol. iii, p. 21; *Chichester Bishops' Acta*, p. 154.
[318] See the discussion by J. H. Round, *The King's Sergeants and Officers of State* (1911), pp. 177–183.
[319] *Suss. Fines*, vol. i, p. 14; *S.A.C.*, vol. li, p. 43; *Chichester Chart.*, p. 118; D. M. Stenton, *Great Roll of the Pipe for the Third and Fourth Years of Richard I* (Pipe Roll Soc., vol. xl) (1926), p. 204; E. Searle, *Lordship and Community* (1974), p. 120; Reaney, *Dict.*, p. 188.
[320] *Suss. Subsidy, 1524–5*, pp. 27, 33, 44, 49.
[321] *S.A.C.*, vol. lxxix, p. 135; P.R.O. S.C. 11/653.
[322] *W. Suss. 1641–2*, p. 141; W. C. Renshaw, *op. cit.*, pp. 1, 4, 9, 11, 12, 13 and *passim*.
[323] *W. Suss. 1641–2*, pp. 20, 168, 175; *Suss. Indictments*, vol. i, p. 67; *Suss. Subsidy, 1524–5*, p. 45; P.R.O. E. 179/191/378, m. 3; *Suss. Wills*, vol. i, p. 17.
[324] J. E. Ray, *op. cit.*, pp. 176, 181; F. Hull, *op. cit.*, pp. 337, 368; L. F. Salzman, *Parish Register of Glynde* (Suss. Record Soc., vol. xxx) (1924), pp. 7, 17; A. Dauzat, *op. cit.*, p. 334; Reaney, *Origins* p. 35; P.R.O. E. 179/235/2; *Suss. Wills*, vol. ii, p. 282. And see p. 10.
[325] Fransson, *op. cit.*, p. 126; *Chichester Chart.*, pp. 268, 350; *Suss. Custumals*, vol. ii, pp. 41, 60; *Lewes Barony Recs.*, pp. 19, 39; Inderwick, *Winchelsea*, p. 207; *3 Suss. Subsidies*, pp. 29, 36, 174, 199, 310; *Hastings Lathe C.R.*, pp. 114, 127; P.R.O. S.C. 11/877; *Suss. Wills*, vol. iii, p. 206.
[326] E. Searle, *Lordship and Community* (1974), pp. 365, 368, 434; *S.A.C.*, vol. lxvi, p. 113; *3 Suss. Subsidies*, p. 317; *Suss. Subsidy, 1524–5*, pp. 153–4; *Suss. Wills*, vol. i, p. 83.
[327] *S.A.C.*, vol. xlv, pp. 164–66, 178; P.R.O. E. 179/225/50, m. 62; *Suss. Wills*, vol. iv, p. 331.
[328] *Suss. Subsidy, 1524–5*, pp. 11, 101, 109, 114, 119, 153, 154.
[329] *Suss. Fines*, vol. i, p. 35; *S.A.C.*, vol. xxii, p. 118; P.R.O., E. 179/225/50, m. 62.

330 Thuresson, *op. cit.*, 138; *3 Suss. Subsidies*, pp. 185, 193, 214, 316; *Lewes Chartulary*, vol. i, p. 182; *Non. Inquis.*, p. 378; P.R.O., S.C. 11/666; *Suss. Fines*, vol. iii, p. 56.
331 *Robertsbridge Surveys*, pp. 25, 141; H.M.C., *Rye MSS.*, p. 132; F. Hull, *op. cit.*, p. 336.
332 Thuresson, *op. cit.*, p. 161.
333 *Non. Inquis.*, p. 359; A. Ponsonby, *Priory and Manor of Lynchmere and Shulbrede* (1920), pp. 40, 134; G. R. Rolston, *Haslemere in History* (1956), p. 36; W. H. Challen, *Parish Register of Cocking*, 1558–1837 (1927), p. 88; *3 Suss. Subsidies*, p. 240.
334 See p. 169.
335 *Suss. Subsidy, 1524–5*, p. 40; P.R.O. E. 179/191/378, m. 2; *P.N. Suss.*, vol. i, p. 121.
336 Lord Leconfield, *Petworth Manor in the 17th Century* (1954), pp. 46, 47, 105; Lord Leconfield, *Sutton and Duncton Manors* (1956), p. 31; *Suss. Wills*, vol. iii, p.295.
337 E. W. D. Penfold, *op. cit.*, pp. 93, 100, 101, 102, 107, 112, 131, 132.
338 P. R. O. E. 179/191/378, m. 2; *West Suss. 1641–2*, p. 25.
339 *Ibid.*, pp. 8, 9, 15, 36, 74, 80, 81, 114–17, 120, 128–29, 136–9, 140, 145, 177, 188.
340 *Ibid.*, pp. 25, 98; R. Garraway Rice, *Parish Register of Horsham* (Suss. Record Soc., vol. xxi) (1915), pp. 93, 293.
341 *West Suss. 1641–2*, pp. 15, 37; P.R.O. E. 179/189/42, m. 26; Thuresson, *op. cit.*, p. 161.
342 D. M. Stenton, *Great Roll of the Pipe for the 4th Year of King John* (Pipe Roll Soc., vol. liii) (1937), p. 143; Fransson, *op. cit.*, p. 97.
343 *Chichester Chart.*, pp. 109, 113, 167, 168.
344 *Boxgrove Chart.*, p. 186; *3 Suss. Subsidies*, p. 126.
345 *Ibid.*, pp. 126, 252; *Battle Custumals*, p. 56; *Non. Inquis.*, p. 394; *Fitzalan Surveys*, p. 17.
346 *Non. Inquis.*, p. 368; *S.A.C.*, vol. xcv, p. 48; P.R.O. E. 179/189/42, m. 19d.
347 *Suss. Custumals*, vol. ii, pp. 96, 98, 115, 134.
348 Reaney, *Dict.*, pp. 352, 356.
349 *Suss. Custumals*, vol. iii, pp. 65, 68.
350 See Cottle, *Dict.*, p. 385.
351 *Suss. Subsidy, 1524–5*, pp. 36–7, 41, 45, 151; *Suss. Wills*, vol. i, p. 244; information on parish registers from Mr F. Leeson.
352 *W. Suss. 1641–2*, pp. 8, 14, 36, 42, 47, 52, 63, 110, 119, 132–4, 137, 167.
353 W. H. Challen, *Parish Register of Cocking, 1558–1837* (1927), *per indice*.
354 *3 Suss. Subsidies*, pp. 54, 128, 152, 158, 272, 273.
355 *Chichester Chart.*, p. 354.
356 R. F. Hunnisett and J. B. Post, *Medieval Legal Records*, p. 372.

[357] *Suss. Subsidy, 1524–5*, pp. 24, 28, 31.
[358] J. E. Ray, *op. cit.*, p. 176.
[359] *W. Suss., 1641–2*, pp. 19, 85; Lane, *Suss. Deeds*, p. 2; *S.A.C.*, vol. xxxii, pp. 7, 8; *Suss. Wills*, vol. i, p. 6.
[360] *S.A.C.*, vol. xx, pp. 4, 8.
[361] *Feudal Aids*, vol. v, p. 165; *Suss. Custumals*, vol. iii, pp. 66–67, 76; *Fitzalan Surveys*, p. 153; H. P. R. Finberg, *Agrarian History of England* (1972), vol. i, part ii, p. 453.
[362] Fransson, *op. cit.*, p. 110.
[363] *Suss. Subsidy, 1524–5*, pp. 32, 44, 50, 76, 78, 79. See also *Suss. Wills*, vol. i, p. 229; vol. ii, p. 18; vol. iii, p. 76; vol. iv, pp. 121, 147.
[364] J. E. Ray, *op. cit.*, pp. 37, 153, 154; *Suss. Indictments*, vol. i, pp. 51, 79, 80, 83; *Chichester Chart.*, p. 202; *Suss. Wills*, vol. iv, p. 357; F. Leeson, "Development of Surnames", *Genealogists' Magazine* (1971), vol. xvi, p. 424.
[365] *W. Suss. 1641–2*, pp. 40, 43, 67, 83, 88, 101, 112, 161, 164–5, 170, 188; *S.A.C.*, vol. xxiv, p. 79; vol. xlii, p. 112; P. S. Godman, *Parish Register of Cowfold* (Suss. Record Soc., vol. xxii) (1916), pp. 7, 52, 58–61, 181, 212; C. H. Wilkie, *op. cit.*, p. 26.
[366] *Surnames of Lancs.*, p. 15.

CHAPTER 5

SURNAMES DERIVED FROM PERSONAL NAMES

The phrase 'personal names' is used here to mean what are generally called 'first', 'given', or 'Christian' names. It is not possible to say what personal names were in widespread use in Sussex at about the time of the Conquest. It is probable that some personal names were at that period much more common in the county than others. The frequency with which some personal names of Old English origin can be found in Sussex, during the 12th and 13th centuries, and the way in which some surnames derived from Old English personal names were each the name of many individuals there from about 1200 onwards, suggests that there are likely to have been some Old English personal names which were in the 11th and 12th centuries numerous and widely distributed in Sussex. There is, however, no effective way of testing this, for the personal names of the great majority of the county's inhabitants at about the time of the Conquest escape us. It is likely that before 1066 there were considerable differences in the personal names in use between one part of England and another. When rather fuller information is available, during the 12th and 13th centuries, it does seem that some personal names of Old English origin were much more common in some English regions than others, but it is uncertain how far this situation can be projected back into the past, and even at these later periods, the evidence about the personal names in use is still very incomplete, especially for the poorer sections of the inhabitants. Domesday lists a small body of landowners in the county, under Edward the Confessor and under William I, but there can be no certainty that at either period landowners' names were typical of the population as a whole. Some sub-tenants named in Domesday as holding land in Sussex under William I had Old English personal names. In some cases these were men who had held land in the county under the Confessor. In some cases, too, they had personal names which were in general use in Sussex during the 12th and 13th centuries, and from which surnames, common there from the 13th century onwards, originated. These included the personal names Aluuinus, Goduinus, Vluuardus and Aluuardus,[1] all of them frequently found in Sussex during the 12th and 13th centuries (when many hereditary surnames developed), and all of them personal names which gave rise to surnames in the county. It is clear that even where landowners were concerned, the Conquest did not produce a complete change in the personal names used. There is a general pattern in the history of personal names in England, taking the country as

301

a whole, during the centuries after 1066, and this can be perceived, despite the scarcity of information about the personal names used by some sections of the population. For a century or more after 1066 a great number and variety of personal names was in use, some of Old English or Scandinavian origin, some names introduced after the Conquest. From the late 12th century onwards, many Old English or Scandinavian personal names tended gradually either to fall out of use altogether, or to become very rare. Some personal names brought in after the Conquest became disused similarly. By the late 13th century, a small number of male personal names had become extremely common, John, William, Richard, Edward, Thomas, for example. Most though not all of these names were ones which had been brought into the country after 1066. Other male personal names had become rare, and by about the middle of the 14th century male personal names, except for the small group which had become very common by the late 13th century, had either fallen into disuse, or were by then very exceptional. The position about male personal names remained largely unchanged from the mid-14th century until the 16th century, with a small number of names being used very frequently indeed, many names in use earlier totally discarded, and some other names being very sparsely employed. During the 16th century the character of personal names began to change in various ways. A much wider range of Biblical names came to be used, for example, mainly because of Puritan influence, and increasing use was made of surnames as Christian names, especially among the gentry. By 1500, very few new surnames were being created, at least in the south and Midlands of England, and these 16th century developments had no noticeable effect on the history of English surnames.

Female personal names in the Middle Ages are less well documented than male ones, but generally seem to have been more varied and more inventive than male ones. The number of surnames derived from female personal names is not very large, but some do occur.[2]

It is not very easy to account for the history of male personal names during the Middle Ages. The popularity of some personal names is understandable. One or two of the names which had become very common by the mid-14th century, such as John or Thomas, for instance, were the names of more than one well known saint; others, such as William, Henry, Richard, or Edward were used by the royal family. It is, however, difficult to understand why so many personal names which were popular in the 12th century, and in some cases later, came to be abandoned, or used very exceptionally, from the 14th century onwards.

The general history of personal names in Sussex during the period when hereditary surnames were evolving, and the history in the county of surnames derived from personal names, has to be seen against this general history of personal names in medieval England. It is not possible to obtain a complete view of the personal names being used in Sussex between the Conquest and about 1200, though this is the period when hereditary surnames were starting to appear. It seems likely that landowners in the county, whether of Norman or English descent, were within a generation or two after 1066 mostly using personal names which had been introduced into England after the Conquest. The 'Cartae' of 1166 for Sussex, which list many of the larger landowners in the county, mention very few men with Old English personal names.[3] Examination of some other sources which list Sussex landholders shows that in the 13th century it was very unusual for major landowners in the county to have Old English personal names.[4] There are a few exceptions, both in the 'Cartae' of 1166 and in other sources, and a few 12th century landowners do appear with Old English first names.[5] It is less easy to discover what the position was for other sections of the community. A list of householders at Battle, about 1110, lists rather more than 100 persons. Miss Cecily Clark has pointed out that, of the male first names in this source, about 40% are Continental forms.[6] Battle was a new foundation, and may not have been typical of Sussex towns. A large number of different sources containing information relating to Sussex has been searched for the present study, and the personal names recorded in these sources as being those of persons who were, so far as can be seen, residents in the county have been examined. It is obvious from this evidence that the number of Old English personal names which continued in use in the county during the 12th and 13th centuries was very large. About 90 different Old English personal names have been discovered in Sussex during the 12th century, and about 75 during the 13th. The personal names found in the 13th century are mostly those already present in the 12th. These figures have been arrived at after eliminating some cases where the origin of particular personal names seem doubtful. There are some cases, especially where Latinised forms are concerned, in which it is difficult to be certain what personal name is involved. Such forms as, for example, Alardus, Walwanus, or Whibertus cannot be assigned an Old English or continental origin with any certainty. It cannot be claimed that the figures given above for Old English names found during the 12th and 13th centuries are the real totals of Old English names in use in the county during those periods. A more comprehensive search than it has been possible to make might yield a few more names, but in any case there are large sections of the population whose personal names are generally not found in the existing sources. In the 12th century, particularly, those whose names are recorded tend to be predominantly either landowners, or clergy, and it seems probable that these groups may have adopted continental personal names earlier than other sections of the population. It is in particular difficult to gain any impression of what the personal names of unfree tenants were during the 12th century, and it is likely that during that period the number of Old English personal names in Sussex was considerably larger than would appear from the figures given above. Such fragmentary evidence as there is for Sussex serfs names in the 12th century suggests that the unfree population then had mostly Old English personal names, but the information is too scanty for any firm conclusions.[7] Early 13th century lists of serfs on several Sussex manors show a minority with personal names of Old English origin.[8] During the early 13th century there are a number of cases where serfs have personal names introduced after the Conquest, but had fathers with Old English personal names.[9] For the middle and late 13th century lists of bond tenants are available for quite a few Sussex manors, located in different parts of the county. These show that it was by then unusual for serfs to have Old English personal names, though many at that time had surnames or bye-names derived from Old English personal names.[10] The evidence for the mid and late 13th century includes the names of many female bond tenants, and from this it is clear that women, as well as men of the servile class, had generally ceased to use Old English personal names. It seems from this evidence that bond tenants had largely ceased to have Old English personal names by the mid 13th century. Though the lack of adequate evidence for the 12th century makes it impossible to be sure of the facts, it seems likely that towards the end of the century serfs largely gave up using Old English personal names, which were only used by bondmen to a very limited extent during the 13th century. Serfs are likely to have abandoned Old English names less rapidly than persons in other classes, and it is probable that by mid 13th century, at the latest, personal names of Old English origin were only being used by a small minority of the Sussex population. In the 1296 lay subsidy role for Sussex, which of course lists taxpayers, and excludes the poorest section of the community, Old English personal names are very scarce. If the two names Edward and Edmund (which remained in general use during the medieval period) are excluded, there are only 32 individuals in the subsidy with Old English personal names, out of more than 7,000 persons listed.[11] Small numbers of Old English personal names appear in the Sussex subsidies for 1327/8 and 1332, and a few more can be found in Sussex sources for the first half of the 14th century.[12] Apart from the names Edward and Edmund, which persist, there are very few examples of Old English personal names in use during the second half of the 14th century in Sussex.[13]

It appears from this evidence, and from the personal names found in the wide range of medieval Sussex sources examined for this study, that already in the first half of the 13th century a minority of the Sussex population had personal names of Old English origin. By the end of the 13th century many Old English personal names had fallen into disuse, and the remainder had become rare with the exception of Edward and Edmund, neither of which was particularly common in Sussex, though both gave rise to surnames in the county. By about 1200 a majority of the

Surnames Derived from Personal Names

Sussex population, so far as can be seen from the available sources, had personal names which had been introduced after the Conquest. By the end of the 13th century, judging from the 1296 subsidy role and from other sources of about the same date, the male personal names which were in common use had become quite few. A small group of about 15 names (John, Thomas, Richard, Henry, etc.) had by then come to be used extremely frequently. Other male personal names had become rare, and many Old English personal names were already disused. During the 14th century this process was carried further, and most Old English names were given up. These factors in the history of personal names in the county must be borne in mind when considering the surnames which arose from personal names in Sussex.

These changes in the personal names employed were not peculiar to Sussex, for similar developments took place in other parts of England, with but minor regional variations. Judging by the evidence of subsidy rolls, rather more Old English personal names remained in use in Sussex during the late 13th century and the first half of the 14th than in most other southern and Midland counties, but the differences between one county and another are not very great. Some northern counties have characteristics of their own, such as the survival during the 13th century of many personal names which were Scandinavian in origin, but in the north of England, too, the general history of personal names was not very different from that which has been outlined above for Sussex.

Three main types of surname derived from personal names can be distinguished: (a) surnames from personal names without inflexion, such as Godwin, Paul, Payne, Gilbert, Herbert, etc. The great majority of surnames derived from personal names found in Sussex, from the 12th century to the present, belong to this type; (b) surnames formed from a personal name with a genitival 's', such as Williams, Roberts, etc. This type has always been rare in Sussex; (c) surnames formed from personal names with the addition of the suffix '-son', Johnson, Williamson, etc. This type of surname, also, has been rare in Sussex, and it is doubtful if any surnames of the type originated in the county. It is intended to deal with each of the three types of surname in turn.

Surnames derived from Personal Names without Inflexion

Surnames from uninflected personal names were already common in Sussex in the late 12th century. The surnames or bye-names of this type which have been noted in the county during the 12th century are preponderantly derived from personal names brought into the country after 1066. A list of surnames of the type concerned found in the county has been compiled from a variety of sources, and about three quarters of the surnames or bye-names involved are from such post-Conquest personal names. The remaining surnames or bye-names are nearly all derived from Old English personal names. There are a few surnames or bye-names from Scandinavian names which are not necessarily imports from Normandy, and there are several names of doubtful origin. It is questionable, however, if the surnames or bye-names present in the sources are fully representative of the names of the type under consideration which were in use in the county at that time. A high proportion of those mentioned in 12th century records were either the more important holders of land, or upper clergy, and were consequently much more likely to be persons of French origin than the average for the whole population. For the 13th century the information is more complete, but by that time the use of Old English personal names was declining. At that period the surnames or bye-names, derived from personal names, found in Sussex were again predominantly ones derived from personal names introduced after the Conquest. Out of all the surnames or bye-names of this category found in the 13th century Sussex sources which have been examined, about three fifths are derived from personal names brought in after 1066. These are figures for number of names, not for numbers of individuals. In the 13th century some surnames or bye-names from Old English personal names had in fact become numerous and widespread in Sussex. For instance, the surname or bye-name Aylwyn, which occurs in a great variety of forms (Ailwyne, Eylwyne, Aldwin, Alwyne, etc.), can be found in different parts of Sussex during the 13th century, and by 1300 was already quite common in the county.[14] This is a surname which could be derived from any of several Old English personal names. The forms which appear are very varied, and at times the surname or bye-name of one individual is found in several, considerably different forms, so that it is often impossible to be sure which personal name, out of several possible ones, gave rise to the surname in any one case.[15] The surname or bye-name Godwin, derived from an Old English personal name which was more common in Sussex during the 12th and 13th centuries than the great majority of Old English names, can similarly be found in most parts of Sussex during the 13th century.[16] Hereward, on the other hand, was little used as a personal name in Sussex during the 12th and 13th centuries, though it is possible that it may have been used rather more widely than appears from the sources, and that it may have been relatively common among those sections of the population which are badly recorded. Very few instances of the personal name in use have been found in Sussex during the 12th and 13th centuries.[17] Despite this, the surname or bye-name Hereward existed there during the 12th century, and was in the 13th century quite numerous in Sussex, and found in most parts of the county.[18] Aylwin, Godwin, and Hereward were all surnames which appear frequently in Sussex in 1300–1500, and later, during the

16th and 17th centuries, all were very numerous in the county. There were a few other surnames or bye-names derived from Old English personal names which were already widespread in the county by 1300, and there were also by the same date many surnames or bye-names (from Old English personal names) which were scarce, and appeared at one or two places in Sussex. Often these rarer cases survived as the hereditary surnames of one or two families, and were still present in Sussex during the 16th and 17th centuries, and later. Despite the fact that by 1200, when the majority of Sussex families were still without hereditary surnames, the use of Old English personal names was declining, there was during the 13th century a sizeable minority of surnames or bye-names in the county (out of the whole body of surnames or bye-names derived from personal names) which were from Old English personal names. This continued to be true at later periods, such as the 16th and 17th centuries. Though there is an obvious connection between the presence in Sussex from the 12th century onwards of many surnames or bye-names derived from personal names introduced after the Conquest and the growing employment in the county of such personal names, it does not seem that in any part of England there was a direct link between the frequency with which any one personal name was in use at the period when hereditary surnames were evolving, and the number of families with surnames from the personal name concerned. The case of the personal name Hereward, mentioned above, is an example of a locally scarce personal name giving rise to a relatively common surname. It is often the case that personal names which were especially common in one region at the time when surnames were evolving gave rise to few or no surnames. The personal name Edmund, for example, was especially common in East Anglia, but gave rise there to fewer surnames than other personal names which were less popular in the region.[19] Even if the evidence about the personal names and surnames of the whole population were more adequate than in fact it is, it must be doubtful whether there would prove to be any very precise relationship between the frequency with which any one personal name occurs during the period when surnames were evolving, and the number of surnames derived from that personal name. This would probably be true for any part of England.

In fact the degree to which many surnames derived from personal names without inflection were common varies considerably from one part of England to another, and while this can be partly explained by difference between regions in the personal names currently used during the period when surnames were arising, there were other factors at work. Some evidence on this has already been put forward about other counties.[20] It is possible to demonstrate the differences between counties or regions by drawing on the evidence of the surnames or bye-names to be found in the subsidy rolls for the late 13th century and the first half of the

14th. These do show great differences from one county to another in the surnames (or bye-names) in use at that time, when in many parts of England a considerable proportion of the population already possessed surnames or bye-names, but when, though some surnames had already been hereditary for several generations, there had not been time for the distribution of surnames to be affected to more than a very limited degree by either migration, or the ramification of individual families. This method has some defects; the subsidy rolls exclude the poorest sections of the community, and so may not give a completely accurate account of the surnames or bye-names in use; individuals were sometimes listed more than once in a subsidy roll, but it is difficult to be sure how much duplication there is; practical considerations of space make it impossible to present the evidence for more than a limited number of counties in a table; and the task of dealing with the manuscript subsidy returns for a county, even for one year, is so time-consuming that it has been necessary to rely on such printed texts of subsidies as are available. Because of these factors there must be some reservations about the complete accuracy of the figures put forward, but it is unlikely that figures obtained from the subsidies seriously misrepresent the position. The figures for the frequency with which some selected surnames or bye-names derived from personal names occur in medieval subsidy returns for some English counties are given below. The need to keep the table to a reasonable size has prevented evidence being given for a greater number of counties, and for more surnames. The names listed in the table have been chosen to include some surnames which were more common in Sussex than in most parts of the country, and consequently are not the same as those used in similar tables which have been published in other volumes of the *Surnames Survey*.[21] Very rare surnames have been excluded, since in such cases the statistics can be much affected, even at an early stage in the development of hereditary surnames, by the ramification of a single family.

It can be seen from the statistics set out in the table that there were substantial differences between counties in the frequency with which some surnames (or bye-names, for it is usually impossible to say what proportion of names were hereditary), can be found in the lay subsidies. It has already been pointed out that this can not be explained simply by differences between counties or regions in the personal names in use. Speaking generally, it does not seem to be that personal names which were very common failed to originate surnames simply because they were so common, and consequently not sufficiently distinctive, though this has been suggested as the reason for the lack of surnames derived from some widely used personal names. In some areas, personal names which were much used gave rise to surnames which were quite numerous. One instance of this is the personal name Godwine, which, as already

Table 1. *Differences between counties in surnames derived from personal names.*[22]

Figures are for the number of individuals bearing each surname listed per *ten thousand individuals in each source. Spelling variants have been consolidated under each name. Surnames of which the origin is uncertain have been excluded from the figures.*

	Suss. 1327	Bucks 1332	Dorset 1327	Kent 1334/5	Lancs. 1332	Leics. 1327	Surr. 1332	Suff. 1327	Warws. 1332
Ailwin (Aylwin, Elwin)	25	10	7	1	0	2	27	18	3
Alard (Adlard, Athelard Aylard)	2	5	0	5	0	0	9	3	1
Alnod (Ailnod, Elnod)	5	0	0	4	0	0	14	3	0
Algar (Elgar)	9	10	1	6	0	2	7	6	0
Andrew	34	20	12	18	0	18	2	24	7
Bartelott (Bartlett)	16	5	0	14	0	0	0	12	0
Daniel	13	0	4	14	0	0	9	9	0
Durrant (Dorrant)	10	21	10	4	0	2	0	6	7
Edrich	9	10	1	4	0	2	0	6	1
Edmund	15	0	4	10	0	2	12	9	7
Gilbert	16	10	7	9	0	15	9	11	10
Goddard	10	0	4	6	0	2	9	1	0
Godwin	24	24	5	16	0	14	18	21	0
Goldwine (Joldwine)	7	0	0	10	0	2	7	5	1
Hammond	28	25	6	51	0	4	29	18	13
Hereward	15	9	2	4	0	2	10	10	15
Osbern	36	14	15	16	0	8	17	24	10
Osmond	6	24	9	1	0	5	14	4	6
Seaman	28	0	2	9	0	0	14	20	3
Willard	1	0	0	0	0	0	0	1	0

described, was a popular personal name in Sussex during the 12th and 13th centuries, and from which a surname widespread in the county was derived. There are other examples. The Old English personal name Saemann was much used in Sussex during the 12th and 13th centuries, and survived into the 14th, though by then scarce in the county,[23] but the surname Seman, derived from it, was widespread in Sussex during the Middle Ages, and later.[24] The small number of male personal names which became very common throughout England produced many surnames, including some which were already numerous, taking the country as a whole, by the end of the 13th century. It is true that many of the uninflected surnames derived from this small group of very common personal names were from hypochoristic forms, and that in some cases individual personal names had several hypochoristic forms, from each of which surnames originated. The hypochoristic forms ('pet-forms'). were presumably the forms actually employed in speech, and the fact that several different hypochoristic forms were often available for a single personal name must in practice have done something to alleviate the situation, existing in England generally from about 1300, of there being a very limited number of male personal names in common use. The fact remains that many very popular personal names did originate surnames which were quite widespread.

In general, it seems to have been true that there was a rough correspondence between the popularity of any one personal name (during the period when surnames from uninflected personal names were evolving), and the frequency with which surnames, derived from the personal name in question, appear in any one area. Most hereditary surnames derived from personal names appear to have developed, so far as the south and Midlands of England are concerned, in the period c. 1200 to c. 1350. This is a period during which changes took place in the body of personal names in general use, as has been described. There were some exceptions to this general rule, both in Sussex, and in other regions. The case of the personal name Edmund, which was very common in East Anglia, but from which very few surnames originated in that part of the country, is one instance. In Sussex, the personal name Osbert was very much used during the 12th, 13th, and 14th centuries, and was more common in the county than in most parts of England,[25] but a surname or bye-name derived from this personal name has been found but once in the county before 1500, in an instance where the surname appears to have been derived from the personal name of a 14th century customary tenant.[26] There is no obvious reason why certain personal names, used a good deal during the 12th, 13th, and 14th centuries failed to produce very many surnames, but it is not to be expected that the development of surnames, not in any of its aspects a particularly regular process, would proceed strictly in accordance with any set of rules.

The preceding remarks about the frequency with which surnames arose from individual personal names apply only where personal names used reasonably often are concerned. Where scarce personal names were involved, it was much more a matter of chance if bye-names came into existence, and if bye-names in turn evolved into hereditary surnames. In some cases rare personal names continued in use in one area for a considerable period, and gave rise there to surnames. For example, the surname Thurgood is derived from a personal name, Scandinavian in origin, which was the name of a landholder in Sussex under the Confessor.[27] The personal name has been found as the name of one individual in the county during the 12th century, and it was probably then rare locally.[28] In the 13th century and the early 14th, the personal name was in use on the manor of South Malling, as the name of small free tenants. Early in the 14th century it also appears at Burwash in the same part of the county.[29] It has not been found elsewhere in Sussex after 1200. The surname Thurgod or Thurgood existed on South Malling manor from the late 13th century. In the case of at least one family a surname appears to have developed from the personal name of a mid or late 13th century tenant of the manor.[30] In the early 14th century the surname was present at Preston (near Beddingham), which is close to South Malling.[31] The only other place in the county where the surname Thurgood has been found during the 13th or 14th centuries is Chichester, where the city drew in migrants from a wide area.[32] It is possible that the Richard Thurgood who is mentioned at Chichester in the late 13th century was the same person as the Richard Thurgot listed at Preston in 1327/8. In this case the surname developed in one part of the county from a rare personal name, which had persisted in the same area but not, so far as can be seen, elsewhere in Sussex.

Another similar example is that of surnames derived from the Old English feminine personal name Godleofu (usually given in the Latinised form Godeleva) The personal name remained in use for a long period in Kent. In Sussex it was rare, so far as can be judged from the scanty evidence for women's names, though it survived in the county into the 16th century.[33] The personal name has been found in Sussex during the 13th century at two places, at Ewhurst in East Sussex, and at Upper Beeding, in the north of the county, near Horsham.[34] In the late 13th and early 14th century the surname derived from this personal name occurs, in the form Godelef or Godeloue, in two parts of Sussex, at Horsham, and in the east around Ewhurst.[35] In this instance too, a rare surname developed from a personal name which survived in two parts of Sussex. The surname was a scarce one, but it persisted in East Sussex, and by the 16th century had ramified in the county to some extent.[36]

The history of the surname Brithmer also shows how the survival of a rare personal name in one area could give rise to a surname. The personal name Brithmer or Bricmar occurs in Sussex during the 11th century, mostly in connection with land at or near Brighton.[37] No examples of the personal name are known from Sussex for the 12th century, but early in the 13th it existed at Southerham and Fletching.[38] It must be presumed that this was a rare name in the county, at least after *c*. 1100. In the late 13th century the surname Brytmere or Brithmer appears at Fletching and at Southerham, two places both in the same part of Sussex.[39] At Southerham it was the surname of several persons, and there at least it is likely to have been hereditary. The surname is listed at Maresfield, which adjoins Fletching, in 1332, but apart from this it has not been found anywhere in the county except Fletching and Southerham before 1400.[40] The persons mentioned with the surname at Southerham were customary tenants. In this case, too, a rare personal name survived until a relatively late date in one area, and produced a surname, which was also rare.

Some other examples could be given of instances where scarce personal names persisted into relatively late periods, in limited areas within the county, and there gave rise to surnames which themselves were at first rare, though in some cases they proliferated later. In most cases where rare personal names persisted until late periods, they did so among the classes of small freeholders and customary tenants. These sections of the community were less rapidly influenced than others in their use of personal names by the introduction after the Conquest of many new names.

One or two surnames may have originated from exotic personal names used by single individuals, possibly aliens. For example, the personal name Ciprian has been found in Sussex as the name of two persons. One of these was a 12th century priest, who was presumably celibate;[41] the other was Cyprian de Newehavene, who was holding land at Littlehampton in the late 13th century[42] (Cyprian's bye-name cannot be from the Sussex place-name Newhaven which was not in use before the 16th century. It was possibly from a harbour in the Selsey area.) Chiprian was in use as a surname or bye-name in 1291 at Winchelsea, which had then just been re-founded, and where the inhabitants had surnames or bye-names from many different parts of Sussex.[43] The surname was very rare, both in Sussex, and in England generally. It seems, however, to have survived, for it still existed in Sussex in the 16th century.[44] The surname Fabian may be a similar case. A single person has been found in the county with Fabian as a personal name, and he was a cleric, at one time vicar of Bexhill,[45] about 1200. No connection can be traced between this clergyman and the individuals who later appear in the county with Fabian as a surname, and as the personal name, though very rare, is known to occur elsewhere in England in the 12th and 13th centuries,[46] it is possible that the surname originated with someone else. Fabian was a surname or bye-name in Sussex from the late 13th century onwards.[47] The surname seems to have been very scarce in Sussex during the Middle Ages, but it too survived, and still existed in the county in the 17th century.[48]

In the case of a few personal names it is possible to perceive reasons for survival to a relatively late period in Sussex. The personal name Saefrith (or Seffrid) was that of two bishops of Chichester in the 12th century. The personal name remained in use in Sussex throughout the 13th century, with most examples being at or near Chichester.[49] There is little doubt that the continued use of the personal name in this area was due to the example of the two diocesan bishops so named. The surname Sefrid or Seffray, derived from the personal name, has first been found in Sussex in the late 13th century. There are further examples of the surname during the 14th and 15th centuries, nearly all from the district around

Chichester.[50] In this case the use by two bishops of a rare Old English personal name, at a late period, led first to the personal name being used fairly often, mostly around Chichester, and then to the development of a surname from the personal name in the same area. The unusual surname Pancras, on the other hand, owes its origin to the presence in Sussex of three churches dedicated to St Pancras. Lewes Priory was dedicated to St Pancras, and so were churches at Chichester and Arlington.[51] Pancras first appears as a surname or bye-name in Sussex at Cocking, in 1296. It has not been found at an early date anywhere else in England, and it is possible that the surname originated exclusively in Sussex.[52] The surname was very rare in medieval Sussex, but it survived, and was present in the 16th century at Horsham, where the surname existed into the 17th century, and elsewhere in West Sussex. At Horsham the surname ramified to some extent during the 16th and 17th centuries.[53] It is possible that the surname has become confused with Pankhurst, which can also be found at Horsham in the 17th century.

In cases such as these it is possible to discover reasons why certain rare personal names gave rise to surnames in the county. There are, however, many instances where uncommon surnames (from uninflected personal names) appear, without it being possible to assign any particular reason for their having originated, and survived. The total number of surnames or bye-names derived from uninflected personal names existing in medieval Sussex was very large, and many failed to survive. More than 160 bye-names, from uninflected personal names, have been found in the county before 1500 which have each been discovered as the name of but one individual, and which have not been found in the county at all after 1500. In a few cases these were the names of aliens. In a few cases, too, the bye-names in question are ones which can be found in adjoining counties, especially in Kent, and their presence in Sussex might be due to individual migration, perhaps temporary, from nearby areas. Allowing for some importation of bye-names, it is clear that there must have been very many bye-names (from uninflected personal names), which failed to develop into hereditary surnames.

Why some such bye-names, out of a large number, evolved into hereditary surnames, and survived through the medieval period, it is generally impossible to decide. No doubt it was often due to the survival of single families, which had acquired uncommon surnames, derived from personal names which were also rare. There are in fact in Sussex a considerable number of surnames from personal names which appear from the way in which early references are distributed to have survived in the county as the hereditary surnames of a single family. It is obviously not possible to discuss all of these in detail, but a few examples will serve to illustrate the history of such surnames.

Allnot

The personal name from which the surname Allnot is derived was in use in Sussex during the 12th and 13th centuries, and has been found in the county as late as 1332. The personal name was not especially scarce, and was not confined to one part of the county, though most of the instances come from East Sussex.[54] During the late 13th and early 14th centuries the surname appears in the part of East Sussex around Seaford (in forms such as Elnot, Aylnoth, Eylnoth, etc.).[55] Isolated examples have been found elsewhere in the county, at and near Sompting;[56] no later examples of the name have been found in the same area, where the name probably did not become hereditary. During the 15th and 16th centuries, the surname existed rather further north than Seaford in East Sussex.[57] (This is probably an instance of the tendency, often found in Sussex surnames, to migrate from the south of the county into the Wealden areas.) In this case the surname seems to have originated in one part of the county, and the early references are so concentrated as to make it very probable that all those with the names (except for the isolated occurences around Sompting) were from one family. The surname still exists in Sussex.

Bensy

The surname Bensy (or Bency), occurs from the later 13th century in a small area near Arundel. The medieval examples of the surname in Sussex are all on manors held by the Fitzalan family. Most of the individuals concerned were serfs, and it is probable that all were. At Binstead and Madehurst the name persisted from the late 13th century to the 15th, leaving little doubt that it was hereditary.[58] The fact that all the medieval instances involve persons of the same class, holding on the same estate, and all in the same small area, suggests strongly that in this case, too, the surname originated in Sussex with one family. The personal name from which the surname is derived has not been found in Sussex, but a diminutive of it (Benceline), does occur, though in a different part of the county. The surname survived near Madehurst in the 16th century.[59]

Botting

Botting is a surname which in Sussex appears to have originated with one family, but which ramified considerably in one part of the county. The surname developed independently elsewhere in England, though it was infrequent. In Sussex it appears during the 14th century in Nuthurst parish, in the north of the county. It has not been discovered anywhere else in Sussex before 1400,[60] but in the 15th century the name occurs at Cowfold, near Nuthurst.[61] The persistence of the name in one area shows that it was hereditary, probably from the early 14th century. The surname survived at Cowfold for many years.[62] At Horsham, a parish which adjoins Nuthurst, the surname was present in the 16th century, and there it became quite numerous.[63] During the 16th and 17th centuries it existed at West Grinstead, which adjoins Nuthurst to the south.[64] In the 16th century the surname began to disperse. It appears at places still in the northern part of Sussex, but more distant, such as East Grinstead and Warnham, and towards the end of the century it spread to more remote parts of the county, such as Winchelsea. During the 17th century the surname was quite widespread in Sussex.[65] The surname Buttyng, which occurs at East Grinstead in the 16th century, is probably a variant of Botting.[66] Botting still survived at Nuthurst in the 17th and 18th centuries.[67] Although it is not possible to link together all the persons named Botting who can be found in Sussex during the medieval period, and in the 16th and 17th centuries, it must be suspected from the way in which the surname gradually dispersed that there was a single family at Nuthurst, which ramified and eventually spread.

There are today a large number of people named Botting in Sussex, and the surname is widely distributed throughout the county. In some cases the presence of the surname in Sussex at the present time may be due to migration from outside the county at relatively recent dates, but it is likely that most of the Sussex Bottings are the descendants of the original Nuthurst family.

Otway

The surname Otway has first been found in Sussex early in the 14th century, when it existed at East Grinstead and Hartfield, two adjoining parishes in the north of the county.[68] It survived at Hartfield for some time during the 14th century, which makes it probable that it was hereditary there.[69] The personal name from which the surname is derived occurs in Sussex during the 13th century, though it seems to have been rare,[70] and was still in use in Surrey in the 14th century.[71] The surname has not been found in any other part of Sussex before the late 14th century, and there seems little doubt that all the persons named Otway who appear in medieval Sussex belonged to one family. The surname still existed in north Sussex in the 17th century.[72] In various forms (Otway, Ottaway, Ottoway) the surname is still present in Sussex, and is now quite widespread in the county. As, however, it arose independently in other counties, this may be partly due to migration.

Sweeting

The surname Sweeting first appears in Sussex as the name of customary tenants on South Malling manor, in the late 13th century. It persisted in the same area in the 14th century, so that it is likely to have been hereditary.[73] The name of Sweatings Lane at Wadhurst (where the Sweetings held land from South Malling manor in the 13th century) is probably derived from the family surname.[74] The surname occurs at Ticehurst, a village adjoining Wadhurst, in the 14th century.[75] The name persisted in Sussex into the 16th and 17th centuries, but does not seem to have increased noticeably in numbers.[76] It survives in the county to the present.

Tomset

The first example of the name Tomset in Sussex is in 1395, at Ewhurst.[77] This is much earlier than any examples known from other counties, or than the references to the surname given in the standard works,[78] and it seems possible that the surname originated exclusively in Sussex. The personal name from which the surname is derived is a hypochoristic form of Thomas. The personal name has not been discovered in Sussex, but this is not surprising, as hypochoristic forms are sparsely represented in medieval sources. The surname survived at Ewhurst throughout the 15th century, leaving little doubt that it had been hereditary there from the late 14th. In the 15th century it also occurred at Burwash, a short distance from Ewhurst, but it has not been found anywhere else before 1500.[79] During the 16th century the surname still persisted at both Ewhurst and Burwash. Those persons who appear with the name during the 15th and 16th centuries all appear to have been yeomen or copyholders.[80] During the 16th century the surname became rather more dispersed, but so far as can be seen it remained confined to the eastern part of East Sussex,[81] and it does not seem to have spread to West Sussex. The Protestation Returns of 1641–42, which list a high proportion of the adult male population of West Sussex, do not record any instances of the surname.

At the present day the surname, in various forms (Tamsett, Tomsett, Thomset, Thompsett, Thomsit, etc.), is quite common in Sussex, still mostly in the east of the county. It can be found today in other parts of England, including the London area, but judging from the evidence of telephone directories (which admittedly do not list the whole population), the surname still occurs more frequently, proportionate to the population, in Sussex than anywhere else in England. In the absence of any known early examples from other parts of the country, it seems likely that the surname originated with a single family in Sussex, and subsequently ramified greatly.

Woolgar

The surname Woolgar (Wolgar, Vulgar, etc.) has first been found in Sussex at the end of the 13th century. The personal name from which the surname is derived is mentioned in Sussex in Domesday,[82] but it has not been discovered in the county during the 12th or early 13th centuries, and must have been rare locally. The surname has never been limited to Sussex, and early examples can be found in other counties. The instances of the surname which have been found in Sussex at the end of the 13th century, and during the first half of the 14th, are all from one part of the county, at and around Steyning.[83] During the second half of the 14th century the surname persists in the same area, though somewhat more dispersed. The survival of the surname over a period in the same small district shows that it had become hereditary.[84] In the late 15th century the surname occurs at Chichester as the surname of a single person, who in fact became mayor of the city,[85] but this is probably simply one of many examples of Chichester having drawn in migrants from the adjoining rural parts; apart from this case, the surname has not been found in Sussex outside the Steyning area before 1500.

In the 16th and 17th centuries the surname Woolgar (etc.) still persisted in the Steyning area. It was to be found in the 17th century at Steyning, and in the adjoining parish of Henfield, both places where it had been in the 14th. In the 16th century the surname also appears at and near Chichester, probably as a result of the descendants of the mayor (already mentioned) proliferating there. Besides this, the surname spread into the parishes east of Steyning and Henfield, such as Edburton (where the name became fairly numerous), Albourne, Woodmancote, and Beeding. Apart from this, there are examples of individuals at more distant places in the county, such as Hastings or Warnham, but even as late as the 17th century the surname was still mainly concentrated around Steyning.[86] It is of course possible that the position may have been affected to some extent by migration into the county from outside. Woolgar was still a surname at Steyning in the 19th century,[87] and it still exists in the Steyning area at the present day. It is now quite a numerous surname in Sussex, and though its present status in the county may owe something to movement from other parts of England, it is likely that it is mainly caused by the ramification of one family originating at Steyning.

It would be possible to discuss many more examples of Sussex surnames which would appear from the evidence to have originated with single families. The instances which have been considered, however, are sufficient to illustrate how a surname originating with a single family could over several centuries increase in numbers, and disperse over a gradually widening area, until in some cases a surname reached considerable numbers in the county. Such developments are one factor in producing the situation, observable in the 16th and 17th centuries, and often earlier, where some surnames are very common in some counties, but rare, or entirely lacking, in others. As has been shown in the case of some of the surnames just discussed, the consequences can still be seen in the distribution of surnames at the present day. In this respect, as in others, the main impression left by the evidence about surnames derived from personal names without inflections is one of the stability and continuity of Sussex surnames. There were of course many bye-names derived from personal names which never became hereditary surnames. There were also many hereditary surnames which existed during the 13th and 14th centuries for several generations, but which subsequently disappeared. The failure of many surnames to survive into the late 14th century is no doubt often due to the heavy mortality during the middle years of that century. Most, however, of the surnames from personal names which are at all common in the county in the 16th and 17th centuries were ones which already had a long history in Sussex before 1500. Even at the present day, despite the growth of seaside resorts, the increase of population, and the migration of many people into the county, most of the Sussex surnames from personal names which were numerous in the county during the 16th and 17th centuries are still common there, and often more numerous there, proportionate to the population, than in other English counties.

SURNAMES FORMED FROM A PERSONAL NAME WITH A GENITIVAL 'S', AND SURNAMES FORMED FROM A PERSONAL NAME WITH THE SUFFIX -SON.

Apart from surnames formed from personal names without inflection, there are two other major types of surname originating from personal names. These are surnames formed from personal names in the genitive (such as Roberts, Williams, Gibbs, etc.), and surnames formed from personal names with the addition of the suffix -son (Williamson, Robertson, Gibson, etc.). Neither of these types has ever been at all as numerous in Sussex as surnames formed from personal names without inflection.

Surnames formed from a personal name with a genitive 's' were very rare in Sussex before 1500, and during the 16th and 17th centuries were still much less common, proportionate to the whole population, than in the South Midland counties. Judging from some printed sources which have been examined for Kent and Surrey, including subsidy rolls, the position in those two counties resembled that in Sussex. No surnames or bye-names of the type in question have been found in Sussex before 1200, and in fact no examples are known from any other county before the late 12th century.[88] In England generally such surnames or bye-names were rare until the late 13th century, even in counties where they later became numerous.[89] In Sussex, a total of 19 individuals with surnames or bye-names of the type have been found for the 13th century in the sources which have been searched for this study.[90] In addition, there are a few doubtful cases.[91] A more extensive search might produce a few more

Surnames Derived from Personal Names 319

instances, but would be unlikely to change the general picture significantly. There are also in Sussex a few 13th century instances of surnames or bye-names found in Latinised forms (in Latin documents) where the surname or bye-name is in the Latin genitive where the sense requires the nominative.[92] These may be translations into a Latin form of Middle English names with a genitive 's'. Similar Latinised forms can be found in other counties at the same period.[93] Two families with names of this type, Andrewes and Rogers, both connected with Ewhurst, seem to have had hereditary surnames during the 13th century.[94]

When the 13th century examples of surnames or bye-names of the type under discussion are examined, two points are obvious. One is that the great majority of the names in question come from the easternmost part of the county, near the Kent border. There are only two examples from West Sussex, both from the immediate vicinity of Chichester, a city which, judging from the surnames present there, was attracting migrants from most other parts of Sussex and from other counties. It seems possible from this that the only part of Sussex where such surnames or bye-names originated was the district on the Kent border, and that the few cases found elsewhere in Sussex are the result of movement from that area. It has not been possible to make a thorough search of Kent sources for the period to ascertain what the position was in that county, but it appears from the Kent lay subsidy for 1334/5[95] that surnames or bye-names formed from a personal name with 's' were then rare in Kent, and were nearly always the names of women. (The circumstances in which relatively large numbers of women came to appear with such names are discussed below.)[96] It is, therefore, doubtful if the position in Sussex can be considered as due either to migration across the county boundary from Kent, or to Kentish habits of name giving having extended into the eastern fringe of Sussex. Judging by the Surrey 1332 lay subsidy, surnames or bye-names in 's' were then very rare in that county too, and they also were almost all womens' names.[97] A more extensive search through Kent and Surrey sources might reveal a rather different position, but it is unlikely that in either of those counties the proportion of surnames or bye-names formed from personal names with 's' was other than very small. It seems likely that East Sussex was an area where names of this type were rather more numerous (though still very few) than in the adjoining parts, either inside or outside Sussex.

The second point that emerges from the small number of 13th century names belonging to this type in Sussex is that none of those who appear with such surnames or bye-names were landowners of substance. So far as can be seen from what information is available about their wealth or status, they were either serfs, or small free tenants.[98] It was suggested many years ago by Professor Eilert Ekwall (not specifically in connection with Sussex) that persons with such names were often people with low status.[99] This point will have to be considered later in discussing the early history of both surnames from personal names in the genitive, and surnames from personal names with '-son'. Here it may be noted that the apparent low status of those with such surnames or bye-names may mean that they are poorly represented in the source material, so that they may have been rather more numerous than might be thought. It is also possible that such names first arose at a rather earlier period than can be seen from the evidence, and that although no examples have been found in Sussex until after 1200, the type could have existed in the county in the late 12th century. Even making full allowance for the defects of the sources, however, it seems clear that in the 13th century the type of name must have been very scarce in the county.

Surnames or bye-names formed from a personal name with 's' were so rare (if womens' names are left aside for the moment) in Sussex, Kent, and Surrey, that it is tempting to suppose that no names of such a category arose in any of the three counties, and that the presence of a very limited number of such names there during the 13th and 14th centuries was entirely due to migration into the region from other parts of England. However, there is no evidence that any of the persons found with names in this category in 13th century Sussex were migrants into the county, and it seems probable that a few such surnames or bye-names were formed within it. This was probably also true of Surrey and Kent.

After 1300 there was no very marked increase in the numbers of surnames or bye-names from a personal name with 's' in Sussex. In some South Midland counties there was a tendency for such names to become much more numerous in the early 14th century, but this was not the case in Sussex, and so far as can be seen from the limited amount of source material examined, Kent, Surrey and Essex seem in this particular to have resembled Sussex. In the Sussex lay subsidy roll for 1332 there are no clear cases of this type of name, though a few doubtful instances, such as Geneys, Pieres, and Remys can be found.[100] A scattering of examples can be found in other 14th century sources for the county, most of them in East Sussex, but it is evident that the type remained very rare.[101] At this period most of those who appeared with names of the type in question were, when their status can be ascertained, serfs or small free tenants. In the 15th century there are still only a small number of cases. They include one or two aliens, whose names may have been Anglicised.[102] By this period surnames or bye-names from a personal name with 's' were not concentrated in any one part of the county, and were those of people very varied in wealth and position.

After 1500 a considerably larger number of surnames in this category can be found in Sussex, probably because better sources are available than for the 15th century. About 3% of all those listed in the 1524–5 lay subsidy for Sussex had names of this type. A few of these were aliens, whose names had probably been Anglicised.[103] Some new surnames, not found in Sussex earlier, appear in the subsidy returns, and it is possible that some of the individuals who are found with names in this category were recent migrants into the county from other parts of England. In the 16th century the proportion of persons with surnames from a personal name with 's' was, judging by the evidence of subsidy returns, much smaller in Sussex than in the south Midlands or in the south-west of England.[104] Neither in the 1524–5 subsidy, nor in other 16th century sources, are surnames of the kind being discussed concentrated in any one part of the county. In the 1641–2 Protestation Returns, which are extant for West Sussex, but not East, some surnames of the type can be seen to have ramified considerably, almost certainly through single families having increased in numbers. There are, for instance, in the Protestation Returns 5 persons named Hoskins, all in the district around Chichester,[105] 26 named Collins, including 9 at Chichester, and several others in adjoining villages,[106] or 8 named Edmondes, mostly at or around Littlehampton.[107] It does not appear, however, that in general surnames of this type had proliferated more than those in other categories.

Three factors complicate any discussion about the origin and distribution of surnames formed from a personal name with a genitive 's'. These are (a) the position of certain womens' names (b) the possibility that some names in 's' are really topographical in origin, and (c) the tendency of surnames in many different categories to acquire an inorganic 's' or 'es', often at relatively late periods such as the 16th and 17th centuries.

Attention was drawn by Dr. P. H. Reaney to the existence in the late 13th century and the 14th of many cases of women having surnames or bye-names formed from occupational terms with a genitival 's',[108] and he suggested that in most cases these were the names of wives or widows, whose names were derived from their husbands' occupations. Examples of women with such names are rare in Sussex. The only clear case in the county is Matilda Candeles, who was very probably the widow of Ralph Candel, and who was a taxpayer at Donnington in 1327/8.[109] Juliana le Prestes, another case (a serf) is likely to have been the priest's servant.[110] In some counties there are at the same period a good many cases of women with surnames or (more probably) bye-names formed from a personal name and 's'. There are some examples in Oxfordshire.[111] In Kent, in the 1334/5 lay subsidy, there are 17 instances of women with surnames or bye-names formed from a personal name and 's'.[112] As against these, there are no certain instances in the source of men with surnames or bye-names formed from a personal name with 's'. The same Kent subsidy also contains many instances of women with surnames or bye-names formed from an occupational term with 's', but again there are no corresponding cases of men with names formed in the same way. It seems very probable that the womens' names concerned, whether formed with a personal name and 's', or an occupational term and 's', were derived from the surnames or bye-names of the husbands of the women concerned. Married women ought not to have been listed as taxpayers, and it is probable that most if not all the women involved were widows. Although the total number of women with such names in the Kent subsidy is small compared with the total number of taxpayers, womens' names tend to be badly recorded, and it is likely that in Kent widows very often had such names. It is probable, too, that such womens' names did not usually become hereditary.

In both Sussex and Surrey, such womens' names can be found much less frequently. In the Surrey 1332 subsidy, a single case has been found of a woman with a surname or bye-name formed from a personal name with 's'.[113] In the same subsidy there are two cases of men with names of the same type.[114] Unfortunately neither of these is a clear example. In the same Surrey subsidy there are a few cases of women with surnames or bye-names formed from an occupational term and 's'.[115] No cases have been found in the subsidy of men with such names. In Sussex there are a very few medieval examples of women with surnames or bye-names formed by a personal name and 's'.[116] As has been mentioned, there is only one clear instance in the county of a woman with an occupational name and 's' before 1400. It seems likely that in Kent it was quite common during the 13th and 14th centuries for wives or widows to have bye-names formed from their husbands' surnames (or bye-names) with a genitive 's' added. It is possible that this did not only occur when the husbands' surnames (or bye-names) were derived from occupational terms or from personal names, but that it also occurred when the husbands' names were in other categories. In the Kent lay subsidy already mentioned there are a number of examples of women with bye-names from topographical terms with a final 's', but it is impossible to be sure if these are derived from topographical terms in the plural, or from husbands' names with a genitive 's'.[117] In Surrey and Sussex, on the other hand, it was much less common for wives or widows to acquire bye-names formed from their husbands' surnames (or bye-names) with a genitive 's' though in both centuries the practice was followed occasionally.

It seems probable that, in England generally, womens' names formed in the way under discussion did not usually become hereditary. Consequently counties (like Kent) where such bye-names were used a good deal did not thereby come to possess a stock of surnames formed from personal names with 's'. How widespread geographically in England the habit of women using such bye-names was, it is impossible to say certainly in the present state of research. The custom certainly existed in the south Midlands, some south-western counties, and London. The position in Essex was similar to that in Kent, judging from the Essex 1327 lay subsidy; in this record there are some instances of women with surnames or bye-names formed from a personal name with 's', and some further examples of women with names formed from an occupational term with 's', while the number of men with names of either type is very small.[118] No examples are known from the north of England, and the practice may have been unknown there, probably because there were other usages in the formation of bye-names for wives and widows.[119] In the regions where the custom prevailed, it seems to have ceased by *c.* 1400, probably because more definite conventions were evolving governing the names used by married women. How far the custom spread through the different social classes is also not clear. It does not seem to have been followed by substantial landowners anywhere, and the many instances involving occupational terms show that it was frequently in use among artisans.

SURNAMES IN 'S' FROM TOPOGRAPHICAL NAMES

One difficulty in determing how common surnames formed from personal names with a genitive 's' were in Sussex (and in adjoining counties) is that some surnames which appear to be in this category are in fact topographical names. In most parts of the country it is possible to find cases of holdings, fields, or other properties which have names derived from the surnames, bye-names, or personal names of tenants. In Sussex the usage of holdings, etc., being given names from the surnames, bye-names, or personal names of tenants has been very general over a long period. Many instances can be found as far back as the 13th century, by which period the practice was well established in the county. In some cases the names of holdings, thus derived from the surnames, bye-names, or personal names of tenants, have themselves later given rise to surnames and some surnames created in this way are difficult to distinguish from surnames formed from a personal name with a genitive 's'. For example, in the late 14th century the surname atte Stevenes or atte Stephenes occurs at Wiston as the name of several persons, all of whom appear to have been related. So far as their status can be discovered, they were unfree tenants of Wiston manor. The same individuals appear in some entries in the court rolls with their names given as Stevenes, without the preposition. In the 15th century the name Stevenes existed at Wiston, and by that period there was nothing to indicate that it was not a surname formed from a personal name with 's', rather than a topographical name derived from the name of a holding.[120] There are other examples of similar names. The surnames atte herrys, at Adamys, at Robynes, and A James all occur in Sussex.[121] Once surnames or bye-names formed in this way have lost the preposition originally attached to them, they cannot be separated from names formed from a personal name with a genitive 's'. It is impossible to say how many of the quite small number of medieval examples of surnames or bye-names from a personal name with 's' arose from surnames or bye-names which were originally topographical, and which were derived from the names of holdings, etc. No doubt surnames such as atte Stevenes, atte herrys, etc., were derived from holdings once held by men either with Stephen, Harry, etc., as personal names, or with Stephen, Harry, etc., as bye-names (or possibly surnames), derived from personal names without inflection. It seems unlikely to be true, however, that all the surnames or bye-names which occur in Sussex during the Middle Ages can be accounted for as either names which were in origin topographical, like the cases just considered, or names brought into the county by migration. It seems likely that a small number of surnames or bye-names were formed in the county from personal names with a genitival 's', perhaps all in the eastern part of Sussex.

INORGANIC 'S' IN SURNAMES

One of the difficulties in deciding what proportion of surnames in any county have been formed from a personal name with a genitival 's' is that some surnames tend to acquire a final 's' or 'es', which is inorganic. This process is not confined to surnames in any one category, nor is it limited to any one part of the country. Examples can be found in surnames of any type, and in most if not all parts of England.[122] The development continues into quite late periods, even into the 17th and 18th centuries. It is in some cases possible to trace in parish registers surnames in all categories which after having existed as hereditary names for centuries without a final 's', acquire one. In 15th century Sussex, there are a fair number of examples of individuals who appear with names (almost certainly hereditary by that date) sometimes with a final 's' or 'es', sometimes without such a termination. For instance, a family called Frank or le Frank were tenants by knight service at Eastbourne in the 13th and 14th centuries; early in the 15th century one of the family occurs with his surname in the form Fraunkes.[123] Richard Repe, mayor of Rye in 1456, also appears as Richard Rypps.[124] John Combe, a Chichester draper, mentioned 1427–40, occurs with his name sometimes as Combe, sometimes as Combes.[125] Thomas Teye (or Taye), a tenant at Amberley in 1418–19, also appears as Thomas Teys.[126] Other examples could be given, from surnames in various categories, and concerning people in differing social classes. From the mid 16th century onwards, it is possible to find many instances in parish registers of individuals, or families, with surnames which are given sometimes without a final 's', sometimes with one. A few examples from Ardingly parish registers will illustrate this. Richard Gibb is listed with his surname in that form in 1656 and 1669, but as Richard Gibbs in 1648;[127] Joan Gibb, probably a member of the same family, occurs in that form in 1670 but as Joan Gibbs in 1672;[128] in the 18th century at Ardingly, one married couple occur in the registers sometimes as Sayer, sometimes as Sayers.[129] Similar cases can be found in the registers of other Sussex parishes.

The tendency for some surnames to acquire an inorganic 's' at relatively late times is no doubt one reason why the proportion of surnames formed from a personal name with 's' is greater in Sussex during the 16th and 17th centuries than might be expected from the quite small number of such surnames or bye-names found in the county before 1500. No doubt the 16th and 17th century position owes something, also, to migration into the county both from other parts of England, and by aliens. It is impossible to say with any accuracy just how much influence either factor had.

Though surnames from a personal name with 's' were much fewer, in proportion to the whole body of surnames, in Sussex than in some other counties, a few surnames in the category had by the 17th century become quite numerous in the county. Adams, for example, ramified at and around Angmering in a part of Sussex where it was already established in the 16th century;[130] Collins became numerous at Chichester,[131] and Edmondes in the Littlehampton area;[132] Roberts, already a common surname in central Sussex in the 16th century, multiplied at Cowfold, in that part of the county;[133] Sayers became common at Horsham, where it had existed in the 16th century.[134] It is probable that the presence of each of these surnames, in some numbers, within one limited area, was due to the ramification of a single family in each case. Despite the proliferation of some individual names in this way, surnames formed from a personal name with 's' were still in the 16th century relatively scarce in Sussex.[135]

SURNAMES FORMED FROM A PERSONAL NAME WITH 'SON'

Surnames formed from a personal name with the suffix 'son' were for long rare in Sussex. In the 1332 subsidy returns for the county, which list about 6,800 taxpayers, there are only 9 certain cases of persons with surnames or bye-names in this form.[136] The 1332 examples are all from the northern part of the county, and all save one are from the northern part of West Sussex. Despite the very small number of examples, a few parishes (Billingshurst, Compton, and Sutton near Petworth) each have two examples. The number of medieval instances to be found in other Sussex material is similarly scanty. In all the other sources which have been searched for this work, there are, excluding people found in the county but known to be aliens, only 28 instances of individuals with surnames or bye-names in the category, and this includes three persons who occur both in 1332, and in other sources. These figures are for examples found between 1200 and 1500. No doubt a more extensive search through manuscript sources would produce a few more cases, but it would be unlikely to alter the position very much. The examples found before 1400 are nearly all in the northern part of Sussex, though there are one or two cases in sea-ports.[137] It is also the case that the surnames or bye-names of this type found before 1400, including those in the 1332 subsidy, include a high proportion that are derived from feminine personal names. The examples which occur between 1400 and 1500 are mostly in ports, but there are some cases in north Sussex, and one or two elsewhere in the county.[138] One of those who appears away from both the ports and the north of the county was a clergyman, and the movements of clergy, mainly determined by ecclesiastical preferment, were governed by different considerations than those of laymen.[139]

One possible explanation of this distribution of surnames or bye-names formed from a personal name and 'son' is that their presence in Sussex was entirely due to migration into the county. The existence of such names in the north of the county could be due to the fact that new land was being cleared in the Wealden parts of the county, and this might have drawn in population from other areas of England. A large estate in north Sussex, centring round Petworth, was held by the Percy family, who also held large estates in the north of England, where surnames in 'son' were numerous, and since there is known to have been interchange between the Percy estates in Sussex and those in the north, this might be one factor involved.[140] There was a good deal of assarting in north Sussex in the 13th and early 14th centuries, and this would account for there being a number of names of the type in the area before 1400. The relatively high position of surnames or bye-names in the category which were from female personal names might be due to there being a larger than average proportion of illegitimate children among those who moved into north Sussex. This, however, is very conjectural, as it does not seem that metronymics were by any means always the names of bastards. As regards the ports, the presence of names in 'son' there could well be due to migration, partly from other parts of England, but mainly from the Continent. This supposition is strengthened by the existence in Sussex, particularly during the 15th century, of many aliens with names in 'son'. These were nearly all either at ports, or in villages adjoining ports. (Aliens were not included in the figures for persons with names in 'son' given above). A list of aliens from the dominions of the Duke of Burgundy (which then included most of the Low Countries), who were resident in Sussex, in 1436, includes 17 aliens with surnames or bye-names formed from a personal name with 'son'. In most cases the names concerned have been Anglicised, and are indistinguishable from ones that originated in England. The aliens involved were all resident at Rye, Winchelsea, or Lewes, except for one (at Hurstpierpoint).[141] Many other aliens occur with surnames or bye-names of the same type in the 15th century alien subsidies for Sussex,[142] and in other sources.[143] Some of the surnames or bye-names which are given as those of aliens appear later in the 15th century as those of natives, very probably the descendants of aliens. For example, Hughson was the name of an alien at Winchelsea in 1436, and Hughson appears as a surname (not apparently that of an alien) at Hastings in 1450.[144] Derykson was the name of an alien in Sussex in 1466–67, and Derykson (or Direckson, Dyrykson) was a surname at and around Rye in the late 15th century and during the 16th.[145] There were some further aliens with surnames or bye-names in 'son' in Sussex during the 16th century. Most of these were from the Low Countries, but some were Scots.[146] By that period aliens with such names were not confined to ports or the vicinity of ports, but were widely distributed through the county.

Besides surnames or bye-names formed from a personal name with 'son', there are in Sussex between *c*. 1200 and 1500 a few instances of surnames or bye-names formed with 'son' and another first element, usually an occupational term, and these ought to be considered here in order to allow all the Sussex evidence for names in 'son' to be set out. In 1200–1500, only six examples have been found in the county of persons with surnames or bye-names formed from a term for occupation or status, and 'son'. In some cases the names concerned seem to have been bye-names describing relationships, rather than stable surnames. Henry le Personesson of Iping, for example, mentioned in 1327–28, seems to have been the son of the parson of Iping,[147] and a Reginald le Smythessone (at Crawley, 1296), had a bye-name which was probably merely descriptive of his parentage.[148] The number of other names formed from an occupational term and 'son' is very small. The name Dameson occurs in the mid 13th century at Chichester, and rather later at Appledram nearby.[149] This is a name of a type which can be found in the south Midlands and south-west England, and its presence in Sussex may be due to migration.[150] The few remaining cases of surnames from an occupational term and 'son' are all ones which are found fairly widely in England, and all could have originated in Sussex, or could have migrated into the county.[151]

There are a few examples with first elements of other types. One name, which became hereditary, had as its first element, unusually, a topographical term. During the 14th century the surname Compsone or Comsone existed at and around Wiston. The surname is only found within a small area, where it persisted, so that it is likely that it was a hereditary surname belonging to a single family. A holding held by persons named Compsone in the 14th century was then described as the tenement 'atte Compe'; it had been held earlier, about 1300, by John de la Compe, who was probably the family's ancestor.[152] The name atte Compe ('at the field') does occur elsewhere in Sussex. Compson survived as a surname at West Sussex.[153]

There are in addition to the names already mentioned a few doubtful cases. The name Beleson or Belson is found at several places in Sussex during the 14th century, and it survives there in the 16th, having evidently become hereditary. This could have originated with a personal name and 'son', but the surname Belsaunt, which is derived from a French personal name, also appears in the county from the 14th century, and Belson could easily have developed from Belsaunt.[154] The name de Amiotesune occurs, as that of one individual, in 13th century Sussex. This could be formed from a personal name with 'son', but if the preposition can be relied upon, the name is a locative one.[155] Myson, found once, in 1392, might be a form of Mayson, but it might also be for the occupational name Mason. William Myson, mentioned in 1392, is probably the same as William Mason, mentioned in the same year.[156] The name Person, which occurs in Sussex from the 13th century, is probably always occupational, from the word 'parson'. Forms such as le Person appear in the county, and an unfree family at Streatham, which had a hereditary surname in the 14th century, had a surname given sometimes as Person, sometimes as Parson.[157] Forms such as Pesson or Peysson seem likely to be variants of Parson or Person. The bye-name Peysson occurs at Alciston, in the 13th century, and the name Parson occurs there at the same period.[158] Rayson, or Rison, which is found in East Sussex during the 13th and 14th centuries, is another doubtful surname. It survived for some time, and was probably hereditary. The surname Ray does occur in Sussex, and might be the first element of Rayson, but this is doubtful.[159] The name Whitsone, which occurs in Sussex but does not seem to have been hereditary there, is possibly a form of the topographical name atte Whitestone (or de la Whyteston), which was also in use in the county. Both Whitsone and de la Whyteston were present in the Arundel area in the 14th century.[160]

By the 16th century a few surnames formed from a personal name and 'son' had already become fairly numerous in the county. These, however, were surnames of which the first element was a common personal name, such as Harrison, Jackson, Johnson, Wilson, etc. In the 1524–25 lay subsidy returns for Sussex,[161] the surnames just mentioned, and a few others, appear repeatedly. So far as can be seen, however, this was not the result of individual families ramifying in Sussex over a period. The occurrences of each individual name in the subsidy are dispersed, and not concentrated within a limited area, as would be expected if a single family had proliferated to the extent that its surname had become numerous. Some of those listed in the 1524–25 subsidy with surnames of this type were certainly aliens, and it must be suspected that many others were migrants from other parts of England, especially since many of the surnames in 'son' given in the subsidy are ones which have not been found in the county before 1500. The proportion of surnames composed of a personal name and 'son' in the 1524–25 subsidy remains very low. There are 11 persons, per thousand individuals listed in the subsidy, with surnames of the type. There are very few surnames in the subsidy formed from an occupational term and 'son' (names such as Clerkson, Smithson, etc.). The ratio of names in 'son' in Sussex, judging by the surnames in the subsidy, was less than in many counties in the south Midlands or East Anglia, and much less than in the north of England generally. Apart from the subsidy returns just mentioned, other 16th century sources suggest that the number of surnames in the category remained small in Sussex.

Subsidy returns are often the best evidence that can be obtained about the general nature of surnames in a county for any one date, but they have disadvantages; in particular, they have the defect that they do not cover the poorest sections of the population, and this means that evidence from subsidies might be misleading here, for it seems possible that names in 'son' were at first in many parts of England mainly those of the poorer elements. However, another source of information suggests that it is improbable that the evidence from the 1524–25 subsidy is seriously misleading. A large number of people from a wide range of social classes were pardoned in Sussex for participation in Cade's revolt, in 1450.[162] Four hundred and twenty-five individuals who are noted as residing in Sussex were pardoned; for 77 of these no rank or occupation is given, but for the rest there is enough to show their social position. They include 22 gentlemen, 109 yeomen, 81 husbandmen, and 73 labourers. There are also 52 who from their occupations might be classed as artisans, 8 merchants or traders, and 3 clerics. Out of all these people, of very mixed position, only one has a surname in 'son'. This information is of course for an earlier date than the subsidy returns just mentioned, but it does show that it is unlikely that there was in Sussex any large body of persons with names in 'son' who fail to appear in the evidence because of their poverty and insignificance.

In the 17th century the proportion of individuals in Sussex with surnames formed from a personal name and 'son' seems to have risen somewhat. In the West Sussex Protestation Returns for 1641–42, which list a high proportion of the adult male population, 17 persons per 1,000 listed had surnames in the category.[163] Unfortunately the corresponding returns for East Sussex have not survived.

In Lancashire, where surnames in 'son' were much more numerous than in Sussex, there is evidence that such surnames were at first usually those of bondmen or small free tenants.[164] The amount of evidence on this point is much smaller in Sussex than in Lancashire, and there are instances of persons in Sussex with names in 'son' whose position and wealth cannot be ascertained. From such evidence as there is, however, it seems that in Sussex, also, such names were mostly those of serfs, or of small free tenants originally.

If surnames or bye-names found in Sussex before 1400 are considered, names in 'son' are those of serfs or of small free tenants in the great majority of cases where the status of the individuals concerned can be discovered. The Comson family, at Wiston, already mentioned, were free tenants there, apparently of no particular wealth.[165] At Amberley, in the late 13th and 14th centuries, there were several small tenants of the manor with names in 'son'.[166] One or two other cases of persons with names in 'son' who were unfree, or small free tenants, occur elsewhere in the county.[167] Out of all the individuals with surnames formed from a personal name with 'son' in the Sussex lay subsidies for 1296, 1327, and 1332, the great majority have small assessments.[168] Only one has an assessment indicating that he might be a substantial freeholder,[169] none of them can have been large landowners. There are inevitably some people with names in the category whose status remains uncertain, but in general it does appear that in Sussex such surnames or by-names were in the 13th and 14th centuries mainly those either of small free tenants, or less frequently, of bondmen.

After this survey of the evidence it is possible to consider the general significance of both surnames with a genitive 's', and surnames in 'son', in Sussex. Neither surnames (or bye-names) formed from a personal name with 's', nor those formed from a personal name with 'son', were at all common in Sussex before 1500. Even in the 16th and 17th centuries both categories remained much less common in the county than in some other parts of England, though rather more numerous, in proportion to the population, than earlier. There are a few surnames or bye-names in 'son', found in Sussex before 1500, in which the first element is an occupational term, or a term of some other nature, but even including these names, it remains that surnames or bye-names in 'son' were rare in medieval Sussex. Some names in 'son' were certainly brought into Sussex by alien immigration, and it is probable that both some names in 'son' found in the county, and some names with a genitive 's', were brought in by movement from other parts of England. It does not seem, however, that the presence of either surnames in 'son', or surnames with a genitive 's' in Sussex can be entirely due to migration. A small number of surnames in both categories do seem to have originated in the county.

So far as can be seen from examining a limited range of sources, the position in Kent and Surrey was very similar to that in Sussex. In Kent there were more cases of women, mostly wives or widows, with bye-names in 's', but this was a type of name which does not usually seem to have become hereditary. In general terms, the situation in the three south-eastern counties seems to have been very similar, both for surnames in 'son', and for surnames in 's', during the 13th and 14th centuries. It has unfortunately not been possible to arrive at any view of the position in Hampshire, because of the lack of published medieval subsidy rolls and similar material for that county.

There is a contrast between the position in Sussex about surnames or bye-names in the two categories under discussion, and some other regions. In some parts of the south Midlands and the south-west, surnames or bye-names composed of a personal name with a genitive 's', after existing as a rare type of name, start to become more numerous in the late 13th century, and during the first half of the 14th become quite common.[170] In these regions surnames or bye-names in 'son' were rare for any period before 1500 (and generally not common thereafter), but some surnames in 'son' did arise, both with personal names as a first element, and with occupational terms as a first element. In the north of England surnames or bye-names in 'son', whether with a personal name or an occupational term as a first element, begin to be common in the late 13th century, and rapidly become more common during the first half of the 14th.[171] So far as can be seen from such research as has been carried out, surnames or bye-names with a genitive 's', whether with a personal name or an occupational term as a first element, were rare in the northern counties, and it seems possible that such names never originated there, the presence of a small number in that region being due to migration. More investigation is, however, needed into the early history of names in 'son' and in 's'.

It has been seen that in Sussex both names in 'son' and names in 's' were originally mainly those of serfs or small freeholders. In Lancashire, names in 'son' were originally mostly those of people in the same social classes.[172] More research covering a large number of counties would be needed to establish that the two types of surname in question were throughout England chiefly the names of those classes in origin. It seems likely, however, that both categories of name were when first formed mainly confined to the two sections of the community just mentioned, and that the reason why each type became much more numerous in the late 13th century and the first half of the 14th is that many members in those classes were then acquiring stable hereditary surnames for the first time. The reason why neither type of surname was at all common in Sussex, Kent, and Surrey is probably that the process of acquiring hereditary surnames had by the late 13th century already proceeded further, and spread further down the social scale, than was the case in most parts of England.[173]

This analysis of the situation still leaves some points unexplained. Detailed research would be needed in more counties to establish just what social classes were adopting names in 'son' and in 's' in different regions, and to clarify in just what parts of the country surnames in a genitive 's' became common, and where surnames in 'son' became common. It is also not clear why, when surnames or bye-names formed from personal names without inflection were already a well established type in the 12th century, widespread geographically and not confined to any one social class, surnames or bye-names formed from personal names with a genitive 's' came into existence at all.

As the origins and distribution of surnames in 's' and in 'son' have been the subject of some controversy it seems worth while putting forward some evidence on the subject, to show how the position in Sussex, and some adjoining counties, differed from that in other regions. Accordingly, tables have been compiled showing the proportion of surnames or byenames in 's' and 'son' found in some medieval tax returns for a number of counties (Table II), and for the proportions in some 16th and 17th century sources (Table III). This method of comparison has some limitations. None of the sources available covers the whole population of any one county, and many of them do not cover complete counties geographically. The use of such material for comparative purposes is somewhat weakened by the fact that the sources used do not necessarily all include the same mixture of people in terms of wealth or social class, and this is a disadvantage when dealing with surnames of types which seem, at least originally, to have been especially connected with particular classes. Despite these factors, the method is the best that can be devised to show the differences between counties where certain categories of names are

Table 2. *Figures are for the numbers of individuals,* per thousand *individuals listed in each source, with surnames or bye-names formed from a personal name with a genitival 's' (column A), and with surnames or bye-names formed from a personal name with 'son' (column B).*[174] *Surnames or bye-names of which the classification is doubtful have not been counted as names in 's' or '-son'. The figures are not for numbers of surnames.*

	A Names in 's'	B Names in '-son'
Bucks. 1332	18	3
Devon 1332	less than 1	less than 1
Dorset 1327	20	less than 1
Essex 1327	2	less than 1
Kent 1334–5	3	less than 1
Lancs. 1332	less than 1	12
Leics. 1327	2	11
Norfolk 1329–30	11	2
Oxon. 1327	38	less than 1
Shropshire 1327	25	8
Staffs. 1327	18	4
Suffolk 1327	3	2
Surrey 1332	less than 1	less than 1
Suss. 1332	less than 1	1
Warws. 1332	48	4
Worcs. 1332	46	3
North Yorks. 1327	2	3

Surnames Derived from Personal Names

Table 3. *Figures are for the numbers of individuals,* per thousand *individuals listed in each source, with surnames formed from a personal name with a genitival 's' (column A), and with surnames formed from a personal name with 'son' (column B). Surnames of which the classification is doubtful have not been counted as names in 's' or '-son'. The figures are not for numbers of surnames.*

	A Names in 's'	B Names in '-son'
Bucks. 1524	77	38
Cornwall 1664	91	4
Devon 1524–25	112	12
Dorset 1662–64	79	10
Durham 1641–42	6	244
Gloucs. 1608	134	8
Hants. 1586	50	9
Herefs. 1663	140	3
Lancs., Salford Hundred, 1642	7	149
Notts. 1641–42	23	93
Oxon. 1641–42	83	3
Rutland 1522	31	43
Shropshire 1672	178	16
Staffs. 1666	58	63
Suffolk 1524	41	30
Surrey 1662–64	49	6
Suss. 1524–25	27	11
Wilts. 1576	95	9
Worcs. 1603	30	14
West Yorks. 1588	8	122

concerned, and it is unlikely that the defects of the sources seriously distort the statistics given. Because of the need to use what material is in print, it has been possible to give figures for a selection of counties only, and not for all. The sources used, however, do come from different regions of England, and should give a general view of the position.

Table II gives figures from a variety of medieval taxation returns, of a period when names in 's' and 'son' were first starting to become numerous in some counties. It can be seen that names in 's' were already more common in the south Midlands, and some southern counties, than elsewhere, while such names were comparatively rare in the south east, Devon, and the north. Names in 'son', on the other hand, were already starting to increase in Lancashire while remaining rare in the other counties listed. Table III shows the position as revealed by some 16th and 17th century sources, from a time when the evolution of hereditary surnames was complete in most parts of the country. It can be seen from this that the proportion of surnames in 's' and 'son' had increased considerably after the dates of the medieval sources used for Table II. This is probably due for the most part to the continuing formation of new surnames in both categories within the counties listed, but the great increase of names in 's' in the counties on the Welsh border probably owes something to migration from Wales. It can be seen that surnames in 's' were very common in the Welsh border, the south Midlands, and some south western counties, while surnames in 'son' were rare in the same areas. Surnames in 'son', on the other hand, were most common, proportionately, in the north, and in parts of the north Midlands. Both types were relatively rare in the south east, with Sussex as a county where both categories were very infrequent.

In many medieval sources which are in Latin, it is common to find individuals described as the son of some person, usually in the standard Latin formula, such as, e.g., *Johannes filius Wilhelmi*. This is common in Sussex during the 12th and 13th centuries, though much less so after about 1300. It is impossible to be certain if such a formula is ever used to translate surnames or bye-names in 'son'. The practices of medieval scribes in translating English names into Latin, or into Latinised forms of English names, are varied, and often do not conform to any fixed rules. No instance has been found in Sussex where it is clear that a Latin phrase, such as *Johannes filius Wilhelmi*, is translating a surname or bye-name in 'son', but it is not possible to be certain that such cases never occur.[175]

METRONYMICS

A small number of surnames and bye-names found in medieval Sussex are derived from feminine personal names. A total of about 50 such names have been noted in the county before 1500. The majority of these were rare, and many have each been discovered as the name of a single individual. It is probable that many of them, like many bye-names from male personal names, never became hereditary. It is sometimes thought that such names arose from illegitimacy, but although this is a possible origin, there is not a great deal of evidence for it. In Sussex, none of the persons who occur with metronymic surnames or bye-names is known to be illegitimate, though as information about parentage is lacking in many cases, this is not conclusive. The proportion of serfs among those people with metronymic surnames or bye-names is rather higher than among the bearers of surnames or bye-names derived from personal names generally, but metronymics were never confined to one particular social class.

Very few metronymics survived to become at all common in Sussex. One of these, Hodierne, is discussed below. Ede, or Eade, which survived for a long period during the 13th and 14th centuries at Edburton, and must have been hereditary there, and which persisted in the villages around Chichester, as the name of serfs and small free tenants, survived to become a fairly numerous name in the county during the 16th and 17th centuries, mainly in West Sussex.[176] The surname still exists in Sussex at the present day. Jenever (Geniver, Jeniver), from a Welsh personal name, appears in the 13th and 14th centuries in the Selsey area, where it seems to have been hereditary in a single family; it still survived in that part of the county in the 15th century. During the 14th century it spread further afield, probably by the dispersal of the family from Selsey and its vicinity; the surname survived into later periods, though never very common in Sussex.[177] Mabbe, from the personal name Mabel, occurs at Lindfield in the 14th century, and survived in East Sussex in the 15th and 16th centuries, probably as the surname of a single family which ramified to some extent in the county.[178] Parnell, or Pernell, was fairly widespread in Sussex from the late 13th century, and persisted in the county into the 16th, though no family with a hereditary surname can be traced. The surname Pennell, which appears in the county in the 16th and 17th centuries, may be a late form of Pernell. Alternatively, however, it may be from the surname Paynell, which was common in Sussex over a long period.[179] These surnames all survived in the county. Many of the rarer names from feminine personal names, however, have been found in Sussex only in one or two examples, and do not seem to have developed into hereditary surnames.

SURNAMES FORMED FROM A PERSONAL NAME WITH 'MAN'

A small category of English surnames is formed by compounds of a personal name with 'man'. It is generally thought that such surnames were originally those of servants, tenants, or vassals, so that, for example, Wattman meant originally 'servant of Watt'; the number of cases where it can be shown that surnames did in fact originate in this way is, however, very small, and the exact circumstances in which the majority of surnames of this type arose must remain uncertain. Such surnames were not confined to any one part of England.[180] A limited number can be found in Sussex, and of these, a few have become fairly numerous. The name Janeman first appears at the end of the 13th century. It existed over a period in East Sussex, around the present town of Newhaven, and must have been hereditary there,[181] but ceased to exist in that area about 1400. During the 14th and 15th centuries the name also occurs at several places in West Sussex.[182] The first element of Janeman is the surname Jan or Jane (from the masculine John, not the feminine Jane) which occurs as a surname in both East and West Sussex during the Middle Ages.[183] In the 16th century the surname Jenman, or Genman, appears in West Sussex. Most of those who appear with the name in Sussex seem to belong to a family who were landowners at North and East Marden, and it is possible that all the persons called Jenman, etc., who are found in Sussex during the 16th and 17th centuries belonged to one family. The surname was quite numerous in the area around Mardon in the 17th century.[184] Although no genealogical links can be established between the bearers of the name Janeman, and those later named Genman or Jenman, the later name Jenman, or Genman, is probably a form of the medieval Janeman. The surname still survives in both East and West Sussex; the forms Jenman and Jemman both exist, but the most usual form today is Janman. Another surname in the category which has become relatively common in the county is Jackman, or Jakeman. This first appears in the county at the end of the 13th century, in north west Sussex. It survived in the same area during the 14th and 15th centuries, and during the 16th and 17th was much more numerous there than in any other part of the county.[185] However, the name occurs from the 14th century both in other parts of West Sussex, and in East Sussex,[186] so that it is unlikely to have originated in the county with a single family. This surname is still at the present day found frequently in both East and West Sussex, usually in the form Jackman, though Jakeman still occurs. Hickman, still a common surname in Sussex at the present day, existed in the county from the late 13th century, but was rare during the Middle Ages, and even in the 16th and 17th centuries.[187] The name seems to have been confined in Sussex to the east before 1500, and to have been absent from West Sussex, though it occurs in other counties. The surname was common in the south Midlands, and its later frequency in Sussex may be due largely to movement into the county. Neither Hick nor Jake has been found as a personal name in Sussex. However, both are hypochoristic forms of common personal names, and such forms do not very often appear in medieval records. Jake does appear as a surname in East Sussex, not far from where some examples of Jakeman are found, but it has not been discovered in the north-east of the county, where Jakeman was most common.[188] Hikke, or Hykke, again, occurs as a surname in East Sussex, near to the area where Hickman also occurs.[189]

No other surnames in this category which can be found in Sussex before 1500 have become common in the county. A few others survived and became hereditary. Chrisman survived over a period in West Sussex, so that it was probably hereditary there. The first element of the name may be from one of several personal names, such as Christopher or Christian.[190] Rickman, or Rykeman, occurs in West Sussex over a long period from the 14th century, and so is likely to have been hereditary there, but seems to have remained rare, though it survives to the present.[191] Walterman existed in one area in the east of the county in the 13th century, all the references being probably to members of a single family.[192] The name Waterman (which is sometimes an occupational, or topographical, surname) is found in the same area later, and there is probably a development of Walterman.[193]

A few surnames which might seem to fall into this category do not in fact belong there. The surnames Bateman (or Batman), Brounman (or Brunman), and Whatman (or Wattman), are all derived from personal names which included the element 'man' as part of the personal name. All three surnames were present in medieval Sussex, though rare in the county.

The Sussex evidence throws little light on how surnames of this type arise. In no case is there proof that people with surnames or bye-names such as Hickman, Janeman, Jakeman, etc., were originally persons who were the servants, tenants, etc., of individuals named Hick, Jane, Jake, etc., though as Hick, Jane, Jake, etc., existed as surnames, that would be quite feasible. The wealth and status of many people who had names of the type are unknown, but from such evidence on the point as is available it does not appear that even where relatively early instances were concerned (that is, occurrences before 1400) those with such surnames or bye-names were always from the poorest part of the community. Judging by the assessments of such people in lay subsidies, that was not always the case. Some individuals with such names were serfs, but others were free tenants. Further, where serfs had such names, it was not certainly the case, in any instance which has been found in Sussex, that the first element of the name was derived from the surname, or the personal name, of the lords of the manors on which the serfs in question resided.

A little light may be thrown on the question by examining some surnames of a similar type, formed from a surname in use, with 'man'. The surname Cadman, or Cademan, is found in connection with land at Slinfold, in north Sussex, in 1285. The name existed at Horsham, which adjoins Slinfold, in the 16th and 17th centuries, and it seems probable that it had survived as a hereditary surname in that area from the 13th century. There are other instances of the surname elsewhere in West Sussex, but it is likely that all the persons named Cadman who occur in medieval Sussex belonged to one family. The first element of the surname Cadman is probably the surname le Cade, which existed in Sussex from the late 13th century onwards. This is a nickname type surname, of uncertain meaning.[194] Cobhamsman occurs, as the name of one person, in East Sussex in 1443, and the surname or bye-name Cobham was present earlier in much the same part of the county.[195] Similarly, the name Kenesman appears at Laughton in 1292 (one example only), and the surname or bye-name Kenne appears in the same part of the county at the same period, and earlier.[196] In each of these cases, it seems that a surname or bye-name in 'man' has been formed with, as the first element, a surname or bye-name in use locally, and surnames or bye-names so formed must be regarded as a type parallel to those formed from a personal name and 'man'. The personal names which are the first elements of names in 'man' were all popular personal names (or hypochoristic forms of such names), and it is not possible to connect the names from a personal name and 'man' with the personal names of particular individuals in any one case. It must, however, be supposed, despite that lack of specific evidence, that the surnames or bye-names in 'man' which occur in Sussex were originally the surnames or bye-names of dependents of the people whose personal names form the first elements of the names in 'man'.

The great majority of surnames derived from personal names do not present any difficulty in determining origins. A small number, however, require explanation.

Judin and Judwin

The surnames which appear in the 16th and 17th centuries as Judwin, Judwin, Judyne, etc., all appear to be derived from forms of the surname Goldwin, which is from an Old English personal name. In the 13th century the surname appears in a variety of forms, Jeldewine, Judewyne, Jeudewyne, Joudewyn, etc. The great majority of examples come from the coastal portion of West Sussex, but there are a few instances from East Sussex.[197] It is evident that these are variants of Goldwine. William Goldewyne, a 13th century tenant of Pagham manor, is also mentioned as William Joldewyne.[198] John Jeldewyne, listed as a taxpayer at Chyngton in 1327/8, is the same as John Geldewyne, listed there in 1332.[199] Richard Goldwyne, mentioned at Poling in the late 13th century, is the same person as Richard Jeudewyn, mentioned there early in the 14th.[200] There is a great variation in the forms encountered, but it seems clear that only one surname is involved. The surname survived in the south of West Sussex from the late 13th century, and was probably hereditary there. By the early 16th century there seems to have been a single family of the name, at Washington. The usual form of the surname at that time was Judwyn. By the 17th century this had become Judin or Judyne.[201] The form Goldwin survived in Sussex into the 16th and 17th centuries, though rare.[202] Both Juden and Goldwin still exist in Sussex at the present day, though both are uncommon.

Goldock

In the 14th century Goldhawk (Goldhauek) was a surname or bye-name in use in north-west Sussex. The name has not been found elsewhere in the county, and was evidently rare.[203] Goldhawk is derived from an Old English personal name, which has not been found in Sussex, though it occurs in Surrey during the 13th century.[204] In the 16th century the surname Goldock (or Goldok), existed in north-west Sussex, in the same area where Goldhawk appears then and earlier.[205] Although no continous pedigree can be traced, there seems little doubt that Goldock is a later form of Goldhawk. Goldock survived in the same part of the county in the 17th century, though by that period it was becoming rather more dispersed.[206] It seems likely that this surname originated with one family.

Hodiern and Odiern

The surname or bye-name Hodierne appears in both East and West Sussex in the 13th century. The surname was scarce, but it survived, and still existed in the county in the 15th century.[207] It was rare in England, but occurs during the 12th century in Norfolk, and during the 14th in Kent and Suffolk.[208] It is derived from a feminine personal name, which usually appears, in a Latinised form, as Hodierna. The personal name has been found in Sussex in the 12th, 13th and 15th centuries.[209] The personal name was in use in Kent in the 14th century.[210] It also occurs in Norfolk in the 12th century, as the name of the wife of a member of a family which held land in both Sussex and Norfolk; this perhaps explains the surname's later appearance in Suffolk.[211]

Ivor and Ivory

The surname Ivory has two distinct origins, and when the surname is found at relatively late periods it is usually impossible to be clear how it originated. In some instances Ivory appears to be from the French place-name Ivry. A Thomas de Ivery was holding land at Southwick in about 1240, and if the preposition in this case can be relied on, this was a locative name.[212] Several people who occur with the surname Ivory or Yvory (without a preposition) in the Southwick area later in the 13th century are likely to have belonged to the same family as Thomas, and so to have had locative names. Judging from the persistence of the name in one area, it was already hereditary around Southwick in the 13th century.[213] It is, however, clear that in Sussex the surname Ivory is sometimes from the personal name Ivor. William Ivory, the Earl of Surrey's bailiff for Lewes Honour in the mid 13th century, was also known as William Ivor.[214] William seems to have been a connection, possibly a brother, of Reginald Ivor, who was the son of a man named Ivor, and who was living in the mid 13th century. Reginald had a son, Robert Ivor, who inherited his father's surname.[215] How confusing the origin of the names Ivor and Ivory is, however, is shown by the fact that Robert is mentioned in one instance as Robert de Ivor, the preposition in this case being evidently added in error (a type of mistake for which there are very many medieval instances, both in Sussex and elsewhere).[216] The possibility of such errors must make it doubtful if the presence of 'de' in the case of Thomas de Ivery can be relied on as a certain indication that his name was locative.

The surname Ivory existed at Rogate in the 14th century; it persisted

Ledgard and Legatt

It is generally held that the surname Legatt (Leggett, Legate, etc.) is derived from the word 'legate', and it has been suggested that the surname was originally given to someone who played the part of a papal legate in a pageant.[218] This may, in fact be the origin of the name in some areas, but in Sussex Legatt seems clearly to have been a variant form of the surname Legard. Legard is from a personal name, which was in use in Sussex during the 13th century.[219] Legard appears as a surname early in the 13th century in and around Boxgrove, east of Chichester. The name survived in that area all through the 13th and 14th centuries, and must have become hereditary there.[220] It also occurs nearby at Chichester.[221] This is probably a case in which a surname originated with a single family in the county. The surname still survived around Chichester and Boxgrove in the 16th century.[222] The surname Legatt or Legate existed from the late 12th century in the Boxgrove area. Two of the earliest bearers of the name, the bothers William and Richard Legatt, are also referred to as William and Richard Legard.[223] They were the sons of Robert Legate, who was living in the late 12th century.[224] It seems clear from this that Legatt and Legard were two variants of a single surname, used by one family, with a hereditary surname from the late 12th century. The surname Legatt has been found at Chichester, in 1296, and in one example at Winchelsea, in 1279, but apart from this it has not been found anywhere in Sussex outside the Boxgrove area before 1500.[225] Legatt still existed around Boxgrove in the 17th century. By that period the surname had dispersed, and was quite widespread in West Sussex.[226] The surname appears in East Sussex in the 16th century, but was rare in that part of the county.[227] At the present day the surname in various forms, Legate, Legat, Leggett, Leggott, etc., is quite numerous in Sussex. The surname Ledger, which is found at Chichester in the 16th century,[228] and which still survives in the county, is another variant of Legard.

A family named De Saint Leger were landowners in Sussex, and in several other counties, from the 12th century. The surnames Ledgard and Legatt, etc., are, however, not connected with the surname of this family.

Salerne

The surname Salerne has been said to be derived from a French place-name,[229] but in fact it is from a personal name. Salernus was the personal name of two persons listed as taxpayers at Knelle, near Beckley in East

Sussex, in 1332.[230] A feminine form of the same personal name, Salerna, is mentioned in the Kent subsidy of 1334/5.[231] By the 14th century the personal name may have been in use over a limited area in East Sussex and West Kent, for no instances of it are known from elsewhere. The first example of Salerne as a surname which has been noted is at Winchelsea, in 1292, when Salerne is given as the name of three persons. In all probability it was by then the hereditary surname of a family in the port.[232] Winchelsea is near to Beckley, where the personal name occurs rather later. During the 14th century Salerne continues as a surname or bye-name in the area around Winchelsea and Beckley.[233] Outside this area a Roger Scalerne or Schalerne is mentioned at Chichester, about 1340–1350,[234] and his name is probably a variant of Salerne, but the surname has not been found anywhere else in Sussex before 1400. The name survived in the area around Beckley in the 15th century.[235] Though it was rare, it was not confined to Sussex, and examples occur in the 14th century in Suffolk.[236]

Till, Tilly, and Tulley

The origin of Till, and of related surnames such as Tilly and Tulley, is complex. Three topographical surnames may have contributed to the modern surname Till. The surname atte Tilthe or atte Tylthe ('at the tilled ground') existed in East Sussex from the 13th century. All the references come from one part of the county, and probably concern one family.[237] A second topographical surname, atte Thele, existed in the north of West Sussex from the late 13th century. All the medieval references to this surname (probably meaning 'at the plank bridge') are from the area around Slinfold, and probably also concern a single family, with a surname hereditary from the late 13th century.[238] The surname is probably from Theale Farm in Slinfold.[239] The surnames Tele and Thiell, which are found in Sussex in the 16th century are probably later forms of atte Thele.[240] A third bye-name, atte Thylle (probably 'at the plank, or platform'), has been found in two isolated cases in Sussex. It is not clear that it was ever hereditary in the county.[241] This name occurs at Wartling in the 15th century, and may be from a locality called Thylle mentioned in 1307 in Warbleton, which is not far from Wartling.[242] Whether any of these topographical names have become Till or Tilly it is not possible to say.

The surname Tille, Tyl, or Tylle has also first been found in Sussex in the late 13th century. Most of the references before 1400 come from Up Marden, West Marden, and Compton, three adjoining townships on the western edge of the county. The surname continued to exist in the same part of the county during the 15th century, and it is evident that there was a family with a hereditary surname in that part from the 13th century.[243]

Isolated examples of Tyl occur elsewhere in West Sussex, but these might concern members of the same family.[244] The name Tylye appears at Compton about 1405, and in this case at least, it is a variant of Tylle, etc.[245]

In addition, however, Tillie, Tyllie, etc. can be found at several other places in both East and West Sussex before 1500. There seem to have been families with Tillie, etc., as a hereditary surname at Wiston and Steyning, at Bersted and Aldingbourne, and around Eastbourne, and there are examples elsewhere. The name was widespread in the county from about 1300.[246] It seems likely that Tillie, Tyly, etc., are variants of the surname which appears as Tille, etc.

It is not easy to be sure how these surnames originate. In Surrey several examples of the surname or bye-name le Tylie (or in one instance of the woman's name la Tilie) have been found during the 14th century.[247] No forms with the article have been discovered in Sussex. The form atte Thylye, found in West Sussex in 1296, appears to be a variant of the topographical name atte Thylle, already mentioned.[248] The surnames Tille, Tillie, and so forth are sufficiently numerous and widespread in Sussex during the 13th and 14th centuries to make it unlikely that they can have been derived from some rare occupation, or from some topographical term which was used for a feature which did not occur frequently. The probability is that Tille, Tillie, etc. are derived from hypochoristic forms of the personal name Matilda, which was one of the more common female personal names at the period when hereditary surnames were evolving in Sussex. It is, however, not possible to be sure that this was the origin of the surnames concerned in all cases. The probability that the surnames under discussion are from Matilda is reinforced by the existence of the surname Tilcock, which is from a diminutive of Matilda,[249] and of the surname Tillet, another diminutive.[250]

During the 16th and 17th centuries the surname Till (or Tyll) survived in the southern part of West Sussex. Nearly all the examples come from the area west and south of Chichester, and it is likely that one family with the name persisted in this district, and that it proliferated to a moderate extent.[251] It has not been found at this period in other parts of the county, outside the south of West Sussex. The surname Tillie (or Tilly, Tylly, etc.) occurs during the 16th century in the same area, to the south and west of Chichester, where Till is also found. Tillie has not been found elsewhere in the county during the 16th century, except for an isolated instance in East Sussex,[252] and it is obviously probable that Till and Tillie in this area share a common origin. In the 17th century Tillie became much more widely distributed over West Sussex.[253] Till, Tilly, and Tillot all survive in Sussex at the present day.

During the 16th and 17th centuries the surname Tully appears in Sussex, where it has not been found before 1500. Most of the examples come from one area, near the boundary between East and West Sussex,

Surnames Derived from Personal Names 343

around Horsham, West Grinstead, and Steyning.[254] In this area the name is a late variant of Tilly, which also existed at the same time in the same part of the county. The surname Tullett, found in a few examples in Sussex during the 17th century, is a variant of Tillet.[255] However, the name Tully has at times other origins, for in East Sussex Tully appears as the name of an alien in 1550, at Ardingly. The surname persisted at Ardingly, and became quite numerous there.[256]

In the 16th century some new surnames derived from personal names appear in Sussex. A few of these may be names which had existed earlier in the county, but had not been recorded in medieval sources, though the presence of most must be due to movement into Sussex from outside. A small number of Welsh surnames first appear in Sussex after 1500, such as Aprece, Apwyliam, Gwynne, Lloyd, Pomphrey, and Price, for example.[257] A few other surnames which first appear in the county during the 16th century are likely to have been brought in by emigration from outside Britain, such as, for instance, Dannet, probably from France,[258] or Derrick, probably from the Low Countries.[259] When, however, the surnames derived from personal names present in Sussex during the 16th and 17th centuries are considered, the small number of new surnames to be found is notable. The great majority of surnames in the category to be found in the county during those two centuries are ones which had already existed there before 1500. In particular, surnames (from personal names) which are at all numerous in the county are usually ones which were already established there before 1500. In the 1524–25 lay subsidy for Sussex very few of the surnames which are recorded as the names of more than a few individuals are ones which cannot be found in the county before 1500. Of the surnames which are given in the subsidy as the names of more than five persons, the only ones which have not been discovered in the county before 1500 are Hosemer, or Osmer, which occurs in East Sussex (probably as the surname of one family), in an area where the personal name from which the surname is derived occurs in the 13th century, so that the surname is probably one which had existed unrecorded before 1500;[260] Hogekyn, which is recorded in 1524 as the surname of six people, all in the Selsey area, and probably all of one family, but which has not been found in the county before 1500, though it is derived from a diminutive of a common personal name;[261] and Liliot (probably from a diminutive of Elisabeth) which was present in the southern part of West Sussex, again probably as the surname of one family.[262] All of these surnames may have been in Sussex for a long period before the 16th century, for medieval sources provide an incomplete record of English surnames, but it is also possible that their presence in the county is due, in each case, to the migration into the county of a single family, which ramified to some extent over a generation or two, without dispersing very much.

In general, the impression made by the surnames derived from personal names present in Sussex during the 16th and 17th centuries is one of continuity with earlier periods. Many surnames of the type surviving in the 16th and 17th centuries, first appear in the county in the 13th or 14th centuries, and in many cases surnames persisted in one area over several centuries. Some examples have aready been mentioned in the course of this chapter. The persistence of common surnames which are found very widely in England generally is not of great significance, for such names must be expected to be present in most parts of the country at any period from the time when hereditary surnames began to evolve, but the survival of rare surnames for several centuries is more noteworthy. It is obviously not possible to consider separately that history of each of the names in the category under discussion, and show how far surnames survived from the Middle Ages into later periods. The history of some surnames already discussed will illustrate the point, and there are many others which could be instanced. The rare surname Luttard (Luthard, Lotterd, etc.) for example, existed in the district around Petworth from the early 14th century, and was still there in the 16th and 17th.[263] The name Walcock existed in Willingdon Hundred in the 14th century, and was still there in the 16th.[264] The rather more common name Whiting survived, over the same period, at and around Poynings.[265] The surname Wolgar (or Woolgar) survived at and near Steyning and Henfield from the late 13th century to the 19th.[266] Similarly, the name Woolvin (Wolvin, Woolfen, Ulvin, etc.), existed at Goring, Ferring, and the surrounding townships from the 13th century to the 17th. Even in the 18th century the surname was still to be found in places only a short distance inland from Goring.[267] Other examples of such continuity could be given.

The continuity in surnames derived from personal names from the Middle Ages into the 16th and 17th centuries, and later, in Sussex is very marked. More recently population movements have brought about changes. Many surnames compounded from a personal name and 'son', for example, are now among the more numerous Sussex surnames. Despite the changes in the county since 1800, however, and the great increase in population, many of the surnames in the category under discussion which were already well established in the county by 1500 are still there today, in many cases in considerable numbers.

There are many further surnames derived from personal names, found in Sussex, including some which have persisted in the county for centuries. Alard, for example, derived from a personal name frequently found in 12th century Sussex, appears during the 13th century as a surname at Winchelsea (where it was already numerous in 1292), Rye, and Pevensey, spread into the adjoining parts of Sussex, and later into Kent, and still remains an established surname in East Sussex.[268] Alfrey, possibly from the personal name Alfred, was the surname of a family at East Grinstead from the 14th century, but it also occurs independently elsewhere in

Sussex. It, too, survives in the county at the present day. Aldrich, or Aldridge, is now a numerous surname in Sussex; it seems to have been rare in the county during the Middle Ages, and even in the 16th century, though it persisted for centuries at West Grinstead. The surname Algar, on the other hand, was already in the 13th century present in both East and West Sussex, with a scattered distribution with suggests that it originated with several distinct families; it survives as a common surname in Sussex to the present. Avery (from a French pronunciation of Alfred) occurs frequently in Hastings Rape during the 14th and 15th centuries, and occasionally in other parts of the county at the same period; the surname was already widespread in the county during the 16th and 17th centuries, and remains common there today. Bartlett (from a diminutive of Batholomew), was in the Middle Ages a surname more common in West than in East Sussex; in the west of the county it was a name borne by both landed families, and serfs; it has survived as a common Sussex surname to the present. It has been suggested that Coleman, or Colman, is an occupational name in Sussex, but no forms have been found which would support that view (such as le Coleman, etc.), and the personal name Coleman can be found in Sussex in the 12th and 13th centuries; it seems more probable, therefore, that the surname Coleman or Colman is from the personal name; the surname was hereditary as that of several different families in Sussex during the Middle Ages, and subsequently was much dispersed in the county.[269] Another surname which has survived as a fairly numerous one in Sussex to the present is Colbran, derived from a personal name which, surprisingly for Sussex, is Scandinavian in origin; the personal name has not been found in use in the county, and the surname may have been brought into the county by migration at some early period, perhaps the 12th or 13th century; the surname was for long mainly in the east of the county, though it existed in the 13th century at Horsham, and survived there for several centuries; it was the name of a landed family at Wartling in the 15th and 16th centuries, and the family name proliferated in that area. The surname Daniel (from the Old Testament personal name which was frequently used in the county during the 12th, 13th, and 14th centuries) was the surname or by-name of a Domesday landholder in Sussex; from the 13th century onwards Daniel appears in several different parts of the county, and it was evidently the hereditary surname of more than one family in Sussex; it survived in the county, and was a fairly common surname there during the 16th and 17th centuries; Daniel as a surname was more common in the south east of England than in other regions. In a similar way the surname Ede, from a hypochoristic form of Edith, occurs in the 13th and 14th centuries as a persistent name at several places in the county, Prinstead, Warnham, and Edburton, for instance, in a way which leaves little doubt that it was the hereditary surname of several families; it survived to become a widely dispersed surname in the county during the 16th and 17th centuries, particularly numerous in the northern part of West Sussex, and it still persists as a surname in Sussex to the present. Ingram, again, is another surname which appears from the 13th century as a name which persists at several places in the county (at Angmering, for example, and around Ninfield), and was clearly the surname of more than one family; it too was a well established surname in Sussex during the 16th and 17th centuries, and survives there now. The personal name from which the surname is derived was much used in Sussex during the 12th and 13th centuries, and was still in use there in the 16th. By the 13th century Osborn (or Osbern) was already a very widespread surname or bye-name in Sussex, and one borne by people of very varying status; by the 16th century it had become one of the more numerous Sussex surnames derived from personal names. The personal name from which the surname comes occurs in the Sussex part of Domesday, but was rare in the county during the 12th and 13th centuries. In this it contrasts with the personal name Osbert, which was used very frequently in the county during the 12th, 13th, and 14th centuries, but which gave rise to a surname which was always rare in Sussex. Paynot (later Pannatt, or Pannett), a surname from a diminutive of an Old French personal name much used in Sussex, and in England generally, during the 12th and 13th centuries, survived in West Sussex from the 13th century; though not especially numerous before 1500, the name proliferated considerably in the 16th and 17th centuries, and in the 1641-42 Protestation Returns for West Sussex there were 24 persons so named; the surname persisted for centuries at and near Angmering. It still survives in Sussex. All these surnames have existed in Sussex over long periods, many of them first appearing in the county in the 13th or early 14th centuries, surviving in much the same areas into the 16th and 17th centuries, and still continuing in Sussex to the present day, often with considerable increases in numbers.

References

[1] J. Morris, *Domesday Book, Suss.* (1976), ff. 18c, 19a, 19b, 20a, 21a, 22c, 24a, 24b, 24d, 26b, 27b, 28d.

[2] See p. 334

[3] H. Hall, *Red Book of the Exchequer* (Rolls Ser., 1896), vol. i, pp. 198-204.

[4] *Book of Fees*, vol. i, pp. 70-73; *Feudal Aids*, vol. v, pp. 128-30.

[5] H. Hall, *op. cit.*, pp. 198-204; *Lewes Chartulary*, vol. i, p. 147; *Great Roll of the Pipe for the 16th Year of Henry II* (Pipe Roll Soc., vol. xv) (1892), pp. 137, 139; D. M. Stenton, *Great Roll of the Pipe for the 2nd Year of King John* (Pipe Roll Soc., vol. l) (1934), p. 247; *Chichester Bishop's Acta*, p. 73.

[6] C. Clark, "Battle c. 1110: An Anthroponymist Looks at an Anglo-Norman New Town", in R. A. Brown, *Proceedings of the Battle Abbey Conference* (1979), vol. ii, p. 28.

[7] *Lewes Chartulary*, vol. ii, p. 46; *Chichester Chart.*, p. 351.

[8] *Suss. Fines*, vol. i, pp. 34–5, 45, 47.

[9] *Suss. Fines*, vol. i, pp. 35, 47, 55. See also *Curia Regis Rolls, 7–8 John*, p. 234.

[10] *Suss. Custumals*, vol. i, pp. 4–11, 13–21, 22–31, 33–9, 42–52, 54–6, 57–61, 71–8, 79–86, 88–9, 90–95, 106–122; vol. ii, 13, 18–21, 23–5, 27–8, 37–9, 40–46, 51–2, 64–66, 67–9, 73–4, 79–83, 88, 91–4, 107, 111–13; *Lewes Barony Recs.*, p. 72; *Chichester Chart.*, pp. 98, 107, 120, 123; *S.A.C.*, vol. liii, pp. 150–55; *3 Suss. Subsidies*, pp. 43, 92, 102–105.

[11] *3 Suss. Subsidies*, pp. 3–105.

[12] *Ibid.*, pp. 109–222, 225–333; *Non. Inquis.*, p. 384; *Feudal Aids*, vol. v, p. 130; *S.A.C.*, vol. liii, p. 153; East Suss. Record Office, Dunn MSS., 5/2; West Suss. Record Office, E.P. VI/194/1: m. 4.

[13] *Hastings Lathe C. R.*, p. 117; *Lewes Barony Recs.*, p. 53; *S.A.C.*, vol. xxiv, p. 67; P.R.O. E 179/225/12. Compare the figures for East Anglia in B. Selten, *The Anglo-Saxon Heritage in Middle English Personal Names*, vol. i, pp. 38–40, and see *Surnames of Oxon.*, pp. 212–15.

[14] *Lewes Barony Recs.*, pp. 15, 27; *3 Suss. Subsidies*, pp. 49, 62, 65, 93; Inderwick, *Winchelsea*, p. 179; *Suss. Fines*, vol. ii, p. 119; *Suss. Custumals*, vol. i, p. 51; vol. ii, pp. 48, 51, 54; *S.A.C.*, vol. lxxxiv, p. 62; L. Fleming, *History of Pagham*, vol. i, p. xxxviii.

[15] Reaney, *Dict.*, pp. 8, 18.

[16] *Boxgrove Chart.*, p. 166; *2 Suss. Subsidies*, pp. 25, 43, 45, 84, 90; *Lewes Barony Recs.*, p. 11; *Suss. Custumals*, vol. i, p. 44; vol. ii, p. 55; L. Fleming, *op. cit.*, vol. i, p. xxxvi.

[17] *Suss. Custumals*, vol. i, pp. 38, 55; *Boxgrove Chart.*, p. 194; *3 Suss. Subsidies*, pp. 30, 32; *Suss. Fines*, vol. i, p. 16.

[18] *Chichester Chart.*, pp. 69, 88, 352, 364; *3 Suss. Subsidies*, pp. 5, 34, 44, 81, 109; *Suss. Fines*, vol. i, pp. 6, 16, 73, 85; *Lewes Barony Recs.*, p. 71; *Lewes Chartulary*, vol. i, pp. 123, 161, 170, 175; *Catalogue of Ancient Deeds*, vol. iv, p. 120; *Book of Fees*, vol. i, p. 72; *Suss. Custumals*, vol. ii, pp. 15, 68, 73; *Great Roll of the Pipe for the 16th Year of Henry II* (Pipe Roll Soc., vol. xv) (1982), p. 139.

[19] Selten, *op. cit.*, pp. 57–62. R. A. McKinley, *Norf. and Suff. Surnames in the Middle Ages* (1975), pp. 127–29.

[20] *Ibid.*; *Surnames of Oxon.* pp. 237–46; *Surnames of Lancs.* pp. 334–337. See also Selten, *op. cit.*, pp. 56–66.

[21] *Surnames of Oxon.* (1977), pp. 240–41; *Surnames of Lancs.* (1981), p. 337.

[22] The following sources have been used: *3 Suss. Subsidies*, pp. 109–222;

A. C. Chibnall, *Early Taxation Returns* (Bucks. Record Soc.) (1966), pp. 2–97; A. Rumble, *Dorset Lay Subsidy Roll of 1327* (Dorset Record Soc., no. vi) (1980); J. P. Rylands, "Exchequer Lay Subsidy Roll", *Miscellanies Relating to Lancs. and Chesh.* (Lancs. and Chesh. Record Soc., vol. xxxi) (1986); W. D. H. Fletcher, "Leics. Lay Subsidy, 1327", *Associated Archaeological Societies Reports and Papers*, vol. xix, pp. 209–312, 447–8, vol. xx, pp. 130–178; *Surr. Taxation Returns* (Surr. Record Soc., vol. xi) (1922, 1932); Anon., *Suff. in 1327* (Suff. Green Books, no. ix) (1906); W. F. Carter, *Lay Subsidy Roll for Warws., for 6 Edward III* (Dugdale Soc., vol. vi) (1926).

[23] *Calendar of Charter Rolls*, vol. ii, p. 169; *Suss. Custumals*, vol. i, pp. 5, 29; L. Fleming, *History of Pagham*, vol. i, p. 41; *3 Suss. Subsidies*, pp. 92, 101, 115; *Boxgrove Chart.*, pp. 171, 172; *Chichester Chartulary*, p. 43; *Chichester Bishop's Acta*, pp. 149, 167; *Great Roll of the Pipe for the 32nd year of Hen. II* (Pipe Roll Soc., vol. xxxvi) (1914), p. 182; *Great Roll of the Pipe for 3rd Year of Henry III* (Pipe Roll Soc., vol. lxxx) (1976), p. 143.

[24] *Ibid.*, p. 137; *3 Suss. Subsidies*, pp. 35, 65, 87, 98, 114, 162, 170, 191, 214, 227, 238, 274, 276, 284; Inderwick, *Winchelsea*, pp. 166, 181, 212, 214; *S.A.C.*, vol. xii, pp. 28, 43; vol. lxxxii, p. 127; vol. lxxxix, pp. 131, 134; *Feudal Aids*, vol. v, p. 164.

[25] Cases are very numerous: see, e.g., *3 Suss. Subsidies*, pp. 13, 46, 52, 180, 181, 185, 217, 287, 294, 298, 314, 330; *Suss. Fines*, vol. i, pp. 21, 35, 42; vol. ii, pp. 12, 29; *Lewes Chartulary*, vol. i, pp. 61, 146–7; vol. ii, p. 40; *Lewes Barony Recs.*, p. 13; *De Lisle and Dudley MSS.*, vol. i, pp. 41, 80; *Chichester Chart.*, pp. 133, 301, 337, 376.

[26] *Suss. Custumals*, vol. i, p. 120.

[27] J. Morris, *op. cit.*, ff. 24d, 27d, 29b.

[28] *Lewes Chartulary*, vol. ii, p. 114.

[29] *3 Suss. Subsidies*, p. 219; *Suss. Custumals*, vol. ii, pp. 99, 100, 127, 128.

[30] *Ibid.*, vol. ii, pp. 98–100, 126.

[31] *3 Suss. Subsidies*, pp. 201, 311.

[32] *Chichester Chart.*, p. 242.

[33] Reaney, *Dict.*, p. 151; *Suss. Subsidy, 1524–5*, p. 146.

[34] *De Lisle and Dudley MSS.*, vol. i, p. 79; *P. N. Suss.*, vol. i, p. 203; a third occurrence, at a place called La Hegeland, may concern Highland Farm, in Horsham: *Suss. Fines*, vol. i, p. 20.

[35] *3 Suss. Subsidies*, pp. 4, 14, 153, 213; *Suss. Fines*, vol. ii, p. 183.

[36] Lane, *Suss. Deeds*, p. 115; *Suss. Subsidy, 1524–5*, pp. 95, 101, 102, 103, 105; *Robertsbridge Surveys*, p. 99.

[37] *Lewes Chartulary*, vol. i, p. 36; vol. ii, p. 50.

[38] *Suss. Fines*, vol. i, p. 26; *Suss. Custumals*, vol. ii, p. 107.

[39] *Ibid.*, vol. ii, pp. 107, 131, 133; *3 Suss. Subsidies*, p. 33.
[40] *Ibid.*, p. 307.
[41] *Boxgrove Chart.*, p. 71.
[42] *Suss. Fines*, vol. ii, p. 112.
[43] Inderwick, *Winchelsea*, p. 177.
[44] J. E. Ray, *Suss. Chantry Records* (Suss. Record Soc., vol. xxxvi) (1931), p. 143.
[45] *Chichester Chart.*, p. 288; *Chichester Bishops' Acta*, pp. 132, 162.
[46] Reaney, *Dict.*, p. 121.
[47] *3 Suss. Subsidies*, p. 31; *S.A.C.*, vol. xii, p. 26; *Fitzalan Surveys*, p. 117.
[48] *W. Suss. 1641–2*, pp. 40, 79, 187.
[49] *Chichester Chart.*, pp. 236, 238; *3 Suss. Subsidies*, pp. 98, 254; *Robertsbridge Charters*, p. 58; *S.A.C.*, vol. li, p. 55; vol. liii, p. 161; *Suss. Custumals*, vol. i, pp. 102–3.
[50] *Ibid.*, vol. i, p. 12; *Fitzalan Surveys*, pp. 169, 170; *3 Suss. Subsidies*, pp. 130, 132, 248; *Chichester Chart.*, p. 294.
[51] *Chichester Bishops' Acta*, p. 95; Reaney, *Dict.*, p. 261; *Lewes Chartulary*, vol. i, pp. 3, 7, 10; *Chichester Chart.*, pp. 94, 126, 129, 130.
[52] *3 Suss. Subsidies*, p. 100.
[53] *Suss. Subsidy, 1524–5*, pp. 25, 81; *Suss. Wills*, vol. ii, p. 341; *Suss. Indictments*, vol. i, p. 4; R. Garraway Rice, *Parish Register of Horsham* (Suss. Record Soc., vol. xxi) (1915), *Per indice*.
[54] E. Searle, *Lordship and Community* (1974), p. 466; C. Clerk, "Battle c. 1100: an anthroponymist looks at an Anglo-Norman New Town", in R. A. Brown, *Proceedings of the Battle Abbey Conference* (1979), vol. ii, pp. 37, 40; *3 Suss. Subsidies*, p. 307; *De Lisle and Dudley MSS.*, vol. i, p. 63; *Chichester Chart.*, p. 40; Reaney, *Dict.*, p. 7.
[55] *3 Suss. Subsidies*, pp. 24, 99, 193, 304.
[56] *Ibid.*, p. 62; Salzman, *Cartulary of Sele*, p. 9.
[57] *Hastings Lathe C.R.*, p. 69; *Suss. Subsidy, 1524–5*, pp. 134, 145; *Suss. Wills*, vol. i, p. 206.
[58] *3 Suss. Subsidies*, pp. 79, 136; *Fitzalan Surveys*, pp. 7, 110, 129, 130.
[59] *De Lisle and Dudley MSS.*, vol. i, p. 69; *Suss. Subsidy, 1524–5*, p. 23.
[60] *3 Suss. Subsidies*, p. 155; P.R.O. E. 179/189/42, m. 2d.
[61] *S.A.C.*, vol. ii, pp. 317, 318.
[62] P. S. Godman, *Parish Register of Cowfold* (Suss. Record Soc., vol. xxii) (1916), *per indice*.
[63] R. Garraway Rice, *op. cit., per indice; Suss. Subsidy, 1524–5*, p. 84; *W. Suss. 1641–2*, pp. 100, 101.
[64] *Suss. Subsidy, 1524–5*, p. 59; *Wiston Archives*, p. 70; *W. Suss. 1641–2*, pp. 90, 91; *Suss. Wills*, vol. ii, p. 233.
[65] *W. Suss. 1641–2*, pp. 148, 175, 190; F. Hull, *Calendar of the White and*

Black Books of the Cinque Ports, pp. 264, 274; Suss. Wills, vol. ii, pp. 221, 260; Wiston Archives, p. 396; S.A.C., vol. xx, p. 172; vol. xxv, p. 131; vol. xxxvi, p. 31; R. P. Crawfurd, Parish Register of East Grinstead (Suss. Record Soc., vol. xxiv) (1917), per indice.

[66] Suss. Subsidy, 1524–5, p. 135.
[67] W. Suss. 1641–2, p. 131. Information from Mr. F. Leeson.
[68] 3 Suss. Subsidies, pp. 188, 299; Lewes Chartulary, vol. i, p. 86.
[69] S.A.C., vol. xcv, p. 48; Hastings Lathe C. R., p. 43; Non. Inquis., p. 378.
[70] Curia Regis Rolls, vol. x, p. 127.
[71] Surr. Taxation Returns (Surr. Record Soc., vol. xi) (1932), p. 72.
[72] W. Suss. 1641–2, pp. 118, 159; Suss. Fines, vol. iii, pp. 202, 226.
[73] Suss. Custumals, vol. ii, pp. 31, 33, 37, 43; 3 Suss. Subsidies, pp. 199, 283, 310.
[74] P. N. Suss., vol. ii, p. 388.
[75] Hastings Lathe C. R., pp. 113, 114; East Suss. Record Office, Dunn MSS., 2/3.
[76] W. Suss. 1641–2, pp. 137, 159; H.M.C., Rye MSS., p. 20.
[77] Hastings Lathe C. R., p. 118.
[78] Reaney, Dict., p. 346, where the first instance cited is 1792.
[79] Hastings Lathe C. R., pp. 106, 148; Robertsbridge Charters, p. 141; Suss. Wills, vol. i, p. 270; vol. ii, p. 131.
[80] Suss. Subsidy, 1524–5, pp. 148, 163; Suss. Wills, vol. i, p. 237; vol. ii, p. 131; Robertsbridge Surveys, p. 71.
[81] Suss. Subsidy, 1524–5, pp. 102, 123, 156; Suss. Wills, vol. i, p. 271; vol. iii, p. 318; vol. iv, p. 362; P. N. Suss., vol. ii, pp. 259, 330. pp. 259, 330.
[82] V. C. H. Suss., vol. i, p. 404.
[83] 3 Suss. Subsidies, pp. 58, 155, 270; De Lisle and Dudley MSS., vol. i, p. 23; S.A.C., vol. lii, p. 19.
[84] Ibid., vol. xii, pp. 30, 32; P.R.O. E. 179/189/42, mm. 16, 24, 24d, 28; West Suss. Record Office, Wiston MSS., 5233(2), d. A form with an inorganic "d" (Wolgard) occurs in 1374: Suss. Custumals, vol. i, p. 105.
[85] Chichester Chart., p. 255; S.A.C., vol. lxxxvii, p. 10; vol. lxxxix, pp. 143, 146, 147.
[86] Suss. Subsidy, 1524–5, pp. 3, 6, 30, 31, 70, 71, 73, 74; W. Suss. 1641–2, pp. 18, 27, 31, 55, 77, 95, 137, 155, 165, 187; S.A.C., vol. ix, p. 84; J. E. Ray, op. cit., p. 33; Suss. Wills, vol. ii, p. 308; Wiston Archives, p. 80; W. H. Challen, Parish Register of Cocking, 1558–1837 (1917), p. 98; C. H. Wilkie, St Andrews, Edburton, Suss.: Copy of the Parish Register Book, 1558–1673 (1884), pp. 1, 6, 7, 16–23, 25, 40–43, 45, 68.
[87] Wiston Archives, p. 222.

Surnames Derived from Personal Names

[88] Selten, *op. cit.*, pp. 52–54; Reaney, *Origins*, pp. 91–92.
[89] *Ibid.*; *Surnames of Oxon.*, pp. 216–8.
[90] *S.A.C.*, vol. lxxxiv, 77; vol. lxxxviii, 25; *De Lisle and Dudley MSS.*, vol. i, p. 110; *Suss. Custumals*, vol. ii, pp. 49, 57, 58, 67; *Lewes Chartulary*, vol. i, p. 123; *Boxgrove Chart.*, p. 177; *Chichester Chart.*, p. 337; *Lewes Barony Recs.*, p. 8; *3 Suss. Subsidies*, pp. 14, 36, 44, 73, 89.
[91] *Ibid.*, pp. 65 (Pachyns), 97 (Mox); *Suss. Fines*, vol. ii, p. 53 (Abbelles); P.R.O., S.C. 11/663 (Abeleys); S.C. 11/877 (Dabbes or Dalbes).
[92] *De Lisle and Dudley MSS.*, vol. i, p. 74 (John Roggeri and William Roggeri), p. 114 (Thomas Alani), p. 117 (Godfrey Alani).
[93] Selten, *op. cit.*, p. 53; *Surnames of Oxon.*, p. 216.
[94] See sources in note 90.
[95] H. A. Hanley and C. W. Chalklin, 'Kent Lay Subsidy Roll of 1334/5', in F. R. H. Du Boulay, *Documents Illustrative of Medieval Kentish Society* (Kent Archaeological Soc.) (1964), vol. xviii.
[96] See p. 321.
[97] *Surr. Taxation Returns* (Surr. Rec. Soc., vol. xi) (1922, 1932), *passim*.
[98] See sources cited in note 90.
[99] E. Ekwall, *Studies on the Genitive of Groups in English*, p. 76.
[100] *3 Suss. Subsidies*, pp. 263, 285, 288, 301, 313.
[101] *Robertsbridge Charters*, pp. 107, 133; *Hastings Lathe C. R.*, p. 12; *Non. Inquis*, pp. 373, 403; *3 Suss. Subsidies*, p. 216; *Chichester Chart.*, p. 354; P.R.O. E. 179/189/42, m. 15; West Suss. Record Office, EP.V1/19A/a, mm. 3d, 9d.
[102] P.R.O. E.179/235/2; E.179/189/94a; *Suss. Fines*, vol. iii, pp. 254, 258, 284.
[103] *Suss. Subsidy, 1524–5*, pp. 4, 6, 92, 100, 131, 153.
[104] *Surnames of Oxon*, p. 231. And see table, p. 333.
[105] *W. Suss. 1641–2*, pp. 19, 36, 79, 155, 164, 179.
[106] *Ibid.*, pp. 50, 51, 54–6, 60, 87–8, 94, 99–101, 105, 109, 168, 177, 183, 187, 192, 199.
[107] *Ibid.*, pp. 59, 115–6, 121, 185, 188, 201. See also *Suss. Wills*, vol. ii, p. 29; vol. iii, p. 166.
[108] Reaney, *Origins*, p. 92.
[109] *Ibid.*, p. 83; *3 Suss. Subsidies*, p. 130.
[110] *Fitzalan Surveys*, p. 29 (1301).
[111] *Surnames of Oxon.*, p. 217.
[112] Hanley and Chalklin, *op. cit.*, pp. 78, 92, 111, 112, 113, 127, 128, 130, 132, 137, 144, 148, 153, 154, 165.
[113] *Surr. Taxation Returns* (Surr. Rec. Soc., vol. xi) (1932), p. 80 (Auicia Hawkines)
[114] *Ibid.*, p. 23 (Thos. Willes, possibly topographical); p. 71 (John Nobis, perhaps a form of Nobbs).

[115] *Ibid.*, pp. 4 (Alice le Roperes), 15 (Agnes Couperes), 47 (Christina Couperes), 53 (Alice le Peyntours), 88 (Johanna Clerkes).
[116] *Suss. Custumals*, vol. ii, p. 67 (Widow Clements); *S.A.C.*, vol. lxxxviii, p. 25 (Alice Nykes); West Suss. Record Office, EP. VI/19A/1, m. 4 (Matilda Makkes).
[117] See, e.g., Hanley and Chalklin, *op. cit.*, p. 81 (Matilda Hokes).
[118] Reaney, *Origins*, pp. 92, 93; *Surnames of Oxon.*, p. 217; A. R. Rumble, *Dorset Lay Subsidy Roll of 1327* (Dorset Record Soc., No. vi) (1980), pp. 108, 123, 125, 131; J. C. Ward, *Medieval Essex Community* (1983).
[119] *Surnames of Lancs.*, p. 358; G. Redmonds, *Yorks.: West Riding* (1973), p. 30; Reaney, *Origins*, p. 313.
[120] *S.A.C.*, vol. liv, pp. 157, 158, 167; West Suss. Record Office, Wiston MSS., 5235; 5236, mm. 1, 1d, 2, 3; 5237, mm. 1, 1d, 2, 5; 5238; 5241, m. 1; 5233 (1); 5233 (2); 5234 (1); 5234 (2); P.R.O. E. 179/189/42, m. 23.
[121] J. E. Ray, *op. cit.*, p. 177; *Suss. Subsidy, 1524–5*, p. 4; West Suss. Record Office, E.P. VI/19A/1, m. 10; P.R.O. E. 179/189/42, m. 22.
[122] *Surnames of Oxon.*, pp. 49–51, 226–27; *Surnames of Lancs.*, pp. 207–210; G. Kristensson, *Studies on Middle English Topographical Terms* (1970), p. 25; *Norf. and Suff. Surnames in the Middle Ages*, pp. 132–3.
[123] *Feudal Aids*, vol. v, pp. 131, 146; *S.A.C.*, vol. lxxxiii, p. 36.
[124] F. Hull, *op. cit.*, p. 35.
[125] *S.A.C.*, vol. lxxxix, pp. 131, 133–5.
[126] West Suss. Record Office, EP. VI/19A/1, mm. 11, 11d.
[127] G. W. E. Loder, *Parish Registers of Ardingly* (Suss. Record Soc., vol. xvii) (1913), pp. 30, 155, 157.
[128] *Ibid.*, pp. 35, 158.
[129] *Ibid.*, pp. 61, 62, 186, 187.
[130] *W. Suss. 1641–2*, pp. 21, 43, 161, 165, 202; *Suss. Subsidy, 1524–5*, p. 75; E. P. W. Penfold, *First Book of the Parish Registers of Angmering* (Suss. Rec. Soc., vol. xviii) (1913), *per indice*; P.R.O. E. 179/191/378, mm. 2, 2d; *Suss. Wills*, vol. iv, p. 153.
[131] *W. Suss. 1641–2*, pp. 51, 54, 55, 56; P.R.O. E. 179/191/380.
[132] *W. Suss. 1641–2*, pp. 59, 115, 116, 121, 185, 188, 201; P.R.O. E. 179/191/378, m. 3d; *Suss. Wills*, vol. ii, p. 29; vol. iii, p. 166.
[133] *W. Suss. 1641–2*, p. 67; *Suss. Subsidy, 1524–5*, pp. 61, 62, 82, 86; J. E. Ray, *op. cit.*, p. 82; P.R.O. E. 179/191/378, m. 3; P. S. Godman, *op. cit., per indice; Suss. Wills*, vol. ii, pp. 40, 342; vol. iv, p. 162.
[134] *Suss. Subsidy, 1524–5*, pp. 81, 84; *W. Suss. 1641–2*, pp. 100, 101; R. Garraway Rice, *Parish Register of Horsham* (Suss. Record Soc., vol. xxi) (1915), *per indice*.
[135] See table, p. 333.

[136] *3 Suss. Subsidies*, pp. 234, 241, 258, 261, 299.
[137] *Ibid.*, pp. 64, 115, 118, 147; *Non. Inquis.*, p. 361; Inderwick, *Winchelsea*, p. 191; West Suss. Record Office, EP. VI/19A/1, m. 3d; *Suss. Fines*, vol. iii, p. 201; L. F. Salzman, *Ministers Accounts of the Manor of Petworth* (1955), pp. 40, 41, 52.
[138] *Suss. Wills*, vol. i, p. 71; F. Hull, *op. cit.*, pp. 79, 102, 103, 114; *S.A.C.*, vol. xviii, p. 28; vol. lxxxvii, p. 22; *Fitzalan Surveys*, pp. 125, 140; *Wiston Archives*, p. 391; *Suss. Custumals*, vol. i, p. 55; P.R.O. E. 179/225/50, mm. 13, 27; West Suss. Record Office, E.P. VI/19A/1, mm. 11, 12; J. E. Ray, *op. cit.*, p. 140; *Suss. Fines*, vol. iii, pp. 273, 290.
[139] J. E. Ray, *loc. cit.*
[140] See p. 5.
[141] *Cal. Pat., 1429–36*, pp. 541, 553, 583, 584, 586, 587.
[142] P.R.O. E. 179/189/94; E. 179/235/2; E. 179/270/10.
[143] *S.A.C.*, vol. lxxi, pp. 199, 202.
[144] *Cal. Pat., 1429–36*, p. 586; *S.A.C.*, vol. xviii, p. 28; *Suss. Subsidy, 1524–5*, p. 23.
[145] *Wiston Archives*, pp. 97, 391; F. Hull, *op. cit.*, pp. 125, 149, 191; P.R.O. E. 179/189/94.
[146] *Suss. Subsidy, 1524–5*, pp. 5, 16, 35, 44, 65, 97, 98, 100, 120, 154, 164, 165; H.M.C., *Rye MSS.*, pp. 1, 37.
[147] *Placita de Banco* (P.R.O. Lists and Indexes, xxxii), vol. ii, p. 671.
[148] *3 Suss. Subsidies*, p. 47; *Suss. Fines*, vol. iii, p. 15.
[149] *S.A.C.*, vol. lxxxix, p. 118; *Battle Custumals*, p. 55.
[150] *Surnames of Oxon.* pp. 235–7; Reaney, *Origins*, p. 84.
[151] *S.A.C.*, vol. x, p. 131; West Suss. Record Office, EP. VI/19A/1, m. 1d; *Suss. Fines*, vol. iii, p. 9.
[152] *3 Suss. Subsidies*, pp. 161, 275; *S.A.C.*, vol. liv, pp. 171, 173; *Non. Inquis.*, p. 387; P.R.O. E. 179/189/42, mm. 20, 22; West Suss. Record Office, Wiston MSS., 5233(2); 5236, m. 2; 5237, mm. 1, 1d, 2; 5241, m. 1.
[153] P.R.O. E. 179/191/380; *3 Suss. Subsidies*, pp. 64, 161, 208; Rubin, *Suss. Phonology*, pp. 22. The name atte Compe occurs at Findon (adjoining Wiston) in 1327, when the name Comsone also occurs there: *3 Suss. Subsidies*, p. 161.
[154] *3 Suss. Subsidies*, pp. 117, 204, 240, 315; *S.A.C.*, vol. xxiv, p. 69; vol. xcv, pp. 50, 54; *Suss. Wills*, vol. ii, p. 25; *Wiston Archives*, p. 164; West Suss. Record Office, EP. VI/19A/1, m.6; East Suss. Record Office, Dunn MSS., 2/19, 2/20; Reaney, *Dict.*, p. 31.
[155] *De Lisle and Dudley MSS.*, vol. i, p. 125.
[156] *Hastings Lathe C.R.*, pp. 11, 114.
[157] *3 Suss. Subsidies*, pp. 24, 141; *Boxgrove Chart.*, p. 185; *Suss. Custumals*, vol. i, pp. 108, 115, 119, 121.

158 *Suss. Custumals*, vol. i, p. 41; *Suss. Fines*, vol. i, p. 136; *Battle Custumals*, p. 40; *P. N. Suss.*, vol. ii, p. 415.
159 *3 Suss. Subsidies*, pp. 16, 51, 210, 322; *Lewes Chartulary*, vol. i, p. 128.
160 *3 Suss. Subsidies*, pp. 137, 248; *Suss. Fines*, vol. ii, p. 197; Rubin, *Suss. Phonology*, p. 137; Reaney, *Dict.*, p. 381.
161 *Suss. Subsidy, 1524–5*.
162 W. D. Cooper, "Participation of Suss. in Cade's Rising", *S.A.C.*, vol. xviii, pp. 23–30; *Cal. Pat., 1446–55*, pp. 339–374.
163 *W. Suss. 1641–2*.
164 *Surnames of Lancs.*, pp. 322–23.
165 See above, p. 327.
166 West Suss. Record Office, EP. VI/19A/1, mm. 1d, 3d, 10, 11.
167 *Battle Custumals*, p. 65; Inderwick, *Winchelsea*, p. 191.
168 *3 Suss. Subsidies*, pp. 64, 115, 118, 147, 234, 241, 258, 261, 299.
169 *Ibid.*, p. 258 (John Sibbesone).
170 *Surnames of Oxon.* pp. 216–32.
171 *Surnames of Lancs.*, pp. 322–25.
172 *Ibid.*, pp. 323–24.
173 See pp. 53–65.
174 The sources used are: Table II, A. C. Chibnall, *Early Taxation Returns* (Bucks. Record Soc.) (1946), pp. 2–97; A. M. Erskine, *Devonshire Lay Subsidy of 1332* (Devon and Cornwall Record Soc., new series, vol. xiv) (1969); A. Rumble, *Dorset Lay Subsidy Roll of 1327* (Dorset Record Soc., no. vi) (1980); J. C. Ward, *Medieval Essex Community* (1983); H. A. Hanley and C. W. Chalklin, *op. cit.*; J. P. Rylands, *op. cit.*; W. D. H. Fletcher, "Leics. Lay Subsidy, 1327", in *Associated Archaeological Socs. Reports and Papers*, vol. xix, pp. 209–312, 447–48; vol. xx, pp. 130–178; P.R.O. E. 179/149/7; P.R.O. E. 179/161/9; W. G. D. Fletcher, "Shropshire Lay Subsidy Roll of 1327", *Transactions Shropshire Archaeological Soc.*, 2nd series, vol. i, (1889), pp. 129–200; vol. iv (1892), pp. 288–388; vol. v (1893), pp. 343–62; vol. viii (1898), pp. 45–60; vol. x (1898), pp. 114–144; vol. xi (1899), pp. 348–90; 3rd ser. vol. v (1905), pp. 56–80; vol. vi (1906), pp. 123–54; vol. vii (1907), pp. 353–74; G. Wrottesley, *Exchequer Subsidy Roll of 1327 (Collections for a History of Staffs.*, vol. vii) (1886); Anon., *Suff. in 1327* (Suff. Green Books, no. ix) (1906); *Surr. Taxation Returns* (Surr. Record Soc., vol. xi), pp. 1–94; *3 Suss. Subsidies*, pp. 225–334; W. F. Carter, *op. cit.*; J. Amphlett, *Lay Subsidy Roll, A.D. 1332-3, and nonarum inquisitiones, 1340, for the county of Worcs.* (Worcs. Hist. Soc., vol. x) (1900), pp. 1–28; J. Parker "Lay Subsidy Rolls, I Edward III", *Miscellanea*, vol. ii (Yorks. Archaeological Soc., vol. lxxiv (1929), pp. 106–71; Table III, A.C. Chibnall and A. V. Woodman, *Subsidy Roll for County of Buckingham, 1524* (Bucks. Record Soc.) (1950); T.

L. Stoate, *Cornwall Hearth and Poll Taxes*, pp. 1–163; T. L. Stoate, *Devon Lay Subsidy Rolls, 1524–7* (1979), and M. M. Rowe, *Tudor Exeter* (Devon and Cornwall Record Soc., new series, vol. xxii) (1977), pp. 35–44; C. A. F. Meekings, *Dorset Hearth Tax Assessments, 1662–64* (1951); H. M. Wood, *Durham Protestations* (Surtees Soc., vol. cxxxv) (1922); J. Smith, *Men and Armour for Glouc.* (1980); C. R. Davey, *Hants. Lay Subsidy Rolls* (Hants. Record Series, vol. iv) (1981); M. A. Faraday, *Herefs. Militia Assessments of 1663* (Camden Soc., 4th series, vol. x) (1972); House of Lords Record Office, Protestation Returns, 1641–2, Salford Hundred, Lancs.; C.S.A. Dobson, *Oxon. Protestation Returns* (Oxon. Record Soc., vol. xxxvi) (1955); J. Cornwall, *County Community under Henry VIII* (Rutland Record Series, vol. i) (1980), pp. 17–86; W. Watkins-Pitchford, *Shropshire Hearth Tax of 1672* (1949); G. Wrottesley, "Lay Subsidy, 256/31, hearth tax", *Collections for a History of Staffs.*, vols. xlv (1921), pp. 44–173; xlvii (1924), pp. 47–256; xlix (1927), pp. 155–242; li (1929), pp. 1–79; Anon., *Suff. in 1524* (Suff. Green Books, no. x) (1910); C. A. F. Meekings, *Surr. Hearth Tax, 1664* (Surr. Record Soc., vol. xvii) (1940); J. Cornwall, *Lay Subsidy Roll, 1524–5* (Suss. Record Soc., vol. lvi) (1956); G. D. Ramsay, *Two 16th Century Taxation Lists* (Wilts. Archaeological and Natural History Soc., vol. x) (1954), pp. 45–159; J. Amphlett, *Lay Subsidy Rolls, A.D. 1603* (Worcs. Historical Soc., vol. xiii) (1901); W. Brigg, "Lay Subsidy, Wapentake of Agbrigg and Morley", *Miscellanea* (Thoresby Soc., vol. xv) (1909), pp. 132–51.

[175] See the discussion in *Surnames of Lancs.*, pp. 328–9.

[176] *Lewes Chartulary*, vol. ii, p. 70; *Wiston Archives*, p. 53; *3 Suss. Subsidies*, pp. 88, 102, 126, 154, 164, 196, 307; L. Fleming, *History of Pagham*, vol. i, p. xxxviii; *Fitzalan Surveys*, pp. 13, 134, 162; West Suss. Record Office, Wiston MSS., 5233 (1); *Suss. Subsidy, 1524–5*, pp. 15, 23, 24, 36, 37, 39, 53, 65, 66, 153; *W. Suss. 1641–2*, pp. 21, 74, 78, 81, 101, 108, 110, 114, 119, 137, 138, 145, 147, 157, 159, 184; J. E. Ray, *op. cit.*, p. 70; *S.A.C.*, vol. lxix, p. 134; P.R.O. E. 179/191/378, mm. 1d, 2; W. H. Challen, *Parish Register of Cocking, 1558–1837* (1927), pp. 34, 46, 47, 64, 65, 103, 113, 114, 122; P. S. Godman, *op. cit.*, pp. 27, 89, 91, 123, 138, 145; *Suss. Wills*, vol. ii, pp. 222, 238; vol. iii, pp. 89, 92–3; vol. iv, p. 294.

[177] *3 Suss. Subsidies*, pp. 86, 132, 248, 302; *S.A.C.*, vol. lxxxix, p. 160; *Suss. Custumals*, vol. i, pp. 13, 118, 140; L. Fleming, *op. cit.*, vol. i, p. 26; *Chichester Chart.*, pp. 67, 246; *Suss. Subsidy, 1524–5*, p. 127; *Suss. Fines*, vol. iii, p. 137

[178] *3 Suss. Subsidies*, p. 181; *Suss. Wills*, vol. ii, p. 106; *S.A.C.*, vol. liv, pp. 88, 92; vol. xcv, p. 54; vol. xcvi, p. 27; *Suss. Subsidy, 1524–5*, pp. 88, 109, 110, 116; *W. Suss. 1641–2*, p. 90.

[179] *Suss. Wills*, vol. i, pp. 42, 100, 365; *3 Suss. Subsidies*, pp. 14, 113, 237,

327; F. Hull, *op. cit.*, pp. 79, 91, 96, 100, 133; *De Lisle and Dudley MSS.*, vol. i, p. 156; *Robertsbridge Surveys*, p. 97; *Suss. Subsidy, 1524–5*, p. 157; *W. Suss. 1641–2*, p. 177; P.R.O. S.C. 11/649, m. 2; West Suss. Record Office, EP. VI/19A/1, m. 1d; Wiston MSS., 5236, m. 1.

[180] Reaney, *Origins*, pp. 192–3, 196–7.

[181] *Non. Inquis.*, p. 384; *3 Suss. Subsidies*, pp. 45, 170, 284; *Hastings Lathe C. R.*, pp. 133, 170.

[182] *3 Suss. Subsidies*, p. 144, 233; *Fitzalan Surveys*, pp. 114, 128; P.R.O. E. 179/189/42, m. 5.

[183] *Hastings Lathe C.R.*, pp. 24, 85; West Suss. Record Office, EP. VI/19A/1, mm. 1, 2, 3d; East Suss. Record Office, Dunn MSS., 16/2; P.R.O. E. 179/189/42, m. 26; L. Fleming, *History of Pagham*, vol. i, p. 62.

[184] *V.C.H. Suss.*, vol. iv, p. 109; *Suss. Wills*, vol. i, pp. 42, 357; vol. ii, p. 72; vol. iii, pp. 196, 197; *S.A.C.*, vol. xxiv, p. 82; vol. lxxvii, pp. 100, 102; *Suss. Indictments*, vol. i, p. 17; *Suss. Subsidy, 1524–5*, pp. 6, 12, 18; *W. Suss. 1641–2*, pp. 9, 47, 52, 55, 56, 65, 79, 93, 123, 143; *Suss. Wills*, vol. ii, p. 124; vol. iv, pp. 186, 187, 257.

[185] *Chichester Chart.*, pp. 213, 348; *Suss. Wills*, vol. iii, p. 64; *Wiston Archives*, pp. 127, 242; *3 Suss. Subsidies*, pp. 139, 258; *Suss. Subsidy, 1524–5*, pp. 31, 39–41; *W. Suss. 1641–2*, pp. 108, 109, 110, 118, 137, 146; R. Garraway Rice, *Parish Register of Horsham* (Suss. Record Soc., vol. xxi) (1915), pp. 351, 370. The names Jokeman and Jukeman, also found in north-west Sussex, seem to be variants of Jakeman: *3 Suss. Subsidies*, p. 93; *Lewes Chartulary*, vol. ii, p. 89; *Chichester Chart.*, p. 220; *Rotuli de Quo Warranto*, pp. 752, 753; *Catalogue of Ancient Deeds*, vol. iii, p. 33.

[186] *Suss. Custumals*, vol. i, p. 116; *S.A.C.*, vol. xlv, p. 177; *V.C.H. Suss.*, vol. iv, p. 144; *Fitzalan Surveys*, p. 170; *Hastings Lathe C.R.*, p. 123; West Suss. Record Office, EP. VI/19A/1, m. 1d; P.R.O. E. 179/189/42, m. 11; E. 179/225/5; E. 179/225/12; E. 179/235/2; *Suss. Subsidy, 1524–5*, p. 113; *W. Suss. 1641–2*, p. 53.

[187] *3 Suss. Subsidies*, pp. 39, 311; *Hastings Lathe C.R.*, pp. 120, 132, 187; *S.A.C.*, vol. xii, p. 37; *Suss. Subsidy, 1524–5*, pp. 14, 88; *W. Suss. 1641–2*, p. 87.

[188] P.R.O. S.C. 11/666.

[189] *Feudal Aids*, vol. v, p. 151; *Hastings Lathe C.R.*, pp. 11, 43, 125, 127; *Placita de Banco* (Public Record Office, Lists and Indexes, no. xxxii), vol. ii, p. 664; East Suss. Record Office, St Audries MSS., /298.

[190] *Non. Inquis.*, p. 366; *Feudal Aids*, vol. v, p. 164; Reaney, *Dict.*, p. 73.

[191] *Fitzalan Surveys*, pp. 139, 169; *Non. Inquis.*, p. 355; *3 Suss. Subsidies*, pp. 122, 129, 154, 245; *W. Suss. 1641–2*, p. 124.

Surnames Derived from Personal Names 357

[192] *3 Suss. Subsidies*, p. 16; Inderwick, *Winchelsea*, p. 209; *S.A.C.*, vol. lxxxiv, p. 75.

[193] *Robertsbridge Charters*, p. 143; *Non. Inquis.*, p. 403; F. Hull, *op. cit.*, p. 339; *Hastings Lathe C.R.*, pp. 49, 114, 138; P.R.O. E. 179/258/21, p. 17; S.C. 11/649, m. 1.

[194] *Suss. Custumals*, vol. ii, pp. 7, 43, 47–8, 51, 55, 59; *Wiston Archives*, p. 86; *3 Suss. Subsidies*, p. 199; *S.A.C.*, vol. liv, p. 153; vol. xcviii, p. 61; *Suss. Subsidy, 1524–5*, pp. 46, 84; R. Garraway Rice, *Parish Register of Horsham* (Suss. Record Soc., vol. xxi) (1915), pp. 8, 11, 118, 360; Reaney, *Dict.*, p. 61.

[195] *3 Suss. Subsidies*, pp. 299, 307; *Hastings Lathe C.R.*, pp. 33, 34.

[196] P.R.O. S.C. 11/877; *Suss. Fines*, vol. i, p. 36; *Suss. Custumals*, vol. ii, p. 134; *Non. Inquis.*, p. 403; *Chichester Chart.*, p. 350.

[197] *3 Suss. Subsidies*, pp. 122, 131, 133, 145, 192, 244, 247; *Placita de Banco* (P.R.O. Lists and Indexes, no. xxxii) vol. ii, p. 666; *V.C.H. Suss..*, vol. iv, pp. 128, 195; *Suss. Custumals*, vol. i, p. 141; *Chichester Chart.*, p. 219; L. Fleming, *History of Pagham*, vol. i, pp. xxxvi, 62; *S.A.C.*, vol. xii, p. 37; vol. li, p. 48; vol. lxxxix, p. 159.

[198] L. Fleming, *op. cit.*, pp. xxxi, xxxvi. See also the form Geudewin (for the personal name Goldwine): *Boxgrove Chart.*, p. 71.

[199] *3 Suss. Subsidies*, pp. 192, 304. See also *Suss. Fines*, vol. iii, p. 178.

[200] *S.A.C.*, vol. lxxxiv, p. 67; *Placita de Banco* (P.R.O. Lists and Indexes, no. xxxii), vol. ii, p. 666.

[201] *Suss. Subsidys, 1524–5*, p. 64; *W Suss. 1641–2*, pp. 190, 197; *Wiston Archives*, p. 237; *Suss. Wills*, vol. iv, p. 310; *Suss. Fines*, vol. iii, pp. 197–8.

[202] *Ibid.*, p. 152; *W Suss. 1641–2*, p. 14.

[203] *3 Suss. Subsidies*, pp. 114, 238.

[204] *Curia Regis Rolls, 15–16 John*, pp. 22, 27; Reaney, *Dict.*, p. 149.

[205] *Suss. Subsidy, 1524–5*, pp. 14, 15, 17, 26, 38; *Suss. Wills*, vol. ii, p. 79; vol. iv, pp. 19, 255.

[206] *Wiston Archives*, p. 137; *W. Suss. 1641–2*, pp. 35, 63, 71, 97; R. Garraway Rice, *op. cit.*, pp. 70, 304; W. H. Challen, *op. cit.*, pp. 27, 29, 31–33, 35.

[207] *Suss. Fines*, vol. i, pp. 71, 73; *Suss. Custumals*, vol. i, p. 29; *De Lisle and Dudley MSS.*, vol. i, p. 151.

[208] Anon., *Suff. in 1327* (Suff. Green Books, no. ix) (1906), p. 76; H. A. Hanley and C. W. Chalklin, *op. cit.*, pp. 91, 112; C. Clark, "Early Personal Names of King's Lynn", *Nomina*, vol. vii, p. 71.

[209] Salzman, *Chartulary of Sele* (1923), p. 89; *De Lisle and Dudley MSS.*, vol. i, p. 90; *Great Roll of the Pipe for the 24th Year of Henry II* (Pipe Roll Soc., vol. xxvii) (1906), p. 90; M. A. Lower, *Dictionary of Family Names* (1860), p. 243; *Suss. Fines*, vol. iii, p. 203.

[210] H. A. Hanley and C. W. Chalklin, *op. cit.*, p. 121; *Non. Inquis.*, p. 396.

[211] W. Farrer, *Honors and Knights Fees*, vol. iii, pp. 141, 147. For other examples, see F. Palgrave, *Rotuli Curiae Regis* (1835), vol. ii, p. 262; *Somerset Rec. Soc.*, vol. v, p. 128.
[212] *Suss. Fines*, vol. i, p. 101.
[213] *3 Suss. Subsidies*, pp. 50, 60, 67.
[214] *Lewes Barony Recs.*, pp. 1, 2, 7, 9; *Lewes Chartulary*, vol. i, p. 99; *S.A.C.*, vol. lxxxiii, p. 50; C. Clark, *op. cit.*, vol. vii, p. 77.
[215] *Lewes Barony Recs.*, pp. 32, 44; *Lewes Chartulary*, vol. ii, p. 33; *Wiston Archives*, p. 205; *Chichester Chart.*, p. 6.
[216] *Suss. Fines*, vol. ii, p. 48; *P. N. Suss.*, vol. i, p. 188.
[217] *3 Suss. Subsidies*, p. 114; *Suss. Subsidy, 1524-5*, pp. 13, 14.
[218] Reaney, *Dict.*, p. 213.
[219] *Suss. Custumals*, vol. i, pp. 96, 97; D. M. Stenton, *Great Roll of the Pipe for the 8th Year of John* (Pipe Roll Soc., vol. lviii) (1942), p. 62; E. P. Ebden, *Great Roll of the Pipe for the 2nd Year of Henry III* (Pipe Roll Soc., vol. lxxvii) (1972), p. 19. The female form Legarda occurs c. 1110: E. Searle, *Lordship and Community* (1974), p. 466.
[220] *Boxgrove Chart.*, pp. 32, 33, 68, 70, 76, 177, 178; *3 Suss. Subsidies*, pp. 96, 97, 123, 125, 245, 249; *S.A.C.*, vol. lxxxix, pp. 122, 126; L. Fleming, *op. cit.*, vol. i, p. 132.
[221] *Non. Inquis.*, p. 353; *Suss. Fines*, vol. iii, p. 269.
[222] *Suss. Subsidy, 1524-5*, pp. 25, 28, 30; *Suss. Wills*, vol. iii, p. 263; *Suss. Fines*, vol. iii, p. 269.
[223] *Boxgrove Chart.*, pp. 32, 33, 68, 70, 72, 75, 76, 107, 156, 177, 178.
[224] *Ibid.*, pp. 24, 30, 62, 156.
[235] *3 Suss. Subsidies*, p. 82; *S.A.C.*, vol. xxxv, p. 91.
[226] *W. Suss. 1641-2*, pp. 10, 15, 29, 101, 116, 122, 127, 133, 142, 149, 173, 176, 191-3, 199, 202; Lord Leconfield, *Sutton and Duncton Manors* (1956), pp. 18, 37, 38.
[227] *Suss. Wills*, vol. iii, p. 124; *Suss. Subsidy, 1524-5*, p. 121.
[228] *Suss. Wills*, vol. i, p. 352.
[229] M. A. Lower, *op. cit.*, p. 301.
[230] *3 Suss. Subsidies*, p. 327.
[231] H. A. Hanley and C. W. Chalkin, *op. cit.*, p. 138.
[232] Inderwick, *Winchelsea*, pp. 157, 158, 159.
[233] *Hastings Lathe C.R.*, p. 122; *S.A.C.*, vol. lxv, p. 47; vol. xcii, p. 142; *Non. Inquis.*, pp. 393, 403; P.R.O. E. 122/147/15; E. 179/225/12; E. 179/225/5; *Suss. Fines*, vol. iii, pp. 196, 208, 217.
[234] *Non. Inquis.*, p. 353; *S.A.C.*, vol. lxxxix, p. 123.
[235] *Hastings Lathe C.R.*, pp. 149, 173, 181, 184; *Suss. Wills*, vol. i, p. 269; vol. iii, p. 31; vol. iv, p. 433; *Cal. Rat. 1441-46*, p. 197; *Suss. Fines*, vol. iii, p. 212, 217.
[236] Anon., *Suff. in 1327* (Suff. Green Books, no. ix) (1906), p. 91.
[237] *3 Suss. Subsidies*, pp. 39, 181, 295, 307; Rubin, *Suss. Phonology*, p. 58.

Surnames Derived from Personal Names 359

[238] *Wiston Archives*, p. 34; W. C. Bolland, *Year Books of Edward II: 8 Edward II* (Selden Soc., vol. xxxvii) (1920), p. 209; *Suss. Custumals*, vol. i, p. 68; *3 Suss. Subsidies*, pp. 65, 147, 160; *Chichester Chart.*, p. 235. And see p. 149.

[239] *P. N. Suss.*, vol. i, p. 160.

[240] J. E. Ray, *op. cit.*, p. 148; *Suss. Subsidies, 1524–5*, p. 39.

[241] *3 Suss. Subsidies*, p. 8; *Feudal Aids*, vol. v, p. 149.

[242] *P. N. Suss.*, vol. ii, p. 435.

[243] *3 Suss. Subsidies*, pp. 111, 234; *Non. Inquis.*, pp. 364, 365; *Fitzalan Surveys*, pp. 114, 139, 155, 156; H. D. Gordon, *History of Harting* (1877), p. 40; *Suss. Fines*, vol. iii, p. 144.

[244] *3 Suss. Subsidies*, p. 63; *Suss. Fines*, vol. iii, p. 200.

[245] *Fitzalan Surveys*, p. 155.

[246] *3 Suss. Subsidies*, pp. 20, 42, 56, 71, 119, 121, 153, 155, 244, 252, 260, 303; *Lewes Chartulary*, vol. i, p. 143; L. Fleming, *op. cit.*, vol. i, pp. xxxvii, lvi; *Suss. Custumals*, vol. iii, p. 130; *S.A.C.*, vol. liii, p. 152; vol. lxxxvii, p. 7; P.R.O. E. 179/189/42, m. 21d; *Suss. Fines*, vol. iii, p. 200.

[247] *Surr. Taxation Returns* (Surr. Record Soc., vol. xi) (1922), pp. 29, 30, 31, 34. Le Tyle occurs as a surname or bye-name in Essex, 1327: J. C. Ward, *Medieval Essex Community* (1983), p. 2.

[248] *3 Suss. Subsidies*, p. 72.

[249] *W. Suss. 1641–2*, pp. 119.

[250] *Ibid.*, pp. 30, 196.

[251] *Ibid.*, pp. 12, 13, 15, 69, 70, 87, 179, 191; *Suss. Subsidy, 1524–5*, pp. 16, 17, 20; *Suss. Wills*, vol. i, pp. 16, 155; vol. ii, p. 88; vol. iv, pp. 278, 317–8; *V.C.H. Suss.* vol. iv, p. 203.

[252] *Ibid.*, vol. i, pp. 176, 331; vol. ii, pp. 12, 205; *Suss. Subsidy, 1524–5*, p. 21; *S.A.C.*, vol. lxxxvii, p. 26; J. E. Ray, *op. cit.*, p. 17; *Robertsbridge Surveys*, p. 115.

[253] *W. Suss. 1641–2*, pp. 26, 27, 43, 58, 80, 88, 95, 96, 141, 152, 175, 177, 178, 194, 197; P.R.O. E. 179/191/378, m. 3d.

[254] *Wiston Archives*, pp. 237–8; *Suss. Wills*, vol. ii, pp. 213, 235; *Suss. Subsidy, 1524–5*, pp. 6, 60, 65, 66, 70, 71, 79, 84–5; *W. Suss. 1641–2*, pp. 91, 111, 112, 190; R. Garraway Rice, *Parish Register of Horsham* (Suss. Record Soc., vol. xxi) (1915), p. 362; C. H. Wilkie, *St Andrew's, Edburton, Suss.: Copy of the Parish Register Book, 1558–1673*, p. 12.

[255] *W. Suss. 1641–2*, pp. 119–20; P. S. Godman, *op. cit.*, pp. 40, 41, 63, 80–86, 89, 153, 198, 200, 225; R. Garraway Rice, *op. cit.*, p. 287.

[256] *P. N. Suss.*, vol. ii, p. 284; G. W. E. Loder, *Parish Registers of Ardingly* (Suss. Record Soc., vol. xvii) (1913), *per indice*.

[257] *Suss. Subsidy, 1524–5*, pp. 19, 23, 25, 59, 70, 154; F. Hull, *op. cit.*, p. 243; J. E. Ray, *op. cit.*, pp. 26, 144; E. Searle, *Lordship and Community* (1974), p. 370; *S.A.C.*, vol. xx, p. 16; vol. xxiv, p. 112;

[258] vol. lxix, p. 119; *Suss. Wills*, vol. i, pp. 112, 167, 293; vol. ii, pp. 25, 136.
[258] H.M.C., *Rye MSS.*, p. 88.
[259] *Suss. Subsidy, 1524–5*, pp. 18, 33, 137, 161; F. Hull, *op. cit.*, p. 191; J. E. Ray, *op. cit.*, p. 189; Lord Leconfield, *Petworth Manor in the 17th Century* (1954), p. 66.
[260] *Suss. Subsidy, 1524–5*, pp. 133, 134; *Robertsbridge Surveys*, p. 11; *S.A.C.*, vol. xli, pp. 31, 34, 37, 39–41; *3 Suss. Subsidies*, p. 10; *Suss. Wills*, vol. iv, p. 25.
[261] *Suss. Subsidys, 1524–5*, pp. 32–33; *Suss. Wills*, vol. ii, p. 167.
[262] *Suss. Subsidy, 1524–5*, pp. 24, 29, 56; *Suss. Wills*, vol. i, p. 5; vol. iii, pp. 272, 326; J. E. Ray, *op. cit.*, p. 36; *S.A.C.*, vol. xxxiii, p. 271; vol. lxxvii, p. 99. Lyllat occurs as the name of an alien in East Suss.: *Suss. Subsidy, 1524–5*, p. 130.
[263] *3 Suss. Subsidies*, pp. 150, 268; *Suss. Subsidy, 1524–5*, pp. 36, 39, 40, 44, 45; *W. Suss. 1641–2*, pp. 137, 185; *Suss. Wills*, vol. i, pp. 243–7.
[264] *3 Suss. Subsidies*, pp. 191, 302; *Suss. Subsidy, 1524–5*, pp. 111, 115, 117, 148; J. E. Ray, *op. cit.*, p. 1; P.R.O., E. 179/225/50, mm. 13, 27; *Suss. Wills*, vol. ii, p. 77.
[265] *3 Suss. Subsidies*, pp. 167, 175, 274, 281; *Suss. Subsidy, 1524–5*, pp. 60, 69, 71, 90, 92, 106, 107; *Suss. Custumals*, vol. i, p. 120; *Non. Inquis.*, p. 385.
[266] See p. 316.
[267] *3 Suss. Subsidies*, pp. 68, 142, 264; *Suss. Custumals*, vol. i, p. 73; vol. iii, pp. 38, 41, 42; *Valor Ecclesiasticus*, vol. i, p. 294; *Suss. Subsidy, 1524–5*, pp. 49, 51, 76, 80; *W. Suss. 1641–2*, p. 111; *Wiston Archives*, pp. 53, 65, 218; *Suss. Wills*, vol. i, p. 218; vol. ii, p. 154; *Suss. Fines*, vol. iii, pp. 12, 239.
[268] See p. 64.
[269] Richard Coleman, mentioned 1219 is the same person as Richard son of Coleman, mentioned 1218: E. P. Ebden, *Great Roll of the Pipe for the 2nd Year of Henry III* (Pipe Roll Soc., vol. lxxvii) (1972), p. 21; P. M. Barnes and others, *Great Roll of the Pipe for the 3rd Year of Henry III* (Pipe Roll Soc., vol. lxxx) (1976), p. 142.

CHAPTER 6

SURNAMES DERIVED FROM NICKNAMES

One of the main categories of English surnames is made up of surnames which originated in the nicknames given to individuals, because of their physical characteristics, morals, habits, methods of speech, and so forth. During the 13th and 14th centuries surnames or bye-names derived from nicknames were very numerous in Sussex. Many of these never became hereditary, and many were always very rare. Out of all the surnames or bye-names derived from nicknames found in Sussex before 1400, just over a third have been found as the name of a single person. In this Sussex was not significantly different from most other southern and Midland counties. (In the north of England, the high proportion of surnames or bye-names derived from place-names created a rather different situation.) It is not surprising that human inventiveness produced an immense variety of nicknames, and it is obvious that new nicknames must have been devised and bestowed very freely. Surnames and bye-names in this category were already very numerous in the 13th century, and it is probably only the defects of the available source material that prevent the discovery of a similarly large body of such surnames and bye-names at earlier periods.

The surnames or bye-names which appear in Sussex during the Middle Ages are so multifarious that it is difficult to give any description which is at all comprehensive. There are names derived from mammals, such as Bat, Beaver, Bull, Catt, Cony, Hart, Hogg, Leppard, Otter, or Steer, from birds, such as Bullfinch (or Bolfin), Crane, Crowe, Dunnock, Fesant, Finch (or Vinch), Nightingale, Peacock, Puttock, Sparrow, Swan, Thrush, and, less certainly, Pink and Puffer, or from fish, such as Fish, Herring, Gurnard, Pilchard, and perhaps Mackerell. There are names, some of them relatively common, from the more obvious physical features of the human form, such as Black, Brown, White, Grey, Long, Short, Grant, and so forth. There are several names from baldness, Ballard and Callow for instance. There are some more imaginative, and generally rarer, names from physical characteristics, such as Beaufront, Blackneck, Fisdelou, Goldeberd, and Sickelfoot, to name a few out of a large number. There is a group of names, including a few which survived to become well established in Sussex, from oaths or ejaculations, such as Bonjour, Godeshalf, Godesmark, Godemefecche, Parfoy, Parmoncorps, or Wardew. Presumably such names arose from the habitual use of the expression concerned by some individual. There is another group, including such names as Blakecherl, Blakeboy, Blakwyght, Bonsergeant,

Goddegroom, Goodehind, Lytelmay, Whitegroom, or Wytemay, which are formed from some word meaning 'man', 'servant', etc., and an adjective. There are a few similar names compounded with the word 'priest', Binprest ('bean priest'),[1] Hoggeprest (a name which was hereditary at and near Amberley),[2] Jakepreyst[3] and Polleprist.[4] The persons so named all seem to have been lay, and these must have originated as nicknames. There are names from favourable or approved aspects of conduct, such as Belamy, Curteys, Fairmaner, Forthright, Goodfellow, Wellkempd, Wise, and Wisdom, and there are names from unfavourable aspects, such as Malvoisin, Malcovenant, Malmains, Milksop, Sleabody ('slybody'), Sleghande ('slyhand'), Sligh, Slogard, and Scorchevileyn. There is a small but interesting group of names which are derived from particular times of the year or festivals, often ones which were important in many Sussex manors as dates on which rent had to be paid, or on which certain types of labour services began. These include Christmas, Hokeday, Masseday, and Pentecost. And besides these, there are a multitude of surnames and bye-names, too varied to describe, and many of such a nature that it is impossible to put forward any plausible conjecture about how they might have arisen.

It is rare, for surnames in any category, to find any evidence which shows how any individual adopted, or was given a particular name, but with surnames in most categories this does not give rise to any special difficulty. With surnames derived from nicknames, however, it is often impossible to be certain what the name originally signified or implied. It must be suspected that some names, such as for example Drinkwater, were ironical when first bestowed, but it is hardly every possible to be sure about this. It is especially difficult to be sure of the significance of some compound surnames, which occur independently in different parts of the country, and which seem, therefore, to be derived from phrases which were in general use over a large area, and which presumably had some generally understood meaning or implication at the period when the surnames concerned arose. For example, the rare name Strokehose existed in the coastal parts of West Sussex during the 13th and 14th centuries. Although no connected pedigree can be traced, the survival of such an unusual name in one area over a period suggests that it was hereditary. The same name, however, can also be found in Kent during the 14th century, and there is no discoverable link between the Kent and Sussex instances.[5] It must be suspected from this that 'strokehose' was a phrase in general use in south-east England, that it conveyed to contemporaries some fairly precise impression of an individual so nicknamed, and that the surname was not merely a soubriquet bestowed on someone who had a habit of stroking his lower garments. A similar case is that of the more common surname Sherewind, which often appears at later periods as Sherwin or Shirwin. During the 13th and 14th centuries this name occurs at several places in Sussex, and the instances are too dispersed to make it likely that all those found with the same name belonged to one family. The name was that of a villein family at Amberley, where it was probably hereditary. In the Amberley manorial records the name was sometimes translated into French as Tranchevent, but presumably this was not the form generally used in speech.[6] The name survived in Sussex, and was present in several parts of the county during the 16th and 17th centuries.[7] Before 1500, however, the name already existed in Dorset, Norfolk, Suffolk, Lancashire, Cumberland, Kent, Worcestershire and Oxfordshire. A more extensive search would no doubt discover examples in further counties.[8] It must be supposed from this that Sherewind was a phrase widely employed in England, probably throughout the country, and that when used as a nickname it was applied to persons with some specific characteristics. Possibly, as suggested by Reaney, it was applied to people who were fast runners. Or, again, the name Spendlove (later Spenlow) can be found during the 13th and 14th centuries in several different parts of Sussex. The name also occurs before 1500 in Norfolk, Suffolk, Lancashire, Bedfordshire, Northumberland, Yorkshire, and Oxfordshire.[9] This surname clearly arose in a number of unrelated families, dispersed across the country. The name survived in many parts, including Sussex. Possibly Spendlove was a nickname for someone who was considered promiscuous, though the exact shade of meaning which the phrase carried in, perhaps, the 13th century is difficult to gauge. The phrase 'spend love' must, however, have been in general use over much, or probably the whole, of England at the period when the surname was coming into being.

These are instances of individual compound surnames derived from nicknames. There is a group of names such as Pullrose, Pluckrose, etc., which are found in many English counties. In Sussex, the names Pullrose and Pluckrose both occur. All the medieval examples of both names which have been found in the county come from one area, in East Sussex around Brighton and Lewes, but the individuals concerned seem too dispersed to be all from one family.[10] Both these names can be found in other counties, and similar surnames or bye-names, such as Shakerose,[11] can be found in some parts of England. Tenements held for a nominal rent of a rose can be found in many parts of England, at least from the 13th century onwards, and this is not at all rare. It is possible that the names Pullrose and Pluckrose may have originated from such holdings, and this seems to be the explanation favoured by Reaney.[12] However, the names do not seem to fit the explanation very well, and the persons who appear in Sussex with both names were in some (and perhaps all) instances villeins, who were unlikely to have held land at such nominal rents (which are typical of free tenure). It is also the case that Pullerose occurs as a ship's name in Sussex customs accounts,[13] though possibly the vessel might have been called after an individual with the surname Pullrose. Mr. Peter McClure has pointed out that names such as Pullrose, etc., may contain allusions to sexual activity.[14] The point here is that such surnames have arisen in widely separated parts of the country, and must consequently have developed from expressions which were in use to a correspondingly wide extent.

There are many other surnames derived from nicknames, to be found in Sussex, which also occur in other counties, sometimes distant ones, in a similar way. Space does not permit a detailed examination of all such cases, but the surnames Breakspear, Drinkwater, Fairweather, Makehait ('make glad'), Pennyfather, Shortfrend, Startup, and Sourmilk, which can all be found in Sussex before 1500, can all be found in other parts of England as well. Though the literal meaning of such names is usually clear, it is often very uncertain what their precise significance was when they were applied as nicknames. Some of these names may well have been ironical. Others, such as Breakspear, may have implications of a sexual character. Where names so widely distributed from an early date are concerned, however, it must be supposed that they are not the chance inventions of some sharp tongued person, nor the product of some one particular incident, but that they originated from widely employed expressions, which in colloquial usage had each a specific meaning. It is probable that each of these names, when first used, conveyed the impression of a person with some clearly defined characteristics. In many cases, however, it is impossible now to estimate accurately the nature of this impression, with whatever allusions or implications may have been attached to it.

There are a great many compound surnames or bye-names in Sussex to which these remarks apply. Many of them were rare names which did not survive after about 1500, and which have left little trace on the county's nomenclature, though a few which have been lost as surnames have given rise to surviving names of fields, farms, etc. A small number of surnames or bye-names which are French linguistically fall into this group. The history of some of these names, mostly those which survived in Sussex over a long period, has been dealt with below.

Similar obscurities exist about the real significance of the quite numerous surnames derived from words for different species of mammals, birds, and fish. It seems likely that in most cases people were given such nicknames because they were considered to possess moral qualities which, by popular belief, were thought to be typical of one particular species. It is, however, difficult at the present day to be sure in all cases just what qualities were generally attributed to any animal. Some beliefs about such matters were probably general throughout the country. Peacocks, for example, seem to have been universally linked with pride, and kites with greed. It is likely that where some creatures were concerned there were purely local opinions and superstitions about various animals, perhaps different from those held in other parts of the country, and it is difficult to discover what these were. Under such circumstances it must often be uncertain why surnames derived from the name of some particular species arose. It is not even clear in all cases what species was involved. In Sussex, for example, there existed the surnames Puffer, apparently from a local word for some species of bird,[15] and Colefish, probably not a name from the type now generally called a coal fish.[16] Even the well known Sussex surname of Hogg, already firmly established in the county by the end of the 15th century, is not necessarily derived from a word for a young pig. The term Hogg was used also to mean a young sheep. As is usually the case, the early instances of Hogg as a surname do not throw any light upon what the word was understood to mean in Sussex when it was employed as a nickname in the 13th century, and its original significance must remain doubtful. It may even be relevant that the word 'hogge' can in Middle English mean a ship, of some type which is not clear.[17] The term 'hogboat' was still being used early in the present century for a type of fishing boat peculiar to the Brighton district.[18]. As most of the medieval instances of the surname Hogg in Sussex occur in the parts of East Sussex near the coast, this might be a possible origin. The name Cog, also derived from a word for a type of ship, appears in Sussex during the 13th and 14th centuries.[19] It is consequently not easy to say what the original significance of many surnames derived from nicknames was.

Two other factors raise questions about surnames in this cateogory. One of these, which concerns a limited number of surnames, is the existence during the 14th and 15th centuries especially, of fictitious characters in certain types of record, mostly men listed as pledges. Fictitious characters are often provided with surnames of the nickname type. Those two well-known legal fictions, John Doe and Richard Roe, appear as pledges in 15th century Sussex, and both William Doo and Richard Doo, listed as pledges in the county at the same period, seem to be fictitious too.[20] Catt appears as a surname in Sussex from the 13th century onwards, and it still survived there in the 16th and 17th, but some 15th century men named Catt seem to be fictitious.[21] Some other instances of surnames derived from nicknames look suspiciously like the names of fictitious characters, but it is at times difficult to be sure.

The second element of doubt also affects a small number of surnames, though one or two of these are ones which had a long history in the county. There is some doubt about whether some surnames are derived from place-names, or from nicknames. The name Chantemerle, for example, could be from a French place-name.[22] The surname existed in Sussex from the mid 13th century. Most of the instances come from the district around Chichester, though not from the city itself, and although there are a few references in East Sussex, they all seem to concern individuals who also appear in the Chichester area. Those involved seem to have been substantial free tenants, probably belonging to the class of franklins.[23] Probably all were from a single family. Forms such as de Chantemerle have not been found in Sussex, and it must be doubtful if the surname there originates from a place-name. Two other compound surnames of French origin about which there are similar doubts are Passeavant and Totemond, both of which could be derived from French place-names.[24] Passeavant was a rare name in medieval Sussex, and does not seem to have survived.[25] There is no indication in the Sussex evidence that the surname originated from a place-name, though that remains possible. Totemund appears at Chichester during the 14th century.[26] It seems probable, however, that this is a later form of the name which appears in the city during the late 12th and the 13th centuries as Tuthome or Tothome. The Latinised form *Toto Mundo* occurs in 1257, and Totemond may have developed from this.[27] If Tuthome, or Tothome, is in fact an earlier form of Totemond, then Totemond is unlikely to be derived from a place-name. A fourth surname which might be locative in origin is Petipas, but only one instance has been found in Sussex, the name does not seem to have survived there, and its origin must be uncertain.[28] Other names with a similar meaning, such as Trottesmale and Trotemenu, can be found in Sussex during the 13th century, but it does not seem that Petipas is a translation of any of these.[29] Although it is impossible to be certain, and locative origins are possible, it seems more likely that all the four names mentioned above are nicknames in origin so far as the Sussex examples are concerned. None of them has been found in the county in a form which is clearly derived from a place-name.

The surnames just considered are all French linguistically. There are a small group of English names about which there may be similar doubts. These include the names Clenewater (? or Clevewater), Hetewater, and Schentewater.[30] The probability is that all these names are topographical. The *Place-names of Sussex* connects Agnes de Clenewater (1327), with the place-name of Clevewaters Farm, in the inland parish of Wivelsfield.[31] Two other instances of the name, neither of which has a preposition, occurs in the coastal area, near Shoreham, some distance from Wivelsfield. This could be due to migration from Wivelsfield, but it is possible that two distinct names are involved. Clenewater may have existed as a surname or bye-name in the Shoreham area, and Agnes' name, perhaps in reality 'Clevewater', may have been mis-spelt. Hetewater and Schentewater are both found in coastal townships, and though neither is preceded by a preposition (de, de la, or atte) which would establish a locative or topographical origin, it seems likely that both names were in fact topographical, and were not derived from nicknames.

Whithorn is another surname with doubtful origins. Reaney suggested that the name might be due to the possession of a notable drinking horn, and this seems feasible if not particularly likely.[32] It is also possible that the name contains a sexual innuendo.[33] A third possibility, however, is that the name is topographical. The surname or bye-name Wodehorn, found in West Sussex, is from one or other of the localities called Woodhorn in that part of the country.[34]

One further complication in considering the origins of surnames from nicknames is that some surnames which apparently fall into this category may in fact not be derived from nicknames. This is true even of a common and apparently straightforward name like Brown, which appears in medieval Sussex as the name of persons very varying in status, from unfree tenants to knights.[35] It was already a common name in the county during the 13th century. Forms such as le Brun show that in some instances the surname was derived from a nickname, presumably for someone with brown hair or complexion.[36] However, Brun occurs as a Christian name in Sussex in the 13th century, and the surname may be derived from a first name in some cases.[37] In addition, in the 15th century an alien named Broun, of unknown nationality, is listed in Sussex.[38] In this instance Broun was probably an Anglicised form of a surname in some other language, probably one which was a cognate form with Brown. The form Atte Broune has been found in one example,[39] but this is probably one of the numerous instances of a preposition being used with a surname in error. The surname Brunecok or Browncock is probably derived from a diminutive of the personal name Brun. Brunecok was in use as a Christian name in Sussex during the 13th century.[40]

Some other surnames have more than one possible origin. Rede (Reede, Reade, etc.) was already a common surname or bye-name in Sussex during the 13th century, and present in many parts of the county. The frequent appearance of forms such as le Rede[41] shows that in many cases the surname was derived from a nickname, for a person with red hair or complexion. So does the use of Latin forms such as *Rubeus* to translate Rede.[42] However, the topographical name atte Rede also existed in the county, and was fairly common there.[43] Even during the 13th and 14th centuries, it is sometimes impossible to be sure what the origin of names like Rede, Read, Ryede, etc., is, and when such names are found at later periods, such as the 16th or 17th centuries, it is usually impossible to be certain of the derivation. The surname Stammer or Stamer similarly has two different origins in Sussex. The name le Stamer existed in West Sussex from the early 14th century. All the instances seem to concern a single family, connected with Prinstead and Marden, on the western edge of the county.[44] This is clearly a surname of the nickname type, meaning 'stammerer'. Some members of the family from Prinstead and Marden also appear at Worthing, and in the 17th century the name Stammer still survived in the Worthing area.[45] Although no connected pedigree can be traced, the probability is that this represents the survival of an hereditary surname in that part of Sussex from about 1300. However, in the 14th century the name de Stammer existed in East Sussex. This is from a local place-name, Stanmer (near Brighton), which occurs as Stamere during the 14th century. It is probable that the several cases of the surname or bye-name Stamer, without any preposition or article, found in East Sussex from the late 13th century are derived from this place-name.[46] The name Stamer found in East Sussex during the 16th century, in much the same area as the medieval occurences, again probably represents the survival in one part of the county of an hereditary surname, derived in this case from a local place-name.[47] The name Stammer, or Stamer, has always been a rare one. Despite this, it had two different origins within one county. The name persisted over a long period in two areas, one in East Sussex, one in West, and because of this it is possible to make a reasonable conjecture what the origins were of surnames which are found at relatively later periods. This would not be possible, had the two versions of the name become more dispersed.

Ferret (Firret, Furet) is another name for which several origins are possible. The obvious derivation is from the mammal so called, and so far as Sussex is concerned this is probably the correct one. It has been suggested that this could be a topographical name, similar to Gravett, Burchet, Naldrett, etc., but forms such as atte Ferret or de la Ferret have not been found.[48] The surnames Feret and Ferret, with varying origins, exist in France,[49] and the relatively large number of French surnames in Sussex means that such an origin seems quite feasible. There is, however, no evidence of French origin. The 13th and 14th century examples of the name in Sussex have all been found at or near Albourne, and probably concern one family.[50] During the 15th century it appears further east in the county. In the late 15th and the 16th centuries several people so named were prominent inhabitants of Winchelsea, and in the 16th century the name occurs elsewhere in the same part of Sussex. It was still present not far from Albourne in the 16th century. The name had spread to the north-west of the county by 1642.[51] The name does occur in other counties at an early period, and it is always possible that some of the later examples in Sussex may have been brought into the county by migration, but it is probable that the spread of the surname in Sussex was due to a gradual dispersal from Albourne.

Such cases show how difficult it often is to be certain about the origins of surnames which may seem, at first sight, to have obvious derivations from nicknames. Though there are corresponding obscurities about the origins of some surnames in other categories, the uncertainties which exist about how surnames derived from nicknames arose make the problems more acute with names of this type.

SURNAMES FROM DIMINUTIVES OF NICKNAMES

There are a number of instances in Sussex where surnames have been formed from diminutives or hypochoristic forms of words which, in unmodified form, have given rise to surnames of the nickname type. Friend is an established Sussex surname, and Frendekyn, also a surname in the county, is from a diminutive of Friend. Love is a surname in the county, and Lovecock and Lovekin both exist there as surnames. There is, of course, nothing surprising in surnames or bye-names developing from diminutives or hypochoristic forms. Surnames arising in this way are very common among surnames derived from personal names, and it would be natural for diminutives to develop from nicknames, which were colloquially used. It is, however, uncertain if surnames which exhibit diminutives or hypochoristic forms are derived from nicknames which existed in such forms before giving rise to surnames, or if surnames which exhibit diminutives or hypochoristic forms have evolved from existing surnames (originally derived from nicknames), which did not themselves exhibit such forms. It is not clear, for instance, if Fynchecok has arisen from a word 'finchcock' already in use as a nickname, or if it has arisen as a form of Finch, already existing as a surname.

There is some evidence which suggests that in such cases some surnames developed through the addition of suffixes which modified existing surnames (derived from nicknames) into diminutives or pet-forms, and that this process sometimes took place after surnames had become stable and hereditary. For example, William Faircock, a late 14th century bondman at Streatham, was also known as William Fair. His holding included a cotage which had been held previously by an earlier William Fayre, presumably an ancestor.[52] In this case Faircock seems to have been formed as a diminutive of the existing, and probably hereditary, surname Fair or Fayre. Possibly William Faircock may have ben so called to distinguish him from the earlier William Fayre. There are other cases where a diminutive or hypochoristic form of a surname appears in an area where the surname in question, not in a diminutive or hypochoristic form, had already existed for some time. For example, the surname Finch (or Fynch, Vinch, etc.) was from the 13th century present in the east of Sussex, where one family named Finch became major landowners (later Earls of Winchelsea). In the late 14th century Fynchecok appears as a surname in the same area.[53] It must be suspected that Fynchecok developed as a pet-form of the existing surname Finch. Similarly Not or Nott was a surname in the east of Sussex from the late 13th century. In the late 14th century Notkyn appears as a surname in the same area. Notkyn was a rare surname, but it survived, and was still present in the same part of Sussex in the 16th century.[54] In the 15th century Notkyng was the name of an alien, from Brabant, living at Lewes,

[55] but as Notkyn can be found considerably earlier in Sussex, the beginnings of the surname in the county cannot be attributed to this immigration. The surname or bye-name Love occurs at Horsham *c.* 1275, and it also appears at other places in the vicinity at about the same date; in the mid 14th century the name Lovekin also occurs at Horsham.[56] The name Lovecok, found at Winchelsea in the 13th century, was probably also a diminutive formed from the surname Love.[57]

The name Merlot, or Marlot, is a more complicated example. The surname Merle has two different origins in Sussex. In some instances it is found in the form de Merle,[58] which is derived from one of the localities now called Marley. The surname in this form occurs at Brede, where it is probably from Marley Farm in that township[59] and some examples may be from Marley Farm, near Battle,[60] or from a locality called Merle at Rackham.[61] Some examples of de Merle are not near any of the Sussex places named Marley, and it is possible that the surname may in some cases have originated from a place-name outside Sussex. In particular, the name de Merle occurs at Annington, near Bramber, which is not very close to any of the Sussex localities just mentioned. However, the name also appears in the form le Merle, in which form it is evidently a surname of the nickname type, from the French word for 'blackbird'.[62] The medieval examples of le Merle were all either at West Firle, or at places very near to Bramber, such as Coombes.[63] The name Merle, often given without any article or preposition, existed in West Firle from about the middle of the 12th century, and it survived there until at least the mid 14th.[64] The name was probably hereditary at West Firle from the mid 12th century. There seems to have been some confusion between the two surnames, de Merle and le Merle, as early as *c.* 1300. This is suggested by the existence of the form de Merle at Annington, and the presence of le Merle, at Coombes nearby, for it must be suspected that, in view of the close proximity of the two places, a single family was involved. When surnames such as Merle or Marley are found at relatively late periods like the 15th and 16th centuries, it is generally not possible to be certain of their origins.[65] It is also difficult to be sure in all cases of the origin of the name Morley in Sussex. This was a widespread surname in West Sussex during the 17th century. One landed family so called is said to have originated in Morley (Lancs.), but the surname may be from one of the Sussex places called Marley,[66] especially as the forms Morley and Marley were at times used interchangeably in surnames.

The surname Merlot has first been found in Sussex about 1220, when it occurs in connection with Yapton. Later in the 13th century the name existed at Coombes (near Bramber), where le Merle was also present, and at two townships near together in West Sussex, Eartham and Walberton.[67] During the 14th century the surname survived at Eartham and Walberton, where it had probably been hereditary from at least *c.* 1270, and it also occured at Steyning and Botolphs, near Coombes, having probably been hereditary in that area (around Bramber) from the late 13th century.[68] Apart from these places, Merlot has been discovered in Sussex before 1400 at Arundel and at Broadwater, but this instance apparently concerns a member of the Merlot family of Annington, in Botolphs.[69] In view of the previous existence of the name le Merle, at Annington, it must seem very probable that Merlot has been formed as a diminutive of the surname Merle. This seems to be a case of a diminutive which is French linguistically being formed in England. Such a diminutive could not have been formed from a locative surname such as de Merle, and it must be supposed that there had been confusion at an early period between le Merle and de Merle. It is unwise to rely too much upon the presence of prepositions or articles in individual cases as evidence for the origins of surnames, and it is likely that in some of the source material articles or prepositions have been used in error here.

Marlot or Merlot continued as a surname at Annington during the 15th century.[70] In the late 14th century Merlot was the name of a family holding land at Shipley, rather further north in West Sussex than Annington. It seems likely that the Shipley family were connected with the Merlots who occur earlier at Annington, but no genealogical link has been established. In the late 14th century the Merlot family of Shipley held lands at Southwick and elsewhere on the coast, not far from Broadwater. This family was still owning land at and near Shipley in the 17th century. The usual spelling of the name during the 16th and 17th centuries was Marlott. The surname survived in Sussex to later periods.[71]

A few other names which appear in Sussex seem to have originated as diminutives or hypochoristic terms of existing surnames in the nickname category. Frendekyn, a rare bye-name which occurs at Pevensey, is probably from Friend, a well established surname in East Sussex.[72] Whitcock, which has not been found in Sussex before 1500, may be from the common surname White, which appears in many parts of the county from the 13th century onwards.[73] Duckel, which was a quite widespread name in Sussex in the late 13th and early 14th centuries, and may have originated exclusively in the county, is said to be a diminutive of Duck, and may have been formed from the surname Duck (le Duk), which existed in the county at the same period.[74] It seems probable that in these cases some surnames have come into existence through the formation of diminutives or hypochoristic terms from existing surnames or bye-names, often from surnames which had been hereditary for several generations.

SURNAMES ESPECIALLY COMMON IN SUSSEX

Very few surnames derived from nicknames have at any time been peculiar to Sussex. Even rare compound surnames or bye-names, such as those discussed earlier in this chapter,[75] frequently occur in other counties as well. There are, however, some surnames in this category which have been over a long period much more numerous in Sussex than in most other parts of England, such as, for example, Blondel (or Blundel), Bost (or Bust), Cobbe, Fest (or Fist), Finch (or Vinch), Fowle (or Vowle, Fougyll, etc.), Friend, Hogge, Love, Peacock, Pentecost, Pollard, Poke (or Pouke, Puck, etc.), Steer, Wisdom, and Wise.[76] All these can be found in other counties, and some, indeed, are names which have been present in most parts of England since the 13th century, but they are all names which have been more numerous in Sussex than in most other counties since before 1500. All these names, too, are ones which appear as dispersed already in several different parts of the county in the late 13th and early 14th centuries, when enough evidence first becomes avialable to form some impression of the way in which individual surnames are distributed. Of course there is no period during the Middle Ages when information is sufficiently copious to provide even an approximately complete view of the incidence of surnames throughout the whole of any county, but it is possible, using late 13th and early 14th century sources, to be sure that by that period some surnames are already widely dispersed. It is consequently unlikely that any of the surnames just listed originated in one family. There are some surnames derived from nicknames which when they first occur in the available sources are confined to a single township, or to several contiguous townships, and in such cases it may reasonably be supposed that each such surname was in origin that of one family. These names are discussed below.[77] Some of them had by the 16th century become quite numerous in the county, but the factors which lead to the surnames of some families multiplying considerably, while those of others remain rare, or die out, require separate consideration. If the surnames listed at the beginning of this paragraph are examined, it can be seen that although all are derived from nicknames of one type or another, they are in most respects very varied. Some are from words for birds or animals, some from terms for physical characteristics, some have other derivations. It is true that a high proportion of these surnames which have long been common in Sussex are monosyllabic, and that certain types of compound names are lacking. There are, for instances as already pointed out, some Sussex surnames which are derived from oaths or similar expressions, but none of these have ever been at all numerous in the county, and those which survived, and which can still be found in the county after about 1500, like Godsmark or Godshalf, for instance, seem to have survived as the surname of a single family, though the families concerned in some cases ramified considerably. There were also a group of compound names such as Litelrolve, Litelwatte, Lytilscot, Petijohn, etc., found in Sussex during the 13th, 14th and 15th centuries. Most though not all of the Sussex instances of names in this group come from one area of the county, the southern part of East Sussex, and there may have been a local habit in that district of forming surnames or bye-names of such a type.[78] (Early examples of such names can be found in other counties, and it is not suggested that the formation of names in this group was unique to Sussex.) There are a fair number of medieval instances of surnames or bye-names in this group, but none of the individual names was ever at all numerous, and none of these names seems to have survived into the 16th century. There are, therefore, some types of surnames derived from nicknames which have not contributed to the set of surnames in the category which were numerous and widely dispersed in Sussex from an early period. Compound surnames in this category tend generally to be rarer from the start than simplex names, to proliferate less, and to become extinct in a higher proportion of cases. There are exceptions, and some compound surnames dervived from nicknames have become numerous, often through the ramification of individual families, but broadly speaking compound surnames of this type are uncommon. If this general tendency is allowed for, and if the absence of certain not very important groups of names is taken into account too, it can be seen that the batch of surnames derived from nicknames which were plentiful and widespread in medieval Sussex were varied in character, and do not have any particular features in common. The surnames or bye-names derived from nicknames which appear in the county during the period before about 1500 are semantically multifarious, but it cannot be said that there was any one semantic type of surname which gave rise to a particularly high proportion of surnames which became very numerous, or to a particularly high proportion of surnames which survived into the 16th century and later.

Some surnames derived from nicknames, including those listed above, have been part of the general body of Sussex surnames for centuries, and in many cases remain so to the present day. It is therefore intended to examine briefly the history of some surnames in this category.

Blundel

The name Blunt (le Blound, *Blundus*) existed in Sussex from the 12th century. One family so named were landowners at West Dean (West Sussex) from the late 12th century onwards, but the name was present in East Sussex, where it existed at Winchelsea over a long period during the 13th century, and was probably hereditary. In the 13th century Blunt appeared in several parts of Sussex, as the name people of varying status, thought it was not numerous.[79] Though the references to Blund are dispersed, most of the 12th and 13th century instances occur in the southern part of West Sussex, around Chichester.

The name Blundell (or Blondell) first appears in Sussex in the same area. The 13th century examples of Blundel (or Blondel) are too scattered for it to be likely that all concern one family, and it is probable that the surname arose independently at several places in West Sussex, perhaps in all cases as a diminutive formed from the existing surname Blund. There are some 13th century references to the name in East Sussex, but these seem to concern an individual who also held land in West Sussex.[80] During the 14th and 15th centuries the surname appears at Chichester, and at several places nereby.[81] Though the medieval examples of the name in Sussex are somewhat dispersed, after 1500 almost all the instances are at Petworth or the parishes to the south of that town. The 1642 Protestation Returns show Blundel as a well-established surname in that area, but nowhere else in West Sussex.[82] It is probable that this situation is due to the name having survived into the 16th century as the surname of a single family, the name having probably existed in some places without having become hereditary, and some families so called and having Blundell as a hereditary name, having died out.

Cobbe

Cobbe has been a widely distributed surname in Sussex from the 13th century onwards. No examples of it have been found in the county before 1200, though instances have been found elsewhere in England at earlier periods. The surname probably originated from a nickname with the meaning 'big, stout'. It has been suggested that the name might originate from a topographical term, but forms such as atte Cobbe have not been found at all in Sussex.[83] By the late 13th century Cobbe was already a widely distributed surname in both East and West Sussex, and the early occurences of the name are too scattered for it to be supposed that all can have sprung from a single family, or even several families. The surname must have been derived from a nickname which was in frequent use throughout the county.[84] The surname did, however, persist over long periods in several areas, suggesting that it had become hereditary as the surname of several distinct families. It existed at Arlington, and at some adjoining places such as Litlington, from the late 13th century onwards, and it was still in the same area in the 17th;[85] it existed in Hurstpierpoint at the end of the 13th century, and was still there in the 16th;[86] there are instances of the name from the 14th century at Icklesham, in the south-east of the county, it appears during the 15th at several places nearby, such as Ore, Wilting, and Hastings, and it was prominent during the 16th at Rye and Winchelsea, which are in the same part of the county;[87] and in West Sussex the name persisted in the area around Bramber and Steyning from the late 13th century, and was still in the same district in the 17th.[88] It seems probable that in each of these areas a family with Cobbe as hereditary surname survived over a long period. This contrasts with the history of some other surnames in the county, for there are cases where surnames which were moderately common in Sussex during the Middle Ages seem to have each survived into the 16th century as the hereditary surname of a single family. During the 16th and 17th centuries Cobbe remained a numerous surname in Sussex. There are many individuals of the name in the 1524-5 subsidy for the county, and in the West Sussex part of the 1641-2 Protestation Returns. There are also many references to the name in some Sussex parish registers, such as those for Horsham.[89] It is still a widespread name in Sussex.

The form Cobby (Cobey, etc.) has first been found in 1332, but apart from this single example, no cases are known in the county until the 15th century. All the instances of Cobby which have been found before 1500 in Sussex, are in the east of the county, but in the 16th century the form occurs frequently in West Sussex too.[90] The form Cobby seems to have developed from Cobbe independently in several different parts of the county. Cobby, too, survives as a Sussex surname.

Fist

The surname Fist (or Fest, Fust, Feist), was presumably given to an aggressive person, or perhaps to someone who was more than usually inclined to come to blows. None of the Sussex instances provide any evidence about the way in which the name was bestowed or acquired, but this obscurity is unfortunately usual where surnames derived from nicknames are involved. The name appears in Sussex during the late 13th and early 14th centuries at a considerable number of separate places, not all in one part of the county, though the surname was more widespread in West Sussex then in East. During the first half of the 14th century the name occurs at Lewes, and it seems likely that it was hereditary there,[91] but it seems subsequently to have died out in East Sussex. Very possibly it disappeared in that part of the county during the population loses of the mid 14th century. In West Sussex the surname existed at Warnham from the late 13th century, and its persistence there indicates that it was hereditary.[92] In the 14th century Fist appeared at Horsham, a parish contiguous to Warnham, from where the surname had probably spread. The surname survived at Horsham for centuries, and eventually became very numerous there. During the 16th and 17th centuries the name was present in several parishes very near to Horsham, such as Shipley, Billingshurst, Itchingfield, and Wisborough. Although it is not possible to trace connected pedigrees, it is probable that the most if not all the persons named Fist, Feist, etc., appearing at and around Horsham were descended from the family so called who first occur at Warnham in the 13th century.[93] If this is so, the family must have proliferated to a great extent, over a period of several centuries. Further south in West Sussex

Fist existed at Wiston in the 14th century. It also appears during the same period at Sullington nearby. Although, again, no connected pedigree can be traced, the surname still survived at Wiston in the 17th and 18th centuries.[94] Besides these instances, the surname occurs at Binstead, near Chichester, in the early 14th century, and at Chichester itself, and at nearby places such as Bosham and Yapton, in the 15th.[95] All this suggests the rise of several families with Fist as a hereditary surname, though probably with the surname eventually disappearing for a time in East Sussex.

During the 17th century there are instances of the name Fist, Feist, etc., in the north west part of East Sussex, at, for example, Crawley, Cowfold, and Hurstpierpoint.[96] The surname was, however, much more common in West Sussex, where it is listed in eleven different places, many of them in the Horsham area, in the Protestant Returns of 1642.[97] The spread of the surname into the western part of East Sussex was probably due to dispersal from Horsham, where it had become very numerous. This is clearly a case of a surname which, unlike many others, not only originated in many different localities in the county, but survived as a hereditary surname in several separate lines throughout the later Middle Ages and into the 16th century, to proliferate considerably at later periods. The forms Feest, Feist, and Feast still survive in Sussex.

Fowle

The surname Fowle (Fugell, Fogell, Vowle, etc.) (from fowl in the sense 'bird') is one which has existed in Sussex from about 1200. The name was never confined to Sussex, and there are early examples in other counties, including Kent, where the name became common, but the surname became exceptionally numerous in Sussex.[98] About 1200 a Fleming called Fugel was the tenant of some marshland near Rye. It is unfortunately not clear whether Fugel was his Christian name or whether it was a bye-name or surname.[99] However, a William Fugel, holding property at Rye early in the 13th century, and possibly a descendant of the Fleming just mentioned, certainly had a surname or bye-name of Fugel.[100] William is the first individual who clearly had Fugel as a surname or bye-name to be discovered in Sussex. In the late 13th century Fugel (Fughel, etc.) occurs as a surname or bye-name at Winchelsea, close to Rye, and at localities in Beckley parish nearby, the parish in which the land held by Fugel the Fleming probably lay. During the 14th century the surname survived in Beckley, and it appeared in the adjoining parishes of Brede and Peasmarsh.[101] The name persisted in the same area during the 15th and 16th centuries. By the 16th it had developed into widely varying forms, Fowle, Fowyll, Fowgyll, Vowle, Voyll, Vugill, and Vugle among others.[102] As late as the 16th century, however, the name of a single family might be spelt in a diversity of forms, often differing substantially. The name of Vugles farm, at Newick, is derived from one of the less common variants of the surname.[103]

An apparently quite separate group of persons named le Foghell or le Fughel were living at East Grinstead, in the north of East Sussex, during the 13th and 14th centuries.[104] During the 15th century Fowle (Fogyll, Foghill, etc.) existed as a surname at Rotherfield, and in the late 15th and 16th centuries it was present at Ticehurst, Etchingham, and Wadhurst, to which places it had apparently spread from Rotherfield.[105] Rotherfield is no great distance either from East Grinstead, or from Beckley and Brede, and the surname may have spread to Rotherfield, and subsequently to adjoining places, from one or other of those localities.

There is also evidence for the surname in two other areas of the county. It existed from the 13th century at several places around Hurstpierpoint, and it was still in the same part of Sussex in the 16th.[106] The surname was also present from the late 13th century at many places around Chichester, though it has not been found in the city itself until the 14th. The name was still very common in the same area in the 16th century.[107] There are so many references to the name in this area that there were probably several families so called with hereditary surnames in that part of the county.

In the cases discussed above, the surname persisted in particular areas sufficiently for it to be reasonably certain that a hereditary surname existed in each instance. In addition, however, there are very many scattered examples of the name in medieval Sussex. Probably in many cases these were individuals with bye-names, which did not become hereditary. By the early 16th century, the surname was very numerous and widespread in the county. In the subsidy returns of 1524–5 it is listed at 18 different places, though a minority of the county's population is assessed in this source.[108] It is in Sussex at the present day in several different forms, Fowle, Fuggle, Fowlie, etc., despite the existence of 'fowl' in general use in modern English. The surname Fogwell, found at the present time in Sussex, and in the Portsmouth district of Hampshire, near the Sussex border, may also be a form of Fowle. Fogwell has the appearance of a surname derived from a place-name, but no place-name from which the surname might have originated has been discovered. Forms such as Fowlie, which exist to-day in both Sussex and Hampshire, have probably arisen through the tendency of a final 'e' to become 'y' or 'ie' in Sussex.[109] Forms such as Fowls, Vowles, Fuggles or Vuggles have not been found in Sussex during the Middle Ages, though Fowls existed in other counties. It is probable that Fowls, Fuggles and similar variants are not patronymics with a genitival 's', but have developed through the acquisition by surnames such as Fowle, Fuggle, etc., of an inorganic 's', probably at a relatively late period.

The name Fowling existed in the early 14th century in East Sussex.

Most of the examples concern Salehurst, where the name was probably hereditary from about 1300. Later in the 14th century the surname appears at Chichester.[110] Fowling is a patronymic, formed from Fugel. It has not been found in use as a Christian name in Sussex. Early examples of Fowling as a surname seem to be confined to Sussex, and it may have been a surname which originated exclusively there.[111] Fowle was in use as a Christian name in the county in 1524, but this is probably an early example of the practive of using surnames as first names, a habit which became more usual among some sections of the population in the second half of the same century.[112] Fowling may have originated in Sussex from the use there of Fugel as a Christian name as, possibly, in the case of the Fleming mentioned above.

Salehurst is in an area where Fowle, etc., was quite a common surname during the Middle Ages.

Fowle is a further instance of a name which originated in the county as the hereditary surname of several distinct families, and which has survived in Sussex up to the present. It has not multiplied very greatly, as a few Sussex surnames have done, and as many names with a similar early history have done in Lancashire and West Yorkshire, but it has persisted as a well established surname in Sussex.

Friend

The surname Friend (usually Frend in early references) is one which has for long been widespread in England. Possibly the name arose through a person being addressed as 'friend', but that is uncertain. In Sussex the name was present from an early period in two areas, one in the south west around Chichester, one in the east near the Kent border. There are a few medieval instances elsewhere; in the 13th century the name was present at and near Midhurst, and during the 14th the name existed at Erringham, near Shoreham, for a sufficiently long period to show that it had become hereditary there, but both around Midhurst and at Erringham the name seems to have died out, probably during the late 14th century. A few isolated examples can be found elsewhere in the county, probably cases in which the name did not become hereditary. Both in the south-west of Sussex, and in the eastern border, the surname survived from the 14th century, to be still present in both areas in the 16th.[113] This persistence of the name in each of the areas concerned shows that the name was hereditary from the 14th century. In fact, some land at Ticehurst remained in the hands of a family called Frend from the late 14th century until the 17th.[114] The early references to the name in East Sussex are sufficiently concentrated geographically to make it likely that all those involved belonged to one family. Most of those so named in East Sussex were small freeholders, or, in the late 16th century, copyholders. In the south-west of the county the early examples are more dispersed, and more than one family may have been involved. Even allowing for this possibility, however, the survival of the surname for a long period in two very limited areas in the county is notable. The name was slightly more dispersed in the 16th century than in the 14th, but it had not spread very much in the intervening years, nor had it increased greatly in numbers. Friend still exists in Sussex at the present day, and has become fairly numerous in the east of the county.

Hogg

Hogg, like Friend, was not a surname confined to Sussex, and there were medieval examples in several other counties, but it became more common in Sussex than in most other parts of England, and it became particularly concentrated in one part of that county. Possibly the name may have been occupational, and not a nickname. Until about 1350 the name was widely distributed in Sussex. Most instances were in East Sussex, and in that half of the county the name was very dispersed. There were, however, a few scattered cases in West Sussex. It is probable that the name was never hereditary in the west, as it seems to have died out there, and was absent from that part of the county for a long period. The Protestation Returns for West Sussex do not list anyone named Hogg, and it is possible that the name disappeared in the western half of the county about the middle of the 14th century, and was still absent 300 years later.[115] In the east of the county, however, the surname persisted. It survived during the 13th and 14th centuries at Southover, near Lewes, and was almost certainly hereditary there.[116] Most medieval instances of the name in Sussex, however, were further east in the county, in places not far from the Kent border. The name occured at Brede and Udimore in the late 13th century, and it continued to exist there, and at other places nearby such as Ore, Rye and Ewhurst during the 14th and 15th centuries, and into the 16th.[117] It is likely that the continued existence of the surname in this limited area was due to the survival there of one family with a hereditary surname. Early in the 15th century Hogg appears in an area rather more to the north-west, at Brightling, Dallington and Frontridge, all places lying close together. The name was still in this part of the county in the 16th century.[118] During the 15th and 16th centuries the surname was also present at Hastings.[119] It is probable that the name's presence both around Brightling, and at Hastings, was due to it having spread from the district around Brede and Udimore. Judging by the 1524–5 subsidy roll, the surname does not seem to have dispersed very much in Sussex by the early 16th century.

It seems possible that the name Hogg survived in Sussex in a single area in the east of the county, and it was there originally the name of one family. The name did exist in other parts of Sussex, but there seems to have died out during the second half of the 14th century. If this is true, it is likely that all the Sussex Hoggs shared a common ancestry. Hogg still survives as a numerous surname in Sussex, mainly in the east of the county.

The surname Hoget existed during the 16th century in East Sussex, in much the same area as Hogg, but it is uncertain if Hoget is a diminutive formed from the surname Hogg. The surname Huget (or Hughet, Hughot), which is from a diminutive of Hugh, occurs in the same part of the county at earlier periods, and Hoget (or Hoggett) may be a later development of Huget,[120] although Hoget etc., may be from the use of the word to mean a young boar or sheep.

Pooke

The surname Pooke (or Puck, Poke, Puke, Pouke) is derived from a word meaning 'goblin' or 'elf'. The term in question is an element in several minor Sussex place-names.[121] It is also an element in some Sussex field names.[122] Pouke Lane, at Chichester, is mentioned about 1266, and a road called Pokestrete at Tottingworth, is mentioned in 1436.[123] These examples of the element are widely distributed throughout Sussex, and it must have been widely used in the county. In Sussex the surname usually occurs before 1500 as Pouke or Puke. Later the form Pook was frequently used. It has been suggested that the form Poke, or le Poke, was an occupational surname, from the trade of making pokes or bags.[124] However, the form Poke is rare in medieval Sussex, and is used for the names of individuals whose surnames also appear in the forms Pouke or Puke; Robert Poke, for example, mentioned at Shermanbury in 1341, is also mentioned as Robert Puke and Robert Pouke.[125] William le Poke, at Wadhurst about 1280–90, is also named as William le Puke.[126] These are the only persons found in Sussex before 1500 with names in the form Poke. At a later period Gilbert Poke, a 16th century copyholder at Robertsbridge, was also referred to as Pooke.[127]

During the 13th century and the first half of the 14th the name Pouke (Puke, etc.) was widely distributed in Sussex. The name existed at Chichester, and in the coastal area south of the city, and it was sufficiently numerous and persistent in this part of the county to make it probable that it was hereditary there from some time in the 13th century.[128] In the 13th century, and for much of the 14th, the surname survived at and around Shermanbury, in central Sussex, where again it was probably hereditary.[129] It occurs in 1332 at Slaugham, not far from Shermanbury, and this may have been due to migration from the Shermanbury district.[130] At Burpham and Storrington, two places close together in the eastern portion of West Sussex, there are some 13th and 14th century examples, and

Pouke may have been hereditary there too. The name was, however, most numerous in the easternmost part of Sussex, near the Kent border. It existed there at a number of places during the 13th, 14th and 15th centuries.[131] At one or two places in this area, such as Wadhurst, the name persisted for several generations, so that it was probably hereditary. It seems likely that all the people named Pouke, etc., found in this part of Sussex during the Middle Ages shared a common descent. There were, in addition, a few scattered instances of the name elsewhere in East Sussex. These may be cases of bye-names which never became hereditary.[132]

In the 16th century Pouke (Poke, etc.) was almost entirely limited in Sussex to the district near the Kent border, where it had been present from the 13th century. There it was quite a numerous surname, and had proliferated considerably.[133] The name also appears at Hailsham, further west in East Sussex.[134] One isolated example has been found near Chichester, but it is doubtful if this was due to the survival of the surname in that quarter, where it had been absent during the 15th century, so far as can be seen from the available sources.[135] Although proof is not possible, it seems likely that Pouke disappeared both in the west of Sussex, and in the Shermanbury district during the late 14th century, and that the surname survived in Sussex in the easternmost part of the county only. Subsequently it ramified considerably there, probably as a result of the descendants of one family multiplying. In the 17th century the Protestation Returns for West Sussex do not include any examples of Pooke, etc., and it is probable that the surname had died out in West Sussex.

At the present day, Pooke is still a widespread surname in East Sussex. It exists in West Sussex, but is less common there. The form Poke is still in use, but is rare. The surname Puckey, found to-day in East Sussex, and also in Hampshire, is probably a late development from Pooke or Puke. Pooke has long been present as a surname in Kent, Hampshire and Dorset, and should not be considered as an exclusively Sussex name.

It is difficult to be certain about the origins of the surname Puckle, found at the present day in East Sussex. It could have originated from a diminutive of Pooke, Puke, etc.,[136] but it must be doubtful if the surname has that derivation in the county. (The name Pusel, found in West Sussex during the 14th century, was probably French in origin.)[137] The name de Pukehol occurs near Battle about 1300.[138] Some land called Pookhole is mentioned at Westfield in 1567, and at the same period there was land called Pookeholde at Burwash. Both these localities are near to Battle, and either could have given rise to the surname de Pukehol.[139] In Sussex Puckle has probably developed from de Pukehol ('goblin's hollow').

Steer

Steer is at the present day one of the more common Sussex surnames. The name was never confined to Sussex; it has long been a common name in Surrey, and there are medieval instances in most counties in the southern half of England. According to Domesday Book, the personal name Sterre was in use in Hampshire in 1086, and this could possibly have been the origin of the surname in some cases. The frequent occurence of forms such as le Ster, however, show that the surname was often, and probably always, derived from a nickname. It may be one of the quite large group of surnames derived from words for species of mammals, birds, fishes, etc. Alternatively, the word may be from the use of the word to mean 'strong' or 'stout'. The widespread use of the nickname in England implies that it must have conveyed some fairly precise image, in a way which was understandable over a wide area, but as is so often the case with surnames derived from nicknames, it is not now possible to be sure what impression such a nickname would have given.

In Sussex Steer (Ster, etc.) can be found during the 13th and 14th centuries in several parts of the county. In the north west there are examples at Lurgashall, Selham, and River, three places all close together.[140] It is probable from the way in which the occurences are concentrated that all the persons involved belonged to one family. Another similar group existed in the coastal part of central Sussex, at Offington, Beeding, Heene, and Sompting, again all places close together, and again it is likely that all those named Steer in this area belonged to a single family.[141] A third group existed at the same period at Chiddingly, Waldron and East Hoathly, three contiguous parishes in East Sussex, and it is likely that here, too, all those in this group belonged to one family.[142] Besides these references, one person named le Ster appears at Chichester in the 13th century, but he may well have been someone who had migrated into the city from one of the areas in which Steer was an established name.[143] It seems probable from this evidence that the surname Steer originated in Sussex with three families, in different, and widely separated, parts of the county. No evidence has been found that any of these families originated through migration into the county from outside, though as the surname existed elsewhere, this might be possible.

During the 15th and 16th centuries, the name Steer persisted in northwest Sussex, at places not far from those where it had been found earlier. It was also still found in the coastal district around Sompting, etc. The appearance of the name in the 16th century at other places not far from this area, such as Albourne, may be due to the gradual dispersal of the surname from the coastal parts around Sompting. In East Sussex the name became more widespread during the 15th and 16th centuries. In the 16th century it still existed in Totnore Hundred, which is quite close to

Chiddingly, but it also occured at more distant places, such as Winchelsea.[144] In the 15th century there are a few references to the name at and near Chichester.[145] The surname still survived in the coastal part of central Sussex after 1600. In the northern part of West Sussex the surname became very widespread, probably chiefly through dispersal from the north west of the county. In some parishes in this part of Sussex, such as Horsham, the name became very numerous.[146] It is probable that this proliferation of the surname in the north of Sussex was mainly due to the natural increase of families named Steer already living in the north-west of the county, and it is probably that most, at least, of the people so named in the north of West Sussex were descended from those named Steer living in that area from the 13th century, though of course there may have been some movement from outside into that part of the county. The increase in the surname in this district is probably to be connected with a growth of population there, expanding mainly by natural increase, and surnames already well established becoming correspondingly more numerous. In the 17th century Steer was still a surname in the coastal portion of central Sussex, though not very numerous.[147] The absence of Protestation Returns for East Sussex makes it difficult to form any general view of the surname's distribution there during the 17th century, but the name did survive there.

At the present day there are still many people named Steer in East Sussex. In West Sussex the surname is rather less common, but it is by no means scarce there. The form Steers exists in East Sussex, and also in Hampshire. This seems to be a variant of relatively recent origin, and it is probably not an example of a patronymic formed with a genitival 's'.[148] It is probably one of the many cases of surnames acquiring an inorganic final 's', after existing for generations without one.

Early in the 16th century the surname Starre can be found in Sussex. No medieval examples have been found in the county, though there are early instances in other parts of England.[149] Starre is usually considered as a name quite distinct from Steer, and there is no reason to doubt that this is generally correct. However, most of the Sussex references to Starre in the 16th century concern Horsham, a parish where Steer had become very common, and this raises the possibility that in Sussex Starre may be a variant of Steer.[150] It has not been possible to find evidence that would show clearly that this is the case, and it is possible that Starre was brought into Sussex by migration.

Wisdom

The surname Wisdom has sometimes been held to be derived from a Devon place-name, but this origin is improbable, and there seems to be no serious doubt that the surname is from a nickname, with the obvious meaning.[151] The surname has never been confined to Sussex, but it has become numerous in one or two places in the county, after having had a long history there.

The examples of Wisdom in Sussex before the mid 14th century are in four groups, geographically, one in the townships lying just to the east of Chichester, a second near Worthing, a third in the north-west of the county, and a fourth at Eastbourne and Pevensey. It is probable that each of these groups originated with a single family, and that in each area the surname was hereditary from the late 13th or early 14th centuries.[152] The group in north west Sussex appears to have survived, for the surname still existed there during the 16th and 17th centuries, and in one or two parishes in that area, such as Cocking and Graffham, it became fairly common.[153] The surname still survived near Chichester in the 17th century, but it is doubtful if it had survived there continuously.[154] In the 15th century the name existed at Amberley, perhaps through migration from the district around Worthing, which is not far away, and during the 16th and 17th centuries it still existed at places adjoining Amberley.[155] In East Sussex, the surname became common in Glynde parish. This is not far from the Eastbourne area, where the surname was present earlier.[156] There are scattered instances of the name elsewhere in Sussex during the 16th and 17th centuries.[157]

It seems probable that in the case of Wisdom, too, that the name originated in Sussex with a few families, not all of which necessarily survived (for the surname may have died out in the Chichester area after the mid 14th century). Though the possibility of migration into the county cannot be excluded, it is likely that the frequency of the name in Sussex during the 16th and 17th centuries was due to the ramification of three or four families. At the present day, Wisdom is still a fairly common surname in East Sussex. In West Sussex it is less common, but it still survives at Chichester.

Wise

The surname Wise, unlike several others dealt with in this chapter, seems to have originated with a considerable number of separate families in Sussex, predominantly from the west of the county. One family, apparently of cottars, existed at Westbourne, in the south-west of the county, in the late 13th and 14th centuries. The name still survived at Westbourne in 1452, but has not been found there subsequently. From its persistence at one place it must have been hereditary, probably from the late 13th century.[158] At Sidlesham, near Selsey, there was a villein family named Wise for a period during the 13th and 14th centuries, for sufficiently long to make it likely that the name was hereditary there, too, but Wise seems to have died out at Sidlesham about the middle of the 14th century.[159] In the late 12th century there was a serf named *Sapiens* at Mundham, which adjoins Sidlesham. This must be a Latinised form of Wise, and it is possible that Wise had been a hereditary surname in this area, borne by an unfree family, from the late 12th century.[160] At Harting and Treyford, two places near together in north west Sussex, Wise was a well established surname from the late 13th century to about 1350, and was the name of a relatively large number of people, but in this area also it seems to have died out after the early 15th century.[161] Elsewhere in West Sussex a bondman named Wise is mentioned at Amberley, about 1350, and during the 14th century the name occurs at Wiston as that of several tenants of the manor there, probably free, but at neither place does the name seem to have survived.[162] Also in the 14th century there were several instances of Wise in the coastal district around Worthing and Shoreham, in some cases as the names of unfree tenants.[163] The references to the name in this area are rather scattered, and it is difficult to know if all the persons named Wise who lived there were related. In this part of Sussex the surname survived. It was present at several places in the 17th century, and it became a common name in Angmering parish, in that area.[164] Amberley and Wiston are near to the coastal district under consideration, and it seems that in the southern part of central Sussex the name Wise was widespread in the 14th century, probably without becoming hereditary in the case of some families, but surviving into the 16th and 17th centuries, and later, in the case of others. It is probable that the surname Wease, listed at West Tarring (on the coast, near Worthing), in 1642, is a variant of Wise. Forms such as le Wes' are found in medieval Sussex.[165] Elsewhere in West Sussex, Wise appears at East Hampnett, near Chichester, in 1327/8, and it was still surviving there, and in the adjoining parish of Boxgrove, in the 16th century. In 1642 the name is listed at Slindon, nearby.[166]

In East Sussex the name was never so widespread. It appears during the 13th and 14th centuries as the name of several tenants of South Malling manor, who were serfs or small free tenants, and who are likely to have all belonged to one family.[167] It also occurs, in one instance, as the name of a serf at Iridge (near Salehurst).[168] The name, however, does not seem to have survived, either at Salehurst, or on South Malling manor, after the mid 14th century.

It will be seen that, despite the complimentary nature of the surname, it is frequently found as the surname or bye-name of bondmen. Other bearers of the name seem to have been small free tenants, and no case has been found in medieval Sussex of a substantial landed family with the name. Surnames derived from nicknames can sometimes be ironical, but here is no evidence that this was so where Wise was concerned. The surname is obviously derived from a nickname widely used in Sussex, especially in the west of the county, among bondmen and small freeholders, presumably as a nickname bestowed on people thought to have a more than average amount of prudence. At the present time, Wise is both a numerous, and widely distributed surname, in East and West Sussex. It is an example of a surname which was already much dispersed by the 14th century, and which probably survived as the hereditary surname of a considerable number of families in the county, despite dying out in some places.

SURNAMES FROM WORDS FOR MAMMALS AND BIRDS

There are, as mentioned at the start of this chapter, many Sussex surnames derived from words for living creatures. Some of these, such as Ferret, Finch, Fowle, Hogg, Merle and Steer have already been mentioned. Others, such as, for example, Jay, Lark, Pye, Sparrow, or Swan, among names from birds, or Bull, Bullock, Buck, Fox, Hart, or Stag, among names from mammals, are surnames found in most parts of England, and were not especially common in Sussex. A few such surnames, however, seem to have originated in each case with one or two families in the county, and there are also a group of surnames from words for exotic or extinct animals.

Some Sussex surnames are derived from words for animal species which became extinct during the early Middle Ages, or earlier. Accurate information about the periods when species died out in particular regions of England is difficult to find, and the history of surnames may at points throw light upon this question. For example, the surname or bye-name Beaver (le Beuer, etc.) existed at Lewes in the mid and late 13th century.[169] The name existed in Kent at the same period.[170] The Sussex names are usually in the form le Bever, and it does not seem possible that they could be from the place-name Belvoir. It is possible that the name might have been hereditary for some time before it can be found in the surviving sources, and in fact it does seem to have been hereditary at Lewes from about 1250. However, the persons named Beaver who appear in the 13th century were not major landowners, and did not belong to a class where hereditary surnames were usual from an early date, and it is improbable that the name can have been hereditary from before the end of the 12th century. Giraldus Cambrensis, writing in connection with a journey in Wales made in 1188, stated that beavers then existed in a single river in Wales, and did not exist in England at all, though they were reported to survive in Scotland.[171] The writer gave a detailed description of beavers in Wales, and seems to have had accurate information about them, but in general he was not an altogether reliable source, and other evidence about the late survival of beavers in England is lacking. It is, of course, possible that the surname may have arisen from an animal which did not exist locally, but about which something was known, perhaps through memories of beavers having existed in Sussex at some time in the past, but it does seem feasible to suppose that beavers may have survived in Sussex, perhaps in the Weald, until the 13th century, though there is no reliable evidence for the presence of beavers in England as late as that.

The surname Beaver survived in East Sussex during the 14th and 15th centuries, probably as the surname of one family.[172] It still existed in the county during the 16th and 17th centuries, but it was rare, and it never seems to have multiplied in Sussex as some other surnames did.[173] The surname Belver, found in Horsham parish in 1524, may be a variant of Beaver, influenced by a belief that the surname was derived from the place-name Belvoir.[174] Both Beaver and Beevor still exist as surnames in Sussex, but neither is at all numerous.

A few other Sussex surnames were derived from species of animal which were probably extinct in the county by the time the surnames in question arose. The name Wolf (le Wlf, Wulf) was in use in several parts of Sussex from the late 13th century. There are a few instances in East Sussex, before 1300, but the name seems to have died out there.[175] In West Sussex Wolf occurs, about 1250-1300, as the name of unfree tenants, at and near Oving (east of Chichester) but here too the name seems to have disappeared about 1300.[176] Apart from these references, however, the surname was present over a long period, from the late 13th century onwards, at a group of places in the central part of West Sussex, Cold Waltham, Petworth, Sullington, Warminghurst, West Chiltington, etc. The places involved are sufficiently far apart for it to be unlikely that a single family was involved. The surname persisted in this part of Sussex for centuries. In 1524 it was still present at Warminghurst, where it was already in 1296. In the 17th century the surname still survived in the same area, though by that time it had become rather more dispersed.[177] Wolf exists to-day in much the same area of West Sussex, though it is now more numerous in the east of the county. As with other animals, there is a lack of detailed information about the regions in England occupied by wolves during the Middle Ages. The animal was probably extinct in England by about 1500, though it survived longer in Scotland.[178] There may have been wolves in the wooded parts of Sussex in the 13th century.

The surnames Pricklove, Trusslove (later Truslow) and Catchlove ('prick wolf, 'bind wolf', and 'chase wolf') can all be found in Sussex during the Middle Ages, and later. All three names can also be found in other parts of England. Though all might be names given to wolf hunters, it is possible, alternatively, that all might be in origin nicknames, bestowed on individuals because of their possession of certain characteristics, possibly boastfulness or aggressiveness.

Though there are uncertainties about the date to which wolves survived in the south of England, it seems clear that bears had been exterminated in the country by the time of the Conquest.[179] Bears, however, seem frequently to have been available for bear-baiting, and for exhibition, so that bears were no doubt seen in the country from time to time, perhaps quite often. Wolves were widely feared as dangerous and destructive carnivores, and the surname Wolf must have originated as a nickname bestowed on men thought to have similar dispositions, but it is less obvious why a man should be nicknamed Bear. (The name does appear as that of a woman, about 1290, but it may have been hereditary by then, or it may have been the surname of the lady's husband.)[180] The name may have been at first a nickname for someone of exceptional physical strength, or for someone whose awkward gait, rough manners, or clumsy movements were thought to resemble those of a bear. Bears, too, had a reputation in folklore for being lustful, and this may account for the name.[181]

In Sussex Michael *ursus*, mentioned in 1214, had a surname or bye-name from the bear.[182] Later in the 13th century the name le Ber appeared in two parts of Sussex. It was the name of several inhabitants of Chichester (who must have been free personally), and of inhabitants (some of them serfs) of two villages close to the city, Boxgrove and Mundham. Besides this, the name occured at North Stoke, rather further from Chichester.[183] Evidently le Ber must have been a nickname current among the peasant population of that district. Its presence in Chichester was probably due to migration into the city from the surrounding villages. It is unlikely that all those concerned belonged to one family, as the name is rather too dispersed in early references. In East Sussex le Ber was from the late 13th century a surname or bye-name around Lewes. Those who occur with the name in early references seem to have been mostly tenants of South Malling manor, which extended into several townships.[184] It is probable that all these people belonged to one family on the manor. Two persons named le Bere listed at Pevensey about 1290, however, do not have any known link with those of the same name on South Malling manor, so that there are likely to have been at least two families so called in East Sussex.[185]

In the 13th century there are a few instances of names such as de Bere or de Bera in Sussex, though it is not clear if these were hereditary.[186] Such names are from one of the places called Bere, Beere, etc. It is impossible to say certainly whether surnames such as Bere or Bear found at later periods were derived in any case from these locative names, or whether they were always from names such as le Ber, which originated as nicknames.

In the 16th century the surnames Bere and Bear were still present around Chichester, and it is probable that this was due to the name which appeared earlier in the form le Ber having survived in that area.[187] The surname was, however, rare in that quarter, and has not been found anywhere else in Sussex at that period. The 1641–2 Protestation Returns for West Sussex list three men named Beare, two of them at Selsey near Chichester, and also one named Bare, a name of which the origin must be in doubt.[188] The surname Beary, listed at Linchmere in 1642, may have developed through the name Beare having acquired a final 'y', like some other Sussex names.[189] The name Bear was always scarce in Sussex, it did not proliferate as some surnames did locally, and although it still exists in Sussex today, it remains very uncommon.

A few other surnames or bye-names in Sussex were drived from words for animals now extinct in England. Wildebor was the name of one individual, at Withyham in the Weald.[190] This name does not seem to have become hereditary in the county. Wild boar were still being hunted in England in the 16th century, and it would not be surprising if there were some in the Weald in the 14th, when the bye-name existed at Withyham. Wildebef was a bye-name in West Sussex during the 14th century, but seems to have gone out of use by about 1400.[191] The surname may not have been derived from feral cattle, but may merely reflect the habit of refering to bulls which were aggressive and out of control as wild. There was a pasture called Wildebef at Willingdon in 1292, and this is probably one of the cases, very numerous in Sussex, of fields or properties being named from the surnames or bye-names of owners and tenants.[192] Wildebor and Wildebef are both among the large number of rare names which were lost between about 1350 and 1400.

A few surnames are derived from words for imported or exotic creatures. The surname or bye-name Fesaunt (Feysant, Faisant) can be found in Sussex during the 13th and 14th centuries, but it is doubious if this can be used as evidence for the presence of such birds locally, though the presence of pheasants in the county by then is quite likely. The first known bearer of the name in Sussex was a John Faisant, mentioned in 1166, but it is not certain that he was resident in the county.[193] The next person found with the name was Thomas le Fesaunt of Dunwich (Suffolk), who was holding land near Eastbourne about 1250.[194] It may be conjectured that he was engaged in fishing or trading along the east coast, and it is not clear whether his nickname was bestowed on him in Sussex, or in East Anglia. Several people who occur in East Sussex in the late 13th and early 14th centuries may have been descended from Thomas, and there are a few examples in West Sussex during the same period, probably not related, but the name seems to have did out in Sussex after about 1350.[195]

By contrast, another name from a species of imported bird, Peacock, has survived in Sussex. Peacocks certainly existed in medieval Sussex, and may have been quite common. Among the labour services of serfs on the manor of Ferring, belonging to the Bishop of Chichester, was the duty of carrying peacocks from Ferring to Chichester, presumably to be eaten at episcopal banquets.[196] Peacocks were evidently a normal part of the poultry kept on this manor, and it is not surprising that Peacock was the name of an unfree tenant at Ferring in 1353.[197] Elsewhere, 5 peacocks kept at Wiston are mentioned in 1357-8.[198] There are scattered examples of the name Peacock (Pocock, Puccock, etc.) in various parts of Sussex during the 13th, 14th and 15th centuries. It is not clear in how many of these cases the name was hereditary,[199] though the references are so dispersed that it is very improbable that all those who appeared with the name were related. The surname must have become hereditary in at least some instances, for it survived in Sussex into the 16th century, so far as can be seen as the name of several families. Fletching parish, where the surname existed in the early 16th century, is near to Uckfield, where the name can be found earlier, and it is probable that a family called Peacock or Pocock had persisted in that area.[200] Another family so called seems to have persisted in the parishes on the Kent border, for the surname survived there from the 14th century to the 16th.[201] However, during the 16th century the name Peacock or Pocock also appears in other parts, in both East and West Sussex, where it cannot be traced before 1500.[202] 17th century references to Peacock are scattered, and the surname, unlike some others never seems to have become at all numerous in any one part of the county.[203] Though the name still survives in Sussex it has not proliferated to any great degree. Peacock is a surname which originated at several different points in the county, had a medieval history which it is difficult to trace systematically, but which involved the survival of more than one family so called, and which has survived to the present in the forms of Peacock and Pocock, to be quite a numerous surname in Sussex.

The surnames Peacock and Pheasant are both from species of birds which, though imported, did exist in Sussex, and were probably already living and breeding in the county by the time that hereditary surnames were first starting to become common there. Another surname which has had a long history in Sussex, Leppard (Lippard, etc.), is derived from an animal which, at the period when hereditary surnames were evolving, can have been seen in the county, if at all, very rarely. The leopard was a charge used in heraldry, which may have made it better known. Exotic creatures were kept in royal menageries, and it is possible that leopards may have been imported through Sussex for such a purpose, but any glimpses of live leopards that the inhabitants of Sussex had must have been few and brief, and it is probable that the origin of the surname should rather be sought in the generally unreliable information given about strange animals in medieval bestiaries. Leppard first appears as a name in Sussex in the late 13th century. Then, and during the early 14th century it was confined to a small area around Laughton, in East Sussex.[204] The status or occupation of some of those concerned cannot be ascertained, but some of those bearing the name at this early period were small free tenants, and it is likely that all the people who appear in Sussex named Leppard before about 1350 were persons of about that condition in life. The concentration of early instances of the name within a very limited district, and the fact that, so far as can be seen, those who appeared with the name were all of much the same status, leaves little doubt that all those involved belonged to one family. The continuity of the surname in one area strongly suggests, also, that the name was hereditary from at least the late 13th century. The name does occur in the 14th century in Essex, where it may well have arisen independently,[205] but the surname was very rare in England as a whole. By the 16th century the surname had become more widespread in Sussex. It was still present at some places not very far from Laughton, such as Barcombe and Newick, but it had spread to places further east, such as Robertsbridge, to an area further west in East Sussex, around Streat, a part of the county where the surname persisted for many years, and to Petworth, in West Sussex, where too the surname continued for a long period during the 16th and 17th centuries.[206] During the late 16th and 17th centuries, the surname became established at Ardingly, where it multiplied considerably.[207] At the same period the surname appeared at a few other places in the county, including Chichester.[208] Forms such as Libbard or Lippard occur at times during the 17th century, but seem to have gone out of use later. At the present time Leppard is a numerous and widely dispersed surname in Sussex. It is also common across the border in Kent, having probably spread to that county from Sussex. Elsewhere in England the name remains very rare. H. B. Guppy, who based his work on surnames found in late 19th century directories, noted Leppard as a common surname only in Sussex.[209] If not entirely a Sussex surname by origin, it is one which seems to have become common nowhere else.

SURVIVAL OF SURNAMES DERIVED FROM NICKNAMES

One of the more general questions that arise when studying the history of surnames concerns the factors which affect the survival and multiplication of names. The category of surnames derived from nicknames is notable for the high proportion of rare surnames which it includes. During the earlier Middle Ages, up to about the middle of the 14th century, there are in this category a very large number of scarce surnames and byenames, including many which have been found in one single example. This is true both in Sussex, and in most if not all other English counties. It is not surprising that a proportion of these has disappeared. Many were rare bye-names which never became hereditary. Others which can be seen to have developed into hereditary surnames were the names of no more than one or two families. Even of the names which became hereditary, many cannot be found after the mid 14th century, and seem to have disappeared in the period between about 1350 and 1450. The period from about the middle of the 14th century was one of heavy population losses, and although there is disagreement about the precise extent of the fall in population, the loss must have been sufficiently large to bring about the extinction of some rare surnames. The country's demographic history explains why many surnames disappear after the mid 14th century, but this still leaves open the question of why some surnames were lost at about that period, while others, no more common as far as can be seen survived and in some instances ramified considerably. Some of the causes involved here are elusive. Genetic factors must have exercised some influence, but it is usually impossible to extract any reliable information about such matters from medieval sources. It is usually not possible to obtain satisfactory evidence on, for example, the numbers of children borne to any one family during successive generations, or to know what the rate of infant mortality was in any family. Economic circumstances must also have had considerable influence. Families with greater resources must have been better fitted to withstand the ravages of pestilence and dearths, if only because they would have been better nourished, than those which were less prosperous. It is, however, often difficult to discover accurately just what the wealth of any family was. These deficiencies in the evidence make it difficult to be sure why some families survived and multiplied, while others disappeared. The survival within a county of surnames which were generally common throughout England cannot be considered as very significant. This applies to a good many occupational surnames, and to many surnames from the more frequently used personal names. It does apply to a few surnames derived from nicknames, mostly names from obvious physical characteristics (names such as White, Black, Long, etc.), but a high proportion of surnames from nicknames are ones which have always been rare. Even some of the rarer surnames developed, independently, in several parts of England, as has already been shown, and it is always possible that the position in Sussex has been affected by migration into the county. It is always possible that there were occasional instances where a scarce surname existed in the county, died out there, and was subsequently re-introduced by migration from elsewhere in England, but such cases are unlikely to have occured frequently. In consequence, the large number of surnames derived from nicknames which were rare ones makes this category particularly suitable for an investigation into the survival, or extinction, of surnames and bye-names.

Since no medieval source lists the whole population, it is not possible to rely on any single piece of evidence to provide an adequate view of the surnames or bye-names in use at any period. However, an index of surnames in this category found in Sussex has been compiled from a large number of printed and manuscript sources. This contains just over 1,000

Surnames Derived from Nicknames

surnames or bye-names, derived from nicknames, which have been found in Sussex between the Conquest and 1650. This figure is for the number of separate names, not for the number of individuals found in the sources utilised. Variant forms of a single surname or bye-name have been counted as one name. It is not claimed that this total is comprehensive. Out of the total number of surnames and bye-names in this category which have been discovered, about 480 have been found in the county before 1350. About 130 names, of the 480, have each been found in Sussex as the name of one individual only, and it is likely that the great majority of names which are found thus, each as the name of a single person, were bye-names which never became hereditary. It would be unwise to be too dogmatic about this, bearing in mind the limitations of the source material, and it is always possible that a few names were rather more numerous, and better established in the county, than can be seen from the extant evidence. There is no doubt, however, that in the 12th and 13th centuries there were large numbers of persons in the county without hereditary surnames, and it is very probable that many of the names found merely as those of single individuals were non-hereditary bye-names. Out of the about 480 surnames found in Sussex before 1350, about 390 have also been discovered in the county between 1500 and 1650. These figures may give a somewhat exaggerated impression of the degree of continuity that prevailed. Some of the names involved are very common ones, which have existed in most parts of England over a long period, and as already mentioned, the possibility that rarer names became extinct, and were later re-introduced, cannot be excluded. Many surnames in this category, however, can be shown to have persisted in one part of the county over a long period. Frequently surnames which first appear in Sussex during the late 13th or early 14th centuries are still present in much the same area in the 16th century. The history of some surnames examined in detail in this chapter illustrates this, and if space permitted many more examples could be given. The general conclusion to be drawn from this evidence is that during the earlier part of the Middle Ages, up to about 1350, the number of surnames or bye-names in this category which were in use in the county were quite large. A considerable number of these names, however, were obviously very rare. Some surnames in this category obviously arose from expressions which were widely used, even if the precise significance attached to them is obscure. There were, however, many bye-names of this type which were always very rare, and which were, perhaps, the product of some chance incident, or of some shaft of wit from a villager. This, of course, is what might be expected from nicknames. Very few names of this type which were well established in the county by about the mid 14th century failed to survive. This includes some surnames which were never at all common, such as, for example, the names Beaver, Ferret, Leppard, Merlot, and Wolf, already discussed.

These remarks are generalisations based on the examination of a large body of evidence, and on tracing the history of many individual surnames in this category. It would be easy to produce many further examples of surnames which have survived from before about 1350, and a smaller number of instances could be cited of surnames which became hereditary in Sussex during the Middle Ages, but which disappeared from the county. For instance, the name Strokehose, already mentioned, occurs at and around Yapton in the 13th and 14th centuries, in a way which strongly suggests that it was hereditary there, and it was probably the name of a single family, but it seems to have disappeared from Sussex about the middle of the 14th century.[210] Belcher, another surname of French origin, existed at and around Fairlight, in the east of Sussex, for some time in the 13th and 14th centuries, long enough for it to be fairly clear that the name was hereditary, but subsequently the name seems to have become extinct in Sussex. It was re-introduced into the county in the 16th century by alien immigration and is to-day quite numerous there.[211] Robinhood (a name probably originating from tales of the legendary outlaw) survived for some time in East Sussex during the 13th and 14th centuries.[212] There is little doubt that this name, too, was hereditary, but it seems to have been lost from the county before 1500. The name Littlewatte ('little Walter') survived for a period at both Pevensey and Hailsham, and was probably hereditary at both from the late 13th century, but it seems to have died out in Sussex in the late 14th century.[213] and indeed seems to have disappeared in England altogether. The name Sickelfoot existed in East Sussex during the 13th and 14th centuries, for a sufficiently long period to suggest that it was hereditary.[214] The bearers of the name were landowners of moderate wealth, and probably all belonged to one family.[215] The name has not been found in the county after 1400. Presumably it originated as a nickname for some individual with a deformed foot.[216] Purfowle, a very rare surname, persisted at Stedham from the 13th century to the 15th and was hereditary there, but seems to have been lost by about 1450. The name is from a word for some unidentified species of bird, possibly the dunlin. Instances of the name have not been found outside Sussex, though the similar name Pingfoghel is found in Kent.[217] Saunzbouche ('mouth-less', perhaps a name applied to one who was dumb or taciturn), was present at and near North Stoke for a sufficiently long period, during the 13th, 14th, and 15th centuries, to show that it had become hereditary there, but again seems to have disappeared. This was another rare surname.[218] It is not known to have survived in England, and as far as can be discovered it does not exist in France at the present day.[219] Taketurn, another very rare name which has not been found outside Sussex, and almost certainly that of one family in the county, persisted at Wellingham during the 13th and 14th centuries, for long enough to leave little doubt it was hereditary, but it has not been found after 1350. Its meaning can only be conjectured, but since the bearers were serfs of South Malling manor, it may have arisen because some labour services on the manor were performed in turn by the bond tenants.[220] Some further examples could be given of surnames derived from nicknames which survived in one part of the county for a sufficiently long and continuous period to make it clear that they had become hereditary, but which failed to survive in Sussex into the 16th century. These would include some further French surnames, such as Mangefer, found around Lewes in the 13th century,[221] or Parfoy, which existed in West Sussex at about the same period.[222] Some of these surnames were probably brought into Sussex by immigration, and were never the names of more than one family in the county in each case, though some can be found in other parts of England as well. There is little doubt that some of the surnames concerned originated in the county, but were always very rare. It is not surprising that some very rare surnames were lost, and in particular it is not surprising that a proportion of names in the category under consideration disappeared during the mid and late 14th century, a period when there was unusually heavy mortality.

What is notable is the large number of surnames derived from nicknames, many of them surnames which were never at all common, to survive from the 13th and 14th centuries into the 16th century and later. When the whole body of surnames in this category found in Sussex is examined, two characteristics seem obvious. One is the great number and variety of the surnames and bye-names in the category which can be found in the county during the Middle Ages, including many names which were rare; the other is the extent to which names, once established as hereditary in the county, tend to survive, and to persist over long periods, often in one limited area. The number of surnames which have survived is too great for all or most of them to be discussed individually. Some examples of surnames which have survived have already been considered, earlier in this chapter. The question which obviously arises is whether any general factors can be observed at work which may have determined the survival or extinction of some groups of names, or whether survival or extinction depended solely on such matters as the genetics of individual families, or the social status or economic circumstances of families, matters which it would be difficult to deal with in any convincing manner in view of the source material.

One group of names of which a relatively high proportion has been lost is that of surnames, derived from nicknames, which are French linguistically. The question of how far such names are the result of migration from French speaking regions on the Continent, and how far they may have originated in England, is considered elsewhere.[223] A total of 177 surnames or bye-names, derived from nicknames, which are French linguistically has been found in Sussex before 1500. During the 16th century a few further names can be discovered, but most of these are the surnames of people listed as aliens, and very few of them persisted in the county. The total includes a few names, such as Chantmerle, for instance, which as already stated have disputable origins. 39 out of the 177 have been found in one example within the county, and it is probable that these were bye-names which did not become hereditary, or were the names of migrants who did not settle permanently. Only 46 of the total of 177 have been found within Sussex during the 16th century in the sources used for this study, though a more intensive investigation might possibly reveal the survival of a few more surnames. The proportion of French surnames to have survived in the county was therefore small. It is also true that even of those surnames which still existed in the county in the 16th century, most remained rare, then and later. A few surnames which are French linguistically have not only survived in the county, but have ramified considerably. The surname Maufe, for example, that of a landed family established in the county from the 12th century, not only survived in Sussex, but increased considerably in numbers.[224] Trenchmere, a name which though French linguistically probably originated in Sussex, survived in several variants, and became moderately common in the county.[225] Cachelove (Catchlowe, Catchlove, Cetchlove, etc.), which appears as the name of an unfree tenant in the Selsey area about 1300, had ramified considerably in the same part of Sussex by the 16th century, and in the 17th was still surviving as a well established surname in West Sussex.[226] The surname Beldam (Beldham, etc.), which occurs around Lewes during the 14th century, was still in the same area in the 16th, but by then it had spread to other parts of Sussex, and was already widely dispersed in the county. The surname still exists in Sussex.[227] The surname is derived from a word which was adopted into Middle English, but this is not known to have taken place until the 15th century. Beldhamland Farm, in Wisborough Green, mentioned in 1623 as Beldam Lands, is probably from this surname (though other explanations have been put forward), in which case it is one of the very numerous instances in Sussex of farms or other holdings having place-names from the surnames of owners or tenants. Beldam does occur[228] at Slinfold and Dunhurst, near Wisborough, in the 16th century. A few other examples could be given of French surnames which have not only survived in Sussex, but have ramified there to some degree, but such cases are exceptional. The great majority of French surnames to be found in Sussex before 1500 were rare, and most remained so.

Apart from French surnames or bye-names, it is difficult to pick out any group of surnames, separated from others in this category on linguistic grounds, which had an exceptionally high, or exceptionally low, rate of survival. Compound names on the whole tend to survive rather less frequently than simplex ones, but this is because many compound names

Surnames Derived from Nicknames

were always rare, and indeed many have been found once only, in the county. One group of compound names, of which many have been lost, is the small collection of surnames or bye-names from oaths, ejaculations, or similar expressions. A total of 17 such surnames has been discovered in Sussex before 1500. 9 of these have each been found as the name of one person in the county only. No more than 4 of these have been found in Sussex after 1500. 3 of these, Godsmark,[229] Godale,[230] and Godeshalf[231] were still rare surnames in Sussex during the 16th century. Godsmark was probably a surname which originated solely in Sussex, and was always a rare surname, but the other two can be found in other parts of England from an early date, and neither was a particularly unusual surname. The fourth surname of the type to survive after 1500, Purdew, had ramified to a moderate extent by the 16th century, but was still not a very common surname.[232] This small group of surnames or bye-names obviously had a low rate of survival, but most of the names involved were always scarce. These four names all survive in Sussex to the present day, but none is really plentiful in the county.

It does not appear that there were any further groups of names in this category which either survived in especially large numbers, or which were particularly likely to disappear. It is more difficult to discover whether the chances of surnames surviving were influenced by the social or economic status of those who bore them. Bondmen are one group which can usually be distinguished from the rest of the population. In practice the demarcation between serfs and free tenants is less clear cut than legal theories might imply. There are instances of bond tenants holding land as lessees, often in addition to their unfree tenements, and there are cases of freemen holding bond tenements, and performing the labour services due from them. So far as economic position is concerned, therefore, the distinction between persons of free and of unfree status is liable to be blurred. There is a further difficulty that serfs are often not denoted as such in subsidy rolls. Nevertheless, bondmen are usually clearly separated in manor court rolls, surveys, and extents, and there are some separate lists of villeins in Sussex subsidy rolls.[233] An index has been compiled from various sources[234] of unfree tenants mentioned in Sussex before 1500. The total number of individuals listed is 1614, and out of these 268, or about 17%, had surnames or bye-names which were derived from nicknames. A considerable number of the surnames or bye-names in question, however, were ones which existed among both the free and the unfree population, and so cannot be used for estimating the rate of survival of surnames used by bondmen. The figures just given are for numbers of individuals, not for numbers of surnames or bye-names. Only 34 surnames or bye-names have been found, which, so far as can be seen from the sources examined, occur up to 1400 as the names of serfs, but not of freemen. After 1400 it becomes increasingly difficult to ascertain what the status of individuals was, and it is also necessary to reckon with the increasing likelihood that families originally unfree had gained their freedom. 22 out of the 34 names in question have not been discovered in the county after 1500, and it is probable that none of these survived in Sussex. The remaining 12 names have been found in the county after 1500, but none was at all numerous there. These figures probably exaggerate the tendency of serfs' names to disappear. Some fairly common surnames can be found in Sussex as the names of both bondmen and freemen. The names Blake, Read, Long, Hore, and Callow, for example, all relatively common surnames, appear in Sussex as the names of both freemen and serfs, and so can not be used to test the rate of survival of bondmens' names. The same is true of a few names which are not generally at all common, but which became well established in Sussex, and persisted there over a long period, such as, for example, Piperwhite, or Catt, both of which existed in Sussex for centuries, and multiplied to some extent, and both of which occur as the names of persons of free and of unfree status. However, after allowing for such factors, which may have tended to make the figures just given misleading to some extent, it does seem that the surnames and byenames in this category borne by the unfree part of the population were significantly less likely to survive than those of freemen.

It is difficult to isolate any other section of the community in the same way. Numbers of small free tenants can be found on many Sussex manors, but it is often uncertain what the economic position of such tenants was, especially because it is generally impossible to be sure whether or not a tenant's holdings on one manor were the total of his lands, or whether he held further tenements elsewhere. A few of the more important landowning families had surnames derived from nicknames. The surname Maufe, which has persisted in Sussex over a long period, is an example. In the great majority of cases, however, the names of the larger landowners fall into other categories, and the question of their survival is discussed elsewhere.[235]

The general impression left by an examination of much evidence regarding the history in Sussex of surnames derived from nicknames is that a great many surnames, many of them rare, which are first evidenced in Sussex sources during the 13th or early 14th centuries, survived into the 16th and 17th centuries, often without migrating very much geographically, and persisted in the county in later periods, often to the present day. This obviously implies a population which was not highly mobile.

An examination of some 16th and 17th century sources for the county does not suggest that there was any great influx of surnames in this category into Sussex in the period 1500–1700. A search through the Sussex returns of the 1524–5 lay subsidy, the surviving Protestation Returns for the county, and some other 16th and 17th century sources has produced a list of 41 surnames, derived from nicknames, which have not been found in the county before 1500 in the material used for this study. A more thorough search through 16th and 17th century evidence, especially parish registers, would no doubt produce some further names. Some of the surnames in this category which have not been found in the county before 1500 occur as the names of single individuals and very few were at all numerous during the 16th and 17th centuries. There are some cases where surnames which, so far as has been discovered, did not arrive in Sussex until after 1500 have ramified, and become relatively common. The name Hobjohn, for example, has not been found in Sussex before the early 16th century, and the surname itself may be one that originated at a relatively late period, but by the 17th century the name was widely distributed in West Sussex, probably through the proliferation of one family. This surname has survived in Sussex to the present day, as Hobgen.[236] This, however, is exceptional. A few other surnames derived from nicknames which did not appear in the county until after 1500 persisted there over long periods. The name Fairmaner, for instance, occurs from the early 16th century as that of a family owning land in West Sussex, on the Hampshire border, and it long survived in that part of the county, but without ramifying significantly.[237] Domesday, a surname of uncertain origin, perhaps from a nickname, perhaps occupational, and a name for which there are early references in East Anglia, has not been found in Sussex before 1500, but it later became an established surname in one part of the county, without becoming very numerous,[238] and survives as a rare surname today. It is, however, more usual during the 16th and 17th centuries to find surnames derived from nicknames (not present in the county before 1500) as the names of one or two individuals, and frequently to find that such surnames have not survived for long in Sussex.

Some comments may be made about the origins and development of certain surnames derived from nicknames.

Friday

The surname Friday has generally been supposed to have originated as a nickname bestowed on someone born on a Friday.[239] This explanation does seem feasible, particularly in view of the existence of surnames derived from major festivals (Christmass, Pentecost, etc.). However, there is some evidence that in Sussex the surname had a topographical origin. Friday occurs as a surname or bye-name in Sussex in 1200. In the late 13th and early 14th centuries the name existed in the Seaford area, where it persisted for long enough to suggest that it was hereditary, and probably the name of one family there. Examples of the name can be found elsewhere in Sussex during the 13th century, but it is doubtful if it was hereditary outside the Seaford area.[240] At Beddingham, which is quite close to Seaford, Fryday was a field name in the 14th century. It is perhaps possible that the field name arose through the land having been held at some earlier time by someone with the surname Friday, but there is no evidence for this, and it seems more likely that the surname was derived from the field name. The field name may have been given to land which was not productive.[241]

Friday was always a rare surname, but it survived, and was still present in the east of the county in the 16th century.[242] It still exists in Sussex at the present day.

Gelding

Gelding is said to be a surname derived from a nickname, with the meaning of 'eunuch'. The early instances of the name cited by Reaney are all from Sussex.[243] Examples of the name can be found in Sussex during the late 13th and 14th centuries, and all come from one district in the more easterly part of the county.[244] All the examples concern one family. It seems clear, however, that Gelding is merely a variant of the widespread surname Golding, a surname derived from a personal name. Thomas Gelding, listed as a taxpayer at Catsfield in 1327/8, is listed at the same place in 1332 as Thomas Golding, and William Gelding, mentioned at Hoo in 1327/8, seems to be the same person as William Goldyng, mentioned in the same area at an earlier date. Golding is a fairly common surname in East Sussex from the 13th century onwards.[245] Another surname from a personal name, Goldwyne, occurs as Geldwyne in East Sussex in some cases.[246] It does not appear that Gelding existed as a distinct surname. The surname Gelding survives in Sussex today, in the form Gilding.

Godsal

The surname Godsal (Goodsole, etc.) is usually said to be derived from the phrase 'good soul'. The orthographically very similar surname Godsell has usually been derived from one or other of the several places named Gadshill, Godshill, or Godsell, in Kent, Hampshire, the Isle of Wight, and Wiltshire.[247] There seems no reason to doubt that these are the correct explanations for the origins of both surnames in many cases. The two surnames have become confused in some parts of the country, and it is difficult to separate them when dealing with surnames which occur at the present day.

The surname Goodsole (also given as Goodsall, Godesole, and Goteshole) existed at and around Burwash, in the eastern part of Sussex near the Kent border, from the late 14th century. It survived in the same area during the 15th and 16th centuries, as the surname of people who seem mostly to have been small freeholders or copyholders, and although no connected pedigree can be traced, the continuous existence of the surname in one part, and the persistent use of the Christian name Stephen with the surname, strongly suggests that all those so named belonged to one family.[248] A Richard de Godeshulle or de Goteshole, mentioned in the same part of Sussex at the end of the 13th century and the early 14th, had what is clearly an earlier form of the same surname, though it is uncertain if he was the ancestor of the persons named Goodsole, etc., who occur later.[249] Richard's surname or bye-name was evidently from a place-name, which must be the present Goodsoal, in Burwash.[250]

From the 16th century onwards it becomes difficult to distinguish between Goodsole, and Godsalve (Godeshalf, etc.) another surname, of different origin, which existed in Sussex over a long period.[251] John Godsall or Godsale, for instance, a mid 16th century tenant at Horsham, is also mentioned as John Godsalve.[252] Godsal (Godsell, Goodsall, etc.), is a surname still frequently found in Sussex.

Moodle

Moodle is a rare surname which has survived in one part of Sussex over a long period. The name le Model appears in the lay subsidies for 1327/8, and 1332, at Sheffield, near Fletching; William le Model, who was holding land at Goring in 1321, was probably the same as the William le Model listed at Sheffield.[253] There are a few other references to the name in Sussex during the Middle Ages,[254] but it survived in the north of the county, and in 1524-5 it occurs, as Modyll, Moodle, or Modle, at Mayfield, and at Greenhurst, near Buxted. These places are not very far from Sheffield, and the surname had evidently survived for some centuries in one part of Sussex, but not, so far as can be seen, anywhere else in the county.[255]

Le Model is probably a form of 'Middle', found as a surname in other counties,[256] with the meaning either of someone who was middling in terms of size, or of someone who was the middle one of three siblings. The name Middle is certainly found in a locative or topographical sense in some parts of England, but forms such as atte Middle or atte Model have not been found in Sussex, despite the county's profusion of topographical surnames. Model is still a Sussex surname, though very rare. The surname Moodley, found in Sussex at the present day, may have developed from forms such as Moodle.

Pentecost and Pankhurst

Pentecost first appears as a surname or bye-name in Sussex in the early 13th century. There are few instances of the name in Sussex before 1500, and it was evidently rare. The name did exist during the 13th and 14th centuries in Surrey, and as some of the Sussex examples come from the north of the county, it is possible that the Sussex Pentecosts were related to those in Surrey. Pentecost was in use as a personal name in Surrey during the 12th century; presumably it was originally a first name bestowed on someone born on the festival so called.[257] By the 16th century the name had become more common. Five persons named Pentecost or Pencost are listed in the Sussex subsidy rolls for 1524, mostly in the north of East Sussex.[258] Pentecost survived as a surname in the county into later centuries, and the name in that form became fairly common in East Sussex.[259]

In some cases, however, the surname evolved into other forms, a process which may have been complicated by confusion with other surnames existing in Sussex. The form Pencost occurs in 1524.[260] The surname Penkehurst appears in 1524, and Pengehurst in 1529, both in the northern part of East Sussex, where Pentecost was to be found, at the same period, and earlier.[261] Penkhurst existed at the same period in West Kent, just across the Sussex border, and it persisted to a later date in East Sussex.[262] The origin of this surname is not clear, especially as it appears in several variants. Henry Penkhurst, a parishioner of Ardingly in the 1560's and 1570's, is recorded in the parish register as Penkhurst, Penkherst, Pynkhurst, and Pankhurst.[263] Penkhurst might be from the East Sussex place-name Penhurst, with a redundant 'k'. The forms Panehurst and Pynherst for the place-name occur in the 13th century. In the 13th and 14th centuries the surname or bye-name de Pynkhurst or de Pynkherst existed at Rudgwick, in West Sussex.[264] This name was probably from the place-name Pinkhurst, in Slinfold parish, which adjoins Rudgwick, though alternatively it could be from Pinkhurst in Surrey. The surname or bye-name de Pyngehurst, listed at Warbleton in 1332, is probably from the place-name Penhurst, which is near to Warbleton.[265] These are all locative surnames or bye-names, and there is no evidence that any of the names such as de Pynkhurst or de Pyngehurst found before 1500 in Sussex had any link with the surname Pentecost. None of the individuals who appear in Sussex during the 16th century with surnames such as Penkhurst, Pengehurst, Pankhurst, Pynkhurst, etc., can be certainly identified as individuals whose name is given as Pentecost, and so far as can be seen the locative surnames such as Penkhurst, Pankhurst, etc., in Sussex at that period are quite distinct from Pentecost. 16th century surnames in forms such as Pencost or Pancost are likely to be variants of locative surnames such as Penkhurst, Pankhurst, etc. Dunstan (or Duncan) Pankherste, a resident in north Sussex under Elizabeth I, also appears as Pancost and Penkeherst.[266]

So far at least as Sussex is concerned, there is no evidence that before 1600 there was any confusion between Pentecost, and the various locative surnames such as Pankhurst or Penkhurst which can be found in the county. The view that the surname Pankhurst is a variant of Pentecost has been put forward in standard works.[267] This opinion is partly based on the belief that the place-name Pankhurst (Surrey) is derived from the surname of John Pentecost. The only evidence cited for this, however, is that John was a taxer, in 1332, in the hundred within which Pankhurst is situated, and this is hardly conclusive. In 1605 Pankhurst in Surrey is mentioned as Pentecost alias Panchurst, but this evidence is too late to be decisive and may be due to a mistaken popular etymology of the place-name, which may have existed for some time unrecorded.[268] At later periods it certainly seems to have been thought that Pankhurst and Pentecost were different forms of the same surname. In 1770, for example, Richard Pankhurst was described as 'Pankhurst alias Penticost'; Richard was a resident at Mayfield, in a part of Sussex where Pentecost and Pankhurst had both existed for centuries.[269] It seems clear that from the 17th century onwards, there was some confusion, both as regards place-names and surnames, between Pankhurst and Pentecost, but this does not seem to extend back to before 1600. Surnames such as Pankhurst, Penkhurst, etc., seem from this evidence to have been locative in origin, though by the 16th century the spelling was so variable that it is impossible to connect such surnames with particular place-names at all certainly. The confusion with Pentecost is a late development.

Pentecost, or Penticost, is still quite a numerous surname in East Sussex at the present day. It still exists at Mayfield, where it has been for centuries.

Pennicod and Pennicott

The surname Pennicod has not been found in Sussex before the early 16th century, when it appears in the north-west of the county. The instances which have been found before 1550 all concern one area, and this makes it likely that those involved were from a single family. Though the surname might have existed for some considerable time unrecorded, it seems possible that it was brought in by the migration into the county of one family, perhaps about 1500.[270] All the 16th century examples which have been found are in the form Pennicod, or Pennycodde.[271] This still seems to have been the usual form in the 17th century, but the forms Pennicott and Pennicorde appear in 1642. In the 17th century the surname was still largely concentrated in the northern part of West Sussex, but it had by then dispersed to some extent, and there are a few cases in the south of West Sussex too.[272] The name still survives in Sussex at the present day, and it is also to be found in south-east Hampshire. The form Pennicod or Pennycodde seems to have disappeared, and the most usual form is now Pennicott, though Pennicard, Penneycard, and Pennycord also occur.

The origin of the name is difficult to determine, especially since no examples are known before 1500. The form Pennicott has the appearance of being derived from a place-name, possibly Pennicott (Devon), but Pennicott is not the form which is found in the earlier examples. Pennicod might possibly be from one of the places called Pencoed or Pencoyd. Alternatively, however, it could be a nickname, similar to Pennyfather. The second element in the name could be from the codfish, but in view of some uses of 'cod', it is possible that the surname originated as a nickname of a lewd character, refering to the male genitals. The later forms may be due to bowdlerising, of a nature found in the case of other surnames.

Peasecod and Peskett

The surname Peasecod (Piscod, Puscod, etc.) is a nickname from the peapod, either for someone who sold or grew peas, or for someone who was thought to resemble a peapod in some way. The name is not confined to Sussex, or to any one English region.[273] The name has first been found in Sussex in 1301, as the name of a serf on the manor of Manwood, which belonged to the Fitzalan family.[274] The name occurs at the same period as the name of a serf at Mileham (Norfolk), on a manor there which also belonged to the Fitzalan family,[275] which suggests that there may have been transfers of tenants on the family's estates between Sussex and Norfolk. There are other 14th century examples of the name in Sussex, all from the southern part of West Sussex.[276] In the 15th century the surname persisted in much the same area.[277] Many of those who appear in Sussex with the name during the 14th and 15th centuries were unfree, and it is possible that name was originally entirely a serf one. The early instances of the name in the county are somewhat dispersed geographically, but most are in places where the Fitzalan family held land, and it is possible that in Sussex the surname originated with a single family who were unfree tenants on the Fitzalan estates.

During the 16th and 17th centuries the surname became more numerous, and rather more dispersed, in West Sussex, but it was still mostly concentrated in the areas where it had been present before 1500. Until after 1600 the form of the name seems generally to have been Pescod or Piscod, but in the 17th century other spellings came into use. The form Pescit occurs in 1642 at Littlehampton, in a part of Sussex where the surname had long existed.[278] From the 17th century onwards Pescod continued in use, and became a fairly common name in Sussex, but spellings such as Peskett came to be used more and more frequently. At the present day, judging from the evidence of telephone directories and other printed directories, Peskett is a rather more numerous form than Pescod in Sussex. Spellings intermediate between the two, such as Pescott, are still in use. Peasecod and Peskett are today quite common names in the Brighton area, now the chief centre of population in the county.

Pescod is another example of a surname which has survived continuously in Sussex over a long period, from at least the beginning of the 14th century to the present. The surname, perhaps originally that of a single family, has in its different variants, ramified very considerably to become quite numerous in the county.

Primmer

Primmer (or Primer) is a surname which has persisted in Sussex for centuries, without increasing very much in numbers. The name has first been found in Sussex in the late 13th century, in the south-west of the county around Bosham. Some, and possibly all, of the people who appear with the name in early references were customary tenants. The name, in fact, originated in much the same area, and in much the same social class, as Pescod, but its history in the county was very different. During the 13th and 14th centuries the name occurs in the forms le Premer and Primer.[279]

A clue about the meaning of the name can be found in the fact that Nicholas le Premir, at East Ashling, 1332, is also mentioned as Nicholas Prinne.[280] Prinn usually means 'first' or 'superior', and Primmer, le Premer, etc., may have had the same significance. The precise context in which the surname arose must remain uncertain; it might have been given to the eldest of several children, or, perhaps, to the most prominent or the most senior of the customary tenants on a manor. Since the early examples of the name were all in one small district of Sussex, it seems likely that all those so named belonged to one family. The Latinised name *Primus*, found in south-west Sussex in the 13th century, may be a translation of Primmer.[281]

During the 15th century, Primmer still survived in south-west Sussex, in the area where it had first appeared, but the surname did spread, and in the late 15th century it occurs in East Sussex.[282] The name was still most numerous in south-west Sussex, around Bosham, in the 16th century, though it also existed in East Sussex. There was evidently a large family so named at Bosham in the 16th century.[283] The name, however, was never at all common, and subsequently seems to have been lost from West Sussex. The 1641–2 Protestation Returns for that half of the county, which provide an almost complete list of the adult male inhabitants, do not include any persons named Primmer, etc. The name did survive in the county, though it remained rare, and did not proliferate to any extent. It is still, in the forms Primmer and Primer, to be found in Sussex at the present day, but it remains quite a scarce name there.

Saxby

Saxby is the name of several places in the east of England, which may have given rise to surnames. A small locality called Saxby exists in West Sussex, near Barnham, but in this case the place-name seems to have been derived from a surname, already in use locally before the place-name arose.[284] The surname Saxby is not, in Sussex, derived from a place-name.

The name Shakespey or Saxepe is listed in the Sussex lay subsidies at Ashurst near West Grinstead, in the late 13th and early 14th centuries.[285] The name has not been found at Ashurst after 1332, but later in the 14th century it was present at Streatham (very near to Ashurst), where it was then hereditary.[286] The surname, however, has not been found in the same area during the 15th century, and may have died out. From the late 13th century the surname existed in Withyham parish, in north-east Sussex, in the form Sakespey and Saxpays. The name survived at Withyham, and must have been hereditary there from the 13th century. It was a well-established surname at Withyham in the 16th century. The Saxbies at Withyham in the 16th century were freeholders, mostly of the yeomen class, and probably were all one family.[287] During the 16th century the surname spread into Rotherfield, East Grinstead, and Hartfield, all places near to Withyham.[288] During the 16th century the usual form of the surname in the Withyham area was Saxbies or Saxpes. Such forms are given during the late 16th and early 17th centuries in the East Grinstead parish register, where there is a succession of entries for the name, but in the register the final 's' is dropped after the early 17th century, and from then on the usual form is Saxby or Saxbee.[289] After about 1500 the name appears further south in East Sussex, around Lewes,[290] probably as a result of dispersal from the Withyham area. Most of those who appear with the name in this part of Sussex were yeomen or husbandmen, and so were of much the same class as those around Withyham. The surname appears in West Sussex in the 17th century, and it may have survived there around Ashurst, though no continuous record of it can be traced.[291] It appears in West Sussex at that time in the form Saxbie or Saxby.

The forms of the surname which are found from about 1600 onwards have all the appearance of being derived from a place-name, but the medieval forms show that this is not the correct derivation. Early forms such as Shakespey are nicknames, with the meaning 'draw sword'. Possibly this may have been a nickname for a quarrelsome or aggressive person. Alternatively it may have been a name for someone who gave instruction in swordsmanship.[292] The name is French linguistically, and may have been brought into Sussex by immigration. Saxby (or Saxbee) remains a Sussex surname to the present day, mostly in the east of the county.

Tranchmere, Trankmore

The surname Tranchmere ('cleave the sea') is one of the many surnames derived from nicknames, of which the literal meaning is clear, but which are obviously used in a metaphorical sense, so that it is difficult to be sure how a surname originated, or what it conveyed to contemporaries at the period when it first came into use. The name Tranchmere is exceptional in that some evidence can be discovered about its early history, and that this throws light upon its original significance. The earliest persons with the name who have been discovered in Sussex are William Trancamare and Alan Trenchemere, a late 12th century shipbuilder and seaman, who built royal ships under Richard I. Alan owned land at Shoreham. He also seems to have been active in East Anglia. It may be inferred from the fact that he built ships for the king that he was a shipwright of high reputation. Very possibly he was well-known for constructing fast ships for cross Channel purposes. It seems clear in any case that his bye-name was originally a nickname arising from his activities as a shipbuilder and seaman. William witnessed one of Alan's charters, and was probably a relative.[293]

Trenchmere remained a surname at Shoreham until the 17th century, and although no connected pedigree can be traced, it is probable that the people called Trenchmere, etc., who lived at Shoreham were Alan's descendants.[294] During the 13th and 14th centuries the surname spread to places on the coast, near Shoreham, such as Hove and Brighton, and to places inland, in the valley of the Adur (which reaches the sea at Shoreham), such as Shermanbury, West Grinstead, and Cowfold.[295] The distribution of the surname in these areas suggests that the spread of the name in Sussex was due to a gradual dispersal of the Trenchmere family of Shoreham. There may have been some confusion with the name Trentemars, which was present at Chichester in the late 12th century, and which survived in that part of the county into the 14th century. Richard Trenemer, listed at Thorney, near Chichester, in 1327/8, is listed as Richard Trentemars in 1332.[296] In the 14th century the name Trenchmere appears at Hastings. The Hastings family held land at Atlingworth, near Shoreham, and were probably a branch of the Shoreham family. The surname still existed at Hastings, in the form Trankmer, about 1500. 15th and 16th century examples of Trankmer at other places in East Sussex are probably due to the ramification of the Hastings family.[297] The surname still survived at Shoreham, and in the adjoining parish of Edburton, in the 17th century.[298] The surname also existed in the 17th century at Horsham, not far from Cowfold and West Grinstead, where it had occured earlier.[299] The usual forms after about 1500 are Tranckmere or Trankmore. The name still survives in Sussex though it has not become at all numerous. Although it is not possible to construct a complete pedigree, it seems probable that all the persons named Trenchmere, Trankmore, etc., found in Sussex are descended from the family which appears at Shoreham from the 12th century onwards. Quite possibly they are all descendants of the original Alan Trenchmere. The surname is not exclusively a Sussex one. There are medieval examples of the name in London, Kent, East Anglia, Dorset and the north of England.[300]

References

[1] *Chichester Chart.*, p. 140; Rubin, *Suss. Phonology*, p. 169.

[2] *3 Suss. Subsidies*, pp. 148, 262; *Non. Inquis.*, p. 351; *S.A.C.*, vol. lxxxii, p. 128; West Suss. Record Office, EP. VI/19A/1, mm. 5, 5d, 10, 10d.

[3] *3 Suss, Subsidies*, 263.

[4] *S.A.C.*, vol. lxii, p. 193.

[5] *3 Suss. Subsidies*, pp. 79, 245; *Non. Inquis.*, p. 351; L. Fleming, *History of Pagham*, vol. i, p. xli; *Boxgrove Chart.*, p. 163; H. A. Hanley and C. W. Chalklin, *op. cit.*, p. 160; *Suss. Fines*, vol. iii, p. 151.

[6] *Suss. Fines*, vol. ii, p. 79; *3 Suss. Subsidies*, pp. 44, 172; *Suss. Custumals*, vol. i, pp. 45, 52, 54, 55; West Suss. Record Office, EP. VI/19A/1, mm. 1, 1d, 2d, 3, 5, 11d, 12. "Sherwyndes' were part of ships' rigging, 14th century: B. Sandahl, *Middle English Sea Terms* (1982), vol. iii, p. 184.

[7] *Suss. Subsidy, 1524–5*, pp. 4, 7, 129; *W. Suss. 1641–2*, p. 187; *S.A.C.*, vol. xx, p. 17; *Valor. Eccl.*, vol. i, p. 298.

[8] Hanley and Chalklin, *op. cit.*, pp. 103, 123; Reaney, *Dict.*, p. 317; W. Rye, *Short Calendar of the Feet of Fines for Norf., for the reigns of Ric. I, John, Hen. III, and Edw. I* (1885), p. 27; East Suff. Record Office, HA 12/C2/7, m. 10; P.R.O. E.179/130/29, m. 2; E.179/161/9, m. 7d; H. E. Salter, *Cartulary of Oseney Abbey* (Oxford Hist. Soc, vol. xcvii) (1934), vol. iv, p. 381–2; *Rotuli Hundredorum* (Rec. Com.) vol. ii, p. 825; W. Farrer, *Lancs. Inquests, Extents and Feudal Aids* (Lancs, and Chesh. Rec. Soc., vol lxx) (1915), vol. iii, p. 90; W. Farrer, *Final Concords of the County of Lanc.* (*ibid.*, vol. l) (1905), part iii, pp. 43, 49; J. W. W. Bund and J. Amphlett, *Lay Subsidy Roll for the County of Worc.* (Worcs. Hist. Soc., vol. i) (1893), pp. 14, 24; A. R. Rumble, *Dorset Lay Subsidy Roll of 1327* (Dorset Rec. Soc., no. 6) (1980), p. 43.

[9] *3 Suss. Subsidies*, pp. 49, 195, 225, 288; P.R.O. E.179/189/42, m. 2; E. 179/130/5, m. 13; J. H. Lumby, *Calendar of Deeds and Papers in Possession of Sir James de Houghton* (Lancs, and Chesh. Rec. Soc., vol. lxxxviii) (1936), pp. 27, 28, 29; Anon., *Suff. in 1327* (Suff. Green

Books, no. ix) (1906), pp. 137, 170, 176; W. Rye, *op. cit.*, p. 42; Reaney, *Dict.*, p. 328; *Rotuli Hundredorum* (Rec. Com), vol. ii, p. 817.

[10] *3 Suss. Subsidies*, pp. 43, 50, 171, 285; *Lewes Barony Recs.*, p. 72.

[11] A. C. Chibnall, *Early Taxation Returns* (Bucks. Rec. Soc. 1946), p. 64. See also the bye-names Coterose, in Suss. (*Suss. Custumals*, vol. ii, p. 56) and Reperose, also Suss. (*S.A.C.*, vol. xcvi, p. 26).

[12] Reaney, *Dict.*, p. 276.

[13] *S.A.C.*, vol. lxxi, pp. 199, 200.

[14] P. McClure, "Interpretation of Middle English Nicknames", *Nomina* (1981), vol. v, p. 99.

[15] See p. 361, 365.

[16] *Non. Inquis.*, pp. 402, 403; *De Lisle and Dudley MSS.*, vol. i, p. 144.

[17] *M.E.D.*

[18] W. D. Parish, *Dictionary of the Suss. Dialect* (1957), p. 60.

[19] *3 Suss. Subsidies*, pp. 68, 152; *Suss. Custumals*, vol. ii, p. 34.

[20] *Hastings Lathe C.R.*, pp. 27, 64, 68, 74, 80, 99, 104.

[21] *Ibid.*, pp. 51, 64, 68.

[22] C. Clark, "Nickname Creation: Some Sources of Evidence", *Nomina* (1981), vol. v, p. 91; M. T. Morlet, *Étude D'Anthroponymie Picarde* (1967), p. 58; P. Erlebach, *Die Zusammengesetzten englischer Zunamen französischer Herkunft* (1979), p. 55; The form de Chauntmerle existed in Dorset: A. Rumble, *Dorset Lay Subsidy Roll of 1327*, pp. 57, 134, 160.

[23] *Chichester Chart.*, pp. 67, 120, 130, 173, 220; *Suss. Fines*, vol. ii, p. 115; *Suss. Custumals*, vol. iii, p. 25; *3 Suss. Subsidies*, pp. 90, 131, 247, 285; *Fitzalan Surveys*, p. 103.

[24] Dauzat, *op. cit.*, p. 465; C. Clarke, *op. cit.*, vol. v, p. 91.

[25] *3 Suss. Subsidies*, pp. 213, 325.

[26] *Boxgrove Chart.*, p. 154; *S.A.C.*, vol. lxx, p. 117; vol. lxxxix, p. 125.

[27] *Ibid.*, vol. li, p. 52; *Suss. Fines*, vol. ii, p. 56; *Lewes Chartulary*, vol. ii, p. 5; L. F. Salzman, *Chartulary of Sele* (1923), pp. 60, 86.

[28] P.R.O. S.C.11/639; Dauzat, *op. cit.*, p. 478.

[29] *3 Suss. Subsidies*, pp. 101, 117 (printed Trotemenn); *V.C.H. Suss.*, vol. iv, p. 58; F. R. H. Du Boulay, *Lordship of Canterbury* (1966), p. 103; Inderwick, *Winchelsea*, p. 184; *Rotuli de Quo Warranto* (Record Commision), p. 750; *Calendar of Inquisitions Post Mortem*, vol. ii, p. 256.

[30] L. Fleming, *Hist. of Pagham*, vol. i, p. 55; *3 Suss. Subsidies*, pp. 41, 44, 180, 282.

[31] *P. N. Suss.*, vol. ii, p. 306.

[32] Reaney, *Dict.*, p. 379.

[33] McClure, *op. cit*, p. 99.

[34] *3 Suss. Subsidies*, p. 246; *P.N. Suss.*, vol. i, pp. 76, 82.

[35] *Chichester Chart.*, p. 255; *Suss. Custumals*, vol. i, pp. 15, 108, 112, 121; vol. iii, p. 36; *3 Suss. Subsidies*, pp. 43, 103.
[36] *Ibid.*, pp. 83, 90, 92; *De Lisle and Dudley MSS.*, vol. i, p. 96.
[37] *3 Suss. Subsidies*, p. 29; Reaney, *Dict., p. 53.*
[38] P.R.O. E.179/235/2.
[39] *Fitzalan Surveys*, p. 22. Possibly Atte Broune could be for atte Burne, with metathesis of "r", since instances of atte Burn are found in Suss.
[40] *3 Suss. Subsidies*, p. 27; *Suss. Custumals*, vol. ii, p. 101; *S.A.C.*, vol. lxxxii, p. 129.
[41] See e.g., *Suss. Custumals*, vol. i, pp. 61, 93, 108; vol. ii, pp. 48, 55, 100, 101; vol. iii, pp. 32, 38, 42, 43; *Non. Inquis.*, p. 377; *3 Suss. Subsidies*, pp. 3, 20, 23, 25, 27, 50 and *passim*.
[42] *Suss. Custumals*, vol. ii, pp. 136, 137.
[43] See p. 195
[44] *3 Suss. Subsidies*, pp. 63, 101, 110, 111, 163, 232, 233, 234; Rubin, *Suss. Phonology*, p. 24.
[45] *W. Suss. 1641–2*, pp. 38, 161.
[46] East Suss. Record Office, Glynde MSS., 1031; Inderwick, *Winchelsea*, p. 170; F. Hull, *Calendar of the White and Black Books of the Cinque Ports* (1966), p. 37.
[47] *Suss. Subsidy, 1524–5*, pp. 24, 141.
[48] Reaney, *Dict.*, p. 126; *P.N. Suss.*, vol. i, p. 18.
[49] Dauzat, *op. cit.*, pp. 252–3.
[50] *3 Suss. Subsidies*, pp. 55, 289; *Chichester Chart.*, p. 298.
[51] *Feudal Aids*, vol. v, p. 163; F. Hull, *op. cit.*, pp. 67, 83, 119, 129, 221; J. E. Ray, *Suss. Chantry Records* (Suss. Record Soc., vol. xxxvi) (1931), p. 12; *Hastings Lathe C. R.*, p. 34; *Suss. Subsidy, 1524–5*, pp. 50, 70, 122; *W. Suss. 1641–2*, pp. 117, 200; P.R.O. S.C.11/649, m.2.
[52] *Suss. Custumals*, vol. i, pp. 108, 115; *3 Suss. Subsidies*, p. 166.
[53] *Hastings Lathe C.R.*, pp. 34, 38–9, 112, 113, 114, 124, 126, 151; *3 Suss. Subsidies*, pp. 14, 44, 76, 210, 211, 216; *S.A.C.*, vol. lxx, p. 19; *Robertsbridge Charters*, pp. 111, 113, 133, 147; *Non. Inquis.*, pp. 352, 370–1.
[54] *Suss Custumals*, vol. ii, p. 61; *Hastings Lathe C.R.*, pp. 3, 6, 16, 122; F. Hull, *op. cit.*, p. 133; *3 Suss. Subsidies*, p. 297; P.R.O. S.C.11/877.
[55] *Cal. Pat, 1429–36*, p. 557.
[56] *Wiston Archives*, pp. 33, 34, 83; *S.A.C.*, vol. lxxxiv, p. 71.
[57] Inderwick, *Winchelsea*, pp. 195, 200.
[58] *Suss. Fines*, vol. i, p. 130; vol. ii, p. 104; vol. iii, pp. 93–4; *De Lisle and Dudley MSS.*, vol. i, p. 83; *3 Suss. Subsidies*, pp. 211, 322; *Fitzalan Surveys*, p. 19; L. F. Salzman, *Chartulary of Sele* (1923), pp. 4, 6, 95.
[59] *P. N. Suss.*, vol. ii, p. 515.

[60] *Ibid.*, vol. ii, p. 498. Marley, in Fernhurst, and Marley, in Peasmarsh, seem unlikely to have given rise to the surname. *Ibid.*, vol. i, p. 20; vol. ii, p. 532.

[61] *Suss. Custumals*, vol, i, p. 129. In the 16th century there was a locality called the Marle at Withyham, but it is not known how old the name is; E. Straker, *Buckhurst Terrier* (Suss. Record Soc., vol. xxxix) (1934), p. 35.

[62] Dauzat, *op. cit.*, p. 430.

[63] *3 Suss. Subsidies*, p. 55, 201, 312.

[64] *Lewes Chartulary*, vol. ii, p. 10; *Chichester Chartulary*, p. 174.

[65] Lane, *Suss. Deeds*, p. 106; P.R.. E.179/225/50, m. 35.

[66] *S.A.C.*, vol. xx, p. 60; Lane, *op. cit.*, p. 92; *W. Suss. 1641–2*, pp. 14, 19, 56, 67, 78, 85, 95–6, 109–10, 133–4, 152.

[67] *Boxgrove Chartulary*, pp. 68, 74, 76; *Chichester Chartulary*, pp. 178, 186; *3 Suss. Subsidies*, pp. 55, 96.

[68] *Ibid.*, pp. 129, 252, 255; *Non. Inquis.*, pp. 351, 355, 375; P.R.O. E.179/189/42, m. 26; *Fitzalan Surveys*, p. 139.

[69] P.R.O. E.179/189/42, m. 19; *Suss. Fines*. vol. iii, pp. 156, 186.

[70] *Feudal Aids*, vol. v, p. 152, 160.

[71] *Calendar of Close Rolls, 1377–81*, pp. 122, 123, 458–9; *S.A.C.*, vol. xli, pp. 95–9; *V.C.H. Suss.*, vol. iv, p. 213; *Suss. Subsidy, 1524–5*, p. 67; *W. Suss. 1641–2*, pp. 105, 153.

[72] *Lewes Chartulary*, vol. i, p. 171.

[73] J. E. Ray, *op. cit.*, p. 17.

[74] *3 Suss. Subsidies*, pp. 52, 79, 137, 176, 181, 253, 291, 294; Reaney, *Dict.*, p. 108. It is difficult to separate the early forms for the name 'Duck' from those for 'Duke'.

[75] See pp. 361–2.

[76] See pp. 373–86, 389, 401.

[77] See pp. 400–1, 403–8.

[78] See, e.g. *3 Suss. Subsidies*, pp. 113, 116, 199, 237, 297, 330; *Lewes Chartulary*, vol. i, pp. 100, 101, 120, 165; *Non. Inquis.*, pp. 378, 403; P.R.O. E.179/225/5; E.179/225/50 mm. 28, 32; S.C.11/663; S.C.11/666; *Suss. Fines*, vol. iii, pp. 214, 222, 254.

[79] *Fitzalan Surveys*, p. 1; *Battle Custumals*, p. 33; D. M. Stenton, *Great Roll of the Pipe for the 7th year of Richard I* (Pipe Roll Soc., vol. xliii) (1928), p. 37; *S.A.C..*, vol. li, p. 64; *3 Suss. Subsidies*, p. 98; *Suss. Fines*, vol. i, pp. 9, 23, 31, 36, 43, 123; vol. ii, pp. 40, 181; *Boxgrove Chart.*, pp. 37, 70; *De Lisle and Dudley MSS.*, vol. i, pp. 35, 76, 118.

[80] *Suss Custumals*, vol. ii, pp. 17, 20; *Chichester Chart.*, pp. 94, 288; *Suss. Fines*, vol. i, p. 111; vol. ii, p. 147; *Boxgrove Chart.*, p. 85; *3 Suss. Subsidies*, p. 247.

[81] *S.A.C.*, vol. xxiv, p. 69; vol. lxxxix, p. 124; *Chichester Chart.*, p. 248; *Fitzalan Surveys*, p. 139.

[82] *Suss. Subsidy, 1524–5*, pp. 38–40; *W. Suss. 1641–2*, pp. 25, 42, 59, 72, 75, 137; *Chichester Chart.*, p. 243; Lord Leconfield, *Sutton and Duncton Manors* (1956), pp. 15, 16, 68; P.R.O. E.179/191/378, m. 2; *Suss. Wills*, vol. i, pp. 72, 188; vol. ii, p. 179; vol. iii, p. 292; vol. iv, pp. 179, 197.

[83] Reaney, *Dict.*, 77; G. Tengvik, *Old English Bye-Names* (1938), pp. 305–6; C. W. Bardsley, *English Surnames* (1969), p. 124. The surname might possibly be from a personal name: G. Tengvik, *op. cit.*, p. 306.

[84] P.R.O. S.C.11/877; *Lewes Barony Recs.*, p. 11; *Chichester Chart.*, pp. 94, 240, 243; *3 Suss. Subsidies.*, pp. 46, 55, 75, 98, 104.

[85] P.R.O. S.C.11/877; *S.A.C.*, vol. xxii, pp. 117–18; vol. liv, pp. 96, 99; Lane, *Suss. Deeds*, p. 56; *Suss. Fines*, vol. iii, p. 224; *Suss. Wills*, vol. i, p. 36.

[86] *Suss. Subsidy, 1524–5*, p. 90; *S.A.C.*, vol. xviii, p. 25; *3 Suss. Subsidies*, p. 46; *Suss. Wills*, vol. iii, p. 20.

[87] *Ibid.*, pp. 213, 214; F. Hull, *op. cit.*, pp. 17, 21, 229, 348; *S.A.C.*, vol. liii, p. 50; H.M.C., *Rye MSS.*, pp. 16, 18; P.R.O. E.179/228/112; E.179/225/5; *Suss. Subsidy, 1524–5*, p. 152; *Suss. Fines*, vol. iii, p. 8.

[88] *W. Suss. 1641–2*, p. 164; *3 Suss. Subsidies*, p. 55; P.R.O. E.179/189/42, mm. 24, 28.

[89] *W. Suss. 1641–2*, pp. 9, 17, 18, 33, 34, 58, 63, 124, 164, 168, 196, 202; *Suss. Subsidy, 1524–5*, pp. 27, 34, 45, 56, 63, 78, 90, 95, 106, 122, 137, 139, 147, 148, 152; R. Garraway Rice, *Parish Register of Horsham* (Suss. Record Soc., vol. xxi) (1915), pp. 162, 354.

[90] *Catalogue of Ancient Deeds*, vol. iii, p. 42; *3 Suss. Subsidies*, p. 299; *Suss. Subsidy, 1524–5*, pp. 27, 34, 45, 56, 63, 78, 90, 106; *Valor Eccl.*, vol. i, p. 298; *S.A.C.*, vol. xlviii, pp. 20, 21; *Suss. Wills*, vol. i, pp. 21, 210, 271; vol. ii, pp. 84, 191; vol iii, pp. 9, 293; J. E. Ray, *op. cit.*, p. 26; West Suss. Record Office, E.P. VI/19A/1, m. 15; P.R.O. E.179/228/112; *Suss. Fines*, vol. iii, p. 288; L. F. Salzman, *Chartulary of Sele*, p. 35; and see p. 17.

[91] *Lewes Chartulary*, vol. ii, p. 95; *3 Suss. Subsidies*, pp. 183, 229.

[92] *Ibid.*, pp. 57, 154, 269; P.R.O. E.179/189/42, m. 4; *Suss. Fines*, vol. ii, p. 113; vol. iii, pp. 71, 97, 292.

[93] *S.A.C.*, vol. xli, p. 141; vol. lxix, p. 139; *Wiston Archives*, p. 86; *Suss. Subsidy, 1524–5*, pp. 66, 67; *W. Suss. 1641–2*, pp. 32, 98, 100–01, 107, 153, 195; R. Garraway Rice, *op. cit., per indice*; *Suss. Fines*, vol. iii, pp. 151, 275; *Suss. Wills*, vol. iii, p. 50.

[94] *3 Suss. Subsidies*, pp. 158, 272; *W. Suss. 1641–2*, p. 197; *Wiston Archives*, p. 30; *S.A.C.*, vol. liv, p. 163; P.R.O. E.179/189/42, m. 23; *Fitzalan Surveys*, pp. 109, 134.

[95] *Feudal Aids*, vol. v, p. 143; *3 Suss. Subsidies*, p. 256; *S.A.C.*, vol. lxxxix, pp. 129, 133, 137–8, 161; *V.C.H. Suss.*, vol. iv, pp. 185, 195; *Suss. Fines*, vol. iii, p. 234.
[96] *S.A.C.*, vol. lviii, pp. 11, 13, 20; P. S. Godman, *Parish Register of Cowfold* (Suss. Record Soc., vol. xxii) (1916), *per indice*, under Feste.
[97] *West Suss. 1641–2*, pp. 26, 32, 38, 59, 98, 100, 101, 107, 153, 173, 174, 195, 197, 202.
[98] Reaney, *Dict.*, p. 133, J. A. H. Murray, *New English Dictionary* (1901), vol. i, part i, p. 500.
[99] *De Lisle and Dudley MSS.*, vol. i, p. 53. The place-name Fowlbrook, in Ewhurst, might be connected with this Fleming. *P. N. Suss*, vol. ii, p. 519.
[100] *Ibid.*, vol. i, p. 68.
[101] *3 Suss. Subsidies*, pp. 14, 210, 322; *Hastings Lathe C.R.*, pp. 133, 150, 170; *Suss. Wills*, vol. iv, p. 58.
[102] *Ibid.*, pp. 32, 150, 158; *Suss. Subsidy, 1524–5*, pp. 157; P.R.O. S.C.11/649, m. 2; F. Hull, *op. cit.*, pp. 210, 213; *Suss. Wills*, vol. i, p. 199; J. S. Cockburn, *Calendar of Assize Records*,(1985), p. 102.
[103] *P. N. Suss*, vol. ii, p. 317.
[104] *Lewes Chartulary*, vol. i, p. 87; *3 Suss. Subsidies*, pp. 35, 229; *Catalogue of Ancient Deeds*, vol. iii, p. 39.
[105] *Robertsbridge Surveys*, pp. 87, 88; *S.A.C.*, vol. xli, pp. 33, 40, 42; *Suss. Subsidy, 1524–5*, p. 124, 134; East Suss. Record Office, Dunn MSS., 1/15, 1/24,–25, 1/31, 1/35, 1/42, 1/49, 1/50, 1/51, 1/52, 1/53, 2/34, 5/3, 20/6; *Suss. Fines*, vol. iii, p. 268; *Suss Wills*, vol. ii, p. 126; vol. iii, p. 75; vol. iv, pp. 25, 223.
[106] *3 Suss. Subsidies*, pp. 46, 176; *Suss. Subsidy, 1524–5*, pp. 71, 90, 106; *Suss. Wills*, vol. i, p. 1; vol. iii, p. 21.
[107] *Ibid.*, pp. 3, 20, 26; *3 Suss. Subsidies*, pp. 91, 92, 111, 119, 129, 230, 231, 232, 233,252; *Feudal Aids*, vol. v, p. 164; *S.A.C.* vol. xxiv, p. 67; vol. lxxxvii, pp. 3–4, 13; vol. lxxix, p. 138; *Suss. Wills*, vol. iv, p. 229.
[108] *Suss. Subsidy, 1524–5*, pp. 3, 10, 20, 26, 45, 71, 88, 90, 97, 106, 121, 124, 134, 139, 143–4, 149, 153, 157.
[109] See p. 17.
[110] *3 Suss. Subsidies*, pp. 212, 221, 324, 333; *Hastings Lathe C.R.*, p. 114; *Robertsbridge Charters*, pp. 110, 116; *Boxgrove Chart.*, p. 154; *S.A.C.*, vol. xxiv, p. 69.
[111] Reaney, *Dict.*, p. 133.
[112] *Suss. Subsidy, 1524–5*, p. 128.
[113] *Ibid.*, pp. 22, 29, 112, 143, 144, 162, 163; *3 Suss. Subsidies*, pp. 24, 93, 101, 122, 143, 163, 267; *Feudal Aids*, vol. v, p. 149; *Hastings Lathe C.R.*, pp. 33–4, 69, 72, 115, 126, 139, 154, 181; *S.A.C.*, vol. li, p. 134; *Robertsbridge Surveys*, p. 84, 85; P.R.O. E.179/189/42, m. 6; E.179/225/50, mm. 19, 29.

[114] *Robertsbridge Surveys*, pp. 84, 85.
[115] *3 Suss. Subsidies*, pp. 15, 47, 51, 114, 177, 210, 217, 322, 328; *Suss. Fines*, vol. ii, p. 12; *Non. Inquis.*, p. 403; *Suss. Custumals*, vol. ii, p. 123; *Catalogue of Ancient Deeds*, vol. iv, p. 96; *Lewes Barony Recs.*, p. 75; P.R.O. E.179/189/42, m. 6; S.C. 11/663.
[116] *3 Suss. Subsidies*, p. 51; *Suss. Fines*, vol. ii, p. 12; *Catalogue of Ancient Deeds*, vol. iv, p. 96.
[117] See sources cited in note 115, and see P.R.O. E.179/228/112; E.179/225/50, m. 26; *Suss. Subsidy, 1524–5*, p. 161; *Hastings Lathe C.R.*, pp. 41, 119.
[118] *S.A.C.*, vol. xviii, p. 26; *Hastings Lathe C.R.*, pp. 161, 188, 193; *Suss. Subsidy, 1524–5*, p. 145; *Suss. Wills*, vol. i, p. 253.
[119] F. Hull, *op. cit.*, pp. 3, 133.
[120] *Suss. Subsidy, 1524–5*, pp. 112, 125, 133, 134; Inderwick, *Winchelsea*, pp. 163, 171; *Hastings Lathe C.R.*, pp. 3, 13; *3 Suss. Subsidies*, pp. 9, 22, 302.
[121] *P.N. Suss.*, vol. i, p. 233; vol. ii, pp. 265, 368, 415.
[122] Lane, *Suss. Deeds*, p. 81; *Robertsbridge Surveys*, pp. 23, 56, 106; *Battle Custumals*, p. 14; *P.N. Suss.* vol. i, pp. 37, 233; *Fitzalan Surveys*, pp. 130, 137.
[123] *Boxgrove Chart.*, p. 88; *Hastings Lathe C.R.*, p. 142. See also the byename Byndepouke (at West Firle, about 1339) (*Chichester Chart.*, p. 195). Compare the bye-name Bindedevel (Reaney, *Origins*, p. 287).
[124] Reaney, *Dict.*, p. 277; J. Glover, *Place-Names of Suss.*, p. 133.
[125] *Non. Inquis.*, p. 391; *3 Suss. Subsidies*, pp. 166, 281.
[126] *P.N. Suss.*, vol. ii, p. 388; *Suss. Custumals*, vol. ii, p. 32.
[127] *Valor Eccl.*, vol. i, p. 350; *Robertsbridge Surveys*, pp. 16, 23.
[128] *3 Suss. Subsidies*, pp. 82, 103, 133; *Suss. Custumals*, vol. i, pp. 6, 31; *Fitzalan Surveys*, p. 20; *Chichester Chart.*, p. 238; *Boxgrove Chart.*, p. 178.
[129] *Non. Inquis.*, p. 391; *Winston Archives*, p. 207; *Suss. Fines*, vol. i, p. 132; vol. ii, p. 114; *3 Suss. Subsidies*, pp. 61, 166. Pook's Farm, at Shermanbury, preserves the name.
[130] *Ibid.*, p. 291.
[131] *Ibid.*, pp. 16, 18, 207, 318; *Suss. Custumals*, vol. ii, pp. 32, 40, 72; *S.A.C.*, vol. xviii, p. 26; *Hastings Lathe C.R.*, pp. 27, 29, 111; *P.N. Suss.*, vol. ii, p. 388.
[132] *3 Suss. Subsidies*, p. 184; *S.A.C.*, vol. xcv, p. 50.
[133] *Suss. Subsidy, 1524–5*, pp. 146, 148, 149, 151, 156, 159; *Valor Eccl.*, vol. i, p. 350; *Robertsbridge Charters*, p. 150; *Robertsbridge Surveys*, pp. 1, 5, 6, 7, 10, 13, 16–17, 23, 35, 45, 181; *Suss. Wills*, vol. i, p. 59; vol. iv, pp. 83, 324.
[134] *Suss. Subsidy, 1524–5*, p. 113.

Surnames Derived from Nicknames

[135] *Ibid.*, p. 25.
[136] Cottle, *Dict.*, p. 304; Reaney, *Dict.*, p. 284.
[137] *3 Suss. Subsidies*, pp. 119, 230, 234. See also the examples of the name le Putel: *ibid.*, p. 141; *Suss. Custumals*, vol. iii, p. 66.
[138] *Battle Custumals*, p. 14.
[139] *Robertsbridge Surveys*, pp. 72, 106.
[140] *Non. Inquis.*, p. 363; *S.A.C.*, vol. lxix, p. 114; *3 Suss. Subsidies*, pp. 140, 257.
[141] *Ibid.*, pp. 63, 161, 164, 276; P.R.O. E.179/189/42, mm. 18, 21.
[142] *3 Suss. Subsidies*, pp. 26, 184, 297; P.R.O. S.C.11/877.
[143] *S.A.C.*, vol. lxxxiv, p. 66.
[144] *Suss. Subsidy, 1524–5*, pp. 13, 15, 71, 74, 80, 103, 117; *Hastings Lathe C.R.*, p. 60; F. Hull, *op. cit.*, p. 136; *Suss. Wills*, vol. ii, p. 81.
[145] *S.A.C.*, vol xii, p. 43; vol. lxxxix, p. 137; vol. xcv, p. 55; vol. xcviii, p. 68; *Fitzalan Surveys*, pp. 157, 160.
[146] *W. Suss. 1641–2*, pp. 9, 60, 81, 95, 98–9, 101, 104, 108–9, 117, 127, 144, 147, 153, 159, 187; R. Garraway Rice, *Parish Register of Horsham* (Suss. Record Soc., vol. xxi) (1915), *per indice*; *Suss. Wills*, vol. ii, p. 343.
[147] *W. Suss. 1641–2*, p. 38, 108.
[148] On such names see p. 318.
[149] Reaney, *Dict.*, p. 332.
[150] *S.A.C.*, vol. xxii, p. 157; R. Garraway Rice, *op. cit.*, p. 35; J. E. Ray, *op. cit.*, pp. 20, 105; *Suss. Subsidy, 1524–5*, pp. 26, 83, 137; *Suss. Wills*, vol. i, p.183; vol. iv, p. 222.
[151] Reaney, *Dict.*, p. 387.
[152] *3 Suss. Subsidies*, p. 63, 95, 131, 149, 191, 250; *Non. Inquis.*, p. 364; *Suss. Custumals*, vol. i, p. 69; *Chichester Chart.*, p. 212; *S.A.C.*, lxxxii, p. 130; P.R.O. S.C.11/666; E.179/189/42, m. 20.
[153] *W. Suss. 1641–2*, pp. 8, 89; *Suss. Subsidy 1524–5*, pp. 9, 11; W. H. Challen, *Parish Register of Cocking, 1558–1837* (1927), pp. 89, 92; P.R.O. E.179/191/378, m. 1.
[154] *W. Suss. 1641–2*, p. 133.
[155] *Ibid.*, p. 102; *Suss. Subsidy, 1524–5*, p. 44; West Suss. Record Office, E.P. VI/19A/1, mm. 11, 12, 15.
[156] L. F. Salzman, *Parish Register of Glynde, Suss., 1558–1812* (Suss. Record Soc., vol. xxx) (1924), *per indice*.
[157] *S.A.C.*, vol. xxv, p. 131.
[158] *Fitzalan Surveys*, pp. 17, 20; *S.A.C.*, vol. lxxxix, p. 139; *3 Suss. Subsidies*, pp. 88, 110.
[159] *Ibid.*, pp. 132, 247; *Suss. Custumals*, vol. i, p. 24; *Chichester Chart.*, p. 219.
[160] *Boxgrove Chart.*, p. 31.
[161] *Non. Inquis.*, p. 360; H. D. Gordon, *History of Harting* (1877), p. 44; *3 Suss. Subsidies*, pp. 84, 112, 113, 114; *Fitzalan Surveys*, p. 156.

[162] P.R.O. E.179/189/42, m. 23; West Suss. Record Office, E.P. VI/19A/1, m. 3d; Wiston MSS, 5234 (2) d; Wiston MSS., 5236, mm. 1d, 3d; Wiston MSS., 5237, m. 1.

[163] *3 Suss. Subsidies*, pp. 168, 265, 282; *Non. Inquis.*, p. 369; P.R.O. E.179/189/42, m. 14.

[164] *W. Suss. 1641–2*, pp. 80, 82, 140; E. W. D. Penfold, *First Book of the Parish Registers of Angmering* (Suss. Record Soc., vol. xviii) (1913), per indice.

[165] *W. Suss. 1641–2*, p. 175; *Suss. Custumals*, vol. ii, p. 51.

[166] *3 Suss. Subsidies*, p. 166; *Suss. Subsidy, 1524–5*, pp. 25, 26; *W. Suss. 1641–2*, p. 158.

[167] *Suss. Custumals*, vol. ii, pp. 51, 129–30, 137.

[168] *3 Suss. Subsidies*, pp. 221, 333; *Robertsbridge Charters*, pp. 110, 128.

[169] *Lewes Chartulary*, vol. i, pp. 99, 144; vol. ii, pp. 4, 5, 23, 70; *Lewes Barony Recs.*, p. 23; *S.A.C.*, vol. vi, p. 218. See also the surname de Beueresford, found in Suss., 13th century: *Suss. Fines*, vol. i, p. 92; *S.A.C.*, vol. xx, p. 4.

[170] *Battle Custumals*, pp. 104, 112. See also Hanley and Chalklin, *op. cit.*, pp. 131, 132.

[171] J. F. Dimock, *Giraldi Cambrensis Itinerarium Kambriae* (1868) (Rolls Series), pp. 114–15.

[172] *3 Suss. Subsidies*, p. 190; P.R.O. E.179/225/5; E.179/225/50, m. 10.

[173] F. Hull, *op. cit.*, p. 219; *W. Suss 1641–2*, p. 20.

[174] *Suss. Subsidy, 1524–5*, p. 65.

[175] *Lewes Chartulary*, vol. i, pp. 142, 147.

[176] *Boxgrove Chart*, p. 192; *3 Suss. Subsidies*, p. 95.

[177] *Ibid.*, pp. 54, 55, 95, 257, 268, 272, 275; *Lewes Chartulary*, vol. ii, p. 77; *Fitzalan Surveys*, p. 108; *Suss. Subsidy, 1524–5*, pp. 43, 59, 67, 92; *W. Suss. 1641–2*, pp. 53, 59, 79, 98, 137, 192. An alien called Wolf is listed at Poynings in 1436; *Cal. Pat., 1429–36*, p. 547.

[178] C. Matheson, "The Grey Wolf", *Antiquity* (1943), vol. xvii, p. 15.

[179] C. Matheson, "Man and Bear in Europe", *Ibid.* (1942), vol. xvi, p. 157.

[180] P.R.O. S.C.11/663.

[181] C. Matheson, "Man and Bear in Europe", *Antiquity* (1942), vol. xvi, p. 153.

[182] P. M. Barnes, *Great Roll of the Pipe for the 16th year of John* (Pipe Roll Soc., vol. lxxiii) (1962), p. 165.

[183] *S.A.C.*, vol. li, p. 61; *Boxgrove Chart.*, pp. 183–5; *Chichester Chart.*, p. 117; *Fitzalan Surveys*, p. 8; *3 Suss. Subsidies*, pp. 97, 126, 127, 249, 251, 267.

[184] *Ibid.*, pp. 30, 37, 299; *Suss. Custumals*, vol. ii, pp. 95, 104, 130.

[185] P.R.O. S.C.11/663.

[186] *Suss. Fines*, vol. ii, p. 54; *Boxgrove Chart*, p. 33.

[187] *Suss. Subsidy, 1524–5*, pp. 21, 23.
[188] *W. Suss. 1641–2*, pp. 126, 150, 151, 164.
[189] *Ibid.*, p. 115. And see p. 17.
[190] *Non. Inquis.*, p. 378; *S.A.C.*., vol. xii, p. 26; *3 Suss. Subsidies*, pp. 187, 300.
[191] *Ibid.*, pp. 126, 249; West Suss. Record Office, E.P. VI/19A/1, m. 9.
[192] *Suss. Custumals*, vol. iii, p. 23.
[193] *Great Roll of the Pipe for the 12th year of Henry II* (Pipe Roll Soc., vol. ix) (1888), p. 92.
[194] *Chichester Chart.*, pp. 156, 157; *Suss. Fines*, vol. ii, p. 36.
[195] H. D. Gordon, *History of Harting* (1877), p. 44; *3 Suss. Subsidies*, pp. 14, 67, 112, 327.
[196] *Suss. Custumals*, vol. i, p. 74.
[197] *Ibid.*, vol. i, p. 77.
[198] *S.A.C.*, vol. liv, p. 154.
[199] *3 Suss. Subsidies*, pp. 68, 184, 217, 330; *De Lisle and Dudley MSS.*, vol. i, pp. 2, 3; *Non. Inquis.*, p. 387; *S.A.C.*, vol. xcvi, p. 28; *Fitzalan Surveys*, p. 114; *Hastings Lathe C.R.*, p. 112; P.R.O. S.C.11/877.
[200] *Suss. Subsidy, 1524–5*, p. 132; *S.A.C.*, vol. xcvi, p. 28.
[201] *Hastings Lathe C.R.*, p. 112; *3 Suss. Subsidies*, pp. 217, 330; *Suss. Subsidy, 1524–5*, p. 142.
[202] *S.A.C.*, vol. lxiv, p. 80; J. E. Ray, *op. cit.*, p. 144; *Suss. Wills*, vol. iv, p. 324.
[203] *W. Suss. 1641–2*, pp. 120, 121, 156; P. S. Godman, *op. cit.*, pp. 99, 101.
[204] *3 Suss. Subsidies*, pp. 26, 28, 184, 297, 310; *Suss. Fines*, vol. ii, p. 156; P.R.O. S.C.11/877. The name de Leoffardi, or de Sancto Leopharde, occurs Petworth, 13th century, but does not seem to be connected.
[205] Reaney, *Dict.*, p. 214; J. C. Ward, *Medieval Essex Community* (1983), p. 5.
[206] *Suss. Subsidy, 1524–5*, pp. 36, 37, 94–6, 103; *Robertsbridge Surveys*, p. 14; *S.A.C.* vol. xxxvi, p. 35; vol. xxxix, pp. 179, 180; *W. Suss. 1641–2*, p. 138; Lord Leconfield, *Petworth Manor in the 17th century* (1954), pp. 47, 108–9, 112; *Suss. Wills*, vol. iii, p. 106.
[207] *S.A.C.*, vol. xxxvi, p. 35; vol. xxxvii, p. 45; G. W. E. Loder, *Parish Registers of Ardingly* (Suss. Record Soc., vol. xvii) (1913), *per indice*.
[208] *W. Suss. 1641–2*, pp. 47, 55.
[209] H. B. Guppy, *Homes of Family Names* (1968), p. 315.
[210] *3 Suss. Subsidies*, p. 79, 245; *Non. Inquis.*, p. 351; L. Fleming, *History of Pagham*, vol. i, p. xli; *Boxgrove Chart.*, pp. 163–64.
[211] *3 Suss. Subsidies*, p. 4; *Suss. Subsidy, 1524–5*, p. 98; P.R.O. E.179/225/5.
[212] *3 Suss. Subsidies*, pp. 33, 236; P.R.O. E.179/225/5; E.179/225/12; the surname also occurs in other counties. See J. Bellamy, *Robin Hood* (1985), p. 135.

[213] Lewes Chartulary, vol. i, p. 165; Non. Inquis., pp. 378, 403; P.R.O. E.179/225/5; S.C.11/663; S.C.11/666.

[214] 3 Suss. Subsidies, pp. 33, 38, 49, 51, 168, 174, 179, 195, 288, 293; Lane, Suss. Deeds, p. 147; Suss. Custumals, vol. ii, p. 134; Non. Inquis., p. 384.

[215] Feudal Aids, vol. v, p. 132; S.A.C., vol. xcviii, p. 157; Lewes Chartulary, vol. i, pp. 55, 93, 99, 168; Calendar of Close Rolls, 1302–7, p. 503; ibid., 1307–13, p. 550.

[216] Compare the Suss. place-name Sicklehatch: P.N. Suss., vol. ii, p. 468.

[217] Suss. Fines, vol. iii, p. 137; Chichester Chart., p. 215; 3 Suss. Subsidies, pp. 99, 116, 240; C. Swainson, Provincial Names and Folklore of British Birds (1885), pp. 193, 202, 203; Fitzalan Surveys, p. 143; Hanley and Chalklin, op. cit., p. 141; Penfogill occurs at Hastings, 16th century, perhaps through migration from Kent: Suss. Wills, vol. ii, p. 275.

[218] 3 Suss. Subsidies, pp. 11, 144; Boxgrove Chart., p. 169; Fitzalan Surveys, pp. 6, 107, 123; Suss. Fines, vol. iii, p. 77; Non. Inquis., p. 367.

[219] This surname is not listed in Dauzat, op. cit.

[220] Suss. Custumals, vol. ii, p. 92; S.A.C., vol. xxi, p. 160; 3 Suss. Subsidies, p. 37; compare the bye-name Takepaine, found in Lewes, 1237: Lewes Chartulary, vol. ii, p. 4.

[221] Lewes Chartulary, vol. i, pp. 104–5, 120, 144; vol. ii, pp. 4, 23; 3 Suss. Subsidies, p. 45; Excerpta e Rotulis Finium, vol. i, p. 44.

[222] 3 Suss. Subsidies, pp. 54, 57, 271; West Suss. Record Office, E.P. VI/19A/1, m. 2d. The name means "by faith", one of the many names from the habitual use of oaths or ejaculations.

[223] See pp. 19.

[224] See p. 46.

[225] See p. 407.

[226] Suss. Custumals, vol. ii, pp. 10, 12; J. E. Ray, op. cit., p. 49; Suss. Subsidy, 1524–5, pp. 3, 28, 31, 40; W. Suss. 1641–2, pp. 158, 171; Suss. Wills, vol. iii, p. 15.

[227] 3 Suss. Subsidies, p. 284; Suss. Subsidy, 1524–5, pp. 26, 48, 91, 92, 101, 102; Suss. Indictments, vol. i, p. 17; J. E. Ray, op. cit., p. 154; Lewes Barony Recs., p. 55; P.R.O. E.179/190/267; Suss. Wills, vol. iv, p. 34.

[228] P.N. Suss., vol. i, p. 131; J. Glover, Place-Names of Sussex, p. 13; Suss. Subsidy, 1524–5, p. 48; Suss. Wills, vol. iv, p. 143.

[229] 3 Suss. Subsidies, pp. 60, 168, 282; Catalogue of Ancient Deeds, vol. iii, p. 29; Wiston Archives, pp. 72, 166; Suss. Indictments, vol. i, p. 76; Suss. Subsidy, 1524–5, pp. 59, 74; W. C. Renshaw, Parish Registers of Cuckfield (Suss. Record Soc., vol. xiii) (1911), p. 40, 56, 57, 75, 195; P.R.O. E.179/189/42, mm. 3, 3d. The surname has been supposed to

have been given to persons who bore the marks of infection with plague (Reaney, *Dict.*, p. 148), but examples cited for the use of the phrase in this sense all date from after 1500, and the name existed before the outbreaks of plague in the mid 14th century.

[230] *Suss. Custumals*, vol. i, p. 110; *Suss. Subsidy, 1524–5*, p. 101; *S.A.C.*, vol. lxiv, p. 72. And see p. 372.

[231] *3 Suss. Subsidies*, p. 62; *Suss. Subsidy, 1524–5*, p. 84; *Lewes Chartulary*, vol. ii, p. 67; D. M. Stenton, *Great Roll of the Pipe for the 8th year of John* (Pipe Roll Soc., vol. lviii) (1942), p. 63; R. Garraway Rice, *Parish Register of Horsham* (Suss. Record Soc., vol. xxi) (1915), pp. 2, 7, 293, 306, 309. And see p. 401.

[232] *Suss. Subsidy, 1524–5*, pp. 16, 22, 24, 28, 32, 33. And see p. 432.

[233] *3 Suss. Subsidies*, pp. 43, 92, 102–105.

[234] *Ibid.*; *Fitzalan Surveys*, pp. 4, 7–8, 10–15, 26–31, 125, 127–30; L. Fleming, *Hist. of Pagham*, vol. i, pp. xxxiv–xxxvi; *Suss. Fines*, vol. i, pp. 34–5, 45, 47, 55, 122, 128–9, 132; vol. ii, pp. 13, 17; *Chichester Chartulary*, pp. 98, 107, 120, 123, 193–4, 345, 351, 354, 357; *Lewes Barony Recs.*, p. 72; *Suss. Custumals*, vol. i, pp. 4–11, 13–31, 33–9, 42–52, 54–61, 65, 71–86, 88–95, 106–22; vol. ii, pp. 11–13, 18–21, 23–5, 37–46, 51–2, 60–1, 64–9, 73–4, 79–83, 88, 91–4, 96, 98, 100, 104, 107, 111–13; vol. iii, pp. 38, 49–53, 62, 65–8, 68–73, 76–8; *Battle Custumals*, pp. 4–9, 19–21, 22–3, 26–7, 32–4, 53, 55–7; *S.A.C.*, vol. liii, pp. 152–5.

[235] See p. 46.

[236] Reaney, *Dict.*, p. 178; *W. Suss. 1641–2*, pp. 64, 88, 102, 121, 138, 176; *S.A.C.*, vol. xxiv, p. 80; *Wiston Archives*, p. 286; W. H. Challen, *Parish Register of Cocking, 1558–1837* (1927), p. 19; R. Garraway Rice, *op. cit.*, pp. 47, 283, 289; R. Garraway Rice, *Transcripts of Suss. Wills* (Suss. Record Soc., vol. xlii) (1937), vol. ii, p. 156.

[237] *V.C.H. Suss.*, vol. vii, pp. 111, 123; *W. Suss. 1641–2*, pp. 9, 65, 171.

[238] R. Garraway Rice, *Parish Register of Horsham* (Suss. Record Soc., vol. xxi) (1915), *per indice*; East Grinstead Parish Registers (transcript by G. M. Smart, at Society of Genealogists). Compare the name Masseday: *3 Suss. Subsidies*, pp. 49, 182.

[239] Reaney, *Dict.*, p. 135.

[240] *3 Suss. Subsidies*, pp. 12, 23, 192; *Suss. Fines*, vol. i, p. 119; D. M. Stenton, *Great Roll of the Pipe for the 2nd year of King John* (Pipe Roll Soc., vol. l) (1934), p. 247.

[241] East Suss. Record Office, Glynde MSS., 991, mm. 1, 3; A. H. Smith, *Place-Name Elements* (1970), vol. i, p. 187.

[242] *Suss. Subsidy, 1524–5*, p. 159.

[243] Reaney, *Dict.*, p. 143; Cottle, *Dict.*, p. 153.

[244] *3 Suss. Subsidies*, pp. 6, 9, 209, 219.

[245] *Ibid.*, pp. 23, 209, 221; *Feudal Aids*, vol. v, p. 132.

[246] *3 Suss. Subsidies*, p. 23, 304. And see p. 338.
[247] Reaney, *Dict.*, p. 148; Cottle, *Dict.*, p. 158.
[248] *Hastings Lathe C.R.*, pp. 32, 73, 111, 149, 150, 158, 166, 200; *S.A.C.*, vol. xviii, p. 26; *Robertsbridge Surveys*, pp. 81, 97, 99; *Suss. Subsidy, 1524–5*, p. 148; East Suss. Record Office, Dunn MSS., 1/23, 2/34, 2/35; *Suss. Wills*, vol. i, p. 236.
[249] *Robertsbridge Charters*, p. 99; *3 Suss. Subsidies*, pp. 167, 281.
[250] *P.N. Suss.*, vol. ii, p. 462.
[251] See p. 5.
[252] *S.A.C.*, vol. xxii, pp. 148, 151; vol. lxxvii, p. 102; J. E. Ray, *op. cit.*, pp. 22, 68.
[253] *3 Suss. Subsidies*, pp. 194, 306; *Suss. Custumals*, vol. iii, p. 45.
[254] *Hastings Lathe C.R.*, p. 119; *Suss. Fines*, vol. iii, p. 133.
[255] *Suss. Subsidy, 1524–5*, pp. 125, 126, 127, 136.
[256] Reaney, *Dict.*, p. 239. See the phonetic evidence given in S. Rubin, *Phonology of the Middle English Dialect of Suss.* (1951), p. 52–61.
[257] *3 Suss. Subsidies*, p. 292; *Surr. Taxation Returns* (Surr. Record Soc., vol. xi) (1922), p. 56; *Curia Regis Rolls, Richard I - 2 John*, p. 170; *Curia Regis Rolls, 11–14 John*, p. 307; *Suss. Fines*, vol. iii, pp. 128, 216, 236, 264; Reaney, *Dict.*, p. 269.
[258] *Suss. Subsidy, 1524–5*, pp. 103, 105, 126, 129, 134.
[259] *S.A.C.*, vol. xxxvi, p. 36; *Wiston Archives*, pp. 295, 405; L. F. Salzman, *Parish Register of Glynde* (Suss. Record Soc., vol. xxx) (1924), p. 56.
[260] *Suss. Subsidy, 1524–5*, p. 129; *Suss. Wills*, vol. ii, p. 297; vol. iv, p. 260.
[261] *Ibid.*, pp. 124, 148.
[262] *S.A.C.*, vol. cxvi, p. 10; G. W. E. Loder, *Parish Registers of Ardingly* (Suss. Record Soc., xvii) (1913), pp. 2, 3, 5, 6, 137, 138.
[263] *Ibid.*, *Suss. Indictments*, vol. i, p. 57.
[264] *P.N. Suss.*, vol. ii, p. 476; *Suss. Fines*, vol. i, p. 69; *De Lisle and Dudley MSS.*, vol. i, p. 25.
[265] *P.N. Suss.*, vol. i, p. 160; J. E. B. Gover and others, *Place-Names of Surr.* p. 260; *3 Suss. Subsidies*, p. 330.
[266] *Suss. Indictments*. vol. i, pp. 1, 3, 42, 85.
[267] Reaney, *Dict.*, p. 269; Cottle, *Dict.*, p. 282.
[268] J. E. B. Gover and others, *Place-Names of Surr.*, p. 116.
[269] *Wiston Archives*, p. 405.
[270] *Suss. Subsidy, 1524–5*, pp. 37, 39.
[271] *Ibid.*; *Wiston Archives*, p. 86; Lord Leconfield, *Petworth Manor in the 17th Century* (1954), p. 85; *Suss. Wills*, vol. iii, p. 65.
[272] *W. Suss. 1641–2*, pp. 8, 37, 113, 119, 120, 137, 139; R. Garraway Rice, *Parish Register of Horsham* (Suss. Record Soc., vol. xxi) (1915), pp. 11, 95, 118, 347, 348; Leconfield, *op. cit.*, p. 73.

[273] Reaney, *Dict.*, p. 267.
[274] *Fitzalan Surveys*, p. 7.
[275] *Ibid.*, p. 37.
[276] *3 Suss. Subsidies*, pp. 141, 144, 265; *Suss. Custumals*, vol. iii, p. 66; *Fitzalan Surveys*, p. 147.
[277] *Feudal Aids*, vol. v, p. 165; *Fitzalan Surveys*, pp. 114, 129.
[278] *Suss. Subsidy, 1524–5*, p. 31; *W. Suss. 1641–2*, pp. 35, 61, 93, 94, 115, 125, 148; Lane, *Suss. Deeds*, p. 19; E. W. D. Penfold, *First Book of the Parish Registers of Angmering* (Suss. Record Soc., vol. xviii) (1913), pp. 76, 97, 102.
[279] *Suss. Custumals*, vol. ii, pp. 17, 20; *3 Suss. Subsidies*, pp. 92, 119, 120, 121, 229, 231.
[280] *Ibid.*, pp. 119, 229.
[281] *S.A.C.*, vol. lxxxiv, p. 60; *Rotuli Hundredorum*, vol. ii, p. 211. It has been suggested that Primer was a name for a dealer in religious texts, or a person of ostentatious piety; C. Clarke, "Early Personal Names of King's Lynn" *Nomina* (1983), vol. vii, p. 74.
[282] *S.A.C.*, vol. lxiv, p. 73; vol. lxxxix, p. 141; vol. xcv, pp. 50, 51.
[283] *Ibid.*, vol xx, p. 147; vol. xlv, p. 170; vol. lxxvii, p. 100; *Suss. Subsidy, 1524–5*, pp. 19, 162; *Suss. Wills*, vol. i, pp. 83, 169, 170, 271; vol. ii, p. 230; vol. iv, p. 304; F. Leeson, "Marriages 1557–1842, from the Parish Registers of Bosham" (1979), at Society of Genealogists.
[284] *P.N. Suss.*, vol. i, p. 138.
[285] *3 Suss, Subsidies*, pp. 65, 159, 274.
[286] *Suss. Custumals*, vol. i, p. 117.
[287] *3 Suss. Subsidies*, p. 30; *S.A.C.*, vol. lxix, p. 123; vol. xcv, p. 56; E. Straker, *Buckhurst Terrier* (Suss. Record Soc., vol. xxxix) (1934), pp. 2, 22, 23, 24, 31, 34, 36.
[288] *Suss. Indictments*, vol. i, p. 19; E. Straker, *op. cit.*, p. 31; *S.A.C.*, vol. cix, p. 25; R. P. Crawfurd, *Parish Register of East Grinstead* (Suss. Record Soc., vol. xxiv) (1917), pp. 4, 11, 42; *Suss. Subsidy, 1524–5*, pp. 130, 137; *Suss. Wills*, vol. ii, p. 261.
[289] Crawfurd, *op. cit.*, pp. 4, 11, 21, 42, 76, 79, 82, 98, 101, 107, 114, 187.
[290] *S.A.C.*, vol. lvi, pp. 1, 2, 11; *Suss. Subsidy, 1524–5*, p. 114; East Suss. Record Office, Dunn MSS., 8/1.
[291] *W. Suss. 1641–2*, pp. 59, 76, 121, 197; J. E. Ray, *op. cit.*, p. 188.
[292] Reaney, *Dict.*, p. 308; Dauzat, *op. cit.*, p. 533.
[293] *Chichester Chart.*, p. 87; *Great Roll of the Pipe for the 16th year of Henry II* (Pipe Roll Soc., vol xv) (1892) p. 135; *Great Roll of the Pipe for the 33rd year of Henry II* (Pipe Roll Soc., vol. xxxvii) (1915), p. 23; B. A. Lees, *Records of the Templars in the 12th century* (1935), p. 240; D. M. Stenton, *Great Roll of the Pipe for the 5th year of Richard I* (Pipe Roll Soc., vol. xli) (1926), p. 150; D. M. Stenton, *Great Roll of the Pipe for the 7th year of Richard I* (Pipe Roll Soc., vol. xliv) (1929),

p. 80; *V.C.H. Suss.*, vol. vi, part i, p. 153; L. F. Salzman, *Chartulary of Sele*, (1923), p. 83.

[294] *S.A.C.*, vol. x, p. 109; *V.C.H. Suss.*, vol. vi, part i, pp. 156–7.

[295] *3 Suss. Subsidies*, p. 42, 65, 160; *S.A.C.*, vol. lxii, p. 139; L. Fleming, *History of Pagham*, vol. i, p. lxxv; *Lewes Chartulary*, vol. ii, p. 54.

[296] *Chichester Chart*, p. 100; *3 Suss. Subsidies*, pp. 118, 235. Trentemars is a French surname ('30 marks'). Compare Quartermars and Cinqmars.

[297] *Lewes Chartulary*, vol. ii, p. 54; *Suss. Subsidy, 1524–5*, p. 96; P.R.O. E.179/225/50, m. 3; S.C.11/649, m. 2.

[298] *V.C.H. Suss.*, vol. vi, part i, p. 157; C. H. Wilkie, *St. Andrews, Edburton, Suss.: Copy of the Parish Register Book, 1558–1673* (1884), pp. 23, 25, 28, 31, 32.

[299] R. Garraway Rice, *Parish Register of Horsham* (Suss. Record Soc., vol. xxi) (1915), p. 45; *S.A.C.* vol. ii, p. 320, 321.

[300] H. A. Hanley and C. W. Chalklin, *op. cit.* p. 93; Anon., *Suff. in 1327* (Suff. Green Books no. ix), pp. 91, 94; J. Jönsjö, *Middle English Nicknames* (1979), vol. i, p. 178; P.R.O. E.179/149/7, m. 67; A. Rumble, *Dorset Lay Subsidy Roll of 1327* (Dorset Record Soc., no. vi) (1980), p. 104; *Somerset Rec. Soc.*, vol. v, p. 110.

CHAPTER 7

SURNAMES OF RELATIONSHIP, AND SURNAMES OF UNEXPLAINED ORIGINS

SURNAMES OF RELATIONSHIP

Surnames of relationship are a small category of names, derived from terms for the differing degree of kinship. Cousins, Brothers or Uncle are examples of surnames in this category. In no part of England were surnames of this type ever more than a small proportion of the the total body of names in use, and in Sussex such names were never at all common. In the 1332 subsidy for the county, for instance, six out of every thousand of all the surnames or bye-names listed fell into this category.[1] However, a few surnames of the type have been present in the county in moderate numbers over a considerable period. For example, the names Cousin, Dobell and Eyr (or Ayer) were already in the 14th century more numerous than the majority of surnames and bye-names in Sussex, and they remained relatively numerous subsequently. Most of the surnames of the type under consideration found in Sussex also occur in other parts of England, and most are ones of which the origins are adequately explained in the standard works of reference.

One or two surnames of the type are worth some brief comments. One of these is the name which is given in 13th and 14th century sources as Fitzleray or fiz le Roy, and which is found at later periods in forms such as Fillery or Fildrey. The name existed in Sussex from the late 13th century. In one early example it seems possible that Fileroy is being used as a Christian name,[2] but in most instances it seems clear that names such as Fitzleray, fiz le Roy, etc., are being used as surnames or bye-names. The name was rare in medieval Sussex, but it was present before 1300 in several different parts of the county, and it is uncertain if all those who appear with the name belonged to one family. One late 13th century individual with the name was a customary tenant.[3] The name can be found in Surrey in the 14th century.[4] The name clearly means 'king's son', but there seems to be no possibility that it is derived from descent from a legitimate son of any king. It is possible that the name has been formed from the surname le Ray, which was fairly common in Sussex over a long period,[5] and which was no doubt originally a nickname, like many other surnames formed from terms for high rank. If the surname originated thus, it might be compared to names such as Clerkson, Smithson, etc., but such names are usually from occupations actually practised. It is also

423

possible that a name like fiz le Roy might have been bestowed simply as a nickname, and this is perhaps the most likely explanation of its origin. A third possibility is that the name originated with the illegitimate issue of kings. King John, in particular, had a number of natural children, about whom little can be discovered. Some of his illegitimate sons are referred to in contemporary sources with the addition to their Christian names of the phrase, *filius regis*.[6] One of John's illegitimate sons, Richard, married the heiress to lands in Kent;[7] Richard's mother appears to have been a sister of Earl William de Warenne.[8] It is possible, therefore, that descendants of one of King John's natural children might have appeared in Sussex, but it has not been possible to connect genealogically any of the people named Fitzleray, etc., with any of John's sons, and the origin of the name must remain uncertain.

There are only a few instances of the surname in Sussex during the 14th and 15th centuries, all from West Sussex, and possibly all concerning one family.[9] The name survived in West Sussex during the 16th and 17th centuries, usually in the form Fillery or Fillary, but it continued to be rare.[10] It still survives in Sussex at the present day, usually in the form Fillery, and has ramified there to some extent.

One other surname of relationship which has persisted in Sussex for a long period is Filleul, a name of French origin meaning 'godson'. The name was never confined to Sussex. It can be found in several other counties, notably Essex, in the 13th and 14th centuries, and it existed as a surname or bye-name in Normandy in the 11th and 12th centuries.[11] The name first appears in Sussex about 1250, when a William Fillol, probably one of an Essex landowning family, obtained land in Sussex. The Fillol family were landholders in Sussex in the 14th century, with estates mostly around Hailsham and Herstmonceux. It is probable that all those found in Sussex with the name belonged to one family.[12] The surname has never been at all common in the county, but it survives there to the present day. It seems probable that all the persons with the surname in Sussex shared a single ancestry, and that this is another case, similar to surnames in other categories, where a surname originated in the county in a single family, though it may have originated independently elsewhere.

None of the other surnames of relationship found in Sussex require particular comment; none was peculiar to the county, and most were surnames which could be found in many other parts of England from the 13th century onwards.

UNIDENTIFIED SURNAMES

Despite the collection of much material on Sussex surnames for the purposes of this work, and despite much evidence on English surnames generally collected by scholars who have compiled dictionaries of surnames, the origins and etymologies of a substantial number of names remain unexplained. There are many instances in the medieval records for the county of names which have been found once only, and of which the origins are unknown. It must be suspected that sometimes, at least, the difficulty of explaining the names concerned is due to scribal errors in the sources having led to names being so badly mangled as to be unrecognisable. This, however, cannot be the explanation for the surnames, of unknown origins, which persisted in the county over generations, which were evidently established there as hereditary surnames, and which in some cases have survived there to the present day. Most unidentified surnames are ones which were always rare, but there are a few which survived in Sussex over long periods, and were of some importance in the history of surnames in the county, yet still defy explanation. Some of these may be names which originated outside England.

Some unidentified names persisted in Sussex for a few generations, evidently as hereditary surnames, but then disappeared from the county, and may well have ceased to exist, like many other surnames which appear briefly in the Middle Ages. For example, the name Armichun (or Armethon or Ernichun), survived in the area south of Chichester during the late 13th century and the first half of the 14th, but has not been found after c.1350.[13] The surname Loredei or Lorday, existed at and near Billingshurst during much the same period. It, too, seems to have been lost in the mid 14th century.[14] Glaion (or Glagon) was the name of a family of small tenants at Barpham, in Angmering, during the 14th century, but again seems to have disappeared about the middle of the century.[15] A few other examples could be given of unidentified names which survived for a few generations, and which seem likely to have been hereditary, but which were subsequently lost.

Some other rare and unexplained names which can be discovered in Sussex during the Middle Ages survived into the 16th century. The name Grugan or Grogan existed in the Selsey area during the late 13th and the 14th centuries;[16] Grogan is generally taken, no doubt correctly in many cases, to be Irish, but it seems improbable that an Irish surname would be found in the rural parts of Sussex in the 13th century. Possibly the name may be French in origin.[17] The name has not been found in Sussex between c.1350 and 1500, but the name Grogen, found in the same part of the county in the 16th century, is probably a later form of the same surname.[18] Grogan is still to be found in Sussex at the present day, but it may now be of Irish origin in some cases. The surname Pralle has first been found in Sussex, in the eastern part of the county, in 1392. It survived in the same area through the 15th century and into the 16th.[19] The surname Dayred existed around Chichester in the 13th and 14th centuries; the name Derett, found at Chichester in 1525, is probably a late form of the same surname.[20] A more common surname than any of these was Scrase (or Scrace, sometimes printed as Stras). The place-name Scrace Bridge, near Haywards Heath, is derived from the surname.[21] The name was fairly widespread in East Sussex from the early 13th century onwards, and seems to have been too dispersed to have been the name of one family.[22] The name occurs as le Scras in one early instance,[23] and this may indicate that the surname originated with a nickname, but it is hazardous to rely upon the presence of the definite article in a single example. The surname survived in Sussex into the 16th and 17th centuries. The 1524-5 subsidy returns show that it was widespread in East Sussex at that time.[24] The surname was still very rare in West Sussex in the 17th century, and only one person so named is listed in the Protestation Returns for West Sussex.[25] The surname still survives in Sussex, as Scrase and Scrace, and is not at all rare, but no explanation can be put forward of its origin.

There are a few other surnames with unexplained origins which have not been found in Sussex before 1500, but which were present in the county after that date, and which have persisted there. The surname Colpoys, (Colpes, Colpas, Colpays, Colpice) has not been found in Sussex before the 16th century. The first instances of it found in Sussex are in the 1524-5 subsidy, where at least nine taxpayers so called are listed; (it is impossible to be sure of the precise number, as some individuals may be assessed at more than one place).[26] This suggests that the name had already been established in the county for some time before 1524. The 16th century references to the name are all from places near the Hampshire border,[27] and this agrees with statements that the name was originally a Hampshire one. The surname did exist at Winchester in the 15th century.[28] The origin of the name has not been explained, though it may be French.[29] 17 people with the name were listed in the West Sussex Protestation Returns, none of them at places very far from the Hampshire border.[30] The surname still survives in Sussex today.

One other surname which has not been found in Sussex before 1500, but which has become fairly common there, is Killick. The surname may possibly be from a place-name, such as Kildwick (West Yorks), or Childwick (Herts). Two persons named Killick are listed in the West Sussex Protestation Returns.[31] The name already existed at Horsham in the 16th century.[32] The surname was probably in origin that of one family in the county, but it has ramified considerably and is now quite numerous there.

Some further surnames or bye-names with uncertain origins can be found in Sussex at various periods, but few of them have ever been more than very rare in the county. Most have only appeared briefly in Sussex, and do not call for any comment. Possibly the origins of some surnames found in Sussex may be elucidated from evidence about their early history in other counties, or from evidence about their origins outside England.

References

[1] See p. 11.
[2] L. Fleming, *History of Pagham*, vol. i, p. 130.
[3] *Ibid*; *Suss. Custumals*, vol. iii, pp. 30, 35; M. T. Martin, *Percy Chartulary*, (Surtees Soc., vol. cxvii) (1911). pp. 364, 393, 466.
[4] *Surr. Taxation Returns*, (Surr. Rec. Soc., no. xxxiii) (1932), pp. 90, 92.
[5] *3 Suss. Subsidies*, pp. 79, 82, 84, 99, 124, 131, 135; Lane, *Suss. Deeds*, pp. 25, 26, 91, 98; *Suss. Custumals*, vol. i, p. 15; *Chichester Chart.*, p. 250. And see p. 234.
[6] *Close Rolls, 1237–42*, p. 511; F. Madden, *Matthei Parisiensis Historia Anglorum*, (Rolls Series) (1866), vol. ii, p. 230.
[7] S. Painter, *Reign of King John*, (1948), pp. 232–3; *Rotuli Litterarum Patentium* (Record Commission) (1835), vol. i, part i, p. 118; *Rotuli Litterarum Clausarum*, (Record Commission) (1833), vol. i, pp. 168, 268.
[8] Painter, *loc. cit.*
[9] *3 Suss. Subsidies*, p. 249; *Suss. Fines*, vol. ii, p. 87; *Fitzalan Surveys*, p. 135.
[10] *Suss. Subsidy, 1524-5*, p. 76; *W.Suss. 1641-2*, p. 139; W. C. Renshaw, *Parish Registers of Cuckfield*, (Suss. Rec. Soc., vol. xiii) (1911), pp. 3, 5, 38, 40, 42, 44, 127, 131, 160.
[11] C. H. Haskins, *Norman Institutions*, (1960), p. 92; J. C. Holt, "Feudal Society and the Family in Early Medieval England", *Trans. Royal Hist. Soc.*, 5th Series, vol. xxxiii (1983), p. 204.
[12] *V.C.H. Suss.*, vol. vii, p. 147; vol. vi, part i, p. 51; vol. ix, p. 139; *3 Suss. Subsidies*, pp. 118, 190, 208, 214, 301, 320; *Suss. Fines*, vol. iii, pp. 25, 33, 64, 135; *Placita de Banco*, (P.R.O. Lists and Indexes, no. xxxii) (1963), vol. ii, pp. 663–4; P.R.O. S.C.11/666.
[13] *3 Suss. Subsidies*, p. 89, 131; *Non Inquis.*, p. 391; *Suss. Custumals*, vol. i, p. 22.
[14] *3 Suss. Subsidies*, pp. 148, 149, 261; *Suss. Custumals*, vol, i, p. 142; *Wiston Archives*, pp. 242, 287–88, 375.
[15] *Non. Inquis*, p. 392; *Suss. Custumals*, vol. iii, pp. 72, 73; *3 Suss. Subsidies*, p. 144, 145, 264. The surname may be from the French place-name Glageon (Nord): I owe this suggestion to Dr Marc Fitch. See M.-T. Morlet, *Étude D'Anthroponymie Picarde* (1967), p. 47.
[16] *3 Suss. Subsidies*, pp. 94, 125, 127, 249, 251.
[17] Dauzat, *op. cit.* p. 310; E. Maclysaght, *Surnames of Ireland*, (1969) p. 110.
[18] *Suss. Subsidy, 1524-5*, p. 55.
[19] *Hastings Lathe C.R.*, pp. 3, 7, 13, 30, 32, 59; *Feudal Aids*, vol. v, p. 150; East Suss. Record Office, Dunn MSS, 16/2; *Suss. Subsidy*,

1524–5, p. 161. The names Pralle, Prail and Praill survive in Suss. The name might be from Prawle (Devon).

[20] *S.A.C.*, vol. lxxxii, p. 128; *Fitzalan Surveys*, p. 27; *Suss. Fines*, vol. i, p. 86; *Suss. Subsidy, 1524–5*, p. 5.

[21] *P. N. Suss*, vol. ii, p. 269.

[22] *Suss. Fines*, vol. ii, p. 45; *Non Inquis.*, p. 381; F. Hull, *op. cit.*, pp. 19, 30, 40; *S.A.C.*, vol. vii, p. 1; vol. xcv, p. 49; *De Lisle and Dudley MSS.*, vol. i, p. 23; *Lewes Chartulary*, vol. ii, pp. 35, 36; *3 Suss. Subsidies*, pp. 229, 288; P.R.O. E.179/189/94; *Hastings Lathe C.R.*, pp. 60, 101.

[23] *3 Suss. Subsidies*, p. 288.

[24] *Suss. Subsidy, 1524–5*, pp. 51, 70, 92, 100, 104, 114, 119, 120, 122, 165; *Suss. Wills*, vol. i, pp. 11, 164; Lane, *Suss. Deeds*, p. 118; *Suss. Indictments*, vol. i, p. 76; *S.A.C.* vol. ix, p. 81; vol. xxv, p. 130; *Wiston Archives*, pp. 157, 160, 203, 247.

[25] *W. Suss. 1641–2*, p. 59.

[26] *Suss. Subsidy, 1524–5*, pp. 7, 12, 17, 18, 20.

[27] *Suss. Indictments*, vol. i, pp. 11, 20; *Cowdray Archives*, vol, i, p. 16; *S.A.C.*, vol. lxxvii, pp. 100, 101.

[28] Maclysaght, *op. cit.*, p. 51; E. O. Blake, *Cartulary of the Priory of St Denis*, (Southampton Rec. Soc.) (1981) vol. i, p. ci.

[29] Dauzat, *op. cit.*, p. 152.

[30] *W. Suss. 1641–2*, pp. 35, 50, 79, 93, 144, 147, 151, 177, 184, 191, 199.

[31] *Ibid.*, pp. 21, 96.

[32] R. Garraway Rice, *Parish Register of Horsham*, (Sussex Rec. Soc., vol. xxi) (1915), pp. 28, 87, 317, 335, 339, 355.

Conclusion

The most significant characteristic of Sussex surnames, taking all the different categories of names together, is the degree of continuity displayed. As late as the 17th century there were in the county a high proportion of surnames which had survived there since before about 1400. It is in particular true that those surnames which were numerous in the county in the 17th and 18th centuries were in the great majority of cases names which had a long history there before 1600. Among the surnames which were common in Sussex at those relatively late periods, there were many instances of surnames which seem likely to have originated in the county with a single family, and to have ramified gradually over a long span of time. The county was of course never at any time sealed off from the introduction of surnames from outside. Between the Conquest and c.1200 some surnames derived from French place-names had been introduced, mostly as the names of landed families, and some of these later proliferated in Sussex. At various times there was movement into the county by families from other parts of England, though there is no evidence of migration on any substantial scale at any period before the mid 18th century, and during the 16th and 17th centuries several factors led to new immigrations from outside England. Movement out of the county into other parts of England is difficult to measure without carrying out detailed research into the position throughout the country, but although there is evidence for some emigration from Sussex, the admittedly limited investigations which it has been possible to carry out have not revealed any information to show that there was a population movement from Sussex on a large scale at any time. The continuity exhibited by Sussex surnames is not surprising when the geographically isolated position of the county is borne in mind.

Some impression of how much continuity there still was in Sussex surnames, even at the end of the 19th century, when the population had been greatly altered by the growth of the south coast resorts, and of some places in central Sussex, can be gained from the work of H.B. Guppy, who made a survey of surnames for the whole of Great Britain, county by county, using as his basic material the names of farmers given in the printed directories current at the end of the 19th century.[1] In Sussex the methods used by Guppy may have tended to exaggerate the element of continuity in surnames, for by confining his attention to farmers' names Guppy excluded the names of most of the inhabitants of the more rapidly growing towns in Sussex. (It should be said that Guppy's object was in any case not to demonstrate how much continuity there was.) Guppy lists 63 surnames which his evidence showed to be 'peculiar names', that is, surnames wholly or mostly confined to the county, so that they did not occur in his material sufficiently often in any other county to be considered as being present in significant numbers.[2] 39 out of the 63 names have been found in Sussex before 1500; a further 15 have been found there during the 16th century, including 6 which have first been found in Sussex in the 1524 subsidy, and which may well have been present there during the 15th century; the remaining 9 names have not been discovered in the county before 1600, but the antecedents of two of these, (Goatcher, and Towes or Towse) are uncertain. This evidence, admittedly based on a group which may not have been accurately representative of the county's whole population, shows that even at the end of the 19th century, many of the names which had originated in Sussex during the Middle Ages were still present there, and were still mostly concentrated within the county, rather than outside it. As this is a list of names 'peculiar to the county', in Guppy's phrase, it naturally does not include names which had migrated into the county from elsewhere in Britain during the 19th century, for such names would obviously tend to be more common in other parts of the country than in Sussex. Though Guppy's evidence fails to show adequately how much movement there had been into the county, it does show that many surnames with a long history in Sussex still survived there.

Some indication of the character of Sussex surnames at the present time (1984) can be obtained from the names in the current Brighton area telephone directory. This covers a large part of the county, though some districts in both East and West Sussex are outside the region covered by the directory. A small part of Surrey is included, but names with Surrey addresses can be left out of consideration here. Although telephone directories do not list the whole population, it is likely that in a prosperous county like Sussex the proportion of people with telephones is large enough for directories to give a resonably accurate sample of the surnames present in the area. The surnames recorded in the directory show how much the nomenclature of the county has been influenced by movements of the population. Out of all the locative surnames given in the directory as the names of more than twenty persons, just under a third could be derived from the names of places in Sussex. This figure must overestimate the proportion of surnames from Sussex place-names, for some of the surnames concerned could be either from Sussex place-names, or from place-names in other counties, and it is obviously likely that in some instances such surnames would be from place-names outside Sussex. On the other hand, some surnames which were certainly from place-names outside Sussex had existed in the county from before 1700.

Conclusion

The surname Baldock (from Baldock, Herts.) now one of the more numerous locative surnames in Sussex, had been in the county since the early 16th century.[3] The surname is one which had already become dispersed in England by c. 1500, probably because of the position of Baldock on the Great North Road, and it is likely that while some of the people named Baldock living in Sussex at the present day may be descended from the persons so named living in Sussex in the 16th century, others may well be descended from more recent migrants into the county. The surname Dimock, still numerous in Sussex, occurs there already in 1332;[4] the surname Evershead, from a Surrey place-name, existed in Sussex from 1327–28,[5] and was already numerous there in the 16th century. The surname Markwick also from a place in Surrey, appears in Sussex in the 15th century, and was already more numerous there than most locative names in the early 16th;[6] Duffield, from Duffield (Derbys.) or Duffield (North Yorks.), another surname already much dispersed in England by 1500, was already well established at East Grinstead by the early 16th century.[7] Many other examples could be given of locative surnames, now numerous in Sussex which are derived from places in other English counties, and which have existed in Sussex from the 16th century, or earlier. Some surnames from French place-names, too, such as Cheney, Cheyney, Daughtrey, or Treagus, now found in Sussex, have a long history there.[8]

Despite this, many locative surnames which are now present in Sussex, and represented by more than a few individuals in the Brighton area telephone directory, are ones which have not been found in the county before 1800. These include many names from the more distant regions of Britain. It has been pointed out earlier that, for example, there are many surnames from Lancashire place-names.[9]

It is less easy to be certain, when dealing with surnames in other categories, to decide which have arrived in the county since, say, 1750. Many of the more common surnames in the telephone directory are occupational names which have been very widespread in England since the 13th century. However, some occupational names to be found frequently in Sussex are ones which arose in other regions. For example, the two surnames Walker and Tucker, both from the craft of bleaching cloth, are names which originated in other parts of England. Walker has not been discovered in Sussex before 1500, though in the early 16th century it was already widespread in the county.[10] One isolated example of Tucker has been found in Sussex in the 14th century,[11] but otherwise the name has not been found in Sussex until the 16th century, when it reappears. Catchpole, another occupational surname now common in Sussex, was a usual term for a peace officer in medieval East Anglia, and gave rise to a surname frequently found in that region from the 13th century onwards. There are also early instances of the surname in

Middlesex. In Sussex, however, the surname has not been found before 1600.

Similarly, the surname derived from personal names now present in the county show the effects of migration from other parts of Britain. Surnames formed from a personal name with the suffix '-son' were very rare in Sussex before 1500, and hardly less scarce during the 16th century,[12] but many surnames of the type are listed in the Brighton directory in large numbers. Besides this some Scots surnames, not found in Sussex before 1600, are now numerous in the county; for instance, the names Buchan, Buchanan, Cameron, Campbell, Carmichael, Cunningham, Dunlop, and Sutherland are all now well represented in Sussex. Names originating in Wales and Ireland, though fewer than Scots ones, are now also present in the county in some numbers. All this evidence might suggest that in Sussex surnames which originated in the county, or which, even if arising elsewhere, had been in the county since such relatively early periods as the 12th and 13th centuries, had been largely replaced by surnames which had migrated into the county since about 1750, as a result of the growth of the south coast resorts, and of places further north in Sussex, such as Crawley, Haywards Heath, or Burgess Hill, whose inhabitants included a considerable proportion of commuters to London. However, although there has certainly been a major influx of names over the last two hundred years or so, very many surnames which have existed in Sussex for long periods, and which in some cases seem likely to have originated there, are still present in the county, some of them rare, some of them today quite numerous. The persistence in the county of some common occupational names, Smith, Baker, etc., or of some of the more common surnames from personal names, is not very significant, for many of these surnames have existed in most parts of England from an early period, but many scarce surnames have survived in Sussex. There are surnames in all the main categories which have existed in Sussex from before 1500, and which are still there today, and these include many which have been discussed in the preceding chapters. Less common occupational names such as Beadle (or Biddle), Blower, Bowker, Capron, Cheeseman, Duke, Shoesmith, or Washer, some of the less common surnames from personal names such as Colbran, Gabriel, Ingram, or Tomsett, some topographical names not national common, such as Funnell, Furlonger, Grover, Heasman, Naldrett, or Streeter, some surnames from nicknames, such as Budgen, Godsmark, Goldring, Leppard, Maufe, Purdew, Peacock, Peasegood, Pentecost, Steer, Vowell (and Fowle, etc.), Wisdom, or Wiseman, and a few surnames from terms for relationship, such as Doubell, Fillery, or Filleul, have all persisted in Sussex to the present day, besides, as already indicated, many surnames possibly from Sussex place-names. The general effect of the population growth in Sussex since *c.* 1750 has been to introduce a great number of new surnames, some of which are now very numerous in the county, but not to obliterate the old established Sussex surnames. If the whole body of surnames listed in the current Brighton telephone directory is considered, the main impressions derived from scrutinising them are, firstly, that there are a very large number of surnames which have not been encountered in Sussex before 1600, some of them ones which have originated outside the British Isles, and secondly, that many surnames with a long history in Sussex are still present in the county, some of them rare, others now quite numerous. This development reflects the population history of Sussex during the 19th and 20th centuries, when parts of the county grew rapidly, while others remained very rural and somewhat isolated.

Some evidence about the nature of the surnames present at Brighton at a point intermediate between the present time and c. 1750 can be gained from a Brighton directory of 1850.[13] The 'general directory' in this work[14] lists about 3,200 people, many of them professional men, retailers, and craftsmen. Out of these, excluding names of firms or companies, rather less than 150 had surnames which could be derived from place-names in Sussex, while about 380 had surnames from place-names outside the county, including some from places outside England. The surnames from outside Sussex include some which had been in the county from a much earlier date, including Baldock, already mentioned, Bradshaw,[15] Burtenshaw,[16] or Seagrave.[17] Even considering that the total number of persons listed is not very large, none of the surnames derived from places outside Sussex was at all numerous in 1850. However, some surnames which had multiplied considerably by 1984, according to the Brighton telephone directory, were already present in 1850. This is true both of locative surnames from places outside Sussex, and of surnames in other categories which seem likely to have originated outside the county. For instance, the surnames Bagnall, Bambridge, Coleby, Featherstone, Harrison, Hemsley, Lloyd, Padwick, Stepney, and Stillwell, all ones which are today to be found in some numbers in the Brighton area telephone directory, are all listed in 1850, though none of them is represented at that date by more than a few individuals. Moderate numbers of people with surnames formed from personal names with '-son', and from personal names with a genitival '-s', are given in the 1850 directory, and a few of the individual surnames, such as Edwards, Phillipps, or Saunders were already becoming quite numerous. About 68 persons per 1,000 listed in the 1850 directory had surnames formed from a personal name with a genitival '-s', and about 27 per 1,000 had surnames formed from a personal name with '-son'. These figures may be compared with the insignificant number of taxpayers with names in either of the two types listed in the Sussex 1332 subsidy,[18] or with the figures of 27 per 1,000 and 11 per 1,000 for names in '-s' and names in '-son' respectively for people listed in the Sussex 1524–5 subsidy.[19] To this it should be added that in 1850 there were a still quite small number of people with surnames beginning with 'Mac-', etc. There had, consequently, been a substantial alteration by 1850 at Brighton in the nature of the surnames derived from personal names in use there.

This evidence all points to considerable changes having been brought about by 1850 in the body of surnames present at Brighton, through migration into the area, mainly from other parts of the British Isles. Brighton is likely to have been more influenced by movements into Sussex in the century before 1850 than the great majority of places in the county. Despite this, there are many surnames in the 1850 directory which can be recognised as ones with a long history in Sussex before that date, many of them well established there before 1500. Occupational names such as, for instance, Cheeseman, Shoesmith, Thatcher, or Thunder, topographical names such as Brooker, Fennell (and Funnell), Heasman, Horsecroft, Penfold, or Stonestreet, surnames from personal names, such as Alfrey, Botting, Elphick, Gabriel, Goodwin, Ingram, Jupp, Leggatt, Pannett, Tomsett, or Tully, or surnames of the nickname type such as Budgen, Cobb, Feist, Morphey, Nightingale, Pentecost, Pocock, Primmer, Saxby, Stent, Tester, Trangmar, or Truslow were still to be found at Brighton in 1850. The evidence from the 1850 directory shows that in the mid 19th century many of the more frequently found surnames at Brighton were ones which had a long history in Sussex, many of them ones to be found in the county during the 13th and 14th centuries, and many of them names which had probably arisen in the county. The body of surnames which had grown up in Sussex before 1500 was still very evident at Brighton in 1850, though mingled with names brought in by population movement. In general terms, this is still true at the present day. There are now in Sussex a great number of surnames brought in since *c.* 1750. Some of the surnames have been in the county for sufficiently long to have ramified considerably, and to have become very numerous in Sussex. Sussex is a county which still had a relatively sparse population at the beginning of the 19th century, and has been influenced by heavy population movements over the last two hundred years to an exceptional degree. During the 19th and 20th centuries Sussex surnames have been more affected by population movement than those of either Lancashire or West Yorkshire, both areas much more heavily industrialised than Sussex. Nevertheless, despite this influx, and despite the presence of many new surnames, some of them at the present time very numerous, very few surnames which were well established in Sussex by the 16th century have been lost from the county. The names of some landed families at one time prominent in the county have, perhaps surprisingly, disappeared from it; the names Lewknor and Bassock are examples. Such losses of old established surnames are, however, exceptional. Many old Sussex surnames still persist in the county to the present day, alongside a large and increasing body of names which have arrived in the county in the last two hundred years.

References

[1] H. B. Guppy, *Homes of Family Names in Great Britain* (1968).
[2] *Ibid.*, p. 380.
[3] *Suss. Subsidy, 1524–5*, p. 142; *Suss. Wills*, vol. iv, p. 232.
[4] *3 Suss. Subsidies*, p. 293. And see p. 104.
[5] *Placita de Banco* (P.R.O. Lists and Indexes, no. xxxii) (1963), vol. ii, p. 662.
[6] *S.A.C.*, vol. xviii, p. 29; *Suss. Fines*, vol. iii, p. 286; *Feudal Aids*, vol. v, pp. 152, 165; *Suss. Subsidy, 1524–5*, pp. 19, 25, 93–5, 103, 128.
[7] *Ibid.*, p. 137.
[8] See pp. 35, 44, 70, 118.
[9] See p. 126.
[10] *Suss. Subsidy, 1524–5*, pp. 3, 27, 33, 94, 95, 102, 106, 116, 128, 147, 149; *Cowdray Archives*, vol. ii, p. 244.
[11] G. Fransson, *Middle English Surnames of Occupation* (1935), p. 101.
[12] See pp. 325–34.
[13] *Court Guide and General Directory of Brighton* (1850), published by Robert Folthorp.
[14] *Ibid.*, pp. 156–235.
[15] See p. 114–5.
[16] See p. 113.
[17] See p. 108.
[18] See p. 332.
[19] See p. 333.

INDEX

Abbeles (Abeleys), surname or byename of, 351
Abbot, surname or bye-name of, 234, 237
Acstede, Roland de (mid 13th century), 85
Adams, surname of, 325
Adamys, at, surname or bye-name of, 199, 323
Adeliza, Queen of England (died 1151), 32, 70
  Jocelin brother of, 70
Adlard, see Alard
Adur River, 119, 242, 407
Agates, surname of, 155
  see Gate
Aguillon, Manasser (*c*. 1150), 45
Aguillon, family of, 45–6, 48, 53
Ailnod, see Alnod
Ailwin, Ailwyne, see Aylwyn
Ak, atte, surname or bye-name of, 203
Akerman, surname or bye-name of, 247
Alan son of Flaald, see Flaald
Alani, Godfrey (? or Alans) (*c*. 1270), 351
Alani, Thomas (? or Alans) (*c*. 1250–70), 351
Alard, Gervase (or Gervase Frendekyn, or Gervase Alard Frendekyn) (*c*. 1290), 65
Alard, personal name of, 64, 303
Alard, (Adlard, Athelard, Aylard), surname or bye-name of, 64–5, 309, 344
Albine, de, Albineia, de, Albiniaco, de, see Aubigny, de
Albourne, 101, 265, 317, 368, 382
Alciston, 177, 178, 248, 328
Alderdynden, Christine de (late 13th cent.), 123
Alderdynden, 123
  see Alerdynden
Aldingbourne, 58–9, 98, 160, 168, 181, 249, 267, 274, 342
Aldret (atte Aldratte, ate Naldrette, ate Nelrette, Naldraate, Aldaret, *de Alneto*), surname or bye-name of, 145–6, 149, 184

Aldrich (Aldridge), surname or bye-name of, 345
Aldrington, 38–9, 57, 166
Aldsworth, 71
Aldwick, 173, 198
Aldwin, see Aylwyn
Aleem, see Leem
Alerdynden, de, surname or bye-name of, 106
  see Alderdynden
Alfred, personal name of, 344
Alfrey, surname or bye-name of, 344, 434
Alfriston, 40
Algar (Elgar), surname or bye-name of, 309, 345
aliens, names of, 6–10, 19–21, 44, 118, 136, 188, 211, 254, 257, 269, 277–8, 282, 320, 325–7, 330, 343, 360, 367, 369, 376, 416
Alkesford, 123
Allnott (Alnod, Ailnod, Elnot, Aylnoth, Eylnoth), surname or bye-name of, 309, 314
Alneto, de, see Aldret
Alta Ripa, Joscelin de (*c*. 1230), 70
Alta Ripa, Robert *de* (*c*. 1140–70), 44, 70
Alta Ripa, Robert de (*c*. 1190–1200), 70
Alta Ripa, William *de* (late 12th century), 44, 70
Alta Ripa, de, Alteriue, de, see Dawtry, Hautrive
Aluuardus, personal name of, 301
Aluuinus, personal name of, 301
Alwyne, see Aylwyn
Amberley, 54, 163, 184, 194, 196, 199, 218, 246, 248–9, 258, 267, 269, 324, 330, 362–3, 384–5
Ambersham, 188
Amiotesune, de, surname or bye-name of, 328
Andrew, surname or bye-name of, 7, 64, 309
Andrewes, surname of, 319
Anglicus, surname of, 20
  see Engleys
Angmering, 72, 252–3, 260, 267, 271, 275, 325, 346, 385, 425

437

Annington, 271, 370–71
Anstee (Anstey), surname of, 126
Antrobus, surname of, 118
Antrobus (Chesh.), 118
Appledram, 242, 272, 327
Aprece, surname of, 343
  see Price
Apwyliam, surname of, 343
Aquila, Gilbert *de* (early 12th century), 43
  see Laigle
Arbalistarius, Hugh (1086), 38
Ardingly, 125, 198, 202, 324, 343, 391, 402
Arkesford, Hen. de (late 13th cent.), 123
Arlington, 161, 189, 251, 262, 313, 374
Armichun (Armethon, Ernichun), surname or bye-name of, 425
artisans, surnames or bye-names of, 14, 62, 323, 329
Arundel, 196, 206, 243, 263, 265–6, 272, 314, 328, 371
Arundel castle, 33
Arundel, Hugh (de Aubigny), Earl of (died 1243), 33
Arundel Rape, 31, 167, 235
Arundel, Richard (Fitzalan), Earl of, (died 1376), 69
Arundel, surname or bye-name of, 97–8, 126
Arundel, William (de Aubigny), Earl of, (died 1176), 4, 19, 32, 51
Ash, surname or bye-name of, 145–6, 183
Ashburner, surname or bye-name of, 153
Ashburnham, 61, 125
Ashfold, 153
Ashington, 39
Ashling, East, 71, 405
Ashling, West, 71
Ashton (in Ringmer), 56, 60
Ashurst (near West Grinstead), 185, 406
Aside, see Lyde, a.
Aspinall, surname of, 126
Assheby, surname or bye-name of, 99
Athelard, see Alard
Atherington, 169, 242
Athoth (or Hother), George (17th century), 158
Atlingworth, 43, 407
Atree, surname of, 201

atterede, see Rode, de la
Atwell, surname of, 155
Aubigny, de, family of, 4, 34, 122
  see Daubenay, Daubeni
  see Arundel, Earls of
Aubigny, family, of Hinton Daubeny (Hants.), 33
Aubigny (Manche), 33
Aubigny, *Nigellus* de (*c.* 1100), 32
Aubigny, Roger de, (late 11th century), 32
Aubigny, see Arundel, Earls of
Aubigny, William de (mid 11th century), 32
Aubigny, William de, *pincerna*, (died 1139), 32
Avenel, – (1166), 51
Avening (Gloucs.), 233
Avening, de, surname or bye-name of, 284
Aveninge, Philip de (1231), 233
Avery, surname or bye-name of, 345
Avesford, John de (1331), 66
Avesford, John Jonesservant de (1331), 66
Awiste, surname or bye-name of, 171
Axsmith, surname of, 229, 245, 253
Ayer (Eyr), surname or bye-name of, 423
Aylard, see Alard
Aylnoth, see Allnot
Aylwyn (Ailwyne, Eylwyne, Elwin, Aldwin, Alwyne), surname or bye-name of, 306, 309
Aytaker, see Eightacre

Bacheler, surname or bye-name of, 258, 276
Backshall, Backshell, see Baxshell
Backshells (in Billingshurst), 136–7
Badby (Nmblnd.), 132
Badby (Northants.), 103
Badbye, Badeby, surname or bye-name of, 103, 117
Badeherste, bye-name of, 127
Badelesmere, surname or bye-name of, 99
Badhurst (in Lindfield), 127
Badlesmere (Kent), 99
Bagnall, surname of, 433
Baker, surname or bye-name of, 221, 222, 223, 224, 226, 257
  see *Pistor*
Balcombe (Baulcombe), surname of, 126

Baldock, surname or bye-name of, 431, 433
Baldock (Herts.), 431
Ballard, surname or bye-name of, 361
Bamber, surname of, 126
Bambridge, surname of, 433
Banister, surname or bye-name of, 258, 276
Bank, surname or bye-name of, 180
Barbor, surname of, 7
Barcombe, 391
Barcombe Hundred, 165
Bardsley, surname of, 126
Bare, surname of, 389
Barker, surname or bye-name of, 224
Barlavington, 271
Barmlinge, Stephen de (c. 1230), 85
Barnham, 406
Barnhorne, 242
Baron, surname or bye-name of, 236
Barpham, 275, 425
Barrarius, bye-name of, 154
Barre, atte, bye-name of, 154
Barre, Walter atte (or le Barrer) (1296), 158
Barrer, bye-name of, 154
Bartelott (Bartlett), surname or bye-name of, 309, 345
Bartholomew, personal name of, 345
Barye (or Larie), Robt. (1327, 1332), 22
Basoches, Adam de (late 12th century), 68
Basoches, Robert de (or de Sedlescombe) (early 13th century), 68
Basochiis, William de (c. 1160), 68
Basok, John (1303), 69
Basok, Laurence (1303), 69
Basokes, Alfred de (early 13th century), 68
Bassingbourne (Cambs.), 103
Bassock, surname of, 50, 68–9, 93, 118, 434
Bassyngeboun, surname of, 103
Bat, surname or bye-name of, 361
Bataille (or Bataylle), surname or bye-name of, 97
Bateman (Batman), surname or bye-name of, 337
Bathurst, surname of, 126
Bathurst (in Warbelton), 127
Bathurst (in Battle), 127
Battersbee, surname of, 118

Battersby (North Yorks.), 118
Battle Abbey, 5, 37, 44, 69
Battle, surname of, 126
Battle, 54, 65, 97, 171, 232, 250, 270, 303, 381
Bauent, le, surname of, 3
see Bavent, de
Baulcombe, see Balcombe
Baverstock (Wilts.), 118
Baxshell (Backshall, Backshell) surname of, 119, 128
Baxter, surname or bye-name of, 226, 258
Bayeux (Calvados), 35
Bayregg, de, surname or bye-name of, 106
Beadle (Bedell, Biddle, Boodle, Bothel), surname or bye-name of, 16, 258, 261–2, 432
beadle, office of, 261
Bear (le Ber, *Ursus*), surname or bye-name of, 388–9
Beary, surname of, 389
Beaufront, surname or bye-name of, 361
Beaumond (or Blamond), Robt. (1327, 1332), 22
Beaver (Beevor, le Bever, Beuer), surname or bye-name of, 361, 386–7, 393
Beche, Isabella de (1265), 85
Beche, Philip de la (? mid 13th century), 85
Beckley, 125, 158, 165, 167, 340–1, 376–7
Beckworth (in Lindfield), 127
see Becworth
Beconsawe, see Burtenshaw
Becworth, de, bye-name of, 127
Bedales (in Lindfield), 295
Beddingham, 183, 311, 399
Bedel, see Beadle
Bedfordshire, surnames or bye-names in, 33, 363
Beedel, Thomas le (1301), 295
Beedel, see Beadle
Beeding, 243, 245, 252, 317, 382
Beeding, Upper, 41, 311
Beeston (Norf.), 5
Beevor, see Beaver
Belamy, surname or bye-name of, 20, 362
Belchamber, surname or bye-name of, 183, 186
Belcher, 394

Beldam (Beldham), surname or bye-name of, 396
Beldam Lands, locality of, 396
Beldhamland Farm, 396
Belechambr (Belechombre), Ric. (*c.* 1280), 186
Belechambre, Walter (*c.* 1330), 186
Belefaunte, surname or bye-name of, 20
Beleson, see Belson
Bellême, Robert de, Count of Bellême, 32
Bellencombre (Seine-Maritime), 186
Bellencumbr', Wm. de (*c.* 1165), 186
Bellingham, surname of, 16, 17, 108
Bellingham (Greater London), 17, 108
Bellingham (Northumberland), 17, 108
see Bellyngham
Bellismo, Robert *de*, see Bellême
Bellower, bye-name of, 229, 244
Bellyngham, Thos. (1486), 108
see Bellingham
Belsaunt, surname or bye-name of, 328
Belson (Beleson), surname or bye-name of, 327–8
Belver, surname of, 387
Belvoir (Leics.), 386
Benceline, personal name of, 314
Benches, field name, 206
Bender, Peter (1227), 282
Bender, surname of, 229
Bennett, surname of, 10
Bensy (Bency), surname or bye-name of, 314
Bepton, 253
Ber, le, see Bear
Bercarius, see Shepherd
Berebruer, surname or bye-name of, 257
Berewerthe, William, atte Byrchette (1436), 65
Berks., landowners in, 267
Berlondere, surname or bye-name of, 153, 159
Bersted, 181, 241, 342
Betchworth (Surr.), 120
Betesfeud, de, surname or bye-name of, 106
Betsworth, surname of, 120
Beueresford, de, surname of, 416
Bever, le, see Beaver
Bevestock, surname of, 118
Bexhill, 75, 149, 192, 242, 265, 312
see Bixle, de

Bexhill Hundred, 260
Bickerstaff (Bickersteth), surname of, 126
Biddle, Bidle, see Beadle
Bidlington, 31, 167–8
Bigenor, de (de Bigenouer), surname of, 5
Bigenor Farm (Egdean), 5
Bignor, 5, 33
Billingham, surname of, 17
Billingham, 17
Billingshurst, 36, 98, 108, 120, 126, 148, 161, 232, 325, 375, 425
Bilsham, 240
Bindevel, bye-name of, 414
Binn (Byn, Byne), surname or bye-name of, 172, 186–7
Binne, la, field name of, 187
Binner, surname or bye-name of, 172
Binprest, surname or bye-name of, 362
Binstead, 196, 275, 314, 376
Birchenestie, atte, surname or bye-name of, 125
Bircher, surname or bye-name of, 155
Birchett (Birket), surname or bye-name of, 145–6, 149, 183
see Burchet
Birdham, 159
Birkenshaw (West Yorks.), 113
Birket, see Birchett
Bishop, surname or bye-name of, 221, 234, 237, 264
Bishopstone, 181
Bixle, Mabel de (? *c.* 1150), 75
Blaber, surname or bye-name of, 259–60
see Blaker
Black, surname or bye-name of, 361
Blacker, see Blaker
Blackheath Hundred (Surr.), 157
Blackland Copse (in Henfield), 125
Blackneck, surname or bye-name of, 361
Blake, surname or bye-name of, 398
Blakeboy, surname or bye-name of, 361
Blakecherl, surname or bye-name of, 361
Blakelond, atte, surname or bye-name of, 125
Blaker, Ric. (or Blaber), (1524–25), 260
Blaker, (Blacker, le Blakyere), surname or bye-name of, 259–60
see Blaber

Index 441

Blakwyght, surname or bye-name of, 361
Blakyster, surname or bye-name of, 259
Blamond, see Beaumond
Blanchard, surname or bye-name of, 20
Blancmoster, Gaudin de, (*c.* 1220–50), 85
Blancmoster, Lucy de (*c.* 1220–1260), 85
  Her father, see Clifton, Reynold de.
Blatchington, West, 266
Blobbere, surname or bye-name of, 294
Blome, surname or bye-name of, 245
Blondel, see Blundel
Bloomer, surname or bye-name of, 245
Blound, le, see Blunt
Blower, surname or bye-name of, 244, 432
Blukefeld, Ralph de (Ralph de Blukefeld *de querceto*) (*c.* 1265), 65
Blundel (Blondel), surname or bye-name of, 372–4
Blunt (le Blound, *Blundus*), surname or bye-name of, 373–4
Boad, see Bode
Boarhunt (Hants.), 102
  see Burhunte
Boddey, Boddie, Boddy, see Bode
Bode, Geoffrey le (or le Bodere) (*c.* 1250), 260
Bode (Boddy) Jn. (1546 and later), 18
Bode (Boad, Body), surname or bye-name of, 260–61
Bodere, le, see Bode
Bodicote, surname of, 118
Bodicote (Oxon.), 118
Bodiham, Henry de (*c.* 1205), 85
Bodiham, Margaret de (*c.* 1205), 85
Bodill, Bodle, see Beadle
Bodlestreet Green, 262
Body, see Bode
Bognor Regis, 196, 198
Bohun family, of Midhurst, 50
Bohun (Bowne), surname of, 93, 118
Bokeselle, de (Bokesull, de, Bokesulle, de), surname of, 127
Bokholte, atte, surname or bye-name of, 125
Bolney, 187, 265
Bolter (Boulter), surname or bye-name of, 276–7
Bolterscombe, 277

Bond (Bound, Bownde, Bunde), surname or bye-name of, 18, 230, 232
Bondy, surname of, 18
Bone, le, surname or bye-name of, 17
Bongard, see Bunger
Bonjour, surname or bye-name of, 361
Bonnick, see Bonwick
Bonsergeant, surname or bye-name of, 361
Bonsire, surname or bye-name of, 20
Bonswick, 133
Bonwick (North Yorks.), 104
Bonwick (Bonwyk, Bonnick), surname of, 104, 117
Bonye (Bonee, Boneye), surname or bye-name of, 17
Boodle, see Beadle
Booker, surname or bye-name of, 258, 276
Booth, surname of, 152
Border, surname or bye-name of, 232
Bordon, Alice (1399), 85
  Her husband, see Stacy, Gilbert
Borer, see Bourer
Boseworth, surname or bye-name of, 103
Bosham, surname of, 98
Bosham, 5, 54, 71, 98, 171, 376, 405
Bost (Bust), surname or bye-name of, 372
Bosworth, Market, or Bosworth, Husbands (Leics.), 103
Botere, le (le Botre), surname or bye-name of, 242
Bothel, see Beadle
Botolphs, 275, 371
Botting, surname or bye-name of, 314–15, 434
  see Buttyng
Boucé (Orne), 40
Bougeselle, surname or bye-name of, 97
Boulter, see Bolter
Boun Mounger, Thomas called (1292), 61
Boure, atte, surname or bye-name of, 172
Bourer (Borer, Bowrer), surname or bye-name of, 172
Bourner, surname or bye-name of, 155, 158
Bover, le (le Bovier), surname or bye-name of, 248

Boverd, surname of, 248
Bowker, surname or bye-name of, 276, 432
Bowne, see Bohun
Bowrer, see Bourer
Bowyer, surname or bye-name of, 248
Boxall (Boxell, Boxhole, Boxsoll), surname of, 119
Boxgrove, 55, 58, 70, 101, 271–2, 340, 385, 388
Boxgrove Priory, 101
Boxholte, 119
Braban, surname of, 94
Brabant, 94, 369
Brabroke, surname of, 114
Bradenex, see Brodnex
Bradshaw, James (1539), 115
Bradshaw, surname of, 114–5, 433
Bradshaw (greater Manchester), 115
Braiosa, Gosbert de (1080), 30
Brakden, see Brickden
Brakepole, de, surname or bye-name of, 96
Brakonshawe, see Burtenshaw
Bramber, 41, 47, 54, 232, 247, 254, 263, 271, 370, 374
Bramber, Rape of, 15, 30, 31, 42
Brambletye, 100
Bramley (near Godalming) (Surr.), 255
Braose, Peter de (1357) (of Wiston), 31
Braose, Philip de (c. 1095 and later), 31, 41, 47
Braose, Thomas de, Peter son of (1357) (of Chesworth), 31
Braose, William de (1086), 29, 30, 31, 39, 41
  Philip father of (? c. 1050), 30
Braose, William de (mid 12th century), 31, 69
Braose, Wm. de (c. 1220–91), 101
Braose, de, surname of, 31, 34, 39
Brapool, 96
Braybrooke (Northants.), 114
Breakspear, surname or bye-name of, 364
Brede, 61, 100, 178–9, 183, 265, 276, 376–7, 379
Brednex, see Brodnex
Bredon, surname of, 114
Bredon (Worcs.), 114
Breedon-on-the-Hill (Leics.), 114
Bregg, see Bridge
Bregger, see Bridger
Brekden, see Brickden

Brekenschawe, see Burtenshaw
Bret (or le Bret), surname or bye-name of, 94
Bretinsha, see Burtenshaw
Bretons, 33
Brewes, surname of, 31
  see Braose
Brewster, surname or bye-name of, 258
Brickden (Brakden, Brikeden, Brekden, Brokeden), surname of, 16
Bricmar, see Brithmer
Bridge (Bregg, Brugge), surname or bye-name of, 141, 155–6, 177, 183
Bridgeman, surname or bye-name of, 141, 147, 152, 174, 179
Bridger (Bregger, Brugger, Brygger), 147, 152, 155–7, 174
Brightling, 37, 267
Brighton, 44, 54, 169, 243, 253, 363, 368, 379, 405, 407, 430–34
Brightwalton (Berks.), 5
Briouze (Orne), 30, 41
Brithmer (Bricmar), personal name of, 311
Brithmer (Brytmere), surname or bye-name of, 311
Brittany, 94
Broadbridge (in Bosham), 71
Broadbridge (in Horsham), 69, 86
Broadwater, 39, 170, 191, 231, 264–5, 271–2, 296, 371
Broadwater, Little, 264, 296
Brocker, surname or bye-name of, 203
Brodnex (Bradenex, Brednex), surname of, 16
Brok, see Brook
Broke, Walkelyn atte (? c. 1370), 57
  see Walklyn, Ralph
Brokeden, see Brickden
Broker, see Brooker
Brokexe, Alexander de, *curtus*, (1292), 65
Brokexe, Sander de, *longus* (1292), 65
Brokexe, de, surname of, 84
Bromham, le, surname or bye-name of, 3
Bromlegh, surname or bye-name of, 99
Brook (Brouk), surname or bye-name of, 141, 145–6, 155, 183
Brooker (Broker), surname or bye-name of, 141, 145–6, 155, 156, 174, 434
Brookman, surname of, 145–6, 174, 179
Brooks, surname or bye-name of, 204
Broomhill, 37, 61

Brouk, see Brook
Brounman (Brunman), surname of, 337
Brown (le Brun, Brown), surname or bye-name of, 361, 367
Browncock (Brunecock), surname of, 367
Browning, Herbertus called (1292), 61
Brugg, see Bridge
Brugger, see Bridger
Brun, le, see Brown
Brun, personal name of, 367
Brunecock, see Browncock
Brunecok, personal name of, 367
Brunman, see Brounman
Brygger, see Bridger
Brygges, surname or bye-name of, 155
Brytmere, see Brithmer
Buchan, surname of, 432
Buchanan, surname of, 432
Buci, Robert de (1086), 40
Buci, Robert de (*c.* 1100–50), 40
Buci, de, family of, 39–40
Buck, surname or bye-name of, 386
see Bukke
Buckholt, 125
Bucks., surnames or bye-names in, 11, 309, 332–3
Bucksteep, 194
Buckwell (in Ashburnham), 125
Buddle, see Bedell
Budgen, surname or bye-name of, 432, 434
Bugsell (in Salehurst), 97, 127–8, 137
Bukherst, surname of, 7
Bukke, Thomas Jonesservant (1401), 66
Bull, surname or bye-name of, 361, 386
Bullfinch (Bolfin), surname or bye-name of, 361
Bullock, surname or bye-name of, 386
Bullocker (Bullockherd, Bullaker), surname of, 248, 253
Bulman, surname or bye-name of, 248
Bulshyne, surname or bye-name of, 248
Buncton, 39, 163
Bungar (Bongard), family of, 10
Burbeach Hundred, 160
Burbridger, surname or bye-name of, 160
Burchet, surname or bye-name of, 368
see Birchett
Burdeville, de, surname of, 93
Burdeville, le, surname of, 3
Burgayn, surname of, 94

Burgess Hill, 432
Burgundy, 94
Burhunte, surname of, (1332), 102
see Boarhunt
Burlands Copse, 159
Burne, atte, surname or bye-name of, 410
Burpham, 260, 275, 380
Bursteye Farm (in Ardingly), 125
Burtenshaw (Byrtemshawe, Brakonshawe, Brekenschawe, Bretinsha, Beconsawe, Buttershawe, Buttinger, Burtinshall), surname of, 113, 114, 433
Burtinshall, see Burtinshaw
Burton, West, 273
Burwash, 61, 138, 274, 311, 316, 381, 401
Bury, 249, 273–4
Bust, see Bost
But, le, Adam called (1291), 83
Buttenshaw, Buttinger, see Burtenshaw
Buttyng, surname of, 315
see Botting
Buxshalls (in Lindfield), 127, 137
Buxted, 123, 245, 401
Byfleet (Surr.), 159
Bylynghurst, surname or bye-name of, 98
Byn, see Binne
Byndepouke, bye-name of, 414
Byrchette, William Berewerthe atte (1436), 65

Cachelove (Catchlowe, Catchlove, Cachelow, Cetchlove), surname or bye-name of, 20, 387, 396
Cade, Jack, revolt of (1450), 14
Cade, surname of, 61, 337
Cadman (Cademan), surname of, 337
Cahagnes (Calvados), 35
Cahaignes, William de (1086), 34, 35
Cahaignes, de (Kaines, de, Keynes, de, Caines, de) surname of, 35
Caine (Kayne), surname of, 74
Caines, de, see Cahaignes, de
Caisned, Ralph de (1086), 35
see Cheney, de
Caisneto, de, see Cheney, de
Cakeham, 243
Calf, Richard (? *c.* 1350), 83
His son, see Loughteburgh, William de
Callaway, surname of, 119

Calle, Richard (or Richeman), 5
Calle, surname or bye-name of, 5
Callow, surname or bye-name of, 361, 398
Calverd, surname or bye-name of, 248
Camberlengus, Camerarius, see Chamberlain
Cambs., surnames from, 103
Cameron, surname of, 432
Camoys, de, surname of, 93
Campagne, place-name of, 159
Campbell, surname of, 432
Campion, see Champion
Campyner, le, surname or bye-name of, 159
Candel, Ralph (*c*. 1320?), 321
Candeler, surname or bye-name of, 174
Candeles, Matilda (1327/8), 321
Candelman, surname or bye-name of, 174
Canner (*cannarius*), surname or bye-name of, 250
Cannere, Ric. le (*c*. 1250), 250
Cannere, Ric. le (? same as above), (1292), 250
Canon, Anfridus (1165–6), 286
Canon, surname or bye-name of, 235, 237
Cantays, persons named (1332), 99 see Kentish
Canterbury, Archbishops of, 4, 106, 148, 237
Capelain, Caplain, Caplin, *Capellanus*, see Chaplain
Capeler, le, see Capper
Capenor, surname or bye-name of, 102
Capenor, (Surr.), 131
Caperon (Capron), surname or bye-name of, 258, 277, 432
Capiere, surname or bye-name of, 174
Caplin, Caplen, surname of, 238
Capman, surname or bye-name of, 174
Capper (le Capeler), surname or bye-name of, 254, 257
Capron, see Caperon
Cardinal, surname or bye-name of, 234
Carectarius, surname or bye-name of, 280
Carker, surname of, 229
Carl (Karl, Kerl) surname or bye-name of, 232–3
Carleford (Carlesford), bye-name of, 128
Carmichael, surname of, 432

Carpentarius, surname or bye-name of, 280
Carr, surname of, 152
Carter, surname or bye-name of, 224, 226
Carver, surname of, 258, 277
Casiere, le, surname or bye-name of, 85 see Caysere
Catchlowe, Catchlove, see Cachelove
Catchpole, surname or bye-name of, 431
Catrik, surname of, 117
Catsfield, 65, 400
Catslands Farm, 61
Catt, surname or bye-name of, 361, 365, 398
Catterick (North Yorks.), 117
Catteslond, surname of, 61
Caumbray, de, surname of, 93
Caysere, Gunnora le (*c*. 1285), 85 see Casiere
Cetchlove, see Cachelove
Chaisneto, John *de* (*c*. 1140–50), 35
Chaisneto, de, see Cheney, de
Chamberlain, (*Camberlengus, Camerarius*), surname or bye-name of, 237
Champagne, 94, 159
Champeneys, surname of, 94
Champion (Campion), surname or bye-name of, 238–9
Chancellor, surname or bye-name of, 237
Chantemerle (Chauntemerle, de), surname or bye-name of, 365–6, 396, 409
Chapel, North, see North Chapel
Chapelayn, Walter (late 13th century), 238
Chaper, surname or bye-name of, 251, 254
see Chipper
Chaplain (Caplain, Chaplin, Chapelain, Capelain, *Capellanus*), surname or bye-name of, 238
Chapman, surname or bye-name of, 174, 221, 224, 226–7
see Chepman
Chappere, surname or bye-name of, 174
Chatfield, surname of, 126
Cheeseman, surname or bye-name of, 258, 277, 432, 434
see Chesman

Index

Cheney, de (Chesney, de; *Caisneto, de*; Kainneto, de; Chenei, de; Cheyni, de; Cheyne; Chenne; *Querceto, de*), family of, 35–6, 93, 431
Cheney, de, see *Querceto, de*; Caisned, de; *Chaisneto, de*
Chepman, Pote called (1292), 61
Cherryman (Cherian, Cheriman, Chiryam, Chyriam), surname of, 177
Cheryman (Chyryam, Chyriam), Thomas (1571 and earlier), 177
Chesh., surnames from, 118
Chesman, John (1373–4), 84
  see Cheeseman
Chesney, de, see Cheney, de
Chesworth, 31
Cheverell, surname of, 114
Cheverell (Wilts.), 114
Cheyne, Cheyney, see Cheney, de
Chichester, Seffrid I, bishop of (1125–45), 312
Chichester, Seffrid II, bishop of (1180–1204), 312
Chichester, Bishops of, 12, 105, 237, 389
Chichester, Earls of, see Arundel, Earls of
Chichester, 12, 18, 33, 38, 43, 64, 66, 70, 98, 100, 104, 114–5, 120, 148, 159–60, 167, 169–70, 172, 178, 185, 192–3, 196, 198, 227, 239, 242, 244, 246, 254, 256, 261–3, 266, 269, 272, 274, 275, 278–9, 281, 311, 313, 317, 319, 321, 324–5, 327, 335, 340–2, 365, 366, 373–4, 376–7, 380–5, 387–9, 407, 425
Chichester Rape, 31, 167
Chiddingfold, surname or bye-name of, 101
Chiddingfold (Surr.), 100, 169–70, see Chuddingfold
Chiddingly, 161, 264, 382
Childerhouse, surname of, 152
Childwick (Herts.), 426
Chilland (Hants.), 102
Chillonde, surname or bye-name of, 102
Chiltington, 208
Chiltington, East, 38
Chiltington, West, 163, 177, 387
Chipper (Chiper), surname or bye-name of, 251
  see Chaper

Chiprian, surname or bye-name of, 312
  see Ciprian
Chitelesbirch, John de (1332), 96
Chittenden (Kent), 113
Chittinden, surname of, 113
Chittlebirch, 96
Chiryam, see Cherryman
Chollington, 49
Chrisman, surname of, 336
Christian, personal name of, 336
Christmas, surname or bye-name of, 362, 399
Christopher, surname of, 336
Chuddingfold, surname or bye-name of, 100
  see Chiddingfold
Church, surname or bye-name of, 183
Churcher, surname or bye-name of, 155, 174
Churchman, surname or bye-name of, 174
Chyngton, 158, 173, 240, 338
Chyriam, Chyryam, see Cherryman, Cheryman
Cinerarius, Gilbert (*c.* 1240), 54
  see Coliere, Robert le
Cinerarius, surname or bye-name of, 281
  see Colebrener
Cinqmars, surname of, 422
Cinque Ports, 236
Cinque Ports, see Hastings, Rye, Winchelsea
Ciprian, personal name of, 312
  see Chiprian
Clanefeld, surname or bye-name of, 102
Clanfield (Hants.), 102
Clapham (near Worthing), 41, 275
Clapham (in Litlington), 190
Clare, surname of, 44
Clarembald (? de St Leger), (Early 12th century), 37
Clay (atte Clee, Cley), surname or bye-name of, 58, 184–5
Cleares, surname of, 44
Clee, atte, see Clay
Clegg, surname of, 126
Clement, Christian name of, 273
Clements, Widow (*c.* 1285), 352
Clenewater (? or Clevewater), surname or bye-name of, 366
Clenewater, Agnes de (1327), 366
Cleopham, Gilbert de (or *de Sancto Audeono*) (1086), 41

446 Index

Clere, Roger de (*c*. 1190 or earlier), 85
  His wife, see Gurnaio, Agnes de
Clere, surname of, 43–4
Cleres (Seine-Maritime), 43
Clerke, surname or bye-name of, 8
Clerkes, Johanna (1332), 352
Clerkson, surname or bye-name of, 328
Clevewater, see Clenewater
Clevewaters Farm, 366
Cley, see Clay
Cliffe (near Lewes), 263, 272
Clifton, Reynold de (*c*. 1200–1220), 85
Climping, 241
Clitheroe, surname of, 126
Clough, surname of, 152
Cobbe (Cobb), surname of, 17, 372, 374–5, 434
Cobby (Cobey), surname or bye-name of, 17, 375
Cobham (Kent), 99
Cobham (Surr.), 99
Cobham (Cobeham), surname or bye-name of, 99, 337
Cobhamsman, surname or bye-name of, 337
Cock, surname or bye-name of, 221, 224, 226, 227
Cockes, de, surname or bye-name of, 199
Cockhaise (in Lindfield), 128
  see Cokkehese
Cocking, 69, 252–3, 270, 274, 313, 384
Cog, le, surname or bye-name of, 241, 365
Cogger (le Coggere), surname or bye-name of, 241, 244
Cogman, surname or bye-name of, 241
Cohen, surname of, 264
Coiner, surname or bye-name of, 262
Cokkehese, surname or bye-name of, 128
Colbran, surname or bye-name of, 345, 432
Colbrook, surname of, 117
  see Colebrook
Coldwaltham, 33, 259, 387
Colebrener, surname or bye-name of, 229, 281
  see *Cinerarius*
Colebrook (Colbrook), surname of, 108, 117
Colebrook (Dev.), 108
Coleby, surname of, 433
Colefish, surname of, 365

Coleman, Ric. (1218–19), 360
Coleman (Colman), surname or bye-name of, 345
Colhook Common, 159
  see Kolhoker
Coliere, Robert le (early 13th century), 54
  see *Cinerarius*, Gilbert
Collier, surname or bye-name of, 258, 277
Collins, surname of, 321, 325
Colpoys (Colpas, Colpays, Colpes, Colpice), surname of, 426
Coltherd, surname or bye-name of, 248
Coltman, surname or bye-name of, 248
Colyn, see Wyn, Colett atte
Combe, Jn. (or Combes), (1427–40), 324
Combe, surname of, 145–6, 149, 183
Comber, surname of, 157–8, 183
Combes, surname or bye-name of, 204
Comes, Simon (*c*. 1096), 47, 48
Comes, Simon (1125–47), 47, 80
Comes, William, (? *c*. 1140), 47, 80
  see Counte, le, Cunte, le
Compe, Jn. de la (*c*. 1300), 327
Compe, atte, holding called, 327
Compe, atte, surname or bye-name of, 8, 172–3, 353
Comper, surname or bye-name of, 172–3
Compton, 325, 341
Comsone, surname or bye-name of, 327, 329, 353
Conier, Thomas le (or le Cunier or Coninger, or *Cunularius*), (*c*. 1250), 262
Conier (Conyer), surname or bye-name of, 262
Coninger, see Conier
Conte, le, see Counte, le
Convers, surname of, 237
Cony, surname or bye-name of, 361
Coombes (near Bramber), 170, 232, 242, 370
Cooper, surname or bye-name of, 221, 224
Copereshurst, surname or bye-name of, 130
Copeshurst, surname or bye-name of, 99
Copner, surname of, 131
Copnor, (Hants.), 102
Copperhurst (Kent), 99
Copshurst (? near Kirdford), 130

Coquus, Robert (1086), 38
Cornelius, Christian name of, 7
Corner, surname or bye-name of, 8
Cornerlye, de, surname or bye-name of, 106
Cornman, bye-name of, 229
Cornw., surnames or bye-names in, 333
Cortesly, 37
Costedell (Costdell, Costell), surname of, 149, 187–8
Costell's Wood, 188
Coteler, surname or bye-name of, 245
Coterose, bye-name of, 409
Cotier, surname or bye-name of, 232
Cotman, surname or bye-name of, 232
Cotterel, surname or bye-name of, 232
Cotur, le, surname or bye-name of, 232
Couerer, surname of, 70
Count, le (Conte, le, Cunte, le, *Comes*), surname of, 47, 235
see *Comes*, Cunte, le
Couperes, Agnes (1332), 352
Couperes, Christina (1332), 352
Court, surname or bye-name of, 183
Courthope, surname or bye-name of, 97
Courtup (in Nuthurst), 97
Cousin, surname or bye-name of, 423
Coventre, John Fuller (1443), 65
Cover, surname of, 70
Covert, Ric. le (1233), 69
Covert, Wm. de (or del Covert), c. 1250–70), 69
Covert, Wm. (died 1494), 69
Covert, de, family of, 50, 69–70, 93, 118
see Cuvert, de
Cowbeech, 197
Cowden (Kent), 100
Cowfold, 119, 275, 314–5, 324, 376, 407
Cowherd (Coward), surname or bye-name of, 248
Cowlishaw, surname of, 126
Cowper, surname or bye-name of, 7
Crabtree, surname of, 152
Cragg, surname of, 152
Cralle, de, surname of, 75
Cralle, 36, 75
Crane, surname or bye-name of, 361
Cras, le, surname or bye-name of, 20
Crawley, surname of, 126, 244, 263, 327, 376, 432
Creall, surname of, 36
see Criol, Cryell, Cruel, de

Crede, surname of, 5
Crede Farm (Bosham), 5
Creep Wood (in Penhurst), 126
Cressi, de, family of, 50, 93
Cresswell (Creswell), place-name of, 159
Cressweller, surname or bye-name of, 159–60
Cressy (Seine-Maritime), 81
Crèvecouer (Calvados), 81
Crevequer, de, family of, 45, 50
Cribelere, Robt. le (*c.* 1290), 281
Criblur, bye-name of, 229
Criel-sur-Mer (Seine-Maritime), 36
Crimsham, 100
Criol, de, family of, 36
Criol, see Creall, Cruel, de, Cryell
Crokked Eight Acres, field name of, 188
Crop, surname of, 126
Crosbie, place-name of, 108
Crosby, surname of, 108
Crossman, surname of, 147
Crouch, surname or bye-name of, 183
Crouherst, Matthew de (late 13th century), 123
Crow, surname or bye-name of, 361
Crowcher, surname or bye-name of, 147, 156, 158
Crowhurst, surname of, 126
Crowhurst (parish), 42, 123
Crowhurst (in Burwash?), 123, 138
Croyden, person named (1332), 100
Croyden (Surr.), 100
Cruce, Andrew *de* (1296, 1327/8), 202
see Holirode, Andrew atte
Cruchese, Thomas le (1296), 202
see Holerode, Thomas
Cruel, Robert de (1086), 35, 36
Cruel, see Criol, de, Cryell, Creall
Crul, William called (1212–22), 83
Cryell, surname of, 36
see Creall, Criol, Cruel, de
Cuckfield, 70, 190, 198, 202, 259–60
Cumberland, surnames or bye-names in, 363
Cunningham, surname of, 432
Cunte, John le (early 13th century), 47
see Counte, le, *Comes*
Cunularius, see Conier
Curtehope, in Laughton, 97
Curteys, surname or bye-name of, 362
Curthup, see Courthope

Cutiller (Cuteler), surname or bye-name of, 245
Cuvert, Richard de (1157), 69
see Covert, de

Dabbes (or? Dalbes), surname or bye-name of, 351
Daber, Hugh (1305–6), 263
Daber, Peter le (or le Dauber) (1266), 262–3
Daber, Peter le (or le Dober), (1296, 1332), 262–3
Daber, see Dauber, Dubbere
Dabney, surname of, 33
Dabredin, see Preston, John
Dacre, surname of, 114
Dacre, place-name of, 114
Dalling, Field (Norf.), 104
Dalling, Wood (Norf.), 104
Dallington, 37, 379
Dallyng, surname or bye-name of, 104
Dameson, surname or bye-name of, 327
Damm, surname of, 152
Dane, de, see Dene, de
Daniel, Roger (1086), 38
Daniel, surname or bye-name of, 309, 345
Daniel, personal name of, 345
see Danyell
Dann, surname of, 202
Danne, atte, see Denne, atte
Dannet, surname of, 343
Danyell, Joan (1447), 86
Danyell, Thomas (1447), 86
see Daniel
Dartnall (Dartnole), surname of, 117
Dash, surname of, 145–6
Daubeney (or Daubene), John (c. 1400), 33
Daubeni, William (1296), 33
Daubeni, Daubeny, Daubigny, surname of, 33, 74
see Aubigny, de
see Arundel, Earls of
Daubeny, Richard (1327), 33
Dauber, Robt. (1332), 263
Dauber (Daber, Dobber, Dober, Dubber), surname or bye-name of, 16, 262–3
Dauber, see Daber, Dubbere
Dauborne, surname of, 74
Daughtery, see Dawtrey
Daughtrey, surname of, see Dawtrey

Daundeville, surname of, 93
Dautre, Dautryue, see Dawtrey
Davye, surname or bye-name of, 8
Dawtrey (Dautre, Daughtrey, Hautriche, de Alteriue, *de Alta Ripa*), surname of, 70–71, 118, 431
see *Alta Ripa, de*
Dayred, surname of, 425
see Derett
Deacon (Dekne), surname or bye-name of, 235, 237
Dean (le Dene, le Dyen, le Doyn), surname or bye-name of, 202, 238
see Dene
Dean, East (West Suss.), 42, 232, 279
Dean, West (West Suss.), 17, 373
Dean, see Westdean, Eastdean
Dekne, see Deacon
Delve, surname of, 183
Dender, see Thunder
Dene, (or de Denne, or de Dane), Amfred de (c. 1200), 219
Dene, atte (de la Dene), surname or bye-name of, 201–2
Dene, (or de Denne), Walter de (c. 1200), 219
Dene, de, surname or bye-name of, 201
Dene, le, surname or bye-name of, 201
Dene, surname or bye-name of, 183, see Dean
Denne, atte (atte Danne), surname or bye-name of, 183, 201–2
Denton, 102, 151, 159, 161, 251
Derett, surname of, 425
see Dayred
Derik, Christian name of, 7
Derrick, surname of, 343
Derykson, Hen. van (1466–67), 327
Derykson (Direckson, Dyrykson), surname of, 327
Devenyssh, surname of, 103
Devon, surnames in, 69, 98, 130, 332–3
Devon, surnames from, 103, 118
Dewhurst, surname of, 126
Dicker (atte Diker, atte Dyker), surname or bye-name of, 161–2
Dicker, the (at Chiddingly), 161
Dicker, the (at Eastbourne), 161
Didling, 50
Dike, de la, (ater Dyke), surname or bye-name of, 162
Dimock, Dimucke, surname of, see Dymmok

Index

Dinder (Dindar), surname or bye-name of, 263
see Thunder
Direckson, see Derykson
Disenhurst, 274
Diva, Boselin *de* (1086), 40
Diva, Hugh *de* (1056–7), 40
Diva, William *de* (1086), 40
Dive, family of, 40, 93
Dives-sur-Mer (Calvados), 40
Dobber, Dober, Dobur, see Dauber, Dubbere
Dobell, surname or bye-name of, 423
see Doubell
Doe, Jn, fictitious person, 365
Domesday, surname of, 399
Dondir, see Thunder
Doneghton, surname of, 64
Donnington, 94, 193–4, 321
Doo, Ric., fictitious person, 365
Doo, Wm, fictitious person, 365
Dorking (Dorcking), surname of, 102, 117
Dorrant, see Durrant
Dorset, surname or bye-name of, 11, 98, 145–6, 224–5, 228, 309, 332–3, 363, 381, 408
Dorset, surnames from, 104
Doubell, surname or bye-name of, 432
see Dobell
Douere, surname or bye-name of, 99
Dover, Ric. de (early 13th century), 424
Dover (Kent), 99
Down, surname or bye-name of, 141, 145–6, 149, 151
Downer, surname of, 145–6, 156, 203
Downes, surname of, 151, 204
Downs, South, 148, 181, 185
Doyn, le, see Dean
Drictneselle, Juliana de (*c*. 1210), 85
Her husbands, see Padiham, Simon de, and Turtellescumbe, Ralph de
Drigsell, near Robertsbridge, 85
Drinkwater, surname or bye-name of, 362, 364
Drogo, Simon son of, see Echingham, Simon de (*c*. 1150)
Drungewick, 232, 284
Dubber, Dubbere, see Dauber
Dubbere, Wm (or le Dobur) (1296), 263
Ducneman, surname or bye-name of, 7
Duck (le Duk), surname or bye-name of, 371

Duckel, surname or bye-name of, 371
Duffield, (Duffill, Dutfield), surname of, 120, 121, 431
Duffield (Derbys.), 120, 431
Duffield (North Yorks.), 120, 431
Duke, surname or bye-name of, 234–5, 432
Dumpford, 50
Duncton, 84, 271
Dunder, see Thunder
Dunhurst, 33, 264, 396
Dunlop, surname of, 432
Dunnock, surname or bye-name of, 361
Dunsfold (Surr.), 284
Dunwich (Suff.), 389
Durdener, surname of, 160
Durh., surnames or bye-names in, 333
Durrant (Dorant), surname or bye-name of, 309
Durrington, 39
le Dyen, see Dean
Dygestre, surname or bye-name of, 258
Dyghere, surname or bye-name of, 258
Dyke, ater, see Dike, de la
Dyker, atte, see Dicker
Dyker (at Hartfield), 161
Dykere, le, surname or bye-name of, 161
Dykerman, surname or bye-name of, 161
Dymmok (Dimock, Dimucke, Dymmook), surname of, 104, 117, 431
Dymock (Glos.), 104
Dyrykson, see Derykson

Eade, see Ede
Earl, surname of, 58, 221, 234
Eartakere, Jn. de (1334–5), 215
Eartham, 370
Easebourne, 167, 169, 252, 267, 271
Easewrithe, East, Hundred, 200
East, surname or bye-name of, 180–82
East Anglia, landowners in, 4, 51
East Anglia, personal names in, 307
East Anglia, surnames or bye-names in, 152, 168, 176, 227, 310, 329, 399, 407–8, 431
see Norf., Suff.
East Anglia, surnames from, 104
Eastbourne, 149, 151, 161, 179, 202, 231, 233, 261, 277, 324, 342, 384, 389
Eastbourne Hundred, 195
Eastdean (East Suss.), 159
see Dean, East (West Suss.)

Eastergate, 275
Eastern England, surnames or bye-names in, 157
Eccles (Greater Manchester), 115
Ecclesden, 162, 262
Echingham, Simon de (*c.* 1150), 49
Echingham, Simon de (*c.* 1190–1230), 49
Echingham, Wm. de (*c.* 1170), 49
Echingham, family of, 49
Echyngham, surname or bye-name of, 97
Edburton, 317, 334, 345, 407
Ede (Eade), surname or bye-name of, 334, 345
Edge, surname of, 152
Edith, personal name of, 345
Edmondes, surname of, 321, 325
Edmund, personal name of, 304, 307, 310
Edmund, surname or bye-name of, 309
Edrich, surname or bye-name of, 309
Edsawe (Edsoll), surname of, 117
Edser, High (Surr.), 117
Edward, personal name of, 302, 304
Edwards, surname of, 433
Egdean, 5
Egle, del, surname of, see Laigle
Eightacre (Eghtacre, Aytakers), surname of, 149, 188, 215
Eillesford, William de (*c.* 1210), 85
  His wife, see Yerceneselle, Mabilia de
Eldred (1086), tenant in chief, 32
Elgar, see Algar
Elizabeth, personal name of, 343
Elm (Nelm), atte, surname or bye-name of, 162
Elmer (de Elmer, de Elmere), surname or bye-name of, 162
Elmer Farm (at Middleton-on-Sea), 162
Elmes (Elmys), surname or bye-name of, 162
Elnod, Elnot, see Allnot
Elphick, surname of, 434
Elsted, 58, 59
Elwin, see Aylwyne
Engelond, surname of, 20
England, kings of, see Henry I
England, queens of, see Adeliza
Engleterre, surname of, 20
Engleys, surname of, 20
English, Janyn (1443), 20

Ermichun, see Armichun
Erringham, 378
Esscotengiis, Inguerranus de (1106), 42
  see Scoteney, Scoteni
Esseta (or Esete), William de (*c.* 1150), 49
Essete, Richard *filius* Hemming de (or Richard de Exsete) (early 12th century), 49
Essete (or Excete), de, family of, 49
Essex, landowners in, 424
Essex, surnames or bye-names in, 81, 98, 157, 175–6, 266, 320, 322, 332, 359, 391
Essex, surnames from, 104
Esterman, Ketel (*c.* 1090), 242
Etchingham, 49, 97, 377
  see Echingham
Étocquingny (Seine-Maritime), 42
Eu, Robert, Count of (1086), 32, 36, 42, 49
Eu, Hen., Count of, (1106), 42
Eu, Jn., Count of (*c.* 1150), 42
Eueresfeud, de, see Eversfield, surname of
Evening, surname or bye-name of, 233, 253
  see Aveninge, de
Eversfield (Everesfeud, de), surname or bye-name of, 106, 123, 126
Eversfield, 123
Evershead (Surr.), 431
Evershead (Evershed, Eversed), surname or bye-name of, 102, 117, 431
Evesk, Elias le (1259), 264
Eveske, Ralph le (1296), 264
  see Vesk
Ewer, le, surname or bye-name of, 194
Ewhurst (near Battle), 100, 187, 200, 236–7, 265, 279, 311, 316, 319, 379, 413
Ewhurst (in Shermanbury), 92
Exceat, 49, 189
Excete, family of, see Essete
Exeter (Devon), 103
Exetter, Excetr', surname or bye-name of, 8, 103
Exsete, Richard de, see Essete, Richard *filius* Hemming de
Eye, surname or bye-name of, 180, 201
Eylnoth, see Allnot
Eylwyne, see Aylwyn
Eyr, see Ayer

Index

Faber, surname or bye-name of, 229
Fabian, personal name of, 312
Fabian, surname or bye-name of, 312
Fagg, Great, 266
Fagg, Sir Jn., bart., (died 1701), 265
Fagg, Jn. (late 16th cent.), 265
Fagg, Wm. (14th cent.), 265
Fagg, Wm. (1473), 265
Fagg (le Fag'), surname or bye-name of, 265–6
Fagger (Vagger), surname or bye-name of, 266
see Fugar
Fair, Wm. (or Faircock) (late 14th cent.), 369
see Fayre
Fairhall (atte Fayrehale, Fairall, Farrall, Feyrall, Fyrral, Verrall, Verrell, Virroll), surname of, 15, 188
Fairlight, 194, 227, 394
Fairmaner, surname of, 362, 399
Fairweather, surname or bye-name of, 364
Faisant, Jn. (1166), 389
Faisant, see Fesaunt
Falesia, Agnes de (*c.* 1180), 85
  Her husband, see Gundevilla, Hugh de
Falesia, Emma de (*c.* 1187), 85
  Her husband, see Sartilleio, Gilbert de
Farables Shaw, 183
Farhall, Farrall, see Fairhall
Farncombe (Surr.), 101
Farncombe, surname of, 126
Farnefold (Farnfold, Farnfeld, Farnford), surname of, 117
Farnthe, persons named (1335), 97
Farrall, see Fairhall
Farrer, Sir William, 39, 51
Fayre, Wm. (? *c.* 1300), 369 see Fair
Fayrehale, atte, see Fairhall
Feast, see Fist
Featherstone, surname of, 433
Fécamp Abbey (Seine-Maritime), 35, 266
Feest, Feist, see Fist
Feilder, see Fielder
Feld, see Field
Felde, la (at Whatlington), 125
Felder, see Fielder
Fell, surname of, 152
Felpham, 241
Fenegle (Fenigle, Funegle), surname of, 189
Feningetrowe, see Vinnetrow

Fenn, surname or bye-name of, 183
Fennell (Vennell), surname of, 189–90, 215, 434
see Fonell
Fenton, surname or bye-name of, 176–7
Fentonman, surname or bye-name of, 176–7
Fernall, surname of, 190
Ferncumbe, surname or bye-name of, 101
Fernhurst, 252, 271
Ferrer (Ferur, Ferour, Ferrour), surname or bye-name of, 229, 244, 247
Ferret (Firret, Furet), surname or bye-name of, 368, 386, 393
Ferring, 54, 72, 238, 344, 389–90
Ferrour, Ferur, see Ferrer
Feryman, surname or bye-name of, 8, 257
Fesaunt, Thomas le (*c.* 1250), 389
Fesaunt (Faisant, Fesant, Feysant), surname or bye-name of, 361, 389–90
Fest, see Fist
Feysall, see Fairhall
Field (Felde, atte, Feld, de la), surname or bye-name of, 125, 141, 145–6, 149, 155, 183
Field Dalling (Norf.), 104
Fielder, (Feilder, Felder, Filder), surname or bye-name of, 141, 147, 152, 155–6
Field Place (in Goring), 125
Field Place (in Warnham), 125
see Feld
Fildrey (Fillery, Fitzleray, fiz le Roi), surname or bye-name of, 423–4, 432
Fileroy, personal name of, 423
Fillol, Wm. (*c.* 1250), 424
Fillol (Filleul), surname or bye-name of, 424, 432
Finch, (Fynch, Vynch), surname or bye-name of, 361, 369, 372, 386
Findon, 97, 162, 173, 198–9, 262, 265, 275, 353
Findone, surname or bye-name of, 97
Finhagh, see Vinall
Finnyng, (Fining, Wynyng), atte, surname or bye-name of, 16, 125
Firle, West, 57, 244, 265, 268–9, 370, 414
see Frog Firle
Firret, see Ferret

Fisdelou, surname or bye-name of, 361
Fish, surname or bye-name of, 361
Fishbourne, 97, 196, 262
Fisher, surname or bye-name of, 224, 228
Fishman, surname of, 229
Fishwick, surname of, 118, 126, 136
Fishwick (Lancs.), 118
Fisschebourne, surname or bye-name of, 97
Fist (Fest, Feast, Fust, Feest, Feist), surname or bye-name of, 372, 375–6, 434
Fittleworth, 71, 186
Fitzalan, John (1243), 33
Fitzalan, William (? late 12th century), 33
Fitzalan, family of, 4–6, 33–4, 55
Fitzalan family, lands of, 4, 314, 404
Fitzleray, see Fildrey
Fitzneal, surname or bye-name of, 215
fitz Ralph, Robert (probably same as Robert son of Ralph de Hastings), 35
fiz le Roi, see Fildrey
Flaald, Alan son of (early 12th century), 33
    William, son of Alan, son of Flaald, (mid 12th cent.), 33
    Walter, son of Alan, son of Flaald, (mid 12th cent.), 33
    See Fitzalan
Flacher, see Flasher
Flameng, see Fleming, le
Flamme, Humphrey (1086), 38
Flanders, 44
Flandrensis, see Fleming, le
Flasher (Flacher, Flusher), surname or bye-name of, 163, 182, 208
Flashman, 163
Flasshe, Jn. atte (1366), 163
Flassher, Jn. atte (1332), 163
Flecchynge, surname or bye-name of, 97
Fleming, le (Flameng, *Flandrensis*), family of, 44
Flemings, 7
Flemmyng, Flemyng, surname or bye-name of, 7, 94
Fleshmonger, William, Rural Dean of Chichester (1535), 254
Fleshmonger, surname of, 254
Fletching, 97, 197, 311, 390, 401
    see Flecchynge

Flexborough Hundred, 158
Floc, Geoffrey de (1086), 35–6
Floc, surname of, 75
Flode, Jn. le, see Floude, de
Flode, Thos. le, see Floude, atte
Flot, surname of, 75
Flote, ate, surname or bye-name of, 58, 243
Flote, le, surname or bye-name of, 243, 244
Flotyere, le, surname or bye-name of, 243
Floude, Jn. de (or le Flode) (1327/8, 1332), 162
Floude, Thos. atte (or le Flode) (1327/8, 1332), 162
Flusher, Flussher, see Flasher
Foghe, John le (? late 12th century), 58
Foghe, John le (c. 1240), 57
Foghe, William le (? early 13th century), 57–8
Foghe (Fogh, Fohe), surname of, 57–8
Fogwell, surname of, 377
    see Fowle
Folkington, 251
Fonell (Funell, Funnell, Furnell, Fournal, Fournell), surname of, 190, 432, 434
Fonnels, surname of, 190
    see Fennell
Forapple, surname of, 183
Forbench, surname of, 149, 191
Ford, Forde, surname or bye-name of, 155–6, 183
Forder, surname or bye-name of, 155–6, 158
Forger, surname or bye-name of, 244, 253
Forlange, atte, bye-name of, 164
Forthright, surname or bye-name of, 362
Foston (Leics.), 5
Fournal, Fournell, see Fonell
Fowlbrook (in Ewhurst), 413
Fowle (Fugell, Fogell, Fowlie, Vowle), surname or bye-name of, 372, 376–8, 386, 432
    see Fogwell, Fugel, Fuggle
Fowle, personal name of, 378
Fowling, surname or bye-name of, 377–8
Fox, surname or bye-name of, 386
Fraelvilla, Ancel *de* (early 12th century), 44
Fraelvilla, Robert *de* (mid 11th century), 44

see Freelvilla, Friville
Fraevilla, Richard de (*c.* 1060), 44
Framfield, 123, 232
France, landowners in, 4
France, place-names in, 3, 4–5, 10, 19, 30–3, 35–7, 40–4, 50, 67–72, 74, 81, 92–4
France, surnames in, 47, 48
France, surnames or bye-names from, 6, 7, 10, 19–21, 343, 431
see French language
Francombe, see Fraunchomme
Frank (Fraunk, Fronk), surname or bye-name of, 230–31, 324
Frant, 97
Fraunchomme (Francombe), surname or bye-name of, 231–2
Fraunkes, surname of, 324
see Frank
Fray, see Free
Frebody, see Freebody
Free (Fray, Frey), surname or bye-name of, 230, 231, 232
see Fry
Freebody (Frebody, Fribody), surname or bye-name of, 230, 231–2, 253
Freeland (Freland, Frilond, Frylond), surname or bye-name of, 153, 230–1
free tenants, surnames or bye-names of, 12, 57–63, 67, 71, 123–4, 197, 234–5, 237, 329–30, 335, 337, 366, 378, 385, 391, 400, 426
see also, yeomen
Freelvilla, Roger *de* (1170), 44
see Fraelvilla, Friville
Freeman, see Freman
Freivill, de, see Friville
Freman (Friman, Fryman), surname or bye-name of, 230–31, 232
French language, surnames or bye-names in, 3, 9, 19–21, 34–5, 45–8, 50, 54, 92, 108, 119, 191, 243, 249, 257, 264, 266, 269, 272, 278, 363–5, 368, 381, 394–6, 406, 422, 424
Frenchmen, in Suss., 9, 119
Frendekyn, Gervase, see Alard, Gervase
Frendekyn, surname or bye-name of, 369, 371
Frensh (Frensch, Frenssh), le, surname of, 94, 106
Frensham (Surr.), 101
Fressenville, Ingelram de (late 12th century), 67

Fressenville, Matilda de (or Meiniers, de) (*c.* 1200), 67
Fretour, see Fruter
Freulleville (Seine-Maritime), 44
Frey, see Free
Fribody, see Freebody
Friday, surname or bye-name of, 399–400
see Fryday
Frie, see Fry
Friend, surname or bye-name of, 369, 371–2, 378–9
Frig, see Fry
Frilond, see Freeland
Friman, see Freman
Friston, 251
Friter, le, see Fruter
Frith (Fryth, Vrythe), surname or bye-name of, 183–4
Friville (*Freivill, de*, Frollouill, Fryvill), family of, 44
see Fraelvilla, Freelvilla
Frog Firle, 49
Frollouill, see Friville
Fronk, see Frank
Frontridge, 250, 379
Fruter (Fretour, le Friter, Frytour), surname of, 16, 251
Fry (Frie, Frye, Frig, Fryg), surname or bye-name of, 230, 232, 258
see Free
Fryday, field name of, 399
see Friday
Frylond, see Freeland
Fryman, see Freman
Fryth, see Frith
Frytour, see Fruter
Fryvill, see Friville
Fugar, surname of, 266
see Fagger
Fugel, personal name of, 376, 378
Fugel, Wm. (early 13th cent.), 376
Fuggle, surname of, 377
Fuggles, surname of, 377
see Fowle
Fulking, 40, 183
Fuller, John (John Fuller Coventre) (1443), 65
Fuller, surname or bye-name of, 227, 256, 258
Fullestr', surname or bye-name of, 258
Funell, Funnell, see Fonell
Funtingdon, 71
Furbour, surname or bye-name of, 7

Furet, see Ferret
Furlonger (Vurlonger), surname of, 149, 156, 164, 182, 432
Furnell, see Fonell
Fust, see Fist
Fynch, see Finch
Fynchecok, surname or bye-name of, 369
Fynegle, see Fenegle
Fynhagh, de, see Vinall
Fynning (in Rogate), 125
Fyntrewe, see Venitroe
Fyrral, see Fairhall

Gabriel, surname or bye-name of, 432, 434
Gadebergh, surname or bye-name of, 124
Gad's Hill (Kent), 400
Galet, surname or bye-name of, 243
Galiot, surname or bye-name of, 243, 253
Gap, surname of, 152
Gardener, surname or bye-name of, 221
Garston, 42
Gascony, 282
Gate, surname or bye-name of, 151, 155, 183
see Agates
Gateborough, 124
Gateman, surname or bye-name of, 179
Gater, surname of, 155
Gauder, see Goater
Geberissh, Gebryge, see Gibbridge
Gelderegg', de, surname or bye-name of, 123
Geldewyne, see Jeldewyne
Gelding, Thomas (or Golding) (1327/8, 1332), 400
Gelding, Wm. (or Goldyng) (1327/8), 400
Gelding, (Gilding), surname or bye-name of, 400
Geldwyne, see Goldwyne
Geneys, surname or bye-name of, 320
Geniver, see Jenever
Genman, see Jenman
gentlemen, surnames of, 14
see landowners
German, serf named (?c. 1280), 85
Germayn, Maud (c. 1285), 85
Gestlyng, surname or bye-name of, 124
see Guestling

Geudewin, personal name of, 357
See Goldwine
Gibb, Joan (or Gibbs) (1670, 1672), 324
Gibb, Ric. (or Gibbs) (1648, 1669), 324
Gibbridge (Geberissh, Gylbrishe, Guybberishe, Gebryge), surname of, 126
Gibbs, surname or bye-name of, 318
Gibson, surname or bye-name of, 318
Gilbert, surname or bye-name of, 305, 309
Gilby (Gilbey, Gylby), surname of, 108, 109
Gilby (Lincs.), 108
Gildewin, son of Savaric (or son of Sanzaver) (early 12th century), 80
Gilding, see Gelding
Gilforde, surname of, 117
see Guildford
Gillridge, 123
Giwerye, atte, see Jewery
Glageon (Nord), 427
Glagon, see Glaion
Glaion (Glagon), surname of, 425
Glasier, surname or bye-name of, 8, 246
see Verrer, le, *Vitrarius*
glass industry in Suss., 9, 10, 169, 246–7
Glaswright (Glaswyrthe, Glasewyrth), surname or bye-name of, 246–7
Gloucs., surnames or bye-names in, 104, 284, 333
Glynde, 159, 183, 269, 384
Glyndere, surname or bye-name of, 159
Goat (in Ringmer), 56
Goater (Goatcher, Gotier, Gauder), surname or bye-name of, 249, 430
Godale, surname or bye-name of, 397
Godalming (Surr.), 101
Godalming Hundred (Surr.), 157
Goddard, surname or bye-name of, 309
Goddegrom, surname or bye-name of, 362
Goddenwick, 128
Godelef (Godeloue), surname or bye-name of, 311
Godemefecche, surname or bye-name of, 361
Godeshalf (Godshalf), surname or bye-name of, 5, 361, 372, 397, 401
see Godsal
Godeshulle, Ric. de (or de Goteshale) (c. 1300), 401
Godesmark, surname or bye-name of, 361

Godesole, Godsal, see Goodsole
Godingewyk, de, bye-name of, 128
Godleofu (Godeleva), personal name of, 311
Godmanneston, surname of, 104
see Godmeston
Godmanstone (Dorset), 104
Godmeston, surname of, 104
see Godmanneston
Godsal, surname or bye-name of, 400–1
Godsall, Jn. (Godsale, Godsalve) (? c. 1550), 401
see Godeshalf
Godsell, surname of, 400
Godsell (Wilts.), 400
Godshalf, see Godeshalf
Godshill (Hants.), 400
Godshill (Isle of Wight), 400
Godsmark, surname or bye-name of, 372, 397, 432
Goduinus, personal name of, 301
see Godwine
Godwin (Goodwin), surname or bye-name of, 142, 305, 306, 309, 434
Godwine, personal name of, 308
see Goduuinus
Golda, Hugh son of (1086), 44
Goldeberd, surname or bye-name of, 361
Goldewyne, Wm. (or Joldewyne), (1279), 338
see Goldwyne
Goldhawk (Goldhauek), surname or bye-name of, 338–9
Golding, surname or bye-name of, 400
see Gelding, Goldyng
Goldock (Goldok), surname of, 338–9
Goldring, surname or bye-name of, 432
Goldspur Hundred, 108
Goldwine (Geldwyne, Joldwine), surname or bye-name of, 309, 400
see Judin
Goldwyne, Ric. (or Jeudewyn) (c. 1300), 338
see Goldewyne
Goldyng, William, de Lem (1292), 56
see Lem, Thomas de, Golding
Goodehind, surname or bye-name of, 362
Goodfellow, surname or bye-name of, 362
Goodsoal (Burwash), 401
Goodsole (Godsal, Goodsall, Godesole, Goteshole), surname or bye-name of, 61, 400–1
Goodwin, see Godwin
Gooseherd (Goshurde, Goushurde), surname or bye-name of, 249
see Gosset, Goushurde
Gore, surname or bye-name of, 183
Goring-on-Sea, 50, 54, 66, 104, 125, 151, 255, 275, 344, 401
Gosden, surname of, 126
Gossatt, Jn. (1525), 249
Gosset, surname of, 249
Goteshole, Ric. de, see Godeshulle
Gotherde, surname or bye-name of, 249
Gotier, see Goater
Goushurde, Alice (1349), 85
Graffham, 384
gramaticus, Philip, (*c.* 1100), 32
Grant, surname or bye-name of, 361
Grashurst, Christina de (13th century), 85
Her husband, see Sperling, Simon
Grashurst, in Icklesham, 85
Gratwick, surname of, 119
Gravely, surname of, 128
Gravelye (in Lindfield), 128
Gravene, surname of, 139
Gravett (Grevett), surname or bye-name of, 150, 163, 184, 368
Gravetye, 98
Greatham, 22, 43
Greatwick, 119
Greener, surname or bye-name of, 158
Greenhalgh, surname of, 126
Greenhurst, 123, 401
Grenatour, see Grevatour
Grenhurst, de, surname of, 123
Grevatour (or atte Grevette) Ric. (1370–73), 163
Grevatour (or atte Grevette), Walter (1370–73), 163
Grevatter (Grevatour, Grevetour), surname or bye-name of, 163–4
Grevette, see Grevatour, Gravett
Grey, surname or bye-name of, 361
Grinstead, surname of, 126
Grinstead, East, 17, 120–21, 149, 166, 239, 268, 315, 344, 377, 406
Grinstead, West, 101, 170, 192, 197, 229, 278, 315, 343, 345, 406–7
Groby (Leics.), 118
Grogan (Grugan), surname or bye-name of, 425
Grogen, surname of, 425

Grombridge, see Grumbridge
Grooby, surname of, 118
Groombridge, 120
Grover, surname or bye-name of, 155, 432
Grugan, see Grogan
Grumbridge (Grombridge), surname of, 120
Guestling, 100, 124, 191, 231, 241
see Gestlyng
Guildford (Surr.), 100, 114, 117
Guldeford, East, 135, 165
Gundevilla, Hugh de (*c*. 1180), 85
His wife, see Falesiam Agnes de
Gundeville, de, surname of, 3, 93
Gundewyne, de, surname or bye-name of, 3
Gurnaio, Awis de (*c*. 1190), 85
Her husband, see Clere, Roger de
Gurnard, surname or bye-name of, 361
Guybberishe, see Gibbridge
Gwynne, surname of, 343
Gybbrishe, see Gibbridge
Gylby, see Gilby
Gyser, surname of, 229

Hacford, surname or bye-name of, 8
Hahewood, atte, bye-name of, 142
Hai, Richard de (early 12th century), 45
Hai, family of, see Hay, Hey
Haia, Ralph *de* (*c*. 1150), 45
Haia, Robert *de* (*c*. 1100), 44–5
Ranulf father of, 45
Richard grandfather of, 45
Haia, Richard *de* (? *c*. 1150), 45
Hailsham, 261, 270, 381, 394, 424
Haiminc, sub-tenant (1066, 1086), 49
Hale, Wm. in the (atte Hale, le Halgh) (1296–1332), 162
Halfbond, surname or bye-name of, 239
Halfknight, surname or bye-name of, 239, 253
Halflord, surname or bye-name of, 239
Halgh, Wm. le, see Hale, in the
Halle, surname of, 7
Halnaker, 98
see Helnaked
Hamer (Lancs.), 164
Hamme, atte, surname or bye-name of, 164, 183
Hammer (Hamer), surname or bye-name of, 164–5, 245, 266–7

Hammond, surname or bye-name of, 309
Hamo, customary tenant (1252), 54
Hamond family (of Battle), 54
Hamper, see Haneper
Hamper (Hanepere, Henepere, le), surname or bye-name of, 164–5, 245, 266–7
Hamper's Lane (Horsham), 267
Hampnett, East, 385
Handhamer, Geof. (1296), 267
Handhamer, bye-name of, 165, 245
Haneholte, atte, surname or bye-name of, 125, 142
Haneper, Robt. (1332), 266
Haneper, Wm. (1332), 267
Haneper, See Hamper
Hanepers, Wm. (1306), 267
Hans, personal name of, 7
Hanshoter, surname of, 160
Hants., landholders in, 32, 43
Hants., personal names in, 382
Hants., services in, 275
Hants., surnames or bye-names in, 43, 120, 157, 163, 184, 186, 226, 229, 230, 239, 251–2, 254, 272, 330, 333, 377, 381, 383, 403, 426
Hants., surnames from, 102
Harberner, surname or bye-name of, 159
Harborne (Harbourne), place-name of, 159
Harborough, surname of, 118
Hardacre (Preston Hundred, Kent), 215
Hardham, 252
Hardwareman, surname of, 7
Haringod (Harengod, Herigaud, Heringaud), family of, 48
Harlot's Wood (in Northiam), 125
Harpeting (or Harpeyng), Peter de (1327, 1332), 93
Harpetinges, see Harpingden
Harpindgen, (Herbertinges, Harpetinges), 38, 93
Harringworth (Northants.), 103–4
Harrison, surname or bye-name of, 10, 328, 433
Harry, see Herry
Harsfold, 253
Hart, surname or bye-name of, 361, 386
Hartfield, 138, 161, 315, 406
Harting, 98, 169, 189, 252, 267–8, 385
see Hertynge

Index

Hartridge (Kent), 99
Haryngworth, surname or bye-name of, 103
Haseling, atte, bye-name of, 142
Haslemere (Surr.), 100
Hastinges, Robert de (1086), 35
Hastingis, Ingerannus de (early 12th century), 35
Hastings, 9, 18, 35–6, 119, 171–2, 236, 261, 269, 317, 327, 374, 379, 407, 418
Hastings, Raimbert de (1106), 35
Hastings Rape, 42, 49, 345
Hastings, Robert son of Ralph de (c. 1128 and earlier) (probably same as Robert fitz Ralph), 35
Hastings, William son of Robert de (1130–31), 35
Hastings, de, surname of, 35, 126
Hatch, surname or bye-name of, 183
Hatmaker, surname or bye-name of, 257
Hauekfeld, atte, bye-name of, 142
Hautriche, see Dawtrey, *Alta Ripa, de*
Hautrive, de (*Alta Ripa, de*, Dautryve, Dawtrey), family of, 44, 93
Hautrive (Orne), 44, 70
Hautyngtot (or Hertherugg), Nichola de (1327, 1332), 92–3
Hawkesborough Hundred, 65
Hawkhurst (in East Hoathly), 197
Hawkines, Avicia (1332), 351
Hay (or Hai), family of, 45
Hay, surname or bye-name of, 183, 191–2
Hay, de (High, le), surname of, 191
Haycroft, atte, bye-name of, 142
Haye, atte (Haye, de la), surname or bye-name of, 191, 216
Haye, de, family of, 44–5
Haye-du-Puits, La (Manche), 44
see Haia
Hayes, surname of, 184
see Hese, atte
Haywards Heath, 426, 432
Hazeldean (near Cuckfield), 202
Hazelhurst (in Ticehurst), 42
Hease, see Hese
Heasman, surname or bye-name of, 432, 434
Heath, surname or bye-name of, 183
Heene, 382
Hegelard, La, see Highland Farm

Hegge, atte, surname or bye-name of, 191–2
Heghehecche, atte, bye-name of, 142
Heighton, South, 251
Held (Hilde), surname or bye-name of, 183
Heldele, atte, bye-name of, 142
Helier (Hellyer), surname or bye-name of, 277
Hellingly, 161
Helnaked, surname of, 98
Hemmingii, Richard *filius*, see Essete, Richard *filius* Hemming de
Hempstead (in Framfield), 123
Hemsley, surname of, 433
Hemsted, de, surname of, 123
Henfeld, de, surname or bye-name of, 128
Henfield (parish), 61, 108, 119, 125, 128, 317, 344
Henfield Wood (in Lindfield), 128
Henhurst Hundred, 18
Henle (Henly), John (1524–25), 18
Henley (in Frant), 18
Henley, place-name of, 18
Henry I, King of England, 32
Henry, personal name of, 18, 302, 305
Henshaw, surname of, 118
Heptonstall, surname of, 118
Herbert, surname or bye-name of, 305
Herbertines, see Harpingden
Herd, surname or bye-name of, 248
Herdman, surname or bye-name of, 248
Herefordshire, surnames or bye-names in, 256, 333
Hereward, personal name of, 306–7
Hereward, surname or bye-name of, 306–7, 309
Herigaud, Heringaud, see Haringod
Herman, personal name of, 7
Herring, surname or bye-name of, 361
Herry, Gilbert (1374), 85
His wife, see Sparwe, Agnes
Herry (Harry), surname of, 218
Herrye, the, field name of, 218
Herrys, atte, surname or bye-name of, 199, 323–4
Herstmonceux, 197, 262, 424
Herterugg, surname or bye-name of, 99
Hertherugg (or Hautyngtot), Nichola de (1327, 1332), 92–3
Hertynge, surname or bye-name of, 98
Hese, Wm. atte, see Hose, Wm. atte

Index

Hese, Wm. de la (1317, 1321), 214
Hese, (Hease), atte, surname or bye-name of, 151, 183–4
see Hayes, Hease
Heser, le, bye-name of, 154
Hetewater, surname or bye-name of, 366
Hethdone, ate, bye-name of, 142
Hey, surname of, 191
Heye, atte, surname or bye-name of, 191
see Hai, Hay
Heyghe, atte, surname or bye-name of, 191
Heyshott, 237, 253
Hickman, surname or bye-name of, 336
Hide, surname or bye-name of, 183
Hidroop's, holding named, 160
High, atte, surname or bye-name of, 192
Highden, 248
Highegate, atte, bye-name of, 142
High Hatch Lane (at Hurstpierpoint), 202
Highland Farm, 348
Hikke (Hykke), surname or bye-name of, 336
Hilde, see Held
Hildershurst, Alice de (mid 13th century), 85
Her husband, see Whatman, Stephen
Hill, surname or bye-name of, 141
Hilldrooper, Wm. (17th century), 160
Hiller, surname of, 157
Hillman, surname or bye-name of, 141, 147, 152
Hinton Daubeni (Hants.), 33
Hoadley Wood (in Ticehurst), 124, 241
Hoathly, East, 197, 382
Hobgen (Hobjohn), surname of, 399
Hodierna, personal name of, 339
Hodierne (Odierne), surname or bye-name of, 334, 339
Hodlegh, surname or bye-name of, 124
Hogekyn, surname of, 343
Hoget (Hoggett), surname or bye-name of, 380
Hogg, surname or bye-name of, 361, 365, 372, 379–80, 386
Hoggeprest, surname or bye-name of, 362
Hoggesflesh, surname or bye-name of, 252
Hokebench, ater, bye-name of, 206

Hokeday, surname or bye-name of, 362
Hoker, see Hooker
Hokes, Matilda (1334–5), 352
Holegrove, atte, bye-name of, 142
Holerode, Thomas (1296), 202
see Cruchere, Thomas le, Holirode
Holgrove Wood, 202
Holibone, surname or bye-name of, 114
Holirode, Andrew atte (1309, 1311), 202
see *Cruce, de*, Holerode
Holirode, atte, bye-name of, 142
Hollingbourne (Kent), 114
Hollington, 37
Holme, surname or bye-name of, 183
Holmes, surname of, 10
Holroyd, surname of, 118
Holstrete, atte, bye-name of, 142
Holter, surname or bye-name of, 155, 156, 183
Holybourne (Hants.), 114
Homwerthe, atte, bye-name of, 142
Homwode, atte, bye-name of, 142
Hone, surname or bye-name of, 18, 83, 192–3
Honer (Honner), surname or bye-name of, 193
Honer, locality, 193
Honess, surname of, 193
Honey, surname of, 18, 193
Honey Bridge, 192
Honey, Jn. (1332), 192
Honeywick, 176
Honickman, surname of, 176
Honney, surname of, 193
Hony, de, surname or bye-name of, 18, 192, 216
see Hune, le, Huny
Hoo, 42, 400
Hook (Houke), surname or bye-name of, 155, 183
Hooker (Hoker), surname or bye-name of, 155
Hope, Jn. at (or Hoppe) (1524–5), 165
Hope, Robt. (or Hoppe) (1524–5), 165
Hope (or Hopper), Thos. (1524–5), 158, 165
Hope (in Beckley), 165, 209
Hoppe, atte, surname of, 165
Hopper, see Hope
Hopper (or Hope), Thos. (1524–5), 158, 165
Hopper, surname or bye-name of, 165

Hoppere, Ric. le (or Hoper) (1327–8, 1332), 165
Hore, surname or bye-name of, 398
Horse, atte, bye-name of, 142
Horsecroft, surname of, 434
Horse Eye (Pevensey), 202
Horsekeeper, surname of, 249
Horseman, surname or bye-name of, 248–9
Horsey (near Eastbourne), 202
Horsham, 22, 66, 69, 104, 120, 153, 163, 165, 168, 170, 172, 177, 190, 193, 198, 230, 241, 249, 253, 255, 264, 266–7, 271, 275, 311, 313, 315, 325, 337, 343, 345, 348, 370, 375, 383, 387, 401, 407, 426
Horsknave, bye-name of, 248
Horstead, Little, 125, 183
Horsted Keynes, 35, 151, 166
Horton (near Shoreham), 242
Hosarius, Robt. (1130), 268
Hosarius, see Hose, Hussey
Hosatus, see Hose, Hussey
Hose, Osbert (or Hussee) (? *c.* 1150), 268
see Husar, Huser, Husyer
Hose, Wm. atte (or atte Hese) (1327–8, 1332), 267
Hose (*Hosarius, Hosatus*), surname or bye-name of, 47, 267–8
Hosee, Hosey, see Hussey
Hoseland, atte, bye-name of, 142
Hosemer, see Osmer
Hosere, Hosier, le, see Husyer, le
Hoskins, surname of, 321
Hoste, atte, bye-name of, 143
Hother (or Athoth), George (17th century), 158
Houghton, 33
Houke, see Hook
Hound (Hants.), 216
Hove, 42, 266, 407
Howel (or Hoel), Daniel (*c.* 1300), 54
Howel, Isabel (1307), 54
Howel, Walter (1307), 54
Howel, William (1307), 54
Huget (Hughet, Hughot), surname or bye-name of, 380
Hugh son of Golda (1086), 44
Hughson, Hugh (1436), 327
Hughson (1450), 327
Huguenots, 6, 9
Huiser, le (Lhuisser), surname or bye-name of, 269

Hunderherst, bye-name of, 143
Hunderlith, bye-name of, 143
Hune, le, surname or bye-name of, 192
Hunna, personal name of, 193
Hunston, 45, 272
Hunt, surname or bye-name of, 224, 228
see *venator*
Hunte, le, see Sperling
Hunts., surnames in, 153
Hunwick (Durh.), 176
Huny, surname or bye-name of, 192
see Hone, Hony
Hurne, surname or bye-name of, 180
Hurst, surname or bye-name of, 183
Hurstpierpoint, 38, 184, 198, 202, 326, 374, 376–7
Husar, Alexander (*c.* 1200), 268
husbandmen, surnames of, 14, 164, 329, 406
Huse, atte (or de la Huse), surname or bye-name of, 267
Huse, see Hose, Hussey
Husee, see Hose, Hussey
Huser, Osbert (c. 1260), 268
see Hose, Osbert
Husewif, surname or bye-name of, 269
Husewif, Christian name of, 269
see Hussey
Hussey (Huse, Husee, Hosey, Hosee, *Hosatus*), family of, 267–9
Hussey, surname or bye-name of, 267–9
see Husewif
Husyer, Robt. le (or le Hosere, le Hosier) (1296, 1316), 268
Huth, Alice atte (1349 or before), 86
Huth, Robert atte (?*c.* 1345) 86
Hyder, surname or bye-name of, 155, 157–8
Hykke, see Hikke

Iardehurst, de, see Yardhurst
Iccombe (Glos.), 104
Ichene, surname or bye-name of, 102
Icklesham, 17, 85, 241, 270, 374
Icoumbe, surname of, 104
Iddesworth, surname or bye-name of, 102
Iden, 97
Idenne, surname or bye-name of, 97
Ideworth (Hants.), 102
Ifield, 159, 170, 201
Iford, 44
Imberhorne, 17
Ingmanthorp, surname of, 104

Ingmanthorpe (West Yorks.), 104
Ingram, surname of, 346, 432, 434
Iping, 252, 286, 327
Ireland, surnames from, 106, 432
Iridge, 385
iron industry in Suss., 9, 228–9, 244
Irysse, le, (Yrisse), surname or bye-name of, 106
Isebrond, personal name of, 7
Isenhurst, 98, 197
Itchen (Hants.), 102
Itchingfield, 375
Ivery, Thomas de (c. 1240), 339
Ivor, Reginald (c. 1250), 339
Ivor, Robt., (or de Ivor) (c. 1260–90), 339
Ivor, Wm. (or Ivory) (c. 1250), 339
Ivor, surname or bye-name of, 339–40
Ivory, surname or bye-name of, 339–40

Jackman (Jakeman), surname or bye-name of, 336
Jackson, surname or bye-name of, 328
Jake, surname or bye name of, 336
Jakeman, see Jackman
Jakepreyst, surname or bye-name of, 362
James, A., surname or bye-name of, 199, 323
Jane (Jan), surname or bye-name of, 335–6
Janeman (Janman), surname or bye-name of, 335
see Jenman
Jardherst, surname or bye-name of, 97
see Yardhurst
Jay, surname or bye-name of, 386
Jeldewine, see Judin
Jeldewyne, Jn. (or Geldewyne) (1327–8, 1332), 338
see Goldwine
Jenever (Jeniver, Geniver), surname or bye-name of, 335
Jenman (Jemman, Genman), surname or bye-name of, 335–6
see Janeman
Jeudewyn, Ric. (early 14th cent.), see Goldwyne
Jeudewyne, see Judin
Jewdwyne, le, surname or bye-name of, 3
Jewery (atte Jewerye, Jewary, Jure, atte, Giwerye), surname or bye-name of, 193–4, 229

Jocelin 'of Louvain', (12th century), 70
John, personal name of, 302, 305
Johnson, surname of, 7, 8, 142, 305, 328
Jokeman, see Jakeman
Joldwine, see Goldwine
Jonhane Rude, Croft called, 169
Jornyman, surname or bye-name of, 257
Joudewyn, see Judin
Judin (Juden, Judwin, Judyne, Judewyne, Jeldewine, Jeudewyne, Joudewyn), surname or bye-name of, 338
see Goldwine
Jukeman, see Jakeman
Julle (or Jully), Wm. (1332), 17
Julle (or Jully), surname of, 17
Jupp, surname of, 434
Jure, see Jewery
Jureman, bye-name of, 229
Justice, surname or bye-name of, 235–6

Kaienes, de, see Cahaignes
Kainneto, de, see Cheney, de
Kant, surname of, 100
see Kent
Karl, see Carl
Kayne, see Caine
Kaynes, Alice de (c. 1265–75), 85
Kaynes, Richard de (c. 1265–75), 85
Kember, surname or bye-name of, 258
Kembestere (Keymestere), surname or bye-name of, 258
Kendal, surname of, 107, 109, 117
Kendall (Cumbria), 107
Kenesman, surname or bye-name of, 337
Kenne, surname or bye-name of, 337
Kent, landowners in, 4, 36, 42, 48, 50, 70
Kent, personal names in, 126, 178, 269, 311, 339, 341
Kent, places in, 99, 100, 113–4, 117–8, 130
Kent, surname or bye-name of, 99, 100
see Kant
Kent, surnames or bye-names in, 11, 12, 36, 52, 97–8, 101, 108, 141, 145, 150–51, 157, 169, 175–6, 198, 215, 224–5, 226, 228, 229, 230, 233, 265–6, 294, 309, 313, 318, 319–20, 321–2, 330, 332, 339, 344, 362, 363, 376, 381, 386, 391, 394, 402, 408, 418

Kent, surnames from, 99, 100
Kenteys, Kentish, surname or bye-name of, 99, 100
see Cantays
Kerl, see Carl
Kerswollere, surname or bye-name of, 206
see Cresweller
Ketel, le, surname or bye-name of, 3
Keverall (Cornw.), 135
Keymestere, see Kemberstere
Keynes, de, see Cahaignes, de
Keysford (in Lindfield), 128
Kildwick (West Yorks.), 426
Killick, surname of, 426
King, surname or bye-name of, 221, 234
Kingston, in Ferring, 94
Kingston near Lewes, 94
Kingston-by-Sea, 39, 93, 244–5
Kirdford, 16, 72, 119, 120, 130, 186, 241, 246, 256
Knelle, at (or Knelle, de), surname or bye-name of, 125
Knelle (in Beckley), 125, 340
Knight (Knyght), surname or bye-name of, 8, 235
Knightly families, surnames or bye-names of, 34–53, 67–72, 92–3, 102–3, 122
Kolhoker, surname or bye-name of, 159
Kyngeston, de, surname of, 94

labourers, surnames or bye-names of, 14, 62, 234, 255, 329
Lachemere, see Lechemere
Ladd, surname or bye-name of, 277, 278
Laigle, de, family of, 43
see *Aquila, de*
Laigle (Orne), 43
Lake, surname of, 7
Lamberhurst (Kent), 99
Lambert, Walter, son of, sub-tenant (1086), 42
Lancing, 39, 61, 164–5, 253, 266–7, 275
Lancs., landowners in, 44
Lancs., place-names in, 164
Lancs., surnames or bye-names in, 11, 12, 23, 47, 115, 121, 126, 145–6, 151, 157, 176, 194, 221–2, 224–6, 231, 255, 276, 309, 329–30, 332–3, 363, 378, 433–4

Lancs., surnames from, 118, 431
landowners, surnames or bye-names of, 13, 14, 259, 265, 267–8, 303, 323–4, 329, 330, 345, 373, 396, 398–9, 424
Lane, Adam atte (late 13th cent.), 189
Lane, Henry in le (1296, 1328), 189
Lane, Robert in le (*c*. 1300), 189
Lardener, surname of, 64
Larie, see Barye
Lark, surname of, 386
Lasher, James (1590), 269
Lasher, surname or bye-name of, 10, 269
Lashmar, surname of, 131
see Lechemere
Lashmer, see Lechemere
Lassher, Laur. (1439–40), 10, 269
see Lusher
Latchmere (Surr.), 100
Laughton, 97, 251, 270, 337, 390–1
Lavant, 71
Layne, see Leyne
Lea, de la, see Lee, atte
Leadbeater (Lidbetter, Lydbeter), surname or bye-name of, 254–5
Leamer, surname of, see Lemmer
Leamland, locality, 116
Lechemere, surname or bye-name of, 100, 101, 131
see Lashmar
Ledes, surname or bye-name of, 99
Ledgard (Legard), surname or bye-name of, 166–7, 340
see Legard
Ledger (Leghere, Legyer), surname of, 167
see Legard, Leger
Lee, atte (de la Lea, ater Legh, de la Lye), surname or bye-name of, 166
Leedes, surname of, 117
see Ledes
Leeds (Kent), 99
Leem (de la Leme, de Lem, Aleem), surname of, 149, 166
see Leme, Lem
Legard, personal name of, 340
Legard, see Ledgard, Legatt
Legarda, personal name of, 358
Legate (Legat, Legatt, Leggett, Leggott, Legard), surname or bye-name of, 340, 434
Legate, Robt. (late 12th cent.), 340
Legatt, Ric. (late 12th cent.), 340
Legatt, Wm. (*c*. 1200), 340

Leger, surname of, 340
  see Ledger
Legge (or Leggy), Robt. (1296, 1327), 17
Legge, surname of, 17
Leggett, Leggott, see Legate
Legh, surname or bye-name of, 183
Legh, atter, see Lee, atte
Leghere, Legyer, see Ledger
Leicester Liberty (Suss.), 240
Leics., places in, 114, 118
Leics., surnames or bye-names in, 224–5, 309, 332
Leics., surnames or bye-names from, 103, 433
Lem, Thomas de (1292), 56
Lem, Thomas (1296), 166
Lem, William Goldyng de (1296), 56
  see Leem
Leme, de la, see Leem
Leme, la, locality, 166
Lemm, surname of, 165
Lemmer, (Leamer, Leymer), surname of, 165–6
Lenarde, surname or bye-name of, 10
Leneslye, de, surname or bye-name of, 106
Leoffardi, de (de Sancto Leopharde), surname or bye-name of, 417
Leppard (Libbard, Lippard), surname or bye-name of, 361, 390, 393, 432
Leucknor, Leukenor, surname of, 103, 117
Leuere, atte, see Lever
Leveque, Ralph (1203), 264
  see Vesk
Lever (atte Leuere), surname or bye-name of, 194
Lever, place-name of, 194
Levyngfolle, personal name of, 7
Lewer, surname or bye-name of, 194
Lewes, de, surname or bye-name of, 97
Lewes, 65, 156, 170, 183, 241, 246, 252, 262–3, 270, 272, 278, 326, 363, 369, 375, 379, 386, 388, 395–6, 418
Lewes Castle, 181
Lewes, honour of, 158, 181, 339
Lewes Priory, 5, 6, 39, 46, 237, 313
Lewes Rape, 4, 29, 109–13, 186
Lewknor, surname of, 434
  see Leucknor
Lewknor (Oxon.), 103
Leymer, see Lemmer
Leyne (Layne), surname of, 148, 182

Lhuissier, see Huissier, le
Libbard, Lippard, see Leppard
Lidbetter, see Leadbetter
Lidgate, atte, surname or bye-name of, 160
Lidgater (Ludgater), surname or bye-name of, 160
Lidhouk (Lydhouk), person named (1332), 102
Ligier, see Lyger
Liliot, surname of, 343
  see Lyllat
Linch, Robt. atte (or Lyncher) (1327–8), 158
Lincher, surname or bye-name of, 155
  see Lyncher
Linchmere, 270–71, 389
Lincs., landowners in, 42
Lindfield, Lindefeld, surname of, 126–27
Lindfield, 119, 127, 137, 188, 295, 325
Lindridge (Kent), 99
Linfield, surname of, 127
Liphook (Hants.), 102
Litelrolve, surname or bye-name of, 372
Litelwatte (Littlewatte), surname or bye-name of, 372, 394
Liteman (Lyteman), surname or bye-name of, 178
Litlington, 18, 189–90, 374
Littlehampton, 312, 321, 325, 404
Lloyd, surname of, 343, 433
Loder, surname of, 158
Lodsworth, 271
Lokear, surname or bye-name of, 8
London, 118
London, surnames or bye-names in, 98, 196, 229–30, 251, 254, 316, 322, 408
Londoners, 118
Long, surname or bye-name of, 361, 389
Lorday (Loredei), surname of, 425
Lote, Wm. atte (or Loteman) (1332), 173
Lote, atte, surname or bye-name of, 18, 158, 177
Loteman, Walter (or de Lotemanesparre, de Lutmannesparr) (1296–1332), 177–8
Loteman (Lutemann, Lutman, Luttman, Ludman, Lydman), surname or bye-name of, 177–8, 182
Lotterd, see Luttard
Lotty, surname or bye-name of, 18

Lotyer, surname or bye-name of, 158
Loughteburgh, William de (late 14th century), 83
  His father, see Calf, Richard
Love, surname or bye-name of, 369, 370, 372
Lovecock, surname or bye-name of, 369–70
Lovekin, surname or bye-name of, 369, 370
Low Countries, surnames or bye-names from, 6, 7, 326–7, 343, 369, 376
  see also Flemings
Lowe, atte, surname or bye-name of, 194
Lower, surname or bye-name of, 194
Loyter, see Luter
Ludgater, see Lidgater
Ludman, see Loteman
Lurgashall, 271, 382
Lusher, surname of, 269
  see Lasher
Luteman, see Loteman
Lutemanesparr', de, bye-name of, 149
  see Loteman
Luter (Lutter, Loyter), surname of, 229–30
Lutman, Luttman, see Loteman
Luttard (Luthard, Lotterd), surname of, 344
Lychepole, le, surname of, 3
Lydbeter, see Leadbetter
Lyde, Mich. a (or Aside) (1327, 1332), 22
Lydman, see Loteman
Lydhouk, see Lidhouk
Lye, de la, see Lee, atte
Lyger (Ligier), surname or bye-name of, 166–7
Lyllat, surname or bye-name of, 360
  see Liliot
Lyminster, 72
Lyncher, Robt. (or atte Linch) (1332), 158
  see Lincher
Lyndregg, surname or bye-name of, 99
Lytelman, surname or bye-name of, 178
Lytelmay, surname or bye-name of, 362
Lyteman, see Liteman
Lytilscot, surname or bye-name of, 372

Mabbe, surname or bye-name of, 335
Mabel, personal name of, 335
Mackerell, surname or bye-name of, 361
Madehurst, 158, 196, 314
Madgwick (Megwik, de, Magicke, Magewike), surname of, 117
Mafey, see Maufe
Magewicke, Magicke, see Madgwick
Maghefeld, surname or bye-name of, 97
  see Mayfield
Maifai, see Maufe
Maister, see Master
Makehait, surname or bye-name of, 364
Makkes, Matilda (1349), 352
Malcovenant, surname or bye-name of, 362
Malfe, see Maufe
Malfed (or Malfeth), William (c. 1130–50), 46
Malfed, William (late 12th century), 46
Malfed (or Maufe), William (early 13th century), 46
Malfei, see Maufe
Malfet (Malfed, Malfei), surname of, 46, 48
  see Maufe
Malling, South, 4, 17, 60, 65, 106, 123, 183, 213, 237, 279, 311, 315–6, 385, 388, 395
Malmains, surname or bye-name of, 362
Malvoisin, surname or bye-name of, 362
Man, surname or bye-name of, 277
Manewode, surname of, 98
Mangefer, surname or bye-name of, 395
Manwood, the, 58, 98, 159, 239, 404
Mapelhurst, surname or bye-name of, 97
Maplehurst, in Ore, 97
Marays, surname of, 58
Marden, 367
Marden, East, 336
Marden, North, 336
Marden, Up, 341
Marden, West, 341
Maresfield, 108, 166, 269, 311
Mariner (Maryner, Marner), surname or bye-name of, 242, 258
Marke, atte, surname or bye-name of, 167
Marker (Merkare, Mirkare), surname or bye-name of, 167

Marker Farm, 167
Markwick, Markewike, surname of, 114, 117, 431
Markwick (Surr.), 114, 431
Marle, the, locality, 411
Marley (in Fernhurst), 411
Marley (in Peasemarsh), 411
Marley Farm (Brede), 370
Marley Farm (Battle), 370
Marley, place-name of, 370
Marlot, Marlott, see Merlot
Marner, see Mariner
Marsh, surname or bye-name of, 183
Marshall, surname or bye-name of, 244, 277
Mascall (Mascold), surname or bye-name of, 277
Mason, Wm., (or Myson) (1392), 328
Masseday, surname or bye-name of, 362, 419
Master (Moster, Muster, Maister), surname or bye-name of, 277
Matilda, personal name of, 342
Maufe, William (early 13th century), see Malfed, William
Maufe (Maufai, Maifai, Malfe, Mafey), surname of, 46–7, 396, 398, 432
see Malfet
Mause, surname of, see Maufe
May (Mey), surname or bye-name of, 258, 278
Maydekin, surname of, 61
Mayfield, 55, 61, 82, 97, 100, 123, 243, 245, 249, 269, 401, 403
see Maghefeld
Mayson, surname or bye-name of, 328
see Myson
Mean, the (Kent), 99
Medested (Medsted, Mested), surname or bye-name of, 102
Medstead (Hants.), 102
Meeching, 242
Megwik, de, see Madgwick
Meiniers, Matilda de (or Fressenville, de) (c. 1200), 67
Meiniers, Rainald de (c. 1200), 67
Mellward, see Millward
Mene, surname or bye-name of, 99
Merchants, surnames or bye-names of, 329
Merewe (Merowe, Merwe), surname or bye-name of, 100, 101
Merewine, surname or bye-name of, 54
Merkare, see Marker

Merke, atte (de la Merke), surname or bye-name of, 167
see Mirke, atte
Merle, surname of, 57, 386
Merle, de, surname or bye-name of, 370–71
Merle, le, surname or bye-name of, 370–71
Merle, locality, 370
Merlot (Marlot), surname or bye-name of, 370–71, 393
Merowe, see Merewe
Merrow (Surr.), 100
Merston, 158
Merwe, see Merewe
Mested, see Medested
Mew, le, surname or bye-name of, 54–5
Mey, see May
Micheldever (Hants.), 102
Middleham, 56, 272
Middlesex, surnames or bye-names in, 432
Middleton-on-Sea, 162
Midhurst, 49, 58, 101, 108, 163, 168, 194–5, 200, 233, 243, 258, 274, 277–8, 378
Midlands, landowners in, 40
Midlands, surnames or bye-names in, 13, 156, 173, 176, 221, 227, 256, 302, 305, 310, 318, 320–2, 327, 329–30, 333–4, 361
Midlands, surnames from, 118
Milby (North Yorks.), 104
Mildeby, surname of, 104
Mildeby, Jn. de (? c. 1170), 133
Mileham (Norf.), 5, 404
miles, William (1086), 38
Milksop, surname or bye-name of, 362
Mill, surname or bye-name of, 141
Miller, surname or bye-name of, 222, 224
Millgroom, surname or bye-name of, 222
Millward (Millard, Milward, Mellward, Mulward), surname or bye-name of, 222, 224, 278
Milne, surname of, 152
Milner, surname or bye-name of, 222
Milton (in Arlington), 251
Mirk, Jn. atte (or de Mirkare), (or de la Merke) (1296–1332), 167
Mirkare, see Marker
Mist (Myst), le, surname of, 55

Index

Model, Wm. le (1321), 401
Model, le, Modyll, Modle, see Moodle
Mogridge (Dev.), 118
Moine, le, see Monk
molendinarius, surname or bye-name of, 280
Molesey (Surr.), 100
Monk (le Moine, Mone, *Monachus*), surname or bye-name of, 235, 238
Montague, surname of, 119
Montbrai (Manche), 33
Montgomeri, Arnulf de (c. 1080), 31
Montgomery, family of (14th century), 32
Montgomery, Roger de, see Shrewsbury, Earl of
Moodle (Model, Modyll, Modle) surname or bye-name of, 401
Moodley, surname of, 401
Moorcroft, surname of, 153
Moorey, see Morey
More, surname or bye-name of, 18, 183
Morey (Moorey), surname of, 18
Morfey (or Morphey, Morphew), surname of, 47, 434
Mori (Mory, Moury), surname or bye-name of, 18
Morley, surname or bye-name of, 370
Morley (Lancs), 370
Morphew, see Morfey
Morphey, surname of, 434
see Maufe
Mortain, Robert, Count of (1086), 32, 40
Mortimer, surname of, 119
Moster, see Master
Mostowe, atte, surname or bye-name of, 277
Mot (de la Mote), surname of, 18
see Motte
Motay, surname of, 18
Mote, le, surname of, 203
Motey, surname of, 18
Moteys, surname of, 18
Motte (Mott), surname of, 18, 145–6, 151, 180, 183
Mottes, surname or bye-name of, 203, 204
Mougridge (Mugeregg), surname of, 118
Mountfield, 15
Moury, see Mori
Mowbray, surname of, 33, 93
Mower, surname or bye-name of, 255

Mox, surname or bye-name of, 351
Mucheldeuere, surname or bye-name of, 102
Mugeregg, Muggeridge, see Mougridge
Mulegroom, bye-name of, 229
see Millgroom
Mulesy, surname or bye-name of, 100
Mulgate, bye-name of, 153
Mulgatere, surname or bye-name of, 153
Mulward, see Millward
Mundham, 15, 274, 286, 385, 388
Muster, see Master
Myson, surname or bye-name of, 328
see Mason, Mayson
Myst, le, see Mist, le

Nabb, surname of, 152
Naldret, surname of, 145–6, 368, 432
see Aldrett
Napper, surname or bye-name of, 58, 252–3
Narford (Norf.), 104
Nash, surname of, 145–6
Nelm, atte, see Elm, atte
Nelrette, ate, see Aldrett, Naldret
Nereford, surname of, 104
Nesse, de, surname or bye-name of, 203
Neston, John a (John a Neston Passhele) (1434), 65
Netherfield, 168
Newehavene, Cyprian de (late 13th cent.), 312
Newhaven, 151, 161, 242, 312, 335
Newick, 125, 377, 391
Newtimber (near Poynings), 270
Nicholas, surname or bye-name of, 8
Nie (Nye), surname or bye-name of, 201
Nightingale, surname or bye-name of, 361, 434
Ninfield, 346
Niweman, Ralph (1305), 56
Niwewyke, ate, surname or bye-name of, 125
see Newick
Noak, surname or bye-name of, 145–6
Nobis, Jn. (1332), 351
Noble, Joan called (c. 1300), 83
Nokes, surname or bye-name of, 203
Norf., landowners in, 5, 6, 32, 35, 48, 51, 104, 122
Norf., personal names in, 339

Norf., surnames or bye-names in, 5, 47, 151, 155, 168, 332, 339, 363, 404
Norlington, 56, 60
Normandy, 41, 260
Normandy, landowners in, 52
Normandy, surnames in or bye-names in, 4, 29, 35–8, 43, 52
North, surname or bye-name of, 145–6, 180–82
Northants., landowners in, 46, 104
Northants., places in, 114
Northants., surnames from, 103
North Chapel, 159, 271
Northern England, personal names in, 305
Northern England, surnames from, 118
Northern England, surnames or bye-names in, 157, 176, 227, 256, 329, 330, 333, 361, 408
Northiam, 125
Northumberland, landowners in, 4
Northumberland, surnames or bye-names in, 363
North-west England, surnames in, 152
Notkyn, surname of, 369–70
Notkyng, surname or bye-name of, 369
Nott (Not), surname or bye-name of, 369
Nottingham, 281
Notts., surnames or bye-names in, 333
Noven Farm (in Lindfield), 128
Novene, atte, surname or bye-name of, 128
Nugent, surname of, 119
Nuthurst (near Cowfold), 97, 296, 314–5
Nutley, surname of, 126
Nutley, 166
Nye, see Nie
Nyetimber (near Pagham), 17, 198
Nykes, Alice (1291), 352

Oak, surname or bye-name of, 145–6, 149, 183
Occupational surnames or bye-names, 62–3, 108
Odierne, see Hodierne
Offington, 42, 243, 382
Okes, surname or bye-name of, 203
Oldham, surname of, 118
Oldham (Greater Manchester), 118
Olecumbe, Robert de (1086), 35, 36
see Ulecumbe, de
Orchard, surname of, 152
Ore, 97, 194, 374

Organmaker, surname or bye-name of, 7, 229
Osbern, surname or bye-name of, 309
Osbert, personal name of, 310, 346
Osbert, surname or bye-name of, 310, 346
Osborn (Osbern), surname or bye-name of, 346
Osmer (Hosemer), surname of, 343
Osmond, surname or bye-name of, 309
Otley, surname of, 114
Otley (Suff.), 114
Otley (West Yorks.), 114
Otter, surname or bye-name of, 361
Otway (Ottaway, Otteway), surname or bye-name of, 315
Ouse River, 183
Oving, 253, 262, 387
Ovingdean, 38, 39
Oxford, 196
Oxherd, surname or bye-name of, 248
Oxman, surname or bye-name of, 248
Oxon., surnames or bye-names in, 11, 24, 145–6, 151, 156, 196, 203, 223–5, 228, 321, 332–3, 363
Oxon., surnames from, 118

Pachyns, surname or bye-name of, 351
Padiham, Simon de (? c. 1200), 85
  His wife, see Drictneselle, Juliana de
Padwick, surname of, 433
Pagham (near Selsey), 4, 17, 58, 172, 181, 189, 193, 198, 214, 237, 247, 274, 338
Pakyn, John (? c. 1445), 86
Pakyn, Potencia (1448–52), 86
Palfrey, surname or bye-name of, 249
Palfreyman, surname or bye-name of, 249
Pallant (ate Palente, de Palenta), surname of, 148
Pallant, the (at Chichester), 148
Palmarius, bye-name of, 54
  see Palmer
Panchurst, Pancost, see Pankhurst
Pancras, surname or bye-name of, 313
Pangdean, 48
Pankeherste, Dunstan or Duncan (Pancost, Penkehurst) (late 16th cent.), 402
Pankhurst, Ric. (or Pentecost) (1770), 403
Pankhurst, surname or bye-name of,

313, 401–3
See Penkhurst, Pynkhurst, Pengehurst
Pankhurst (Surr.), 403
Pannatt, Pannett, see Paynot
Parcertes, Wm. (1166), see Tarcortais, Wm. (*c.* 1150–70)
Parfoy, surname or bye-name of, 361, 395
Parham, 22, 43, 163, 252, 275
Parker, surname or bye-name of, 225, 227
Parkminster (earlier Picknoll, Pyteknolle), 92
Parmoncorps, surname or bye-name of, 361
Parnell (Pernell), surname or bye-name of, 335
see Pennell
Parr, Paul van (1456–7), 136
Parr (Merseyside), 118
Parre, surname of, 118
Parry, surname or bye-name of, 204
Parson, see Person
Parstepe, surname or bye-name of, 99
Passeavant, surname or bye-name of, 366
Passhele, John a Neston (1434), 65
Pastheap (Kent), 99
Patcham, 96
Paul, surname or bye-name of, 305
Paxhill (in Lindfield), 119, 128
Payne, surname or bye-name of, 305
Paynell, surname or bye-name of, 335
Paynot (Pannatt, Pannett), surname or bye-name of, 346, 434
Peacock, surname or bye-name of, 361, 372, 389–90, 432
Pearley (Perly), surname of, 117
see Purlye
Peasecod (Peasegood, Peskett, Pescott, Piscod, Puscod), surname or bye-name of, 5, 404–5, 432
Peasemarsh, 376
Peckden, surname of, 128
Pegden, 128
Peghedenn, de (Pehedenn, de), bye-name of, 128
Pelham, surname of, 103, 117
Pelham (Herts.), 103
Pencoed, place-name of, 404
Pencost, see Pankhurst, Pentecost
Pencoyd, place-name of, 404
Pende, surname or bye-name of, 158

Pendere, surname or bye-name of, 158
Pendlebury, surname of, 126
Pendleton, surname of, 126
Penfogill, surname of, 418
Penfold, surname of, 153, 434
Pengehurst, surname of, 402
Penhurst, 126, 168, 402
Penketh (Lancs.), 176
Penketh, surname of, 176
Penkethman, surname of, 176
Penkhurst, Hen. (or Penkherst, Pynkhurst, or Pankhurst) (*c.* 1560–80), 402
Penkhurst (Penkehurst), surname of, 402
see Pankhurst, Pynkhurst, Pinkhurst
Pennell, surname of, 335
see Parnell, Paynell
Pennicod (Pennicott, Pennycodde, Pennicard, Penneycard, Pennycord), surname of, 403–4
Pennicott (Dev.), 404
Pennyfather, surname or bye-name of, 364, 404
Penshurst (Kent), 117
Pentecost, Jn. (1332), 403
Pentecost, personal name of, 402
Pentecost, surname or bye-name of, 362, 372, 399, 401–3, 432, 434
Pepperhams (Surr.), 100
Perching, 40, 183
Perci, Ric. de (died 1244), 70
Percy, family of, 4, 5, 6, 46, 70, 93, 104, 122, 326
Periere, see Perryer
Perley, see Purlye, Pearley
Pernell, see Parnell
Perour, Jn. le (or Purie, or atte Purye) (1296–13289), 167
Perour, see Perryer
Perry (atte Perye, atte Purie, atte Pyrye, Pirie), surname of, 145–6, 167, 183
Perryer (Peryer, Periere, Perur, Perour, Purier), surname or bye-name of, 145–6, 167–8
Perryman, surname of, 145
Persevent, bye-name of, 229
Person (Parson, le Person), surname or bye-name of, 328
see Pesson, Peysson
Persones, atte, surname or bye-name of, 199
Personeson, Henry le (1327–8), 286, 327
Perur, Peryer, see Perryer

Pescit, Pescud, Pescott, Peskett, see Peasecod
Pesson, surname or bye-name of, 328
  see Person, Peysson
Peter, surname of, 7
Petersfield (Hants.), 252
Petevyne, surname or bye-name of, 94
  see Peytevyn, Poitevin
Petijohn, surname or bye-name of, 372
Petipas, surname or bye-name of, 366
Petreponte (or Petraponte), Robt. de (1086 and later), 38–9
Petroponte, see Pierrepoint
Petroponte (or Petraponte), Godfrey de (1086 and later), 38–9
Petroponte, Robt. de (c. 1060, ? same as preceding), 39
Petroponte, Wm. de (c. 1100), 39
Pett, 194
Petworth, 5, 10, 100, 104, 148, 186, 253, 255–6, 264, 267, 271, 273, 326, 344, 374, 387, 391, 417
Petworth, honour of, 4, 6, 44, 70, 105, 122
Pevensel, Drogo de (early 12th century), 49
Pevensey, Wm. of (c. 1120), 40
  Ric. son of (c. 1170), 40
Pevensey, 40, 168–9, 188, 190, 194–5, 202, 270, 344, 371, 384, 388, 394
Pevensey, Rape of, 38
Peyntours, Alice le (1332), 352
Peysson, surname or bye-name of, 328
  see Person, Pesson
Peytevyn, surname or bye-name of, 94
  see Petevyne, Poitevin
Pheasant, see Fesaunt
Phillipps, surname of, 433
Phisicon, surname or bye-name of, 257
Picard (Pycard), surname or bye-name of, 94
Picardy, 94
Picknoll, see Parkminster
Pickup, surname of, 126
Pictavinus, see Poitevin
Piddinghoe, 38, 93
Pieres, surname or bye-name of, 320
Pierrepoint, de (*Petroponte, de*; Perpond), family of, 38, 93
  see *Petroponte, de*
Pigherde, Wm. (or le Porcher) (c. 1300), 249
Pighurde, Robt. (or le Porcher) (c. 1300), 249
  see Porcher, le
Pikewoll, Wm., see Pitknolle, Wm.
Pilchard, surname or bye-name of, 361
Pilcher, Ric. (or Pulcher) (1430–31), 270
Pilcher (Pulcher, Pullchare), surname or bye-name of, 269–70
Pilecherestrete, at Lewes, 270
Pilter, surname or bye-name of, 270
Pincerna, Aluredus (1086), 40
  William son of, see Pevensey, Wm. of,
Pingfoghel, surname or bye-name of, 394
Pink, surname or bye-name of, 361
Pinkhurst (in Slinfold), 402
Pinkhurst (Surr.), 402
Piperwhite, surname or bye-name of, 398
Pipperham, surname or bye-name of, 100
Pirie, see Perry
piscator, surname or bye-name of, 280
Piscod, see Peasecod
Pistor, Jn. (John Pistor Witegrom) (1292), 65
Pitknolle (or Pikewoll), Wm. (1327, 1332), 92
Plaiz, Hugh de (c. 1150), 44
Plaiz, Ralph de (c. 1140), 44
Plaiz, family of, 44
Platt, surname of, 152
Playden, 44
Pluckrose, surname or bye-name of, 363
Plumeresden, see Plummerdene
Plummerden, 128
Plummerdene, de (Plumeresden, de) surname or bye-name of, 128
Plymouth (Devon), 130
Pockford (Surr.), 100
Pocock, surname of, 434
  see Peacock
Pointel, Ralph (1160), 41
Pointel, Robert (1220), 42
Pointel (Orne), 41
Pointell, family of, 41–3
Pointell, see Puintel, Puntel, Pyntel
Poitevin, Roger the, 32
  see Petevyne, Peytevyn
Poitou, 32, 94
Poke (Pocke, Pouke, Puck), surname or bye-name of, 372, 380
Poke (or Pooke), Gilbert (1535), 380

Poke (or Puke, Pouke), Robt. (1341), 380
Poke (or le Puke), Wm. (*c.* 1280–90), 380
Poke, see Pooke
Pokeford, surname or bye-name of, 100
Pokestrete (Tottingworth), 380
Polesworth (Warws.), 103
Poling, 72, 271, 338
Pollard, surname or bye-name of, 372
Polleprest, surname or bye-name of, 362
Pollingfold (Surr.), 100
Pollyngfold (Polyngfold), surname or bye-name of, 100, 101
Polton, surname or bye-name of, 99
Poltreuysh, see Sengeltone, Ric. de
Polyngfold, Polyngefold, see Pollyngfold
Pomfrett, surname of, 107
Pomphrey, surname of, 343
Pontefract (West Yorks.), 107
Ponyng (or Ponyghe), surname or bye-name of, 97
Pookeholde, land called (Burwash), 381
Pookhole, land called (Westfield), 381
Pook's Farm (Shermanbury), 414
Pope, surname or bye-name of, 234, 240
Porcarius, bye-name of, 249
see Swynherde
Porcher, Robt. le (*c.* 1300), 249
Porcher, Wm. le (*c.* 1300), 249
Porcher, surname or bye-name of, 249
see Pighurde
Porchester, surname of, 117
Portchester (Hants.), 117
Portreve (Portriffe), surname or bye-name of, 270
Portreve, John le (early 14th cent.), 270
Portslade, 259
Portsmouth (Hants.), 43, 377
Posterne, atte (or Posterne, de), surname of, 61, 83
Pote, Christian name of, 212
Poteman, Christian name of, 178–9
Poteman, Stephen (1327/8), 178
Potman (Poteman), surname or bye-name of, 178–9
Potman's Farm, locality, 179
Potmanshill, locality, 179
Potman's Land, locality, 179
Potte, atte (de la Potte), surname or bye-name of, 179
Potte, le (at Willingdon), 179

Potter, Steph. (1332), 179
see Poteman
Potter, surname or bye-name of, 179
Pottere, Reynold le (1292), 56
see Renaud, Simon
Poucher, surname or bye-name of, 257
Pouke, see Pooke
Pouke Lane (Chichester), 380
Poulesworth, surname of, 103
Poulton (Kent), 99
Poynings, Adam de (*c.* 1140), 48
Wm. son of, 48
Jn. son of (? same person as John de Poynings), 48
Poynings, Adam de (*c.* 1170), 48
Poynings, Jn. de (*c.* 1145), 48
Poynings, Michael de (*c.* 1210–30), 48
Poynings, family of, 48
Poynings, 48, 97, 344, 416
Poynings, see Puninges
Pralle (Prail, Praill), surname of, 425, 428
Pratte (Prat), surname of, 17
Praty, surname of, 17
Prawle (Dev.), 428
Premer, le, see Primmer
Premir, Nic. le (or Prinne) (1332), 405
Presbiter, see Priest
Prestes, Juliana de (1301), 321
Prestes, atte, surname or bye-name of, 199–200
Preston, John, alias Dabredin (1572–75), 9
Preston (near Hove), 42, 233
Preston Court (in Beddingham), 311
Preston, East, 100, 232, 273–5
Preston Hundred (Kent), 215
Preston, West, 232
Price, surname of, 243
see Aprece
Pricklove, surname of, 64, 387
Priest (Prest), surname or bye-name of, 235, 237–8
Primmer (le Premer, le Premir, Primer), surname or bye-name of, 405, 434
Prince, surname or bye-name of, 234, 239
Prinne, see Premir, le
Prinstead, 345, 367
Prior, surname or bye-name of, 237
Puccock, see Peacock
Puck, see Poke
Puckey, surname of, 381
Puckle, surname of, 381

Puffer, surname or bye-name of, 361, 365
Puggesley, surname of, 114
Pugsley (Dev.), 114
Puintel, Wm. de (c. 1100), 41
see Pointel
Pukehol, de, surname or bye-name of, 381
Pulborough, 44, 102, 108, 163, 168, 177, 203, 232, 251–2, 265
Pulcher, Pullchare, see Pilcher
Pullerose, ship's name of, 363
Pullrose, surname or bye-name of, 363–4
Punctello, Robt. *de* (1093), 41
see Pointel
Puninges, Rainald de (or Rainald son of Renner son of Reidi) (late 11th century), 48
William son of, 48
see Poynings
Puntel, Adam (1199–1200), 42
see Pointel
Purdew, surname or bye-name of, 397, 432
Purfowle, surname or bye-name of, 394
Purley (Surr.), 100
Purlye (Pearly, Perly), surname or bye-name of, 100, 101
see Pearley
Purye, Jn. atte, or Purie, see Perour, Jn. le
Puryere, see Perryer
Puscod, see Peasecod
Pusel, surname or bye-name of, 381
Putel, le, surname or bye-name of, 415
Puttock, surname or bye-name of, 361
Pycard, see Picard
Pye, surname or bye-name of, 386
Pyecombe, 101, 295
Pyngehurst, de, surname or bye-name of, 402
Pynherst, see Penhurst
Pynkhurst, de (Pynkherst, de), surname or bye-name of, 402
Pyntel (or Pointel), surname of, 42
see Pointel
Pypelor, surname of, 5
Pyrieman, surname or bye-name of, 179
Pyrye, atte, see Perry
Pyteknolle, see Parkminster

Quarer, Henry de la (1270), 54
Quarer, Jn. de la (c. 1250), 54
Jn. son of, 54
Quarer, Wm. de la (early 13th century), 54
Quatermars, surname of, 422
Querceto, Ralph *de* (c. 1100), 35
Querceto, Ralph, de Blukefeld *de* (c. 1265), 65
Querceto, de, see Cheney, de
Quernbetere, bye-name of, 229
Quernbites, field name of, 281
Quesnay, le (Seine-Maritime), 35

Rackham, 58, 249, 370
Racton, 253
Rainald son of Renner son of Reidi, see Puninges, Rainald de
Rainald, Wm. son of, sub-tenant (1086), 48
Ralph (? de Buci), sub-tenant (1086), 39
Ray, le surname or bye-name of, 20, 328, 423
see Roy, le
Rayson (Rison), surname or bye-name of, 328
Rea, surname or bye-name of, 201
see Ree
Read, surname or bye-name of, 398
see Rede, Reed
Reader, see Reder
Redbridger, see Rombrydger
Rede, Mich de la (or atte Rode) (1327, 1332), 195
Rede, Robt. (1332), 130
Rede, Wm. at (1474), 200
Rede (Reade, Reede, Ryede, *Rubeus*, le Rede), surname or bye-name of, 367
Rede, atte, see Rude, atte, Reed
Rede, the, field name of, 195, 200
Redeland, field name of, 195
Redelande, Ric. atte (1363), 195
Redelond, land called, at Selham, 195
Reder (Reader), surname or bye-name of, 168–9
Redes, Wm. at (1514–15), 200
Redland (Redlands), place-name of, 159
Redlondere, surname or bye-name of, 153, 159
Ree, Jn. at (or at Trice) (1525), 201
Ree, Michael atte (or atte Rye) (1327, 1332), 201
Ree, atte, surname or bye-name of, 201
see Rea

Reed (a Reede, atte Rede, atte Read, atte Ryde, de la Ride, atte Rode, atte Rude), surname or bye-name of, 168–9, 195–6, 367
see Rede, Rude, atte
Reeve, see Reve
Reidi, Rainald son of Renner son of, see Puninges, Rainald de
Reigate (Surr.), 101
Reigate Hundred (Surr.), 157
Reinbert, sub-tenant (1086), 49
Remys, surname or bye-name of, 320
Renaud, Simon (1296), 56
see Pottere, Reynold le
Renfield (Renefeud), surname of, 100, 117
Renville (Kent), 100
Repe, Ric. (or Rypps) (1456), 324
Reperose, bye-name of, 409
Repyer, surname or bye-name of, 8
Reve (Reeve), surname or bye-name of, 278
Reygate, surname or bye-name of, 101
Rice Bridge, 160
Ricford, surname of, 113–4
Richard, personal name of, 126, 302, 305
Rickford (Surr.), 114
Rickford (Somers.), 134
Rickman (Rykeman), surname or bye-name of, 336
Ridding, surname of, 152
Ride, de la, see Reed
Ridgebridge (Surr.), 160
Rie, atte (or atte Rye), surname or bye-name of, 201
Rigden (Riggeden, de), surname of, 126
Rilands, surname of, 152
Ringmer, 183, 195
Ringmer Hundred, 170
Ripe, 151, 251
Ripecherl, bye-name of, 229
Ripon, place-name of, 160
Ripreue, surname or bye-name of, 282
Risbrigger (Rusbridger), surname or bye-name of, 160
Risebridge (Ess.), 160
Risebridge (Surr.), 160
Rison, see Rayson
River, 256, 382
Robard, surname or bye-name of, 8
Robert, sub-tenant (1086; ? same as Robert *Salvagius*), 39

Roberts, surname or bye-name of, 318, 305, 325
Robertsbridge, 85, 165, 187, 380, 391
Robertsbridge Abbey, 54, 69
Robertsbridge Hundred, 158, 273
Robertson, surname or bye-name of, 318
Robinhood, surname or bye-name of, 394
Robynes, at, surname or bye-name of, 199, 323
Roddelond, Jn. atte (1327/8), 195
see Rued, atte
Rode, Michael atte, see Rede, de la
Rode, Wm. de la (or atterede) (1304 and earlier), 195
Rode, atte, see Reed
Rodmell, 93
Roe, Ric., fictitious person, 365
Rogate, de la, surname or bye-name of, 125
Rogate, 100, 101, 125, 169, 252, 330–40
Rogers, surname of, 319
Roggeri, Jn. (? or Rogers) (*c.* 1220), 351
Rombrydger, see Rumbryger
Roofer, surname of, 230
Roper, surname or bye-name of, 258, 278
Roperes, Alice le (1332), 352
Rother (eastern), River, 165
Rother (western), River, 252
Rotherfield, 167, 377, 406
Rottingdean, 39, 49, 50
Roy, le, surname or bye-name of, 20
see Ray, le
Rubeus, see Rede
Rude, atte (de la Rude), surname or bye-name of, 168–9
Rude, see Jonhane Rude
Rude, field name of, 195
Rude, atte, see Reed, Rued, atte, Rede, atte
Rudere, surname or bye-name of, 210
Rudgwick, 33, 197, 253, 255, 402
Rued, Jn. atte (1332), 195
see Roddelond, atte
Rumboldswyke, 43
Rumbridge (Hants.), 207
Rumbridge, 160
Rumbryger (Rombrydger, Redbridger), surname or bye-name of, 160
Rusbridger, see Risbrigger
Rusper, 253

Russell, Robert (1266), 85
  His wife, see Wogham, Matilda de
Rustington, 58, 59
Rutland, surnames or bye-names in, 333
Ryde, atte, see Reed
Rye, 6, 9–10, 61, 108, 119, 169, 172, 179, 201, 260, 265–6, 269–70, 324, 326–7, 344, 374, 376, 379
Rye, Michael atte, see Ree, atte
Rye, de, see Rie, de
Rye, atte (or de la Rye) surname of, 169
  see Rie, atte
Ryede, see Rede
Ryer, surname or bye-name of, 169
Rykeman, see Rickman
Ryman, Gillian (1499), 86
Ryman, John (? *c*. 1490), 86
Ryponder, surname or bye-name of, 160
Rypps, see Repe
Rysebrigger, surname or bye-name of, 153

Sacerdos, see Priest
Sacher, see Shotter
Sacker, surname or bye-name of, 271
  see Saker
Sadler, surname or bye-name of, 278
Saefrith (Seffrid), personal name of, 312
Saemann, personal name of, 309
  see Seman
Saier, see Sayer
St. George, de, family of, 50, 93
St. Georges de Bohun (Manche), 50
St. John, de, family of, 45
St. Leger, Geoffrey de (*c*. 1170), 37
St. Leger, Geoffrey de (early 13th century), 37
St. Leger, Jn. de (*c*. 1190), 37
St. Leger, Rainald (or Reginald) de (mid 12th century), 37
  Goddard, brother of, 37
  Thomas, brother of, 37
St. Leger, Robert de (1086), 35, 37
St. Leger, Roger de (*c*. 1190), 75
St. Leger, Thomas de (1166), 37
St. Leger, William de (early 12th century), 37
St. Leger, William de (mid 12th century), 37
St. Leger, William de (late 12th century, ? same as preceding), 37

St. Leger, family of, 37, 93, 340
St. Leger, see Clarembald
Saint Leger-aux-Bois (Seine-Maritime), 37
St. Owen (or *Sancto Audeono, de,* Seyntoweyn), family of, 41
St. Owen-sur-Maire (Orne), 41
  see *Sancto Audeono, de*
Saker, surname or bye-name of, 271
  see Sacker, Shotter
Sakespey, see Saxby
Saleherste, Roger de (*c*. 1260), 237
Salehurst, 18, 97, 128, 137, 200, 214, 270, 385, 378
Salerna, personal name of, 341
Salerne, surname or bye-name of, 340–41
  see Scalerne
Salernus, personal name of, 340–41
Salford Hundred (Lancs.), 146, 333
Salt, le, surname or bye-name of, 240
Salt (Staffs.), 240
Salt trade, 240–41
Salter (Sealter, Selter, Silter, Syltere), surname or bye-name of, 240–41
Salvagius (or *Silvaticus, Silvatinus*), Robert (late 11th century), 39
Salvagius, Robert (1150), 39
Salvagius (or le Sauvage), Robert (13th century), 39
Sancto Audeono, Gilbert *de* (or Cleopham, de) (1086), 41
  see St. Owen
Sancto Leodegario, de, see St. Leger
Sancto Leopharde, de, see Leoffardi, de
Sande, surname of, 145–6, 149, 151
Sandes, surname of, 151
  see Sandys
Sandlake, near Battle, 270
Sandys (Sandis), surname or bye-name of, 203, 204
  see Sandes
Sansaver, Ralph (*c*. 1170), 47
  William father of, 47
  Hugh, grandfather of, 47
Sansaver, family of, 47
Saper, Sapper, see Soper
Sapiens, see Wise
Sartilleio, Gilbert *de* (*c*. 1187), 85
  His wife, see Falesia, Emma de
Satcher, see Shotter
Saunders, surname of, 433
Saunzbouche, surname or bye-name of, 394

Savage (le Sauvage, *Silvaticus, Salvagius*), family of, 39
  see *Salvagius*
Savaric, Gildewin son (or son of Sanzaver), (early 12th century), 80
Saxby (near Barnham), 406
Saxby (Shakespey, Sakespey, Saxepe, Saxpes, Saxbee, Saxbie), surname or bye-name of, 406, 434
Saxby, place-name of, 406
Sayer (Saier or Sayers), surname or bye-name of, 7, 325
Scalerne, Roger (or Schalerne) (*c*. 1340–50), 341
Scardeville, de (Scarfield), family of, 50, 71–2, 93, 118
Scardevyle, Wm. (early 15th century), 71
Scarisbrick, surname of, 126
Scarvilla (? Calvados), 81
Schentewater, surname or bye-name of, 366
Schepman, surname or bye-name of, 242, 247
Scheppurd, see Shepperd
Scheter, Robt. le (1249), 271
Schipwerght, Jn. le (late 13th century), 243
  see Shipwright
Schottere, see Shotter
Schurte, atte, see Shurte, atte
Scoles, surname of, 152
Scorchevileyn, surname or bye-name of, 362
Scoteigni, Peter de (1211–12), 42
Scoteigni, Thomas de (1212), 43
Scoteigni, Walter de (*c*. 1170–80), 42
Scoteigni, Wm. de (1212), 43
Scoteigny, Lambert de (1160 and later), 42
Scoteney, Benedict (1327/8), 43
  see Esscotengiis, Scoteni
Scoteney, Ric. (1357), 43
Scoteney, Walter (1259), 43
Scoteney, Wm. (*c*. 1260), 43
Scoteney, Wm. (1327/8), 43
Scoteni, Engerranus de (*c*. 1150), 42
  see Esscotengiis, Scoteney
Scotenie, Walter de (1292), 43
Scotenye, John de (1292), 43
Scotenye, Simon de (1292), 43
Scotiniis, Henry de (*c*. 1216), 43
Scotland Farm (Steyning), 138
Scotland, personal name of, 126

Scotland, places in, 108
Scotland, surname of, 126
Scotney, Ingelram de (early 12th century), 42
Scotney, Peter de (? 1200), 42
Scotney, family of, 42
  see Esscotengiis, de
Scots, surnames or bye-names of, 327, 432
Scrace Bridge, 426
Scrase (Scrace), surname or bye-name of, 426
Scutt (or Scute), surname of, 64
Seaford, 42, 251, 263–4, 268, 270, 279, 314, 399
Seagrave (Segrove), surname or bye-name of, 108–9, 114, 117, 433
Seagrave (Leics.), 108
Sealter, see Salter
Seaman, surname of, 309
  see Saemann
Sedelscomb, surname or bye-name of, 96
Sedgewick, surname of, 126
Sedlescombe, Robert de, see Basoches, Robert de
Sedlescombe, 18, 42–3, 50, 68–9, 96
See, Philip atte (1327/8), (1332), 150–1
See, Wm. atte (1332), 151
See, atte (Sea), surname or bye-name of, 150–1, 155
Seer, surname or bye-name of, 155
Seffrid, see Saefrith
Sefrid (Seffray), surname or bye-name of, 312
Segrom, surname or bye-name of, 242, 253
Segrove, see Seagrave
Selde, atte (*de Selda*), surname or bye-name of, 196
Sele, 41
Sele Priory, 54
Selham, 195, 382
Selsey, 71, 159, 242, 248, 274, 279, 312, 335, 343, 384, 389, 396, 425
Selter, see Salter
Sengeltone, Ric. de, called Poltreuysh (*c*. 1300), 83
Sepherde, see Shepherd
Septemmolendinis, surname or bye-name of, 36
Sept Mueles, William de (1086), 35, 36
serfs, surnames and bye-names of, 5, 12–13, 17, 20, 42, 53–7, 67, 82, 85,

105–8, 123–4, 147, 171, 181, 197, 199, 235–8, 261, 268, 303–4, 314–5, 321, 328–30, 334–5, 337, 345, 363, 369, 384–5, 387–8, 390, 395, 396–7, 404–5
servants, surnames of, 62, 105
Setene, atte (or de la Setent), surname of, 58
Seton, de, surname of, see Setene, atte
Sevenoaks (Kent), 100
Sevenok, surname or bye-name of, 100, 102
Seyntoweyn (St. Owen, *Sancto Audeono, de*), family of, 41
see St. Owen
Shakerose, surname or bye-name of, 363
Shakespey, see Saxby
Shamele, atte (de la Shamele), surname or bye-name of, 159
Shamell, le, locality, 159
Shamler (Shambler), surname or bye-name of, 159
Shawe, surname or bye-name of, 183
Sheffield, 401
Shelley, surname of, 126
Shepare, see Shepper
Shepherd (Sepherde, Schephurd, *Bercarius*), surname or bye-name of, 247
Shepper (Shepare, Shupper), surname or bye-name of, 247–8
Sheppestre, surname or bye-name of, 247
Sherer, surname or bye-name of, 64, 263
Sherewind (Sherwin, Shirwin), surname or bye-name of, 362–3
see Tranchevent, Scherewyndes
Sheriff, surname or bye-name of, 235–6
Sherman, surname or bye-name of, 7, 263
Shermanbury, 39, 92, 380–1, 407, 414
Sherrington, 49
Sherter, Jn. (1385), 169
Sherter (le Shurtare), surname or bye-name of, 169–70
Sherwyndes (rigging), 408
Shipley, 164, 371, 375
Shipman, surname or bye-name of, 242
Shipwright (Sipwergte, Shipwerghte, Schipwerght), surname or bye-name of, 243
Shittere (Shieter), surname or bye-name of, 271
see Scheter, Shuiter
Shobeham, Robert de (13th century), 85
His wife, see Suttone, Rose de
Shoddington (Kent), 100
Shoesmith (Showersmith), surname or bye-name of, 58, 245, 253, 432, 434
Shoesmith's Wood, 245
Shoker, surname of, 229
Shoreham, 22, 183, 235, 244, 259–60, 265, 366, 378, 385, 407
Short, surname or bye-name of, 361
Shorter, surname or bye-name of, 169–70, 271
see Sherter, Shottere
Shortfrend, surname or bye-name of, 364
Shorthose, surname or bye-name of, 170
Shotcher, Ric. (or Sotcher, Satcher, Sacher) (1663), 271
Shottenden (Kent), 100
Shotter (Schottere, Satcher, Sacher, Shotyer, Shotcher, Sotcher), surname or bye-name of, 170, 270–1
see Saker, Scheter, Shittere
Shottere, Wm. (or Shorter) (1441–4), 210
Showersmith, see Shoesmith
Shrewsbury, Hugh (de Montgomeri) Earl of, (died 1098), 31
Shrewsbury, Roger (de Montgomery), Earl of (1086), 31, 32
Roger father of, 31
Shripney, 181
Shropshire, landowners in, 33
Shropshire, surnames or bye-names in, 146, 204, 332–3
Shuiter, surname or bye-name of, 271
see Shittere
Shuper, see Shepper
Shurtare, le, see Sherter, Shorter
Shurte, ate (or atte Schurte), surname or bye-name of, 169
Sibbesone, Jn. (1332), 354
Sickelfoot, surname or bye-name of, 361, 394
Sicklehatch (Heathfield), 418
Sidlesham, 148, 171, 192, 242, 261, 275, 384–5
Sidyngebourn, surname or bye-name of, 100
Silter, see Salter
Silvatinus, Silvaticus, see *Salvagius*

Index

Sinderford (atte Synderford), surname or bye-name of, 197
Singleton, 71
Singleton, surname of, 126
Sipwerte, see Shipwright
Sittingbourne (Kent), 100
Skardefeld, see Scarfield
Skardevile, see Scardeville
Skarvile, see Scardeville
Skeppere, surname or bye-name of, 243
  see Skypard
Skipper, see Skypper, Skeppere
Skypard, Wm. (or Skeppere) (late 14th century), 243
Skypard, surname or bye-name of, 243
  see Skeppere
Skypper (Skipper), surname or bye-name of, 243, 244
Slater, surname or bye-name of, 170
  see Slutter
Slaugham, 69, 380
Sleabody, surname or bye-name of, 362
Sleghande, surname or bye-name of, 362
Sligh, surname or bye-name of, 362
Slindon, 167, 186, 249, 385
Slinfold, 197, 255, 337, 341, 396, 402
Slogard, surname or bye-name of, 362
Slutte, atte, surname or bye-name of, 170
Slutter (Slytter), surname or bye-name of, 170
Slutter (or Slater), Edward (c. 1550), 170
Slytter, see Slutter
Smith, surname or bye-name of, 221, 222, 223, 225, 226, 227, 228, 244, 257
Smithers, surname or bye-name of, 328
Smyth, William (1473), 84
Smythessone, Reginald le (1296), 327
Socknersh, 37
Sodyngton, surname or bye-name of, 100
  see Sotiton
Sokernershe, William de (c. 1220–50), 37
  see Swokenerse
Sole, surname or bye-name of, 145–6, 149, 183
Somarsall, surname of, 114
Someres, atte, surname or bye-name of, 200
  see Somneres, Sumners

Somerley, 192
Somerset, surnames or bye-names in, 155, 157, 206
Somershall (Derbys.), 114
Somneres, surname or bye-name of, 200
  see Someres, atte, Sumners
Sompting, 39, 164, 187, 264, 267–8, 275, 314, 382
Sondre, de le, see Soundry, Sundre
Soper (Saper, Sapper), surname or bye-name of, 278
Sotcher, see Shotter
Sotiton, Sotyngton, surname or bye-name of, 100
  see Sodyngton
Sounde, atte, surname of, 183, 184, 213
Sounde, the, at Beddingham, 183
Soundere, surname or bye-name of, 213
Soundre (de la Sondre, Soundry), surname or bye-name of, 83, 149, 196–7
  see Sundre
Sourmilk, surname or bye-name of, 364
South, surname or bye-name of, 180–82
Southampton (Hants.), 239, 272
Southerham, 56, 311
southern England, personal names in, 305
southern England, surnames or bye-names in, 156, 173, 176, 302, 310, 361
Southman, surname or bye-name of, 180
Southover, 248, 379
south-west England, surnames or bye-names in, 13, 118, 150, 227, 321–2, 327, 330, 334
Southwick, 47, 97, 275, 339, 371
Southwyk, persons named (1335), 97
Soweden, surname or bye-name of, 234
Sparre (atte Sparre, de la Sparre), surname of, 148, 182
Sparrow, surname or bye-name of, 361, 386
Sparwe, Agnes (1374), 85
  Her husband, see Herry, Gilbert
Spendlove (Spenlow), surname or bye-name of, 363
Sperling, Simon, le Hunte (13th century), 85
  His wife, see Grashurst, Christina de

Spicer, surname or bye-name of, 225, 228, 278
Spracligh, surname or bye-name of, 100
Spreakley (Surr.), 101
Squibb, surname of, 64
Squire, surname or bye-name of, 239
Stack (atte Stak, le Stak, de la Stake), surname or bye-name of, 171
Stacker (Staker, Stakyar), surname or bye-name of, 83, 171, 182
Stacy, Gilbert (1399), 85
His wife, see Bordon, Alice
Staffs., surnames or bye-names in, 224–5, 332–3
Stag, surname or bye-name of, 386
Stak, atte, Stake, de la, see Stack
Staker, Stakyar, see Stacker
Stalker (Stawker), surname of, 171
Stammer (le Stamer), surname or bye-name of, 367
Stammer, de, surname or bye-name of, 367–8
Stanbourne, Henry Jonesservant de (1331), 66
Standbynorth, surname of, 183
Stanleygh, de, surname of, 123
Stanleygh (? in Mayfield), 123
Stanmer, 368
Stanstreet, surname of, 153
Staple (Stapley), Nicholas (1597), 18
Staple, surname or bye-name of, 155, 183
Stapler, surname or bye-name of, 155
Starre, surname of, 383
Startup, surname or bye-name of, 364
Stawker, see Stalker
Stearman, see Sterman
Stedham, surname or bye-name of, 98
Stedham, 253, 394
Stedman, surname or bye-name of, 249, 258
Steeper, surname of, 230, 253
Steer (le Ster), surname or bye-name of, 258, 361, 372, 382–3, 386, 432
Steers, surname or bye-name of, 383
Stent, surname of, 434
Stephenes, atte
see Stevenes, atte
Stepney, surname of, 433
Ster, le, see Steer
Sterman (Steresman, Stearman), surname or bye-name of, 242
see Esterman
Sterse, personal name of, 382

Steryngman, surname or bye-name of, 242
Stevenes, atte (or atte Stephenes), surname of, 199, 323–4
Steyning, 46, 101, 117, 138, 200, 255, 263–6, 274–5, 317, 342, 344, 371, 374
Stile (Style), surname or bye-name of, 8, 183
Stillwell, surname of, 433
Stilton (Cambs.), 103
Stiltone, surname or bye-name of, 103
Stisted (Ess.), 104
Stistede, surname of, 104
Stock, surname or bye-name of, 183
Stodherd, surname or bye-name of, 249
Stoke, North, 388, 394
Stoke, West, 271
Stone, surname or bye-name of, 183
Stonestreet, surname of, 434
Storrington, 58, 59, 185, 260, 275, 380
Stradwick, see Strudwick
Stras, see Scrase
Streat, 58, 59, 188, 391
Streater, see Streeter
Streatham, 57, 61, 108, 265–6, 328, 369, 406
Street, atte, surname or bye-name of, 155
Streeter (Streater), surname or bye-name of, 155–6, 205, 432
Stridwicke, see Strudwick
Stringer, Thomas (1524), 255
Stringer, surname or bye-name of, 255
Stringersland Farm, 255
Strodewyke, Strodwyke, see Strudwick
Strokehose, surname or bye-name of, 362, 394
Strudder, bye-name of, 249
Strudgwick, 16, 120
Strudwick (Stradwick, Stridwicke, Strodewyke), surname of, 16, 120, 126
Style, see Stile
Suffolk, landowners in, 38
Suff., surnames or bye-names in, 11, 145–6, 151, 198, 224–5, 231, 309, 332–3, 339, 341, 363
Sullington, 69, 86, 163, 185, 252, 376, 387
Sumners, surname or bye-name of, 200
see Someres, atte, Somneres
Sundre, Peter atte (or le Sundre) (1296), 162

Sundre, atte, surname of, 162
  see Soundre
Surrey, Isabel (de Warenne), countess of (1148–*c.* 1203), 30, 186
Surrey, Jn., 7th Earl of, 339
Surrey, Wm. (de Warenne), 1st Earl of, 29, 31
  Rodolfus, brother of, 29
Surrey, William (de Warenne), 2nd Earl of, 29, 30
Surrey, William (de Warenne), 3rd Earl of, 30
Surrey, Wm. (de Warenne), 6th Earl of, 30, 424
Surr., landowners in, 4, 69
Surr., places in, 114, 117, 120
Surr., personal names in, 338
Surr., surnames or bye-names in, 11, 12, 16, 52, 97–8, 120, 141, 145–6, 149–51, 156–7, 159, 163, 169–70, 175–6, 184, 195, 200, 224–6, 229–30, 251–3, 255, 271, 284, 309, 330, 332–3, 382, 402
Surr., surnames from, 100–102, 120, 431
Sussex, Earls of, see Arundel, Earls of
Sutherland, surname of, 432
Sutor, surname or bye-name of, 272
Sutton (near Petworth), 325
Suttone, Rose de (13th century), 85
  Her husband, see Shobeham, Robert de
Swan, surname or bye-name of, 361, 386
Sweatings Lane, at Wadhurst, 316
Sweeting, surname or bye-name of, 315
Swokenerse, Roger de (*c.* 1195), 37
  see Sokenershe
Swyft, surname of, 61
Swynherde, surname or bye-name of, 249
  see Porcarius
Syltere, see Salter
Synderford, atte, see Sinderford

Taillebois, surname of, 257
Taillour, John (1443–5), 84
Taillour (Taylor), surname of, 7, 221–3, 225–8, 257
Takepaine, bye-name of, 418
Taketurn, surname or bye-name of, 394
Talcourteys, land called, 79
Talcurtes, Adam (1228), 46
Talcurtes, Philip (1230), 46
Talcurtes, surname of, 53
  see Tartcurteis
Tamsett, see Tomset
Tandridge Hundred (Surr.), 157
Tanner, surname or bye-name of, 221, 225
Tapene, surname or bye-name of, 272
Tapener (Tapner, Taupener, le Taupenyr, *tapinarius*), surname or bye-name of, 272
tapinarius, Robt. (1202), 272
Tapper, surname of, 16
Tapper, see Tupper
Tarcortais, William (*c.* 1150–70), 46
  see Talcurtes
Tarring, West, 170, 251, 267, 272, 385
Tartcurteis (Talecurteys, Talcurtes, Tardcorteys), family of, 46
Taupener, see Tapener
Taupenyr, Walter le (*c.* 1250), 272
Taverner, surname or bye-name of, 258, 278
Tay, surname or bye-name of, 204
  see Tye, Teye
Teal, surname of, 197
Teele, surname of, 197
Tele, surname or bye-name of, 197, 341
  see Thele, Thiell
Tervell, surname of, 119
Tesselyn, surname or bye-name of, 76
Testard, William called (1279), 83
Tester, surname of, 434
textor, surname or bye-name of, 280
Teye, Thomas (Teys, Taye) (1418–19), 324
Tezelinus, sub-tenant (1086), 40
  William son of, 40
Thakeham, 163, 170, 185, 210
Thatcher (Thetcher, Theccer), surname or bye-name of, 279, 434
Theale Farm, 197, 341
Theccer, see Thatcher
Thele, surname or bye-name of, 83, 149, 182, 197, 341
  see Tele, Thiell
Thetcher, see Thatcher
Thiell, surname or bye-name of, 341
  see Tele, Thele
Thomas, personal name of, 302, 305, 316
Thomset, Thompsett, Thomsit, see Tomset
Thonder, see Thunder
Thonderscrofth, field name of, 264

Thorney, 407
Thorney Island, 167
Thornhill, surname or bye-name of, 199
Threle (Threll, Thrale, Threel, Thrule), surname or bye-name of, 232–3
Thrower (Trewer, Trower), surname or bye-name of, 255–6
Thrush, surname or bye-name of, 361
Thunder, Thomas (1435), 263
Thunder (Dender, Dinder, Dunder, Tunder, Thonder), surname of, 16, 263–4, 434
Thunders Hill, 264
Thunderyscrosse, field name of, 264
Thundre, Wm. le (late 13th cent.), 263
see Tundur
Thurgood, Ric. (late 13th cent.), 311
Thurgood (Thurgod), surname or bye-name of, 310–11
Thurgot, Ric. (1327/8), 311
Thylle, atte (atte Thyleye), surname or bye-name of, 341, 342
Thylle, locality of, 341
Ticchurst, 17, 42, 58 9, 65, 124, 241, 269, 316, 377–8
Tickner, surname of, 126
Tilcock, surname of, 342
Till (Tille, Tilly, Tillie, Tylye, Tyl, Tylle), surname or bye-name of, 341–3
Tillet (Tullett), surname of, 342–3
Tillington, 100
Tillot, surname of, 342
Tilly, see Till, Tulley
Tilthe, atte (atte Tylthe), surname or bye-name of, 341
Tisted, East or West (Hants.), 102
see Tysted
Tockenham (Wilts.), 104
Tokenham, surname of, 104
Tomset (Tamsett, Thomset, Thompsett, Thomsit), surname or bye-name of, 316, 432, 434
Topere, le, see Topper
Topp, atte, surname or bye-name of, 273
Topper (le Topere), surname or bye-name of, 273
see Tupper
Tortington, 196
Totemond, surname or bye-name of, 366
see Tuthome
Tothome, *Toto-Mundo*, see Tuthome

Totnore Hundred, 382
Tottingworth, 187, 380
Toundour, see Thunder
Towes (Towse), surname of, 430
Townsend, surname of, 152–3
townspeople, surnames of, 64–5
Tracie, surname of, 119
Tragoose, see Tregose
Trancamare, Wm. (late 12th cent.), 407
see Tranchmere, Trenchemere, Trankmer
Tranchemier, Isabell (1321–29), 85
Her husband, see Trenchemer, Robert
Tranchevent, surname or bye-name of, 363
see Sherewind
Trandilgrenes, locality, 198
Trandle, Jn. ate (1327/8), 173–4, 198
Trandle, see Trendle
Trandleman, Jn. (1327/8), see Trandle, Jn. ate
Trangmar, surname of, 434
see Trankmer
Treagoose, Treagus, see Tregose
Tree, surname of, 201
Tregoose, surname of, 81
Tregos, de (Treigoz, Tresgos, de), family of, 50, 93
Tregos, surname of, 81
Tregose (Tragoose, Treagoose, Treagus), surname of, 118, 431
Tregose (Cornw.), 81
Tregoss (Cornw.), 81
Treisgoz, see Tregos
Trenchemer, Robert (? c. 1320), 85
His wife, see Tranckemier, Isabel
Trenchemere, Alan (late 12th cent.), 407
see Trancamare, Tranchmere
Trenchmere (Trankmore, Trancamare, Trenchmere), surname or bye-name of, 20, 396, 407–8
Trendelgrof, field name of, 198
Trendle, John (1560), 198
see Trunell, Tronell, Trandle
Trendle (Trandle, Trindle, Trendell, at Trendlee), surname or bye-name of, 17, 198–9
Trendlefield, field name of, 198
Trenemer, see Trentemars
Trentemars, Ric. (or Trenemer) (1327/8, 1332), 407
Trentemars, surname or bye-name of, 407, 422

Index

Treport (Seine-Maritime), 39
Tresgos, see Tregos
Trewer, see Thrower
Treyford, 44, 385
Trice, Tryce, surname or bye-name of, 201
Trice, see Ree, at
Trindle, see Trendle
Troisgotz (Manche), 81
Tronell, Jn. (1560), 198
  see Trendle, Trunell
Trotemenu, surname or bye-name of, 366
Troton, persons named (1332), 98
Trott (Trot), surname or bye-name of, 274
Trotteman, surname or bye-name of, 274
Trottesmale, surname or bye-name of, 366
Trotton, 98
Trowell (Trouel, Truell), surname of, 108
Trowell (Notts.), 108
Trower, see Thrower
Truell, see Trowell
Trumpet, surname or bye-name of, 229, 282
Trumpeter, surname or bye-name of, 282
Trundle, the (earthwork), 198
Trunell, Jn. (1560), 198
  see Trendle, Tronell, Trandle
Trunell, surname of, 198–9
Truslow (or Trusweller), Jn. (17th century), 160
Trusslove (Truslow), surname or bye-name of, 207, 387, 434
Trussman, surname of, 229
Trusweller, see Truslow
Tryce, see Trice
Tryse, de, surname or bye-name of, 201
  see Ree, atte
Tucker, surname or bye-name of, 227, 256, 431
Tugmore (in Hartfield), 138
Tullett, see Tillet
Tulley (Tilley), surname or bye-name of, 342–3, 434
  see Till
Tunder, see Thunder
Tundur, Wm. le (late 13th cent.), 263
  see Thundre
Tuperforlang, le field name of, 273

Tupherd, surname or bye-name of, 273
Tuppard, surname or bye-name of, 273
Tupper (le Tupere), surname or bye-name of, 16, 258, 273–4
  see Topper, Tapper
Turgis, surname of, 58
Turgisius, sub-tenant (1086), 83
Turner, surname or bye-name of, 225
Turtellescumbe, Ralph de (c. 1210), 85
  His wife, see Drictneselle, Juliana de
Tuthome (Tothome, *Toto Mundo*), surname or bye-name of, 366
  see Totemond
Twaincherch, de, surname of, 64
Twineham, 69, 187
Tye, surname or bye-name of, 145–6, 149, 183
Tyl, Tylle, Tylye, see Till
Tyle, le, surname or bye-name of, 359
Tyler, surname of, 10
Tylthe, atte, see Tilthe, atte
Tyrel, Olive (1275), 85
  Her husband, see Acstede, Roland de
Tyrel, Thomas (? c. 1240), 85
Tysted, surname or bye-name of, 102
  see Tisted

Uckfield, 258, 390
Udimore, 17, 43, 61, 172, 179, 231, 379
Ugborough, 277
Ulcombe (Kent), 36
Ulecumbe, de, surname of, 36
  see Olecumbe, de
Ulvin, see Woolvin
Underley, 203
Upperton (near Eastbourne), 270
Up Waltham, 58, 71
Ursus, see Bear

Vacher, surname or bye-name of, 248, 290
Vagger, see Fagger
Varncombe, 101
Venator, surname or bye-name of, 280
  see Hunt
Venele, de la, see Lane, in the
Venella, de, see Lane, atte, Lane, in the
Venitroe (Fyntrewe, Vennetree), surname of, 15
Vennel, see Fennell
Vennells, surname of, 190

Vennetree, see Venitroe
Verall, Gilbvert (1524), 188
Verral, Verrall, Verell, see Fairhall
Verrer, le, bye-name of, 246–7
  see Glasier, Vitrarius
Vesk, Jn., M.P., (1445, 1447), 265
Vesk, Master Jn. (1376), 264
Vesk, Ralph (1332), 264
Vesk, Ralph (1341), 264
Vesk (Evesk, Leveque), surname or bye-name of, 264
  see Evesk, Leveque
Vesseler, surname of, 230, 253
vicecomes, Gilbert (1086), 38
Vicecomes, see Sheriff
Vilers, de, family of, 44
Vinall (Finhagh, Fynhagh de, Vynhagh, Vynall, Vynawe), surname of, 15
Vinch, see Finch
Vinehall, 15
Vinnetrow (Feningetrowe), 15
Virroll, see Fairhall
Vitrarius, bye-name of, 246–7
  see Glasier, Verrer, le
Vluuardus, personal name of, 301
Vowle, Vogll, see Fowle
Vrythe, see Frith
Vuggles, surname of, 377
  see Fowle
Vughes Farm (Newick), 377
Vugill, Vugle, see Fowle, Fuggle, Fugel
Vulgar, see Woolgar
Vurlonger, see Furlonger
Vynagh, Vynall, Vynawe, see Vinall

Wadhurst, 56, 61, 100, 138, 241, 245, 269, 316, 377, 380–81
Wakeford, surname of, 102, 117
  see Walkeford
Waker, surname or bye-name of, 256
  see Walker
Walberton, 260, 370
Walcock, surname of, 344
Waldron, 246, 382
Walecot, de, surname or bye-name of, 99
Wales, personal names from, 385
Wales, surnames or bye-names in, 334
Wales, surnames from, 343, 432
Walilonde, Mabel de (c. 1230), 85
  Her husband, see Barmlinge, Stephen de
Walilonde, Robert de (? c. 1200), 85
Walkeford, surname or bye-name of, 102

Walker, surname or bye-name of, 225, 226–7, 256, 431
  see Waker
Walkford (Hants.), 102
  see Wakeford
Walklyn, Ralph (1374), 57
  see Broke, Walkelyn atte
Walksted, see Walsted
Walle, Jn. de la (or Wllere) (1266), 158
Walshe, Alice (c. 1487), 86
Walshe, Ralph (? c. 1480), 86
Walstead (in Lindfield), 128
Walsted (Walksted), surname of, 128
Walter son of Lambert, sub-tenant (1086), 42
Walterman, surname or bye-name of, 336–7
  see Waterman
Waltham, Cold, see Cold Waltham
Waltham, Up, see Up Waltham
Walwanus, personal name of, 303
Wancy, le, surname of, 3
Wancy, de, family of, 45, 93
Warbleton, 75, 188, 194, 341, 402
Ward, surname or bye-name of, 225, 279
Wardew, surname or bye-name of, 361
Warenne, de, family of, 4, 34, 44, 51, 104, 122, 186
Warenne, Rainald de (c. 1150), 30
Warenne, Ralph de (c. 1145), 30
Warenne, Reginald de (c. 1150)
  see Warenne, Rainald de
Warenne, Rodolfus de (c. 1050)
Warenne, William de (1086), 35, 38, 48
Warenne, Wm. de, son of Rainald (c. 1200), 30
Warenne (Seine-Maritime), 30
Warenne, see Surrey, Earls of
Warminghurst, 261, 274–5, 387
Warner (le Wasenner, le Wariner), surname or bye-name of, 279
Warnham, 125, 149, 315, 317, 345, 375
Warningcamp, 259, 271, 275
Wartling, 37, 159, 173, 262, 341, 345
Warws., surnames or bye-names in, 11, 145, 198, 203, 224–5, 309, 332
Warws., surnames from, 103, 118
Washer, surname or bye-name of, 258, 275–6, 432
Washingham, 248
Washington, surname of, 126
Washington, 162, 185, 199, 238, 254–5, 267, 279, 338

Index

Wastel, Geoffrey (c. 1167), 19
Waterer, surname of, 149, 153, 155, 173
Wateringbury (Kent), 100
Waterman, surname or bye-name of, 336
   see Walterman
Wateryngbury, surname or bye-name of, 100
Watevill, family of, 36–7
Watevill, Robert de (1197), 36
Wateville, William de (1086), 35–7
Watt, surname of, 335
Watteville (Eure), 36
Wattman, surname or bye-name of, 335
   see Whatman
Weald, the, 1, 9, 96, 98, 123, 157, 184, 229, 247, 264, 277, 314, 326, 387, 389
Wease, surname of, 385
   see Wise
Weaver (Wever), surname or bye-name of, 7, 227
Webb, surname or bye-name of, 225, 227
Webbys, A, surname or bye-name of, 199–200
Webster, surname or bye-name of, 225, 227, 258
Welle, atte (Wyle, atte, Wylle, atte, Wille, atte), surname or bye-name of, 25, 172, 183
Weller, surname of, 152, 155–6
Wellingham, 59, 60, 394
Wellkempd, surname or bye-name of, 362
Wellman, surname or bye-name of, 152
Wells, surname of, 155
Welsh Marches, landowners in, 4
Welsh Marches, surnames or bye-names in, 334
Wenbregg, person named (1332), 100
Wepham, 275
West, family of, 181
West, surname or bye-name of, 180–82
Westbourne, 272, 384
Westdean (East Suss.), 49, 189
   see Dean, West (West Suss.)
Westergate, 169
Westfield, 381
Westham, 190, 270
Westmoston, 38
Westre, surname or bye-name of, 180, 213
Westres, Jn. (1524), 213

Wever, see Weaver
Whalesborne Hundred, 169
Whamm (atte Whamme, atte Whame), surname of, 149, 182
Whatlington, 125, 172, 218
Whatman, Stephen (mid 13th century), 85
   His wife, see Hilderhurst, Alice de
Whatman (Wattman), surname of, 337
Wheeler, surname or bye-name of, 279
Whibertus, personal name of, 303
Whitbread, surname or bye-name of, 279
Whitcher (Whicchere, le Wuchere, Wycher), surname or bye-name of, 172
Whitcock, surname of, 371
White, surname or bye-name of, 361, 371
Whitegroom, surname or bye-name of, 362
Whitestone, atte (de la Whytestone), surname or bye-name of, 328
Whithorn, surname or bye-name of, 366
Whiting, surname of, 344
Whitlok, surname of, 5
Whitsone, surname or bye-name of, 328
Whytestone, de la, see Whitestone, atte
Wickens (Kent), 100
Wiggonholt, 252
Wigmore, surname of, 114
Wigmore (Kent), 114
Wigperry, 98
Wikenden, surname of, 117
Wildebef, bye-name of, 389
Wildebef, field name of, 389
Wildebor, bye-name of, 389
Wiley, surname of, 26
   see Wyley
Willard, surname or bye-name of, 309
Wille, atte, see Welle, atte
Willer (Willar, Wyliar, Wyllere), surname or bye-name of, 172
Willes, Thomas (1332), 351
Willesham, surname of, 61
Willey, surname of, 26
   see Wyley
William son of Rainald (1086), see Rainald, William son of
William son of Techeline (c. 1100), 40
William, sub-tenant (1086), (? Wm. de St. Leger), 37

William, personal name of, 302
Williams, surname or bye-name of, 142, 305, 318
Williamson, surname or bye-name of, 7, 305, 318
Willingdon, 55, 149, 166, 179, 389
Willingdon Hundred, 344
Wilmington, 189, 190
Wilson, surname or bye-name of, 328
Wilteschyre (Wylcher), surname of, 104
see Wiltshire
Wilting, 124, 171–2, 374
Wilton, John (1403), 66
Wilton, William Jonesservant (1403), 66
Wilts., landowners in, 215, 267
Wilts., surnames or bye-names in, 146, 323
Wilts., surnames from, 104, 114, 117, 118
Wiltshire, surname of, 117
see Wilteschyre
Win Bridge, 100
Winccstr' (Wynchestr'), surname or bye-name of, 102
Winchelse (or Wynchelese), surname or bye-name of, 97
Winchelsea, Andrew of (c. 1200), 64
Winchelsea, Earls of, 369
Winchelsea, 43, 61, 64–5, 130, 172, 183, 241–2, 250–1, 263, 270, 278, 294, 312, 315, 326, 340–41, 344, 368–70, 373–4, 376, 383
Winchester, Odo of (1086), 32
Eldred, ? brother of, 32
Winchester (Hants.), 102, 426
see Wincestr'
Winder (Wynder), surname or bye-name of, 155, 171–2, 182
Winder, place-name of, 171
Winstanley, surname of, 126
Wisborough Green, 10, 138, 148, 177–8, 375, 396
Wisdom, surname or bye-name of, 362, 372, 383–4, 432
Wise, Denise la (c. 1285), 85
Wise, le, serf named (before c. 1285), 85
Wise (*Sapiens*), surname or bye-name of, 85, 362, 372, 384–6
Wiseman, surname or bye-name of, 432
Wiske (Wyseke, Wyske, Wysky), surname of, 18, 83
Wister, surname of, 149, 171

Wiston, 13, 17, 31, 168, 185, 199, 206, 243, 264–5, 267, 279, 323, 327, 329, 342, 353, 376, 385, 390
Witegrom, John Pistor (1292), 65
Withyham, 120, 123, 164, 389, 406, 411
Wittering, 160, 172, 192–3
Wivelsfield, 158, 201, 366
Wllere, Jn. le (or de la Walle) (1266), 158
Wodehorn, surname or bye-name of, 367
see Woodhorn
Wodetaller, surname or bye-name of, 257
Wodeward, William (1395), 84
Wogham (or Woham), Matilda de (1266), 85
Her husband, see Russell, Robert
Wolf (Wulf), surname or bye-name of, 387, 388, 393, 416
Wolgar, see Woolgar
Wolvin, Wolvyn, see Woolvin
Wood, surname or bye-name of, 183
Wood Dalling (Norf.), 104
Woodhorn, place-name of, 367
see Wodehorn
Woodmancote, 70, 79
Woodmancote (near Steyning), 317
Woolgar, Thos. (1500), 317
Woolgar (Wolgar, Vulgar), surname or bye-name of, 316–7, 344
Woolvin (Wolvin, Wolvyn, Woolfen, Ulvin), surname or bye-name of, 54, 344
Worcs., places in, 114
Worcs., surnames in, 145–6, 156, 243, 332–3, 363
Worth (near Crawley), 125, 263
Worth, atte, surname or bye-name of, 125
Worth Farm (Little Horstead), 125
Worthing, 39, 41, 191, 266, 277, 367, 384–5
Wotton Hundred (Surr.), 157
Wright, surname or bye-name of, 225, 280
Wringar, bye-name of, 229
Wuchere, le, see Whitcher
Wulf, see Wolf
Wych, atte, surname or bye-name of, 172
Wycher, see Whitcher
Wyckham (in Steyning), 46
Wydesparre, bye-name of, 149

Wyke, de, surname of, 61
Wykyng, surname or bye-name of, 100
Wylcher, see Wilteschyre
Wyldereve, bye-name of, 229
Wyle, Wm. atte (1306), 17
  see Wylye, Wm.
Wyle, atte, see Welle, atte
Wyley, surname of, 26
  see Wiley
Wyliar, see Willer
Wylle, atte, see Welle, atte
Wyllere, see Willer
Wyltyng, surname of, 124
  see Wilting
Wylye, Wm. (1296), 17
  see Wyle, Wm. atte
Wyn, Colett atte (1440), 9
Wyn, atte, surname or bye-name of, 172, 211
Wynchelese, see Winchelse
Wynchestr', see Wincestr'
Wynde, atte (Wynne, atte Wyne), surname or bye-name of, 83, 171–2
Wynder, Thos. (1439–40), 9
Wynder, Thomas, 211
Wynder, see Winder
Wyndham, 187
Wynyng, atte, see Finnyng, atte
Wyseke, atte, see Wiske
Wyske, see Wiske

Wysky, see Wiske
Wyssere, le, surname or bye-name of, 159
Wysshe, atte, surname or bye-name of, 159
Wytemay, surname or bye-name of, 362

Yapton, 162, 171, 196, 242, 370, 376, 394
Yardhurst (Iardherst, de), surname or bye-name of, 106
Yardhurst, 97
yeomen, surnames or bye-names of, 14, 18, 238, 255, 329, 406
  see free tenants
Yerceneselle, Mabilia de (c. 1210), 85
  Her husband, see Eillesford, William de
Yorks., landowners in, 4, 5, 43, 46, 70–1, 105
Yorks., surnames or bye-names in, 121, 145, 157, 176, 224–5, 255, 332–3, 363, 378, 434
Yorks., surnames from, 104, 118
Yqual, le, bye-name of, 233
Yrisse, see Irysse

Zouch, family of, 104